ELIZABETHAN AND
JACOBEAN TRAGEDIES

THE NEW MERMAIDS

General Editor
BRIAN GIBBONS
Professor of English Literature,
University of Zurich

Previous General Editors
PHILIP BROCKBANK
BRIAN MORRIS
ROMA GILL

Elizabethan and Jacobean Tragedies

Introduced by
BRIAN GIBBONS

THE SPANISH TRAGEDY
DOCTOR FAUSTUS
SEJANUS HIS FALL
WOMEN BEWARE WOMEN
THE WHITE DEVIL
'TIS PITY SHE'S A WHORE

ERNEST BENN LIMITED

First published in this form 1984
by Ernest Benn Limited
Sovereign Way, Tonbridge, Kent, TN9 1RW
© Ernest Benn Limited 1984

Printed in Great Britain by
Richard Clay (The Chaucer Press) Ltd,
Bungay, Suffolk

ISBN 0-510-00166-1

NOTE

NEW MERMAIDS are modern-spelling, fully annotated editions of important English plays. Each play in this anthology is also available individually, with a critical introduction, biography of the author, discussions of dates and sources, textual details, and a bibliography. The reader is recommended to consult these editions for fuller information.

CONTENTS

ABBREVIATIONS

ed.	editor
O.E.D.	*The Oxford English Dictionary*
om.	omit
s.d.	stage direction
s.p.	speech prefix
Tilley	M. P. Tilley, *A Dictionary of the Proverbs in England in the Sixteenth and Seventeenth Centuries,* Ann Arbor, 1950

Names of periodicals abbreviated:

E.L.H.	*English Literary History*
E.S.	*English Studies*
E & S	*Essays and Studies*
J.E.G.P.	*Journal of English and Germanic Philology*
M.L.N.	*Modern Language Notes*
M.L.R.	*Modern Language Review*
N & Q	*Notes & Queries*
P.M.L.A.	*Publications of the Modern Language Association of America*
P.Q.	*Philological Quarterly*
R.E.S.	*Review of English Studies*
S.P.	*Studies in Philology*
T.L.S.	*The Times Literary Supplement*

INTRODUCTION

THE SIX PLAYS in this New Mermaid volume have been chosen to represent the tragic drama of the English Renaissance from about 1590 to about 1630. There are two plays from the early phase, *Dr Faustus* (c. 1589) and *The Spanish Tragedy* (c. 1587-90), a period which also saw Shakespeare's earliest plays. There are two from the first decade of the Jacobean age, *Sejanus* (1603), in which Shakespeare acted and which is in part Jonson's response to *Julius Caesar*, and *The White Devil* (1612), in which echoes from the language and situations of Shakespeare's major tragedies are apparent. The last two plays span the remaining decades of major dramatic activity of the age, *Women Beware Women* (1621), and *'Tis Pity She's a Whore* (1632). They can be read as a chronological sequence, and many strands connect later plays to earlier ones; but although it is valuable to analyse, in quasi-Darwinian terms, a process of evolution in dramatic technique and dramatic poetry, it is also possible to arrange the plays in many other patterns according to their subject matter, styles, and their thematic concerns.

Several of the plays give close attention to Courts as social and as political institutions; they explore the inter-dependence of public and private morality and focus attention on the systems by which power is distributed and exercised. Factually speaking politics in the Renaissance was dominated by men, but there were some striking exceptions to this rule — Lucrezia Borgia, for instance, on the one hand, Elizabeth I on the other. The interest in women as individuals in prominent social and political circles is an important feature of the drama of the age, and more generally the representation of women in these plays, depicted as they are with penetrating insight, becomes the more interesting as it shows itself alert to the constricting social and ideological images imposed upon them. Love, as a tragic experience, plays a subordinate role in the first three plays in the collection but is given greater prominence in the last three. Here we may infer that the impact of Shakespeare has been too powerful for the dramatists to ignore. Webster, Middleton, and Ford bring their own complex dramatic thinking to the question of the relationship between love and death, but they cannot forget Shakespeare, especially in *Romeo, Hamlet and Othello*. The last three plays in the present collection show a peculiar self-consciousness about the arts of dramatic narrative and dramatic poetry; they often deliberately call attention to episodes or images from predecessors, partly to make use of their inherent power and partly to establish variant emphases or contrasting views. This kind of allusiveness can be traced in the relationship of *'Tis Pity* to *Romeo and Juliet,* of *Sejanus* to *Julius Caesar,* or in the development of such recurrent roles as the malcontent, the revenger, the corrupt ruler. Indeed a particulaly profitable exercise, and one which the present selection of plays is partly designed to encourage, is to read the plays in the present volume alongside a related selection of Shakespearean tragedies — *Titus, Romeo, Caesar, Hamlet, Othello, Macbeth.* Alternatively, the extraordinary appetite for the variety and extremity of experience which distinguishes Elizabethan and Jacobean dramatists can be studied by combining, as a whole or in part, the present volume of tragedies with its companion New Mermaid volume of Elizabethan and Jacobean comedies. Yet readers of the present volume of tragedies may justly feel that substance and satisfaction in abundance may be gained from this volume alone, and it is to this view that we may now address ourselves.

*   *   *

The rediscovery in twentieth century theatre of the virtues of a non-realistic drama, and of acting and production techniques which aim not for 'photographic' accuracy in simulating actuality, but for the representation of imaginative truth, has allowed dramatists to repossess for the theatre stories and experiences which had become, in the interim, the exclusive province of poetry and the novel. Only a theatre which preserves the sense of artifice, pretence, make-believe, of the actor as at once himself and the character he portrays, can depict with full power the metaphysical experience and the epic-scale historical experience represented in Elizabethan drama. It was thus that Milton could conceive of writing his *Paradise Lost* originally as a play. Both *Dr Faustus* and *The Spanish Tragedy* frame their human stories with the supernatural. In Marlowe's tragedy good and bad angels can share the stage with the human hero, and Mephistopheles, while never ceasing to be a spirit in eternal torment, can simultaneously stand in human form as a dignified, elegant and ironic companion to Faustus. This awesome doubleness is also represented through the whole mode of theatre in which alienation effects are of the essence. Mephistopheles makes a memorable reply to Faustus when asked how he is out of hell,

Why this is hell, nor am I out of it. (I.iii, 76).

Faustus cannot as yet comprehend this reply; but an audience is directed to perceive the double sense of the action, for what can be seen and physically performed is shadowed, as it were, by a more important action not bound by the constraints of the body or the feeble yardstick of human time, understanding and emotion. Consequently Marlowe identifies the artifice of theatre — illusory and, at its lowest, two-dimensionally tawdry and crude — with human life and the world we live in. In the episodes involving the Emperor and the Pope, or in the pageant of the seven deadly sins, the rough and ready vigour of popular pageant-art is adapted wryly, to reinforce the mocking degradation which is Faustus' only reward. The vitality of these shows derives from popular festivals, in themselves not without double sense.

The questioning — we may term it the dialectical treatment — of the issue of judgement is apparent in every aspect of the play, particularly its use of contrasting modes abruptly juxtaposed to one another. In one version of the ending, immediately after our deeply moving and fearful experience of the last, damned moments of Faustus' life, the scholars enter and find the gruesome shreds of his body, torn in pieces by the devils and scattered all over the stage. Here the audience is offered two opposed views of his death: the human being is suddenly no more than a broken puppet, what was alive moments before in the passionate play, now is valueless bric-a-brac, like theatre props seen back-stage the morning after. Does this revoltingly barbaric dismemberment express Marlowe's hostility to a medieval dogma and iconography which he thought intolerable for its exploitation of superstition, credulity and fear? Or does it awaken in an audience trained in the Chistian tradition a proper awe at the reality of damnation?

In *The Spanish Tragedy* there are also, as in *Dr Faustus,* supernatural figures, Revenge and the Ghost of Andrea; they are the first to enter; as they make their way to their seats they converse almost as if they were two real noble spectators with reserved seats in the Lords' Room. The audience will watch them watching the human drama from above, signifying their supernatural status and rendering them invisible and inaccessible to the human characters below. In the middle of the play Andrea upbraids Revenge for having fallen asleep and having allowed his influence to be withdrawn from the action below; but Revenge reassures him

Content thyself, Andrea: though I sleep,
Yet is my mood soliciting their souls; . . .
Nor dies Revenge although he sleep awhile (III.xv, 19-20, 23)

and Revenge makes an effort to explain his scheme. We recognise the parallel between the playwright and Fate itself, as the spectacular dumb-show is now performed with a commentary by Revenge to

help Andrea imagine
    What 'tis to be subject to destiny. (III.xv, 28)
Revenge is allowed to go back to sleep (Kyd has an excellent sense of
humour: what is vitally interesting to mortals is to Revenge as
tedious as a dull play). The representation of the supernatural in
Kyd's play, by contrast with Marlowe's, is almost devoid of Christian ideas or terms, and derives from pagan Roman times and the
drama of Seneca; but *The Spanish Tragedy*, like *Dr Faustus*, has at its
centre a human hero. He is great in his capacity for passion, both in
love of his son and desire for justice, and it is the power of human
feeling in the play, not the representation of the supernatural, that is
its main claim to greatness.

    To make such a claim is to accept the high rhetorical style of the
great speeches in the play, not as artificial and mechanical, but as for-
mally organised to create and generate emotion like arias in grand
opera. The formality of the language has the same function and proceeds upon the same principle as the stagecraft and design of the
dramatic narrative: it represents imaginatively, rather than attempting to simulate the actuality of spontaneous utterance. Furthermore
the great speeches of passion in the play are founded in experiences
central to humanity and integral to an idea of what it is to be a father,
a citizen, a man of honour, faced with a son's murder, then with a
ruler indifferent to atrocity, and finally with the dawning possiblity
of a universe blankly meaningless. In these speeches Hieronymo
discovers the successive layers of his own nature as the stings of a
hostile destiny torture him:
    Where shall I run to breathe abroad my woes,
    My woes whose weight hath wearied the earth?
    Or mine exclaims, that have surcharged the air
    With ceaseless plaints for my deceased son?
    The blustering winds, conspiring with my words,
    At my lament have moved the leafless trees,
    Disrobed the meadows of their flowering green,
    Made mountains marsh with spring-tides of my tears,
    And broken through the brazen gates of hell. (III.vii, 1-9).
There is madness in this speech, emerging through distorted hyper-
bole which is at once expressive and generative of passion; the
dynamic pulse of passion takes over from thr rational faculty in
speech, and the images in the final two lines supplant, with surreal
dream forms, the rational forms that precede them, just as the image
of blustering wind announces a tempest.
    Hieronymo's madness is depicted in disordered speech, but the
passion he feels is clearly not disproportionate to his suffering.
Hieronymo reaches the limits of human suffering and the resources

of human speech to express it. He glimpses and touches the border of the superhuman but he cannot cross it or comprehend it; the audience watch Revenge and Andrea as they in turn, immune to the cries of Hieronymo, work out a larger and more intricate and also quite endless pattern: for the final moments of the play consist in the departure of the Ghost of Andrea and Revenge to another 'theatre' hidden from the audience.

REVENGE (*To* ANDREA)
>Then haste we down to meet thy friends and foes:
>To place thy friends in ease, the rest in woes.
>For here, though death hath end their misery,
>I'll there begin their endless tragedy. (IV.v, 45-8).

Perhaps here the tragic vision of Kyd is closest to Marlowe's: Revenge relies on human nature and human institutions to produce the play's intricate web of misery, fear and destruction; but in the *Spanish Tragedy* there is no answer to the deep need of the characters for justice, no answer to the demand they make for meaning, in their own lives and in the world as a whole. In both plays the questions, however, have a fierce directness engaging us politically as well as philosophically: their expression through drama ensures that they are given a properly human complexity.

The Spanish Tragedy, perhaps the earliest in date, and some would argue first in quality of all the non-Shakespearian plays of the age, has at last (in 1982) been given a full-scale production by a modern professional dramatic company, an event to which its New Mermaid editor, J. R. Mulryne, could only look forward with faint hope in 1970. At that time Mulryne declared his faith in the play as a work that needed to be seen on stage for its full stature to be recognised: he wrote that the play has 'too often been discussed for its historical significance . . . What is most remarkable in fact is not Kyd's debt to the past nor even what his play holds for development in the future by others, but the extent to which it is already a moving, successful stage-play in its own right. More noticeable than the display of academically correct rhetorical devices is the extraordinary range of dramatic styles Kyd employs'. Now that the production for which Mulryne hoped has finally come, audiences clearly agree that *The Spanish Tragedy* deserves its palace in the professional repertoire, and it may be hoped that once this famous work comes to be thought of as a script for performance, readers will recognise its full theatrical stature.

Although we speak readily enough of reading a play, really this is not the same kind of activity as reading a lyric poem or a novel by, say, George Eliot. With novels and poems, certainly, imaginative participation is required on the part of the reader who needs to have sensitivity to language as well as to feeling and ideas: but when we approach a play there is an additional dimension to be kept constantly in mind. Theatre in its immediate reality must be physical. Action is performed by animate bodies, watched by spectators. Theatre is a visual art, like painting, but also a temporal art like music. Eric Bentley in his book *The Life of the Drama* meditates on the paradox that although the great works of theatre present spiritual and political experience in their full nakedness, they must present this nakedness by means of the body. 'And though a philosopher may represent the body as a mere shadow of a more substantial spiritual reality, and a playwright may follow him in this, our crude retort is inevitably that the shadow is itself pretty substantial. "Can spirit set to a leg? No. Or an arm? No." . . . though the great nakednesses of the theatre are spiritual, the immediate reality of theatre is aggressively physical, corporeal.'

Together with this uninhibited appetite for the physical and corporeal elements of theatre—gesture, action, spectacle, properties and special effects—the Elizabethan dramatists of the first rank persistently explored the creative possibilities of the structure of the stage and theatre itself. Metaphors integrate the play, and their prominence in the verbal dialogue is reflected and extended in action and stage-image. There is often a counterpoint between the different expressive modes, verbal and visual, through which a play's central metaphors are expressed. An awareness of the fact of playing, of the performance itself, is often incorporated as a metaphor within the particular play.

So habitual are these methods of composition for Elizabethan dramatists that it is tempting to suppose sometimes that a playwright visualised the action, scene by scene (like the choreographer of a ballet) and only when this part of the design was complete came to compose the dialogue. Certainly this robust design of the plays, in terms of telling visual action and spectacle, is a source of pleasure and dramatic energy for an audience. Against the action as we see it the dramatist often counterpoints the speeches of the characters: in Shakespeare's *Titus Andronicus,* for instance, the mutilated daughter of Titus is brought on stage, bleeding and speechless, her tongue having been torn out. As the audience gazes at this terrible spectacle it listens to the speeches of her brothers who try to articulate their reactions, and at the same time it sees the suffering as wordless agony. The action of this tragedy is based on a series of increasingly appalling spectacles of human misery and iniquity, in which the audience compares its own powers of response with those of the hero.

Titus Andronicus has many affinities with *The Spanish Tragedy,* and in neither play is it possible, even for a reader, to ignore the central importance of spectacle (we may think of Heironimo discovering his murdered son hanging in the arbour, or of Hieronimo later biting out his tongue in full view of the audience, or of the spectacular multiple killings at the end). The point that stage-action is centrally important is made more forcibly therefore by considering a play often dismissed as unsuited for the theatre and better read in the study, Jonson's *Sejanus,* which has indeed yet to receive a full-scale modern production.

Of the plays in the present selection *Sejanus* is certainly the most restrained in its use of the resources of theatre and it has the plainest dramatic narrative. It does not seek to involve the audience in intimate personal identification with particular, fully drawn characters. However engrossing a purely literary reading of it may be, nevertheless *Sejanus* is designed as a coherent visual spectacle. It is a performed metaphor of the horror of systematised and institutionalised tyranny, not just literary but also a physically embodied experience.

At the play's beginning the character Sejanus, risen to great power under the favour of the Emperor Tiberius, has his success ascribed to the power of Fortune, worshipped as a goddess in ancient Rome. In Jonson's time, after Machiavelli, it was possible to conceive of the goddess Fortune as a metaphor for something all too prosaic though still inhuman. Jonson makes his play give maximum exposure to the amoral forces latent in the system of Court Patronage, which was practiced by absolutist European rulers in his own day as well as in classical Rome. The play's first scenes accordingly demonstrate an idea: that this system is vicious as a system: as well as depicting most of the individuals in it as corrupt. The twentieth century spectator needs little persuading that to contemplate bureaucracy can induce disgust. Our guides here, Silius and Sabinus, express the author's *implicit* directions as to how this first scene is to be played, and a reader who realises the full importance of these unobtrusive but vital directions can quickly recognise the visual design. The chief characters, Sejanus, Drusus, and Tiberius, as the *explicit* printed stage directions dictate, each make entrances surrounded by flatterers and henchmen, provoking obsequious gestures and ripples of ingratiating movement among the rival groups of courtiers already on stage. Jonson also gives detailed stage directions within the dialogue itself, as when Silius comments on the courtiers' reaction to Sejanus as he enters:

Now observe the stoops,/The bendings and the falls. (I.i, 175-6)

Jonson makes such gesture and movement a metaphor for the moral and political corruption of this manipulative society, yet the episode is a clear stage action which has independent authenticity, as itself. Jonson's dramaturgy here is based on the moral as well as artistic conviction that physical signs tell moral truths; his convictions inspire the forceful shaping of choreographic rhythm as well as the emphasis on particular acts—such as Drusus slapping Sejanus' face, or Livia, in the very next scene, actually painting her face: metaphor for a corrupt flattering society, but also discomfittingly a historical fact in ancient Rome, in Jacobean England, and in modern society.

The great scene in the Senate in Act III.i (anticipating political show trials of the present century) climaxes with a brave and scornful act by the victim Silius, as he stabs himself to death. Growing political terror in Rome soon yields news of dark omens; but this purely verbal report of off-stage events is succeeded by a remarkable spectacle that the audience is shown: Jonson directs that a full Roman ceremony be performed on stage, before the image of the goddess Fortune. The audience watch as she, amazingly, turns away her face from the contemptuous suppliant Sejanus. The play's climax turns on the arrival of a series of letters, a simple stage device of ancient origin but one that here displays and reinforces the violence of an impersonal system, more remorseless than the passionate act of any individual human being. The displeasure of Tiberius with Sejanus is read out from a letter and the extraordinary spectacle of the Senators shifting their places away from Sejanus, like leaves falling from a tree, will recall with ironic increment of spectacular effect the show trial of Silius in III.i. This half-farcical shifting of places away from the tainted ex-favourite is an ominous anticipation and a stage-action metaphor for the physical dismemberment he is soon to suffer off-stage. As Terentius reports, old men, virgins, widows, mothers, exultant at the fall of Sejanus, dismember his body:

> These digging out his eyes, those with his brain
> Sprinkling themselves, their houses and their friends;
> Others are met, having ravished thence an arm,
> And deal small pieces of the flesh for favours;
> These with a thigh; this hath cut off his hands (V.vi, 822-6).

The People's passion is thus satiated, at least for the time being, yet below the surface Jonson's irony works savagely. The fall of Sejanus chages nothing; Rome's system of tyrannical rule remains unaltered. The whole dramatisation — narrative, characterisation, stage-action — is disciplined and shaped to express this single, fiercely honest, unpalatable truth.

In Webster's *The White Devil* a feature common to the plays so far discussed is given exceptional prominence: it is the act of observing.

An important consideration for a dramatist is that he must manipulate the point of view from which an audience is shown events. He must ask himself when to prepare them for a scene with advance information, so that they know more than any of the characters, or can share with one or several characters information that the others do not have; or when, on the contrary, it will be better to give the audience a surprise. What then, he may ask, can be achieved by making an audience self-conscious of overhearing or seeing extremely private and intimate events in the lives of the play's characters? These may be important elements in an audience's experience of a play, though since a spectator watches art, a representation of real life, not the thing itself, his sense of guilt is combined with a healthful distancing. Nevertheless it is as well to recognise the darker pleasures a spectator enjoys from watching violence, and in a certain sense participating in forbidden experience. Part of the experience of the spectator in watching the horrible events of *The White Devil*, and *'Tis a Pity She's a Whore* — or *Othello* — is fascination with the evil characters and perverse impulses; some answering impulse within us responds and is tempted to recognise and identify with them.

The conventional character the 'malcontent', because those at Court suppose him of little account, is made privy to many dark plots and ugly desires. Deprived of wealth and rank and honour, to his other humiliations is added a sordid insight into the human heart. Having no other path to preferment he must serve superiors whom he despises. Thus, himself a forced victim of manipulation, he must in turn manipulate. Witty ingenuity produces wry jesting from the malcontent, but his schemes bring to the surface disease concealed within. Flamineo in *The White Devil* is an exceptionally complex, perhaps partly incoherent, version of this character-type who persistently acts out roles in front of other characters, the better to manipulate them, but seems never to be really free of his own thoughts and feelings behind his assorted masks. In his first big scene (I.ii) we can observe him striving to excite erotically the melancholy self-obsessed Brachiano, who desires Flamineo's already-married sister Vittoria. Flamineo adopts a pose at once prurient and despising towards women and sex, stessing women's supposedly greater sexual libidinousness beneath their coyness. He proffers Brachiano several gross sexual metaphors ('buttery hatch', 'great barriers moulting feathers', 'Dutch doublet') with evident pornographic purpose. Brachiano implicitly invites more with his brief replies: he drinks it in. A moment later Flamineo uses a variant technique to inflame the husband Camillo with images of his wide's adultery. Just before she comes in he tells of a trick pair of spectacles which produce multiple images:

> now should you wear a pair of these spectacles, and see your wife tying her shoe, you would imagine twenty hands were taking up your wife's clothes   (I.ii, 100-102).

When Vittoria herself enters, this suggestion still remains as an after-image (to continue the ocular figure) and Flamineo goes on to play a further risky trick on Camillo, by holding a double conversation with Vittoria: half, directed at Camillo, seemingly urging her to reconcilement with her husband, half, privately to her, arranging an assignation with Brachiano. (This episode is a variant on a key scene in Shakespeare's *Othello* in which the malcontent Iago persuades Othello to spy on a meeting he arranges with Cassio. The audience can hear the innocuous conversation, but Othello is out of earshot and must rely on Iago's word that Cassio will be seen exultant at having cuckolded the Moor: cf. *Othello* IV.i, 100ff.) A few moments later Flamineo again is a contriver, stage-managing the encounter between the love-sick Brachiano and Vittoria; with the maid Zanche Flamineo watches the lovers in their embraces, contributing half-sympathetic, half-lewd commentary. Vittoria is his sister, but there is no certainty about Flamineo's personal emotional involvement here, and it is true that the images have a certain self-conscious quality. Flamineo's own erotic excitement could be faked, part of his role; yet the role is prurient and voyeuristic: to what extent can he, or we, remain unaffected by such imaginings?

A character or group very frequently observes others in a play; the act may be innocent — to admire, simply to explain behaviour — or it may be critical, satirical; it may be an act of espionage, or engrossing as a voyeuristic pleasure or a dream. There are many such overhearings and acts of spying in *The White Devil*: Francisco covertly observes Lodovico secretly sprinkle Brachiano's helmet with poison, though others who are present do not see it; Brachiano's protracted death agony is watched for a time by Francisco and Flamineo; Lodovico watches the love-making of Zanche and Francisco:

> Mark her I prithee — she simpers like the suds
> A collier hath been washed in   (V.iii, 238-9)

There are bizarre episodes representing dream-like experience; Brachiano watches the conjuror's dumb shows (II.ii) and Flamineo watches Brachiano's ghost which *'throws earth upon him and shows him the skull'* (V.iv), a deadly omen. Flamineo sado-masochistically watches Vittoria and Zanche exult over him as he lies feigning death agony:

There's a plumber laying pipes in my guts — it scalds (V.v, 143)

Not long after, in grave mood, he in turn watches her die and describes the process while his own life ebbs swiftly away. In some of these episodes an audience may find a disconcerting reflection of their own absorption in looking at scenes of intimate distress, pleasure and disgust.

At the end of both *Women Beware Women* and *'Tis Pity*, after an audience has been drawn deeply into the intensely private drama involving the principal characters, a spectacular catastrophe erupts to expose everything to an astonished society, hitherto unaware of the evil at its core. In *Women Beware Women*, a play in which Middleton traces first the tentative, then cumulatively corrosive, process by which materialist appetite gnaws away the quick of spiritual life, the catastrophe comes in a sumptuous and brilliant court festival, in which a richly robed company watch a lavish masque. This luxurious display, celebrating the wealth for which the characters have sold their humanity, suddenly splits apart to reveal death behind the hollow disguise. The familiar mythological figures and emblems of the masque suddenly recover their original literal reality: Danae's golden shower really burns to death, Cupid's arrows actually kill. The dramatist presents through a fantastic theatre form an exactly appropriate judgement of each punished character: the tired metaphors of classical myth are renewed by being made actual, so paradoxically affirming the supremacy of the moral and spiritual. The grotesque trick of the contrived killings is not simply ludicrous but also a fit medium to annihilate the perversity and inhumanity that has raged; the public outcry on stage from the society witnessing the events causes us, another audience, to reconsider at a distance what has hitherto absorbed us. The masque shows what, morally, the characters have become, and an audience, shocked by the sudden horror, also recognises that a fierce affirmation is being expressed.

In *'Tis Pity*, too, we can see poetic imagery, having become over-familiar, being made new by being given literal force. Giovanni expresses himself in the metaphorical language of the love sonnet, but intends literally to act out the hyperbolic trajectory of absolute commitment to love. He expresses his love like an old-fashioned Elizabethan sonneteer of the 1580s or like Shakespeare's Romeo, but with an important difference: however much it may contradict social and doctrinal norms, he insists that his love, though incestuous, is overpowering and therefore cannot be unnatural. The love sonnet-teer's narcissism, Ford would imply, is analogous to incest: for he makes his beloved only the occasion for thinking about himself, her image adored as it reflects himself, his union with her a transcendent duplication of himself. As a treatment of love poetry and love tragedy the play is thus highly self-conscious, its allusiveness ironic and pointed. Ford gives the lovers the persuasiveness of youth and romantic idealism, they affirm joyous fulfilment, but the love they feel is incestuous. An audience is thus confronted with a dilemma, since it cannot readily reconcile itself to incest as beautiful, true and good. Such treatment of an audience first awakens their unthinking stock responses and then confuses and reverses them. Giovanni, at the end, despairing and driven mad by isolation and fear of persecution, fulfils his oath to the letter, and confronts his family and society with his sister's heart, torn out and spitted on the point of his dagger. From the outside, from a public conventional perspective, brother and sister appear surrealistically perverse and absurd; from within, from the privileged intimate perspective which the play affords us, Giovanni and Annabella can be sympathised with, and we may believe them honest and true to their lonely faith. From one point of view they are guilty of crime and sinful, from another an audience can recognise that the questions they fearlessly raise are not answered.

Giovanni's act confirms him as unnatural in the shocked eyes of society, but it is a society that has refused to listen to him, and has imposed psychological exile and finally madness on him. Literary metaphors of love are acceptable to society, but on the strict assumption that they are not to be confused with real life. An Elizabethan sonnet image, the central emblem of lyric tragedy, thus to be presented literally! To live by the idealising hyperboles of love poetry in the world, turning life into art, means madness and death. Giovanni and his sister cannot and will not conform to the ground rules. They have too much heart, we might say, following Ford's own cruel but serious punning.

In an important respect Ford's play can be thought of as inverting the structure of *Women Beware Women*, for Middleton's achievement is that, while depicting human personality and behaviour with such precision and analytic insight that we think of his plays almost as a form of psychological experimentation, nevertheless his conclusion is the very reverse of Ford's; for Middleton makes apparent in a character's deepest being, irreversible changes which are without doubt evil, and are so recognised by the characters themselves. Livia and Isabella are presented with subtle and detailed attention to the ripples of feeling and the cross-currents of reaction they experience from moment to moment; analysis of the play's dialogue will show how important rhythm and tone are in registering small shifts and adjustments whereby a character chooses to accommodate others, as well as when an obviously distressing or hostile manner is deliberately prolonged. These women have powerful emotions which they have no intention of suppressing; their wilfulness is an act of bold self-assertion; they are interesting not only because they are intelligent and articulate but because they have the strength to know their own natures. They cannot act other than sinfully but they will not flinch finally from recognising what they have become. Their emotional honesty is morally admirable, however damnable their behaviour may be. Isabella's tragic stature is undoubtedly equal in depth to, though distinctly unlike, that of a male tragic hero. She is seen with the piercing, clear, yet dispassionate art that is uniquely Middleton's in the drama of the age.

*   *   *

In this introduction there has been space to touch upon only a few of the issues explored in the plays, and many more topics remain for the reader to discover and study for himself: especially the dramatic poetry. Each play is a major work of art that repays study in isolation, but they share many structural and stylistic features, and to begin to compare and contrast them is to be drawn at once into an imaginatively and intellectually absorbing experience.

BRIAN GIBBONS

The Spanish Tragedy

THOMAS KYD

Edited by

J. R. MULRYNE

ABBREVIATIONS

1592   the octavo-in-fours edition of *The Spanish Tragedy* printed in that year.

1594   the octavo-in-fours of that year.

1602   the quarto of that year.

Barish   Jonas A. Barish, 'The Spanish Tragedy, or The Pleasures and Perils of Rhetoric', in *Elizabethan Theatre*, Stratford-upon-Avon Studies 9, ed. Harris, London, 1966, pp. 59-86.

Boas   *Works of Thomas Kyd*, Oxford, 1901.

Bowers   Fredson T. Bowers, *Elizabethan Revenge Tragedy*, Princeton, 1940.

Cairncross   Andrew S. Cairncross ed., *The First Part of Hieronimo and The Spanish Tragedy* (Regents Renaissance Drama Series), London, 1967.

Clemen   Wolfgang Clemen, *English Tragedy before Shakespeare*, London, 1967.

Edwards   Philip Edwards ed., *The Spanish Tragedy* (The Revels Plays), London, 1959.

Freeman   Arthur Freeman, *Thomas Kyd: Facts and Problems*, Oxford, 1967.

Johnson   S. F. Johnson, 'The Spanish Tragedy, or Babylon Revisited'.

Joseph   Bertram Joseph ed., *The Spanish Tragedy* (The New Mermaids), London, 1964.

McIlwraith   A. K. McIlwraith ed., *Five Elizabethan Tragedies* (The World's Classics), Oxford, 1938.

Schick   J. Schick ed., *The Spanish Tragedy* (The Temple Dramatists), London, 1898.

2

THE

SPANISH TRAGE-

die, Containing the lamentable
end of *Don Horatio*, and *Bel-imperia*:
with the pittifull death of
olde *Hieronimo*.

Newly corrected and amended of such grosse faults as
passed in the first impression.

AT LONDON
Printed by *Edward Allde*, for
Edward White.

[DRAMATIS PERSONAE

GHOST OF ANDREA
REVENGE
KING OF SPAIN
CYPRIAN, DUKE OF CASTILE, *his brother*
LORENZO, *the Duke's son*
BEL-IMPERIA, *Lorenzo's sister*
GENERAL *of the Spanish Army*

VICEROY OF PORTUGAL
PEDRO, *his brother*
BALTHAZAR, *his son*
ALEXANDRO ⎫
VILLUPPO ⎬ *Portuguese noblemen*
AMBASSADOR *of Portugal*

HIERONIMO, *Knight Marshal of Spain*
ISABELLA, *his wife*
HORATIO, *their son*

PEDRINGANO, *servant to Bel-imperia*
SERBERINE, *servant to Balthazar*
CHRISTOPHIL, *servant to Lorenzo*
BAZULTO, *an old man*

Page *to Lorenzo*, Three Watchmen, Messenger, Deputy, Hangman,
Maid *to Isabella*, Two Portuguese, Servant, Three Citizens, Portuguese Nobles, Soldiers, Officers, Attendants, Halberdiers

Three Knights, Three Kings, a Drummer *in the first Dumb-show*,
Hymen, Two Torch-bearers *in the second Dumb-show*

In the 'Additions':
PEDRO ⎫
JAQUES ⎬ *Hieronimo's servants*
BAZARDO, *a Painter*]

4

THE SPANISH TRAGEDY

Act I, Scene i

Enter the Ghost of ANDREA, *and with him* REVENGE

ANDREA
When this eternal substance of my soul
Did live imprisoned in my wanton flesh,
Each in their function serving other's need,
I was a courtier in the Spanish court.
My name was Don Andrea, my descent,   5
Though not ignoble, yet inferior far
To gracious fortunes of my tender youth:
For there in prime and pride of all my years,
By duteous service and deserving love,
In secret I possessed a worthy dame,   10
Which hight sweet Bel-imperia by name.
But in the harvest of my summer joys
Death's winter nipped the blossoms of my bliss,
Forcing divorce betwixt my love and me.
For in the late conflict with Portingale   15
My valour drew me into danger's mouth,
Till life to death made passage through my wounds.

---

8 *prime* spring-time
8 *pride* the most flourishing condition (*O.E.D.*)
10 *possessed* made love to
11 *hight* was called
13 *nipped* destroyed by frost
14 *divorce* separation
15 *Portingale* Portugal

---

1 ff. These opening lines were often parodied in later Elizabethan plays.
   Edwards quotes Beaumont's *The Knight of the Burning Pestle* (first
   performed 1607), V, i: 'When I was mortal, this my costive corpse/Did
   lap up figs and raisins in the Strand.'
10–11 *In secret . . . by name* The details of this intrigue are never made
   plain, perhaps to avoid an unfavourable estimate of Bel-imperia.
   It is, however, mentioned again at II, i, 45–8, III, x, 54–5 and III,
   xiv, 111-12. Its clandestine nature anticipates the Horatio / Bel-imperia
   relationship, making for one more parallel between Andrea and Horatio.

5

When I was slain, my soul descended straight
To pass the flowing stream of Acheron:
But churlish Charon, only boatman there,   20
Said that my rites of burial not performed,
I might not sit amongst his passengers.
Ere Sol had slept three nights in Thetis' lap
And slaked his smoking chariot in her flood,
By Don Horatio, our Knight Marshal's son,   25
My funerals and obsequies were done.
Then was the ferryman of hell content
To pass me over to the slimy strond,
That leads to fell Avernus' ugly waves:
There, pleasing Cerberus with honeyed speech,   30
I passed the perils of the foremost porch.
Not far from hence, amidst ten thousand souls,
Sat Minos, Aeacus, and Rhadamanth,
To whom no sooner 'gan I make approach,
To crave a passport for my wandering ghost,   35

19 *Acheron* a river of the lower world, identified here with Styx
   where Charon was ferryman
23 *Sol* the sun
23 *Thetis* daughter of Nereus, a Homeric sea-god; here, the sea
24 *slaked* extinguished the flame of
24 *her flood* the sea
28 *strond* shore
29 *fell* cruel, deadly
29 *Avernus* the lake near Puteoli thought to serve as entrance to the
   underworld
30 *Cerberus* the monstrous three-headed dog, guardian of the underworld
31 *porch* place of entry
33 *Minos, Aeacus, Rhadamanth* judges of the underworld
35 *passport* safe-conduct, letters of protection

18 ff. This description of the underworld derives from *Aeneid* book VI,
   though Kyd has altered the details of Vergil's description. For a full
   discussion see Boas, pp. 394-5.
25 *Knight Marshal* a legal official of the English royal household 'who
   had judicial cognizance of transgressions "within the king's house and
   verge", i.e. within a radius of twelve miles from the king's palace'
   (*O.E.D.*, Marshal sb. 6b). Hieronimo's judicial responsibilities are
   insisted upon even before Horatio's murder.

But Minos, in graven leaves of lottery,
Drew forth the manner of my life and death.
'This knight,' quoth he, 'both lived and died in love,
And for his love tried fortune of the wars,
And by war's fortune lost both love and life.'   40
'Why then,' said Aeacus, 'convey him hence,
To walk with lovers in our fields of love,
And spend the course of everlasting time
Under green myrtle trees and cypress shades.'
'No, no,' said Rhadamanth, 'it were not well   45
With loving souls to place a martialist:
He died in war, and must to martial fields,
Where wounded Hector lives in lasting pain,
And Achilles' Myrmidons do scour the plain.'
Then Minos, mildest censor of the three,   50
Made this device to end the difference:
'Send him,' quoth he, 'to our infernal king,
To doom him as best seems his majesty.'
To this effect my passport straight was drawn.
In keeping on my way to Pluto's court,   55
Through dreadful shades of ever-glooming night,
I saw more sights than thousand tongues can tell,
Or pens can write, or mortal hearts can think.
Three ways there were: that on the right-hand side
Was ready way unto the foresaid fields   60
Where lovers live and bloody martialists,
But either sort contained within his bounds.

---

46 *martialist* warrior
49 *Achilles' Myrmidons* followers of the warrior Achilles in Homer;
   killers of Hector (l.48)
49 *scour* range speedily over
50 *censor* judge
52 *infernal* underworld
53 *doom* give judgment on
55 *Pluto* king of the underworld
56 *ever-glooming* always dark and threatening
62 *his* its own

---

36 *graven leaves of lottery* not clear. Lots are drawn in Vergil to settle
   where the dead will spend the after-life, but here it seems that
   Minos is, additionally, reading from some account of Andrea's past.
   Edwards comments: '*Drew forth* (l.37) is best interpreted literally and
   we must suppose that Minos draws from his urn the lottery slip on
   which was engraved the manner of life which Andrea has by now
   fulfilled, i.e., what has been his lot'.

The left-hand path, declining fearfully,
Was ready downfall to the deepest hell,
Where bloody Furies shakes their whips of steel,   65
And poor Ixion turns an endless wheel;
Where usurers are choked with melting gold,
And wantons are embraced with ugly snakes,
And murderers groan with never-killing wounds,
And perjured wights scalded in boiling lead,   70
And all foul sins with torments overwhelmed.
'Twixt these two ways I trod the middle path,
Which brought me to the fair Elysian green,
In midst whereof there stands a stately tower,
The walls of brass, the gates of adamant.   75
Here finding Pluto with his Proserpine,
I showed my passport, humbled on my knee;
Whereat fair Proserpine began to smile,
And begged that only she might give my doom.
Pluto was pleased, and sealed it with a kiss.   80
Forthwith, Revenge, she rounded thee in th'ear,
And bade thee lead me through the gates of horn,
Where dreams have passage in the silent night.

63 *declining* sloping down
64 *downfall* precipice, gulf
65 *Furies* mythical avengers of crime
66 *Ixion* punished on a treadmill for seeking Hera's love
70 *wights* persons
73 *Elysian green* Elysium is the abode of the blessed in the after-life;
     Vergil places it in the underworld
75 *adamant* very hard stone; diamond
76 *Proserpine* the Greek Persephone, consort of Dis (or Pluto),
     queen of the underworld
77 *humbled on my knee* kneeling in humility
79 *doom* sentence
81 *rounded* whispered
82 *horn* ed. (Hor: *1592*)

63–71 Lorenzo and his confederates are doomed to this region of hell at
     the play's end, while Horatio, Bel-imperia and Hieronimo take the
     alternative path (for lovers and martialists). See IV, v, 17 ff.
82 *gates of horn* The gate of horn in *Aeneid* VI (modelled on Homer)
     is the gate through which *true* dreams or visions pass, as against the
     ivory gate of *false* dreams; a prediction that the purposes of Revenge
     will be fulfilled.

No sooner had she spoke but we were here,
I wot not how, in twinkling of an eye. 85

REVENGE
Then know, Andrea, that thou art arrived
Where thou shalt see the author of thy death,
Don Balthazar, the prince of Portingale,
Deprived of life by Bel-imperia.
Here sit we down to see the mystery, 90
And serve for Chorus in this tragedy.

Act I, Scene ii

Enter SPANISH KING, GENERAL, CASTILE, HIERONIMO

KING
Now say, Lord General, how fares our camp?

GENERAL
All well, my sovereign liege, except some few
That are deceased by fortune of the war.

KING
But what portends thy cheerful countenance,
And posting to our presence thus in haste? 5
Speak man, hath fortune given us victory?

GENERAL
Victory, my liege, and that with little loss.

KING
Our Portingals will pay us tribute then?

GENERAL
Tribute and wonted homage therewithal.

KING
Then blest be heaven, and guider of the heavens, 10
From whose fair influence such justice flows.

---

85 *wot* know
90 *mystery* events yet to be revealed, of a special significance
1 *camp* army in the field
5 *posting* speeding
8 *Portingals* Portuguese
8 *tribute* tribute-money

86–9 The audience's knowledge that these events will take place has an
important bearing on their attitude to the action and the characters in the
main play.
1–21 The opening lines of this scene have a calculated air of light
optimism and even complacency: ironic in view of our knowledge
that catastrophe is to follow.

CASTILE

> *O multum dilecte Deo, tibi militat aether,*
> *Et conjuratae curvato poplite gentes*
> *Succumbunt: recti soror est victoria juris.*

KING

Thanks to my loving brother of Castile.   15
But General, unfold in brief discourse
Your form of battle and your war's success,
That adding all the pleasure of thy news
Unto the height of former happiness,
With deeper wage and greater dignity   20
We may reward thy blissful chivalry.

GENERAL

Where Spain and Portingale do jointly knit
Their frontiers, leaning on each other's bound,
There met our armies in their proud array:
Both furnished well, both full of hope and fear,   25
⁓Both menacing alike with daring shows,
Both vaunting sundry colours of device,
Both cheerly sounding trumpets, drums and fifes,
Both raising dreadful clamours to the sky,
That valleys, hills, and rivers made rebound,   30
And heaven itself was frighted with the sound.
Our battles both were pitched in squadron form,

13 *poplite* ed. (*poplito 1592*)
16 *unfold* explain
20 *deeper wage* richer reward
21 *chivalry* skill in arms
23 *bound* boundary
25 *furnished* equipped
27 *vaunting* displaying proudly
27 *colours of device* heraldic banners
32 *battles* forces
32 *squadron form* in a square formation

12–14 'O one much loved of God, for thee the heavens contend, and the united peoples fall down on bended knee: victory is sister to just rights.' Boas indicates the lines are adapted from Claudian's *De Tertio Consulatu Honorii*, 96–8.

22–84 The General's account of the battle (in accordance with Kyd's narrative patterning) expands that of Andrea at I, i, 15 ff., and anticipates both the distorted version by Villuppo (I, iii, 59 ff.) and Horatio's corrective account at I, iv, 9 ff. It serves both as 'good theatre' in the elaborate theatrical vein enjoyed by Elizabethans, and also to establish an unbiased perspective on events from which the rest of the plot springs.

Each corner strongly fenced with wings of shot;
But ere we joined and came to push of pike,
I brought a squadron of our readiest shot   35
From out our rearward to begin the fight:
They brought another wing to encounter us.
Meanwhile, our ordnance played on either side,
And captains strove to have their valours tried.
Don Pedro, their chief horsemen's colonel,   40
Did with his cornet bravely make attempt
To break the order of our battle ranks:
But Don Rogero, worthy man of war,
Marched forth against him with our musketeers,
And stopped the malice of his fell approach.   45
While they maintain hot skirmish to and fro,
Both battles join and fall to handy blows,
Their violent shot resembling th'ocean's rage,
When, roaring loud, and with a swelling tide,
It beats upon the rampiers of huge rocks,   50
And gapes to swallow neighbour-bounding lands.
Now while Bellona rageth here and there,
Thick storms of bullets rain like winter's hail,
And shivered lances dark the troubled air.
         Pede pes et cuspide cuspis;   55
    Arma sonant armis, vir petiturque viro.

33 *fenced* defended, reinforced
33 *wings of shot* soldiers carrying firearms placed on the outer edges
    of the formation
34 *push of pike* hand-to-hand fighting
38 *ordnance* ed. (ordinance *1592*) heavy artillery
38 *played* directed their fire
40 *colonel* ed. (Corlonell *1592*) three syllables
41 *cornet* a squadron of cavalry
45 *malice* danger, harm
47 *handy* hand-to-hand
48 *shot* shooting, exchange of fire (presumably at close quarters)
50 *rampiers* ramparts
51 *neighbour-bounding* neighbouring, on its margin
52 *Bellona* Roman goddess of war
53 *rain* ed. (ran *1592*)   54 *dark* darken
56 *Arma* ed. (*Anni 1592*)   56 *armis* ed. (*annis 1592*)

55–6 'Foot against foot and spear against spear, arms ring on arms and
    man is assailed by man.' Boas says the Latin is taken partly from
    Statius (*Thebais*, viii. 399) and, quoting Schick, partly structured on
    analogies in Vergil and Curtius.

On every side drop captains to the ground,
And soldiers, some ill-maimed, some slain outright:
Here falls a body scindered from his head,
There legs and arms lie bleeding on the grass,   60
Mingled with weapons and unbowelled steeds,
That scattering overspread the purple plain.
In all this turmoil, three long hours and more,
The victory to neither part inclined,
Till Don Andrea with his brave lanciers   65
In their main battle made so great a breach
That, half dismayed, the multitude retired:
But Balthazar, the Portingales' young prince,
Brought rescue, and encouraged them to stay.
Here-hence the fight was eagerly renewed,   70
And in that conflict was Andrea slain—
Brave man at arms, but weak to Balthazar.
Yet while the prince, insulting over him,
Breathed out proud vaunts, sounding to our reproach,
Friendship and hardy valour joined in one   75
Pricked forth Horatio, our Knight Marshal's son,
To challenge forth that prince in single fight.
Not long between these twain the fight endured,
But straight the prince was beaten from his horse,
And forced to yield him prisoner to his foe: 80
When he was taken, all the rest they fled,
And our carbines pursued them to the death,

---

58 *ill-maimed* badly injured
59 *scindered* sundered
62 *purple* blood-red, covered in blood
65 *lanciers* (two syllables) lancers
70 *Here-hence* as a result of this (*O.E.D.*, 1)
72 *man at arms* specifically, a mounted soldier
73 *insulting* exulting
74 *sounding to* tending to, inferring (*O.E.D.*, 5a)
76 *Pricked forth* spurred on
80 *him* himself
82 *carbines* presumably soldiers carrying these weapons (*O.E.D.* has no example)

---

72 A reminiscence, in keeping with the heroic manner of these lines, of references to defeated warriors in Homer.

Till, Phoebus waning to the western deep,
Our trumpeters were charged to sound retreat.

KING

Thanks good Lord General for these good news;   85
And for some argument of more to come,
Take this and wear it for thy sovereign's sake.

Give him his chain

But tell me now, hast thou confirmed a peace?

GENERAL

No peace, my liege, but peace conditional,
That if with homage tribute be well paid,   90
The fury of your forces will be stayed:
And to this peace their viceroy hath subscribed,

Give the KING *a paper*

And made a solemn vow that, during life,
His tribute shall be truly paid to Spain.

KING

These words, these deeds, become thy person well.   95
But now, Knight Marshal, frolic with thy king,
For 'tis thy son that wins this battle's prize.

HIERONIMO

Long may he live to serve my sovereign liege,
And soon decay unless he serve my liege.

A tucket afar off

KING

Nor thou, nor he, shall die without reward.   100
What means the warning of this trumpet's sound?

GENERAL

This tells me that your grace's men of war,
Such as war's fortune hath reserved from death,
Come marching on towards your royal seat,
To show themselves before your majesty,   105
For so I gave in charge at my depart.
Whereby by demonstration shall appear,

83   *Phoebus* the sun
83   *waning* ed. (wauing *1592*)
83   *deep* the sea
86   *argument* token
89   *but* except
91   *stayed* restrained, halted
92   *subscribed* signed his name
96   *frolic* rejoice, be happy
99   *decay* fail in health and fortune
101 *the* ed. (this *1592*)

That all (except three hundred or few more)
Are safe returned and by their foes enriched.

The Army enters; BALTHAZAR, *between* LORENZO *and* HORATIO,
captive

KING
A gladsome sight! I long to see them here.   110
They enter and pass by
Was that the warlike prince of Portingale,
That by our nephew was in triumph led?
GENERAL
It was, my liege, the prince of Portingale.
KING
But what was he that on the other side
Held him by th'arm as partner of the prize?   115
HIERONIMO
That was my son, my gracious sovereign,
Of whom, though from his tender infancy
My loving thoughts did never hope but well,
He never pleased his father's eyes till now,
Nor filled my heart with overcloying joys.   120
KING
Go let them march once more about these walls,
That staying them we may confer and talk
With our brave prisoner and his double guard.
Hieronimo, it greatly pleaseth us,
That in our victory thou have a share,   125
By virtue of thy worthy son's exploit.
Enter [the Army] again
Bring hither the young prince of Portingale:
The rest march on, but ere they be dismissed,

120 *overcloying* causing surfeit, satiating
122 *staying* stopping

---

108 This calm writing-off of 300 men perhaps underlines what we know
to be the false complacency of the Spanish court. Compare the opening
speeches of *Much Ado.*
109 s.d. The double entry of the army (here and after 1.126) complements
the high verbal flourish of the General's speech and extends the air of
martial grandeur and confidence; it also permits the theatrical display
so dear to Elizabethans.
111 ff. Kyd's very strong sense of dramatic structure brings the three principal antagonists together at their first entry; the later enmity between
Lorenzo and Horatio is visually suggested by each laying claim to the
prisoner Balthazar.

　　We will bestow on every soldier
　　Two ducats, and on every leader ten,   130
　　That they may know our largess welcomes them.
　　　　Exeunt all [the Army] but BALTHAZAR, LORENZO, HORATIO
　　Welcome, Don Balthazar, welcome, nephew,
　　And thou, Horatio, thou art welcome too.
　　Young prince, although thy father's hard misdeeds,
　　In keeping back the tribute that he owes,   135
　　Deserve but evil measure at our hands,
　　Yet shalt thou know that Spain is honourable.

BALTHAZAR
　　The trespass that my father made in peace
　　Is now controlled by fortune of the wars;
　　And cards once dealt, it boots not ask why so.   140
　　His men are slain, a weakening to his realm,
　　His colours seized, a blot unto his name,
　　His son distressed, a corsive to his heart:
　　These punishments may clear his late offence.

KING
　　Ay, Balthazar, if he observe this truce,   145
　　Our peace will grow the stronger for these wars.
　　Meanwhile live thou, though not in liberty,
　　Yet free from bearing any servile yoke;
　　For in our hearing thy deserts were great,
　　And in our sight thyself art gracious.   150

BALTHAZAR
　　And I shall study to deserve this grace.

KING
　　But tell me, for their holding makes me doubt,
　　To which of these twain art thou prisoner?

129–31 (lineation ed. We . . . ducats / And . . . know / Our . . them
　　1592)
131 *largess* money and gifts bestowed by a king
139 *controlled* brought to an end
140 *boots* profits　　　　142 *colours* standards, flags
143 *distressed* taken prisoner
143 *corsive* corrosive (a destructive substance)
144 *clear* erase　　　　144 *late* previous, past
152 *their holding* the way they hold you

152 ff. Clemen (p. 101) points out that the scene from this point corre-
　　sponds to the familiar Elizabethan 'tribunal scene' in which a dispute
　　between two nobles is arbitrated by the king. (Compare e.g. *Richard II*,
　　I, i.) Kyd's handling of this conventional situation is much more
　　flexible dramatically than that of his predecessors.

LORENZO
    To me, my liege.
HORATIO   To me, my sovereign.
LORENZO
    This hand first took his courser by the reins.   155
HORATIO
    But first my lance did put him from his horse.
LORENZO
    I seized his weapon, and enjoyed it first.
HORATIO
    But first I forced him lay his weapons down.
KING
    Let go his arm, upon our privilege.   [*They*] *let him go*
    Say, worthy prince, to whether didst thou yield?   160
BALTHAZAR
    To him in courtesy, to this perforce:
    He spake me fair, this other gave me strokes;
    He promised life, this other threatened death;
    He wan my love, this other conquered me;
    And truth to say I yield myself to both.   165
HIERONIMO
    But that I know your grace for just and wise.
    And might seem partial in this difference,
    Enforced by nature and by law of arms
    My tongue should plead for young Horatio's right.
    He hunted well that was a lion's death,   170
    Not he that in a garment wore his skin:
    So hares may pull dead lions by the beard.
KING
    Content thee, Marshal, thou shalt have no wrong;
    And for thy sake thy son shall want no right.
    Will both abide the censure of my doom?   175
LORENZO
    I crave no better than your grace awards.

159 *privilege* the king's prerogative
160 *whether* which of the two
164 *wan* won
167 *partial* guilty of favouritism
175 *censure of my doom* the outcome of my judgment

170–2 Hieronimo argues that Horatio deserves credit as the true con-
    queror of Balthazar. The reference in l.171 derives, as Edwards shows,
    from the Fourth Fable of Avian concerning an ass who disports him-
    self in a lion's skin he has found. Line 172 is proverbial; even timid hares
    may beard a *dead* lion.

HORATIO
　Nor I, although I sit beside my right.

KING
　Then by my judgment thus your strife shall end:
　You both deserve and both shall have reward.
　Nephew, thou took'st his weapon and his horse,　　　180
　His weapons and his horse are thy reward.
　Horatio, thou didst force him first to yield,
　His ransom therefore is thy valour's fee:
　Appoint the sum as you shall both agree.
　But nephew, thou shalt have the prince in guard,　　185
　For thine estate best fitteth such a guest:
　Horatio's house were small for all his train.
　Yet in regard thy substance passeth his,
　And that just guerdon may befall desert,
　To him we yield the armour of the prince.　　　　　190
　How likes Don Balthazar of this device?

BALTHAZAR
　Right well my liege, if this proviso were,
　That Don Horatio bear us company,
　Whom I admire and love for chivalry.

KING
　Horatio, leave him not that loves thee so.　　　　195
　Now let us hence to see our soldiers paid,
　And feast our prisoner as our friendly guest.　　　*Exeunt*

Act I, Scene iii

Enter VICEROY, ALEXANDRO, VILLUPPO [, *Attendants*]

VICEROY
　Is our ambassador despatched for Spain?

ALEXANDRO
　Two days, my liege, are passed since his depart.

VICEROY
　And tribute payment gone along with him?

177　*sit beside* forgo (Edwards)　　　188　*in regard* since
189　*that* in order that
189　*guerdon* reward
190　*him* Horatio

187　Horatio's social standing (like Hieronimo's) is emphatically lower
　　than that of Lorenzo and Bel-imperia (and of course Balthazar).
　　See also II, iv, 61 and III, x, 57.

ALEXANDRO

Ay my good lord.

VICEROY

Then rest we here awhile in our unrest,   5
And feed our sorrows with some inward sighs,
For deepest cares break never into tears.
But wherefore sit I in a regal throne?
This better fits a wretch's endless moan.

Falls to the ground

Yet this is higher than my fortunes reach,   10
And therefore better than my state deserves.
Ay, ay, this earth, image of melancholy,
Seeks him whom fates adjudge to misery:
Here let me lie, now am I at the lowest.
  Qui jacet in terra, non habet unde cadat.   15
  In me consumpsit vires fortuna nocendo,
  Nil superest ut jam possit obesse magis.
Yes, Fortune may bereave me of my crown:
Here, take it now; let Fortune do her worst,
She will not rob me of this sable weed: 20
O no, she envies none but pleasant things.
Such is the folly of despiteful chance!
Fortune is blind and sees not my deserts,
So is she deaf and hears not my laments:

9 s.d. follows l.11 in *1592*
10 'My circumstances are even worse than this suggests.'
11 *state* condition, situation
20 *sable weed* black costume
21 *envies* feels ill-will towards
22 *despiteful* malicious

5 ff. The Viceroy's speech contrasts with the self-congratulation of the
  Spanish King, and anticipates Hieronimo's similar grief over the loss
  of a son. Clemen (p. 269) draws attention to Kyd's dramatically-alert
  transformation in these lines of the standard 'lament speech'. Compare
  the King's lines in *Richard II*, III, ii, 144 ff.
12 *image of melancholy* Melancholy is the bodily 'humour' (responsible for a
  person's temperament) that corresponds to the element earth, one of
  the four elements (the others are air, fire and water) that make up all
  created things.
15–17 'If one lies on the ground, one has no further to fall. Towards me
  Fortune has exhausted her power to injure; there is nothing further
  that can happen to me.' The first line is borrowed from Alanus de
  Insulis, *Lib. Parab.*, cap. 2, l.19, the second from Seneca's *Agamemnon*
  l.698, while the third is probably Kyd's own composition. (See W. P.
  Mustard, *PQ*, V (1926), 85–6.)

And could she hear, yet is she wilful mad,　　　　25
And therefore will not pity my distress.
Suppose that she could pity me, what then?
What help can be expected at her hands,
Whose foot is standing on a rolling stone,
And mind more mutable than fickle winds?　　　　30
Why wail I then, where's hope of no redress?
O yes, complaining makes my grief seem less.
My late ambition hath distained my faith,
My breach of faith occasioned bloody wars,
Those bloody wars have spent my treasure,　　　35
And with my treasure my people's blood,
And with their blood, my joy and best beloved,
My best beloved, my sweet and only son.
O wherefore went I not to war myself?
The cause was mine, I might have died for both:　40
My years were mellow, his but young and green,
My death were natural, but his was forced.

ALEXANDRO
No doubt, my liege, but still the prince survives.

VICEROY
Survives! ay, where?

ALEXANDRO
In Spain, a prisoner by mischance of war.　　　45

VICEROY
Then they have slain him for his father's fault.

ALEXANDRO
That were a breach to common law of arms.

---

25 *wilful mad* deliberately closed to reason
29 *is* ed. (*not in 1592*)
30 *mutable* ever-changing
33 *distained* sullied
35, 36 *treasure* Edwards says tri-syllabic: 'treas-u-er'
42 *forced* against the course of nature
46 *fault* crime, wrongdoing

23–30 In the emblem books, Fortune is normally depicted as blind,
sometimes as deaf, and frequently as standing on a rolling sphere;
all to express her lack of discrimination and changeableness. The
Viceroy's complaint of Fortune contributes to the play's preoccupation
with justice and retribution. Lines 33–42 are the Viceroy's attempt to
construct a rational (and therefore 'just') explanation for what has
happened, and so to rationalise Fortune.

VICEROY
They reck no laws that meditate revenge.
ALEXANDRO
His ransom's worth will stay from foul revenge.
VICEROY
No, if he lived the news would soon be here.   50
ALEXANDRO
Nay, evil news fly faster still than good.
VICEROY
Tell me no more of news, for he is dead.
VILLUPPO
My sovereign, pardon the author of ill news,
And I'll bewray the fortune of thy son.
VICEROY
Speak on, I'll guerdon thee whate'er it be: 55
Mine ear is ready to receive ill news,
My heart grown hard 'gainst mischief's battery;
Stand up I say, and tell thy tale at large.
VILLUPPO
Then hear that truth which these mine eyes have seen.
When both the armies were in battle joined,   60
Don Balthazar, amidst the thickest troops,
To win renown did wondrous feats of arms:
Amongst the rest I saw him hand to hand
In single fight with their Lord General;
Till Alexandro, that here counterfeits   65
Under the colour of a duteous friend,
Discharged his pistol at the prince's back,
As though he would have slain their general.
But therewithal Don Balthazar fell down,
And when he fell, then we began to fly: 70
But had he lived, the day had sure been ours.

---

48 *reck* heed
49 *stay* restrain
53 *author* one who transmits; or one who lends his authority to,
   vouches for
54 *bewray* reveal
55 *guerdon* reward
57 *mischief* misfortune
66 *colour* pretence

---

48 That revenge was by nature lawless was the accepted Elizabethan
   attitude (see Bowers, esp. pp. 3-14).

ALEXANDRO
O wicked forgery! O traitorous miscreant!
VICEROY
Hold thou thy peace! But now, Villuppo, say,
Where then became the carcase of my son?
VILLUPPO
I saw them drag it to the Spanish tents.   75
VICEROY
Ay, ay, my nightly dreams have told me this.
Thou false, unkind, unthankful, traitorous beast,
Wherein had Balthazar offended thee,
That thou shouldst thus betray him to our foes?
Was't Spanish gold that bleared so thine eyes   80
That thou couldst see no part of our deserts?
Perchance because thou art Terceira's lord,
Thou hadst some hope to wear this diadem,
If first my son and then myself were slain:
But thy ambitious thought shall break thy neck.   85
Ay, this was it that made thee spill his blood,
                    Take the crown and put it on again
But I'll now wear it till thy blood be spilt.
ALEXANDRO
Vouchsafe, dread sovereign, to hear me speak.
VICEROY
Away with him, his sight is second hell;
Keep him till we determine of his death.   90
                    [*Exeunt Attendants with* ALEXANDRO]
If Balthazar be dead, he shall not live.
Villuppo, follow us for thy reward.   *Exit* VICEROY
VILLUPPO
Thus have I with an envious, forged tale

---

72 *forgery* falsehood, fabrication
72 *miscreant* villain, rascal
83 *diadem* ed. (Diadome *1592*)
93 *envious* malicious

---

82 *Terceira's lord* Boas says that Alexandro was apparently *Capitão
    Donatario* of Terceira, an island in the Azores group, and would
    because of this position enjoy virtually despotic powers. The title was
    given to the first discoverers and colonisers of overseas territories and
    was hereditary.
93–5 The villain's explicit confession seems awkward to modern readers;
    it remained a convention widely acceptable in the Elizabethan theatre.
    Compare e.g. Flamineo in *The White Devil*, IV, ii, 242–6.

Deceived the king, betrayed mine enemy,
And hope for guerdon of my villainy.   *Exit*   95

Act I, Scene iv

Enter HORATIO *and* BEL-IMPERIA

BEL-IMPERIA
Signior Horatio, this is the place and hour
Wherein I must entreat thee to relate
The circumstance of Don Andrea's death,
Who, living, was my garland's sweetest flower,
And in his death hath buried my delights.   5
HORATIO
For love of him and service to yourself,
I nill refuse this heavy doleful charge.
Yet tears and sighs, I fear will hinder me.
When both our armies were enjoined in fight,
Your worthy chevalier amidst the thick'st,   10
For glorious cause still aiming at the fairest,
Was at the last by young Don Balthazar
Encountered hand to hand: their fight was long,
Their hearts were great, their clamours menacing,
Their strength alike, their strokes both dangerous.   15
But wrathful Nemesis, that wicked power,
Envying at Andrea's praise and worth,
Cut short his life, to end his praise and worth.
She, she herself, disguised in armour's mask,

---

7 *nill* will not
9 *enjoined* joined
10 *chevalier* a lady's cavalier or gallant
16 *Nemesis* the goddess of retribution, especially exercised by the gods
   against human presumption
17 *Envying at* regarding with ill-will

6–43 Horatio's account of the battle gives the personal angle, as against
   the General's more objective description. Contrast the emotionalism
   of many lines in this speech with the General's technicalities (esp.
   I, ii, 32 ff.).
11 'always aiming at the most outstanding achievements in honour of his
   glorious cause' (the love for Bel-imperia that inspired him).
19–20 Kyd probably refers to *Aeneid*, II, ll.615–16, as Boas suggests, but
   though Pallas (Athene) is there mentioned, it is Juno who is 'ferro
   accincta', 'girt with steel'.

(As Pallas was before proud Pergamus)   20
Brought in a fresh supply of halberdiers,
Which paunched his horse, and dinged him to the ground.
Then young Don Balthazar with ruthless rage,
Taking advantage of his foe's distress,
Did finish what his halberdiers begun,   25
And left not till Andrea's life was done.
Then, though too late, incensed with just remorse,
I with my band set forth against the prince,
And brought him prisoner from his halberdiers.

BEL-IMPERIA
Would thou hadst slain him that so slew my love.   30
But then was Don Andrea's carcase lost?

HORATIO
No, that was it for which I chiefly strove,
Nor stepped I back till I recovered him:
I took him up, and wound him in mine arms,
And welding him unto my private tent,   35
There laid him down, and dewed him with my tears,
And sighed and sorrowed as became a friend,
But neither friendly sorrow, sighs nor tears
Could win pale Death from his usurpéd right.
Yet this I did, and less I could not do: 40
I saw him honoured with due funeral.

---

20 *Pallas* Athene, patroness of Athens, and one of the divinities
   associated with the Greeks at Troy
20 *Pergamus* Troy
21 *halberdiers* soldiers carrying halberds, weapons that are a com-
   bination of spear and battle-axe, the head being mounted on a
   long pole
22 *paunched* stabbed in the belly
22 *dinged* thrust, struck
27 *just remorse* righteous indignation and pity
34 *wound* embraced
35 *welding* carrying

21–6 Andrea is overwhelmed by superior numbers, not killed in fair
   combat (see Bel-imperia's comment, ll.73–5). *I Hieronimo* also lays
   stress on the dishonourable way Balthazar brought about Andrea's
   death (scene xi; and see Cairncross, pp. xviii and 49).

This scarf I plucked from off his lifeless arm,
And wear it in remembrance of my friend.

BEL-IMPERIA

I know the scarf, would he had kept it still,
For had he lived he would have kept it still,   45
And worn it for his Bel-imperia's sake:
For 'twas my favour at his last depart.
But now wear thou it both for him and me,
For after him thou hast deserved it best.
But, for thy kindness in his life and death,   50
Be sure while Bel-imperia's life endures,
She will be Don Horatio's thankful friend.

HORATIO

And, madam, Don Horatio will not slack
Humbly to serve fair Bel-imperia.
But now, if your good liking stand thereto,   55
I'll crave your pardon to go seek the prince,
For so the duke your father gave me charge.   *Exit*

BEL-IMPERIA

Ay, go Horatio, leave me here alone,
For solitude best fits my cheerless mood.
Yet what avails to wail Andrea's death,   60
From whence Horatio proves my second love?
Had he not loved Andrea as he did,
He could not sit in Bel-imperia's thoughts.
But how can love find harbour in my breast,
Till I revenge the death of my beloved?   65

---

42 *lifeless* ed. (liveless *1592*)
47 *favour* a gift given to a lover to be worn as a token of affection

---

42 *This scarf* 'Scarves' or 'handkerchers' and sometimes gloves were
worn as ladies' favours (see 1.47) by knights on the battlefield (compare
the 'pledges' Troilus and Cressida exchange: see *TC*, IV, iv and V, ii).
When Horatio wears the scarf (see ll.48, 49) he becomes visually
Andrea's representative; if this scarf is the 'bloody handkercher' that
Hieronimo takes from the dead Horatio's body (see II, v, 51 and III,
xiii, 86–9) then it also serves as a visual link between the twin revenges,
for Andrea and Horatio.

60–8 Bel-imperia's love for Horatio may strike us as sudden, unmotiv-
ated and even (ll.66–8) unpleasantly mixed with calculation. Partly
this is a matter of dramatic convention (the early plays were not greatly
concerned with psychological probability) and partly an item in Kyd's
developing portrait of Bel-imperia as a formidable woman, decisively
able to control and direct her emotions. Her decision is also of course
vital in joining the two revenges.

Yes, second love shall further my revenge.
I'll love Horatio, my Andrea's friend,
The more to spite the prince that wrought his end.
And where Don Balthazar, that slew my love,
Himself now pleads for favour at my hands,   70
He shall in rigour of my just disdain
Reap long repentance for his murderous deed.
For what was't else but murderous cowardice,
So many to oppress one valiant knight,
Without respect of honour in the fight?   75
And here he comes that murdered my delight.

Enter LORENZO *and* BALTHAZAR

LORENZO
Sister, what means this melancholy walk?
BEL-IMPERIA
That for a while I wish no company.
LORENZO
But here the prince is come to visit you.
BEL-IMPERIA
That argues that he lives in liberty.   80
BALTHAZAR
No madam, but in pleasing servitude.
BEL-IMPERIA
Your prison then belike is your conceit.
BALTHAZAR
Ay, by conceit my freedom is enthralled.
BEL-IMPERIA
Then with conceit enlarge yourself again.
BALTHAZAR
What if conceit have laid my heart to gage?   85
BEL-IMPERIA
Pay that you borrowed and recover it.

71 *disdain* indignation (*O.E.D.*, **sb. 2**)
74 *oppress* overwhelm with numbers (*O.E.D.*, **1b**)
82 *conceit* fancy, imagination
83 *enthralled* enslaved
84 *enlarge* set free
85 *laid . . . to gage* given as a pledge, placed in pawn

77–89 This stichomythia or line-by-line dialogue is a dramatic convention
   deriving from Seneca.

BALTHAZAR
I die if it return from whence it lies.
BEL-IMPERIA
A heartless man, and live? A miracle!
BALTHAZAR
Ay lady, love can work such miracles.
LORENZO
Tush, tush, my lord, let go these ambages,   90
And in plain terms acquaint her with your love.
BEL-IMPERIA
What boots complaint, when there's no remedy?
BALTHAZAR
Yes, to your gracious self must I complain,
In whose fair answer lies my remedy,
On whose perfection all my thoughts attend,   95
On whose aspect mine eyes find beauty's bower,
In whose translucent breast my heart is lodged.
BEL-IMPERIA
Alas, my lord, these are but words of course,
And but device to drive me from this place.
She, in going in, lets fall her glove, which HORATIO, *coming out,*
                              takes up
HORATIO
Madam, your glove.   100
BEL-IMPERIA
Thanks good Horatio, take it for thy pains.
BALTHAZAR
Signior Horatio stooped in happy time.
HORATIO
I reaped more grace than I deserved or hoped.
LORENZO
My Lord, be not dismayed for what is passed,

---

90 *ambages* oblique, roundabout ways of speaking
92 *What boots complaint* What point is there in pleading your love?
96 *aspect* form, appearance
98 *words of course* conventional phrases
99 *device* ed. (deuise *1592*)

---

99 s.d. This rather awkward piece of stage-action may be intended to
   underline the part accident plays in the linked process of 'revenge'.
   Compare the direction 'a letter falleth' (III, ii, 23) and the letter written
   by Pedringano which finds its way by chance into Hieronimo's hands at
   III, vii, 19 ff.

You know that women oft are humorous;   105
These clouds will overblow with little wind;
Let me alone, I'll scatter them myself.
Meanwhile let us devise to spend the time
In some delightful sports and revelling.

HORATIO
The king, my lords, is coming hither straight,   110
To feast the Portingale ambassador:
Things were in readiness before I came.

BALTHAZAR
Then here it fits us to attend the king,
To welcome hither our ambassador,
And learn my father and my country's health.   115

Enter the Banquet, Trumpets, *the* KING, *and* AMBASSADOR

KING
See Lord Ambassador, how Spain entreats
Their prisoner Balthazar, thy viceroy's son:
We pleasure more in kindness than in wars.

AMBASSADOR
Sad is our king, and Portingale laments,
Supposing that Don Balthazar is slain.   120

BALTHAZAR
[*Aside*] So am I slain by beauty's tyranny.
[*To him*] You see, my lord, how Balthazar is slain:
I frolic with the Duke of Castile's son,
Wrapped every hour in pleasures of the court,
And graced with favours of his majesty.   125

KING
Put off your greetings till our feast be done;
Now come and sit with us and taste our cheer.
                         [*They*] *sit to the banquet*
Sit down young prince, you are our second guest;
Brother sit down and nephew take your place;

105 *humorous* temperamental
113 *fits* befits
118 *pleasure* take pleasure

---

115 s.d. *the Banquet, Trumpets* another opportunity for display, underlining
     the proud, self-confident society of the Spanish court. A full-scale
     occasion is evidently intended (not just a buffet-type banquet often
     used on the Elizabethan stage) for they 'sit to the banquet' (l.127 s.d.)
     and remain seated to watch Hieronimo's entertainment.
121 This aside hints the trouble that is breeding under the surface appear-
     ance of order.

Signior Horatio, wait thou upon our cup,   130
For well thou hast deservéd to be honoured.
Now, lordings, fall to; Spain is Portugal,
And Portugal is Spain, we both are friends,
Tribute is paid, and we enjoy our right.
But where is old Hieronimo, our marshal?   135
He promised us, in honour of our guest,
To grace our banquet with some pompous jest.

Enter HIERONIMO *with a* Drum, *three* KNIGHTS, *each* [*with*] *his*
scutcheon: then he fetches three KINGS, [*the* KNIGHTS] *take their*
crowns and them captive

Hieronimo, this masque contents mine eye,
Although I sound not well the mystery.
HIERONIMO
The first armed knight, that hung his scutcheon up,   140
     He takes the scutcheon and gives it to the KING
Was English Robert, Earl of Gioucester,
Who when King Stephen bore sway in Albion,
Arrived with five and twenty thousand men
In Portingale, and by success of war
Enforced the king, then but a Saracen,   145
To bear the yoke of the English monarchy.
KING
My lord of Portingale, by this you see
That which may comfort both your king and you,
And make your late discomfort seem the less.
But say, Hieronimo, what was the next?   150
HIERONIMO
The second knight, that hung his scutcheon up,
     He doth as he did before

137 *pompous jest* stately entertainment
137 s.d. *Drum* a drummer
137 s.d. *scutcheon* shield with armorial bearings
139 *sound* understand, fathom
139 *mystery* significance, hidden meaning
142 *Albion* England

135 ff. Hieronimo's entertainment appeals to English patriotism at a moment
(the 1580s or very early 90s) when Spain was the arch-enemy; theatre-
goers would have expected some patriotic flourish. The history is
popular rather than academic; for a full discussion of Kyd's sources
and of his errors concerning the earls of Gloucester and Kent and the
duke of Lancaster see Boas, pp. 397–8, Edwards, p. 26 fn. and Freeman,
pp. 55 ff.

Was Edmund, Earl of Kent in Albion,
When English Richard wore the diadem;
He came likewise, and razed Lisbon walls,
And took the King of Portingale in fight: 155
For which, and other suchlike service done,
He after was created Duke of York.

KING

This is another special argument,
That Portingale may deign to bear our yoke,
When it by little England hath been yoked.   160
But now Hieronimo, what were the last?

HIERONIMO

The third and last, not least in our account,
                                    Doing as before

Was as the rest a valiant Englishman,
Brave John of Gaunt, the Duke of Lancaster,
As by his scutcheon plainly may appear.   165
He with a puissant army came to Spain,
And took our King of Castile prisoner.

AMBASSADOR

This is an argument for our viceroy,
That Spain may not insult for her success,
Since English warriors likewise conquered Spain,   170
And made them bow their knees to Albion.

KING

Hieronimo, I drink to thee for this device,
Which hath pleased both the ambassador and me;
Pledge me Hieronimo, if thou love the king.
                          Takes the cup of HORATIO
My lord, I fear we sit but over-long,   175
Unless our dainties were more delicate:
But welcome are you to the best we have.
Now let us in, that you may be despatched,
I think our council is already set.
                                    Exeunt omnes

158 *special* particular, appropriate (*O.E.D.*, 5)
158 *argument* illustration, proof
166 *puissant* powerful
169 *insult* boast
172 *device* show, masque (see l.138)
174 s.d. *of* from
176 *Unless* unless it were that

Act I, Scene v

ANDREA
   Come we for this from depth of underground,
   To see him feast that gave me my death's wound?
   These pleasant sights are sorrow to my soul,
   Nothing but league, and love, and banqueting!
REVENGE
   Be still Andrea, ere we go from hence,   5
   I'll turn their friendship into fell despite,
   Their love to mortal hate, their day to night,
   Their hope into despair, their peace to war,
   Their joys to pain, their bliss to misery.

Act II, Scene i

Enter LORENZO and BALTHAZAR

LORENZO
   My lord, though Bel-imperia seem thus coy,
   Let reason hold you in your wonted joy:
   'In time the savage bull sustains the yoke,
   In time all haggard hawks will stoop to lure,
   In time small wedges cleave the hardest oak,   5
   In time the flint is pierced with softest shower'—
   And she in time will fall from her disdain,
   And rue the sufferance of your friendly pain.

6 *fell despite* cruel hatred
1 *coy* disdainful, unresponsive
3 *sustains* undergoes, has to submit to (*O.E.D.*, 9)
4 *haggard* wild, untrained
4 *stoop to lure* swoop down to the lure, a dead bird, or feathers made
   to resemble a bird, used for training hawks
5 *wedges* wedge-shaped pieces of metal used in felling trees
8 *rue* pity   8 *sufferance* patient endurance

1 ff. The Andrea—Revenge exchange serves to maintain the audience's
   sense of irony: Revenge plays up (ll.6 ff.) the antitheses of love and
   hate, hope and despair, bliss and misery that underlie it.
3–6 Lorenzo argues in the sonneteering vein extremely popular at this
   date, actually quoting, almost word for word, a sonnet in Thomas
   Watson's *Hecatompathia* (entered for publication 1582). The lines
   represent conventional notions about the courtship of reluctant ladies,
   and therefore deliberately adopt the artifices of up-to-date poetry on
   the subject. Line 3 is recalled in *Much Ado* (I, i, 258) as Don Pedro
   prophesies that even Benedick will fall victim to love.

BALTHAZAR

'No, she is wilder, and more hard withal,
Than beast, or bird, or tree, or stony wall'.   10
But wherefore blot I Bel-imperia's name?
It is my fault, not she, that merits blame.
My feature is not to content her sight,
My words are rude and work her no delight.
The lines I send her are but harsh and ill,   15
Such as do drop from Pan and Marsyas' quill.
My presents are not of sufficient cost,
And being worthless all my labour's lost.
Yet might she love me for my valiancy;
Ay, but that's slandered by captivity.   20
Yet might she love me to content her sire;
Ay, but her reason masters his desire.
Yet might she love me as her brother's friend;
Ay, but her hopes aim at some other end.
Yet might she love me to uprear her state;   25
Ay, but perhaps she hopes some nobler mate.
Yet might she love me as her beauty's thrall;
Ay, but I fear she cannot love at all.

13 *feature* form, bearing (not merely the face)
13 *to* such as to
16 *Pan and Marsyas* each of these gods, in different stories, challenged Apollo to contests in flute-playing; neither could match his skill and both were punished
16 *quill* either a musical pipe or a pen; Kyd appears to use both senses here
19 *valiancy* valour
20 *slandered* brought into disrepute (*O.E.D.*, v, 2)
25 *uprear her state* improve her social position
27 *beauty's* ed. (beauteous *1592*)

9–10 Balthazar quotes (with variation) the lines of Watson's sonnet that follow those quoted by Lorenzo. (The original reads: 'More fierce is my sweet loue, more hard withall, / Then Beast, or Birde, then Tree, or Stony wall.') The two young men are showing their familiarity with contemporary poetry.
11–28 Balthazar's speech became famous, and was often parodied. The parodists, like modern readers, are no doubt reacting against this highly artificial and self-conscious way of dramatising indecision and self-doubt. Balthazar must of course be at least half-ridiculous here, being excessively in love, and being in any case a weak nature.

LORENZO
My lord, for my sake leave these ecstasies,
And doubt not but we'll find some remedy.   30
Some cause there is that lets you not be loved:
First that must needs be known, and then removed.
What if my sister love some other knight?
BALTHAZAR
My summer's day will turn to winter's night.
LORENZO
I have already found a stratagem,   35
To sound the bottom of this doubtful theme.
My lord, for once you shall be ruled by me:
Hinder me not whate'er you hear or see.
By force or fair means will I cast about
To find the truth of all this question out.   40
Ho, Pedringano!
PEDRINGANO   [*Within*] Signior!
LORENZO   *Vien qui presto.*

Enter PEDRINGANO

PEDRINGANO
Hath your lordship any service to command me?
LORENZO
Ay, Pedringano, service of import.
And not to spend the time in trifling words,
Thus stands the case: it is not long thou know'st,   45
Since I did shield thee from my father's wrath,
For thy conveyance in Andrea's love,
For which thou wert adjudged to punishment.
I stood betwixt thee and thy punishment;
And since, thou know'st how I have favoured thee.   50
Now to these favours will I add reward,
Not with fair words, but store of golden coin,
And lands and living joined with dignities,

29 *ecstasies* unreasoning passions (Edwards)
36 *sound the bottom* discover the exact features (the metaphor is
   from 'sounding' a waterway to detect snags and shallows)
41 *Vien qui presto* Come here quickly (Italian)
41 *qui* ed. (*que 1592*)
47 *conveyance* secret or underhand dealing
52 *store* abundance

29 *ecstasies* Lorenzo's word shows that Kyd meant Balthazar's speech
   to be delivered in an exaggerated fashion.

If thou but satisfy my just demand.
Tell truth and have me for thy lasting friend.   55
PEDRINGANO
Whate'er it be your lordship shall demand,
My bounden duty bids me tell the truth,
If case it lie in me to tell the truth.
LORENZO
Then, Pedringano, this is my demand:
Whom loves my sister Bel-imperia?   60
For she reposeth all her trust in thee—
Speak man, and gain both friendship and reward:
I mean, whom loves she in Andrea's place?
PEDRINGANO
Alas, my lord, since Don Andrea's death,
I have no credit with her as before,   65
And therefore know not if she love or no.
LORENZO
Nay, if thou dally then I am thy foe,   [*Draws his sword*]
And fear shall force what friendship cannot win.
Thy death shall bury what thy life conceals.
Thou diest for more esteeming her than me.   70
PEDRINGANO
O, stay, my lord.
LORENZO
Yet speak the truth and I will guerdon thee,
And shield thee from whatever can ensue,
And will conceal whate'er proceeds from thee:
But if thou dally once again, thou diest.   75
PEDRINGANO
If Madam Bel-imperia be in love—
LORENZO
What, villain, ifs and ands?

                              [*Offers to kill him*]

PEDRINGANO
O stay my lord, she loves Horatio.

                              BALTHAZAR *starts back*

58 *it lie in me* I am able to
71 *stay* wait, hold off
72 *guerdon* reward

---

77 *ifs and ands* 'ifs and ifs' (and used to mean 'if'). A strong theatrical
  moment (as Lorenzo lunges at Pedringano) that Nashe may be remembering in his preface to Greene's *Menaphon*, where he writes of
  'translators' who are content 'to bodge up a blank verse with ifs and
  ands'.

LORENZO
What, Don Horatio our Knight Marshal's son?
PEDRINGANO
Even him my lord.   30
LORENZO
Now say but how know'st thou he is her love,
And thou shalt find me kind and liberal:
Stand up, I say, and fearless tell the truth.
PEDRINGANO
She sent him letters which myself perused,
Full-fraught with lines and arguments of love,   85
Preferring him before Prince Balthazar.
LORENZO
Swear on this cross that what thou say'st is true,
And that thou wilt conceal what thou hast told.
PEDRINGANO
I swear to both by him that made us all.
LORENZO
In hope thine oath is true, here's thy reward,   90
But if I prove thee perjured and unjust,
This very sword whereon thou took'st thine oath,
Shall be the worker of thy tragedy.
PEDRINGANO
What I have said is true, and shall for me
Be still concealed from Bel-imperia.   95
Besides, your honour's liberality
Deserves my duteous service even till death.
LORENZO
Let this be all that thou shalt do for me:
Be watchful when, and where, these lovers meet,
And give me notice in some secret sort.   100
PEDRINGANO
I will my lord.
LORENZO
Then shalt thou find that I am liberal.
Thou know'st that I can more advance thy state
Than she, be therefore wise and fail me not.
Go and attend her as thy custom is,   105

85 *fraught* loaded
87 *this cross* his sword-hilt
90 *In hope* in the faith that
91 *unjust* false, dishonest   100 *in sort* by some secret means
103 *advance thy state* improve your social position and your finances

Lest absence make her think thou dost amiss.

Exit PEDRINGANO

Why so: *tam armis quam ingenio:*
Where words prevail not, violence prevails;
But gold doth more than either of them both.
How likes Prince Balthazar this stratagem?   110

BALTHAZAR

Both well, and ill: it makes me glad and sad:
Glad, that I know the hinderer of my love,
Sad, that I fear she hates me whom I love.
Glad, that I know on whom to be revenged,
Sad, that she'll fly me if I take revenge.   115
Yet must I take revenge or die myself,
For love resisted grows impatient.
I think Horatio be my destined plague:
First, in his hand he brandished a sword,
And with that sword he fiercely waged war,   120
And in that war he gave me dangerous wounds,
And by those wounds he forced me to yield,
And by my yielding I became his slave.
Now in his mouth he carries pleasing words,
Which pleasing words do harbour sweet conceits,   125
Which sweet conceits are limed with sly deceits,
Which sly deceits smooth Bel-imperia's ears,
And through her ears dive down into her heart,
And in her heart set him where I should stand.
Thus hath he ta'en my body by his force,   130
And now by sleight would captivate my soul:
But in his fall I'll tempt the destinies,
And either lose my life, or win my love.

107 *tam . . . ingenio* by equal parts of force and skill
125 *sweet conceits* pleasing figures of speech
126 *limed with* made into traps with (from bird-lime, a gluey substance used to catch birds)
127 *smooth* seduce, flatter (compare *O.E.D.*, v, 5a)
131 *sleight* trickery
132 *in his fall* in causing his downfall

111–33 Clemen (pp. 106–7) usefully comments: 'the lack of substance in this repetitive style of his, tediously amplified by antithesis and other rhetorical figures, is exactly in keeping with the irresolute, dependent, puppet-like role that Balthazar is to sustain in the play.' His speech here parallels and complements his lines on Bel-imperia (ll.9 ff.) near the scene's beginning.

LORENZO

Let's go, my lord, your staying stays revenge.
Do you but follow me and gain your love: 135
Her favour must be won by his remove.   *Exeunt*

Act II, Scene ii

Enter HORATIO *and* BEL-IMPERIA

HORATIO

Now, madam, since by favour of your love
Our hidden smoke is turned to open flame,
And that with looks and words we feed our thoughts
(Two chief contents, where more cannot be had),
Thus in the midst of love's fair blandishments,   5
Why show you sign of inward languishments?

PEDRINGANO *showeth all to the* PRINCE *and* LORENZO, *placing them in secret [above]*

BEL-IMPERIA

My heart, sweet friend, is like a ship at sea:
She wisheth port, where riding all at ease,
She may repair what stormy times have worn,
And leaning on the shore, may sing with joy   10
That pleasure follows pain, and bliss annoy.
Possession of thy love is th'only port,
Wherein my heart, with fears and hopes long tossed,
Each hour doth wish and long to make resort;
There to repair the joys that it hath lost,   15
And sitting safe, to sing in Cupid's choir
That sweetest bliss is crown of love's desire.

3 *thoughts* ed. (though *1592*) wishes, imaginings
4 *contents* sources of contentment
7 *friend* love (a common Elizabethan sense)
9 *may* ed. (mad *1592*)
15 *repair* restore
16 *sing* celebrate
17 *is* which is
17 *1592* has s.d. '*Balthazar* above'; Edwards suggests, convincingly, that this is a note by the author to clarify the earlier direction (l.6) and need not be repeated

6 s.d. Balthazar and Lorenzo watch the lovers from the upper-stage or balcony. Edwards is, I think, correct in arguing that *1592*'s 'Balthazar aboue.' after l.17 is an author's clarification; like him I transfer the 'above' to the end of the present direction.

BALTHAZAR
  O sleep mine eyes, see not my love profaned;
  Be deaf, my ears, hear not my discontent;
  Die, heart, another joys what thou deservest.   20
LORENZO
  Watch still mine eyes, to see this love disjoined;
  Hear still mine ears, to hear them both lament;
  Live, heart, to joy at fond Horatio's fall.
BEL-IMPERIA
  Why stands Horatio speechless all this while?
HORATIO
  The less I speak, the more I meditate.   25
BEL-IMPERIA
  But whereon dost thou chiefly meditate?
HORATIO
  On dangers past, and pleasures to ensue.
BALTHAZAR
  On pleasures past, and dangers to ensue.
BEL-IMPERIA
  What dangers and what pleasures dost thou mean?
HORATIO
  Dangers of war and pleasures of our love.   30
LORENZO
  Dangers of death, but pleasures none at all.
BEL-IMPERIA
  Let dangers go, thy war shall be with me,
  But such a war as breaks no bond of peace.
  Speak thou fair words, I'll cross them with fair words;
  Send thou sweet looks, I'll meet them with sweet looks;   35
  Write loving lines, I'll answer loving lines;
  Give me a kiss, I'll countercheck thy kiss:
  Be this our warring peace, or peaceful war.
HORATIO
  But gracious madam, then appoint the field
  Where trial of this war shall first be made.   40

20 *joys* enjoys   23 *fond* foolish, besotted
33 *war* ed. (warring *1592*)
34 *cross* meet, complement (a punning reference to cross meaning
    thwart, go counter to, is intended)
37 *countercheck* oppose, take countering action against

18 ff. The antithetical speeches by the lovers and those watching them is
one of Kyd's more obvious ways of insisting on dramatic irony. Bel-
imperia's description of the bower (ll.42 ff.) is also obviously and
grimly ironic.

BALTHAZAR

Ambitious villain, how his boldness grows!

BEL-IMPERIA

Then be thy father's pleasant bower the field,
Where first we vowed a mutual amity:
The court were dangerous, that place is safe.
Our hour shall be when Vesper gins to rise, 45
That summons home distressful travellers.
There none shall hear us but the harmless birds:
Happily the gentle nightingale
Shall carol us asleep ere we be ware,
And singing with the prickle at her breast, 50
Tell our delight and mirthful dalliance.
Till then each hour will seem a year and more.

HORATIO

But, honey sweet, and honourable love,
Return we now into your father's sight:
Dangerous suspicion waits on our delight. 55

LORENZO

Ay, danger mixed with jealous despite
Shall send thy soul into eternal night.   *Exeunt*

Act II, Scene iii

Enter KING *of Spain, Portingale* AMBASSADOR, DON CYPRIAN, *etc.*

KING

Brother of Castile, to the prince's love
What says your daughter Bel-imperia?

CASTILE

Although she coy it as becomes her kind,
And yet dissemble that she loves the prince,
I doubt not, I, but she will stoop in time. 5

42 *bower* an arbour, or enclosed garden-seat, covered with branches
of trees, plants etc. Cf. II, iv, 53 s.d. and note
45 *Vesper* the evening star or Venus
46 *distressful travellers* weary labourers ('travel' and 'travail' were
closely linked in Elizabethan use)
48 *Happily* haply, perhaps
50 *prickle* thorn
56 *jealous* ed. (jealous *1592*) watchful, suspicious; metre requires
three syllables
3 *coy it* affects disinclination
3 *as becomes her kind* as it is a woman's nature to do
5 *stoop* become obedient; and compare II, i, 4 and note

And were she froward, which she will not be,
Yet herein shall she follow my advice,
Which is to love him or forgo my love.

KING
Then, Lord Ambassador of Portingale,
Advise thy king to make this marriage up,   10
For strengthening of our late-confirmed league;
I know no better means to make us friends.
Her dowry shall be large and liberal:
Besides that she is daughter and half-heir
Unto our brother here, Don Cyprian,   15
And shall enjoy the moiety of his land,
I'll grace her marriage with an uncle's gift.
And this it is: in case the match go forward,
The tribute which you pay shall be released,
And if by Balthazar she have a son,   20
He shall enjoy the kingdom after us.

AMBASSADOR
I'll make the motion to my sovereign liege,
And work it if my counsel may prevail.

KING
Do so, my lord, and if he give consent,
I hope his presence here will honour us   25
In celebration of the nuptial day—
And let himself determine of the time.

AMBASSADOR
Will't please your grace command me aught beside?

KING
Commend me to the king, and so farewell.
But where's Prince Balthazar to take his leave?   30

AMBASSADOR
That is performed already, my good lord.

KING
Amongst the rest of what you have in charge,
The prince's ransom must not be forgot;
That's none of mine, but his that took him prisoner,
And well his forwardness deserves reward: 35
It was Horatio, our Knight Marshal's son.

---

6 *froward* perverse, refractory
16 *moiety* a half-share
22 *make the motion* put the proposal
35 *forwardness* enterprise, zeal

AMBASSADOR
  Between us there's a price already pitched,
  And shall be sent with all convenient speed.
KING
  Then once again farewell, my lord.
AMBASSADOR
  Farewell, my Lord of Castile and the rest.   *Exit*   40
KING
  Now, brother, you must take some little pains
  To win fair Bel-imperia from her will:
  Young virgins must be ruled by their friends.
  The prince is amiable, and loves her well,
  If she neglect him and forgo his love,   45
  She both will wrong her own estate and ours.
  Therefore, whiles I do entertain the prince
  With greatest pleasure that our court affords,
  Endeavour you to win your daughter's thought:
  If she give back, all this will come to naught.   *Exeunt*   50

Act II, Scene iv

Enter HORATIO, BEL-IMPERIA, *and* PEDRINGANO

HORATIO
  Now that the night begins with sable wings
  To overcloud the brightness of the sun,
  And that in darkness pleasures may be done,
  Come Bel-imperia, let us to the bower,
  And there in safety pass a pleasant hour.   5
BEL-IMPERIA
  I follow thee my love, and will not back,
  Although my fainting heart controls my soul.
HORATIO
  Why, make you doubt of Pedringano's faith?

37 *pitched* agreed
42 *will* wilfulness
49 *thought* ed. (thoughts *1592*)
50 *give back* 'turn her back on us' (Edwards), refuse
 1 *sable* black
 7 *controls* oppresses, masters (the heart's fearfulness struggles
    against the soul's wishes)

1–5 An Elizabethan audience would immediately feel the irony of
invoking night, associated with evil, to watch over the relationship.
The ironies are strengthened in the next lines; see esp. ll.16–19.

BEL-IMPERIA
    No, he is as trusty as my second self.
    Go Pedringano, watch without the gate,   10
    And let us know if any make approach.

PEDRINGANO
    [*Aside*] Instead of watching, I'll deserve more gold
    By fetching Don Lorenzo to this match.

                                    Exit PEDRINGANO

HORATIO
    What means my love?

BEL-IMPERIA   I know not what myself.
    And yet my heart foretells me some mischance.   15

HORATIO
    Sweet say not so, fair fortune is our friend,
    And heavens have shut up day to pleasure us.
    The stars thou see'st hold back their twinkling shine,
    And Luna hides herself to pleasure us.

BEL-IMPERIA
    Thou hast prevailed, I'll conquer my misdoubt,   20
    And in thy love and counsel drown my fear.
    I fear no more, love now is all my thoughts.
    Why sit we not? for pleasure asketh ease.

HORATIO
    The more thou sit'st within these leafy bowers,
    The more will Flora deck it with her flowers.   25

BEL-IMPERIA
    Ay, but if Flora spy Horatio here,
    Her jealous eye will think I sit too near.

HORATIO
    Hark, madam, how the birds record by night,
    For joy that Bel-imperia sits in sight.

BEL-IMPERIA
    No, Cupid counterfeits the nightingale,   30
    To frame sweet music to Horatio's tale.

HORATIO
    If Cupid sing, then Venus is not far:
    Ay, thou art Venus or some fairer star.

---

10 *without* outside   13 *match* meeting
19 *Luna* the moon   23 *asketh* needs, requires
28 *record* sing
31 *frame* adapt, compose

32–5 *Venus . . . Mars* Aphrodite (Venus) was unfaithful to her husband
    Hephaestus with Ares (Mars) the god of war.

BEL-IMPERIA
If I be Venus, thou must needs be Mars,
And where Mars reigneth, there must needs be wars. 35
HORATIO
Then thus begin our wars: put forth thy hand,
That it may combat with my ruder hand.
BEL-IMPERIA
Set forth thy foot to try the push of mine.
HORATIO
But first my looks shall combat against thine.
BEL-IMPERIA
Then ward thyself: I dart this kiss at thee. 40
HORATIO
Thus I retort the dart thou threw'st at me.
BEL-IMPERIA
Nay then, to gain the glory of the field,
My twining arms shall yoke and make thee yield.
HORATIO
Nay then, my arms are large and strong withal:
Thus elms by vines are compassed till they fall. 45
BEL-IMPERIA
O let me go, for in my troubled eyes
Now may'st thou read that life in passion dies.
HORATIO
O stay a while and I will die with thee,
So shalt thou yield and yet have conquered me.
BEL-IMPERIA
Who's there? Pedringano! We are betrayed! 50

35 *wars* ed. (war *1592*); rhyme requires the plural form
37 *ruder* rougher, coarser
40 *ward* guard, shield
44 *withal* ed. (with *1592*)
50 *Who's there? Pedringano!* ed. (Whose there *Pedringano? 1592*)

43–5 Edwards shows that Horatio here inverts a familiar saying about
the elm (usually an emblem of friendship: the vine holds up the tree
in its embraces); taken with the double meaning in 'die' (a common
sexual pun), it becomes obvious that Kyd wishes to emphasise the
sensuality of the moment, thus making the ironies more emotionally
charged. The literal sense of l.48 does of course come about; a somewhat heavy-handed irony.

Enter LORENZO, BALTHAZAR, SERBERINE, PEDRINGANO, *disguised*

LORENZO
My lord, away with her, take her aside.
O sir, forbear, your valour is already tried.
Quickly despatch, my masters.

They hang him in the arbour

HORATIO
What, will you murder me?

LORENZO
Ay, thus, and thus; these are the fruits of love.   55

They stab him

BEL-IMPERIA
O save his life and let me die for him!
O save him, brother, save him, Balthazar:
I loved Horatio, but he loved not me.

BALTHAZAR
But Balthazar loves Bel-imperia.

LORENZO
Although his life were still ambitious proud,   60
Yet is he at the highest now he is dead.

BEL-IMPERIA
Murder! murder! Help, Hieronimo, help!

LORENZO
Come, stop her mouth, away with her.

Exeunt, [leaving HORATIO'S *body]*

---

52 *tried* tested, proved. The thought of Horatio's martial prowess
still rankles with Lorenzo
60 *ambitious proud* ambitious for a position that would satisfy his
pride

---

53 s.d. Whether a stage-tree was used for this purpose remains unclear;
Isabella (IV, ii, 6 ff.) seems to refer to a tree; Hieronimo says (IV, iv,
111) he found Horatio 'hanging on a tree'; the author of the Fourth
Addition thinks very specifically of a tree (see ll.60 ff.). But editors
may well be right in arguing that the arbour illustrated on the title-page
of the 1615 edition (a trellis-work arch with a seat in it) may have been
decorated with leaves and branches, and so have served as both arbour
and tree.

Act II, Scene v

Enter HIERONIMO *in his shirt, etc.*

HIERONIMO

What outcries pluck me from my naked bed,
And chill my throbbing heart with trembling fear,
Which never danger yet could daunt before?
Who calls Hieronimo? Speak, here I am.
I did not slumber, therefore 'twas no dream,   5
No, no, it was some woman cried for help,
And here within this garden did she cry,
And in this garden must I rescue her.
But stay, what murderous spectacle is this?
A man hanged up and all the murderers gone,   10
And in my bower to lay the guilt on me.
This place was made for pleasure not for death.

                He cuts him down

Those garments that he wears I oft have seen—
Alas, it is Horatio, my sweet son!
Oh no, but he that whilom was my son.   15
O was it thou that calledst me from my bed?
O speak, if any spark of life remain:
I am thy father. Who hath slain my son?
What savage monster, not of human kind,
Hath here been glutted with thy harmless blood,   20
And left thy bloody corpse dishonoured here,
For me, amidst this dark and deathful shades,
To drown thee with an ocean of my tears?

1 s.d. *shirt* nightshirt
1 *naked bed* a transferred epithet; the sleeper is naked (or lightly clothed).
   Edwards says the phrase was familiar
15 *whilom* in the past, till now
22 *this* an accepted plural form at this date

1 s.d. For a description of probable stage-practice here see Fourth
   Addition ll.135–9.
1–33 Hieronimo's soliloquy, perhaps the most famous of the play,
   is one which, as Clemen (p. 102) points out, 'is not only spoken but
   acted', carrying its own internal 'stage-directions', a technique followed,
   and made more subtle, by Shakespeare.
12 continuing the pleasure / death irony of II, ii and II, iv.
13 ff. Good direction and acting can make the moment of discovery
   deeply poignant. Kyd's words may seem absurdly simple here, but he is
   surely right not to overload Hieronimo's speech with rhetoric.

O heavens, why made you night to cover sin?
By day this deed of darkness had not been.   25
O earth, why didst thou not in time devour
The vild profaner of this sacred bower?
O poor Horatio, what hadst thou misdone,
To leese thy life erè life was new begun?
O wicked butcher, whatsoe'er thou wert,   30
How could thou strangle virtue and desert?
Ay me most wretched, that have lost my joy,
In leesing my Horatio, my sweet boy!

Enter ISABELLA

ISABELLA
My husband's absence makes my heart to throb—
Hieronimo!   35
HIERONIMO
Here, Isabella, help me to lament,
For sighs are stopped and all my tears are spent.
ISABELLA
What world of grief! My son Horatio!
O where's the author of this endless woe?
HIERONIMO
To know the author were some ease of grief,   40
For in revenge my heart would find relief.
ISABELLA
Then is he gone? and is my son gone too?
O, gush out, tears, fountains and floods of tears;
Blow, sighs, and raise an everlasting storm:
For outrage fits our cursed wretchedness.   45
HIERONIMO   *by Bel-imperia cf. p.42-69*
Sweet lovely rose, ill plucked before thy time,
Fair worthy son, not conquered, but betrayed:
I'll kiss thee now, for words with tears are stayed.
ISABELLA
And I'll close up the glasses of his sight,
For once these eyes were only my delight.   50

26 *in time* at the due moment
27 *vild* vile   29 *leese* lose
29 *was new begun* had entered a new phase; perhaps the reference is
to Horatio's new life as a prominent citizen after his success in
war   39 *author* the one responsible
45 *outrage* passionate behaviour (*O.E.D.*, sb. 2)   48 *with* by
48 *stayed* ed. (stainde *1592*) stopped
49 *glasses of his sight* his eyes

HIERONIMO
    See'st thou this handkercher besmeared with blood?
    It shall not from me till I take revenge.
    See'st thou those wounds that yet are bleeding fresh?
    I'll not entomb them till I have revenged.
    Then will I joy amidst my discontent,   55
    Till then my sorrow never shall be spent.
ISABELLA
    The heavens are just, murder cannot be hid:
    Time is the author both of truth and right,
    And time will bring this treachery to light.
HIERONIMO
    Meanwhile, good Isabella, cease thy plaints,   60
    Or at the least dissemble them awhile:
    So shall we sooner find the practice out,
    And learn by whom all this was brought about.
    Come Isabel, now let us take him up,
                         They take him up
    And bear him in from out this cursed place.   65
    I'll say his dirge, singing fits not this case.
    O aliquis mihi quas pulchrum ver educat herbas

51 *handkercher* hankderchief, small scarf
60 *plaints* complaints, sorrowing   62 *practice* plot
66 *dirge* funeral song or hymn (from *dirige*, the first word of a Latin
    antiphon in the office for the dead)
67 *ver educat* ed. (*var educet 1592*)

51–2 For the possible origin of this 'handkercher' see I, iv, 42 note.
57–9 Isabella's words are a common Elizabethan axiom (see Tilley M1315),
    skilfully used by Kyd to contrast with Hieronimo's complete bewilder-
    ment.
67–80 'Let someone bind for me the herbs which beautiful spring fosters,
    and let a salve be given for our grief; or let him apply juices, if there are
    any that bring forgetfulness to men's minds. I myself shall gather
    anywhere in the great world whatever plants the sun draws forth into
    the fair regions of light; I myself shall drink whatever drug the wise-
    woman devises, and whatever herbs incantation assembles by its
    secret power. I shall face all things, death even, until the moment our
    every feeling dies in this dead breast. And so shall I never again, my
    life, see those eyes of yours, and has everlasting slumber sealed up your
    light of life? I shall perish with you; thus, thus would it please me to go
    to the shades below. But none the less I shall keep myself from yielding
    to a hastened death, lest in that case no revenge should follow your death'.
    The passage, which contains reminiscences of Lucretius, Vergil and
    Ovid, is 'a *pastiche*, in Kyd's singular fashion, of tags from classical
    poetry, and lines of his own composition' (Boas).

HIERONIMO *sets his breast unto his sword*
Misceat, et nostro detur medicina dolori;
Aut, si qui faciunt animis oblivia, succos
Praebeat; ipse metam magnum quaecunque per orbem	70
Gramina Sol pulchras effert in luminis oras;
Ipse bibam quicquid meditatur saga veneni,
Quicquid et herbarum vi caeca nenia nectit:
Omnia perpetiar, lethum quoque, dum semel omnis
Noster in extincto moriatur pectore sensus.	75
Ergo tuos oculos nunquam, mea vita, videbo,
Et tua perpetuus sepelivit lumina somnus?
Emoriar tecum: sic, sic juvat ire sub umbras.
At tamen absistam properato cedere letho,
Ne mortem vindicta tuam tum nulla sequatur.	80
Here he throws it from him and bears the body away

Act II, Scene vi

ANDREA
Brought'st thou me hither to increase my pain?
I looked that Balthazar should have been slain;
But 'tis my friend Horatio that is slain,
And they abuse fair Bel-imperia,
On whom I doted more than all the world,	5
Because she loved me more than all the world.

REVENGE
Thou talk'st of harvest when the corn is green:
The end is crown of every work well done;
The sickle comes not till the corn be ripe.
Be still, and ere I lead thee from this place,	10
I'll show thee Balthazar in heavy case.

69 *animis oblivia* ed. (*annum oblimia 1592*)
70 *metam magnum quaecunque* ed. (*metum magnam quicunque 1592*)
71 *effert* ed. (*effecit 1592*)
72 *veneni* ed. (*veneri 1592*)
73 *herbarum vi caeca nenia* ed. (*irraui euecaeca menia 1592*)
75 *pectore* ed. (*pectora 1592*)
80 *tum* ed. (*tam 1592*)
2 *looked* expected, hoped
5 *On* ed. (Or *1592*)
11 *in heavy case* in a sad state

1 ff. One effect of the Andrea–Revenge exchange is to maintain an
audience's detachment, threatened by the emotion-laden events of the
past scenes.

Act III, Scene i

Enter VICEROY *of Portingale*, NOBLES, VILLUPPO

VICEROY
Infortunate condition of kings,
Seated amidst so many helpless doubts!
First we are placed upon extremest height,
And oft supplanted with exceeding heat,
But ever subject to the wheel of chance;   5
And at our highest never joy we so,
As we both doubt and dread our overthrow.
So striveth not the waves with sundry winds
As Fortune toileth in the affairs of kings,
That would be feared, yet fear to be beloved,   10
Sith fear or love to kings is flattery.
For instance, lordings, look upon your king,
By hate deprived of his dearest son,
The only hope of our successive line.

1 NOBLEMAN
I had not thought that Alexandro's heart   15
Had been envenomed with such extreme hate:
But now I see that words have several works,
And there's no credit in the countenance.

1 s.d. NOBLES, VILLUPPO ed. (*Nobles, Alexandro, Villuppo 1592*)
1 *Infortunate* ill-used by Fortune
2 *Seated* placed
2 *helpless* for which there is no help
2 *doubts* fears   4 *heat* fury
10 *would be* wish-to be   11 *Sith* since
12 *lordings* lords
14 *successive line* line of succession
15 s.p 1 NOBLEMAN ed. (*Nob. 1592*)
17 *words have several works* i.e. what a man does may not always
   reflect what he says
18 *no credit in* no point in trusting

1–11 A common theme in Elizabethan writing (see e.g. *Richard II,*
   III, ii, 155 ff.) and with parallels also in Seneca (see *Agamemnon,*
   57–73).
5 *the wheel of chance* the common Elizabethan figure to describe the
   cycle of achievement and failure in human (and especially political)
   life: kings rise to the top of the wheel in prosperity and fall, inevitably,
   to its lowest point in defeat and death.

VILLUPPO
No, for, my lord, had you beheld the train
That feigned love had coloured in his looks,   20
When he in camp consorted Balthazar,
Far more inconstant had you thought the sun,
That hourly coasts the centre of the earth,
Than Alexandro's purpose to the prince.

VICEROY
No more, Villuppo, thou hast said enough,   25
And with thy words thou slay'st our wounded thoughts.
Nor shall I longer dally with the world,
Procrastinating Alexandro's death:
Go some of you and fetch the traitor forth,
That as he is condemned he may die.   30

Enter ALEXANDRO *with a* NOBLEMAN *and* HALBERTS

2 NOBLEMAN
In such extremes will naught but patience serve.

ALEXANDRO
But in extremes what patience shall I use?
Nor discontents it me to leave the world,
With whom there nothing can prevail but wrong.

2 NOBLEMAN
Yet hope the best.

ALEXANDRO   'Tis Heaven is my hope.   35

21 *consorted* associated with, kept company with
24 *purpose* attitude, relationship
30 s.d. HALBERTS halberdiers; see I, iv, 21 note
31 s.p. 2 NOBLEMAN ed. (*Nob. 1592*)
34 *With . . . wrong* i.e. Since all I ever meet is injustice

19–20 'if you had seen the false appearance [of friendship] that pretended
love had counterfeited in his face.' 'Train' literally means 'treachery';
Villuppo uses the word to describe the false appearance of love (a
treacherous mask) Alexandro is accused of wearing.

23 *That hourly . . . earth* 'that with a regular motion (in a precise number
of hours) circles this earth, the centre of the universe.' Kyd writes
in terms of the old cosmology; the sun's (apparent) circling often
served as a metaphor for constancy.

32–7 Alexandro's sense of life's injustices anticipates much that Hieronimo
has to say in the next scene: part of the 'overlapping' technique Kyd
uses so successfully (see III, ii, 3 ff.).

As for the earth, it is too much infect
To yield me hope of any of her mould.

VICEROY

Why linger ye? bring forth that daring fiend,
And let him die for his accursed deed.

ALEXANDRO

Not that I fear the extremity of death,   40
For nobles cannot stoop to servile fear,
Do I, O king, thus discontented live.
But this, O this, torments my labouring soul,
That thus I die suspected of a sin,
Whereof, as heavens have known my secret thoughts,   45
So am I free from this suggestion.

VICEROY

No more, I say! to the tortures! when!
Bind him, and burn his body in those flames,
                              They bind him to the stake
That shall prefigure those unquenched fires
Of Phlegethon prepared for his soul.   50

ALEXANDRO

My guiltless death will be avenged on thee,
On thee, Villuppo, that hath maliced thus,
Or for thy meed hast falsely me accused.

VILLUPPO

Nay, Alexandro, if thou menace me,
I'll lend a hand to send thee to the lake   55
Where those thy words shall perish with thy works—
Injurious traitor, monstrous homicide!

Enter AMBASSADOR

AMBASSADOR

Stay, hold a while,
And here, with pardon of his majesty,
Lay hands upon Villuppo.

36 *infect* infected
37 *To yield . . . mould* i.e. to allow me to place any faith in anyone
   born and brought up there
46 *suggestion* false accusation (*O.E.D.*, 3)
47 *when!* an impatient exclamation
50 *Phlegethon* the mythical river of hell whose waves were of fire
52 *maliced* entertained malice (*O.E.D.*, v, 2)
53 *meed* reward, advantage
55 *lake* the lake of Acheron in hell, into which Phlegethon (l.50)
   flows

VICEROY   Ambassador,   60
What news hath urged this sudden entrance?

AMBASSADOR
Know, sovereign lord, that Balthazar doth live.

VICEROY
What say'st thou? liveth Balthazar our son?

AMBASSADOR
Your highness' son, Lord Balthazar, doth live;
And, well entreated in the court of Spain,   65
Humbly commends him to your majesty.
These eyes beheld, and these my followers;
With these, the letters of the king's commends,
                              Gives him letters
Are happy witnesses of his highness' health.
                    The VICEROY *looks on the letters, and proceeds*

VICEROY
[*Reads*] 'Thy son doth live, your tribute is received,   70
Thy peace is made, and we are satisfied.
The rest resolve upon as things proposed
For both our honours and thy benefit.'

AMBASSADOR
These are his highness' farther articles.
                              He gives him more letters

VICEROY
Accursed wretch, to intimate these ills   75
Against the life and reputation
Of noble Alexandro! Come, my lord,
Let him unbind thee that is bound to death,
To make a quital for thy discontent.
                              They unbind him

58–61 lineation ed. (Stay . . . Maiestie,/Lay . . . *Villuppo.*/Embassa-
    dour . . . entrance? *1592*)
61 *entrance* three syllables   68 *commends* greetings
69 s.d. VICEROY ed. (*King 1592*)
72 *resolve upon* decide upon 75 *intimate* make known, announce publicly
77 *Come, my lord*, ed. (come my lord vnbinde him. *1592*)
79 *quital* requital, recompense

77 *Come, my lord 1592* adds 'vnbinde him', but this gives the line thirteen
    syllables. The extra words may have been included into the text from a
    stage-direction placed too early (and not cancelled when the direction
    at l.79 was added), or they may result from a compositor's anticipation
    of that direction. Edwards must be right to omit them.
79 s.d. Villuppo unbinds Alexandro as the text directs; 'they unbind him'
    is used to mean 'he is unbound'.

ALEXANDRO

Dread lord, in kindness you could do no less,   80
Upon report of such a damned fact.
But thus we see our innocence hath saved
The hopeless life which thou, Villuppo, sought
By thy suggestions to have massacred.

VICEROY

Say, false Villuppo, wherefore didst thou thus   85
Falsely betray Lord Alexandro's life?
Him, whom thou knowest that no unkindness else,
But even the slaughter of our dearest son,
Could once have moved us to have misconceived.

ALEXANDRO

Say, treacherous Villuppo, tell the king,   90
Wherein hath Alexandro used thee ill?

VILLUPPO

Rent with remembrance of so foul a deed,
My guilty soul submits me to thy doom:
For not for Alexandro's injuries,
But for reward and hope to be preferred,   95
Thus have I shamelessly hazarded his life.

VICEROY

Which, villain, shall be ransomed with thy death,
And not so mean a torment as we here
Devised for him who thou said'st slew our son,
But with the bitterest torments and extremes   100
That may be yet invented for thine end.

                    ALEXANDRO *seems to entreat*

Entreat me not, go, take the traitor hence.

                         Exit VILLUPPO [*guarded*]

And, Alexandro, let us honour thee
With public notice of thy loyalty.
To end those things articulated here   105
By our great lord, the mighty King of Spain,

80 *in kindness* by your nature (as a king)
81 *fact* deed
82 *our* my
84 *suggestions* false accusations
89 *misconceived* suspected, formed a wrong opinion of
91 *Wherein* ed. (Or wherein *1592*)
93 *doom* judgment
98 *mean* moderate
105 *articulated* contained in the proposals (or articles) sent by the
   King of Spain (see l.74)

We with our Council will deliberate.
Come, Alexandro, keep us company.   *Exeunt*

Act III, Scene ii

Enter HIERONIMO

HIERONIMO
    O eyes, no eyes, but fountains fraught with tears;
    O life, no life, but lively form of death;
    O world, no world, but mass of public wrongs,
    Confused and filled with murder and misdeeds!
    O sacred heavens! if this unhallowed deed,   5
    If this inhuman and barbarous attempt,
    If this incomparable murder thus
    Of mine, but now no more my son,
    Shall unrevealed and unrevengéd pass,
    How should we term your dealings to be just,   10
    If you unjustly deal with those that in your justice trust?
    The night, sad secretary to my moans,
    With direful visions wake my vexed soul,
    And with the wounds of my distressful son
    Solicit me for notice of his death.   15
    The ugly fiends do sally forth of hell,
    And frame my steps to unfrequented paths,
    And fear my heart with fierce inflamed thoughts.
    The cloudy day my discontents records,
    Early begins to register my dreams   20
    And drive me forth to seek the murderer.

  1 *fraught* filled
  2 *lively form of death* death with the appearance of life
  4 *Confused* disordered   12 *secretary* confidant
  13 *wake* plural for singular; Edwards compares solicit (l.15) and
     drive (l.21)
  14 *distressful* causing distress, or distressed
  18 *fear* frighten

  1 ff. When Bobadil and Matthew discuss plays (in *Everyman in his
    Humour*, I, iv) they reserve their highest (clownish) praise for this
    speech; and thus convey Jonson's scorn for Kyd's 'conceited' oratorical
    style (Jonson may himself have acted Hieronimo). Sympathetic modern
    critics think otherwise: Clemen's analysis (pp. 271–5) shows the speech
    as 'a masterpiece of rhetorical art. Its structure and proportions are
    worked out with an almost mathematical exactness, and a variety of
    stylistic figures are harmoniously dovetailed in order to make a powerful
    emotional impact.'

Eyes, life, world, heavens, hell, night, and day,
See, search, show, send some man, some mean, that may—
                                    A letter falleth

What's here? a letter? tush, it is not so!
A letter written to Hieronimo!   *Red ink*   25
[*Reads*] ' For want of ink, receive this bloody writ.
Me hath my hapless brother hid from thee:
Revenge thyself on Balthazar and him,
For these were they that murderéd thy son.
Hieronimo, revenge Horatio's death,   30
And better fare than Bel-imperia doth.'
What means this unexpected miracle?
My son slain by Lorenzo and the prince!
What cause had they Horatio to malign?
Or what might move thee, Bel-imperia,   35
To accuse thy brother, had he been the mean?
Hieronimo, beware, thou art betrayed,
And to entrap thy life this train is laid.
Advise thee therefore, be not credulous:
This is devised to endanger thee,   40
That thou by this Lorenzo shouldst accuse,
And he, for thy dishonour done, should draw
Thy life in question, and thy name in hate.
Dear was the life of my beloved son,
And of his death behoves me be revengéd: 45
Then hazard not thine own, Hieronimo,
But live t'effect thy resolution.
I therefore will by circumstances try
What I can gather to confirm this writ,
And, hearkening near the Duke of Castile's house,   50

23 *See . . . may*— ed. (See . . . some man, / Some . . . may: *1592*)
23 *mean* means, way   26 '*For* ed. (*Bel.* For *1592*)
26 *writ* writing, document
27 *hapless* luckless; perhaps 'attended with ill-luck'
32 *What* ed. (*Hiero* What *1592*)
34 *malign* hate   38 *train* plot, trap
47 *t'effect thy resolution* to bring about what you have resolved
48 *by circumstances* by observing how they act; by gathering circum-
   stantial evidence

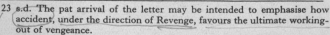

23 s.d. The pat arrival of the letter may be intended to emphasise how
   accident, under the direction of Revenge, favours the ultimate working-
   out of vengeance.
25 *Red ink* probably an author's note that the letter should be seen to have
   been written in red.

Close if I can with Bel-imperia,
To listen more, but nothing to bewray.

Enter PEDRINGANO

Now Pedringano!
PEDRINGANO   Now, Hieronimo!
HIERONIMO
Where's thy lady?
PEDRINGANO   I know not; here's my lord.

Enter LORENZO

LORENZO
How now, who's this? Hieronimo?
HIERONIMO   My lord.   55
PEDRINGANO
He asketh for my lady Bel-imperia.
LORENZO
What to do, Hieronimo? The duke my father hath
Upon some disgrace awhile removed her hence;
But if it be aught I may inform her of,
Tell me, Hieronimo, and I'll let her know it.   60
HIERONIMO
Nay, nay, my lord, I thank you, it shall not need.
I had a suit unto her, but too late,
And her disgrace makes me unfortunate.
LORENZO
Why so, Hieronimo? use me.
HIERONIMO
O no, my lord, I dare not, it must not be,   65
I humbly thank your lordship.
LORENZO   Why then, farewell.
HIERONIMO
My grief no heart, my thoughts no tongue can tell.

                                                  Exit

LORENZO
Come hither, Pedringano, see'st thou this?
PEDRINGANO
My lord, I see it, and suspect it too.
LORENZO
This is that damned villain Serberine,   70
That hath, I fear, revealed Horatio's death.

---

51 *Close* meet; come to an understanding
52 *bewray* disclose   64 *use me* put your suit to me

PEDRINGANO
My lord, he could not, 'twas so lately done;
And since, he hath not left my company.

LORENZO
Admit he have not, his condition's such,
As fear or flattering words may make him false.   75
I know his humour, and therewith repent
That e'er I used him in this enterprise.
But Pedringano, to prevent the worst,
And 'cause I know thee secret as my soul,
Here, for thy further satisfaction, take thou this,   80
                              Gives him more gold
And hearken to me. Thus it is devised:
This night thou must, and prithee so resolve,
Meet Serberine at Saint Luigi's Park—
Thou know'st 'tis here hard by behind the house.
There take thy stand, and see thou strike him sure,   85
For die he must, if we do mean to live.

PEDRINGANO
But how shall Serberine be there, my lord?

LORENZO
Let me alone, I'll send to him to meet
The prince and me, where thou must do this deed.

PEDRINGANO
It shall be done, my lord, it shall be done,   90
And I'll go arm myself to meet him there.

LORENZO
When things shall alter, as I hope they will,
Then shalt thou mount for this: thou know'st my mind.
                              Exit PEDRINGANO
Che le Ieron!

74 *condition* nature, temperament   76 *humour* disposition
83 *Saint Luigi's* ed. (S. *Liugis 1592*)
88 *Let me alone* leave it to me
93 *mount* rise (socially); with a punning reference to 'mounting'
   the gallows, as he does; cf. II, iv, 60–1 on Horatio's similar rise
94–7 lineation ed. (Goe . . . forthwith, / Meet . . . Parke, / Behinde . . .
   boy. *1592*)

94 *Che le Ieron!* unexplained; perhaps, as Boas suggests, a corruption
   of the page's name. Freeman (p. 68) offers the suggestion that 'Che le'
   is equivalent to Italian 'chi là' (Who [is] there?) and Ieron either the
   page's name or an abbreviation of Hieronimo; in the latter case the
   phrase would be prompted by Lorenzo's hearing a noise. This suggestion seems rather implausible dramatically.

Enter PAGE

PAGE   My lord?
LORENZO   Go, sirrah, to Serberine,
And bid him forthwith meet the prince and me   95
At Saint Luigi's Park, behind the house,
This evening, boy.
PAGE   I go, my lord.
LORENZO
But, sirrah, let the hour be eight o'clock.
Bid him not fail.
PAGE   I fly, my lord.   *Exit*
LORENZO
Now to confirm the complot thou hast cast   100
Of all these practices, I'll spread the watch,
Upon precise commandment from the king,
Strongly to guard the place where Pedringano
This night shall murder hapless Serberine.
Thus must we work that will avoid distrust,   105
Thus must we practise to prevent mishap,
And thus one ill another must expulse.
This sly enquiry of Hieronimo
For Bel-imperia breeds suspicion,
And this suspicion bodes a further ill.   110
As for myself, I know my secret fault;
And so do they, but I have dealt for them.
They that for coin their souls endangered,
To save my life, for coin shall venture theirs:
And better it's that base companions die,   115
Than by their life to hazard our good haps.
Nor shall they live, for me to fear their faith:

96 *Saint Luigi's* ed. (*S. Liugis 1592*)
100 *complot* conspiracy
100 *cast* devised
101 *practices* deceits, plots
101 *spread the watch* position the constables
105 *distrust* suspicion
106 *practise* scheme
107 *expulse* expel
108–9 lineation ed. (This . . . suspition, *one line 1592*)
115 *it's* ed. (its *1592*) 115 *base companions* low-bred vulgar fellows
116 *good haps* good fortune, security
117 *fear their faith* be apprehensive about their keeping faith

105–19 a speech full of sentiments typical of the Elizabethan 'Machiavellian'.

I'll trust myself, myself shall be my friend,
For die they shall, slaves are ordained to no other end.

Exit

Act III, Scene iii

Enter PEDRINGANO *with a pistol*

PEDRINGANO
Now, Pedringano, bid thy pistol hold,
And hold on, Fortune! once more favour me;
Give but success to mine attempting spirit,
And let me shift for taking of mine aim!
Here is the gold, this is the gold proposed: 5
It is no dream that I adventure for,
But Pedringano is possessed thereof.
And he that would not strain his conscience
For him that thus his liberal purse hath stretched,
Unworthy such a favour may he fail,   10
And, wishing, want, when such as I prevail.
As for the fear of apprehension,
I know, if need should be, my noble lord
Will stand between me and ensuing harms;
Besides, this place is free from all suspect.   15
Here therefore will I stay and take my stand.

Enter the WATCH

1 WATCH
I wonder much to what intent it is
That we are thus expressly charged to watch.
2 WATCH
'Tis by commandment in the king's own name.
3 WATCH
But we were never wont to watch and ward   20
So near the duke his brother's house before.

119 *slaves* mean, worthless fellows
  1 *hold* be true, function properly
  2 *hold on* continue, be consistent
  4 *let me shift* leave it to me
  7 *is possessed thereof* actually has the gold in his grasp
 10 *fail* be unsuccessful, fall into poverty
 15 *suspect* suspicion
 20 *watch and ward* patrol, keep guard. 'Originally part of the legal
    definition of the duties of a sentinel' (Edwards)

2 WATCH
    Content yourself, stand close, there's somewhat in't.

                    Enter SERBERINE

SERBERINE
    Here, Serberine, attend and stay thy pace,
    For here did Don Lorenzo's page appoint
    That thou by his command shouldst meet with him.   25
    How fit a place, if one were so disposed,
    Methinks this corner is, to close with one.
PEDRINGANO
    Here comes the bird that I must seize upon;
    Now, Pedringano, or never, play the man!
SERBERINE
    I wonder that his lordship stays so long,   30
    Or wherefore should he send for me so late?
PEDRINGANO
    For this, Serberine, and thou shalt ha't.

                                        Shoots the dag

    So, there he lies, my promise is performed.

                    The WATCH

1 WATCH
    Hark gentlemen, this is a pistol shot.
2 WATCH
    And here's one slain; stay the murderer.   35
PEDRINGANO
    Now by the sorrows of the souls in hell,
                        He strives with the WATCH
    Who first lays hand on me, I'll be his priest.
3 WATCH
    Sirrah, confess, and therein play the priest;
    Why hast thou thus unkindly killed the man?
PEDRINGANO
    Why? because he walked abroad so late.   40

22 *close* concealed
23 *stay thy pace* cease walking
27 *close with* grapple with, attack at close quarters (*O.E.D.*, v, 13)
32 s.d. *dag* a heavy pistol
35 *stay* arrest
37 *I'll be his priest* i.e. I'll be there at his death; I'll make an end of him
39 *unkindly* inhumanly, against nature
40 *abroad* out of doors

3 WATCH
　　Come sir, you had been better kept your bed,
　　Than have committed this misdeed so late.
2 WATCH
　　Come, to the marshal's with the murderer!
1 WATCH
　　On to Hieronimo's! help me here
　　To bring the murdered body with us too.   45
PEDRINGANO
　　Hieronimo? carry me before whom you will,
　　Whate'er he be I'll answer him and you.
　　And do your worst, for I defy you all.   *Exeunt*

Act III, Scene iv

Enter LORENZO *and* BALTHAZAR

BALTHAZAR
　　How now, my lord, what makes you rise so soon?
LORENZO
　　Fear of preventing our mishaps too late.
BALTHAZAR
　　What mischief is it that we not mistrust?
LORENZO
　　Our greatest ills we least mistrust, my lord,
　　And inexpected harms do hurt us most.   5
BALTHAZAR
　　Why tell me Don Lorenzo, tell me man,
　　If aught concerns our honour and your own.
LORENZO
　　Nor you nor me, my lord, but both in one;
　　For I suspect, and the presumption's great,
　　That by those base confederates in our fault   10
　　Touching the death of Don Horatio,
　　We are betrayed to old Hieronimo.
BALTHAZAR
　　Betrayed, Lorenzo? tush, it cannot be.
LORENZO
　　A guilty conscience, urged with the thought

43 *Come*, ed. (Come *1592*)
2 *preventing* forestalling
3 *mistrust* 'suspect the existence of or anticipate the occurrence of
　　[something evil]' (*O.E.D.*, v, 3)
5 *inexpected* ed. (in expected *1592*)
10 *confederates in our fault* partners in crime

Of former evils, easily cannot err: 15
I am persuaded, and dissuade me not,
That all's revealed to Hieronimo.
And therefore know that I have cast it thus—

[*Enter* PAGE]

But here's the page. How now, what news with thee?
PAGE
My lord, Serberine is slain.   20
BALTHAZAR
Who? Serberine, my man?
PAGE
Your highness' man, my lord.
LORENZO
Speak page, who murdered him?
PAGE
He that is apprehended for the fact.
LORENZO
Who?   25
PAGE
Pedringano.
BALTHAZAR
Is Serberine slain, that loved his lord so well?
Injurious villain, murderer of his friend!
LORENZO
Hath Pedringano murdered Serberine?
My lord, let me entreat you to take the pains   30
To exasperate and hasten his revenge
With your complaints unto my lord the king.
This their dissension breeds a greater doubt.
BALTHAZAR
Assure thee, Don Lorenzo, he shall die,
Or else his highness hardly shall deny.   35
Meanwhile I'll haste the Marshal-Sessions,
For die he shall for this his damned deed.

Exit BALTHAZAR

18 *cast it thus* laid these plans
24 *fact* deed, crime
31 *exasperate* make harsher
32 *complaints* outcries, statements of grievance
33 *doubt* fear
35 *hardly shall deny* either 'refuse only with difficulty' or (as Edwards suggests) 'show harshness in denying me'

LORENZO   *Bal.*

Why so, this fits our former policy,
And thus experience bids the wise to deal:
I lay the plot, he prosecutes the point;   40
I set the trap, he breaks the worthless twigs,
And sees not that wherewith the bird was limed.
Thus hopeful men, that mean to hold their own,
Must look like fowlers to their dearest friends.
He runs to kill whom I have holp to catch,   45
And no man knows it was my reaching fatch.
'Tis hard to trust unto a multitude,
Or anyone, in mine opinion,
When men themselves their secrets will reveal.

Enter a MESSENGER *with a letter*

Boy!   50
PAGE
My lord?
LORENZO
What's he?
MESSENGER   I have a letter to your lordship.
LORENZO
From whence?
MESSENGER   From Pedringano that's imprisoned.
LORENZO
So he is in prison then?
MESSENGER   Ay, my good lord.
LORENZO
What would he with us? He writes us here   55
To stand good lord and help him in distress.
Tell him I have his letters, know his mind,
And what we may, let him assure him of.
Fellow, begone: my boy shall follow thee.

Exit MESSENGER

40 *prosecutes the point* brings about the goal aimed at
42 *limed* caught in bird-lime   45 *holp* helped
46 *reaching* penetrating, designing
46 *fatch* stratagem (equals 'fetch', *O.E.D* , sb.1, 2)
55–6 lineation ed. (What . . . vs? / He . . . distres. *1592*)
56 *stand good lord* act as good lord and protector

38–49 another typical speech of Machiavellian 'policy', where the main
    aim was to manipulate others.

This works like wax; yet once more try thy wits.   60
Boy, go convey this purse to Pedringano,
Thou knowest the prison, closely give it him,
And be advised that none be there about.
Bid him be merry still, but secret;
And though the Marshal-Sessions be today,   65
Bid him not doubt of his delivery.
Tell him his pardon is already signed,
And thereon bid him boldly be resolved;
For, were he ready to be turned off
(As 'tis my will the uttermost be tried)   70
Thou with his pardon shalt attend him still.
Show him this box, tell him his pardon's in't,
But open't not, and if thou lov'st thy life,
But let him wisely keep his hopes unknown;
He shall not want while Don Lorenzo lives.   75
Away!
PAGE   I go my lord, I run.
LORENZO
But sirrah, see that this be cleanly done.   *Exit* PAGE
Now stands our fortune on a tickle point,
And now or never ends Lorenzo's doubts.
One only thing is uneffected yet,   80
And that's to see the executioner.
But to what end? I list not trust the air
With utterance of our pretence therein,
For fear the privy whispering of the wind
Convey our words amongst unfriendly ears,   85
That lie too open to advantages.
E quel che voglio io, nessun lo sa,
Intendo io: quel mi basterà.   *Exit*

60 *works like wax* follows my design (as wax is easily moulded and
    formed)
62 *closely* secretly   63 *be advised* take care
68 *boldly be resolved* feel completely assured
69 *turned off* hanged (the prisoner is 'turned off' the support he
    stands on and so hanged; see III, vi, 104 s.d.)
73 *and if* if   75–6 lineation ed. (*one line 1592*)
77 *cleanly* efficiently   78 *tickle* precarious, finely-balanced
79 *doubts* fears   82 *list not* have no wish to
83 *pretence* design, intention
86 *advantages* taking advantage, getting the upper hand
87–8 *E quel . . . basterà* ed. (*Et quel que voglio Ii nessun le sa,/Intendo
    io quel mi bassara. 1592*) 'And what I wish, no one knows; *I*
    understand, that suffices me'

Act III, Scene v

Enter BOY *with the box*

PAGE

My master hath forbidden me to look in this box, and by my
troth 'tis likely, if he had not warned me, I should not have
had so much idle time; for we men's-kind in our minority are
like women in their uncertainty: that they are most forbidden, they will soonest attempt. So I now. By my bare   5
honesty, here's nothing but the bare empty box. Were it not
sin against secrecy, I would say it were a piece of gentleman-
like knavery. I must go to Pedringano, and tell him his
pardon is in this box; nay, I would have sworn it, had I not
seen the contrary. I cannot choose but smile to think how   10
the villain will flout the gallows, scorn the audience, and
descant on the hangman, and all presuming of his pardon
from hence. Will't not be an odd jest, for me to stand and
grace every jest he makes, pointing my finger at this box, as
who would say, 'Mock on, here's thy warrant'. Is't not a   15
scurvy jest that a man should jest himself to death? Alas,
poor Pedringano, I am in a sort sorry for thee, but if I should
be hanged with thee, I cannot weep.   *Exit*

Act III, Scene vi

Enter HIERONIMO *and the* DEPUTY

HIERONIMO
Thus must we toil in other men's extremes,
That know not how to remedy our own;
And do them justice, when unjustly we,

1 s.p. PAGE ed. (*not in 1592*)
3 *minority* while still boys   4 *uncertainty* fearfulness
11 *flout* jest at   12 *descant on* hold forth about
16 *scurvy* bitter, base
1 s.d. DEPUTY 'the official title of the assistant to the Knight
Marshal' (Edwards)
1 *extremes* difficulties, hardships

1 ff. This speech, and that at III, vii, 10 ff., is crucial to an understanding
of Hieronimo's outlook at this stage in the play. Both speeches show,
against hostile critics, Hieronimo's deep concern for justice (and not
merely vengeance), together with his frustration at Heaven's apparent
deafness.

For all our wrongs, can compass no redress.
But shall I never live to see the day　　　　　　　5
That I may come, by justice of the heavens,
To know the cause that may my care allay?
This toils my body, this consumeth age,
That only I to all men just must be,
And neither gods nor men be just to me.　　　　10

DEPUTY
Worthy Hieronimo, your office asks
A care to punish such as do transgress.

HIERONIMO
So is't my duty to regard his death
Who when he lived deserved my dearest blood.
But come, for that we came for, let's begin,　　　15
For here lies that which bids me to be gone.

Enter OFFICERS, BOY, *and* PEDRINGANO, *with a letter in his hand,*
bound

DEPUTY
Bring forth the prisoner, for the court is set.

PEDRINGANO
Gramercy, boy, but it was time to come;
For I had written to my lord anew
A nearer matter that concerneth him,　　　　　20
For fear his lordship had forgotten me.
But sith he hath remembered me so well—
Come, come, come on, when shall we to this gear?

HIERONIMO
Stand forth, thou monster, murderer of men,
And here, for satisfaction of the world,　　　　25
Confess thy folly and repent thy fault,
For there's thy place of execution.

7 *know the cause* experience the circumstance
8 *toils* burdens　　　　8 *consumeth age* wears out my life
13 *regard* care about, concern myself with
14 *deserved* merited my spilling
15 ed. (But come, for that we came for lets begin, *1592*)
18 *Gramercy* an exclamation of relief
20 *nearer* of greater concern, more serious
23 *gear* business
25 *for satisfaction of* to convince, demonstrate to

16 *here* Hieronimo touches his head or heart. Or possibly (as Boas thinks)
he refers to the bloody handkercher.

PEDRINGANO

    This is short work! Well, to your marshalship
    First I confess, nor fear I death therefore,
    I am the man, 'twas I slew Serberine.   30
    But sir, then you think this shall be the place
    Where we shall satisfy you for this gear?

DEPUTY

    Ay, Pedringano.

PEDRINGANO   Now I think not so.

HIERONIMO

    Peace, impudent, for thou shalt find it so:
    For blood with blood shall, while I sit as judge,   35
    Be satisfied, and the law discharged.
    And though myself cannot receive the like,
    Yet will I see that others have their right.
    Despatch, the fault's approvéd and confessed,
    And by our law he is condemned to die.   40

HANGMAN

    Come on sir, are you ready?

PEDRINGANO

    To do what, my fine officious knave?

HANGMAN

    To go to this gear.

PEDRINGANO

    O sir, you are too forward; thou wouldst fain furnish me
    with a halter, to disfurnish me of my habit. So I should go   45
    out of this gear, my raiment, into that gear, the rope. But,
    hangman, now I spy your knavery, I'll not change without
    boot, that's flat.

HANGMAN

    Come sir.

PEDRINGANO

    So then, I must up?   50

29 *therefore* 'therefor' may be the correct reading
32 *gear* action, behaviour
39 *approvéd* proved, shown openly
43 *this gear* i.e. hanging
44 *forward* presumptuous
44–8 prose ed. (O sir . . . habit. / So . . . rope. / But . . . flat. *1592*)
45 *habit* clothes
47–8 *without boot* without compensation, without some amends
    (*O.E.D.*, sb. 19)

---

45 *disfurnish me of my habit* Pedringano refers to the custom of giving the
hangman his victim's clothes.

HANGMAN
No remedy.

PEDRINGANO
Yes, but there shall be for my coming down.

HANGMAN
Indeed, here's a remedy for that.

PEDRINGANO
How? be turned off?

HANGMAN
Ay, truly; come, are you ready? I pray, sir, despatch, the   55
day goes away.

PEDRINGANO
What, do you hang by the hour? If you do, I may chance to
break your old custom.

HANGMAN
Faith, you have reason, for I am like to break your young
neck.   60

PEDRINGANO
Dost thou mock me, hangman? Pray God I be not preserved
to break your knave's pate for this.

HANGMAN
Alas, sir, you are a foot too low to reach it, and I hope you
will never grow so high while I am in the office.

PEDRINGANO
Sirrah, dost see yonder boy with the box in his hand?   65

HANGMAN
What, he that points to it with his finger?

PEDRINGANO
Ay, that companion.

HANGMAN
I know him not, but what of him?

PEDRINGANO
Dost thou think to live till his old doublet will make thee a
new truss?   70

HANGMAN
Ay, and many a fair year after, to truss up many an honester
man than either thou or he.

---

54 *turned off* be thrust off the support and so hang
55 *despatch* work quickly
55-6 as prose ed. (I . . . ready / I . . . away. *1592*)
57 *by the hour* at set times
67 *companion* fellow
70 *truss* a close-fitting jacket (*O.E.D.*, sb. 3a); to 'truss up' (l.71) is to
hang

PEDRINGANO

What hath he in his box, as thou think'st?

HANGMAN

Faith, I cannot tell, nor I care not greatly. Methinks you
should rather hearken to your soul's health.   75

PEDRINGANO

Why, sirrah hangman, I take it that that is good for the body
is likewise good for the soul; and it may be, in that box is
balm for both.

HANGMAN

Well, thou art even the merriest piece of man's flesh that
e'er groaned at my office door.   80

PEDRINGANO

Is your roguery become an 'office' with a knave's name?

HANGMAN

Ay, and that shall all they witness that see you seal it with a
thief's name.

PEDRINGANO

I prithee, request this good company to pray with me.

HANGMAN

Ay marry sir, this is a good motion; my masters, you see   85
here's a good fellow.

PEDRINGANO

Nay, nay, now I remember me, let them alone till some other
time, for now I have no great need.

HIERONIMO

I have not seen a wretch so impudent!
O monstrous times, where murder's set so light;   90
And where the soul that should be shrined in heaven,
Solely delights in interdicted things,
Still wandering in the thorny passages
That intercepts itself of happiness.
Murder, O bloody monster, God forbid   95
A fault so foul should 'scape unpunished.

75 *hearken to* care for
74–5 as prose ed. (Faith . . . greatly. / Me thinks . . . health. *1592*)
85 *motion* suggestion, idea
93 *Still* always, for ever

81 *Is your . . . 'office'* Pedringano mocks the high-sounding 'office' used to
   describe the hangman's low-born ('knave's') occupation.
94 Edwards explains 'which prevent it (the soul) from attaining happiness.'
   A more natural construction would arise if 'That' were a misprint
   for 'And', making 'soul' the subject of 'intercepts'; there are, however,
   no grounds for emendation.

Despatch and see this execution done—
This makes me to remember thee, my son.

Exit HIERONIMO

PEDRINGANO
Nay soft, no haste.
DEPUTY
Why, wherefore stay you? Have you hope of life?   100
PEDRINGANO
Why, ay.
HANGMAN
As how?
PEDRINGANO
Why, rascal, by my pardon from the king.
HANGMAN
Stand you on that? then you shall off with this.

He turns him off

DEPUTY
So, executioner. Convey him hence,   105
But let his body be unburied:
Let not the earth be choked or infect
With that which heaven contemns, and men neglect.

Exeunt

Act III, Scene vii

Enter HIERONIMO

HIERONIMO
Where shall I run to breathe abroad my woes,
My woes whose weight hath wearied the earth?

---

99 *soft* wait a moment
104 *Stand you on that?* Do you depend on that? The hangman then
     refers to the literal sense of 'stand'
108 *heaven* ed. (heauens *1592*)
 1 s.p. HIERONIMO ed. (*not in 1592*)
 1 *breathe abroad* give expression to

---

104 s.d. The property which has already done duty as an arbour may have
     again been used here (stripped, perhaps, of its leaves and branches)
     to effect this second hanging. But see II, iv, 53 s.d. and note.
 1–9 Hieronimo's language, and the implied stage-action, may seem
     exaggerated and over-theatrical to modern readers; the speech is,
     however, very nicely calculated for stage-delivery and may be played
     with restraint, while the wording very effectively conveys Hieronimo's
     total preoccupation with his son's death.

Or mine exclaims, that have surcharged the air
With ceaseless plaints for my deceased son?
The blustering winds, conspiring with my words,   5
At my lament have moved the leafless trees,
Disrobed the meadows of their flowered green,
Made mountains marsh with spring-tides of my tears,
And broken through the brazen gates of hell.
Yet still tormented is my tortured soul   10
With broken sighs and restless passions,
That winged mount, and hovering in the air,
Beat at the windows of the brightest heavens,
Soliciting for justice and revenge;
But they are placed in those empyreal heights,   15
Where, counter-mured with walls of diamond,
I find the place impregnable; and they
Resist my woes, and give my words no way.

Enter HANGMAN *with a letter*

HANGMAN
O lord sir, God bless you sir, the man sir,
Petergade sir, he that was so full of merry conceits—   20
HIERONIMO
Well, what of him?
HANGMAN
O lord sir, he went the wrong way, the fellow had a fair
commission to the contrary. Sir, here is his passport; I pray
you sir, we have done him wrong.
HIERONIMO
I warrant thee, give it me.   25
HANGMAN
You will stand between the gallows and me?
HIERONIMO
Ay, ay.

3 *exclaims* cries
11 *passions* sufferings, protesting cries
15 *empyreal* of the highest heaven; the dwelling-place of God
16 *counter-mured* having two walls, one within the other
20 *Petergade* the hangman's bungling attempt at 'Pedringano'
20 *conceits* jests
22-3 *fair commission* proper written authority

10-18 Hieronimo's sense of thwarted right, and the apparent indifference
of 'the brightest heavens', are main elements in our sympathy for his
cause. His state of mind predicts, if briefly and unsubtly, the baffled and
thwarted questioning of Hamlet.

HANGMAN
  I thank your Lord Worship.

                                   Exit HANGMAN

HIERONIMO
  And yet, though somewhat nearer me concerns,
  I will, to ease the grief that I sustain,   30
  Take truce with sorrow while I read on this.
  'My lord, I writ as mine extremes required,
  That you would labour my delivery;
  If you neglect, my life is desperate,
  And in my death I shall reveal the troth.   35
  You know, my lord, I slew him for your sake;
  And as confederate with the prince and you,
  Won by rewards and hopeful promises,
  I holp to murder Don Horatio too.'
  Holp he to murder mine Horatio?   40
  And actors in th' accursed tragedy
  Wast thou, Lorenzo, Balthazar and thou,
  Of whom my son, my son deserved so well?
  What have I heard, what have mine eyes beheld?
  O sacred heavens, may it come to pass   45
  That such a monstrous and detested deed,
  So closely smothered, and so long concealed,
  Shall thus by this be vengéd or revealed!
  Now see I what I durst not then suspect,
  That Bel-imperia's letter was not feigned.   50
  Nor feigned she, though falsely they have wronged
  Both her, myself, Horatio and themselves.

32 *writ* ed. (write *1592*)
32 *extremes* extreme position, predicament
34 *desperate* despaired of, without hope
37 *as* ed. (was *1592*)
47 *closely smothered* kept a close secret

---

32 *writ* The past tense (see textual gloss) must be correct; Pedringano
    refers to his *previous* letter.
37 *as confederate* Edwards's correction ('as' for 'was') gives good sense and
    syntax; Joseph's retention of 'was' on the grounds that three separate
    statements are involved is possible but strained.
45 ff. Hieronimo accepts that coincidences indicate Heaven's wish to bring
    about justice; a weakened form of the mediaeval belief in Fortune as
    God's servant.
50-1 *was not feigned. Nor feigned she* 'He is relieved of two doubts [see
    III, ii, 37–52], whether or not Bel-imperia really wrote the letter, and if
    so whether or not she was telling the truth.' (McIlwraith.)

Now may I make compare, 'twixt hers and this,
Of every accident; I ne'er could find
Till now, and now I feelingly perceive,   55
They did what heaven unpunished would not leave.
O false Lorenzo, are these thy flattering looks?
Is this the hónour that thou didst my son?
And Balthazar, bane to thy soul and me,
Was this the ransom he reserved thee for?   60
Woe to the cause of these constrained wars,
Woe to thy baseness and captivity,
Woe to thy birth, thy body and thy soul,
Thy cursed father, and thy conquered self!
And banned with bitter execrations be   65
The day and place where he did pity thee!
But wherefore waste I mine unfruitful words,
When naught but blood will satisfy my woes?
I will go plain me to my lord the king,
And cry aloud for justice through the court,   70
Wearing the flints with these my withered feet,
And either purchase justice by entreats
Or tire them all with my revenging threats.   *Exit*

Act III, Scene viii

Enter ISABELLA *and her* MAID

ISABELLA
So that, you say, this herb will purge the eye,
And this the head?

54 *accident;* ed. (accident, *1592*) happening, occurrence (relating to
   Horatio's death)
54 *find* understand   55 *feelingly* vividly, with feeling
59 *bane* poison, cause of ruin   61 *constrained* forced, unnecessary
65 *banned* cursed   69 *plair* complain, plead
 1 *purge* cleanse, heal
 2-3 lineation ed. (*one line 1592*)

53-6 'Now I can check on every happening, by using the two letters;
   I could never be sure till now — but now I see very vividly — that
   they committed this crime which Heaven must and will punish.'
   Edwards, I take it, is correct in keeping (and giving greater weight to)
   1592's stop after 'accident'.
69-73 Hieronimo's impulse is to seek justice through the approved
   channels; only if he is thwarted will he take matters into his own hands.
 1-5 These lines may conceivably have suggested Ophelia's flower-lore
   in madness.

Ah, but none of them will purge the heart:
No, there's no medicine left for my disease,
Nor any physic to recure the dead. 5

She runs lunatic

Horatio! O, where's Horatio?

MAID

Good madam, affright not thus yourself
With outrage for your son Horatio:
He sleeps in quiet in the Elysian fields.

ISABELLA

Why, did I not give you gowns and goodly things, 10
Bought you a whistle and a whipstalk too,
To be revenged on their villainies?

MAID

Madam, these humours do torment my soul.

ISABELLA

My soul! poor soul, thou talks of things
Thou know'st not what—my soul hath silver wings, 15
That mounts me up unto the highest heavens;
To heaven, ay, there sits my Horatio,
Backed with a troop of fiery cherubins,
Dancing about his newly-healed wounds,
Singing sweet hymns and chanting heavenly notes, 20
Rare harmony to greet his innocence,
That died, ay died a mirror in our days.
But say, where shall I find the men, the murderers,
That slew Horatio? Whither shall I run
To find them out that murdered my son? *Exeunt* 25

---

5 *recure* recover, restore to health
8 *outrage* outrageous behaviour, passion
9 *Elysian fields* the place of the blessed in the afterworld
11 *whipstalk* whip-handle; used, presumably, in a child's game
13 *humours* uncontrolled fancies
21 *greet* honour (*not*, as the context shows, 'welcome'); Edwards compares (*O.E.D.*, 3e) Spenser's use of the word to mean 'to offer congratulations'
22 *mirror* model of excellence

14–22 Isabella's language here, perhaps only to secure pathos, is distinctly Christian in its description of the after-life, in contrast to the Vergilian language of most other references. Edwards has shown that Kyd's writing here may be indebted to Thomas Watson's elegy on Walsingham, published in 1590.

Act III, Scene ix

BEL-IMPERIA *at a window*

BEL-IMPERIA
What means this outrage that is offered me?
Why am I thus sequestered from the court?
No notice? Shall I not know the cause
Of this my secret and suspicious ills?
Accursed brother, unkind murderer,   5
Why bends thou thus thy mind to martyr me?
Hieronimo, why writ I of thy wrongs,
Or why art thou so slack in thy revenge?
Andrea, O Andrea, that thou sawest
Me for thy friend Horatio handled thus,   10
And him for me thus causeless murdered.
Well, force perforce, I must constrain myself
To patience, and apply me to the time,
Till heaven, as I have hoped, shall set me free.
                    Enter CHRISTOPHIL
CHRISTOPHIL
Come, Madam Bel-imperia, this may not be.   *Exeunt*   15

Act III, Scene x

Enter LORENZO, BALTHAZAR, *and the* PAGE

LORENZO
Boy, talk no further, thus far things go well.
Thou art assured that thou sawest him dead?
PAGE
Or else my lord I live not.
LORENZO   That's enough.
As for his resolution in his end,
Leave that to him with whom he sojourns now.   5
Here, take my ring and give it Christophil,

2 *sequestered* kept apart, secluded
3 *No notice* kept in ignorance
4 *suspicious* arousing suspicion
5 *unkind* unnatural
6 *bends* applies
12 *force perforce* of necessity
13 *apply me to the time* accept things as they are
4 *resolution* courage

And bid him let my sister be enlarged,
And bring her hither straight.   *Exit* PAGE
This that I did was for a policy
To smooth and keep the murder secret,   10
Which as a nine-days' wonder being o'erblown,
My gentle sister will I now enlarge.

BALTHAZAR
And time, Lorenzo, for my lord the duke,
You heard, enquired for her yester-night.

LORENZO
Why, and, my lord, I hope you heard me say   15
Sufficient reason why she kept away.
But that's all one. My lord, you love her?

BALTHAZAR   Ay.

LORENZO
Then in your love beware, deal cunningly,
Salve all suspicions; only soothe me up;
And if she hap to stand on terms with us,   20
As for her sweetheart, and concealment so,
Jest with her gently: under feigned jest
Are things concealed that else would breed unrest.
But here she comes.

Enter BEL-IMPERIA

Now, sister—

BEL-IMPERIA   Sister? No!
Thou art no brother, but an enemy,   25
Else wouldst thou not have used thy sister so:
First, to affright me with thy weapons drawn,
And with extremes abuse my company;
And then to hurry me, like whirlwind's rage,
Amidst a crew of thy confederates,   30
And clap me up where none might come at me,

---

7 *enlarged* set free
9 *policy* stratagem, cunning purpose
10 *smooth* avoid difficult consequences
19 *Salve* allay
19 *soothe me up* agree with me
20 *stand on terms* argue, prove difficult
24 *Now* ed. (*Lor.* Now *1592*)
24–5 lineation ed. (But . . . comes. / Now Sister. / Sister . . . enemy. *1592*)
28 *extremes* harsh behaviour
31 *clap me up* lock me up, unceremoniously

Nor I at any, to reveal my wrongs.
What madding fury did possess thy wits?
Or wherein is't that I offended thee?

LORENZO
Advise you better, Bel-imperia,   35
For I have done you no disparagement;
Unless, by more discretion than deserved,
I sought to save your honour and mine own.

BEL-IMPERIA
Mine honour! why, Lorenzo, wherein is't
That I neglect my reputation so,   40
As you, or any, need to rescue it?

LORENZO
His highness and my father were resolved
To come confer with old Hieronimo,
Concerning certain matters of estate,
That by the viceroy was determined.   45

BEL-IMPERIA
And wherein was mine honour touched in that?

BALTHAZAR
Have patience, Bel-imperia; hear the rest.

LORENZO
Me next in sight as messenger they sent,
To give him notice that they were so nigh:
Now when I came, consorted with the prince,   50
And unexpected, in an arbour there,
Found Bel-imperia with Horatio—

BEL-IMPERIA
How then?

LORENZO
Why then, remembering that old disgrace,
Which you for Don Andrea had endured,   55
And now were likely longer to sustain,

36 *disparagement* dishonour, humiliation
48 *next in sight* standing nearby

---

37 'unless it were that, showing more concern and foresight than you
    deserved . . . '
44–5 Edwards, citing *O.E.D.*, explains: 'concerning certain matters about
    possessions which the viceroy had given up.' 'determined' might,
    however, mean more simply 'decided' or 'specified', and 'matters of
    estate' might mean 'matters of importance', 'state-matters'.
54 *that old disgrace* See I, i, 10–11 and note.

By being found so meanly accompanied,
Thought rather, for I knew no readier mean,
To thrust Horatio forth my father's way.

BALTHAZAR
And carry you obscurely somewhere else,   60
Lest that his highness should have found you there.

BEL-IMPERIA
Even so, my lord? And you are witness
That this is true which he entreateth of?
You, gentle brother, forged this for my sake,
And you, my lord, were made his instrument: 65
A work of worth, worthy the noting too!
But what's the cause that you concealed me since?

LORENZO
Your melancholy, sister, since the news
Of your first favourite Don Andrea's death,
My father's old wrath hath exasperate.   70

BALTHAZAR
And better was't for you, being in disgrace,
To absent yourself, and give his fury place.

BEL-IMPERIA
But why had I no notice of his ire?

LORENZO
That were to add more fuel to your fire,
Who burnt like Aetna for Andrea's loss.   75

BEL-IMPERIA
Hath not my father then enquired for me?

LORENZO
Sister, he hath, and thus excused I thee.
                              He whispereth in her ear
But, Bel-imperia, see the gentle prince;
Look on thy love, behold young Balthazar,
Whose passions by thy presence are increased;   80
And in whose melancholy thou may'st see
Thy hate, his love; thy flight, his following thee.

---

57 *meanly* by a man of low rank
64 *forged* devised and executed this course of action; with an ironic
   hint of the modern sense of deceit
70 *exasperate* made harsher
72 *give his fury place* allow his wrath to expend itself harmlessly
75 *Aetna* the volcano in Sicily

---

57 *so meanly accompanied* Horatio's inferior social standing is frequently
   emphasised.

BEL-IMPERIA
Brother, you are become an orator—
I know not, I, by what experience—
Too politic for me, past all compare,   85
Since last I saw you; but content yourself,
The prince is meditating higher things.
BALTHAZAR
'Tis of thy beauty, then, that conquers kings;
Of those thy tresses, Ariadne's twines,
Wherewith my liberty thou hast surprised;   90
Of that thine ivory front, my sorrow's map,
Wherein I see no haven to rest my hope.
BEL-IMPERIA
To love and fear, and both at once, my lord,
In my conceit, are things of more import
Than women's wits are to be busied with.   95
BALTHAZAR
'Tis I that love.
BEL-IMPERIA   Whom?
BALTHAZAR   Bel-imperia.
BEL-IMPERIA
But I that fear.
BALTHAZAR   Whom?
BEL-IMPERIA   Bel-imperia.
LORENZO
Fear yourself?
BEL-IMPERIA   Ay, brother.
LORENZO   How?
BEL-IMPERIA   As those
That what they love are loath and fear to lose.

---

89 *twines* threads, cords
90 *surprised* captured
91 *front* forehead
94 *In my conceit* to my mind, in my judgment
98-9 lineation ed. (*one line 1592*)

---

85 *Too politic* refers to the 'orator' (who has become too cunning), and not
   to 'experience'.
89 *Ariadne's* Kyd probably has in mind here Arachne, the Lydian weaver
   whom Athene changed to a spider; Ariadne, daughter of King Minos
   of Crete, did, however, use a thread in guiding Theseus through the
   labyrinth. Neither is especially apt here.
91 *sorrow's map* the forehead was supposed to reflect feelings; it is a 'map'
   because Balthazar seeks its aid in discovering the success of his proposal.

BALTHAZAR

  Then, fair, let Balthazar your keeper be.   100

BEL-IMPERIA

  No, Balthazar doth fear as well as we:

  Et tremulo metui pavidum junxere timorem,

  Et vanum stolidae proditionis opus.   *Exit*

LORENZO

  Nay, and you argue things so cunningly,

  We'll go continue this discourse at court.   105

BALTHAZAR

  Led by the loadstar of her heavenly looks,

  Wends poor oppressed Balthazar,

  As o'er the mountains walks the wanderer,

  Incertain to effect his pilgrimage.   *Exeunt*

Act III, Scene xi

Enter two PORTINGALES, *and* HIERONIMO *meets them*

1 PORTINGALE

  By your leave, sir.

HIERONIMO

  Good leave have you: nay, I pray you go,

  For I'll leave you; if you can leave me, so.

2 PORTINGALE

  Pray you, which is the next way to my lord the duke's?

HIERONIMO

  The next way from me.

1 PORTINGALE   To his house, we mean.   5

HIERONIMO

  O, hard by, 'tis yon house that you see.

2 PORTINGALE

  You could not tell us if his son were there?

102 *Et* ed. (*Est 1592*)
106 *loadstar* a star to steer by, usually in reference to the pole-star
109 *Incertain to effect* with no confidence of being able to complete
  3 *me, so* ed. (me so *1592*)
  4 *next* nearest

102-3 'They yoked craven fear to trembling dread: and that a fruitless
  work of doltish treason'. It is difficult to make of these lines a more than
  very general sense.
1-8 Hieronimo's inconsequential talk, like Hamlet's 'wild and whirling
  words', is meant to convey the tension he is suffering under. The
  'Third Addition', inserted after l.1, much expands this state of mind.

HIERONIMO
   Who, my lord Lorenzo?
1 PORTINGALE   Ay, sir.
              He goeth in at one door and comes out at another
HIERONIMO   O, forbear,
   For other talk for us far fitter were.
   But if you be importunate to know   10
   The way to him, and where to find him out,
   Then list to me, and I'll resolve your doubt.
   There is a path upon your left-hand side,
   That leadeth from a guilty conscience
   Unto a forest of distrust and fear,   15
   A darksome place, and dangerous to pass:
   There shall you meet with melancholy thoughts,
   Whose baleful humours if you but uphold,
   It will conduct you to despair and death;
   Whose rocky cliffs when you have once beheld,   20
   Within a hugy dale of lasting night,
   That, kindled with the world's iniquities,
   Doth cast up filthy and detested fumes,
   Not far from thence, where murderers have built
   A habitation for their cursed souls,   25
   There, in a brazen cauldron, fixed by Jove
   In his fell wrath upon a sulphur flame,
   Yourselves shall find Lorenzo bathing him
   In boiling lead and blood of innocents.
1 PORTINGALE
   Ha, ha, ha!
HIERONIMO   Ha, ha, ha!   30
   Why, ha, ha, ha! Farewell, good, ha, ha, ha!
                                                      Exit
2 PORTINGALE
   Doubtless this man is passing lunatic,

8–9 lineation ed. (*one line 1592*)
10 *be importunate* insist
18 *baleful humours* evil tendencies, habits of mind
18 *uphold* persist in
21 *hugy* huge, profound
22 *kindled* set on fire   27 *fell* cruel
30–1 lineation ed. (*one line 1592*)
32 *passing* exceedingly

---

13 Compare I, i, 63–71 and note. Lorenzo is, according to Hieronimo, in
'the deepest hell'.

Or imperfection of his age doth make him dote.
Come, let's away to seek my lord the duke.

[Exeunt]

Act III, Scene xii

Enter HIERONIMO, *with a poniard in one hand, and a rope in the
other*

HIERONIMO

Now sir, perhaps I come and see the king,
The king sees me, and fain would hear my suit:
Why, is not this a strange and seld-seen thing,
That standers-by with toys should strike me mute?
Go to, I see their shifts, and say no more.　　　　　　　　5
Hieronimo, 'tis time for thee to trudge:
Down by the dale that flows with purple gore
Standeth a fiery tower; there sits a judge
Upon a seat of steel and molten brass,
And 'twixt his teeth he holds a fire-brand,　　　　　　　10
That leads unto the lake where hell doth stand.
Away, Hieronimo, to him be gone:
He'll do thee justice for Horatio's death.
Turn down this path, thou shalt be with him straight;
Or this, and then thou need'st not take thy breath.　　　15
This way or that way? Soft and fair, not so:
For if I hang or kill myself, let's know

33　*imperfection of his age* decrepitude, the declining powers of old age
1　s.d. *poniard* dagger
3　*seld* seldom
4　*toys* trifles; trivial business
5　*shifts* tricks
6　*trudge* get moving (*not* slowly)
7　*purple* blood-red
11　*leads* shows the way to
14　*straight* right away
17　*kill* stab

1　s.d. Hieronimo carries, as Boas remarks, 'the stock "properties" of a
would-be suicide' in Elizabethan drama.
7 ff. Hieronimo's search for justice takes place in a landscape that directly
recalls Andrea's search for a resting-place in the afterworld (see I, i);
Kyd is anxious to draw out the analogies between the two quests.
14–15　*this path . . . Or this* by killing himself with poniard or rope. Schick
points out that ll.14–19 present the same ideas as the last three lines
of the Latin dirge (II, v, 78–80).

Who will revenge Horatio's murder then?
No, no! fie, no! pardon me, I'll none of that:
    He flings away the dagger and halter
This way I'll take, and this way comes the king; 20
    He takes them up again
And here I'll have a fling at him, that's flat;
And, Balthazar, I'll be with thee to bring,
And thee, Lorenzo! Here's the king; nay, stay,
And here, ay here; there goes the hare away.

   Enter KING, AMBASSADOR, CASTILE, *and* LORENZO

KING
Now show, Ambassador, what our viceroy saith: 25
Hath he received the articles we sent?
HIERONIMO
Justice, O, justice to Hieronimo.
LORENZO
Back, see'st thou not the king is busy?
HIERONIMO
O, is he so?
KING
Who is he that interrupts our business? 30
HIERONIMO
Not I. Hieronimo, beware: go by, go by.
AMBASSADOR
Renowned king, he hath received and read
Thy kingly proffers, and thy promised league,
And, as a man extremely overjoyed
To hear his son so princely entertained, 35
Whose death he had so solemnly bewailed,
This for thy further satisfaction
And kingly love, he kindly lets thee know:
First, for the marriage of his princely son
With Bel-imperia, thy beloved niece, 40
The news are more delightful to his soul,
Than myrrh or incense to the offended heavens.

---

21 *that's flat* I have made up my mind
22 *I'll . . . bring* I'll get even with you
24 *there . . . away* Edwards explains the phrase refers to losing
  something one has tried to achieve or hold: Hieronimo sees the
  king passing by, preoccupied by business
31 *go by, go by* beware, don't get into trouble

25–30 Hieronimo is thwarted by the day-to-day preoccupations of court
  business; as he foresaw at ll.1–5.

In person, therefore, will be come himself,
To see the marriage rites solemnised;
And, in the presence of the court of Spain,   45
To knit a sure, inexplicable band
Of kingly love, and everlasting league,
Betwixt the crowns of Spain and Portingale,
There will he give his crown to Balthazar,
And make a queen of Bel-imperia.   50

KING
Brother, how like you this our viceroy's love?

CASTILE
No doubt, my lord, it is an argument
Of honourable care to keep his friend,
And wondrous zeal to Balthazar his son;
Nor am I least indebted to his grace,   55
That bends his liking to my daughter thus.

AMBASSADOR
Now last, dread lord, here hath his highness sent
(Although he send not that his son return)
His ransom due to Don Horatio.

HIERONIMO
Horatio! who calls Horatio?   60

KING
And well remembered, thank his majesty.
Here, see it given to Horatio.

HIERONIMO
Justice, O justice, justice, gentle king!

KING
Who is that? Hieronimo?

HIERONIMO
Justice, O, justice! O my son, my son,   65
My son, whom naught can ransom or redeem!

46 *inexplicable* ed. (inexecrable *1592*) which cannot be untied
52 *argument* demonstration, proof
56 *bends* directs   58 *that* in order that

---

46 *inexplicable* *1594*'s reading, unique in that text for the extent of its
   departure from the earlier edition, is here preferred to *1592*'s 'inexecrable', on grounds of meaning. Edwards points out that *1594* might have
   been set up from a copy of *1592* which contained a corrected forme of
   inner G (and this reading); the sole surviving copy of *1592* would on
   that supposition contain an *uncorrected* inner G.
62 The King alone seems unaware that Horatio is dead; an extremely
   implausible situation.

LORENZO

    Hieronimo, you are not well-advised.

HIERONIMO

    Away, Lorenzo, hinder me no more,
    For thou hast made me bankrupt of my bliss.
    Give me my son, you shall not ransom him!   70
    Away! I'll rip the bowels of the earth,

                    He diggeth with his dagger

    And ferry over to th' Elysian plains,
    And bring my son to show his deadly wounds.
    Stand from about me!
    I'll make a pickaxe of my poniard,   75
    And here surrender up my marshalship:
    For I'll go marshal up the fiends in hell,
    To be avenged on you all for this.

KING

    What means this outrage?
    Will none of you restrain his fury?   80

HIERONIMO

    Nay, soft and fair: you shall not need to strive,
    Needs must he go that the devils drive.   *Exit*

KING

    What accident hath happed Hieronimo?
    I have not seen him to demean him so.

LORENZO

    My gracious lord, he is with extreme pride,   85
    Conceived of young Horatio his son,
    And covetous of having to himself
    The ransom of the young prince Balthazar,
    Distract, and in a manner lunatic.

KING

    Believe me, nephew, we are sorry for't: 90
    This is the love that fathers bear their sons.
    But, gentle brother, go give to him this gold,
    The prince's ransom; let him have his due.
    For what he hath Horatio shall not want:
    Haply Hieronimo hath need thereof.   95

---

70 *you . . . him* i.e., from death
72 *th'Elysian plains* see III, viii, 9 and note
74–5 lineation ed. (*one line 1592*)
79 *outrage* violent outburst
79–80 lineation ed. (*one line 1592*)
83 *happed* happened to
84 *demean him* behave himself   95 *Haply* perhaps

LORENZO
> But if he be thus helplessly distract,
> 'Tis requisite his office be resigned,
> And given to one of more discretion.

KING
> We shall increase his melancholy so.
> 'Tis best that we see further in it first;   100
> Till when, ourself will exempt the place.
> And brother, now bring in the ambassador,
> That he may be a witness of the match
> 'Twixt Balthazar and Bel-imperia,
> And that we may prefix a certain time,   105
> Wherein the marriage shall be solemnised,
> That we may have thy lord the viceroy here.

AMBASSADOR
> Therein your highness highly shall content
> His majesty, that longs to hear from hence.

KING
> On, then, and hear you, Lord Ambassador.   *Exeunt*   110

Act III, Scene xiii

Enter HIERONIMO *with a book in his hand*

HIERONIMO
> *Vindicta mihi!*
> Ay, heaven will be revenged of every ill,
> Nor will they suffer murder unrepaid:

100 *see further in it* examine the business further
  1 s.p. HIERONIMO ed. (*not in 1592*)

---

101 *ourself will exempt the place* I have retained the 1592 reading despite
  difficulties over the meaning of 'exempt' and despite the line's being
  one syllable short. The latter difficulty may not be a real one: the line
  would *act* perfectly well as it stands. 'Exempt' I take to mean something
  like 'hold in suspense': the King will avoid the indignity, for Hieronimo,
  of replacing him (Lorenzo's suggestion at 11.96–8), and instead will
  continue the crown's judicial functions without an active Knight
  Marshal. Collier's emendation, 'execute', is attractive in that it presents
  the same idea more explicitly.
  1 s.d. Hieronimo carries a copy of Seneca, as later quotations show.
  1 *Vindicta mihi* Hieronimo quotes the Biblical admonition 'vengeance is
  mine; I will repay, saith the Lord' (Romans xii. 19), a statement much
  used by Elizabethan writers to reserve the execution of vengeance to
  God. The next four lines expand this attitude.

Then stay, Hieronimo, attend their will,
For mortal men may not appoint their time. 5
'*Per scelus semper tutum est sceleribus iter.*'
Strike, and strike home, where wrong is offered thee;
For evils unto ills conductors be,
And death's the worst of resolution.
For he that thinks with patience to contend 10
To quiet life, his life shall easily end.
'*Fata si miseros juvant, habes salutem;*
Fata si vitam negant, habes sepulchrum.'
If destiny thy miseries do ease,
Then hast thou health, and happy shalt thou be; 15
If destiny deny thee life, Hieronimo,
Yet shalt thou be assured of a tomb;
If neither, yet let this thy comfort be,
Heaven covereth him that hath no burial.
And to conclude, I will revenge his death! 20
But how? not as the vulgar wits of men,
With open, but inevitable ills,
As by a secret, yet a certain mean,
Which under kindship will be cloaked best.

---

4 *attend their will* await Heaven's pleasure
9 *death's . . . resolution* death is the worst that can follow bold conduct
10 *contend* strive, make one's way
21 *vulgar* common
22 *inevitable* inevitably successful   22 *ills* ill practices
23 *mean* course of action
24 *kindship* kindness   24 *cloaked* hidden

---

6 'The safe way for crimes is through (further) crimes'. Hieronimo reads from the Seneca he holds in his hand (the Latin is an adaptation of Seneca's *Agamemnon*, l.115). Prompted by the Senecan tag, he reflects that Lorenzo will probably try to secure his own safety by adding a crime against himself to the crime against Horatio (see ll.10–11). It is this reflection that prompts his abandoning the argument for Christian patience of the first five lines.
12–13 Again Hieronimo reads from Seneca (here *Troades*, ll.511–12). The next four lines give a loose translation.
18 *neither* Presumably Hieronimo means neither health nor tomb.
22–3 rather clumsily expressed. Hieronimo means perhaps that simple-minded men ('vulgar wits') seek vengeance by methods which are bold and obvious ('open'), yet despite this effective; he, however, will use subtlety, though the subtlety will not endanger his plan's effectiveness. The main contrast is between crude force and the witty devices Hieronimo is considering.

Wise men will take their opportunity,   25
Closely and safely fitting things to time.
But in extremes advantage hath no time;
And therefore all times fit not for revenge.
Thus therefore will I rest me in unrest,
Dissembling quiet in unquietness,   30
Not seeming that I know their villainies;
That my simplicity may make them think
That ignorantly I will let all slip—
For ignorance, I wot, and well they know,
Remedium malorum iners est.   35
Nor aught avails it me to menace them,
Who, as a wintry storm upon a plain,
Will bear me down with their nobility.
No, no, Hieronimo, thou must enjoin
Thine eyes to observation, and thy tongue   40
To milder speeches than thy spirit affords,
Thy heart to patience, and thy hands to rest,
Thy cap to courtesy, and thy knee to bow,
Till to revenge thou know, when, where and how.
                                        A noise within
How now, what noise? what coil is that you keep?   45

                    Enter a SERVANT

SERVANT
   Here are a sort of poor petitioners,
   That are importunate, and it shall please you, sir,
   That you should plead their cases to the king.

26 *Closely* with subtlety   26 *time* opportunity
32 *simplicity* apparently undesigning behaviour
38 *nobility* noble rank   44 s.d. *follows l.45 in 1592*
45 *what coil . . . keep?* what is all that noise you are making?
46 *sort* group, company   47 *and* if

27–8 'But' here means 'only'; Hieronimo says that only crises ('extremes')
   exclude the possibility of waiting for a favourable moment ('advantage');
   revenge, being considered and deliberate, requires that one waits one's
   opportunity.
29–33 Hieronimo's proposed stealth need not conflict with his sense that
   Heaven prompts and supports him (see e.g. IV, i, 32–4 and III, vii,
   45–56). Johnson (p. 29) quotes Calvin's remark that in dealing with the
   wicked 'God shewed himself a revenger by little and little, and as
   it were faire and softly' (i.e. stealthily).
35 'is an unskilful antidote to evils.' A further quotation from Seneca
   (adapted from *Oedipus* l.515) but not, I think, read from the book.

HIERONIMO
  That I should plead their several actions?
  Why, let them enter, and let me see them.   50

          Enter three CITIZENS *and an* OLD MAN

1 CITIZEN
  So, I tell you this, for learning and for law,
  There's not any advocate in Spain
  That can prevail, or will take half the pain
  That he will, in pursuit of equity.
HIERONIMO
  Come near, you men, that thus importune me.   55
  [*Aside*] Now must I bear a face of gravity,
  For thus I used, before my marshalship,
  To plead in causes as corregidor.—
  Come on sirs, what's the matter?
2 CITIZEN   Sir, an action.
HIERONIMO
  Of battery?
1 CITIZEN   Mine of debt.
HIERONIMO   Give place.   60
2 CITIZEN
  No sir, mine is an action of the case.
3 CITIZEN
  Mine an *ejectione firmae* by a lease.
HIERONIMO
  Content you sirs, are you determined
  That I should plead your several actions?
1 CITIZEN
  Ay sir, and here's my declaration.   65
2 CITIZEN
  And here is my band.

  49 *actions* cases in law
  58 *corregidor* advocate. Strictly, Edwards notes, the chief magistrate
      of a Spanish town
  61 *action of the case* An action not within the limited jurisdiction
      of the Common Pleas needed a special writ to cover it. These
      special writs were known as 'actions of trespass on the case' or
      'actions on the case' (Edwards)
  62 *ejectione firmae* 'a writ to eject a tenant from his holding before
      the expiration of his lease' (Edwards). Kyd's 'by a lease' is
      difficult to account for
  62 *firmae* ed. (firma *1592*)
  65 *declaration* in law, the plaintiff's statement of claim
  66 *band* bond; the special writ referred to at l.61 and note

3 CITIZEN   And here is my lease.
                                        They give him papers

HIERONIMO
    But wherefore stands yon silly man so mute,
    With mournful eyes and hands to heaven upreared?
    Come hither, father, let me know thy cause.
SENEX
    O worthy sir, my cause, but slightly known,   70
    May move the hearts of warlike Myrmidons
    And melt the Corsic rocks with ruthful tears.
HIERONIMO
    Say, father, tell me what's thy suit?
SENEX
    No sir, could my woes
    Give way unto my most distressful words,   75
    Then should I not in paper, as you see,
    With ink bewray what blood began in me.
HIERONIMO
    What's here? 'The humble supplication
    Of Don Bazulto for his murdered son.'
SENEX
    Ay sir.
HIERONIMO No sir, it was my murdered son,   80
    O my son, my son, O my son Horatio!
    But mine, or thine, Bazulto, be content.
    Here, take my handkercher, and wipe thine eyes,
    Whiles wretched I in thy mishaps may see
    The lively portrait of my dying self.   85
                              He draweth out a bloody napkin
    O no, not this: Horatio, this was thine,
    And when I dyed it in thy dearest blood,

---

67 *silly* simple, pitiable
71 *Myrmidons* Achilles' followers; a Thessalian tribe noted for their
    fierceness
72 *Corsic* of Corsica; Seneca's *Octavia* (II.i. in Newton's ed., 1581)
    has a reference to the 'craggy corsicke rockes' among which
    Seneca lived in exile
77 *blood* passion
80-1 lineation ed. (my murdred sonne, oh my sonne. / My sonne . . .
    Horatio. 1592)
85 *lively* living

78-9 Shakespeare uses similar parallels (of sons who have lost fathers)
    in *Hamlet*. Hieronimo's shame (see ll.95 ff.) parallels Hamlet's after
    watching the First Player act the tale of Priam.

This was a token 'twixt thy soul and me
That of thy death revenged I should be.
But here, take this, and this—what, my purse?—   90
Ay, this, and that, and all of them are thine;
For all as one are our extremities.

1 CITIZEN
O see the kindness of Hieronimo!

2 CITIZEN
This gentleness shows him a gentleman.

HIERONIMO
See, see, O see thy shame, Hieronimo,   95
See here a loving father to his son!
Behold the sorrows and the sad laments
That he delivereth for his son's decease!
If love's effects so strives in lesser things,
If love enforce such moods in meaner wits,   100
If love express such power in poor estates—
Hieronimo, whenas a raging sea
Tossed with the wind and tide, o'erturneth then
The upper billows, course of waves to keep,
Whilst lesser waters labour in the deep,   105
Then sham'st thou not, Hieronimo, to neglect
The sweet revenge of thy Horatio?
Though on this earth justice will not be found,
I'll down to hell, and in this passion
Knock at the dismal gates of Pluto's court,   110
Getting by force, as once Alcides did,

90 *this* this coin   92 *extremities* extreme sufferings
100 *meaner* of lower social rank
102 *whenas* ed. (when as *1592*)
103 *o'erturneth* ed. (ore turnest *1592*)
109 *passion* suffering, deep emotion
110 *Pluto* god of the underworld
111 *Alcides* Heracles or Hercules, who in his twelfth labour descended
     to the underworld and conquered Cerberus

102–7 A difficult passage to explain. Hieronimo may mean that in storm
       conditions (i.e. in a time of grief) the surface of the sea is driven into
       great waves (the response of the 'upper waters' to the grief-storm),
       while other and less majestic waters ('lesser waters') are troubled too.
       I think Hieronimo sees himself as, in social standing, equivalent to the
       'upper billows' and is ashamed he has not kept his 'course of waves';
       the Old Man has responded as lesser waters should. (For an alternative
       explanation, reversing the roles, see Edwards.) 'In the deep' need not
       mean 'in the depths' but merely 'in the sea'.

A troop of Furies and tormenting hags
To torture Don Lorenzo and the rest.
Yet lest the triple-headed porter should
Deny my passage to the slimy strond,   115
The Thracian poet thou shalt counterfeit:
Come on, old father, be my Orpheus,
And if thou canst no notes upon the harp,
Then sound the burden of thy sore heart's grief,
Till we do gain that Proserpine may grant   120
Revenge on them that murdered my son.
Then will I rent and tear them thus and thus,
Shivering their limbs in pieces with my teeth.

Tear the papers

1 CITIZEN
O sir, my declaration!

Exit HIERONIMO *and they after*

2 CITIZEN
Save my bond!   125

Enter HIERONIMO

2 CITIZEN
Save my bond!
3 CITIZEN
Alas, my lease! it cost me ten pound,
And you, my lord, have torn the same.
HIERONIMO
That cannot be, I gave it never a wound;
Show me one drop of blood fall from the same: 130
How is it possible I should slay it then?
Tush, no; run after, catch me if you can.

Exeunt all but the OLD MAN

---

114 *triple-headed porter* the three-headed monstrous dog Cerberus,
    guardian of the underworld   115 *slimy strond* see I, i, 27–9
116 *Thracian poet* Orpheus (see next note)
117 *Orpheus* the legendary poet and master of music who followed his
    dead wife Eurydice to the underworld and induced Persephone
    (Proserpine) by his playing to let her go (see following lines)
119 *burden* the theme or refrain of a song   122 *rent* rend

---

120–1 The audience knows that Proserpine has already granted his request
    (I, i, 78 ff.).
132 The similarity to Hamlet's behaviour after the killing of Polonius is
    striking (*Hamlet*, IV, ii). Hieronimo's mistaking the Old Man in the
    following lines is perhaps more acceptable to modern taste, as a way of
    expressing obsession, than Hamlet's vision of the Ghost in the Closet
    scene.

BAZULTO *remains till* HIERONIMO *enters again, who, staring him in the face, speaks*

HIERONIMO
    And art thou come, Horatio, from the depth,
    To ask for justice in this upper earth?
    To tell thy father thou art unrevenged,   135
    To wring more tears from Isabella's eyes,
    Whose lights are dimmed with over-long laments?
    Go back my son, complain to Aeacus,
    For here's no justice; gentle boy be gone,
    For justice is exiled from the earth;   140
    Hieronimo will bear thee company.
    Thy mother cries on righteous Rhadamanth
    For just revenge against the murderers.
SENEX
    Alas my lord, whence springs this troubled speech?
HIERONIMO
    But let me look on my Horatio.   145
    Sweet boy, how art thou changed in death's black shade!
    Had Proserpine no pity on thy youth,
    But suffered thy fair crimson-coloured spring
    With withered winter to be blasted thus?
    Horatio, thou art older than thy father;   150
    Ah ruthless fate, that favour thus transforms!
SENEX
    Ah my good lord, I am not your young son.
HIERONIMO
    What, not my son? thou, then, a Fury art,
    Sent from the empty kingdom of black night
    To summon me to make appearance   155
    Before grim Minos and just Rhadamanth,
    To plague Hieronimo that is remiss,
    And seeks not vengeance for Horatio's death.

137 *lights* eyes
138 *Aeacus* a judge of the underworld; see I, i, 33
142 *cries on* pleads to
142 *Rhadamanth* a judge of the underworld; see I, i, 33
149 *blasted* blighted
151 *fate* ed. (Father *1592*)
151 *favour* appearance, looks
153 *Fury* avenging spirit
156 *Minos* the third judge of the underworld; 'grim' appears to
    contradict the estimate of Minos given at I, i, 50

SENEX

   I am a grieved man, and not a ghost,
   That came for justice for my murdered son.   160

HIERONIMO

   Ay, now I know thee, now thou nam'st thy son;
   Thou art the lively image of my grief:
   Within thy face my sorrows I may see.
   Thy eyes are gummed with tears, thy cheeks are wan,
   Thy forehead troubled, and thy muttering lips   165
   Murmur sad words abruptly broken off
   By force of windy sighs thy spirit breathes;
   And all this sorrow riseth for thy son:
   And selfsame sorrow feel I for my son.
   Come in old man, thou shalt to Isabel;   170
   Lean on my arm: I thee, thou me shalt stay,
   And thou, and I, and she, will sing a song,
   Three parts in one, but all of discords framed—
   Talk not of cords, but let us now be gone,
   For with a cord Horatio was slain.   *Exeunt* 175

Act III, Scene xiv

Enter KING *of* SPAIN, *the* DUKE, VICEROY, *and* LORENZO,
BALTHAZAR, DON PEDRO, *and* BEL-IMPERIA

KING

   Go brother, it is the Duke of Castile's cause,
   Salute the viceroy in our name.

CASTILE   I go.

VICEROY

   Go forth, Don Pedro, for thy nephew's sake,
   And greet the Duke of Castile.

PEDRO   It shall be so.

KING

   And now to meet these Portuguese,   5
   For as we now are, so sometimes were these,

161 *thy* ed. (my *1592*)
162 *lively* living
171 *stay* sustain, prop up
174 *cords* punning on the musical 'chord' and cord meaning rope
1–2 lineation ed. (*as prose 1592*)

6–7 Freeman (pp. 53–4) says that 'western Indies' here refers to Portuguese Brazil, a prize taken by Spain during the quarrels with Portugal of
the late sixteenth century.

Kings and commanders of the western Indies.
Welcome, brave viceroy, to the court of Spain,
And welcome all his honourable train.
'Tis not unknown to us, for why you come,   10
Or have so kingly crossed the seas:
Sufficeth it, in this we note the troth
And more than common love you lend to us.
So is it that mine honourable niece,
(For it beseems us now that it be known)   15
Already is betrothed to Balthazar,
And by appointment and our condescent
To-morrow are they to be married.
To this intent we entertain thyself,
Thy followers, their pleasure and our peace.   20
Speak, men of Portingale, shall it be so?
If ay, say so; if not, say flatly no.

VICEROY

Renowned king, I come not as thou think'st,
With doubtful followers, unresolved men,
But such as háve upon thine articles   25
Confirmed thy motion and contented me.
Know sovereign, I come to solemnise
The marriage of thy beloved niece,
Fair Bel-imperia, with my Balthazar—
With thee, my son; whom sith I live to see,   30
Here take my crown, I give it her and thee;
And let me live a solitary life,
In ceaseless prayers,
To think how strangely heaven hath thee preserved.

KING

See brother, see, how nature strives in him!   35
Come, worthy viceroy, and accompany

9 *train* company, followers
12 *troth* loyalty
17 *condescent* agreement
20 *their* i.e. Bel-imperia and Balthazar   26 *motion* proposal
34 *strangely* wonderfully
35 *nature strives in him* he weeps

11 This looks like an absurd error, though Freeman (p. 12) suggests that
the play may be set in Seville, frequently the seat of the Spanish court;
in this case a Portuguese deputation might well travel partly by sea
(via Cadiz).

Thy friend with thine extremities;
A place more private fits this princely mood.

VICEROY

Or here or where your highness thinks it good.

Exeunt all but CASTILE *and* LORENZO

CASTILE

Nay stay, Lorenzo, let me talk with you.   40
See'st thou this entertainment of these kings?

LORENZO

I do, my lord, and joy to see the same.

CASTILE

And knowest thou why this meeting is?

LORENZO

For her, my lord, whom Balthazar doth love,
And to confirm their promised marriage.   45

CASTILE

She is thy sister?

LORENZO   Who, Bel-imperia?
Ay, my gracious lord, and this is the day
That I have longed so happily to see.

CASTILE

Thou wouldst be loath that any fault of thine
Should intercept her in her happiness.   50

LORENZO

Heavens will not let Lorenzo err so much.

CASTILE

Why then, Lorenzo, listen to my words:
It is suspected and reported too,
That thou, Lorenzo, wrong'st Hieronimo,
And in his suits towards his majesty   55
Still keep'st him back, and seeks to cross his suit.

LORENZO

That I, my lord—?

CASTILE

I tell thee son, myself have heard it said,
When, to my sorrow, I have been ashamed
To answer for thee, though thou art my son.   60
Lorenzo, knowest thou not the common love

37 *extremities* extreme emotions
41 *entertainment* greeting, hospitable reception
46–8 lineation ed. (She . . . Sister? / Who . . . Lord, / And . . . see.
    1592).
50 *intercept* obstruct
56 *cross* interrupt, prevent   61 *common* widespread

King is ignorant of tricks what is going on. around H or Horat.

And kindness that Hieronimo hath won
By his deserts within the court of Spain?
Or seest thou not the king my brother's care
In his behalf, and to procure his health?   65
Lorenzo, shouldst thou thwart his passions,
And he exclaim against thee to the king,
What honour were't in this assembly,
Or what a scandal were't among the kings
To hear Hieronimo exclaim on thee?   70
Tell me, and look thou tell me truly too,
Whence grows the ground of this report in court?

LORENZO
My lord, it lies not in Lorenzo's power
To stop the vulgar, liberal of their tongues:
A small advantage makes a water-breach,   75
And no man lives that long contenteth all.

CASTILE
Myself have seen thee busy to keep back
Him and his supplications from the king.

LORENZO
Yourself, my lord, hath seen his passions,
That ill beseemed the presence of a king;   80
And for I pitied him in his distress,
I held him thence with kind and courteous words,
As free from malice to Hieronimo
As to my soul, my lord.

CASTILE
Hieronimo, my son, mistakes thee then.   85

LORENZO
My gracious father, believe me so he doth.
But what's a silly man, distract in mind,
To think upon the murder of his son?
Alas, how easy is it for him to err!
But for his satisfaction and the world's,   90
'Twere good, my lord, that Hieronimo and I
Were reconciled, if he misconster me.

66 *passions* laments, complaints
67 *exclaim against* denounce
74 *vulgar, liberal* ed. (vulgar liberall *1592*) common people, free with
75 *advantage* opportunity (for exploitation), weakness
75 *water-breach* a gap in wall or dyke caused by water-pressure
80 *ill beseemed* fitted ill with
87 *silly* simple, poor
92 *misconster* misconstrue, wilfully misinterpret

CASTILE

Lorenzo, thou hast said; it shall be so;
Go one of you and call Hieronimo.

Enter BALTHAZAR *and* BEL-IMPERIA

BALTHAZAR

Come, Bel-imperia, Balthazar's content,　　　　95
My sorrow's ease and sovereign of my bliss,
Sith heaven hath ordained thee to be mine;
Disperse those clouds and melancholy looks,
And clear them up with those thy sun-bright eyes,
Wherein my hope and heaven's fair beauty lies.　　　100

BEL-IMPERIA

My looks, my lord, are fitting for my love,
Which new begun, can show no brighter yet.

BALTHAZAR

New kindled flames should burn as morning sun.

BEL-IMPERIA

But not too fast, lest heat and all be done.
I see my lord my father.

BALTHAZAR　　　　　　Truce, my love;　　　　105
I will go salute him.

CASTILE　　　　　　　Welcome, Balthazar,
Welcome brave prince, the pledge of Castile's peace;
And welcome Bel-imperia. How now, girl?
Why com'st thou sadly to salute us thus?
Content thyself, for I am satisfied;　　　　110
It is not now as when Andrea lived,
We have forgotten and forgiven that,
And thou art graced with a happier love.
But Balthazar, here comes Hieronimo,
I'll have a word with him.　　　　115

---

102 *no brighter* ed. (brighter *1592*)
105-7 lineation ed. (I see . . . Father. / Truce . . . him. / Welcome . .
　　　Prince, / The . . . peace: *1592*)
109 *sadly* with serious looks

---

102 *no brighter* *1594*'s emendation (*1592* omits 'no') must be right; *1592*
　　makes sense ('there's time for them to get brighter') but asks Bel-
　　imperia to be coyly encouraging, an improbable attitude here.
110-13 yet another reference to the disapproval felt for Bel-imperia's
　　liaison with Andrea (see I, i, 10-11 and note).

Enter HIERONIMO *and a* SERVANT

HIERONIMO
And where's the duke?
SERVANT   Yonder.
HIERONIMO   Even so:
What new device have they devised, trow?
Pocas palabras! mild as the lamb,
Is't I will be revenged? No, I am not the man.
CASTILE
Welcome Hieronimo.   120
LORENZO
Welcome Hieronimo.
BALTHAZAR
Welcome Hieronimo.
HIERONIMO
My lords, I thank you for Horatio.
CASTILE
Hieronimo, the reason that I sent
To speak with you, is this.
HIERONIMO   What, so short?   125
Then I'll be gone, I thank you for't.
CASTILE
Nay, stay, Hieronimo—go call him, son.
LORENZO
Hieronimo, my father craves a word with you.
HIERONIMO
With me sir? why, my lord, I thought you had done.
LORENZO
[*Aside*] No, would he had.
CASTILE   Hieronimo, I hear   130
You find yourself aggrieved at my son
Because you have not access unto the king,
And say 'tis he that intercepts your suits.

116–17 lineation ed. (*one line 1592*)
117 *device* plot
117 *trow?* do you think?
118 *Pocas palabras* few words (Spanish)
128 s.p. LORENZO ed. (*not in 1592*)
130–1 lineation ed. (No, . . . had. / Hieronimo . . . Sonne, *1592*)
133 *intercepts* obstructs, thwarts

117–19 Hieronimo now feels threatened, like Hamlet later, by plots ('devices') on all sides.

HIERONIMO
  Why, is not this a miserable thing, my lord?
CASTILE
  Hieronimo, I hope you have no cause,   135
  And would be loath that one of your deserts
  Should once have reason to suspect my son,
  Considering how I think of you myself.
HIERONIMO
  Your son Lorenzo! whom, my noble lord?
  The hope of Spain, mine honourable friend?   140
  Grant me the combat of them, if they dare:
                                  Draws out his sword
  I'll meet him face to face, to tell me so.
  These be the scandalous reports of such
  As love not me, and hate my lord too much.
  Should I suspect Lorenzo would prevent   145
  Or cross my suit, that loved my son so well?
  My lord, I am ashamed it should be said.
LORENZO
  Hieronimo, I never gave you cause.
HIERONIMO
  My good lord, I know you did not.
CASTILE   There then pause,
  And for the satisfaction of the world,   150
  Hieronimo, frequent my homely house,
  The Duke of Castile, Cyprian's ancient seat,
  And when thou wilt, use me, my son, and it.
  But here, before Prince Balthazar and me,
  Embrace each other, and be perfect friends.   155
HIERONIMO
  Ay marry, my lord, and shall.
  Friends, quoth he? see, I'll be friends with you all:
  Specially with you, my lovely lord;
  For divers causes it is fit for us
  That we be friends—the world is suspicious,   160
  And men may think what we imagine not.

141 *the combat of them* the right to meet them in (hand-to-hand) combat
144 *love* ed. (loues *1592*)
145 *prevent* forestall, obstruct
146 *cross* thwart
149–50 lineation ed. (There . . . world *one line 1592*)
151 *homely* welcoming, hospitable, 'home-like'
153 *use* make use of, ask the services of

BALTHAZAR
  Why, this is friendly done, Hieronimo.
LORENZO
  And thus I hope old grudges are forgot.
HIERONIMO
  What else? it were a shame it should not be so.
CASTILE
  Come on, Hieronimo, at my request;   165
  Let us intreat your company today.

                    Exeunt [*all but* HIERONIMO]

HIERONIMO
  Your lordship's to command.—Pha! keep your way:
  Chi mi fa più carezze che non suole,
  Tradito mi ha, o tradir vuole.   *Exit*

Act III, Scene xv

            Ghost [*of* ANDREA] *and* REVENGE

ANDREA
  Awake, Erichtho! Cerberus, awake!
  Solicit Pluto, gentle Proserpine;
  To combat, Acheron and Erebus!
  For ne'er by Styx and Phlegethon in hell
    5
  Nor ferried Charon to the fiery lakes

163 *thus* ed. (that *1592*)
167 *Pha!* an exclamation of contempt or disgust
168 *Chi . . . suole* ed. (*Mi. Chi mi fa? Pui Correzza Che non sule 1592*)
169 *Tradito . . . vuole* ed. (*Tradito viha otrade vule. 1592*)
  1 s.d. Ghost ed. (Enter *Ghoast 1592*)
  1 s.p. ANDREA ed. (*Ghost 1592 throughout this scene*)
  1 *Erichtho* ed. (*Erictha 1592*) 'the Thessalian sorceress' (Schick)
  3 *Acheron* ed. (*Achinon 1592*) see III, i, 55 and note
  3 *Erebus* ed. (*Ericus 1592*) primaeval darkness, child of chaos
  4 *ne'er* ed. (neere *1592*)
  4 *Styx and Phlegethon* rivers of the underworld
  4 *in hell* (*end of l.3 in 1592*)   6 *Charon* see I, i, 20 and note at I, i, 19

168-9 'He who gives me more caresses than usual has betrayed me or.
    wishes to betray me.'
  4-7 I accept Edwards's supposition that a line has dropped out after l.4
    (he suggests it might have been something like 'Was I distressed with
    outrage sore as this'). Only on this basis can the passage be made to
    give reasonable sense.

Such fearful sights, as poor Andrea sees!
Revenge, awake!

REVENGE

Awake? for why?

ANDREA

Awake, Revenge, for thou art ill-advised   10
To sleep away what thou art warned to watch!

REVENGE

Content thyself, and do not trouble me.

ANDREA

Awake, Revenge, if love, as love hath had,
Have yet the power or prevalence in hell!
Hieronimo with Lorenzo is joined in league, —   15
And intercepts our passage to revenge:
Awake, Revenge, or we are woe-begone!

REVENGE

Thus worldlings ground, what they have dreamed, upon.
Content thyself, Andrea: though I sleep,
Yet is my mood soliciting their souls;   20
Sufficeth thee that poor Hieronimo
Cannot forget his son Horatio.
Nor dies Revenge although he sleep awhile,

7 *sees!* ed. (see? *1592*)
11 *To sleep* ed. (Thsleep *1592*)
11 away ed. (away, *1592*)
11 *sleep away* sleep out
11 *watch* stay awake
14 *prevalence* ed. (preuailance *1592*)
17 *begone* ed. (degone *1592*)
20 *mood* Edwards thinks 'anger' just possible; a more general **sense**
   such as 'attitude', 'purposes' seems required

---

8 ff. The repetitions of 'Awake' may seem crude, and there is considerable
   suspicion that the text of this scene as a whole is a debased one (see
   Edwards, esp. pp. xxxiii and xxxviii–xxxix), yet the action does have
   dramatic point in giving emphatic expression to Andrea's sense that
   vengeance is becoming less and less probable — even Hieronimo seems
   to have betrayed the cause (see l.15). Elizabethans would have understood the scene as referring to the 'worldling's' (see l.18) faithless
   supposition that delay is equivalent to the abandoning of God's (or
   Revenge's) purposes.
11 *away* Edwards may be correct in accepting Hawkins's emendation
   'awake!' in place of *1592*'s 'away'; but the text makes good sense as it
   stands and I see no compelling grounds for emendation.
18 *worldlings . . . upon* 'mortals base their beliefs on what they have merely
   dreamed (or fancied)'.

For in unquiet, quietness is feigned,
And slumbering is a common worldly wile.   25
Behold, Andrea, for an instance how
Revenge hath slept, and then imagine thou
What 'tis to be subject to destiny.

Enter a Dumb Show [*; they act and exeunt*]

ANDREA
Awake, Revenge, reveal this mystery.
REVENGE
The two first, the nuptial torches bore,   30
As brightly burning as the mid-day's sun;
But after them doth Hymen hie as fast,
Clothed in sable, and a saffron robe,
And blows them out, and quencheth them with blood,
As discontent that things continue so   35
ANDREA
Sufficeth me; thy meaning's understood;
And thanks to thee and those infernal powers
That will not tolerate a lover's woe.
Rest thee, for I will sit to see the rest.
REVENGE
Then argue not, for thou hast thy request.   40

Exeunt

Act IV, Scene i

Enter BEL-IMPERIA *and* HIERONIMO

BEL-IMPERIA
Is this the love thou bear'st Horatio?
Is this the kindness that thou counterfeits?
Are these the fruits of thine incessant tears?
Hieronimo, are these thy passions,
Thy protestations and thy deep laments,   5
That thou wert wont to weary men withal?
O unkind father, O deceitful world!

29 *reveal this mystery* explain the secret meaning of this action (the
   dumb show)
32 *Hymen* god of marriage
32 *hie* run
33 *sable* black
33 *saffron* yellow, the usual colour of Hymen's robe
 4 *passions* passionate exclamations
 7 *unkind* unnatural

With what excuses canst thou show thyself,
With what...............................
From this dishonour and the hate of men?—   10
Thus to neglect the loss and life of him
Whom both my letters and thine own belief
Assures thee to be causeless slaughtered.
Hieronimo, for shame, Hieronimo,
Be not a history to after times   15
Of such ingratitude unto thy son.
Unhappy mothers of such children then—
But monstrous fathers, to forget so soon
The death of those, whom they with care and cost
Have tendered so, thus careless should be lost.   20
Myself a stranger in respect of thee,
So loved his life, as still I wish their deaths;
Nor shall his death be unrevenged by me,
Although I bear it out for fashion's sake:
For here I swear in sight of heaven and earth,   25
Shouldst thou neglect the love thou shouldst retain
And give it over and devise no more,
Myself should send their hateful souls to hell,
That wrought his downfall with extremest death.

HIERONIMO
But may it be that Bel-imperia   30
Vows such revenge as she hath deigned to say?
Why then, I see that heaven applies our drift

---

9 *With what* . . . ed. (With what dishonour, and the hate of men
    1592)
15 *history* example, tale   20 *tendered* cared for, cherished
21 *in respect of* compared to
24 *bear it . . . sake* 'make a pretence of accepting the situation for the
    sake of appearances' (Edwards)
27 *devise* plot   29 *extremest* most cruel
32 *applies our drift* blesses our enterprise (drift, 'what we are
    driving at')

---

9 The dots represent material presumed lost when the *1592* compositor
    inadvertently included in l.9 the last six words of l.10 (see textual
    gloss above). The first two words (as printed) may be either the correct
    first words of the (now missing) l.9 or a mistaken repeat of the beginning
    of l.8. Bungling of some kind has certainly taken place, and since the
    true original cannot be recovered it seems best to indicate this by
    inserting dots.
17–20 an incomplete sentence; just plausible dramatically as reflecting in
    its lack of grammatical structure Bel-imperia's unsettled state of mind.

And all the saints do sit soliciting
For vengeance on those cursed murderers.
Madam 'tis true, and now I find it so;   35
I found a letter, written in your name,
And in that letter, how Horatio died.
Pardon, O pardon, Bel-imperia,
My fear and care in not believing it,
Nor think I thoughtless think upon a mean   40
To let his death be unrevenged at full;
And here I vow, so you but give consent,
And will conceal my resolution,
I will ere long determine of their deaths
That causeless thus have murdered my son.   45

BEL-IMPERIA
Hieronimo, I will consent, conceal;
And aught that may effect for thine avail
Join with thee to revenge Horatio's death.

HIERONIMO
On then; whatsoever I devise,
Let me entreat you, grace my practices.   50
For why, the plot's already in mine head.
Here they are.

Enter BALTHAZAR *and* LORENZO

BALTHAZAR   How now, Hieronimo?
What, courting Bel-imperia?

HIERONIMO   Ay, my lord,
Such courting as, I promise you,
She hath my heart, but you, my lord, have hers.   55

LORENZO
But now, Hieronimo, or never,
We are to entreat your help.

39 *care* caution
40 *thoughtless* unconcerned
44 *determine of* bring about
47 *avail* assistance
50 *grace* support, involve yourself in
51 *For why* because
52–61 lineation ed. (Heere . . . are. / How . . . *Bel-Imperia*. / I . . . you
      / She . . . hers. / But . . . helpe. / My . . . me. / For . . . you. / It . . .
      Embassadour. *1592*)

52 ff. Kyd here allows his actors an excellent opportunity for expressing,
      through hypocritical politeness, the tensions between the three men.

HIERONIMO   My help?
Why, my good lords, assure yourselves of me,
For you have given me cause,
Ay, by my faith have you.

BALTHAZAR   It pleased you   60
At the entertainment of the ambassador
To grace the king so much as with a show:
Now were your study so well furnished,
As, for the passing of the first night's sport,
To entertain my father with the like,   65
Or any such-like pleasing motion,
Assure yourself it would content them well.

HIERONIMO
Is this all?

BALTHAZAR
Ay, this is all.

HIERONIMO
Why then I'll fit you; say no more.   70
When I was young I gave my mind
And plied myself to fruitless poetry:
Which though it profit the professor naught,
Yet is it passing pleasing to the world.

LORENZO
And how for that?

HIERONIMO   Marry, my good lord, thus—   75
And yet, methinks, you are too quick with us—
When in Toledo there I studied,
It was my chance to write a tragedy—
See here my lords—   *He shows them a book*
Which long forgot, I found this other day.   80
Now would your lordships favour me so much
As but to grace me with your acting it—
I mean each one of you to play a part—

62 *grace* honour
63 *furnished* stocked
66 *motion* entertainment
70 *I'll fit you* (a) 'I'll provide you what you need' (b) 'I'll pay you
out' or 'I'll punish you as you deserve' (Edwards)
73 *professor* the man who 'professes' or practises it
76 *too quick* too pressing; perhaps with a pun on quick meaning alive

76 unclear. Perhaps the line is meant to convey that Hieronimo's anger
is only just under control.

Assure you it will prove most passing strange
And wondrous plausible to that assembly.   85

BALTHAZAR
What, would you have us play a tragedy?

HIERONIMO
Why, Nero thought it no disparagement,
And kings and emperors have ta'en delight
To make experience of their wits in plays!

LORENZO
Nay, be not angry good Hieronimo,   90
The prince but asked a question.

BALTHAZAR
In faith, Hieronimo, and you be in earnest,
I'll make one.

LORENZO
And I another.

HIERONIMO
Now my good lord, could you entreat   95
Your sister Bel-imperia to make one?
For what's a play without a woman in it?

BEL-IMPERIA
Little entreaty shall serve me, Hieronimo,
For I must needs be employed in your play.

HIERONIMO
Why, this is well; I tell you lordings,   100
It was determined to have been acted
By gentlemen and scholars too
Such as could tell what to speak.

84 *strange* remarkable, wonderful
85 *plausible* agreeable
87 *disparagement* loss of dignity
89 *experience* trial   92 *and* if
101 *determined* intended, arranged
103 *could tell* knew, were skilful

87 *Nero* Hieronimo is correct in indicating that the Roman emperor Nero
    patronised plays and acted in them himself; at the same time he was
    associated with violence and deeds of blood, and the audience would no
    doubt pick up the allusion. Balthazar's nervousness (l.155) is fully
    justified.
103–5 *what to speak . . . how to speak* not clear. Balthazar may mean only
    that courtiers are as skilled as 'gentlemen and scholars' in these matters.
    Some contrast may be intended between scholars who are good at
    invention and courtiers who are good at elocution.

BALTHAZAR
　　And now it shall be played by princes and courtiers,
　　Such as can tell how to speak,　　　　　　　　　　105
　　If, as it is our country manner,
　　You will but let us know the argument.
HIERONIMO
　　That shall I roundly. The chronicles of Spain
　　Record this written of a knight of Rhodes:
　　He was betrothed, and wedded at the length　　110
　　To one Perseda, an Italian dame,
　　Whose beauty ravished all that her beheld,
　　Especially the soul of Soliman,
　　Who at the marriage was the chiefest guest.
　　By sundry means sought Soliman to win　　　115
　　Perseda's love, and could not gain the same.
　　Then gan he break his passions to a friend,
　　One of his bashaws whom he held full dear;
　　Her had this bashaw long solicited,
　　And saw she was not otherwise to be won　　120
　　But by her husband's death, this knight of Rhodes,
　　Whom presently by treachery he slew.
　　She, stirred with an exceeding hate therefore,
　　As cause of this slew Soliman;
　　And to escape the bashaw's tyranny　　　　　125
　　Did stab herself: and this the tragedy.
LORENZO
　　O excellent!
BEL-IMPERIA　　But say, Hieronimo,
　　What then became of him that was the bashaw?

---

107 *argument* plot, narrative　　　108 *roundly* plainly; at once
114 *was* ed. (*way 1592*)　　　117 *break* disclose, confess
118 *bashaws* pashas, Turkish officers of high rank; courtiers
127–8 lineation ed. (O excellent. / But . . . him/That . . . Bashaw? *1592*)

---

107 *let us know the argument* Apparently we should think of the play as
　　unscripted: Hieronimo will sketch in the plot and on that basis the
　　actors will improvise their own lines. Kyd avoids repeating the 'argu-
　　ment' (or plot) by providing the King with a written copy (IV, iii,
　　6–7; IV, iv, 9–10). The 'abstracts' referred to at l. 141 would perhaps
　　outline the play's narrative a little more fully.
108–40 The playlet of Soliman and Perseda, as well as providing the mech-
　　anism of disaster, represents several of the main relationships of the
　　larger play.

HIERONIMO
Marry thus: moved with remorse of his misdeeds,
Ran to a mountain-top and hung himself.   130
BALTHAZAR
But which of us is to perform that part?
HIERONIMO
O, that will I my lords, make no doubt of it:
I'll play the murderer, I warrant you,
For I already have conceited that.
BALTHAZAR
And what shall I?   135
HIERONIMO
Great Soliman the Turkish emperor.
LORENZO
And I?
HIERONIMO
Erastus the knight of Rhodes.
BEL-IMPERIA
And I?
HIERONIMO
Perseda, chaste and resolute.   140
And here, my lords, are several abstracts drawn,
For each of you to note your parts,
And act it, as occasion's offered you.
You must provide a Turkish cap,
A black mustachio and a fauchion.   145
                    Gives a paper to BALTHAZAR.
You with a cross like to a knight of Rhodes.
                    Gives another to LORENZO
And madam, you must attire yourself
                    He giveth BEL-IMPERIA *another*
Like Phoebe, Flora, or the Huntress,
Which to your discretion shall seem best.
And as for me, my lords, I'll look to one;   150
And, with the ransom that the viceroy sent
So furnish and perform this tragedy,
As all the world shall say Hieronimo
Was liberal in gracing of it so.

---

134 *conceited* envisaged, formed a conception of
141 *abstracts* outlines   141 *drawn* drawn up, written out
145 *fauchion* a broad curved sword (also spelled 'falchion')
148 *Huntress* Diana, goddess of hunting
150 *look to* prepare   154 *gracing* setting it out, adorning it

BALTHAZAR
  Hieronimo, methinks a comedy were better.   155
HIERONIMO
  A comedy?
  Fie, comedies are fit for common wits:
  But to present a kingly troop withal,
  Give me a stately-written tragedy,
  Tragedia cothurnata, fitting kings,   160
  Containing matter, and not common things.
  My lords, all this must be performed,
  As fitting for the first night's revelling.
  The Italian tragedians were so sharp of wit,
  That in one hour's meditation   165
  They would perform anything in action.
LORENZO
  And well it may; for I have seen the like
  In Paris, 'mongst the French tragedians.
HIERONIMO
  In Paris? mass, and well remembered!
  There's one thing more that rests for us to do.   170
BALTHAZAR
  What's that, Hieronimo? forget not anything.
HIERONIMO
  Each one of us must act his part
  In unknown languages,

156–7 lineation ed. (A . . . wits *one line 1592*)
158 *kingly troop* royal audience
160 *Tragedia cothurnata* in ancient Athens tragedy performed by an
    actor wearing buskins (thick-soled boots); the most serious kind
    of drama
160 *cothurnata* ed. (*cother nato 1592*)
161 *matter* substance, serious content
170 *rests* remains   173 *unknown* i.e. not in our own tongue

164–6 The reference is to the performers of the *Commedia dell' Arte*,
    who improvised plays from scenarios.
172 ff. It is not clear whether the 'sundry languages' will ever have been
    used on stage. The note to the reader at IV, iv, 10 s.d. seems to suggest
    they were, and that the present text of the playlet is a translation,
    perhaps expanded, from the original. Since the audience has already
    heard the play's 'argument' they might well have been content to
    listen to 'unknown languages', provided they were not given too much
    of them and provided the action that accompanied them was highly
    explicit and stylised.

That it may breed the more variety.
As you, my lord, in Latin, I in Greek,   175
You in Italian; and for because I know
That Bel-imperia hath practised the French,
In courtly French shall all her phrases be.

BEL-IMPERIA
You mean to try my cunning then, Hieronimo.

BALTHAZAR
But this will be a mere confusion,   180
And hardly shall we all be understood.

HIERONIMO
It must be so, for the conclusion
Shall prove the invention and all was good.
And I myself in an oration,
And with a strange and wondrous show besides,   185
That I will have there behind a curtain,
Assure yourself, shall make the matter known.
And all shall be concluded in one scene,
For there's no pleasure ta'en in tediousness.

BALTHAZAR
[*Aside to* LORENZO] How like you this?   190

LORENZO
Why, thus my lord,
We must resolve to soothe his humours up.

BALTHAZAR
On then Hieronimo, farewell till soon.

HIERONIMO
You'll ply this gear?

LORENZO   I warrant you.
                                   Exeunt all but HIERONIMO
HIERONIMO   Why so.
Now shall I see the fall of Babylon,   195

179 *cunning* skill   183 *invention* basic idea
185 *show* tableau (in fact Horatio's body)
185–6 transposed in *1592*   192 *We must resolve* (ends *l.191 in 1592*)
192 *soothe . . . up* indulge his whims
194 *ply this gear* carry out this business
194–5 lineation ed. (*one line in 1592*)

185 *strange and wondrous show* Horatio's body: the emblem that justifies
    and explains the whole elaborate business.
195 *fall of Babylon* Johnson (pp. 24 ff.) explains that the Geneva Bible
    (in use at Kyd's date of writing) uses 'Babel' both for the Tower of
    Babel and for the wicked city of Babylon: the two would be closely
    associated in the audience's mind. For the destruction of Babylon see
    Isaiah xiii, Jeremiah li, and Revelation xviii.

Wrought by the heavens in this confusion.
And if the world like not this tragedy,
Hard is the hap of old Hieronimo.

Exit

Act IV, Scene ii

Enter ISABELLA *with a weapon*

ISABELLA

Tell me no more! O monstrous homicides!
Since neither piety nor pity moves
The king to justice or compassion,
I will revenge myself upon this place
Where thus they murdered my beloved son.   5

She cuts down the arbour

Down with these branches and these loathsome boughs
Of this unfortunate and fatal pine:
Down with them, Isabella, rent them up
And burn the roots from whence the rest is sprung.
I will not leave a root, a stalk, a tree,   10
A bough, a branch, a blossom, nor a leaf,
No, not an herb within this garden-plot.
Accursed complot of my misery,
Fruitless for ever may this garden be!
Barren the earth, and blissless whosoever   15
Imagines not to keep it unmanured!
An eastern wind commixed with noisome airs
Shall blast the plants and the young saplings;
The earth with serpents shall be pestered,
And passengers, for fear to be infect,   20
Shall stand aloof, and, looking at it, tell,
'There, murdered, died the son of Isabel.'
Ay, here he died, and here I him embrace:

1 s.d. ISABELLA ed. (*not in 1592*)
7 *unfortunate* ominous
8 *rent* rend, tear
13 *complot* plot
16 *unmanured* uncultivated, barren
17 *noisome* pestilent
20 *passengers* passers-by
20 *infect* infected

5 s.d. Isabella may merely strip the leaves and branches from the arbour;
    or she may topple a property tree if one was used. See II, iv, 53 s.d.
    and note.

See where his ghost solicits with his wounds
Revenge on her that should revenge his death.   25
Hieronimo, make haste to see thy son,
For sorrow and despair hath cited me
To hear Horatio plead with Rhadamanth:
Make haste, Hieronimo, to hold excused
Thy negligence in pursuit of their deaths,   30
Whose hateful wrath bereaved him of his breath.
Ah nay, thou dost delay their deaths,
Forgives the murderers of thy noble son,
And none but I bestir me—to no end.
And as I curse this tree from further fruit,   35
So shall my womb be cursed for his sake;
And with this weapon will I wound the breast,

She stabs herself

The hapless breast that gave Horatio suck.

[Exit]

Act IV, Scene iii

Enter HIERONIMO; *he knocks up the curtain*
Enter the DUKE OF CASTILE

CASTILE
How now Hieronimo, where's your fellows,
That you take all this pain?
HIERONIMO
O sir, it is for the author's credit
To look that all things may go well.
But, good my lord, let me entreat your grace   5

27 *cited* summoned
28 *Rhadamanth* one of the judges of the underworld
29 *hold excused* to *have* it held excused
34 *me—to* ed. (me to *1592*)
 1 *fellows* fellow actors

32–4 Even Isabella is deceived by Hieronimo's plan of stealthy and
    circumspect revenge.
37 s.d., 38 s.d. The stage has to be cleared, though there is no one to
    remove Isabella's body. Presumably she stumbles off, wounded.
 1 s.d. Hieronimo probably hangs a curtain over one of the large entrance-
    doors at the rear of the Elizabethan stage. We can, it seems clear, take
    it that there was no permanent inner-stage, at least at this theatre,
    since such a stage would have been the obvious place to use on this
    occasion, and stage-carpentry would have been unnecessary.

To give the king the copy of the play:
This is the argument of what we show.

CASTILE
I will, Hieronimo

HIERONIMO
One thing more, my good lord.

CASTILE
What's that?   10

HIERONIMO
Let me entreat your grace
That, when the train are passed into the gallery,
You would vouchsafe to throw me down the key.

CASTILE
I will, Hieronimo.   *Exit* CASTILE

HIERONIMO
What, are you ready, Balthazar?   15
Bring a chair and a cushion for the king.

Enter BALTHAZAR *with a chair*

Well done, Balthazar; hang up the title.
Our scene is Rhodes—what, is your beard on?

BALTHAZAR
Half on, the other is in my hand.

HIERONIMO
Despatch for shame, are you so long?   20

                                               Exit BALTHAZAR

Bethink thyself, Hieronimo,
Recall thy wits, recompt thy former wrongs
Thou hast received by murder of thy son;
And lastly, not least, how Isabel,

---

7 *argument* plot, narrative
20 *Despatch* hurry   22 *recompt* call to memory

12–13 It would seem natural to use the upper stage for the King and
courtiers watching the play; subsequent action shows, however, that
all the actors remained on the main stage. The 'gallery' must refer to
the 'hall' or 'long gallery' of a large Elizabethan house. 'Throw down' is
explained by Edwards as 'throw the key down [on the floor] for me.'

17–18 *title . . . scene* There is some evidence that Elizabethan theatres
used both title-boards and locality-labels to give audiences information
they might otherwise miss.

18–19 *beard . . . Half on* Kyd deliberately, and with some finesse, makes
the play-occasion as authentic as possible, and so provides the greatest
degree of contrast between the surface normality and the horror to
come: an intensification of the play's continuing irony.

Once his mother and thy dearest wife,   25
All woe-begone for him, hath slain herself.
Behoves thee then, Hieronimo, to be revenged.
The plot is laid of dire revenge:
On then, Hieronimo, pursue revenge,
For nothing wants but acting of revenge.   30

Exit HIERONIMO

Act IV, Scene iv

Enter SPANISH KING, VICEROY, *the* DUKE OF CASTILE, *and their*
train

KING
Now, Viceroy, shall we see the tragedy
Of Soliman the Turkish emperor,
Performed of pleasure by your son the prince,
My nephew Don Lorenzo, and my niece.
VICEROY
Who, Bel-imperia?   5
KING
Ay, and Hieronimo, our marshal,
At whose request they deign to do't themselves:
These be our pastimes in the court of Spain.
Here, brother, you shall be the book-keeper:
This is the argument of that they show.   10

He giveth him a book

Gentlemen, this play of Hieronimo, in sundry languages, was
thought good to be set down in English more largely, for the
easier understanding to every public reader.

Enter BALTHAZAR, BEL-IMPERIA, *and* HIERONIMO

BALTHAZAR
Bashaw, that Rhodes is ours, yield heavens the honour,
And holy Mahomet, our sacred prophet;
And be thou graced with every excellence
That Soliman can give, or thou desire.
But thy desert in conquering Rhodes is less   15

---

3 *of pleasure* at their pleasure
9 *book-keeper* in the Elizabethan theatre referring to the book-
holder and prompter

10 s.d. See IV, i, 172 ff. and note.

Than in reserving this fair Christian nymph,
Perseda, blissful lamp of excellence,
Whose eyes compel, like powerful adamant,
The warlike heart of Soliman to wait.

KING

See, Viceroy, that is Balthazar, your son,   20
That represents the emperor Soliman:
How well he acts his amorous passion.

VICEROY

Ay, Bel-imperia hath taught him that.

CASTILE

That's because his mind runs all on Bel-imperia.

HIERONIMO

Whatever joy earth yields betide your majesty.   25

BALTHAZAR

Earth yields no joy without Perseda's love.

HIERONIMO

Let then Perseda on your grace attend.

BALTHAZAR

She shall not wait on me, but I on her:
Drawn by the influence of her lights, I yield.
But let my friend, the Rhodian knight, come forth,   30
Erasto, dearer than my life to me,
That he may see Perseda, my beloved.

Enter [LORENZO *as*] ERASTO

KING

Here comes Lorenzo; look upon the plot,
And tell me, brother, what part plays he?

BEL-IMPERIA

Ah, my Erasto, welcome to Perseda.   35

LORENZO

Thrice happy is Erasto that thou liv'st—
Rhodes' loss is nothing to Erasto's joy;
Sith his Perseda lives, his life survives.

16 *reserving* preserving, protecting
18 *adamant* the loadstone (which had magnetic properties)
19 *wait* attend on her
29 *lights* eyes
33 *plot* synopsis and cast-list
37 *to* compared to

20–4 Kyd takes some pains to see that the audience is aware of the parallels
between the actor and his assumed part.

BALTHAZAR
    Ah, bashaw, here is love between Erasto
    And fair Perseda, sovereign of my soul.   40
HIERONIMO
    Remove Erasto, mighty Soliman,
    And then Perseda will be quickly won.
BALTHAZAR
    Erasto is my friend, and while he lives
    Perseda never will remove her love.
HIERONIMO
    Let not Erasto live to grieve great Soliman.   45
BALTHAZAR
    Dear is Erasto in our princely eye.
HIERONIMO
    But if he be your rival, let him die.
BALTHAZAR
    Why, let him die: so love commandeth me.
    Yet grieve I that Erasto should so die.
HIERONIMO
    Erasto, Soliman saluteth thee,   50
    And lets thee wit by me his highness' will,
    Which is, thou shouldst be thus employed.

                                              Stab him
BEL-IMPERIA   *Ay me,*
    Erasto! see, Soliman, Erasto's slain!
BALTHAZAR
    Yet liveth Soliman to comfort thee.
    Fair queen of beauty, let not favour die,   55
    But with a gracious eye behold his grief,
    That with Perseda's beauty is increased,
    If by Perseda his grief be not released.
BEL-IMPERIA
    Tyrant, desist soliciting vain suits;
    Relentless are mine ears to thy laments,   60
    As thy butcher is pitiless and base,
    Which seized on my Erasto, harmless knight.
    Yet by thy power thou thinkest to command,
    And to thy power Perseda doth obey:
    But were she able, thus she would revenge   65

52 *Ay me*, ed. (*begins l.53 in 1592*)
55 *favour* i.e. your love
58 *Perseda his* ed. (*Persedaes 1592*) 'his' must be heavily elided, as
     the *1592* spelling indicates

Thy treacheries on thee, ignoble prince: *Stab him*
And on herself she would be thus revenged   *Stab herself*

KING
Well said, old marshal, this was bravely done!

HIERONIMO
But Bel-imperia plays Perseda well.

VICEROY
Were this in earnest, Bel-imperia,   70
You would be better to my son than so.

KING
But now what follows for Hieronimo?

HIERONIMO
Marry, this follows for Hieronimo:
Here break we off our sundry languages
And thus conclude I in our vulgar tongue.   75
Haply you think, but bootless are your thoughts,
That this is fabulously counterfeit,
And that we do as all tragedians do:
To die today, for fashioning our scene,
The death of Ajax, or some Roman peer,   80
And in a minute starting up again,
Revive to please to-morrow's audience.
No, princes; know I am Hieronimo,
The hopeless father of a hapless son,
Whose tongue is tuned to tell his latest tale,   85
Not to excuse gross errors in the play.
I see your looks urge instance of these words;
Behold the reason urging me to this:
                                        Shows his dead son
See here my show, look on this spectacle.

75 *vulgar tongue* the vernacular, our everyday speech
76 *Haply* perhaps
76 *bootless* unavailing
77 *fabulously counterfeit* acted in fiction only
79 *for . . . scene* ed. (for (fashioning our scene) *1592*) enacting our
    play
85 *latest* last
87 *instance* explanation, what lies behind (these words)
89 *show* tableau, spectacle

68 *Well said* The King refers to Hieronimo's success in composing the
    piece: 'Well done'.
76-86 The fiction—fact relationship, stated very simply here by Kyd,
    became a topic for much more subtle exploration by Shakespeare and
    later Elizabethan dramatists.

Here lay my hope, and here my hope hath end; 90
Here lay my heart, and here my heart was slain;
Here lay my treasure, here my treasure lost;
Here lay my bliss, and here my bliss bereft;
But hope, heart, treasure, joy, and bliss,
All fled, failed, died, yea, all decayed with this. 95
From forth these wounds came breath that gave me life;
They murdered me that made these fatal marks.
The cause was love, whence grew this mortal hate
The hate, Lorenzo and young Balthazar,
The love, my son to Bel-imperia. 100
But night, the coverer of accursed crimes,
With pitchy silence hushed these traitors' harms
And lent them leave, for they had sorted leisure
To take advantage in my garden-plot
Upon my son, my dear Horatio: 105
There merciless they butchered up my boy,
In black dark night, to pale dim cruel death.
He shrieks, I heard, and yet methinks I hear,
His dismal outcry echo in the air.
With soonest speed I hasted to the noise, 110
Where hanging on a tree I found my son,
Through-girt with wounds, and slaughtered as you see.
And grieved I, think you, at this spectacle?
Speak, Portuguese, whose loss resembles mine:
If thou canst weep upon thy Balthazar, 115
'Tis like I wailed for my Horatio.
And you, my lord, whose reconciled son
Marched in a net, and thought himself unseen,
And rated me for brainsick lunacy,
With 'God amend that mad Hieronimo!'— 120
How can you brook our play's catastrophe?
And here behold this bloody handkercher,
Which at Horatio's death I weeping dipped

---

102 *harms* their malicious actions   103 *sorted* sought out
112 *Through-girt* pierced through
118 *Marched in a net* kept himself concealed, practised deceit; a proverbial phrase
119 *rated* berated

---

96 *From forth . . . life* i.e. *my* life-breath left me when these wounds were
made in my son's body.
117 *reconciled* presumably to Hieronimo (see III, xiv, 130–64).
119–20 Compare Lorenzo's advice to the King at III, xii, 85–9 and 96–8.

Within the river of his bleeding wounds:
It as propitious, see I have reserved,   125
And never hath it left my bloody heart,
Soliciting remembrance of my vow
With these, O these accursed murderers:
Which now performed, my heart is satisfied.
And to this end the bashaw I became   130
That might revenge me on Lorenzo's life,
Who therefore was appointed to the part,
And was to represent the knight of Rhodes,
That I might kill him more conveniently.
So, Viceroy, was this Balthazar, thy son —   135
That Soliman which Bel-imperia
In person of Perseda murdered—
Solely appointed to that tragic part
That she might slay him that offended her.
Poor Bel-imperia missed her part in this: 140
For though the story saith she should have died,
Yet I of kindness, and of care to her,
Did otherwise determine of her end;
But love of him whom they did hate too much
Did urge her resolution to be such.   145
And princes, now behold Hieronimo,
Author and actor in this tragedy,
Bearing his latest fortune in his fist:
And will as resolute conclude his part
As any of the actors gone before.   150
And, gentles, thus I end my play:
Urge no more words; I have no more to say.
                         He runs to hang himself

KING

O hearken, Viceroy! Hold, Hieronimo!
Brother, my nephew and thy son are slain!

---

125 *propitious* of good omen; a token prompting to due revenge
140 *missed her part* strayed from her assigned part
153 *Hold, Hieronimo!* cd. (holde *Hieronimo, 1592*) wait, Hieronimo;
     'hold' in *1592* might mean 'arrest'

130–52 This may be over-explicit; but audiences are notoriously slow at
     registering the action of plays, especially when they have more than one
     group of actors to watch, as is the case with Hieronimo's playlet and
     its audience.

VICEROY

We are betrayed! my Balthazar is slain!   155
Break ope the doors, run, save Hieronimo.

[They break in, and hold HIERONIMO]

Hieronimo, do but inform the king of these events;
Upon mine honour thou shalt have no harm.

HIERONIMO

Viceroy, I will not trust thee with my life,
Which I this day have offered to my son.   160
Accursed wretch,
Why stayest thou him that was resolved to die?

KING

Speak, traitor; damned, bloody murderer, speak!
For now I have thee I will make thee speak—
Why hast thou done this undeserving deed?   165

VICEROY

Why hast thou murdered my Balthazar?

CASTILE

Why hast thou butchered both my children thus?

HIERONIMO

O, good words!
As dear to me was my Horatio
As yours, or yours, or yours, my lord, to you.   170
My guiltless son was by Lorenzo slain,
And by Lorenzo and that Balthazar

161 *Accursed wretch*, ed. (*begins l.162 in 1592*)
168 *O, good words* ed. (*begins l.169 in 1592*)
172 *by* i.e. by the deaths of

---

156 The doors have been locked by Castile, as Hieronimo requested
(IV, iii, 12–13). The attendants 'break in' from off-stage and guard
Hieronimo.

165–7 and 179–82 Edwards finds the questions at these points an 'extraordinary inconsistency', since Hieronimo has already 'told [the king]
everything'. He accounts for the inconsistency by supposing (with
Schücking) that IV, iv, 153–201 represents 'an alternative ending
to the play', replacing Hieronimo's long speech (ll.73–152), and
requiring therefore the brief explanation at ll.169 ff. Edwards makes
out a good case, but the inconsistency may be less glaring than at first
appears, for at l.179 the King is asking Hieronimo to discuss his confederates (Bel-imperia principally), which he has not yet done in
detail; Hieronimo refuses to break the vow he swore to Bel-imperia at
IV, i, 42–5 (see ll.187–8). The King's earlier questioning, and that of
the Viceroy and Castile, might be explained as the result of grief-
stricken bewilderment and not mere redundancy; they have not taken
in what Hieronimo has said.

    Am I at last revenged thoroughly,
    Upon whose souls may heavens be yet avenged
    With greater far than these afflictions.   175

CASTILE
    But who were thy confederates in this?

VICEROY
    That was thy daughter Bel-imperia;
    For by her hand my Balthazar was slain:
    I saw her stab him.

KING   Why speak'st thou not?

HIERONIMO
    What lesser liberty can kings afford   180
    Than harmless silence? then afford it me:
    Sufficeth I may not, nor I will not tell thee.

KING
    Fetch forth the tortures.
    Traitor as thou art, I'll make thee tell.

HIERONIMO   Indeed,
    Thou may'st torment me, as his wretched son   185
    Hath done in murdering my Horatio,
    But never shalt thou force me to reveal
    The thing which I have vowed inviolate.
    And therefore in despite of all thy threats,
    Pleased with their deaths, and eased with their revenge,   190
    First take my tongue, and afterwards my heart.
                      [He bites out his tongue]

KING
    O monstrous resolution of a wretch!
    See, Viceroy, he hath bitten forth his tongue
    Rather than to reveal what we required.

CASTILE
    Yet can he write.   195

KING
    And if in this he satisfy us not,

---

184 *Indeed* ed. (*begins l.185 in 1592*)

---

191 s.d. Barish (p. 82) thinks this action 'betrays the final despair at the
    uselessness of talk, the beserk resolve to have done with language
    forever.' Johnson (p. 34) says it 'serves to identify Hieronimo as ad-
    mirably stoic' since his action imitates Zeno of Elea, the famous Stoic,
    who under torture 'bit off his own tongue, and spat it out in the tor-
    mentors' face' (quoting William Baldwin's *Treatise of Morall Philosophie*,
    9th ed., 1579).

We will devise th'extremest kind of death
That ever was invented for a wretch.
> *Then he makes signs for a knife to mend his pen*

CASTILE
O, he would have a knife to mend his pen.
VICEROY
Here; and advise thee that thou write the troth.   200
KING
Look to my brother! save Hieronimo!
> *He with a knife stabs the* DUKE *and himself*
What age hath ever heard such monstrous deeds?
My brother, and the whole succeeding hope
That Spain expected after my decease!
Go bear his body hence, that we may mourn   205
The loss of our beloved brother's death;
That he may be entombed, whate'er befall:
I am the next, the nearest, last of all.

VICEROY
And thou, Don Pedro, do the like for us;
Take up our hapless son, untimely slain: 210
Set me with him, and he with woeful me,
Upon the main-mast of a ship unmanned,
And let the wind and tide haul me along
To Scylla's barking and untamed gulf,
Or to the loathsome pool of Acheron,   215
To weep my want for my sweet Balthazar:
Spain hath no refuge for a Portingale.

The trumpets sound a dead march, the KING *of* SPAIN *mourning
after his brother's body, and the* VICEROY *of* PORTINGALE *bearing
the body of his son*

200 *advise thee* be advised, take care
201 s.p. KING ed. (*not in 1592?*)
213 *haul* drive; hale; possibly, suggests Edwards, a word with nautical
    associations for Kyd
214 *gulf* ed. (greefe *1592*)
215 *Acheron* see I, i, 19 and note   216 *my want for* my loss of
217 s.d. VICEROY OF PORTINGALE ed. (*King of Portingale 1592*)

202–4 Patriotic feelings may be involved here: English audiences would be
    delighted by Spain's discomfiture.
214 *Scylla's . . . gulf* Scylla was one of a pair of dangerous rocks (the other
    was Charybdis) between Italy and Sicily; Joseph says that Homer
    refers to Scylla, the goddess of the rock, as 'barking', while later
    writers described her as accompanied by barking dogs.

Act IV, Scene v

Ghost [of ANDREA] *and* REVENGE

ANDREA
Ay, now my hopes have end in their effects,
When blood and sorrow finish my desires:
Horatio murdered in his father's bower,
Vild Serberine by Pedringano slain,
False Pedringano hanged by quaint device,   5
Fair Isabella by herself misdone,
Prince Balthazar by Bel-imperia stabbed,
The Duke of Castile and his wicked son
Both done to death by old Hieronimo,
My Bel-imperia fallen as Dido fell,   10
And good Hieronimo slain by himself:
Ay, these were spectacles to please my soul.
Now will I beg at lovely Proserpine,
That, by the virtue of her princely doom,
I may consort my friends in pleasing sort,   15
And on my foes work just and sharp revenge.
I'll lead my friend Horatio through those fields
Where never-dying wars are still inured:
I'll lead fair Isabella to that train
Where pity weeps but never feeleth pain: 20
I'll lead my Bel-imperia to those joys
That vestal virgins and fair queens possess;
I'll lead Hieronimo where Orpheus plays,

1 s.p. ANDREA ed. (*Ghoast. 1592 throughout this scene*)
1 s.d. *Ghost* ed. (*Enter Ghoast 1592*)
4 *Vild* vile   5 *quaint* cunning
6 *misdone* slain
14 *doom* judgment
15 *consort* accompany, treat
18 *inured* carried on
19 *train* company
22 *vestal virgins* virgins consecrated to the Roman goddess Vesta,
     and vowed to chastity
23 *Orpheus* see III, xiii, 117 and note

1–2 Compare Revenge at II, vi, 7–8.
10 *as Dido fell* Vergil (*Aeneid* IV) records that Dido killed herself after
     Aeneas's departure from Carthage. The legend Vergil adapted also
     speaks of Dido as a suicide, killing herself to avoid marriage with
     Iarbas.

Adding sweet pleasure to eternal days.
But say, Revenge, for thou must help, or none,   25
Against the rest how shall my hate be shown?

REVENGE

This hand shall hale them down to deepest hell,
Where none but Furies, bugs and tortures dwell.

ANDREA

Then, sweet Revenge, do this at my request;
Let me be judge, and doom them to unrest: 30
Let loose poor Tityus from the vulture's gripe,
And let Don Cyprian supply his room;
Place Don Lorenzo on Ixion's wheel,
And let the lover's endless pains surcease—
Juno forgets old wrath, and grants him ease;   35
Hang Balthazar about Chimaera's neck,
And let him there bewail his bloody love,
Repining at our joys that are above;
Let Serberine go roll the fatal stone,
And take from Sisyphus his endless moan;   40
False Pedringano for his treachery,
Let him be dragged through boiling Acheron,
And there live, dying still in endless flames,
Blaspheming gods and all their holy names.

REVENGE

Then haste we down to meet thy friends and foes: 45
To place thy friends in ease, the rest in woes.
For here, though death hath end their misery,
I'll there begin their endless tragedy.   *Exeunt*

---

28 *bugs* bugbears, horrors
32 *supply his room* take his place
34 *the lover* Ixion, who had tried to seduce Juno
34 *surcease* cease
36 *Chimaera* a fire-breathing monster of Greek mythology, with
     head of a lion, body of a goat, tail of a dragon
40 *Sisyphus* a legendary king of Crete, condemned for his misdeeds
     to roll a large stone eternally uphill in the underworld
43 *still* continually, for ever
47 *end* ended

---

32 *Don Cyprian* the Duke of Castile; he had frowned on Andrea's
     relationship with Bel-imperia (see II, i, 45–8).

APPENDIX: THE 'ADDITIONS'

First printed in 1602 and there incorporated into the original text of the play, the so-called 'Additions' to *The Spanish Tragedy* comprise in all some 320 lines. Of the five additional passages, the first, second and fifth are brief and of slight importance; the third is a more sustained and accomplished piece, and the fourth is the well-known Painter scene, which amplifies in a striking manner the theme of Hieronimo's grief, and provides a remarkable opportunity for an actor to portray madness. Despite the excellence of some of the writing, however, there can be little doubt that inclusion of these scenes in an acting version would have the effect of upsetting the rhythm of Kyd's play.

It is most unlikely in fact that the 1602 text, including the 'Additions', was ever performed in its existing state. It is, for one thing, exceptionally long. It is more likely that the additional passages were intended to replace parts of Kyd's text which were felt by 1602 to be either old-fashioned or weak. Pavier, the publisher of this new edition, may have received from the theatre or from some intermediary, authorised or not, portions of the new copy; he would then incorporate them as best he could into an example of *1592*. Some support for this theory comes from the rough, or at the least 'free', state of the verse in the additional passages; we may suspect that some kind of printer's bungling has taken place.

The author of the 'Additions' is unknown. Ben Jonson was, we know, paid for revisions to *The Spanish Tragedy*, but those we have are rather unlike his characteristic work, and there are problems (of dating mainly) about connecting Henslowe's payment to Jonson with the printing of *1602*. Jonson, it is true, may have adapted his style to suit the play he was editing; but equally plausible is the suggestion that the lines are the work of another author, and that Jonson's revision of the play has unfortunately never reached print. Webster, Shakespeare and Dekker are among writers suggested as alternative authors, but the case for any one of them, or for other contemporaries, is not a strong one.

Scenes added to
THE SPANISH TRAGEDY
in the edition of 1602

First Addition, between II, v, 45 and 46

[For outrage fits our cursed wretchedness.]
Ay me, Hieronimo, sweet husband speak.
HIERONIMO
He supped with us tonight, frolic and merry,
And said he would go visit Balthazar
At the duke's palace: there the prince doth lodge.
He had no custom to stay out so late,   5
He may be in his chamber; some go see.
Roderigo, ho!

Enter PEDRO *and* JAQUES

ISABELLA
Ay me, he raves. Sweet Hieronimo!
HIERONIMO
True, all Spain takes note of it.
Besides, he is so generally beloved   10
His majesty the other day did grace him
With waiting on his cup: these be favours
Which do assure he cannot be short-lived.
ISABELLA
Sweet Hieronimo!
HIERONIMO
I wonder how this fellow got his clothes?   15
Sirrah, sirrah, I'll know the truth of all:
Jaques, run to the Duke of Castile's presently,
And bid my son Horatio to come home:
I and his mother have had strange dreams tonight.
Do you hear me, sir?
JAQUES   Ay, sir.

2 *frolic* frolicsome, gay
7 *Roderigo, ho!* (ends l.6 in *1602*)
10 *generally* by everyone
13 *assure* ensure, prove
13 *he* ed. (me *1602*)
17 *presently* at once

11–12 See I, iv, 130.

HIERONIMO   Well sir, begone.   20
 Pedro, come hither: knowest thou who this is?

PEDRO
 Too well, sir.

HIERONIMO
 Too well? Who? Who is it? Peace, Isabella:
 Nay, blush not, man.

PEDRO   It is my lord Horatio.

HIERONIMO
 Ha, ha! Saint James, but this doth make me laugh, 25
 That there are more deluded than myself.

PEDRO
 Deluded?

HIERONIMO
 Ay, I would have sworn myself within this hour
 That this had been my son Horatio,
 His garments are so like.   30
 Ha! are they not great persuasions?

ISABELLA
 O, would to God it were not so!

HIERONIMO
 Were not, Isabella? Dost thou dream it is?
 Can thy soft bosom entertain a thought
 That such a black deed of mischief should be done 35
 On one so pure and spotless as our son?
 Away, I am ashamed.

ISABELLA   Dear Hieronimo,
 Cast a more serious eye upon thy grief:
 Weak apprehension gives but weak belief.

HIERONIMO
 It was a man, sure, that was hanged up here;   40
 A youth, as I remember: I cut him down.
 If it should prove my son now after all—
 Say you, say you, light! Lend me a taper,
 Let me look again. O God!
 Confusion, mischief, torment, death and hell,   45

20–4 lineation ed. (*prose in 1602*)
30–1 lineation ed. (*one line 1602*)
31 *persuasions* evidences, means of persuasion
36 *pure* ed. (*poore 1602*)
37 *Dear Hieronimo* ed. (*begins l.38 in 1602*)
39 *apprehension* understanding, grasp of what's happening
44 *O God!* ed. (*begins l.45 in 1602*)

Drop all your stings at once in my cold bosom,
That now is stiff with horror; kill me quickly:
Be gracious to me, thou infective night,
And drop this deed of murder down on me;
Gird in my waste of grief with thy large darkness,   50
And let me not survive to see the light
May put me in the mind I had a son.

ISABELLA

O, sweet Horatio. O, my dearest son!

HIERONIMO

How strangely had I lost my way to grief!
[Sweet lovely rose, ill plucked before thy time,]

Second Addition, replacing III, ii, 65 and part of 66

[LORENZO

Why so, Hieronimo? use me.]

HIERONIMO

Who, you, my lord?
I reserve your favour for a greater honour;
This is a very toy my lord, a toy.

LORENZO

All's one, Hieronimo, acquaint me with it.

HIERONIMO

I'faith, my lord, 'tis an idle thing.   5
I must confess, I ha' been too slack,
Too tardy. Too remiss unto your honour.

LORENZO

How now, Hieronimo?

HIERONIMO

In troth, my lord, it is a thing of nothing,
The murder of a son, or so: 10
A thing of nothing, my lord.

[LORENZO   Why then, farewell.]

48 *infective* bearing infection
50 *Gird in* confine, limit
50 *waste* a vast, empty area (with a play on 'waist')
 3 *toy* trifle, trivial thing
5–7 lineation ed. (*prose in 1602*)

Third Addition, between III, xi, 1 and 2

[1 PORTINGALE
  By your leave, sir.]
HIERONIMO
  'Tis neither as you think, nor as you think,
  Nor as you think: you're wide all:
  These slippers are not mine, they were my son Horatio's.
  My son, and what's a son? A thing begot
  Within a pair of minutes, thereabout: 5
  A lump bred up in darkness, and doth serve
  To ballace these light creatures we call women;
  And, at nine moneths' end, creeps forth to light.
  What is there yet in a son
  To make a father dote, rave or run mad?   10
  Being born, it pouts, cries, and breeds teeth.
  What is there yet in a son? He must be fed,
  Be taught to go, and speak. Ay, or yet?
  Why might not a man love a calf as well?
  Or melt in passion o'er a frisking kid,   15
  As for a son? Methinks a young bacon
  Or a fine little smooth horse-colt
  Should move a man as much as doth a son:
  For one of these in very little time
  Will grow to some good use, whereas a son,   20
  The more he grows in stature and in years,
  The more unsquared, unbevelled he appears,
  Reckons his parents among the rank of fools,
  Strikes care upon their heads with his mad riots,
  Makes them look old before they meet with age: 25

  2 *wide* wide of the mark, quite wrong
  4 *A thing begot* ed. (*begins l.5 in 1602*)
  7 *ballace* ballast, weigh down
  8 *moneths* months (metre requires a dissyllable)
  11 *breeds teeth* cuts teeth
  13 *go* walk
  16 *young bacon* piglet

  13. *Ay, or yet?* Hieronimo means 'Yes, or what else?', 'What can I add?'
  22 *unsquared, unbevelled* Boas says 'uneven and unpolished': the author
      of this Addition has in mind the rough manners of young bloods.
      'Bevelling' is a decorative process in carpentry performed with a 'bevel'
      or 'bevel-square'.

This is a son:
And what a loss were this, considered truly?
Oh, but my Horatio
Grew out of reach of these insatiate humours:
He loved his loving parents,   30
He was my comfort, and his mother's joy,
The very arm that did hold up our house: —
Our hopes were stored up in him,
None but a damned murderer could hate him.
He had not seen the back of nineteen year,   35
When his strong arm unhorsed the proud Prince Balthazar,
And his great mind, too full of honour,
Took him unto mercy,
That valiant but ignoble Portingale.
Well, heaven is heaven still,   40
And there is Nemesis and Furies,
And things called whips,
And they sometimes do meet with murderers:
They do not always 'scape, that's some comfort.
Ay, ay, ay, and then time steals on: 45
And steals, and steals, till violence leaps forth
Like thunder wrapped in a ball of fire,
And so doth bring confusion to them all.
[Good leave have you: nay, I pray you go,]

26–30 lineation ed. (This . . . truly. / O . . . of these / Insatiate . . .
    parents, *1602*)
29 *insatiate humours* unsatisfied whims and caprices
35 *the back of* i.e. he was still nineteen
38 *unto* ed. (vs to *1602*)
38–9 lineation ed. (*one line 1602*)
41 *Nemesis* a personification of the gods' anger at human presump-
    tion, and their punishment of it
41 *Furies* legendary avengers of crime in ancient Greece
45–7 lineation ed. (I, . . . steales, and steales / Till . . . thunder /
    Wrapt . . . fire, *1602*)
48 *confusion* destruction

36–9 The syntax is unclear at this point. Presumably l.39 simply expands
    'the proud Prince Balthazar' (l.36). Should l.39 follow l.36 immedi-
    ately?

Fourth Addition, between III, xii and xiii

Enter JAQUES *and* PEDRO

JAQUES
I wonder, Pedro, why our master thus
At midnight sends us with our torches' light,
When man and bird and beast are all at rest,
Save those that watch for rape and bloody murder?

PEDRO
O Jaques, know thou that our master's mind   5
Is much distraught since his Horatio died,
And now his aged years should sleep in rest,
His heart in quiet; like a desperate man,
Grows lunatic and childish for his son:
Sometimes, as he doth at his table sit,   10
He speaks as if Horatio stood by him;
Then starting in a rage, falls on the earth,
Cries out 'Horatio, where is my Horatio?'
So that with extreme grief and cutting sorrow,
There is not left in him one inch of man: 15
See, where he comes.

Enter HIERONIMO

HIERONIMO
I pry through every crevice of each wall,
Look on each tree, and search through every brake,
Beat at the bushes, stamp our grandam earth,
Dive in the water, and stare up to heaven,   20
Yet cannot I behold my son Horatio.
How now, who's there, sprites, sprites?

PEDRO
We are your servants that attend you, sir.

HIERONIMO
What make you with your torches in the dark?

PEDRO
You bid us light them, and attend you here.   25

HIERONIMO
No, no, you are deceived, not I, you are deceived:

12 *starting* starting up
17 *crevice* (creuie *1602*)
18 *brake* thicket
22 *sprites, sprites?* ed. (sprits, sprits? *1602*) spirits, demons
24 *What make you* What are you doing? What is your purpose?

Was I so mad to bid you light your torches now?
Light me your torches at the mid of noon,
Whenas the sun-god rides in all his glory:
Light me your torches then.

PEDRO   Then we burn daylight.   30

HIERONIMO

Let it be burnt: night is a murderous slut,
That would not have her treasons to be seen;
And yonder pale-faced Hecate there, the moon,
Doth give consent to that is done in darkness;
And all those stars that gaze upon her face,   35
Are aglets on her sleeve, pins on her train;
And those that should be powerful and divine,
Do sleep in darkness when they most should shine.

PEDRO

Provoke them not, fair sir, with tempting words:
The heavens are gracious, and your miseries   40
And sorrow makes you speak you know not what.

HIERONIMO

Villain, thou liest, and thou doest naught
But tell me I am mad: thou liest, I am not mad.
I know thee to be Pedro, and he Jaques.
I'll prove it to thee, and were I mad, how could I?   45
Where was she that same night when my Horatio
Was murdered? She should have shone: search thou the
    book.
Had the moon shone, in my boy's face there was a kind of
    grace,
That I know (nay, I do know) had the murderer seen him,

29 *Whenas* when
30 *burn daylight* a phrase meaning to waste time; here used also in the literal sense
33 *Hecate* ed. (Hee-cat *1602*) in Greek thought a goddess associated with night and the lower world; Elizabethans associated her with the moon. Here, two syllables only
36 *aglets* ed. (aggots *1602*) spangles ('properly, the ornamental tags of laces', Edwards)
36 *pins* spangles, ornaments
41 *And sorrow* ed. (*ends l.40 in 1602*)
47 *Was murdered* ed. (*ends l.46 in 1602*)
47 *book* almanac, recording the phases of the moon
49 *That I know* ed. (*ends l.48 in 1602*)

45 *prove it* i.e. prove the Heavens negligent in the matter of Horatio's murder.

His weapon would have fallen and cut the earth,   50
Had he been framed of naught but blood and death.
Alack, when mischief doth it knows not what,
What shall we say to mischief?

Enter ISABELLA

ISABELLA
Dear Hieronimo, come in a-doors.
O, seek not means so to increase thy sorrow.   55
HIERONIMO
Indeed, Isabella, we do nothing here;
I do not cry; ask Pedro, and ask Jaques;
Not I indeed, we are very merry, very merry.
ISABELLA
How? be merry here, be merry here?
Is not this the place, and this the very tree,   60
Where my Horatio died, where he was murdered?
HIERONIMO
Was—do not say what: let her weep it out.
This was the tree, I set it of a kernel,
And when our hot Spain could not let it grow,
But that the infant and the human sap   65
Began to wither, duly twice a morning
Would I be sprinkling it with fountain water.
At last it grew, and grew, and bore and bore,
Till at the length
It grew a gallows, and did bear our son.   70
It bore thy fruit and mine: O wicked, wicked plant.
                        One knocks within at the door
See who knock there.
PEDRO   It is a painter, sir.
HIERONIMO
Bid him come in, and paint some comfort,
For surely there's none lives but painted comfort.
Let him come in. One knows not what may chance: 75

51 *framed* made, created
61 *died* ed. (hied *1602*)
69 *Till . . . length* ed. (*begins l.70 in 1602*)
74 *painted* false, merely apparent

64 ff. *our hot Spain* a much stronger sense of actual locality than in Kyd's
    text.

God's will that I should set this tree—but even so
Masters ungrateful servants rear from naught,
And then they hate them that did bring them up.

Enter the PAINTER

PAINTER
  God bless you, sir.
HIERONIMO
  Wherefore? why, thou scornful villain,   80
  How, where, or by what means should I be blessed?
ISABELLA
  What wouldst thou have, good fellow?
PAINTER   Justice, madam.
HIERONIMO
  O ambitious beggar, wouldst thou have that
  That lives not in the world?
  Why, all the undelved mines cannot buy   85
  An ounce of justice, 'tis a jewel so inestimable:
  I tell thee,
  God hath engrossed all justice in his hands,
  And there is none, but what comes from him.
PAINTER
  O then I see   90
  That God must right me for my murdered son.
HIERONIMO
  How, was thy son murdered?
PAINTER
  Ay sir, no man did hold a son so dear.
HIERONIMO
  What, not as thine? that's a lie
  As massy as the earth: I had a son,   95

76 *but even so* ed. (*begins l.77 in 1602*)
80 *Wherefore?* Why?
85 *undelved* unworked
87 *I tell thee* ed. (*begins l.88 in 1602*)
88 *engrossed* taken up
90 *O then I see* ed. (*begins l.91 in 1602*)
95 *massy* huge, weighty

76–7 The dash in l.76 represents the anguished question implied in the
    preceding phrase: 'Can it also be God's will that it should grow to
    such terrible uses?'
90–4 The writer of this Addition develops Kyd's device of including a
    surrogate for Hieronimo, 'The lively portrait of my dying self' (III,
    xiii, 85).

Whose least unvalued hair did weigh
A thousand of thy sons: and he was murdered.

PAINTER

Alas sir, I had no more but he.

HIERONIMO

Nor I, nor I: but this same one of mine
Was worth a legion: but all is one.   100
Pedro, Jaques, go in a-doors: Isabella go,
And this good fellow here and I
Will range this hideous orchard up and down,
Like to two lions reaved of their young.
Go in a-doors, I say.   105

Exeunt [ISABELLA, PEDRO, JAQUES]
The PAINTER *and he sits down*

Come, let's talk wisely now. Was thy son murdered?

PAINTER

Ay sir.

HIERONIMO

So was mine. How dost take it? Art thou not sometimes
mad? Is there no tricks that comes before thine eyes?

PAINTER

O Lord, yes sir.   110

HIERONIMO

Art a painter? Canst paint me a tear, or a wound, a groan, or
a sigh? Canst paint me such a tree as this?

PAINTER

Sir, I am sure you have heard of my painting, my name's
Bazardo.

HIERONIMO

Bazardo! afore God, an excellent fellow! Look you sir, do   115
you see, I'd have you paint me in my gallery, in your oil
colours matted, and draw me five years younger than I am.
Do you see sir, let five years go, let them go, like the marshal
of Spain. My wife Isabella standing by me, with a speaking
look to my son Horatio, which should intend to this or some   120

100 *all is one* no matter
103 *range* walk up and down
104 *reaved* bereft, robbed
116 *me in my* ed. (me my *1602*)
117 *matted* perhaps 'made dull or matt'; but Boas may be right in
     suggesting 'set in a mat or mount'
119 *speaking* eloquent, full of meaning
120 *intend to* signify

such like purpose: 'God bless thee, my sweet son': and my
hand leaning upon his head, thus, sir, do you see? may it
be done?

PAINTER
Very well sir.

HIERONIMO
Nay, I pray mark me sir. Then sir, would I have you paint   125
me this tree, this very tree. Canst paint a doleful cry?

PAINTER
Seemingly, sir.

HIERONIMO
Nay, it should cry: but all is one. Well sir, paint me a youth
run through and through with villains' swords, hanging
upon this tree. Canst thou draw a murderer?   130

PAINTER
I'll warrant you sir, I have the pattern of the most notorious
villains that ever lived in all Spain.

HIERONIMO
O, let them be worse, worse: stretch thine art, and let their
beards be of Judas his own colour, and let their eyebrows
jutty over: in any case observe that. Then sir, after some   135
violent noise, bring me forth in my shirt, and my gown under
mine arm, with my torch in my hand, and my sword reared
up thus: and with these words:
    What noise is this? who calls Hieronimo?
May it be done?   140

PAINTER
Yea sir.

HIERONIMO
Well sir, then bring me forth, bring me through alley and
alley, still with a distracted countenance going along, and
let my hair heave up my night-cap. Let the clouds scowl,
make the moon dark, the stars extinct, the winds blowing,   145
the bells tolling, the owl shrieking, the toads croaking, the
minutes jarring, and the clock striking twelve. And then at

127 *Seemingly* in illusion
131 *pattern* model, portrait
134 *Judas . . . colour* red (Judas Iscariot was alleged to be red-haired)
135 *jutty* project
142 s.p. HIERONIMO ed. (*not in 1602*)
147 *jarring* ed. (iering *1602*) ticking away

135–9 These lines may provide us with a good indication of Elizabethan
practice in staging the first lines of II, v in the main play.

last, sir, starting, behold a man hanging: and tottering, and
tottering as you know the wind will weave a man, and I
with a trice to cut him down. And looking upon him by the   150
advantage of my torch, find it to be my son Horatio. There
you may show a passion, there you may show a passion.
Draw me like old Priam of Troy, crying 'The house is a-fire,
the house is a-fire as the torch over my head!' Make me
curse, make me rave, make me cry, make me mad, make me   155
well again, make me curse hell, invocate heaven, and in the
end leave me in a trance; and so forth.

PAINTER
And is this the end?

HIERONIMO
O no, there is no end: the end is death and madness! As I
am never better than when I am mad, then methinks I am a   160
brave fellow, then I do wonders: but reason abuseth me, and
there's the torment, there's the hell. At the last, sir, bring me
to one of the murderers, were he as strong as Hector, thus
would I tear and drag him up and down.

He beats the PAINTER *in, then comes out again with a book in his
hand*

Fifth Addition, replacing IV, iv, 168 to 190

[CASTILE
Why hast thou butchered both my children thus?]

HIERONIMO
But are you sure they are dead?

CASTILE   Ay, slave, too sure.

HIERONIMO
What, and yours too?

VICEROY
Ay, all are dead, not one of them survive.

148 *tottering* dangling, swinging to and fro
149 *weave* weave about, make him swing (*O.E.D.* does not give this
    transitive sense)
150 *with a trice* instantly
151 *advantage* assistance
152 *show* ed. (*not in 1602*)
161 *brave* glorious, splendid
161 *abuseth* deceives

153-7 The closeness of these lines to the First Player's speech (*Hamlet*
    II, ii) is intriguing.

HIERONIMO
Nay then, I care not, come, and we shall be friends:
Let us lay our heads together; 5
See here's a goodly noose will hold them all.

VICEROY
O damned devil, how secure he is.

HIERONIMO
Secure, why dost thou wonder at it?
I tell thee Viceroy, this day I have seen revenge,
And in that sight am grown a prouder monarch 10
Than ever sat under the crown of Spain:
Had I as many lives as there be stars,
As many heavens to go to as those lives,
I'd give them all, ay, and my soul to boot,
But I would see thee ride in this red pool. 15

CASTILE
Speak, who were thy confederates in this?

VICEROY
That was thy daughter Bel-imperia,
For by her hand my Balthazar was slain:
I saw her stab him.

HIERONIMO   Oh, good words:
As dear to me was my Horatio, 20
As yours, or yours, or yours, my lord, to you.
My guiltless son was by Lorenzo slain,
And by Lorenzo, and that Balthazar,
Am I at last revenged thoroughly,
Upon whose souls may heavens be yet revenged 25
With greater far than these afflictions.
Methinks since I grew inward with revenge,
I cannot look with scorn enough on death.

KING
What, dost thou mock us, slave? Bring tortures forth.

7 *secure* confident
9 *revenge* ed. (reueng'd *1602*)
14 *to boot* in addition
19 *Oh, good words:* ed. (*begins l.20 in 1602*)
27 *inward with* closely acquainted with
29 *tortures* instruments of torture

HIERONIMO

   Do, do, do, and meantime I'll torture you.   30
   You had a son, as I take it: and your son
   Should ha' been married to your daughter:
   Ha, was't not so? You had a son too,
   He was my liege's nephew. He was proud,
   And politic. Had he lived, he might ha' come   35
   To wear the crown of Spain, I think 'twas so:
   'Twas I that killed him; look you, this same hand,
   'Twas it that stabbed his heart; do you see, this hand?
   For one Horatio, if you ever knew him, a youth,
   One that they hanged up in his father's garden,   40
   One that did force your valiant son to yield,
   While your more valiant son did take him prisoner.

VICEROY

   Be deaf my senses, I can hear no more.

KING

   Fall heaven, and cover us with thy sad ruins.

CASTILE

   Roll all the world within thy pitchy cloud.   45

HIERONIMO

   Now do I applaud what I have acted.
          Nunc iners cadat manus.
   Now to express the rupture of my part,
   [First take my tongue, and afterward my heart.]

END

35 *ha'* ed. (a *1602*)
47 *iners cadat* ed. (*mers cadae 1602*)
48 *the . . . part* the breaking-off of my role

31–3 Hieronimo speaks first to the viceroy and then ('your daughter')
    to Castile. The son (l.33) is Lorenzo.
47 'Now let my hand fall idle'.

Doctor Faustus

CHRISTOPHER MARLOWE

Edited by
ROMA GILL

ABBREVIATIONS

I have followed the usual practice in referring to the seventeenth-century editions of *Dr. Faustus*. 'A' indicates substantial agreement among all the A texts which are referred to separately on occasion as A1 (1604), A2 (1609), and A3 (1611); the six B texts (1616, 1619, 1620, 1624, 1628, and 1631) are similarly distinguished. Modern editions consulted are referred to as follows:

Boas   *The Tragical History of Doctor Faustus*, edited by F. S. Boas (1923)

Bullen   *The Works of Christopher Marlowe*, edited by A. H. Bullen (1885)

Greg   *Marlowe's 'Dr. Faustus' 1604–1616: Parallel Texts*, edited by W. W. Greg (1950)

Jump   *Doctor Faustus*, edited by John D. Jump (1962)

Other works frequently referred to are:

EFB   The English *Faust Book*, the name often given to Marlowe's source [*The Historie of the damnable life, and deserved death of Doctor Iohn Faustus*, translated by P. F. (1592)]

Kocher   P. H. Kocher, *Christopher Marlowe* (Chapel Hill, 1946)

Quotations from other plays by Marlowe are taken from the edition of R. H. Case *et al.* (1930–33); those from Shakespeare's plays are from the London edition [edited by John Munro (1958)].

The Tragicall Histor
of the Life and Death
of Doctor FAVSTVS.

With new Additions.

Written by *Ch. Mar.*

Printed at London for *John Wright*, and are to be sold at his shop without Newgate, 1624.

[DRAMATIS PERSONAE

Chorus
Dr. John Faustus
Wagner, *his servant, a student*
Valdes,
Cornelius, } *his friends, magicians*
Three Scholars, *students under* Faustus
An Old Man

Pope Adrian
Raymond, *King of Hungary*
Bruno, *the rival pope*
Cardinals of France *and* Padua
The Archbishop of Rheims

Charles V, *Emperor of Germany*
Martino,
Frederick, } *knights at the Emperor's court*
Benvolio,
Duke of Saxony

Duke of Vanholt
Duchess of Vanholt

Robin, *also called the* Clown
Dick
A Vintner
A Horse-courser
A Carter
The Hostess *at an inn*

The Good Angel
The Bad Angel
Mephostophilis
Lucifer
Belzebub
Spirits *presenting* The Seven Deadly Sins
Alexander the Great
Alexander's Paramour
Darius, *King of Persia*
Helen of Troy

Devils, Bishops, Monks, Soldiers *and* Attendants]

145

PROLOGUE

Enter CHORUS

CHORUS

Not marching in the fields of Thrasimene,
Where Mars did mate the warlike Carthagens,
Nor sporting in the dalliance of love
In courts of kings, where state is overturned,
Nor in the pomp of proud audacious deeds,   5
Intends our Muse to vaunt his heavenly verse:
Only this, Gentles – we must now perform
The form of Faustus' fortunes, good or bad.
And now to patient judgements we appeal,
And speak for Faustus in his infancy.   10
Now is he born, of parents base of stock,
In Germany, within a town called Rhode:
At riper years to Wittenberg he went,
Whereas his kinsmen chiefly brought him up;
So much he profits in divinity,   15
The fruitful plot of scholarism graced,
That shortly he was graced with doctor's name,

---

12 *Rhode* ed. (Rhodes Qq) Roda, since 1922 Stadtroda, in central
Germany
14 *Whereas* where
16 A (*not in* B) A credit to the rich academic discipline
17 *graced* At Cambridge a new Doctor of Divinity was enrolled in
the Book of Grace

Prologue 1–6
The Prologue speaks of plays already performed, but it is not clear
whether these were written by Marlowe or, more generally, are part of
the company's repertoire. In either case there is no trace of the first,
showing the victory of the Carthaginians under Hannibal at Lake
Trasimene (217 B.C.) If Marlowe's own plays are meant, 11.3–4 must
refer to *Edward II* and 1.5 to *Tamburlaine*. A masculine Muse (1.6) is
unusual but not unknown (*cf.* 'Lycidas', 19–21); yet Shakespeare, comparing himself with 'that Muse Stirred by a painted beauty to his verse',
(Sonnet XXI), clearly alludes to a rival poet. It seems to me that 'Muse'
here means simply 'Poet' and that the Chorus is speaking on behalf of
the actors.
13 *Wittenberg* Hamlet's university, and Luther's; the home of scepticism.
But this Wittenberg is, in all outward appearances, Marlowe's Cambridge.

Excelling all, whose sweet delight disputes
In th' heavenly matters of theology.
Till, swollen with cunning, of a self-conceit,   20
His waxen wings did mount above his reach,
And, melting, heavens conspired his overthrow:
For, falling to a devilish exercise,
And glutted now with learning's golden gifts,
He surfeits upon cursed necromancy: 25
Nothing so sweet as magic is to him,
Which he prefers before his chiefest bliss:
And this the man that in his study sits.

Exit

18 *whose sweet delight disputes* A (and sweetly can dispute B) whose
     great pleasure is in argument
20 *cunning* knowledge; usually knowledge misapplied;
     self-conceit pride in his own abilities
21–2 Icarus flew too near the sun on wings of wax; they melted and
     he fell into the sea
27 *chiefest bliss* i.e. hope of salvation

Act I, Scene i

FAUSTUS

Settle thy studies, Faustus, and begin
To sound the depth of that thou wilt profess;
Having commenced, be a divine in show,
Yet level at the end of every art,
And live and die in Aristotle's works.
Sweet *Analytics*, 'tis thou hast ravished me:
Bene disserere est finis logices.
Is to dispute well logic's chiefest end?
Affords this art no greater miracle?
Then read no more, thou hast attained that end;
A greater subject fitteth Faustus' wit.
Bid *on kai me on* farewell; Galen come:
Seeing, *ubi desinit philosophus, ibi incipit medicus.*

2 *profess* specialize in, study and teach
3 *commenced* graduated; a Cambridge term;
   in show in appearance; show that you are indeed a student of theology
4 Consider the purpose of every discipline
12 *on kai me on* being and not being
13 Since the doctor starts where the philosopher leaves off; Aristotle,
   de sensu, 436a

1–36 Jump has pointed out that for the first part of Faustus' soliloquy
   Marlowe seems to owe a debt to Lyly:
   Philosophie, Phisicke, Divinitie, shal be my studie. O yᵉ hidden
   secrets of Nature, the expresse image of morall vertues, the equall
   balaunce of Justice, the medicines to heale all diseases, how they
   beginne to delyght me. The *Axiomaes* of *Aristotle*, the *Maxims* of
   Justinian, the *Aphorismes* of *Galen*, have sodaynelye made such a
   breache into my minde that I seeme onely to desire them which did
   onely earst detest them.
                                        Euphues (1579), ed. Bond, i,241
5–7 Aristotle had been the dominant figure in the university curriculum
   since the thirteenth century, but in Marlowe's day his supremacy was
   challenged by Petrus Ramus (1515–72) whose ideas were defended in
   Cambridge by William Temple. *Analytics* is the name give to two of
   Aristotle's works on the nature of proof in argument, but the definition
   of logic in 1.7 comes in fact from Ramus' *Dialecticae*. Ramus, his ideas
   and his violent death, are displayed in Marlowe's *Massacre at Paris.*
12 *on kai me on* Bullen (Oncaymaeon A₁; Oeconomy A₂, ₃, B) The later
   A texts were trying to make sense out of A₁'s apparent gibberish which
   Bullen recognized as a transliteration of Aristotle's Greek phrase.

148

Be a physician Faustus, heap up gold,
And be eternized for some wondrous cure.   15
Summum bonum medicinae sanitas:
The end of physic is our body's health.
Why Faustus, hast thou not attained that end?
Is not thy common talk sound aphorisms?
Are not thy bills hung up as monuments,   20
Whereby whole cities have escaped the plague,
And thousand desperate maladies been cured?
Yet art thou still but Faustus, and a man.
Couldst thou make men to live eternally,
Or, being dead, raise them to life again,   25
Then this profession were to be esteemed.
Physic farewell! Where is Justinian?
Si una eademque res legatur duobus,
Alter rem, alter valorem rei etc.
A petty case of paltry legacies!   30
Exhereditare filium non potest pater nisi . . .
Such is the subject of the Institute,
And universal body of the law.
This study fits a mercenary drudge,
Who aims at nothing but external trash,   35
Too servile and illiberal for me.
When all is done, divinity is best:
Jerome's Bible Faustus, view it well:
Stipendium peccati mors est: ha! *Stipendium, etc*
The reward of sin is death? That's hard.   40

15 *eternized* immortalized
16 Aristotle, *Nicomachean Ethics*, 1094.a.8
19 *aphorisms* medical precepts; after the *Aphorisms* of Hippocrates
20 *bills* prescriptions
28–9 If one and the same thing is bequeathed to two persons, one
    should have the thing itself, the other the value of the thing;
    Justinian, *Institutes*, ii,20
31 A father cannot disinherit his son unless . . .; Justinian, ii,13
38 *Jerome's Bible* the Vulgate, prepared mainly by St Jerome; but
    the texts Faustus quotes are not in the words of the Vulgate
39 Romans, vi, 23

---

14 *heap up gold* The association of gold and the medical profession is an
    old one; Shakespeare mentions the use of gold for 'Preserving life in
    med'cine potable' (2 *Henry IV*, IV.v, 162). Faustus, however, is think-
    ing of the profit to be gained – like Chaucer's Physician in *The Canter-*
    bury Tales:
        For gold in phisik is a cordial,
        Therefore he lovede gold in special
                        Prologue, 444–5

Si peccasse negamus, fallimur, et nulla est in nobis veritas:
If we say that we have no sin, we deceive ourselves, and there
is no truth in us. Why then, belike, we must sin, and so con-
sequently die.
Ay, we must die an everlasting death.   45
What doctrine call you this? *Che sarà, sarà:*
What will be, shall be. Divinity adieu!
These metaphysics of magicians,
And necromantic books are heavenly;
Lines, circles, signs, letters and characters!   50
Ay, these are those that Faustus most desires.
O what a world of profit and delight,
Of power, of honour, of omnipotence,
Is promised to the studious artisan!
All things that move between the quiet poles   55
Shall be at my command: emperors and kings,
Are but obeyed in their several provinces,
Nor can they raise the wind, or rend the clouds;
But his dominion that exceeds in this,
Stretcheth as far as doth the mind of man: 60
A sound magician is a mighty god;
Here Faustus, try thy brains to gain a deity.

Enter WAGNER

Wagner, commend me to my dearest friends,
The German Valdes and Cornelius,
Request them earnestly to visit me.   65
WAGNER
    I will sir.

Exit

FAUSTUS
    Their conference will be a greater help to me,
    Than all my labours, plod I ne'er so fast.

Enter the ANGEL *and* SPIRIT

41 I John, i, 8
48 *metaphysics* supernatural sciences
50 *signs* ed. (scenes A; *not in* B) (see note on I.iii, 8–13)
54 *artisan* craftsman
55 *quiet poles* the poles of the universe, quiet because unmoving
57 *several* respective
58 A (*not in* B)
59 *this* this art, magic
61 *a mighty god* A (a demi-god B)
62 *Faustus, try thy brains to gain* A (tire, my brains, to get B)
68 s.d. *Spirit* (see note on II.i, 96)

GOOD ANGEL

O Faustus, lay that damned book aside,
And gaze not on it lest it tempt thy soul,　　　　70
And heap God's heavy wrath upon thy head:
Read, read the Scriptures; that is blasphemy.

BAD ANGEL

Go forward Faustus in that famous art
Wherein all nature's treasury is contained:
Be thou on earth as Jove is in the sky,　　　　75
Lord and commander of these elements.

Exeunt ANGELS

FAUSTUS

How am I glutted with conceit of this!
Shall I make spirits fetch me what I please?
Resolve me of all ambiguities?
Perform what desperate enterprise I will?　　　　80
I'll have them fly to India for gold;
Ransack the ocean for orient pearl,
And search all corners of the new-found-world
For pleasant fruits, and princely delicates.
I'll have them read me strange philosophy,　　　　85
And tell the secrets of all foreign kings:
I'll have them wall all Germany with brass,
And make swift Rhine, circle fair Wittenberg:
I'll have them fill the public schools with silk,
Wherewith the students shall be bravely clad.　　　　90
I'll levy soldiers with the coin they bring,
And chase the Prince of Parma from our land,
And reign sole king of all our provinces.
Yea, stranger engines for the brunt of war,

77 *glutted with conceit* drunk with the thought
84 *delicates* delicacies
89 *public schools* university lecture rooms;
　　silk Dyce (skill Qq). In Marlowe's day undergraduates were
　　ordered to dress soberly
90 *bravely* smartly
92 *Prince of Parma* Spanish governor-general of the Netherlands,
　　1579–92
94 *engines* machines;
　　brunt assault

75 *Jove* The names of pagan deities were frequently attributed to the
　　Christian God; there is special force in this, coming from the Bad
　　Angel.
87 *wall . . . brass* Friar Bacon, in Greene's *Friar Bacon and Friar Bungay*
　　(before 1592) intended to 'circle England round with brass' (ii,178)
　　when his magic schemes reached fruition.

Than was the fiery keel at Antwerp's bridge,   95
I'll make my servile spirits to invent.
Come German Valdes and Cornelius,
And make me blest with your sage conference.

Enter VALDES *and* CORNELIUS

Valdes, sweet Valdes, and Cornelius!
Know that your words have won me at the last   100
To practise magic and concealed arts;
Yet not your words only, but mine own fantasy,
That will receive no object for my head,
But ruminates on necromantic skill.
Philosophy is odious and obscure;   105
Both law and physic are for petty wits;
Divinity is basest of the three,
Unpleasant, harsh, contemptible and vile.
'Tis magic, magic that hath ravished me.
Then gentle friends, aid me in this attempt,   110
And I, that have with concise syllogisms
Gravelled the pastors of the German church
And made the flowering pride of Wittenberg
Swarm to my problems, as th'infernal spirits
On sweet Musaeus when he came to hell,   115
Will be as cunning as Agrippa was,
Whose shadows made all Europe honour him.

VALDES
Faustus, these books, thy wit, and our experience
Shall make all nations to canonise us.

101 *concealed* occult
102–4 A (*not in* B) Not your advice alone, but my own imagination has
    won me to this, allowing me to think of nothing else while it con-
    templates the possibilities of black magic
107–8 A (*not in* B)
111 *concise syllogisms* A$_{1,2}$ (subtle syllogisms A$_3$, B) trenchant argument
112 *Gravelled* confounded, perplexed
114 *problems* topics of scholarly debate

95 A bridge across the Scheldt, constructed by the Duke of Parma in the
    blockade of Antwerp, was attacked and destroyed by a fire-ship in April
    1585.
115 *Musaeus* A legendary pre-Homeric bard often confused (as perhaps here)
    with Orpheus: *Aeneid* vi,667–8 describes Musaeus in the Elysian fields
    and *Georgics* iv tells of spirits swarming round Orpheus in the Under-
    world.
116–7 Henry Cornelius Agrippa von Nettesheim (1486–1535), magician
    and necromancer, was famous for his reputed power of invoking shades
    of the dead.

As Indian Moors obey their Spanish lords   120
So shall the spirits of every element
Be always serviceable to us three;
Like lions shall they guard us when we please,
Like Almaine rutters with their horsemen's staves,
Or Lapland giants trotting by our sides;   125
Sometimes like women or unwedded maids,
Shadowing more beauty in their airy brows,
Than have the white breasts of the Queen of Love.
From Venice shall they drag huge argosies,
And from America the golden fleece,   130
That yearly stuffs old Philip's treasury,
If learned Faustus will be resolute.

FAUSTUS
Valdes, as resolute am I in this,
As thou to live, therefore object it not.

CORNELIUS
The miracles that magic will perform,   135
Will make thee vow to study nothing else.
He that is grounded in astrology,
Enriched with tongues, well seen in minerals,
Hath all the principles magic doth require:
Then doubt not Faustus but to be renowned,   140
And more frequented for this mystery,
Than heretofore the Delphian oracle.
The spirits tell me they can dry the sea,
And fetch the treasure of all foreign wrecks;
Yea, all the wealth that our forefathers hid,   145

120 *Moors* dark-skinned natives; here specifically American Indians
124 Like German cavalry with lances
129 *argosies* treasure ships
130–31 America, whose richness is compared to the golden fleece
    sought by Jason and the Argonauts, paid annual tribute to Philip
    of Spain
134 *object it not* don't raise such objections
137 *grounded in* well schooled in
138 *well seen in minerals* informed about the properties of minerals
141 More sought after for practising this art
142 *Delphian oracle* the oracle of Apollo at Delphi

---

125 *Lapland giants* On another occasion Marlowe refers to the inhabitants
    of the polar regions in this way: 'tall and sturdy men, Giants as big as
    hugy Polypheme'. (2 *Tamburlaine*, I.i, 37–8)
138 *tongues* Greek and Hebrew were desirable for those who would converse
    with spirits, but Latin was the recognized common language: 'Thou art
    a scholar: speak to it Horatio.' *Hamlet*, I.i, 42

Within the massy entrails of the earth:
Then tell me, Faustus, what shall we three want?

FAUSTUS
Nothing Cornelius! O this cheers my soul!
Come, show me some demonstrations magical,
That I may conjure in some lusty grove,   150
And have these joys in full possession.

VALDES
Then haste thee to some solitary grove,
And bear wise Bacon's and Abanus' works,
The Hebrew Psalter, and New Testament;
And whatsoever else is requisite,   155
We will inform thee ere our conference cease.

CORNELIUS
Valdes, first let him know the words of art,
And then, all other ceremonies learnt,
Faustus may try his cunning by himself.

VALDES
First I'll instruct thee in the rudiments,   160
And then wilt thou be perfecter than I.

FAUSTUS
Then come and dine with me, and after meat
We'll canvass every quiddity thereof:
For ere I sleep, I'll try what I can do:
This night I'll conjure though I die therefore. 165

Exeunt omnes

146 *massy* solid
150 *lusty* A₁ (little A₂,₃; bushy B)
163 *canvass every quiddity* explore every detail; *quiddity* is a scholastic
   term denoting the essence of a thing, that which makes it what it is

153–4 *wise Bacon's and Abanus' works* Roger Bacon (1214?–94), protagonist
   of Greene's *Friar Bacon and Friar Bungay*, was an Oxford philosopher
   popularly supposed to have dabbled in black magic. Abanus is perhaps
   Pietro d'Abano (?1250–1316), Italian humanist and physician, also
   believed to have been a conjuror. As well as the works of these two,
   which would supply formulae for incantation, Faustus would need
   certain Psalms (especially 22 and 51) and the opening words of St.
   John's Gospel for his conjuring.
160 *rudiments* 'all that which is called vulgarly the vertue of worde, herbe, &
   stone: which is used by unlawful charmes, without natural causes . . .
   such kinde of charmes as commonlie daft wives use'.
   James I, *Daemonologie* (Edinburgh, 1597), p.11

Act I, Scene ii

Enter two SCHOLARS

1 SCHOLAR
   I wonder what's become of Faustus, that was wont to make
   our schools ring with *sic probo*.
2 SCHOLAR
   That shall we presently know; here comes his boy.

Enter WAGNER

1 SCHOLAR
   How now sirra, where's thy master?
WAGNER
   God in heaven knows.   5
2 SCHOLAR
   Why, dost not thou know then?
WAGNER
   Yes, I know, but that follows not.
1 SCHOLAR
   Go to sirra, leave your jesting, and tell us where he is.
WAGNER
   That follows not by force of argument, which you, being
   licentiates, should stand upon, therefore acknowledge your   10
   error, and be attentive.
2 SCHOLAR
   Then you will not tell us?
WAGNER
   You are deceived, for I will tell you: yet if you were not
   dunces, you would never ask me such a question. For is he

---

2 *sic probo* I prove it thus; a term from scholastic disputation
3 *presently* at once
10 *licentiates* graduates; holders of a degree permitting them to study
    for higher (master's or doctor's) degrees

---

14 *dunces* blockheads. The followers of Duns Scotus were commonly known
    as Dunses, but since it is Wagner who indulges in the characteristic
    Scotist cavilling it seems likely that he applies the word to the scholars
    in its modern sense.

not *corpus naturale*? And is not that *mobile*? Then wherefore   15
should you ask me such a question? But that I am by nature
phlegmatic, slow to wrath, and prone to lechery – to love, I
would say – it were not for you to come within forty foot
of the place of execution, although I do not doubt but to
see you both hanged the next sessions. Thus having tri-   20
umphed over you, I will set my countenance like a precisian,
and begin to speak thus: Truly my dear brethren, my master
is within at dinner, with Valdes and Cornelius, as this wine,
if it could speak, would inform your worships: and so the
Lord bless you, preserve you, and keep you, my dear   25
brethren.

Exit

1 SCHOLAR
Nay then, I fear he is fallen into that damned art, for which
they two are infamous through the world.
2 SCHOLAR
Were he a stranger, and not allied to me, yet should I grieve
for him. But come, let us go and inform the Rector, and   30
see if he by his grave counsel can reclaim him.
1 SCHOLAR
I fear me, nothing will reclaim him now.
2 SCHOLAR
Yet let us see what we can do.   *Exeunt*

---

19 *place of execution* the dining room; Wagner continues to make
   comic capital out of the phrase
21 *precisian* Puritan
30 *Rector* Head of the university

---

15 *corpus . . . mobile* a natural body and as such capable of movement.
   Aristotle's *corpus naturale seu mobile* was the current scholastic definition
   of the subject matter of physics.
27–31 B prints these lines as verse, altering the first to read 'O Faustus, then
   I fear that which I have long suspected'. The flatness of the verse,
   coming at the end of a scene of fairly pithy prose, casts some doubt on
   B's authenticity; there is, moreover, no reason why the Scholar should
   have 'long suspected' Faustus of necromantic proclivities.

Act I, Scene iii

Thunder. Enter LUCIFER *and four* DEVILS *above.*
FAUSTUS *to them, with this speech*

FAUSTUS
Now that the gloomy shadow of the earth,
Longing to view Orion's drizzling look,
Leaps from th'antarctic world unto the sky,
And dims the welkin, with her pitchy breath:
Faustus, begin thine incantations,   5
And try if devils will obey thy hest,
Seeing thou hast prayed and sacrificed to them.
Within this circle is Jehovah's name,
Forward and backward anagrammatised:
Th'abbreviated names of holy saints,   10
Figures of every adjunct to the heavens,
And characters of signs and erring stars,
By which the spirits are enforced to rise:
Then fear not Faustus, but be resolute
And try the uttermost magic can perform.   15

---

s.d. *Thunder . . . above* B (*not in* A)
  2 *Orion's drizzling look* the rainy constellation of Orion
 11 *adjunct* heavenly body fixed to the firmament (see note on II.ii,
     35–66)
 12 *characters* symbols; *signs and erring stars* signs of the Zodiac and
     planets

---

  1 *shadow of the earth* A (shadow of the night B) 'the night also, is no other
     thing but the shadow of the earth', La Primaudaye, *The French Academie*,
     III, xxxvii.
  3 Marlowe seems to have thought that night advances from the southern
     hemisphere.
  7 *prayed and sacrificed.* A period of prayer and sacrifice, a kind of spiritual
     preparation, was a pre-requisite for conjuring.
8–13 Before he began his conjuring the magician would draw a circle
     round himself, inscribing on the periphery certain signs (of the zodiac,
     for instance) and the tetragrammaton, the four Hebrew letters of the
     Divine Name. This was not only part of the invocation; so long as the
     circle was unbroken and the magician stayed inside it, no evil spirit
     could harm him.

(Thunder)

Sint mihi dei Acherontis propitii, valeat numen triplex Jehovae;
ignei, aerii, aquatici, terreni spiritus salvete! Orientis princeps,
Belzebub inferni ardentis monarcha, et Demogorgon, propi-
tiamus vos, ut appareat, et surgat Mephostophilis.

(Dragon)

Quid tu moraris? Per Jehovam, Gehennam, et consecratam   20
aquam, quam nunc spargo; signumque crucis quod nunc facio;
et per vota nostra, ipse nunc surgat nobis dicatus Mephostophilis.

Enter a DEVIL

I charge thee to return, and change thy shape,
Thou art too ugly to attend on me:
Go and return an old Franciscan friar,   25
That holy shape becomes a devil best.   *Exit* DEVIL
I see there's virtue in my heavenly words!
Who would not be proficient in this art?
How pliant is this Mephostophilis,
Full of obedience and humility,   30

---

17 *terreni* ed. (*not in* Qq) Faustus would call the spirits of all four
   elements
18 *Belzebub* Marlowe's form of the name has been retained because
   at certain points (e.g. II.i, 12) this suits better with the metre than
   the more commonly used Hebraic Beëlzebub
20 *Quid tu moraris* Ellis (quod tumeraris Qq)

23–4 The wary magician always stipulated from the beginning that
   a pleasing shape should be assumed

16–22 'May the gods of Acheron look with favour upon me. Away with
the spirit of the three-fold Jehovah. Welcome, spirits of fire, air, water
and earth. We ask your favour, O prince of the East, Belzebub, monarch
of burning hell, and Demogorgon, that Mephostophilis may appear
and rise. Why do you delay? By Jehovah, Gehenna, and the holy water
which I now sprinkle, and the sign of the cross which I now form, and
by our vows, may Mephostophilis himself now rise, compelled to obey
us'.

   Rejecting the Christian Trinity, Faustus turns to the infernal counter-
part (the prince of the East is Lucifer–see Isaiah, xiv, 12) He hails the
spirits of the elements: 'they make them believe, that at the fall of
Lucifer, some spirits fell in the aire, some in the fire, some in the water,
some in the lande' (*Daemonologie*, p.20). The name of Mephostophilis
(Marlowe's spelling is retained) was not, it seems, known before the
Faustus story; A. E. Taylor, in a letter to *T.L.S.* (6th December 1917)
suggests it might be glossed as the Greek *me faustopheles* – no true friend
to Faustus. Many versions of invocations to the devil express similar
surprise and impatience at his delay, after which the conjuror redoubles
his efforts. The sign of the cross had a double function; a powerful
charm to overcome diabolic disobedience, it also protected the conjuror
from injury by any spirit that might appear.

Such is the force of magic and my spells.
Now Faustus, thou art conjuror laureate
That canst command great Mephostophilis.
Quin redis, Mephostophilis, fratris imagine!

Enter MEPHOSTOPHILIS

MEPHOSTOPHILIS
Now Faustus, what wouldst thou have me do?   35
FAUSTUS
I charge thee wait upon me whilst I live
To do whatever Faustus shall command:
Be it to make the moon drop from her sphere,
Or the ocean to overwhelm the world.
MEPHOSTOPHILIS
I am a servant to great Lucifer,   40
And may not follow thee without his leave;
No more than he commands, must we perform.
FAUSTUS
Did not he charge thee to appear to me?
MEPHOSTOPHILIS
No, I came now hither of mine own accord.
FAUSTUS
Did not my conjuring speeches raise thee? Speak!   45
MEPHOSTOPHILIS
That was the cause, but yet *per accidens*:
For when we hear one rack the name of God,
Abjure the Scriptures, and his saviour Christ,
We fly in hope to get his glorious soul;
Nor will we come unless he use such means,   50
Whereby he is in danger to be damned:
Therefore the shortest cut for conjuring
Is stoutly to abjure the Trinity,
And pray devoutly to the prince of hell.

32–4 A (*not in* B)
34 Why do you not return, Mephostophilis, in the likeness of a friar
46 *per accidens* as it appeared; what the conjuring represented was the
   real cause
47 *rack* violate
53 *the Trinity* A (all godliness B)

38–9 Faustus would share these powers with the enchanters of classical
   literature (see Kocher, p. 141).
44 What Kocher (p. 160) calls the 'doctrine of voluntary ascent' is fairly
   well established in witchcraft.
47 *rack* Jump notes 'torment by anagrammatizing', but Mephostophilis
   has just explained that this is not necessary. 'Take the name of the
   Lord in vain' might be a better interpretation.

FAUSTUS
So Faustus hath already done, and holds this principle: 55
There is no chief but only Belzebub,
To whom Faustus doth dedicate himself.
This word 'damnation' terrifies not him,
For he confounds hell in Elysium:
His ghost be with the old philosophers. 60
But leaving these vain trifles of men's souls,
Tell me, what is that Lucifer thy lord?
MEPHOSTOPHILIS
Arch-regent and commander of all spirits.
FAUSTUS
Was not that Lucifer an angel once?
MEPHOSTOPHILIS
Yes Faustus, and most dearly loved of God. 65
FAUSTUS
How comes it then that he is prince of devils?
MEPHOSTOPHILIS
O, by aspiring pride and insolence,
For which God threw him from the face of heaven.
FAUSTUS
And what are you that live with Lucifer?
MEPHOSTOPHILIS
Unhappy spirits that fell with Lucifer, 70
Conspired against our God with Lucifer,
And are for ever damned with Lucifer.
FAUSTUS
Where are you damned?
MEPHOSTOPHILIS
In hell.
FAUSTUS
How comes it then that thou art out of hell? 75

---

59 *confounds hell in Elysium* makes no distinction between the Christian
concept of hell and the pagan (Greek) notion of the after-life in Elysium.
Marlowe has already coupled the two: 'Hell and Elysium swarm with
ghosts of men' (1 *Tamburlaine*, V.ii, 403). Nashe may be referring to
either of these passages when he scorns the writers that 'thrust Elisium
into hell' (Preface to Greene's *Menaphon* (1589), ed. McKerrow, iii, 316).
60 *old philosophers* those who shared his disbelief in an eternity of punishment; the line seems to come from a saying of Averroes, '*sit anima mea
cum philosophis*' (*cf*. J. C. Maxwell, *N & Q*, CXIV (1949), 334–5; J. M.
Steadman, *N & Q*, CCVII (1962), 327–9.)

MEPHOSTOPHILIS
Why this is hell, nor am I out of it.
Think'st thou that I, who saw the face of God,
And tasted the eternal joys of heaven,
Am not tormented with ten thousand hells,
In being deprived of everlasting bliss?   80
O Faustus, leave these frivolous demands,
Which strike a terror to my fainting soul.

FAUSTUS
What, is great Mephostophilis so passionate
For being deprived of the joys of heaven?
Learn thou of Faustus manly fortitude,   85
And scorn those joys thou never shalt possess.
Go bear these tidings to great Lucifer,
Seeing Faustus hath incurred eternal death,
By desperate thoughts against Jove's deity:
Say he surrenders up to him his soul,   90
So he will spare him four and twenty years,
Letting him live in all voluptuousness,
Having thee ever to attend on me,
To give me whatsoever I shall ask;
To tell me whatsoever I demand: 95
To slay mine enemies, and aid my friends,
And always be obedient to my will.
Go, and return to mighty Lucifer,
And meet me in my study, at midnight,
And then resolve me of thy master's mind.   100

MEPHOSTOPHILIS
I will Faustus.   *Exit*

91 *So* On condition that

76–80 Caxton, while locating hell 'in the most lowest place, moste derke,
and most vyle of the erthe', stressed that it is a state as well as a place;
the sinner is like a man 'that had a grete maladye, so moche that he
shold deye, and that he were brought in to a fair place and plesaunt
for to have Joye and solace; of so moche shold he be more hevy and
sorowful' (*The Mirrour of the World* (1480), ii, 18). Marlowe's concept
of hell at this point may be compared with Milton's; like Mephostophilis,
Satan cannot escape.

for within him Hell
He brings, and round about him, nor from Hell
One step, no more than from himself can fly
By change of place.
                                    Paradise Lost, iv, 20–23.

Mephostophilis' account of the torment of deprivation is translated
from St. John Chrysostom: '*si decem mille gehennas quis dixerit, nihil
tale est quale ab illa beata visione excidere*' (see John Searle, *T.L.S.*, 15th
February 1936).

FAUSTUS

Had I as many souls as there be stars
I'd give them all for Mephostophilis.
By him, I'll be great emperor of the world,
And make a bridge through the moving air   105
To pass the ocean with a band of men;
I'll join the hills that bind the Afric shore,
And make that country continent to Spain,
And both contributory to my crown.
The emperor shall not live, but by my leave,   110
Nor any potentate of Germany.
Now that I have obtained what I desired
I'll live in speculation of this art
Till Mephostophilis return again.   *Exit*

Act I, Scene iv

Enter WAGNER *and the* CLOWN

WAGNER

Come hither sirra boy.

107 *hills . . . shore* The hills on either side of the straits of Gibraltar
which, if joined, would unite Africa and Europe into a single
continent

Act I, Scene iv. It is not easy to account for all the variants between A and
B in this scene. A's *pickadevants* (1.3) is supported against B's *beards*
by the imitation of this in the anonymous *Taming of A Shrew.* The
'French crowns' passage (11.26–9) has hitherto been rejected on
historical grounds (but see note below) and Greg discards the 'kill-
devil' lines (35–9) with the argument that these are borrowed from
Looking Glass for London (see Introduction p. xvii). Two passages in
the A Text were almost certainly interpolated by the comedians. When
the devils have vanished the Clown comments:

> What, are they gone? A vengeance on them, they have vile long
> nails; there was a he-devil and a she-devil; I'll tell you how you
> shall know them: all he-devils has horns, and all she-devils has
> clifts and cloven feet.

At Wagner's promise of the power of metamorphosis the Clown is at
first disapproving and then lewdly appreciative:

> How? A Christian fellow to a dog, or a cat, a mouse or a rat? No,
> no, sir, if you turn me into anything, let it be in the likeness of a
> little pretty frisking flea, that I may be here and there and every-
> where. O I'll tickle the pretty wenches' plackets, I'll be amongst
> them i'faith.

CLOWN

Boy? O disgrace to my person! Zounds, boy in your face!
You have seen many boys with such pickadevants, I am sure.

WAGNER

Sirra, hast thou no comings in?

CLOWN

Yes, and goings out too, you may see sir.   5

WAGNER

Alas poor slave, see how poverty jests in his nakedness. The
villain is bare and out of service, and so hungry, that I know
he would give his soul to the devil, for a shoulder of mutton,
though it were blood-raw.

CLOWN

Not so neither! I had need to have it well roasted, and good   10
sauce to it, if I pay so dear, I can tell you.

WAGNER

Sirra, wilt thou be my man and wait on me? And I will
make thee go, like *Qui mihi discipulus*.

CLOWN

What, in verse?

WAGNER

No slave, in beaten silk, and stavesacre,   15

CLOWN

Stavesacre? That's good to kill vermin; then, belike, if I
serve you, I shall be lousy.

WAGNER

Why, so thou shalt be, whether thou dost it or no: for sirra,

---

 3 *pickadevants* A (beards B) beards fashionably cut to a small
   point (French *pic à devant*)
 4 *comings in* earnings, income
 5 *goings out* expenses; but the Clown makes the word serve two
   functions, pointing also to his tattered clothing
 7 *out of service* out of a job
13 *Qui mihi discipulus* You who are my pupil; the opening words of
   a didactic Latin poem by the schoolmaster William Lily which
   would be familiar to every grammar school boy

---

15 *beaten silk, and stavesacre* 'In effect Wagner promises to dress his servant
   (or rather to dress him down) in silk—and adds that plenty of Keating's
   powder will be needed' (Greg). Gold or silver was hammered into silk
   as a kind of embroidery; *stavesacre* was a preparation from delphinium
   seeds used for killing fleas. It has been suggested that the Clown's
   stavesacre is a comic corruption of what Wagner actually said. But the
   A Clown interpolates here 'Knavesacre? Ay, I thought that was all the
   land his father left him: do you hear, I would be sorry to rob you of your
   living'. Whether this has any authority or not, it shows that Wagner's
   word must have been *stavesacre;* a script writer would not use the same
   kind of joke twice.

if thou dost not presently bind thyself to me for seven years,
I'll turn all the lice about thee into familiars, and make them 20
tear thee in pieces.

CLOWN

Nay sir, you may save yourself a labour, for they are as
familiar with me, as if they paid for their meat and drink, I
can tell you.

WAGNER

Well sirra, leave your jesting, and take these guilders. 25

CLOWN

Gridirons, what be they?

WAGNER

Why, French crowns.

CLOWN

Mass, but for the name of French crowns a man were as
good have as many English counters.

WAGNER

So, now thou art to be at an hour's warning, whensoever, 30
and wheresoever the devil shall fetch thee.

CLOWN

Here, take your guilders again, I'll none of 'em.

WAGNER

Not I, thou art pressed, prepare thyself, for I will presently
raise up two devils to carry thee away: Baliol and Belcher!

CLOWN

Let your Balio and your Belcher come here, and I'll knock 35

20 *familiars* familiar spirits, diabolic personal attendants
23 they treat me as contemptuously as if they were customers at an
inn who pay for what they consume
29 *counters* worthless tokens
33 *pressed* enlisted; the taking of money was a token of enrolment for
military service
34 *Baliol* A (Banio B) probably a corruption of Belial
35 *knock* thump, beat

26-9 French crowns, legal tender in England in the 16th and early 17th
centuries, were easily counterfeited. Marlowe himself is reported in the
Baines' Libel as having boasted 'That he had as good Right to Coine as
the Queen of England and that . . . he ment, through the help of a
Cunninge stamp maker to Coin ffrench Crownes pistoletes and English
shillinges'. Among government measures to stop the flood of false coins
was a proclamation of 1587 urging all who were offered such pieces to
strike a hole in them (See Ruding, *Annals of the Coinage of Britain*,
(1817), i, 192 ff); perhaps the Clown refers to the holes in the coins when
he describes them as *gridirons*. (See H. E. Cain, 'Marlowe's "French
Crowns"', *M.L.N.*, XLIX (1934), 380-84.) The money market
under James was less troubled by this kind of counterfeiting, and the
passage may have been omitted from B because it was no longer meaning-
ful.

them, they were never so knocked since they were devils.
Say I should kill one of them, what would folks say? 'Do ye
see yonder tall fellow in the round slop, he has killed the
devil!' So I should be called kill-devil all the parish over.

Enter two DEVILS *and the* CLOWN
runs up and down crying

WAGNER
How now sir, will you serve me now?   40
CLOWN
Ay good Wagner, take away the devil then.
WAGNER
Spirits away!   *Exeunt* [DEVILS]
          Now sirra, follow me.
CLOWN
I will sir; but hark you master, will you teach me this
conjuring occupation?
WAGNER
Ay sirra, I'll teach thee to turn thyself to a dog, or a cat, or   45
a mouse, or a rat, or anything.
CLOWN
A dog, or a cat, or a mouse, or a rat? O brave, Wagner.
WAGNER
Villain, call me Master Wagner, and see that you walk
attentively, and let your right eye be always diametrally
fixed upon my left heel, that thou may'st *quasi vestigias*   50
nostras insistere.
CLOWN
Well sir, I warrant you.   *Exeunt*

Act II, Scene i

Enter FAUSTUS *in his study*

FAUSTUS
Now Faustus must thou needs be damned
And canst thou not be saved?
What boots it then to think on God or heaven?

38 *tall* brave;
    round slop baggy trousers
49 *diametrally* diametrically
50–51 *quasi vestigias nostras insistere* as it were tread in our footsteps;
    the construction is false (for *vestigiis nostris*) but this may be
    intentional

Away with such vain fancies and despair,
Despair in God, and trust in Belzebub.   5
Now go not backward: no, Faustus, be resolute,
Why waverest thou? O, something soundeth in mine ears:
'Abjure this magic, turn to God again'.
Ay, and Faustus will turn to God again.
To God? He loves thee not: 10
The God thou servest is thine own appetite
Wherein is fixed the love of Belzebub:
To him, I'll build an altar and a church,
And offer luke-warm blood of new-born babes.

Enter the two ANGELS

GOOD ANGEL
Sweet Faustus, leave that execrable art.   15
FAUSTUS
Contrition, prayer, repentance – what of these?
GOOD ANGEL
O they are means to bring thee unto heaven.
BAD ANGEL
Rather illusions, fruits of lunacy,
That make men foolish that do trust them most.
GOOD ANGEL
Sweet Faustus, think of heaven, and heavenly things.   20
BAD ANGEL
No Faustus, think of honour and of wealth.

                                        Exeunt ANGELS
FAUSTUS
Wealth!
Why, the signory of Emden shall be mine:
When Mephostophilis shall stand by me
What god can hurt me? Faustus thou art safe.   25
Cast no more doubts; Mephostophilis, come
And bring glad tidings from great Lucifer.

9–10 *Ay . . . God* A (*not in* B)
23 *signory of Emden* governorship of Emden – a port on the mouth of
   the Ems, at this time trading extensively with England
25 *god* A (power B)

---

15 Before this line B inserts:
     Evil Angel Go forward Faustus, in that famous art.
   The line exactly repeats I.i, 73, and this alone makes it suspect. Furthermore, the inconsistency of the speech heading (*Evil* instead of *Bad*) points
   to some kind of tinkering with the text. The same inconsistency is to be
   found at II.ii, 17, but here B has borrowed the line and its heading from A.

Is't not midnight? Come Mephostophilis,
Veni, veni Mephostophilis.

Enter MEPHOSTOPHILIS

Now tell me what saith Lucifer thy lord? 30

MEPHOSTOPHILIS
That I shall wait on Faustus whilst he lives,
So he will buy my service with his soul.

FAUSTUS
Already Faustus hath hazarded that for thee.

MEPHOSTOPHILIS
But now thou must bequeath it solemnly,
And write a deed of gift with thine own blood; 35
For that security craves Lucifer.
If thou deny it I must back to hell.

FAUSTUS
Stay Mephostophilis, and tell me,
What good will my soul do thy lord?

MEPHOSTOPHILIS
Enlarge his kingdom. 40

FAUSTUS
Is that the reason why he tempts us thus?

MEPHOSTOPHILIS
Solamen miseris, socios habuisse doloris.

FAUSTUS
Why, have you any pain that torture others?

MEPHOSTOPHILIS
As great as have the human souls of men.
But tell me Faustus, shall I have thy soul? 45
And I will be thy slave and wait on thee,
And give thee more than thou hast wit to ask.

FAUSTUS
Ay Mephostophilis, I'll give it him.

MEPHOSTOPHILIS
Then Faustus, stab thine arm courageously,
And bind thy soul, that at some certain day 50

29 Come, O come Mephostophilis
33 *hazarded* jeopardized
42 In Chaucer's version: 'Men seyn, "to wrecche is consolacioun
   To have an-other felawe in his peyne".' *Troilus and Criseyde*, i,
   708–9.

---

40 'Satan's chiefest drift & main point that he aimeth at, is the inlargement
   of his owne kingdom, by the eternall destruction of man in the life to
   come', James Mason, *The Anatomie of Sorcerie* (1612), p. 55.

Great Lucifer may claim it as his own,
And then be thou as great as Lucifer.

FAUSTUS

Lo Mephostophilis, for love of thee
           [*stabs his arm*]
Faustus hath cut his arm, and with his proper blood
Assures his soul to be great Lucifer's,   55
Chief lord and regent of perpetual night.
View here this blood that trickles from mine arm,
And let it be propitious for my wish.

MEPHOSTOPHILIS

But Faustus,
Write it in manner of a deed of gift.   60

FAUSTUS

Ay, so I will.
            [*writes*]
      But Mephostophilis,
My blood congeals, and I can write no more.

MEPHOSTOPHILIS

I'll fetch thee fire to dissolve it straight.

                        Exit

FAUSTUS

What might the staying of my blood portend?
Is it unwilling I should write this bill?   65
Why streams it not, that I may write afresh?
'Faustus gives to thee his soul': ah, there it stayed!
Why should'st thou not? Is not thy soul thine own?
Then write again: 'Faustus gives to thee his soul'.

      Enter MEPHOSTOPHILIS *with the*
           Chafer of Fire

MEPHOSTOPHILIS

See Faustus here is fire, set it on.   70

FAUSTUS

So, now the blood begins to clear again:
            [*writes again*]
Now will I make an end immediately.

MEPHOSTOPHILIS

What will not I do to obtain his soul!

54 *proper* own
69 s.d. *Chafer* portable grate
70 *set it on* 'set his blood in a saucer on warm ashes'. *EFB*,vi.
71 Greg observes that no earthly fire will liquefy congealed blood

FAUSTUS

Consummatum est: this bill is ended,
And Faustus hath bequeathed his soul to Lucifer.   75
But what is this inscription on mine arm?
Homo fuge! Whither should I fly?
If unto God, he'll throw me down to hell.
My senses are deceived, here's nothing writ:
O yes, I see it plain, even here is writ   80
Homo fuge! Yet shall not Faustus fly.

MEPHOSTOPHILIS

I'll fetch him somewhat to delight his mind.

Exit

Enter DEVILS, *giving crowns and rich apparel*
to FAUSTUS: *they dance, and then depart:*
Enter MEPHOSTOPHILIS

FAUSTUS

What means this show? Speak Mephostophilis.

MEPHOSTOPHILIS

Nothing Faustus, but to delight thy mind,
And let thee see what magic can perform.   85

FAUSTUS

But may I raise such spirits when I please?

MEPHOSTOPHILIS

Ay Faustus, and do greater things than these.

FAUSTUS

Then Mephostophilis, receive this scroll.
A deed of gift, of body and of soul:
But yet conditionally, that thou perform   90
All covenants and articles between us both.

MEPHOSTOPHILIS

Faustus, I swear by hell and Lucifer,
To effect all promises between us made.

FAUSTUS

Then hear me read it Mephostophilis.
On these conditions following: 95
First, that Faustus may be a spirit in form and substance.

74 *Consummatum est* It is finished; the last words of Christ on the
cross: St. John, xix,30
77 *Homo fuge* Fly, O man   78 *God* A (heaven B)
88 A gives Faustus another line before this one: 'Then there's
enough for a thousand souls.'

96 *spirit* A spirit, to the Elizabethans, was usually an evil one, a devil (see
Shakespeare, Sonnet CXLIV); according to some theologians, who
followed Aquinas, God could have no mercy on a devil who was *ipso*
facto incapable of repenting. See II.ii, 13–15.

Secondly, that Mephostophilis shall be his servant, and at
his command.
Thirdly, that Mephostophilis shall do for him, and bring
him whatsoever.   100
Fourthly, that he shall be in his chamber or house invisible.
Lastly, that he shall appear to the said John Faustus, at all
times, in what form or shape soever he please.
I, John Faustus of Wittenberg, doctor, by these presents, do
give both body and soul to Lucifer, Prince of the East, and   105
his minister Mephostophilis, and furthermore grant unto
them, that four and twenty years being expired, the articles
above written inviolate, full power to fetch or carry the said
John Faustus, body and soul, flesh, blood, or goods, into
their habitation wheresoever.   110
                          By me John Faustus

MEPHOSTOPHILIS
Speak Faustus, do you deliver this as your deed?
FAUSTUS
Ay, take it, and the devil give thee good on't.
MEPHOSTOPHILIS
Now Faustus, ask what thou wilt.
FAUSTUS
First will I question with thee about hell: 115
Tell me, where is the place that men call hell?
MEPHOSTOPHILIS
Under the heavens.
FAUSTUS
Ay, so are all things else; but whereabouts?
MEPHOSTOPHILIS
Within the bowels of these elements,
Where we are tortured, and remain for ever.   120
Hell hath no limits, nor is circumscribed
In one self place; but where we are is hell,
And where hell is, there must we ever be.
And to be short, when all the world dissolves,
And every creature shall be purified,   125
All places shall be hell that is not heaven.
FAUSTUS
I think hell's a fable.
MEPHOSTOPHILIS
Ay, think so still, till experience change thy mind.

---

104 *these presents* the legal articles
119 *these elements* the four elements below the sphere of the moon
122 *one self place* one particular place

FAUSTUS

Why, dost thou think that Faustus shall be damned?

MEPHOSTOPHILIS

Ay, of necessity, for here's the scroll   130
In which thou hast given thy soul to Lucifer.

FAUSTUS

Ay, and body too, but what of that?
Think'st thou that Faustus is so fond to imagine,
That after this life there is any pain?
No, these are trifles, and mere old wives' tales.   135

MEPHOSTOPHILIS

But I am an instance to prove the contrary:
For I tell thee I am damned, and now in hell.

FAUSTUS

Nay, and this be hell, I'll willingly be damned.
What, sleeping, eating, walking and disputing?
But leaving this, let me have a wife, the fairest maid in   140
Germany, for I am wanton and lascivious, and cannot live
without a wife.

MEPHOSTOPHILIS

How, a wife? I prithee Faustus, talk not of a wife.

FAUSTUS

Nay sweet Mephostophilis, fetch me one, for I will have one.

MEPHOSTOPHILIS

Well, thou wilt have one; sit there till I come;   145
I'll fetch thee a wife in the devil's name.   [*Exit*]

Enter with a DEVIL *dressed like a woman, with fireworks*

MEPHOSTOPHILIS

Tell me Faustus, how dost thou like thy wife?

FAUSTUS

A plague on her for a hot whore! No, I'll no wife.

MEPHOSTOPHILIS

Marriage is but a ceremonial toy,
And if thou lovest me think no more of it.   150
I'll cull thee out the fairest courtesans,
And bring them every morning to thy bed:
She whom thine eye shall like, thy heart shall have,
Were she as chaste as was Penelope,

133 *fond foolish*
151 *cull pick*
154 *Penelope* wife of Ulysses, renowned for her fidelity to a lost husband

139–47 A gives the fuller text here; the abrupt change to prose, in both
versions, suggests that another author has taken over.

As wise as Saba, or as beautiful 155
As was bright Lucifer before his fall.
Hold, take this book, peruse it thoroughly:
The iterating of these lines brings gold;
The framing of this circle on the ground
Brings thunder, whirlwinds, storm and lightning: 160
Pronounce this thrice devoutly to thyself,
And men in harness shall appear to thee,
Ready to execute what thou command'st.

FAUSTUS
Thanks Mephostophilis; yet fain would I have a book
wherein I might behold all spells and incantations, that I 165
might raise up spirits when I please.

MEPHOSTOPHILIS
Here they are in this book. *There turn to them*

FAUSTUS
Now would I have a book where I might see all characters
and planets of the heavens, that I might know their motions
and dispositions. 170

MEPHOSTOPHILIS
Here they are too. *Turn to them*

FAUSTUS
Nay, let me have one book more, and then I have done,
wherein I might see all plants, herbs and trees that grow
upon the earth.

MEPHOSTOPHILIS
Here they be. 175

FAUSTUS
O thou art deceived.

MEPHOSTOPHILIS
Tut I warrant thee. *Turn to them*
Exeunt

---

155 *Saba* the Queen of Sheba, who confronted Solomon with 'hard
questions', I Kings, x
162 *harness* armour
170 *dispositions* situations

163–76 B allows no investigation of the magic book, ending the episode
abruptly with Faustus' thanks:

Thanks Mephostophilis for this sweet book.
This will I keep as chary as my life.

Although the sudden switch in A from verse to prose suggests another
author, or even an after-thought, B's anticipation of II.ii, 172 is equally
suspicious.

Act II, Scene ii

Enter FAUSTUS *in his study*
and MEPHOSTOPHILIS

FAUSTUS
When I behold the heavens then I repent
And curse thee wicked Mephostophilis,
Because thou hast deprived me of those joys.

MEPHOSTOPHILIS
'Twas thine own seeking Faustus, thank thyself:
But think'st thou heaven is such a glorious thing?   5
I tell thee Faustus, it is not half so fair
As thou, or any man that breathes on earth.

FAUSTUS
How prov'st thou that?

MEPHOSTOPHILIS
'Twas made for man; then he's more excellent.

FAUSTUS
If heaven was made for man, 'twas made for me: 10
I will renounce this magic and repent.

Enter the two ANGELS

GOOD ANGEL
Faustus repent, yet God will pity thee.

BAD ANGEL
Thou art a spirit, God cannot pity thee.

FAUSTUS
Who buzzeth in mine ears I am a spirit?
Be I a devil yet God may pity me,   15
Yea, God will pity me if I repent.

---

4 B (*not in* A)
13 (see note on II.i, 96)
14 *buzzeth* whispers
15 *Be I* This could mean either 'Even if I am' or else 'Even though
I were'

Act II, Scene ii. Both texts seem to have lost a scene here; the Elizabethans
would never take two characters off the stage to bring them on again
immediately. Boas suggests a comic interlude with Wagner, Greg an
episode in preparation for II.iii, showing the Clown stealing one of
Faustus' conjuring books and determining to leave Wagner's service.
But the Clown of I.iv seems to me to be a different kind of comedian
from the Robin of the subsequent comic scenes.

EVIL ANGEL

    Ay, but Faustus never shall repent.   *Exeunt* ANGELS

FAUSTUS

    My heart's so hardened I cannot repent!
    Scarce can I name salvation, faith, or heaven,
    But fearful echoes thunders in mine ears,   20
    'Faustus, thou art damned': then swords and knives,
    Poison, guns, halters and envenomed steel
    Are laid before me to dispatch myself:
    And long ere this, I should have done the deed,
    Had not sweet pleasure conquered deep despair.   25
    Have not I made blind Homer sing to me
    Of Alexander's love, and Oenon's death?
    And hath not he, that built the walls of Thebes
    With ravishing sound of his melodious harp,
    Made music with my Mephostophilis?   30
    Why should I die then, or basely despair?
    I am resolved! Faustus shall not repent.
    Come Mephostophilis let us dispute again,
    And reason of divine astrology.
    Speak, are there many spheres above the moon?   35
    Are all celestial bodies but one globe,
    As is the substance of this centric earth?

MEPHOSTOPHILIS

    As are the elements, such are the heavens,
    Even from the moon unto the empyreal orb,
    Mutually folded in each other's spheres,   40

---

17 (see note on II.i, 15)
22 *halters* hangman's ropes
24 *done the deed* B (slain myself A)
39 B (*not in* A)

---

27 *Alexander . . . death* Alexander, Homer's name for Paris son of Priam,
    fell in love with Oenone before he encountered Helen; wounded in the
    Trojan War, he was carried to Oenone and died at her feet, whereupon
    she stabbed herself.
28–9 At the sound of Amphion's harp the stones were so affected that
    they rose of their own accord to form the walls of Thebes.
35–62 The Faustus of Marlowe's source was an astrologer–a calendar-
    maker and weather-forecaster–rather than an astronomer, and although
    Mephostophilis promises to teach him about the planets the approach
    is unscientific and the information a miscellaneous jumble. Marlowe's
    protagonist has the questioning mind of the Renaissance student, and
    the answers he is given accord with the sceptical authorities of the day
    (See Kocher, pp. 214–23, and F. R. Johnson, 'Marlowe's Astronomy
    and Renaissance Skepticism', *E.L.H.*, XIII (1946), iv). The Ptolemaic

And jointly move upon one axletree,
Whose termine is termed the world's wide pole.
Nor are the names of Saturn, Mars or Jupiter,
Feigned, but are erring stars.

FAUSTUS

But have they all one motion, both *situ et tempore*?   45

MEPHOSTOPHILIS

All move from east to west in four and twenty hours, upon
the poles of the world, but differ in their motions upon the
poles of the zodiac.

FAUSTUS

These slender questions Wagner can decide!
Hath Mephostophilis no greater skill?   50
Who knows not the double motion of the planets?
That the first is finished in a natural day, the second thus:

42 *termine* boundary (astronomical)
45 *situ et tempore* in direction and in time
49 *questions* B (trifles A)

---

system, as yet unshaken by Copernicus, held that the universe was
composed of concentric spheres with the earth (*this centric earth*) as
the innermost. Beyond the earth was the sphere of the Moon, and
further out still the spheres of the six other *erring stars* or planets:
Mercury, Venus, Sun, Mars, Jupiter, Saturn. The eighth was the
firmament, or sphere of the fixed stars, which Marlowe, admitting only
nine spheres (1.59) identified with the *Primum Mobile*, the first moving
thing which imparted movement to all the rest. The ninth sphere
(tenth, if the *Primum Mobile* was allowed to be separate from the
firmament) was the immoveable empyrean (*the empyreal orb*).

35–44 Faustus asks first for confirmation of the number of spheres beyond
the Moon and whether in fact these do form a single ball. Mephostophilis replies that just as the four elements enclose each other (earth is
surrounded by water, water by air, and air by fire), so each sphere or
heaven is circled round by the ones beyond it, and all rotate upon a
single axletree. Saturn, Mars and the other planets are individually
recognizable and are called *erring* or wandering stars to distinguish
them from the fixed stars joined to the firmament.

45–56 'Do all the planets move at the same speed and in the same direction?'
is Faustus' next question. He is told that the planets have two movements: a daily east to west rotation round the earth governed by the
Primum Mobile, and a slower, individual turning from west to east.
Caxton (*Mirrour of the World*, (1480), i.13) explains that each planet is
like a fly crawling on a wheel; if the fly crawls in one direction and the
wheel turns in the opposite, the fly may be said to have two movements.
Faustus knows this well enough, and proceeds to detail with reasonable
accuracy the different times taken by the planets in their individual
revolutions—the farthest from the earth, naturally, taking the longest.
The figures usually given are: Saturn 29½ years; Jupiter 11¾ years;
Mars 1 year 11 months; Sun 1 year; Venus 7½ months; and Mercury
3 months.

Saturn in thirty years; Jupiter in twelve; Mars in four; the
Sun, Venus and Mercury in a year; the Moon in twenty-
eight days. These are freshmen's suppositions. But tell me,   55
hath every sphere a dominion or intelligentia?

MEPHOSTOPHILIS
Ay.

FAUSTUS
How many heavens, or spheres, are there?

MEPHOSTOPHILIS
Nine: the seven planets, the firmament, and the empyreal
heaven.   60

FAUSTUS
But is there not *coelum igneum? et cristallinum?*

MEPHOSTOPHILIS
No Faustus, they be but fables.

FAUSTUS
Resolve me then in this one question: why are not conjunctions, oppositions, aspects, eclipses, all at one time,
but in some years we have more, in some less?   65

MEPHOSTOPHILIS
Per inaequalem motum, respectu totius.

FAUSTUS
Well, I am answered. Now tell me who made the world?

MEPHOSTOPHILIS
I will not.

FAUSTUS
Sweet Mephostophilis, tell me.

55 *suppositions* A (questions B) elementary facts given to first year
undergraduates for them to build an argument on

56-7 The next question at issue relates to a theory first propounded by
Plato and developed in the Middle Ages, that each planet was guided
by an angelic spirit, commonly called the *intelligence*:

> Let mans Soule be a Spheare, and then, in this,
> The intelligence that moves, devotion is,
>   Donne, 'Good Friday, Riding Westwards'

Mephostophilis affirms the *intelligence*, but the theory was never really
accepted by scientists.

58-62 Faustus seems to return to his earlier query about the number of
spheres or heavens. Aristotle accounted for eight, but another was
added by the early Church Fathers who postulated the *empyreal heaven*
which was the abode of God, unmoving and shining with a piercing,
stainless light. Mephostophilis contradicts the current belief that there
were still more celestial spheres, the *coelum igneum* and *coelum cristallinum* (heavens of fire and crystal). Both these were added to the
Aristotelian concept of the universe (the latter by Ptolemy) and Marlowe
was not alone in denying their existence. Pierre de La Primaudaye,
whose *French Academie* (vol. III) is a possible source for Marlowe's
astronomical knowledge, shares this doubt.

MEPHOSTOPHILIS
Move me not Faustus.   70
FAUSTUS
Villain, have not I bound thee to tell me anything?
MEPHOSTOPHILIS
Ay, that is not against our kingdom.
This is: thou art damned, think thou on hell.
FAUSTUS
Think, Faustus, upon God, that made the world.
MEPHOSTOPHILIS
Remember this!   75
                                                              Exit

FAUSTUS
Ay, go accursed spirit to ugly hell:
'Tis thou hast damned distressed Faustus' soul.
Is't not too late?

                       Enter the two ANGELS

BAD ANGEL
Too late.
GOOD ANGEL
Never too late, if Faustus will repent.   80
BAD ANGEL
If thou repent, devils will tear thee in pieces.
GOOD ANGEL
Repent, and they shall never raze thy skin.
                                              Exeunt ANGELS

70 *Move* Vex
82 *raze* graze

63-6 Mephostophilis' answer to the next question sounds like a quotation
from some astronomical textbook. Faustus asks about the behaviour
of the planets, using technical but well-known astronomical terms:
conjunctions are the apparent joinings together of two planets, while
oppositions describes their relationships when most remote:

> Therefore the love which us doth bind,
> But Fate so enviously debarrs,
> Is the Conjunction of the Mind,
> And Opposition of the Stars.
>   Marvell, 'The Definition of Love'.

Any position between the two extremes of conjunction and opposition
was termed an *aspect*. To astrologers the differing situations and
relations of the planets all have some particular significance—hence the
horoscope. Faustus is finally told what he already knows: that the
heavenly bodies do not all move at the same speed, and that for this
reason ('through an irregular motion so far as the whole is concerned',
1.66) there are more eclipses etc. in some years than in others.

FAUSTUS
O Christ my saviour, my saviour,
Help to save distressed Faustus' soul.

Enter LUCIFER, BELZEBUB, *and* MEPHOSTOPHILIS

LUCIFER
Christ cannot save thy soul, for he is just; 85
There's none but I have interest in the same.

FAUSTUS
O what art thou that look'st so terribly?

LUCIFER
I am Lucifer, and this is my companion prince in hell.

FAUSTUS
O Faustus, they are come to fetch thy soul!

BELZEBUB
We are come to tell thee thou dost injure us. 90

LUCIFER
Thou call'st on Christ contrary to thy promise.

BELZEBUB
Thou should'st not think on God.

LUCIFER
Think on the devil.

BELZEBUB
And his dam too.

FAUSTUS
Nor will I henceforth: pardon me in this, 95
And Faustus vows never to look to heaven,
Never to name God, or to pray to him,
To burn his scriptures, slay his ministers,
And make my spirits pull his churches down.

LUCIFER
So shalt thou show thyself an obedient servant, 100
And we will highly gratify thee for it.

BELZEBUB
Faustus, we are come from hell in person to show thee some
pastime: sit down and thou shalt behold the Seven Deadly
Sins appear to thee in their own proper shapes and likeness.

FAUSTUS
That sight will be as pleasing unto me as Paradise was to 105
Adam the first day of his creation.

84 *Help* B (Seek A)
86 *interest in* legal claim on
97–9 A (*not in* B)

LUCIFER

Talk not of Paradise or creation, but mark the show.
Go Mephostophilis, fetch them in.

Enter the SEVEN DEADLY SINS

BELZEBUB

Now Faustus, examine them of their several names and
dispositions.   110

FAUSTUS

That shall I soon: what art thou, the first?

PRIDE

I am Pride; I disdain to have any parents: I am like to
Ovid's flea, I can creep into every corner of a wench: sometimes, like a periwig, I sit upon her brow; next, like a neck-
lace, I hang about her neck; then, like a fan of feathers, I   115
kiss her lips; and then, turning myself to a wrought smock,
do what I list. But fie, what a smell is here! I'll not speak
another word unless the ground be perfumed, and covered
with cloth of arras.

FAUSTUS

Thou art a proud knave indeed: what art thou, the second?   120

COVETOUSNESS

I am Covetousness, begotten of an old churl in a leather
bag; and might I now obtain my wish, this house, you and
all should turn to gold, that I might lock you safe into my
chest. O my sweet gold!

FAUSTUS

And what art thou, the third?   125

ENVY

I am Envy, begotten of a chimney-sweeper, and an oyster-
wife: I cannot read, and therefore wish all books burnt. I
am lean with seeing others eat: O that there would come a
famine over all the world, that all might die, and I live
alone, then thou shouldst see how fat I'd be. But must thou   130
sit, and I stand? Come down, with a vengeance.

---

113 *Ovid's flea* The poet of 'The Song of the Flea' (probably medieval
but attributed to Ovid) envies the flea for its freedom of movement
over his mistress' body
116 *wrought* embroidered
117 *another word* A (a word more for a king's ransom B); B anticipates
the words of Sloth (below, 157–8)
119 *cloth of arras* tapestry; woven at Arras in Flanders and used for
wall-hangings
121 *leather bag* the miser's purse
126–7 *begotten . . . wife* 'and therefore black and malodorous' (Wheeler)

FAUSTUS

Out, envious wretch! But what art thou, the fourth?

WRATH

I am Wrath: I had neither father nor mother; I leapt out
of a lion's mouth when I was scarce an hour old, and ever
since have run up and down the world with these case of   135
rapiers, wounding myself when I could get none to fight
withal: I was born in hell, and look to it, for some of you
shall be my father.

FAUSTUS

And what art thou, the fifth?

GLUTTONY

I am gluttony; my parents are all dead, and the devil a   140
penny they have left me, but a small pension, and that buys
me thirty meals a day, and ten bevers: a small trifle to
suffice nature. I come of a royal pedigree: my father was a
gammon of bacon, and my mother was a hogshead of claret
wine. My godfathers were these: Peter Pickled-Herring and   145
Martin Martlemass-Beef: O but my godmother, she was a
jolly gentlewoman, and well beloved in every good town and
city; her name was Mistress Margery March-Beer. Now
Faustus, thou hast heard all my progeny, wilt thou bid me
to supper?   150

FAUSTUS

No, I'll see thee hanged, thou wilt eat up all my victuals.

GLUTTONY

Then the devil choke thee.

FAUSTUS

Choke thyself, Glutton; what art thou, the sixth?

SLOTH

Hey ho! I am Sloth: I was begotten on a sunny bank, where
I have lain ever since, and you have done me great injury   155
to bring me from thence; let me be carried thither again by
Gluttony and Lechery. Hey ho, I'll not speak a word more
for a king's ransom.

135 *these case* A case of rapiers is in fact a pair
142 *bevers* snacks
146 *Martlemass-Beef* Meat, salted to preserve it for winter, was hung
up to Martinmas (November 11th)
147-8 *a jolly ... city* A (an ancient gentlewoman B)
148 *March-Beer* a rich ale, made in March and left to mature for at
least two years
149 *progeny* lineage (obsolete)
154-7 *where ... Lechery* A (*not in* B)

FAUSTUS
  And what are you Mistress Minx, the seventh and last?
LECHERY
  Who I? I sir? I am one that loves an inch of raw mutton,   160
  better than an ell of fried stockfish: and the first letter of
  my name begins with Lechery.
LUCIFER
  Away to hell, away, on piper.   *Exeunt the* SEVEN SINS
FAUSTUS
  O how this sight doth delight my soul.
LUCIFER
  But Faustus, in hell is all manner of delight.   165
FAUSTUS
  O might I see hell, and return again safe, how happy were
  I then.
LUCIFER
  Faustus, thou shalt, at midnight I will send for thee;
  Meanwhile peruse this book, and view it throughly,
  And thou shalt turn thyself into what shape thou wilt.   170
FAUSTUS
  Thanks mighty Lucifer:
  This will I keep as chary as my life.
LUCIFER
  Now Faustus, farewell.
FAUSTUS
  Farewell, great Lucifer: come Mephostophilis.
                        Exeunt omnes, several ways

162 *begins with Lechery* A common form of jest: 'Her name begins
    with Mistress Purge', Middleton, *The Family of Love*, II.iii, 53
169 *throughly* thoroughly
172 *chary* carefully
174 s.d. *several ways* in different directions

160–1 *loves . . . stockfish* Most editors are reticent about the meaning of this
    line and content themselves with pointing out that *mutton* is frequently
    used to mean 'prostitute'. Greg observes that such an interpretation
    cannot apply where Lechery is *Mistress Minx*, and he adds 'but this
    indelicate subject need not be pursued. Ward by omitting the passage
    showed that he understood it'. Lechery is saying in effect that she prefers
    a small quantity of virility to a large extent of impotence. *Stock-fish*, a
    long dried-up piece of cod, is a common term of abuse, indicating
    impotence: 'he was begot between two stockfishes', *Measure for
    Measure*, III.ii, 98.

Act II, Scene iii

Enter the CLOWN [ROBIN]

CLOWN
What, Dick, look to the horses there till I come again. I have
gotten one of Doctor Faustus' conjuring books, and now
we'll have such knavery, as't passes.

Enter DICK

DICK
What, Robin, you must come away and walk the horses.
ROBIN
I walk the horses! I scorn't, 'faith, I have other matters in   5
hand, let the horses walk themselves and they will. [*reads*]
'A *per se* a; t. h. e. the; o *per se* o; deny orgon, gorgon'. Keep
further from me, O thou illiterate and unlearned ostler.
DICK
'Snails, what hast thou got there? A book? Why, thou canst
not tell ne'er a word on't.   10
ROBIN
That thou shalt see presently: keep out of the circle, I say,
lest I send you into the hostry with a vengeance.
DICK
That's like, 'faith: you had best leave your foolery, for an
my master come, he'll conjure you, 'faith.
ROBIN
My master conjure me? I'll tell thee what, an my master   15
come here, I'll clap as fair a pair of horns on's head as e'er
thou sawest in thy life.
DICK
Thou needest not do that, for my mistress hath done it.
ROBIN
Ay, there be of us here, that have waded as deep into matters,
as other men, if they were disposed to talk.   20

II.iii. A's version of this scene is printed in the Appendix
   3 *as't passes* as beats everything
   7 *per se* by itself; a by itself spells a
     deny orgon, gorgon Robin is struggling to read the 'Demogorgon'
     of Faustus' invocation
   9 *'Snails* By God's nails
  12 *hostry* hostelry, inn
  13 *That's like* A likely chance
  19 *matters* affairs; 'I meddle with no tradesman's matters, nor
     women's matters', *Julius Caesar*, I.i, 23

DICK

A plague take you, I thought you did not sneak up and down
after her for nothing. But I prithee tell me, in good sadness,
Robin, is that a conjuring book?

ROBIN

Do but speak what thou'lt have me to do, and I'll do't: if
thou'lt dance naked, put off thy clothes, and I'll conjure thee   25
about presently; or if thou'lt go but to the tavern with me,
I'll give thee white wine, red wine, claret wine, sack, muscadine, malmsey and whippincrust, hold belly hold, and we'll
not pay one penny for it.

DICK

O brave! Prithee, let's to it presently, for I am as dry as a   30
dog.

ROBIN

Come then, let's away.   *Exeunt*

CHORUS I

Enter the CHORUS

CHORUS

Learned Faustus,
To find the secrets of astronomy,
Graven in the book of Jove's high firmament,
Did mount him up to scale Olympus' top;
Where sitting in a chariot burning bright,   5
Drawn by the strength of yoked dragons' necks,
He views the clouds, the planets, and the stars,
The tropics, zones, and quarters of the sky,
From the bright circle of the horned moon,
Even to the height of *Primum Mobile:*   10

---

22 *in good sadness* seriously
27 *sack* strong, light-coloured wine from Spain
  muscadine muscatel; strong sweet wine from the muscat grape
28 *malmsey* another strong sweet wine
  whippincrust a spiced wine; corruption of hippocras
  hold belly hold a belly-full
7–19 B (*not in* A)
8 *tropics* of Cancer and Capricorn
  zones Four circles (the two tropics and two polar circles) divide
  the world into five zones; this technical word is used by La Primaudaye (*French Academie*, III, xvii)
9–10 From the innermost to the outermost sphere; everywhere,
  that is, except to the empyrean
10 *Primum Mobile* (see note on II.ii, 35–62)

And whirling round with this circumference,
Within the concave compass of the pole,
From east to west his dragons swiftly glide,
And in eight days did bring him home again.
Not long he stayed within his quiet house,   15
To rest his bones after his weary toil,
But new exploits do hale him out again,
And mounted then upon a dragon's back,
That with his wings did part the subtle air,
He now is gone to prove cosmography,   20
That measures coasts and kingdoms of the earth:
And as I guess will first arrive at Rome,
To see the Pope and manner of his court,
And take some part of holy Peter's feast,
The which this day is highly solemnized.   *Exit*   25

Act III, Scene i

Enter FAUSTUS *and* MEPHOSTOPHILIS

FAUSTUS

Having now, my good Mephostophilis,
Passed with delight the stately town of Trier,
Environed round with airy mountain tops,
With walls of flint, and deep entrenched lakes,
Not to be won by any conquering prince;   5
From Paris next, coasting the realm of France,
We saw the river Main fall into Rhine,
Whose banks are set with groves of fruitful vines.
Then up to Naples, rich Campania,
With buildings fair, and gorgeous to the eye,   10
Whose streets straight forth, and paved with finest brick,
Quarter the town in four equivalents;
There saw we learned Maro's golden tomb,

---

11 *this circumference* i.e. the Primum Mobile
25 *this day* June 29th is the Feast of St. Peter
 9 *Campania EFB* led Marlowe into this erroneous identification of
    Naples with Campagna
10 *With* ed. (Whose Qq)
11 *Whose* ed. (The Qq)
    straight forth in straight lines
13–15 Virgil (Publius Virgilius Maro) was buried in Naples in 19 B.C.
    and posthumously acquired some reputation as a magician. His
    tomb stands at the end of the promontory of Posilippo between
    Naples and Pozzuoli and legend ascribes the tunnel running
    through this promontory to his magic art.

The way he cut an English mile in length
Thorough a rock of stone in one night's space: 15
From thence to Venice, Padua and the rest,
In midst of which a sumptuous temple stands,
That threats the stars with her aspiring top,
Whose frame is paved with sundry coloured stones,
And roofed aloft with curious work in gold.   20
Thus hitherto hath Faustus spent his time.
But tell me now, what resting place is this?
Hast thou, as erst I did command,
Conducted me within the walls of Rome?

MEPHOSTOPHILIS
I have my Faustus, and for proof thereof,   25
This is the goodly palace of the Pope:
And 'cause we are no common guests,
I choose his privy chamber for our use.

FAUSTUS
I hope his holiness will bid us welcome.

MEPHOSTOPHILIS
All's one, for we'll be bold with his venison.   30
But now my Faustus, that thou may'st perceive,
What Rome contains for to delight thine eyes,
Know that this city stands upon seven hills,
That underprop the groundwork of the same:
Just through the midst runs flowing Tiber's stream,   35
With winding banks that cut it in two parts;
Over the which four stately bridges lean,
That make safe passage to each part of Rome.
Upon the bridge called Ponte Angelo
Erected is a castle passing strong,   40
Where thou shalt see such store of ordinance,
As that the double cannons forged of brass
Do match the number of the days contained
Within the compass of one complete year:

16 *rest* A (east B)
17 *midst* A (one B)
23 *erst* earlier
35–6 B (*not in* A)
42 *double cannons* cannons of very high calibre

17–20 St. Mark's in Venice; details (supplied by *EFB*) of the mosaics
and the gilded roof are accurate, but unless the nearby campanile is
meant the *aspiring top* exists only in the dramatist's imagination. (See
Introduction p. xiv)
39–40 The Ponte Angelo was built in A.D. 135 by Hadrian; his mausoleum
faces the bridge but never stood on it.

Besides the gates, and high pyramides　　　　　45
That Julius Caesar brought from Africa.

FAUSTUS

Now by the kingdoms of infernal rule,
Of Styx, of Acheron, and the fiery lake
Of ever-burning Phlegethon, I swear,
That I do long to see the monuments　　　　　50
And situation of bright-splendent Rome.
Come therefore, let's away.

MEPHOSTOPHILIS

Nay, stay my Faustus, I know you'd see the Pope,
And take some part of holy Peter's feast,
The which in state and high solemnity,　　　　　55
This day is held through Rome and Italy,
In honour of the Pope's triumphant victory.

FAUSTUS

Sweet Mephostophilis, thou pleasest me;
Whilst I am here on earth, let me be cloyed
With all things that delight the heart of man.　　　　　60
My four and twenty years of liberty
I'll spend in pleasure and in dalliance,
That Faustus' name, whilst this bright frame doth stand,
May be admired through the furthest land.

MEPHOSTOPHILIS

'Tis well said Faustus, come then stand by me　　　　　65
And thou shalt see them come immediately.

FAUSTUS

Nay stay my gentle Mephostophilis,
And grant me my request, and then I go.
Thou knowest within the compass of eight days,
We viewed the face of heaven, of earth and hell:　　　　　70

---

51 *situation* lay-out
55 *in state and* B₂ (this day with B₁)
64 *admired* wondered at

45–6 *pyramides . . . Africa* the obelisk; in fact this was brought from Helio-
　　polis by the Emperor Caligula in the first century A.D. The plural form
　　pyramides (here stressing the need to pronounce the final syllable) is
　　also used as a singular by Marlowe in *The Massacre at Paris*, ii, 43–6.
57 *victory* This must be the victory over Bruno the usurper; but no addi-
　　tional pretext should be needed for a feast on St. Peter's day. A reads
　　simply:
　　　　Where thou shalt see a troup of bald-pate friars,
　　　　Whose *summum bonum* is in belly-cheer.
　　There are only the vestiges of a banquet scene in A.

So high our dragons soared into the air,
That, looking down, the earth appeared to me
No bigger than my hand in quantity.
There did we view the kingdoms of the world,
And what might please mine eye, I there beheld.   75
Then in this show let me an actor be,
That this proud Pope may Faustus' cunning see.

MEPHOSTOPHILIS
Let it be so my Faustus, but first stay,
And view their triumphs, as they pass this way;
And then devise what best contents thy mind,   80
By cunning in thine art to cross the Pope,
Or dash the pride of this solemnity;
To make his monks and abbots stand like apes,
And point like antics at his triple crown:
To beat the beads about the friars' pates,   85
Or clap huge horns upon the cardinals' heads:
Or any villainy thou canst devise,
And I'll perform it Faustus: hark, they come:
This day shall make thee be admired in Rome.

Enter the CARDINALS *and* BISHOPS, *some bearing crosiers, some the
pillars;* MONKS *and* FRIARS *singing their procession: Then the*
POPE, *and* RAYMOND King of Hungary, *with* BRUNO *led in chains*

POPE
Cast down our footstool.

RAYMOND   Saxon Bruno stoop,   90
Whilst on thy back his holiness ascends
Saint Peter's chair and state pontifical.

BRUNO
Proud Lucifer, that state belongs to me:
But thus I fall to Peter, not to thee.

POPE
To me and Peter shalt thou grovelling lie,   95
And crouch before the papal dignity:
Sound trumpets then, for thus Saint Peter's heir,
From Bruno's back ascends Saint Peter's chair.
                              A Flourish while he ascends

77 *cunning* B₄ (coming B₁)
79 *triumphs* procession
81 *cunning* B₄ (coming B₁)
84 *antics* clowns
89 s.d. *pillars* Wolsey substituted portable pillars for the silver
    maces usually carried by cardinals
    procession office sung in a religious procession

Thus, as the gods creep on with feet of wool,
Long ere with iron hands they punish men,   100
So shall our sleeping vengeance now arise,
And smite with death thy hated enterprise.
Lord Cardinals of France and Padua,
Go forthwith to our holy consistory,
And read amongst the statutes decretal,   105
What by the holy council held at Trent,
The sacred synod hath decreed for him
That doth assume the papal government,
Without election and a true consent:
Away, and bring us word with speed.   110

1 CARDINAL
We go my Lord.
                                        Exeunt CARDINALS

POPE
Lord Raymond!
            [*The* POPE *and* RAYMOND *converse*]

FAUSTUS
Go, haste thee gentle Mephostophilis,
Follow the cardinals to the consistory;
And as they turn their superstitious books,   115
Strike them with sloth, and drowsy idleness;
And make them sleep so sound, that in their shapes,
Thyself and I may parley with this Pope,
This proud confronter of the Emperor,
And in despite of all his holiness   120
Restore this Bruno to his liberty,
And bear him to the states of Germany.

MEPHOSTOPHILIS
Faustus, I go.

FAUSTUS   Dispatch it soon:
The Pope shall curse that Faustus came to Rome.
                        Exeunt FAUSTUS *and* MEPHOSTOPHILIS

BRUNO
Pope Adrian, let me have some right of law: 125
I was elected by the Emperor.

POPE
We will depose the Emperor for that deed,

99–100 Proverb: 'God comes with leaden (woolen) feet but strikes
    with iron hands' (Tilley, G 270)
104 *consistory* meeting place of the papal senate
106 The Council of Trent met, with interruptions, between 1545 and
    1563
107 *synod* general council

And curse the people that submit to him;
Both he and thou shalt stand excommunicate,
And interdict from Church's privilege,   130
And all society of holy men:
He grows too proud in his authority,
Lifting his lofty head above the clouds,
And like a steeple overpeers the Church.
But we'll pull down his haughty insolence;   135
And as Pope Alexander, our progenitor,
Trod on the neck of German Frederick,
Adding this golden sentence to our praise:
That Peter's heirs should tread on emperors,
And walk upon the dreadful adder's back,   140
Treading the lion, and the dragon down,
And fearless spurn the killing basilisk:
So will we quell that haughty schismatic,
And by authority apostolical
Depose him from his regal government.   145

BRUNO
Pope Julius swore to princely Sigismund,
For him, and the succeeding popes of Rome,
To hold the emperors their lawful lords.

POPE
Pope Julius did abuse the Church's rites,
And therefore none of his decrees can stand.   150
Is not all power on earth bestowed on us?
And therefore though we would we cannot err.
Behold this silver belt, whereto is fixed
Seven golden keys fast sealed with seven seals,
In token of our seven-fold power from heaven,   155
To bind or loose, lock fast, condemn, or judge,
Resign, or seal, or whatso pleaseth us.
Then he, and thou, and all the world shall stoop,
Or be assured of our dreadful curse,
To light as heavy as the pains of hell.   160

Enter FAUSTUS *and* MEPHOSTOPHILIS
like the cardinals

130 *interdict* officially debarred
136 *progenitor* predecessor
136–7 Pope Alexander III (1159–81) compelled the Emperor
      Frederick Barbarossa to accept his supremacy
142 *basilisk* a mythical beast whose glance was fatal
154 *keys* ed. (seals B) symbolic of St. Peter's keys
157 *Resign* Unseal; the word has the force of Latin *resignare*

MEPHOSTOPHILIS
    Now tell me Faustus, are we not fitted well?
FAUSTUS
    Yes Mephostophilis, and two such cardinals
    Ne'er served a holy pope as we shall do.
    But whilst they sleep within the consistory,
    Let us salute his reverend Fatherhood.   165
RAYMOND
    Behold my Lord, the cardinals are returned.
POPE
    Welcome grave fathers, answer presently,
    What have our holy council there decreed
    Concerning Bruno and the Emperor,
    In quittance of their late conspiracy   170
    Against our state, and papal dignity?
FAUSTUS
    Most sacred patron of the Church of Rome,
    By full consent of all the synod
    Of priests and prelates, it is thus decreed:
    That Bruno and the German Emperor   175
    Be held as lollards and bold schismatics,
    And proud disturbers of the Church's peace.
    And if that Bruno by his own assent,
    Without enforcement of the German peers,
    Did seek to wear the triple diadem,   180
    And by your death to climb Saint Peter's chair,
    The statutes decretal have thus decreed,
    He shall be straight condemned of heresy,
    And on a pile of faggots burnt to death.
POPE
    It is enough: here, take him to your charge,   185
    And bear him straight to Ponte Angelo,
    And in the strongest tower enclose him fast.
    Tomorrow, sitting in our consistory,
    With all our college of grave cardinals,
    We will determine of his life or death.   190
    Here, take his triple crown along with you,
    And leave it in the Church's treasury.
    Make haste again, my good lord cardinals,
    And take our blessing apostolical.

176 *lollards* heretics; originally followers of Wyclif
179 *enforcement of* compulsion from
189 *college* official title for the body of cardinals forming the pope's
    council

MEPHOSTOPHILIS
  So, so, was never devil thus blessed before!   195
FAUSTUS
  Away sweet Mephostophilis, be gone,
  The cardinals will be plagued for this anon.
            Exeunt FAUSTUS *and* MEPHOSTOPHILIS [*with* BRUNO]
POPE
  Go presently, and bring a banquet forth,
  That we may solemnize Saint Peter's feast,
  And with Lord Raymond, King of Hungary,   200
  Drink to our late and happy victory.   *Exeunt*

Act III, Scene ii

A Sennet while the Banquet is brought in; and then enter
                FAUSTUS *and* MEPHOSTOPHILIS
                in their own shapes

MEPHOSTOPHILIS
  Now Faustus come, prepare thyself for mirth,
  The sleepy cardinals are hard at hand,
  To censure Bruno, that is posted hence,
  And on a proud-paced steed, as swift as thought,
  Flies o'er the Alps to fruitful Germany,   5
  There to salute the woeful Emperor.
FAUSTUS
  The Pope will curse them for their sloth today,
  That slept both Bruno and his crown away.
  But now, that Faustus may delight his mind,
  And by their folly make some merriment,   10
  Sweet Mephostophilis, so charm me here,
  That I may walk invisible to all,
  And do whate'er I please, unseen of any.
MEPHOSTOPHILIS
  Faustus thou shalt, then kneel down presently:
      Whilst on thy head I lay my hand,   15
      And charm thee with this magic wand:
      First wear this girdle, then appear
      Invisible to all are here:
      The planets seven, the gloomy air,

---

s.d. *Sennet* A flourish on the trumpets, usually heralding a ceremonious
     entrance

Hell, and the Furies' forked hair,   20
Pluto's blue fire, and Hecat's tree,
With magic spells so compass thee,
That no eye may thy body see.
So Faustus, now for all their holiness,
Do what thou wilt, thou shalt not be discerned.   25

FAUSTUS

Thanks Mephostophilis: now friars take heed,
Lest Faustus make your shaven crowns to bleed.

MEPHOSTOPHILIS

Faustus no more: see where the cardinals come.
Sound a sennet. Enter POPE *and all the* LORDS
Enter the CARDINALS *with a book*

POPE

Welcome Lord Cardinals: come sit down.
Lord Raymond, take your seat. Friars attend,   30
And see that all things be in readiness,
As best beseems this solemn festival.

1 CARDINAL

First, may it please your sacred Holiness,
To view the sentence of the reverend synod,
Concerning Bruno and the Emperor?   35

POPE

What needs this question? Did I not tell you,
Tomorrow we would sit i'th'consistory,
And there determine of his punishment?
You brought us word even now, it was decreed,
That Bruno and the cursed Emperor   40
Were by the holy council both condemned
For loathed lollards and base schismatics:
Then wherefore would you have me view that book?

1 CARDINAL

Your Grace mistakes; you gave us no such charge.

POPE

Deny it not, we all are witnesses   45
That Bruno here was late delivered you
With his rich triple crown to be reserved,
And put into the Church's treasury.

20 *forked hair* the forked tongues of the snakes which form the hair of the
   Furies
21 *Pluto's blue fire* the sulphurous smoke of hell
   Hecat's tree perhaps the gallows tree, since Hecate was also Trivia,
   goddess of cross-roads where the gallows was set up. Boas may be
   right in thinking that *tree* ought to be *three*, in allusion to the triple form
   of the deity (Luna in Heaven, Diana on Earth and Hecate or Proserpina
   in Hell).

AMBO CARDINALS

  By holy Paul we saw them not.

POPE

  By Peter, you shall die,   50

  Unless you bring them forth immediately:

  Hale them to prison, lade their limbs with gyves:

  False prelates, for this hateful treachery,

  Cursed be your souls to hellish misery.

                [Exeunt CARDINALS *with some* FRIARS]

FAUSTUS

  So, they are safe: now Faustus, to the feast;   55

  The Pope had never such a frolic guest.

POPE

  Lord Archbishop of Rheims, sit down with us.

ARCHBISHOP

  I thank your Holiness.

FAUSTUS

  Fall to! The devil choke you an you spare.

POPE

  Who's that spoke? Friars, look about!   60

  Lord Raymond, pray fall to; I am beholding

  To the Bishop of Milan, for this so rare a present.

FAUSTUS

  I thank you sir.   *Snatch it*

POPE

  How now? Who snatched the meat from me?

  Villains, why speak you not?   65

  My good Lord Archbishop, here's a most dainty dish,

  Was sent me from a cardinal in France.

FAUSTUS

  I'll have that too.   *[Snatch it]*

POPE

  What lollards do attend our Holiness,

  That we receive such great indignity?   70

  Fetch me some wine.

FAUSTUS

  Ay, pray do, for Faustus is a-dry.

POPE

  Lord Raymond, I drink unto your grace.

FAUSTUS

  I pledge your grace.   *[Snatch cup]*

POPE

  My wine gone too! Ye lubbers, look about   75

49 *Ambo* Both

And find the man that doth this villainy,
Or by our sanctitude you all shall die.
I pray my lords have patience at this troublesome banquet.

ARCHBISHOP
Please it your Holiness, I think it be some ghost crept out of
purgatory, and now is come unto your Holiness for his   80
pardon.

POPE
It may be so:
Go then command our priests to sing a dirge,
To lay the fury of this same troublesome ghost.
Once again my lord, fall to.   85

The POPE *crosseth himself*

FAUSTUS
How now? Must every bit be spiced with a cross?
Nay then, take that.

FAUSTUS *hits him a box of the ear*

POPE
O, I am slain! Help me my lords!
O come and help to bear my body hence:
Damned be this soul for ever for this deed.   90

Exeunt the POPE *and his train*

MEPHOSTOPHILIS
Now Faustus, what will you do now? For I can tell you,
you'll be cursed with bell, book and candle.

FAUSTUS
Bell, book and candle; candle, book and bell,
Forward and backward, to curse Faustus to hell.

Enter the FRIARS *with Bell, Book and Candle for the Dirge*

---

83 *dirge* corruption of *dirige*, the antiphon at Matins in the Office for
the dead, hence any requiem mass; correctly used here but not
at line 102 below

86–7 The A pope is allowed to cross himself three times, with a warning
from Faustus on each occasion:

> *The Pope crosseth himself*
> What, are you crossing of yourself?
> Well, use that trick no more, I would advise you.
> *Cross again*
> Well, there's the second time; aware the third,
> I give you fair warning.
> *Cross again, and* FAUSTUS *hits him a box of the ear*

This sounds to me like a comedian's expansion.

1 FRIAR

Come brethren, let's about our business with good devotion.   95
                                                         Sing this
> *Cursed be he that stole his Holiness' meat from the table.*
>   *Maledicat Dominus.*
> *Cursed be he that struck his Holiness a blow on the face.*
>   *Maledicat Dominus.*
> *Cursed be he that took Friar Sandelo a blow on the pate.*   100
>   *Maledicat Dominus.*
> *Cursed be he that disturbeth our holy dirge.*
>   *Maledicat Dominus.*
> *Cursed be he that took away his Holiness' wine.*
>   *Maledicat Dominus*   105
[FAUSTUS *and* MEPHOSTOPHILIS] *beat the* FRIARS, *fling
    fireworks among them, and Exeunt*

Act III, Scene iii

Enter CLOWN [ROBIN] *and* DICK, *with a Cup*

DICK

Sirra Robin, we were best look that your devil can answer
the stealing of this same cup, for the vintner's boy follows
us at the hard heels.

ROBIN

'Tis no matter, let him come; an he follow us, I'll so conjure
him, as he was never conjured in his life, I warrant him: let   5
me see the cup.

Enter VINTNER

DICK

Here 'tis—yonder he comes! Now Robin, now or never show
thy cunning.

VINTNER

O, are you here? I am glad I have found you. You are a
couple of fine companions! Pray, where's the cup you stole   10
from the tavern?

---

97 *Maledicat Dominus* May the Lord curse him
III,iii. A's version of this scene is printed in the Appendix
  3 *at the hard heels* close on our heels

---

106 A concludes the scene with the formal '*Et omnes sancti, Amen*' (and all
    the saints, Amen). From lines 100 and 102, however, it seems that
    Faustus is making a nuisance of himself; this and the stage direction
    suggests that the scene comes to a sharp and undignified end.

ROBIN

How, how? We steal a cup! Take heed what you say; we look
not like cup-stealers, I can tell you.

VINTNER

Never deny't, for I know you have it, and I'll search you.

ROBIN

Search me? Ay, and spare not—hold the cup Dick—come,   15
come, search me, search me.

[VINTNER *searches* ROBIN]

VINTNER

Come on sirra, let me search you now.

DICK

Ay, ay, do, do—hold the cup Robin—I fear not your searching; we scorn to steal your cups, I can tell you.

[VINTNER *searches* DICK]

VINTNER

Never outface me for the matter, for sure the cup is between   20
you two.

ROBIN

Nay, there you lie, 'tis beyond us both.

VINTNER

A plague take you, I thought 'twas your knavery to take it
away. Come, give it me again.

ROBIN

Ay much! When, can you tell? Dick, make me a circle, and   25
stand close at my back, and stir not for thy life. Vintner,
you shall have your cup anon—say nothing Dick! *O per se,
o; Demogorgon, Belcher and Mephostophilis!*

Enter MEPHOSTOPHILIS

MEPHOSTOPHILIS

You princely legions of infernal rule,
How am I vexed by these villains' charms!   30
From Constantinople have they brought me now,
Only for pleasure of these damned slaves.

[*Exit* VINTNER]

ROBIN

By lady sir, you have had a shrewd journey of it. Will it

---

20 *outface . . . matter* brazen it out with me
22 *beyond us both* out of our hands; the Clowns have succeeded in
   juggling with the cup so that neither holds it
25 *Ay . . . tell* derisive comments
33 *shrewd* tiresome

please you to take a shoulder of mutton to supper, and a
tester in your purse, and go back again?   35

DICK

Ay, I pray you heartily sir, for we called you but in jest, I
promise you.

MEPHOSTOPHILIS

To purge the rashness of this cursed deed,
First, be thou turned to this ugly shape,
For apish deeds transformed to an ape.   40

ROBIN

O brave, an ape! I pray sir, let me have the carrying of him
about to show some tricks.

MEPHOSTOPHILIS

And so thou shalt: be thou transformed to a dog, and carry
him upon thy back. Away, be gone!

ROBIN

A dog? That's excellent: let the maids look well to their   45
porridge-pots, for I'll into the kitchen presently: come
Dick, come.

Exeunt the two CLOWNS

MEPHOSTOPHILIS

Now with the flames of ever-burning fire,
I'll wing myself, and forthwith fly amain
Unto my Faustus, to the great Turk's court.   *Exit*   50

CHORUS 2

Enter CHORUS

CHORUS

When Faustus had with pleasure ta'en the view
Of rarest things and royal courts of kings,
He stayed his course, and so returned home,
Where such as bare his absence but with grief—
I mean his friends and near'st companions—   5
Did gratulate his safety with kind words;
And in their conference of what befell,
Touching his journey through the world and air,
They put forth questions of astrology,
Which Faustus answered with such learned skill,   10
As they admired and wondered at his wit.
Now is his fame spread forth in every land:

---

35 *tester* sixpence; a slang term
Chorus 2 Not to be found in B, this Chorus preceded the Clowns' scene
   with the goblet in A

Amongst the rest, the Emperor is one,
Carolus the fifth, at whose palace now
Faustus is feasted 'mongst his noblemen.   15
What there he did in trial of his art,
I leave untold, your eyes shall see performed.

Act IV, Scene i

Enter MARTINO *and* FREDERICK *at several doors*

MARTINO

What ho, officers, gentlemen,
Hie to the presence to attend the Emperor!
Good Frederick, see the rooms be voided straight,
His Majesty is coming to the hall;
Go back, and see the state in readiness.   5

FREDERICK

But where is Bruno, our elected Pope,
That on a fury's back came post from Rome?
Will not his grace consort the Emperor?

MARTINO

O yes, and with him comes the German conjuror,
The learned Faustus, fame of Wittenberg,   10
The wonder of the world for magic art;
And he intends to show great Carolus,
The race of all his stout progenitors;
And bring in presence of his Majesty,
The royal shapes and warlike semblances   15
Of Alexander and his beauteous paramour.

FREDERICK

Where is Benvolio?

MARTINO

Fast asleep I warrant you.
He took his rouse with stoups of Rhenish wine
So kindly yesternight to Bruno's health,   20
That all this day the sluggard keeps his bed.

FREDERICK

See, see, his window's ope; we'll call to him.

14 *Carolus* Charles V, Emperor 1519–56
 2 *presence* audience chamber
 3 *voided straight* cleared instantly
 5 *state* throne
15 *warlike* heroic
19 *took his rouse* had a heavy drinking session; *cf. Hamlet*, I.iv, 8–10
    stoups measures

MARTINO
  What ho, Benvolio!

  Enter BENVOLIO *above at a window, in his nightcap;*
                              buttoning

BENVOLIO
  What a devil ail you two?

MARTINO
  Speak softly sir, lest the devil hear you: 25
  For Faustus at the court is late arrived,
  And at his heels a thousand furies wait,
  To accomplish whatsoever the doctor please.

BENVOLIO
  What of this?

MARTINO
  Come, leave thy chamber first, and thou shalt see   30
  This conjuror perform such rare exploits,
  Before the Pope and royal Emperor,
  As never yet was seen in Germany.

BENVOLIO
  Has not the Pope enough of conjuring yet?
  He was upon the devil's back late enough;   35
  And if he be so far in love with him
  I would he would post with him to Rome again.

FREDERICK
  Speak, wilt thou come and see this sport?

BENVOLIO
  Not I.

MARTINO
  Wilt thou stand in thy window, and see it then?   40

BENVOLIO
  Ay, and I fall not asleep i'th'meantime.

MARTINO
  The Emperor is at hand, who comes to see
  What wonders by black spells may compassed be.

BENVOLIO
  Well, go you attend the Emperor; I am content for this
  once to thrust my head out at a window: for they say, if a   45
  man be drunk overnight, the devil cannot hurt/him in the
  morning: if that be true, I have a charm in my head, shall
  control him as well as the conjuror, I warrant you.
                          [*Exeunt* FREDERICK *and* MARTINO]

  ────────────────────

  23 s. d. *buttoning* buttoning up his clothes; the intransitive use of
     the verb is rare

Act IV, Scene ii

A Sennet. CHARLES *the* GERMAN EMPEROR, BRUNO,
SAXONY, FAUSTUS, MEPHOSTOPHILIS, FREDERICK, MARTINO,
and ATTENDANTS
[BENVOLIO *remains in the window*]

EMPEROR
    Wonder of men, renowned magician,
    Thrice-learned Faustus, welcome to our court.
    This deed of thine, in setting Bruno free
    From his and our professed enemy,
    Shall add more excellence unto thine art,   5
    Than if by powerful necromantic spells,
    Thou could'st command the world's obedience:
    For ever be beloved of Carolus.
    And if this Bruno thou hast late redeemed,
    In peace possess the triple diadem,   10
    And sit in Peter's chair, despite of chance,
    Thou shalt be famous through all Italy,
    And honoured of the German Emperor.
FAUSTUS
    These gracious words, most royal Carolus,
    Shall make poor Faustus to his utmost power,   15
    Both love and serve the German Emperor,
    And lay his life at holy Bruno's feet.
    For proof whereof, if so your grace be pleased,
    The doctor stands prepared, by power of art,
    To cast his magic charms, that shall pierce through   20
    The ebon gates of ever-burning hell,
    And hale the stubborn furies from their caves,
    To compass whatsoe'er your grace commands.
BENVOLIO
    'Blood, he speaks terribly; but for all that, I do not greatly
    believe him; he looks as like a conjuror as the Pope to a   25
    costermonger.
EMPEROR
    Then Faustus, as thou late didst promise us,
    We would behold that famous conqueror,
    Great Alexander, and his paramour,
    In their true shapes, and state majestical,   30
    That we may wonder at their excellence.

IV.ii. A's version of this scene is printed in the Appendix
  29 *paramour* Alexander's wife, Roxana

FAUSTUS
  Your Majesty shall see them presently.
  Mephostophilis, away!
  And with a solemn noise of trumpets' sound,
  Present before this royal Emperor,   35
  Great Alexander and his beauteous paramour.
MEPHOSTOPHILIS
  Faustus I will.

                                                              Exit

BENVOLIO
  Well master doctor, an your devils come not away quickly,
  you shall have me asleep presently: zounds, I could eat
  myself for anger, to think I have been such an ass all this   40
  while, to stand gaping after the devil's governor, and can
  see nothing.
FAUSTUS
  I'll make you feel something anon, if my art fail me not.
  My lord, I must forewarn your Majesty,
  That when my spirits present the royal shapes   45
  Of Alexander and his paramour,
  Your grace demand no questions of the king,
  But in dumb silence let them come and go.
EMPEROR
  Be it as Faustus please, we are content.
BENVOLIO
  Ay, ay, and I am content too: and thou bring Alexander and   50
  his paramour before the Emperor, I'll be Actaeon, and turn
  my self to a stag.
FAUSTUS
  And I'll play Diana, and send you the horns presently.
Sennet. Enter at one door the EMPEROR ALEXANDER, *at the other*
DARIUS: *they meet,* DARIUS *is thrown down,* ALEXANDER *kills him;*
takes off his crown, and offering to go out, his PARAMOUR *meets*
him, he embraceth her, and sets DARIUS' *crown upon her head; and*
coming back, both salute the EMPEROR, *who leaving his state,*
offers to embrace them, which FAUSTUS *seeing, suddenly stays him.*
          Then trumpets cease, and music sounds
  My gracious lord, you do forget yourself;
  These are but shadows, not substantial.   55

44–8 The A Text (see Appendix) makes it plain that the Emperor is to be
     shown spirits in the forms of Alexander and his paramour — hence the
     need for silence.
51 *Actaeon* As punishment for coming upon Diana and her nymphs
     bathing, Actaeon was turned into a stag, and his own hounds tore
     him to pieces.

EMPEROR

O pardon me, my thoughts are so ravished
With sight of this renowned emperor,
That in mine arms I would have compassed him.
But Faustus, since I may not speak to them,
To satisfy my longing thoughts at full,   60
Let me this tell thee: I have heard it said,
That this fair lady, whilst she lived on earth,
Had on her neck a little wart or mole;
How may I prove that saying to be true?

FAUSTUS

Your Majesty may boldly go and see.   65

EMPEROR

Faustus I see it plain,
And in this sight thou better pleasest me,
Than if I gained another monarchy.

FAUSTUS

Away, be gone.   *Exit* SHOW
See, see, my gracious lord, what strange beast is yon, that   70
thrusts his head out at window?

EMPEROR

O wondrous sight! See, Duke of Saxony,
Two spreading horns most strangely fastened
Upon the head of young Benvolio.

SAXONY

What, is he asleep, or dead?   75

FAUSTUS

He sleeps my lord, but dreams not of his horns.

EMPEROR

This sport is excellent: we'll call and wake him.
What ho, Benvolio!

BENVOLIO

A plague upon you, let me sleep awhile.

EMPEROR

I blame thee not to sleep much, having such a head of thine   80
own.

SAXONY

Look up Benvolio, 'tis the Emperor calls.

BENVOLIO

The Emperor? Where? O zounds my head!

EMPEROR

Nay, and thy horns hold, 'tis no matter for thy head, for
that's armed sufficiently.   85

FAUSTUS

Why, how now sir knight? What, hanged by the horns? This

is most horrible! Fie, fie, pull in your head for shame, let
not all the world wonder at you.

BENVOLIO

Zounds doctor, is this your villainy?

FAUSTUS

O say not so sir: the doctor has no skill,   90
No art, no cunning, to present these lords,
Or bring before this royal Emperor
The mighty monarch, warlike Alexander.
If Faustus do it, you are straight resolved
In bold Actaeon's shape to turn a stag.   95
And therefore my lord, so please your Majesty,
I'll raise a kennel of hounds shall hunt him so,
As all his footmanship shall scarce prevail
To keep his carcase from their bloody fangs.
Ho, Belimote, Argiron, Asterote!   100

BENVOLIO

Hold, hold! Zounds, he'll raise up a kennel of devils, I
think, anon: good my lord, entreat for me: 'sblood, I am
never able to endure these torments.

EMPEROR

Then good master doctor,
Let me entreat you to remove his horns,   105
He has done penance now sufficiently.

FAUSTUS

My gracious lord, not so much for injury done to me, as
to delight your Majesty with some mirth, hath Faustus
justly requited this injurious knight; which being all I
desire, I am content to remove his horns. Mephostophilis,   110
transform him—and hereafter sir, look you speak well of
scholars.

BENVOLIO

Speak well of ye! 'Sblood, and scholars be such cuckold-
makers to clap horns of honest men's heads o' this order,
I'll ne'er trust smooth faces and small ruffs more. But an I be 115
not revenged for this, would I might be turned to a gaping
oyster, and drink nothing but salt water.

EMPEROR

Come Faustus, while the Emperor lives,
In recompense of this thy high desert,
Thou shalt command the state of Germany,   120
And live beloved of mighty Carolus.

Exeunt omnes

98 *footmanship* skill in running
115 *smooth . . . ruffs* beardless scholars in academic dress

Act IV, Scene iii

Enter BENVOLIO, MARTINO, FREDERICK, *and* SOLDIERS

MARTINO
    Nay sweet Benvolio, let us sway thy thoughts
    From this attempt against the conjuror.
BENVOLIO
    Away, you love me not, to urge me thus.
    Shall I let slip so great an injury,
    When every servile groom jests at my wrongs,   5
    And in their rustic gambols proudly say,
    'Benvolio's head was graced with horns today'?
    O may these eyelids never close again,
    Till with my sword I have that conjuror slain.
    If you will aid me in this enterprise,   10
    Then draw your weapons, and be resolute:
    If not, depart: here will Benvolio die,
    But Faustus' death shall quit my infamy.
FREDERICK
    Nay, we will stay with thee, betide what may,
    And kill that doctor if he come this way.   15
BENVOLIO
    Then gentle Frederick, hie thee to the grove,
    And place our servants and our followers
    Close in an ambush there behind the trees.
    By this (I know) the conjuror is near,
    I saw him kneel and kiss the Emperor's hand,   20
    And take his leave, laden with rich rewards.
    Then soldiers boldly fight; if Faustus die,
    Take you the wealth, leave us the victory.
FREDERICK
    Come soldiers, follow me unto the grove;
    Who kills him shall have gold and endless love.   25
                    Exit FREDERICK *with the* SOLDIERS
BENVOLIO
    My head is lighter than it was by th'horns,

6 *proudly* insolently
13 *But* Unless
18 *Close* Hidden
19 *By this* By this time

But yet my heart's more ponderous than my head,
And pants until I see that conjuror dead.

MARTINO
Where shall we place ourselves Benvolio?

BENVOLIO
Here will we stay to bide the first assault.　　　　　　　30
O were that damned hell-hound but in place,
Thou soon should'st see me quit my foul disgrace.

Enter FREDERICK

FREDERICK
Close, close, the conjuror is at hand,
And all alone, comes walking in his gown.
Be ready then, and strike the peasant down.　　　　　　35

BENVOLIO
Mine be that honour then: now sword strike home,
For horns he gave, I'll have his head anon.

Enter FAUSTUS *with the false head*

MARTINO
See, see, he comes.

BENVOLIO　　　　　　　No words; this blow ends all,
Hell take his soul, his body thus must fall.

　　　　　　　　　　　　　　　　　[Strikes FAUSTUS*]*

FAUSTUS
O!　　　　　　　　　　　　　　　　　　　　　　　　40

FREDERICK
Groan you master doctor?

BENVOLIO
Break may his heart with groans: dear Frederick see,
Thus will I end his griefs immediately.

　　　　　　　　　　　　　　　　　[Cuts off his head]

MARTINO
Strike with a willing hand; his head is off.

BENVOLIO
The devil's dead, the furies now may laugh.　　　　　　45

FREDERICK
Was this that stern aspect, that awful frown,
Made the grim monarch of infernal spirits,
Tremble and quake at his commanding charms?

MARTINO
Was this that damned head, whose heart conspired
Benvolio's shame before the Emperor?　　　　　　　　50

31 *in place* on the spot

BENVOLIO
    Ay, that's the head, and here the body lies,
    Justly rewarded for his villainies.
FREDERICK
    Come, let's devise how we may add more shame
    To the black scandal of his hated name.
BENVOLIO
    First, on his head, in quittance of my wrongs,   55
    I'll nail huge forked horns, and let them hang
    Within the window where he yoked me first,
    That all the world may see my just revenge.
MARTINO
    What use shall we put his beard to?
BENVOLIO
    We'll sell it to a chimney-sweeper; it will wear out   60
    ten birchen brooms, I warrant you.
FREDERICK
    What shall eyes do?
BENVOLIO
    We'll put out his eyes, and they shall serve for buttons to
    his lips, to keep his tongue from catching cold.
MARTINO
    An excellent policy: and now sirs, having divided him,   65
    what shall the body do?   [FAUSTUS stands up]
BENVOLIO
    Zounds, the devil's alive again!
FREDERICK
    Give him his head for God's sake.
FAUSTUS
    Nay keep it: Faustus will have heads and hands,
    Ay, all your hearts to recompense this deed.   70
    Knew you not, traitors, I was limited
    For four and twenty years to breathe on earth?
    And had you cut my body with your swords,
    Or hewed this flesh and bones as small as sand,
    Yet in a minute had my spirit returned,   75
    And I had breathed a man made free from harm.
    But wherefore do I dally my revenge?
    Asteroth, Belimoth, Mephostophilis!

            Enter MEPHOSTOPHILIS *and other* DEVILS

    Go, horse these traitors on your fiery backs,
    And mount aloft with them as high as heaven,   80

70 *Ay, all* ed. (I call B)

Thence pitch them headlong to the lowest hell:
Yet stay, the world shall see their misery,
And hell shall after plague their treachery.
Go Belimoth, and take this caitiff hence,
And hurl him in some lake of mud and dirt: 85
Take thou this other, drag him through the woods,
Amongst the pricking thorns and sharpest briers,
Whilst with my gentle Mephostophilis,
This traitor flies unto some steepy rock,
That, rolling down, may break the villain's bones,   90
As he intended to dismember me.
Fly hence, dispatch my charge immediately.

FREDERICK
Pity us gentle Faustus, save our lives.

FAUSTUS
Away!

FREDERICK
He must needs go that the devil drives.   95

      Exeunt SPIRITS *with the* KNIGHTS

Enter the ambushed SOLDIERS

1 SOLDIER
Come sirs, prepare yourselves in readiness,
Make haste to help these noble gentlemen;
I heard them parley with the conjuror.

2 SOLDIER
See where he comes, dispatch, and kill the slave.

FAUSTUS
What's here? An ambush to betray my life!   100
Then Faustus try thy skill: base peasants stand!
For lo, these trees remove at my command,
And stand as bulwarks 'twixt yourselves and me,
To shield me from your hated treachery:
Yet to encounter this your weak attempt,   105
Behold an army comes incontinent.

FAUSTUS *strikes the door, and enter a* DEVIL *playing on a drum,*
after him another bearing an ensign: and divers with weapons,
MEPHOSTOPHILIS *with fireworks; they set upon the* SOLDIERS
and drive them out

          [*Exit* FAUSTUS]

95 A well known proverb (Tilley, D 278)
106 *incontinent* without delay

Act IV, Scene iv

Enter at several doors, BENVOLIO, FREDERICK, *and* MARTINO,
their heads and faces bloody, and besmeared with mud and dirt;
all having horns on their heads

MARTINO
　What ho, Benvolio!
BENVOLIO
　Here, what Frederick, ho!
FREDERICK
　O help me gentle friend; where is Martino?
MARTINO
　Dear Frederick here,
　Half smothered in a lake of mud and dirt,　　　　　　　5
　Through which the furies dragged me by the heels.
FREDERICK
　Martino see, Benvolio's horns again!
MARTINO
　O misery! How now, Benvolio?
BENVOLIO
　Defend me heaven! Shall I be haunted still?
MARTINO
　Nay, fear not man, we have no power to kill.　　　　　10
BENVOLIO
　My friends transformed thus! O hellish spite,
　Your heads are all set with horns.
FREDERICK　　　　　　　　　　　　You hit it right,
　It is your own you mean; feel on your head.
BENVOLIO
　Zounds, horns again!
MARTINO　　　　　　　　Nay, chafe not man, we all are sped.
BENVOLIO
　What devil attends this damned magician,　　　　　　15
　That spite of spite, our wrongs are doubled?
FREDERICK
　What may we do, that we may hide our shame?
BENVOLIO
　If we should follow him to work revenge,
　He'd join long asses' ears to these huge horns,
　And make us laughing-stocks to all the world.　　　　20
MARTINO
　What shall we do then dear Benvolio?

10 *kill* This suggests a pun on *haunted/hunted* in the preceding line

BENVOLIO
    I have a castle joining near these woods,
    And thither we'll repair and live obscure,
    Till time shall alter these our brutish shapes:
    Sith black disgrace hath thus eclipsed our fame,   25
    We'll rather die with grief, than live with shame.

                         Exeunt omnes

Act IV, Scene v

Enter FAUSTUS *and the* HORSE-COURSER

HORSE-COURSER
    I beseech your worship accept of these forty dollars.
FAUSTUS
    Friend, thou canst not buy so good a horse for so small a
    price: I have no great need to sell him, but if thou likest
    him for ten dollars more, take him, because I can see thou
    hast a good mind to him.   5
HORSE-COURSER
    I beseech you sir, accept of this; I am a very poor man, and
    have lost very much of late by horse-flesh, and this bargain
    will set me up again.
FAUSTUS
    Well, I will not stand with thee; give me the money. Now,
    sirra, I must tell you, that you may ride him o'er hedge and   10
    ditch, and spare him not; but: do you hear, in any case ride
    him not into the water.
HORSE-COURSER
    How sir, not into the water? Why, will he not drink of all
    waters?
FAUSTUS
    Yes, he will drink of all waters, but ride him not into the   15

---

  24 *Till time shall alter EFB* explains that the knights were condemned
     to wear the horns for a month
  26 'It is better to die with honour than live with shame' (Tilley,
     H 576)
IV.v. A's version of this scene is printed in the Appendix
s.d. *Horse-courser* Horse-dealer; a reputation for dishonesty has always
     attached to such traders
   9 *stand with thee* haggle over it
  11 *in any case* whatever happens
  12 *not into the water* Running water (but not the stagnant water of a
     ditch) dissolves a witch's spell
 13–14 *drink of all waters* go anywhere; 'I am for all waters', *Twelfth*
     Night, IV.ii, 57

water; o'er hedge and ditch, or where thou wilt, but not
into the water. Go bid the ostler deliver him unto you, and
remember what I say.

HORSE-COURSER

I warrant you sir; O joyful day! Now am I a made man for
ever.   *Exit*   20

FAUSTUS

What art thou, Faustus, but a man condemned to die?
Thy fatal time draws to a final end;
Despair doth drive distrust into my thoughts.
Confound these passions with a quiet sleep:
Tush, Christ did call the thief upon the cross;   25
Then rest thee, Faustus, quiet in conceit.

                                          He sits to sleep

                Enter the HORSE-COURSER, *wet*

HORSE-COURSER

O what a cozening doctor was this! I riding my horse into
the water, thinking some hidden mystery had been in the
horse, I had nothing under me but a little straw, and had
much ado to escape drowning. Well, I'll go rouse him, and   30
make him give me my forty dollars again. Ho, sirra doctor,
you cozening scab! Maister doctor awake, and rise, and give
me my money again, for your horse is turned to a bottle of
hay. Maister doctor—

                                        He pulls off his leg

Alas, I am undone, what shall I do? I have pulled off his leg!   35

FAUSTUS

O help, help, the villain hath murdered me!

HORSE-COURSER

Murder or not murder, now he has but one leg, I'll out-run
him, and cast this leg into some ditch or other.   [*Exit*]

FAUSTUS

Stop him, stop him, stop him!—ha, ha, ha, Faustus hath
his leg again, and the horse-courser a bundle of hay for his   40
forty dollars.

                    Enter WAGNER

How now Wagner, what news with thee?

26 *in conceit* in this thought
27 *cozening* cheating
32 *Maister* Here, and in the succeeding comic scenes, the author
    attempts to indicate dialectal pronunciation
33 *bottle* truss

WAGNER
If it please you, the Duke of Vanholt doth earnestly entreat your company, and hath sent some of his men to
attend you with provision fit for your journey.   45

FAUSTUS
The Duke of Vanholt's an honourable gentleman, and one
to whom I must be no niggard of my cunning. Come away.
Exeunt

Act IV, Scene vi

Enter CLOWN [ROBIN], DICK,
HORSE-COURSER, *and a* CARTER

CARTER
Come my masters, I'll bring you to the best beer in Europe.
What ho hostess! Where be these whores?

Enter HOSTESS

HOSTESS
How now, what lack you? What, my old guests, welcome.

ROBIN
Sirra Dick, dost thou know why I stand so mute?

DICK
No Robin, why is't?   5

ROBIN
I am eighteenpence on the score; but say nothing, see if she
have forgotten me.

HOSTESS
Who's this, that stands so solemnly by himself? What, my
old guest!

ROBIN
O hostess, how do you? I hope my score stands still.   10

HOSTESS
Ay, there's no doubt of that, for methinks you make no
haste to wipe it out.

DICK
Why hostess, I say, fetch us some beer.

HOSTESS
You shall presently. Look up into th'hall there, ho!   *Exit*

---

2 *whores* 'A cup of ale without a wench, why alas, 'tis like an egg
without salt, or a red herring without mustard', *Looking Glass for London*, II,278–80
14 *Look . . . ho* The Hostess calls to her servants

DICK

Come sirs, what shall we do now till mine hostess comes?   15

CARTER

Marry sir, I'll tell you the bravest tale how a conjuror served me; you know Doctor Fauster?

HORSE-COURSER

Ay, a plague take him. Here's some on's have cause to know him. Did he conjure thee too?

CARTER

I'll tell you how he served me. As I was going to Wittenberg   20
t'other day, with a load of hay, he met me, and asked me what he should give me for as much hay as he could eat. Now, sir, I, thinking that a little would serve his turn, bade him take as much as he would for three farthings. So he presently gave me my money, and fell to eating, and as I am   25
a cursen man, he never left eating, till he had eat up all my load of hay.

ALL

O monstrous, eat a whole load of hay!

ROBIN

Yes, yes, that may be; for I have heard of one, that h'as eat a load of logs.   30

HORSE-COURSER

Now sirs, you shall hear how villainously he served me: I went to him yesterday to buy a horse of him, and he would by no means sell him under forty dollars; so sir, because I knew him to be such a horse, as would run over hedge and ditch, and never tire, I gave him his money. So when I had   35
my horse, Doctor Fauster bade me ride him night and day, and spare him no time; 'But', quoth he, 'in any case ride him not into the water'. Now sir, I, thinking the horse had had some quality that he would not have me know of, what did I but rid him into a great river, and when I came just in   40
the midst, my horse vanished away, and I sat straddling upon a bottle of hay.

ALL

O brave doctor!

HORSE-COURSER

But you shall hear how bravely I served him for it. I went me home to his house, and there I found him asleep; I kept   45
a-hallowing and whooping in his ears, but all could not wake him. I, seeing that, took him by the leg, and never

26 *cursen* Christian; the dialectal form of christened
29 *h'as* he has

rested pulling, till I had pulled me his leg quite off, and
now 'tis at home in mine hostry.

ROBIN

And has the doctor but one leg then? That's excellent, for   50
one of his devils turned me into the likeness of an ape's face.

CARTER

Some more drink hostess!

ROBIN

Hark you, we'll into another room and drink awhile, and
then we'll go seek out the doctor.

Exeunt omnes

Act IV, Scene vii

Enter the DUKE OF VANHOLT, *his* DUCHESS,
FAUSTUS, *and* MEPHOSTOPHILIS

DUKE

Thanks master doctor, for these pleasant sights. Nor know
I how sufficiently to recompense your great deserts in erect-
ing that enchanted castle in the air; the sight whereof so
delighted me, as nothing in the world could please me more.

FAUSTUS

I do think myself, my good lord, highly recompensed in   5
that it pleaseth your grace to think but well of that which
Faustus hath performed. But gracious lady, it may be that
you have taken no pleasure in those sights; therefore I pray
you tell me, what is the thing you most desire to have: be
it in the world, it shall be yours. I have heard that great-   10
bellied women do long for things are rare and dainty.

LADY

True, master doctor, and since I find you so kind, I will
make known unto you what my heart desires to have; and
were it now summer, as it is January, a dead time of the
winter, I would request no better meat, than a dish of ripe   15
grapes.

FAUSTUS

This is but a small matter: go Mephostophilis, away.

Exit MEPHOSTOPHILIS

Madam, I will do more than this for your content.

Enter MEPHOSTOPHILIS *again with the grapes*

IV.vii. A's version of this scene does not include the intrusion of the
    Clowns (32 ff)

Here, now taste ye these; they should be good for they
come from a far country, I can tell you.   20

DUKE

This makes me wonder more than all the rest, that at this
time of the year, when every tree is barren of his fruits,
from whence you had these ripe grapes.

FAUSTUS

Please it your grace, the year is divided into two circles over
the whole world, so that when it is winter with us, in the   25
contrary circle it is likewise summer with them, as in
India, Saba, and such countries that lie far east, where they
have fruit twice a year. From whence, by means of a swift
spirit that I have, I had these grapes brought as you see.

LADY

And trust me, they are the sweetest grapes that e'er I   30
tasted.

                    The CLOWNS *bounce at the gate, within*

DUKE

What rude disturbers have we at the gate?
Go pacify their fury, set it ope,
And then demand of them, what they would have.
                    They knock again, and call out to talk with FAUSTUS

A SERVANT

Why, how now masters? What a coil is there! What is   35
the reason you disturb the Duke?

DICK

We have no reason for it, therefore a fig for him.

SERVANT

Why saucy varlets, dare you be so bold?

HORSE-COURSER

I hope sir, we have wit enough to be more bold than
welcome.   40

SERVANT

It appears so; pray be bold elsewhere, and trouble not the
Duke.

DUKE

What would they have?

24–8 The relevant circles would be the northern and southern hemi-
    spheres, but the author appears to be thinking in terms of east
    and west; *EFB* evades the matter while providing the detail of
    the twice-yearly fruit
27 *Saba* Sheba
31 s.d. *bounce* beat
35 *coil* din
37 *reason . . . fig* Dick makes the not uncommon pun on reason/raisin

SERVANT
    They all cry out to speak with Doctor Faustus.

CARTER
    Ay, and we will speak with him.   45

DUKE
    Will you sir? Commit the rascals.

DICK
    Commit with us! He were as good commit with his father,
    as commit with us.

FAUSTUS
    I do beseech your grace let them come in,
    They are good subject for a merriment.   50

DUKE
    Do as thou wilt Faustus, I give thee leave.

FAUSTUS
    I thank your grace.

Enter the CLOWN [ROBIN], DICK, CARTER, *and* HORSE-COURSER

              Why, how now my good friends?
    'Faith, you are too outrageous, but come near,
    I have procured your pardons: welcome all.

ROBIN
    Nay sir, we will be welcome for our money, and we will   55
    pay for what we take: what ho! Give's half a dozen of beer
    here, and be hanged.

FAUSTUS
    Nay, hark you, can you tell me where you are?

CARTER
    Ay, marry can I, we are under heaven.

SERVANT
    Ay, but sir sauce-box, know you in what place?   60

HORSE-COURSER
    Ay, ay, the house is good enough to drink in. Zounds, fill
    us some beer, or we'll break all the barrels in the house, and
    dash out all your brains with your bottles.

FAUSTUS
    Be not so furious: come, you shall have beer.

---

46 *Commit* Take to prison; through frequent collocations such as 'commit
    adultery' the word came to have the sense of 'fornicate', which Dick
    assumes in the next line.
55ff The Clowns believe that, as they promised at the end of IV.vi, they
    have simply stepped into 'another room', whereas it would appear that
    Faustus, by his magic spells, has brought them unawares to the court
    of Vanholt.

My lord, beseech you give me leave awhile,   65
I'll gage my credit, 'twill content your grace.

DUKE

With all my heart, kind doctor, please thyself:
Our servants, and our court's at thy command.

FAUSTUS

I humbly thank your grace: then fetch some beer.

HORSE-COURSER

Ay, marry, there spake a doctor indeed, and 'faith I'll drink   70
a health to thy wooden leg for that word.

FAUSTUS

My wooden leg? What dost thou mean by that?

CARTER

Ha, ha, ha, dost thou hear him Dick? He has forgot his leg.

HORSE-COURSER

Ay, ay, he does not stand much upon that.

FAUSTUS

No 'faith, not much upon a wooden leg.   75

CARTER

Good Lord, that flesh and blood should be so frail with
your worship! Do not you remember a horse-courser you
sold a horse to?

FAUSTUS

Yes, I remember one I sold a horse.

CARTER

And do you remember you bid he should not ride into the   80
water?

FAUSTUS

Yes, I do very well remember that.

CARTER

And do you remember nothing of your leg?

FAUSTUS

No, in good sooth.

CARTER

Then I pray remember your curtsy.   85

FAUSTUS

I thank you sir.   *[He bows to the company]*

---

66 *gage* stake

---

73 ff The writer plays on the literal and metaphorical (=bow) uses of *leg*.
In line 74 the Horse-courser says, in effect, that Faustus does not
stand much upon ceremony.

85 *curtsy* (curtesie B) One of B's meanings is lost in modernizing the word
either as 'courtesy' or as 'curtsy'; the latter seems preferable since
it sustains the joke.

CARTER

'Tis not so much worth; I pray you tell me one thing.

FAUSTUS

What's that?

CARTER

Be both your legs bedfellows every night together?

FAUSTUS

Would'st thou make a colossus of me, that thou askest me   90
such questions?

CARTER

No truly sir, I would make nothing of you, but I would fain
know that.

Enter HOSTESS *with drink*

FAUSTUS

Then I assure thee certainly they are.

CARTER

I thank you, I am fully satisfied.   95

FAUSTUS

But wherefore dost thou ask?

CARTER

For nothing sir—but methinks you should have a wooden
bedfellow of one of 'em.

HORSE-COURSER

Why, do you hear sir, did not I pull off one of your legs
when you were asleep?   100

FAUSTUS

But I have it again now I am awake: look you here sir.

ALL

O horrible! Had the doctor three legs?

CARTER

Do you remember sir, how you cozened me and eat up my
load of—

FAUSTUS *charms him dumb*

DICK

Do you remember how you made me wear an ape's—   105

HORSE-COURSER

You whoreson conjuring scab, do you remember how you
cozened me with a ho—

---

87 *'Tis not so much worth* Faustus' bow is not worth much as an
   indication of whether or not he has a wooden leg
90 *colossus* gigantic statue; the Colossus at Rhodes straddled the
   entrance to the harbour; *cf. Julius Caesar*, I.ii, 135–6

ROBIN

Ha' you forgotten me? You think to carry it away with your
hey-pass and re-pass: do you remember the dog's fa—

Exeunt CLOWNS

HOSTESS

Who pays for the ale? Hear you maister doctor, now you   110
have sent away my guests, I pray who shall pay me for my
a—

Exit HOSTESS

LADY

My lord,
We are much beholding to this learned man.

DUKE

So are we, madam, which we will recompense   115
With all the love and kindness that we may;
His artful sport drives all sad thoughts away.

Exeunt

Act V, Scene i

Thunder and lightning: Enter DEVILS *with covered dishes:*
MEPHOSTOPHILIS *leads them into* FAUSTUS' *study. Then
enter* WAGNER

WAGNER

I think my master means to die shortly,
For he hath given to me all his goods;
And yet, methinks, if that death were near,
He would not banquet, and carouse, and swill
Amongst the students, as even now he doth,   5
Who are at supper with such belly-cheer,
As Wagner ne'er beheld in all his life.
See where they come: belike the feast is ended.   *Exit*

---

109 *hey-pass and re-pass* abracadabra

1–8 At this point B gives Wagner a prose speech containing the gist of
A's verse but adding:

> he hath made his will, and given me his wealth, his house, his
> goods, and store of golden plate; besides two thousand duckets
> ready coined.

Most editors conflate the two, but it seems to me that a choice must
be made; A's version, I think, is preferable, if only because by omitting
mention of the will it avoids repetition at V.ii, 18*ff*.

Enter FAUSTUS, MEPHOSTOPHILIS, *and two or three* SCHOLARS

1 SCHOLAR
Master Doctor Faustus, since our conference about fair
ladies, which was the beautifullest in all the world, we have   10
determined with ourselves, that Helen of Greece was the
admirablest lady that ever lived: therefore, master doctor,
if you will do us so much favour, as to let us see that peerless
dame of Greece, we should think ourselves much beholding
unto you.   15
FAUSTUS
Gentlemen,
For that I know your friendship is unfeigned,
And Faustus' custom is not to deny
The just requests of those that wish him well:
You shall behold that peerless dame of Greece,   20
No otherways for pomp and majesty,
Than when Sir Paris crossed the seas with her,
And brought the spoils to rich Dardania:
Be silent then, for danger is in words.
          Music sound: MEPHOSTOPHILIS *brings in* HELEN; *she*
                    passeth over the stage
2 SCHOLAR
Too simple is my wit to tell her praise,   25
Whom all the world admires for majesty.
3 SCHOLAR
No marvel though the angry Greeks pursued
With ten years' war the rape of such a queen,
Whose heavenly beauty passeth all compare.

___

23 *Dardania* Troy; in fact the city built by Dardanus on the Helles-
   pont, but the name is often transferred to Troy

___

13–14 *peerless dame of Greece* Here both texts anticipate Faustus at 1.20, and
      then both add 'whom all the world admires for majesty', thereby
      anticipating the Second Scholar's remark at 1.26. Greg, who detects
      revision in prompt-book at this point, suggests that the speech was
      written as part of this revision and copied by B from A. The revision
      must have been very careless. To my mind it seems more likely that
      the confusion is due to the A reporter.
24 s.d. *passeth over* It would appear that the character was instructed to
      move from one side of the yard, across the stage, and out at the other
      side of the yard, instead of entering by the stage doors (*cf.* Allardyce
      Nicoll, 'Passing Over the Stage', *Shakespeare Survey*, XII (1959),
      pp. 47–55).

1 SCHOLAR

Since we have seen the pride of Nature's works,   30
And only paragon of excellence,
Let us depart, and for this glorious deed
Happy and blest be Faustus evermore.

FAUSTUS

Gentlemen farewell; the same I wish to you.

                      Exeunt SCHOLARS

Enter an OLD MAN

OLD MAN

O gentle Faustus, leave this damned art,   35
This magic, that will charm thy soul to hell,
And quite bereave thee of salvation.
Though thou hast now offended like a man,
Do not persever in it like a devil;
Yet, yet, thou hast an amiable soul,   40
If sin by custom grow not into nature:
Then, Faustus, will repentance come too late,
Then thou art banished from the sight of heaven;
No mortal can express the pains of hell.
It may be this my exhortation   45
Seems harsh, and all unpleasant; let it not,
For, gentle son, I speak it not in wrath,
Or envy of thee, but in tender love,

35–51 A's version of the Old Man's speech is printed in the Appendix
39 *persever* Accented on the second syllable
40–41 Your soul is still capable of being loved, so long as sin does not become habitual and thus part of your nature

---

25–33 In the B Text the Scholars' comments are as follows:
       2 SCHOLAR
       Was this fair Helen, whose admired worth
       Made Greece with ten years' war afflict poor Troy?
       3 SCHOLAR
       Too simple is my wit to tell her worth,
       Whom all the world admires for majesty.
       1 SCHOLAR
       Now we have seen the pride of Nature's work
       We'll take our leaves, and for this blessed sight,
       Happy and blest be Faustus evermore.

Greg attributes the superiority of A's version to Marlowe's having revised the lines. I doubt this; the multiple repetitions and other weaknesses sound more like very bad reporting–although I confess I cannot see how this fits in with any theory about the nature of the B text.

And pity of thy future misery;
And so have hope, that this my kind rebuke,   50
Checking thy body, may amend thy soul.

FAUSTUS
Where art thou Faustus, wretch, what hast thou done?
Damned art thou Faustus, damned; despair and die!
                            MEPHOSTOPHILIS *gives him a dagger*
Hell claims his right, and with a roaring voice
Says 'Faustus come, thine hour is almost come',   55
And Faustus now will come to do thee right.
                            [FAUSTUS *goes to use the dagger*]

OLD MAN
O stay, good Faustus, stay thy desperate steps!
I see an angel hover o'er thy head,
And with a vial full of precious grace,
Offers to pour the same into thy soul;   60
Then call for mercy, and avoid despair.

FAUSTUS
O friend, I feel
Thy words to comfort my distressed soul:
Leave me awhile, to ponder on my sins.

OLD MAN
Faustus I leave thee, but with grief of heart,   65
Fearing the enemy of thy hapless soul.   *Exit*

FAUSTUS
Accursed Faustus, where is mercy now?
I do repent, and yet I do despair;
Hell strives with grace for conquest in my breast:
What shall I do to shun the snares of death?   70

MEPHOSTOPHILIS
Thou traitor Faustus, I arrest thy soul
For disobedience to my sovereign lord.
Revolt, or I'll in piecemeal tear thy flesh.

FAUSTUS
I do repent I e'er offended him;
Sweet Mephostophilis, entreat thy lord   75
To pardon my unjust presumption,
And with my blood again I will confirm
The former vow I made to Lucifer.

53 A (*not in* B)
66 *enemy* B (ruin A);
    hapless B (hopeless A)
67 *where is mercy now* A (wretch, what hast thou done B)
73 *Revolt* Turn again to your allegiance
74 B (*not in* A)

MEPHOSTOPHILIS

Do it then quickly with unfeigned heart,
Lest greater dangers do attend thy drift.   80

FAUSTUS

Torment, sweet friend, that base and crooked age,
That durst dissuade me from thy Lucifer,
With greatest torment that our hell affords.

MEPHOSTOPHILIS

His faith is great, I cannot touch his soul;
But what I may afflict his body with,   85
I will attempt, which is but little worth.

FAUSTUS

One thing, good servant, let me crave of thee,
To glut the longing of my heart's desire,
That I may have unto my paramour,
That heavenly Helen, which I saw of late,   90
Whose sweet embracings may extinguish clear
Those thoughts that do dissuade me from my vow,
And keep mine oath I made to Lucifer.

MEPHOSTOPHILIS

This, or what else my Faustus shall desire,
Shall be performed in twinkling of an eye.   95

Enter HELEN *again, passing over between two* CUPIDS

FAUSTUS

Was this the face that launched a thousand ships,
And burnt the topless towers of Ilium?
Sweet Helen, make me immortal with a kiss:
Her lips suck forth my soul, see where it flies!

79 *quickly* A (Faustus B)
80 *drift* drifting; also purpose
81 *base and crooked age* A (base and aged man B)
91 *embracings* A (embraces B)
93 *mine oath* A (my vow B)
97 *Ilium* Troy

96–104 In these lines Marlowe is repeating his own memorable phrases:
    Helen, whose beauty summoned Greece to arms,
    And drew a thousand ships to Tenedos.
            2 *Tamburlaine*, II.iv, 87–8
    And he'll make me immortal with a kiss.
            Dido, IV.iv, 123
    So thou wouldst prove as true as Paris did,
    Would, as fair Troy was, Carthage might be sacked,
    And I be called a second Helena.
            Dido, V.i, 146–8

Come Helen, come, give me my soul again.   100
Here will I dwell, for heaven is in these lips,
And all is dross that is not Helena.

Enter OLD MAN

I will be Paris, and for love of thee,
Instead of Troy shall Wittenberg be sacked;
And I will combat with weak Menelaus,   105
And wear thy colours on my plumed crest;
Yea, I will wound Achilles in the heel,
And then return to Helen for a kiss.
O, thou art fairer than the evening's air,
Clad in the beauty of a thousand stars: 110
Brighter art thou than flaming Jupiter,
When he appeared to hapless Semele;
More lovely than the monarch of the sky
In wanton Arethusa's azured arms;
And none but thou shalt be my paramour.   115
                              Exeunt [FAUSTUS *and* HELEN]
OLD MAN
Accursed Faustus, miserable man,
That from thy soul exclud'st the grace of heaven,
And fliest the throne of His tribunal seat!

Enter the DEVILS

Satan begins to sift me with his pride,
As in this furnace God shall try my faith: 120
My faith, vile hell, shall triumph over thee!
Ambitious fiends, see how the heavens smiles
At your repulse, and laughs your state to scorn!
Hence hell, for hence I fly unto my God.   *Exeunt*

---

102 s.d. This direction, and the Old Man's final speech (116–24) are
   missing from B
111–12 The sight of Jupiter in all his divine splendour was too much for
   mortal eyes, and Semele was consumed by the fire of his brightness.
113–14 No myth has been traced linking the sun-god with Arethusa; the
   nymph was changed into a fountain, and perhaps Marlowe is referring
   to the reflection of the sun in blue waters.

Act V, Scene ii

Thunder. Enter LUCIFER, BELZEBUB, *and* MEPHOSTOPHILIS

LUCIFER
    Thus from infernal Dis do we ascend
    To view the subjects of our monarchy,
    Those souls which sin seals the black sons of hell,
    'Mong which as chief, Faustus, we come to thee,
    Bringing with us lasting damnation,   5
    To wait upon thy soul; the time is come
    Which makes it forfeit.
MEPHOSTOPHILIS   And this gloomy night,
    Here in this room will wretched Faustus be.
BELZEBUB
    And here we'll stay,
    To mark him how he doth demean himself.   10
MEPHOSTOPHILIS
    How should he, but in desperate lunacy?
    Fond worldling, now his heart-blood dries with grief,
    His conscience kills it, and his labouring brain,
    Begets a world of idle fantasies,
    To overreach the devil; but all in vain: 15
    His store of pleasures must be sauced with pain.
    He and his servant Wagner are at hand,
    Both come from drawing Faustus' latest will.
    See where they come.

Enter FAUSTUS *and* WAGNER

FAUSTUS
    Say Wagner, thou hast perused my will,   20
    How dost thou like it?
WAGNER   Sir, so wondrous well,
    As in all humble duty, I do yield
    My life and lasting service for your love.
FAUSTUS
    Gramercies Wagner.   [*Exit* WAGNER]

---

1 *Dis* The Underworld; an alternative name for Pluto and extended
   to his kingdom

Act V, Scene ii. Textually the most vexed portion of the play. The infernal
    conclave (ll. 1–23), the interview with Mephostophilis (11.85–96), and
    the visions of heaven and hell (11.97–130) are found only in the B Text.
    If the first two are indeed Marlowe's, the play takes on a quite different
    nature from that indicated by the first and last soliloquies.

Enter the SCHOLARS

Welcome gentlemen.

1 SCHOLAR

Now worthy Faustus, methinks your looks are changed.   25

FAUSTUS

Ah, gentlemen!

2 SCHOLAR

What ails Faustus?

FAUSTUS

Ah my sweet chamber-fellow, had I lived with thee, then
had I lived still, but now must die eternally. Look sirs,
comes he not, comes he not?   30

1 SCHOLAR

O my dear Faustus, what imports this fear?

2 SCHOLAR

Is all our pleasure turned to melancholy?

3 SCHOLAR

He is not well with being over-solitary.

2 SCHOLAR

If it be so, we'll have physicians, and Faustus shall be cured.

3 SCHOLAR

'Tis but a surfeit sir, fear nothing.   35

FAUSTUS

A surfeit of deadly sin, that hath damned both body and
soul.

2 SCHOLAR

Yet Faustus, look up to heaven, and remember God's mercy
is infinite.

FAUSTUS

But Faustus' offence can ne'er be pardoned. The serpent   40
that tempted Eve may be saved, but not Faustus. Ah gentlemen, hear with patience, and tremble not at my speeches;
though my heart pants and quivers to remember that I
have been a student here these thirty years—O would I had
never seen Wittenberg, never read book—and what wonders   45
I have done, all Germany can witness, yea, all the world—
for which Faustus hath lost both Germany and the world
—yea, heaven itself—heaven, the seat of God, the throne of
the blessed, the kingdom of joy; and must remain in hell

38–39 *God's mercy is infinite* ed. (God's mercies are infinite A; mercy is
infinite B) B's reading, with the addition of A's *God's* (omitted, perhaps,
by the censoring editor) is the more appropriate; Faustus is being
reminded that God's power of forgiveness is boundless, not that his
blessings are without number

for ever. Hell, ah hell, for ever! Sweet friends, what shall   50
become of Faustus, being in hell for ever?

2 SCHOLAR

Yet Faustus, call on God.

FAUSTUS

On God, whom Faustus hath abjured? On God, whom
Faustus hath blasphemed? Ah my God–I would weep,
but the devil draws in my tears. Gush forth blood instead   55
of tears, yea, life and soul. O, he stays my tongue! I would
lift up my hands, but see, they hold 'em, they hold 'em.

ALL

Who Faustus?

FAUSTUS

Why, Lucifer and Mephostophilis: ah gentlemen, I gave
them my soul for my cunning.   60

ALL

God forbid!

FAUSTUS

God forbade it indeed, but Faustus hath done it. For the
vain pleasure of four and twenty years hath Faustus lost
eternal joy and felicity. I writ them a bill with mine own
blood: the date is expired, this is the time, and he will fetch   65
me.

1 SCHOLAR

Why did not Faustus tell us of this before, that divines
might have prayed for thee?

FAUSTUS

Oft have I thought to have done so, but the devil threatened
to tear me in pieces if I named God, to fetch me body and   70
soul if I once gave ear to divinity; and now 'tis too late.
Gentlemen, away: lest you perish with me.

2 SCHOLAR

O what may we do to save Faustus?

FAUSTUS

Talk not of me, but save yourselves and depart.

3 SCHOLAR

God will strengthen me. I will stay with Faustus.   75

1 SCHOLAR

Tempt not God, sweet friend, but let us into the next room,
and there pray for him.

54–5 'No not so much as their eyes are able to shed teares (thretten and
torture them as ye please) while first they repent (God not permitting
them to dissemble their obstinacie in so horrible a crime'. *Daemonologie*,
p. 81.

FAUSTUS

    Ay, pray for me, pray for me; and what noise soever you
hear, come not unto me, for nothing can rescue me.

2 SCHOLAR

    Pray thou, and we will pray, that God may have mercy upon   80
thee.

FAUSTUS

    Gentlemen, farewell. If I live till morning, I'll visit you:
if not, Faustus is gone to hell.

ALL

    Faustus, farewell.   *Exeunt* SCHOLARS

MEPHOSTOPHILIS

    Ay Faustus, now thou hast no hope of heaven,   85
    Therefore despair, think only upon hell;
    For that must be thy mansion, there to dwell.

FAUSTUS

    O thou bewitching fiend, 'twas thy temptation,
    Hath robbed me of eternal happiness.

MEPHOSTOPHILIS

    I do confess it Faustus, and rejoice: 90
    'Twas I that, when thou wert i'the way to heaven,
    Damned up thy passage; when thou took'st the book,
    To view the Scriptures, then I turned the leaves
    And led thine eye.
    What, weep'st thou? 'Tis too late, despair, farewell: 95
    Fools that will laugh on earth, must weep in hell.   *Exit*

Enter the GOOD ANGEL, *and the* BAD ANGEL *at several doors*

GOOD ANGEL

    O Faustus, if thou hadst given ear to me,
    Innumerable joys had followed thee.
    But thou didst love the world.

BAD ANGEL   Gave ear to me,
    And now must taste hell's pains perpetually.   100

GOOD ANGEL

    O what will all thy riches, pleasures, pomps,
    Avail thee now?

BAD ANGEL   Nothing but vex thee more,
    To want in hell, that had on earth such store.
    Music while the throne descends

GOOD ANGEL

    O thou hast lost celestial happiness,
    Pleasures unspeakable, bliss without end.   105
    Hadst thou affected sweet divinity,
    Hell, or the devil, had had no power on thee.

Hadst thou kept on that way, Faustus, behold,
In what resplendent glory thou hadst sat
In yonder throne, like those bright shining saints,   110
And triumphed over hell; that hast thou lost,
And now, poor soul, must thy good angel leave thee:
The jaws of hell are open to receive thee.
                        Exit [*the throne ascends*]
            Hell is discovered

BAD ANGEL

Now Faustus, let thine eyes with horror stare
Into that vast perpetual torture-house.   115
There are the furies tossing damned souls
On burning forks; there bodies boil in lead;
There are live quarters broiling on the coals,
That ne'er can die; this ever-burning chair,
Is for o'er-tortured souls to rest them in;   120
These, that are fed with sops of flaming fire,
Were gluttons, and loved only delicates,
And laughed to see the poor starve at their gates:
But yet all these are nothing: thou shalt see
Ten thousand tortures that more horrid be.   125

FAUSTUS

O, I have seen enough to torture me.

BAD ANGEL

Nay, thou must feel them, taste the smart of all:
He that loves pleasure, must for pleasure fall.
And so I leave thee Faustus, till anon,
Then wilt thou tumble in confusion.   *Exit*   130
            The clock strikes eleven

FAUSTUS

Ah Faustus,
Now hast thou but one bare hour to live,
And then thou must be damned perpetually.
Stand still, you ever-moving spheres of heaven,
That time may cease, and midnight never come.   135
Fair nature's eye, rise, rise again and make
Perpetual day; or let this hour be but
A year, a month, a week, a natural day,

134–7 *Cf. Edward II*, V.i, 64–8:
    Continue ever, thou celestial sun;
    Let never silent night possess this clime:
    Stand still you watches of the element;
    All times and seasons, rest you at a stay,
    That Edward may be still fair England's king.

That Faustus may repent, and save his soul.
O lente, lente currite noctis equi!   140
The stars move still, time runs, the clock will strike,
The devil will come, and Faustus must be damned.
O I'll leap up to my God! Who pulls me down?
See, see where Christ's blood streams in the firmament!
One drop would save my soul, half a drop. Ah my Christ— 145
Rend not my heart for naming of my Christ;
Yet will I call on him: O spare me Lucifer!
Where is it now? 'Tis gone, and see where God
Stretcheth out his arm, and bends his ireful brows:
Mountains and hills, come, come, and fall on me,   150
And hide me from the heavy wrath of God.
No, no!
Then will I headlong run into the earth:
Earth, gape! O no, it will not harbour me.
You stars that reigned at my nativity,   155
Whose influence hath allotted death and hell,
Now draw up Faustus like a foggy mist
Into the entrails of yon labouring cloud,
That when you vomit forth into the air,
My limbs may issue from your smoky mouths,   160
So that my soul may but ascend to heaven.
                          The watch strikes
Ah, half the hour is past; 'twill all be past anon!
O God,

140 Gallop slowly, slowly, you horses of the night
143 *my God* A (heaven B)
144 A (*not in* B)
148 *it* the vision of God; the momentary yielding to terror and the
     devil banishes even this remote vision of mercy
148–9 *see where . . . brows* A (see a threatening arm, an angry brow B)
151 *God* A (heaven B)

---

140 The final and most famous irony of the play. The line is from Ovid's
     Amores, I.xiii, 40, where the poet longs for never-ending night in the
     arms of his mistress.
150–51 'And they shall say to the mountains, Cover us; and to the hills,
     Fall on us', Hosea, x,8 (See also Revelations, vi,16 and Luke, xxiii,3);
     Looking Glass for London has the same idea:
        Hell gapes for me, heaven will not hold my soule,
        You mountaines shroude me from the God of truth . . .
        Cover me hills, and shroude me from the Lord. 11.2054–5,9.
155–61 Faustus prays the stars, whose positions at his birth ordained this
     fate, to suck him up into a cloud as a fog or mist is drawn up, and then
     in a storm expel his body in order that his soul may be saved. Instead of
     So that at 1.61 B reads 'But let'; Greg suggests that the B editor 'felt
     that A's text smacked too much of a bargain with heaven'.

If thou wilt not have mercy on my soul,
Yet for Christ's sake, whose blood hath ransomed me,   165
Impose some end to my incessant pain:
Let Faustus live in hell a thousand years,
A hundred thousand, and at last be saved.
O, no end is limited to damned souls!
Why wert thou not a creature wanting soul?   170
Or why is this immortal that thou hast?
Ah, Pythagoras' *metempsychosis*—were that true,
This soul should fly from me, and I be changed
Unto some brutish beast.
All beasts are happy, for when they die,   175
Their souls are soon dissolved in elements;
But mine must live still to be plagued in hell.
Cursed be the parents that engendered me!
No Faustus, curse thyself, curse Lucifer,
That hath deprived thee of the joys of heaven.   180
                              The clock striketh twelve
It strikes, it strikes! Now body turn to air,
Or Lucifer will bear thee quick to hell.
                              Thunder and lightning
O soul, be changed into little water drops,
And fall into the ocean, ne'er be found.

                    Enter the DEVILS

My God, my God! Look not so fierce on me!   185
Adders, and serpents, let me breathe awhile!
Ugly hell gape not! Come not Lucifer;
I'll burn my books—ah Mephostophilis!   *Exeunt with him*

Act V, Scene iii
Enter the SCHOLARS

1 SCHOLAR
Come gentlemen, let us go visit Faustus,
For such a dreadful night was never seen

163–4 *O God . . . soul* A (O, if my soul must suffer for my sin B)
182 *quick* living
183 little A (small B)
V.iii. This scene is not in the A Text

---

172 *Pythagoras' metempsychosis* The theory of the transmigration of souls,
   attributed to Pythagoras, whereby the human soul at the death of the
   body took on some other form of life.
188 *I'll burn my books* All magicians who renounced their art made a solemn
   act of disposing of their books of magic; *cf. The Tempest*, V.i, 56–7.

Since first the world's creation did begin;
Such fearful shrieks, and cries were never heard.
Pray heaven the doctor have escaped the danger.   5

2 SCHOLAR
O help us heaven! See, here are Faustus' limbs,
All torn asunder by the hand of death.

3 SCHOLAR
The devils whom Faustus served have torn him thus:
For 'twixt the hours of twelve and one, methought
I heard him shriek and call aloud for help: 10
At which self time the house seemed all on fire,
With dreadful horror of these damned fiends.

2 SCHOLAR
Well Gentlemen, though Faustus' end be such
As every Christian heart laments to think on;
Yet for he was a scholar, once admired   15
For wondrous knowledge in our German schools,
We'll give his mangled limbs due burial,
And all the students clothed in mourning black,
Shall wait upon his heavy funeral.   *Exeunt*

EPILOGUE

Enter CHORUS

CHORUS
Cut is the branch that might have grown full straight,
And burned is Apollo's laurel bough,
That sometime grew within this learned man.
Faustus is gone: regard his hellish fall,
Whose fiendful fortune may exhort the wise   5
Only to wonder at unlawful things:
Whose deepness doth entice such forward wits,
To practise more than heavenly power permits.

                                            [*Exit*]

Terminat hora diem, terminat author opus

FINIS

16 *schools* universities
19 *heavy* sorrowful

Terminat . . . opus The hour ends the day, the author ends his work.
The origin is unknown, and it seems likely that the line was appended
to the play by the printer and not by Marlowe.

APPENDIX

Major variants in the A Text

Act II, Scene iii

Enter ROBIN *the Ostler with a book in his hand*

ROBIN

O this is admirable! Here I ha' stolen one of Doctor Faustus'
conjuring books and, 'faith, I mean to search some circles
for my own use. Now will I make all the maidens in our
parish dance at my pleasure stark naked before me, and so
by that means I shall see more than e'er I felt or saw yet.   5

Enter RALPH, *calling* ROBIN

RALPH

Robin, prithee come away. There's a gentleman tarries to
have his horse, and he would have his things rubbed and
made clean; he keeps such a chafing with my mistress about
it, and she has sent me to look thee out. Prithee come away.

ROBIN

Keep out, keep out, or else you are blown up, you are dis-   10
membered, Ralph; keep out, for I am about a roaring piece
of work.

RALPH

Come, what dost thou with that same book? Thou canst not
read.

ROBIN

Yes, my master and mistress shall find that I can read, he   15
for his forehead, she for her private study; she's born to
bear with me, or else my art fails.

RALPH

Why Robin, what book is that?

ROBIN

What book? Why, the most intolerable book for conjuring
that e'er was invented by any brimstone devil.   20

RALPH

Canst thou conjure with it?

2 *circles* magicians' circles; but the sexual overtones are obvious
11 *roaring* wild and dangerous
19 *intolerable* Robin probably means incomparable

232

ROBIN

I can do all these things easily with it: first, I can make thee
drunk with hippocras at any tavern in Europe for nothing
– that's one of my conjuring works.

RALPH

Our master parson says that's nothing.   25

ROBIN

True Ralph, and more Ralph, if thou hast any mind to
Nan Spit our kitchen maid, then turn her and wind her
to thy own use, as often as thou wilt, and at midnight.

RALPH

O brave, Robin, shall I have Nan Spit, and to mine own use?
On that condition I'll feed thy devil with horse-bread as   30
long as he lives, of free cost.

ROBIN

No more, sweet Ralph; let's go and make clean our boots
which lie foul upon our hands, and then to our conjuring,
in the devil's name.   *Exeunt*

Act III, Scene iii

Enter ROBIN *and* RALPH *with a silver goblet*

ROBIN

Come Ralph, did not I tell thee we were made for ever by
this Doctor Faustus' book? *Ecce signum*, here's a simple
purchase for horse-keepers; our horses shall eat no hay
as long as this lasts.

RALPH

But Robin, here comes the vintner.   5

ROBIN

Hush, I'll gull him supernaturally. Drawer, I hope all is
paid. God be with you. Come, Ralph.

VINTNER

Soft, sir, a word with you. I must yet have a goblet paid
from you ere you go.

ROBIN

I, a goblet, Ralph! I, a goblet! I scorn you; and you are   10
but a etc. I, a goblet! Search me.

---

2 *Ecce signum* Behold the proof; a catchword fairly frequent among
the Clowns; *cf. I Henry IV*, II.iv, 149
simple purchase piece of clear profit
6 *gull* trick
11 *etc.* This probably indicated that the Clown was to fill in with any
comic terms of abuse that came to his mind

VINTNER

I mean so, sir, with your favour.   [*Searches him*]

ROBIN

How say you now?

VINTNER

I must say somewhat to your fellow. You sir!

RALPH

Me, sir! Me, sir! Search your fill.   [VINTNER *searches him*]   15
Now sir, you may be ashamed to burden honest men with
a matter of truth.

VINTNER

Well, t'one of you hath this goblet about you.

ROBIN

You lie, drawer, 'tis afore me. Sirra, you, I'll teach ye to
impeach honest men. Stand by. I'll scour you for a goblet.   20
Stand aside, you had best. I charge you in the name of
Belzebub – look to the goblet Ralph.

VINTNER

What mean you sirra?

ROBIN

I'll tell you what I mean.   *He reads*
Sanctobulorum Periphrasticon – nay, I'll tickle you, vintner –   25
look to the goblet Ralph – *Polypragmos, Belseborams framanto*
pacostiphos tostu Mephostophilis etc.

         Enter MEPHOSTOPHILIS : *sets squibs at their backs:*
                    they run about

VINTNER

O nomine Domine, what meanest thou Robin? thou hast no
goblet.

RALPH

Peccatum peccatorum, here's thy goblet, good Vintner.   30

ROBIN

Misericordia pro nobis, what shall I do? Good devil, forgive
me now, and I'll never rob thy library more.

                    Enter to them MEPHOSTOPHILIS

MEPHOSTOPHILIS

Vanish villains, th'one like an ape, another like a bear, the
third an ass, for doing this enterprise.
Monarch of hell, under whose black survey   35

20 *scour you* settle you, polish you off

28–32 The dog-Latin marks the Clowns' attempts to protect themselves
    from the devil; 'Nominus patrus, I bless me from thee' *Looking Glass*
    for London, line 1698.
33–49 These lines must constitute an alternative ending to the scene.

Great potentates do kneel with awful fear,
Upon whose altars thousand souls do lie,
How am I vexed with these villains' charms!
From Constantinople am I hither come,
Only for pleasure of these damned slaves   40

ROBIN
How, from Constantinople? You have had a great journey.
Will you take sixpence in your purse to pay for your supper
and be gone?

MEPHOSTOPHILIS
Well, villains, for your presumption, I transform thee into
an ape, and thee into a dog, and so be gone.   *Exit*   45

ROBIN
How, into an ape? That's brave! I'll have fine sport with
the boys, I'll get nuts and apples enow.

RALPH
And I must be a dog.

ROBIN
I'faith, thy head will never be out of the potage pot.
                                                Exeunt

Act IV, Scene ii

Enter EMPEROR, FAUSTUS, *and a* KNIGHT *with* ATTENDANTS

EMPEROR
Master Doctor Faustus, I have heard strange report of thy
knowledge in the black art, how that none in my empire,
nor in the whole world can compare with thee for the rare
effects of magic. They say thou hast a familiar spirit by
whom thou canst accomplish what thou list. This therefore   5
is my request: that thou let me see some proof of thy skill,
that mine eyes may be witnesses to confirm what mine ears
have heard reported; and here I swear to thee, by the honour
of mine imperial crown, that whatever thou dost, thou shalt
be no ways prejudiced or endamaged.   10

KNIGHT
I'faith, he looks much like a conjuror.   *Aside*

FAUSTUS
My gracious sovereign, though I must confess myself far
inferior to the report men have published and nothing
answerable to the honour of your imperial Majesty, yet for

13–14 *nothing answerable to* in no way worthy of

that love and duty binds me thereunto, I am content to do   15
whatsoever your majesty shall command me.

EMPEROR

Then Doctor Faustus, mark what I shall say.
As I was sometime solitary set
Within my closet, sundry thoughts arose
About the honour of mine ancestors;   20
How they had won by prowess such exploits,
Got such riches, subdued so many kingdoms,
As we that do succeed, or they that shall
Hereafter possess our throne, shall,
I fear me, never attain to that degree   25
Of high renown and great authority;
Amongst which kings is Alexander the Great,
Chief spectacle of the world's pre-eminence,
The bright shining of whose glorious acts
Lightens the world with his reflecting beams;   30
As when I hear but motion made of him,
It grieves my soul I never saw the man.
If, therefore, thou, by cunning of thine art,
Canst raise this man from hollow vaults below,
Where lies entombed this famous conqueror,   35
And bring with him his beauteous paramour,
Both in their right shapes, gesture and attire
They used to wear during their time of life,
Thou shalt both satisfy my just desire,
And give me cause to praise thee whilst I live.   40

FAUSTUS

My gracious lord, I am ready to accomplish your request
so far forth as by art and power of my spirit I am able to
perform.

KNIGHT

I'faith, that's just nothing at all.   *Aside*

FAUSTUS

But if it like your Grace, it is not in my ability to present   45
before your eyes the true substantial bodies of those two
deceased princes, which long since are consumed to dust.

KNIGHT

Ay, marry master doctor, now there's a sign of grace in you,
when you will confess the truth.   *Aside*

FAUSTUS

But such spirits as can lively resemble Alexander and his   50

28 *pre-eminence* pre-eminent men; *cf.* the two uses of 'nobility'
31 *motion* mention
37 *gesture* manner

paramour shall appear before your Grace, in that manner
that they best lived in, in their most flourishing estate; which
I doubt not shall sufficiently content your imperial Majesty.

EMPEROR

Go to, master doctor, let me see them presently.

KNIGHT

Do you hear, master doctor? You bring Alexander and his   55
paramour before the Emperor.

FAUSTUS

How then sir?

KNIGHT

I'faith, that's as true as Diana turned me to a stag.

FAUSTUS

No sir, but when Actaeon died, he left the horns for you.
Mephostophilis, begone!   60

Exit MEPHOSTOPHILIS

KNIGHT

Nay, and you go to conjuring, I'll be gone.

Exit KNIGHT

FAUSTUS

I'll meet with you anon for interrupting me so—Here they
are, my gracious lord.

Enter MEPHOSTOPHILIS *with* ALEXANDER *and his* PARAMOUR

EMPEROR

Master doctor, I heard this lady, while she lived, had a wart
or mole in her neck. How shall I know whether it be so or no? 65

FAUSTUS

Your Highness may boldly go and see.

EMPEROR

Sure these are no spirits but the true substantial bodies of
those two deceased princes.

Exit ALEXANDER [*and* PARAMOUR]

FAUSTUS

Will't please your Highness now to send for the knight that
was so pleasant with me here of late?   70

EMPEROR

One of you call him forth.

Enter the KNIGHT *with a pair of horns on his head*

EMPEROR

How now sir knight? Why, I had thought thou hadst been

58 *Diana . . . stag* (see note on IV.ii, 51)
62 *meet with you anon* get even with you soon
70 *pleasant* facetious

a bachelor, but now I see thou hast wife, that not only gives
thee horns, but makes thee wear them. Feel on thy head.

KNIGHT

Thou damned wretch and execrable dog,   75
Bred in the concave of some monstrous rock!
How dar'st thou thus abuse a gentleman?
Villain, I say, undo what thou hast done.

FAUSTUS

O, not so fast sir, there's no haste but good. Are you
remembered how you crossed me in my conference with   80
the Emperor? I think I have met with you for it.

EMPEROR

Good master doctor, at my entreaty release him; he hath
done penance sufficient.

FAUSTUS

My gracious lord, not so much for the injury he offered me
here in your presence, as to delight you with some mirth,   85
hath Faustus worthily requited this injurious knight; which
being all I desire, I am content to release him of his horns:
and, sir knight, hereafter speak well of scholars. Mephostophilis, transform him straight. Now my good lord, having
done my duty, I humbly take my leave.   90

EMPEROR

Farewell master doctor; yet ere you go, expect from me a
bounteous reward.

Exit EMPEROR [KNIGHT *and* ATTENDANTS]

Act IV, Scene v

FAUSTUS

Now, Mephostophilis, the restless course
That time doth run with calm and silent foot,
Shortening my days and thread of vital life,
Calls for the payment of my latest years.
Therefore sweet Mephostophilis, let us   5
Make haste to Wittenberg.

MEPHOSTOPHILIS   What, will you go
On horseback, or on foot?

---

76 *concave* hollow; the same expression is in 2 *Tamburlaine*, II.ii, 89
79 *no haste but good* Proverb (Tilley, H 199)
84 *injury* insult
IV.v. At the end of the court scene Faustus and Mephostophilis
  apparently remain on stage for the scene that follows

FAUSTUS   Nay, till I am past
This fair and pleasant green, I'll walk on foot.

Enter a HORSE-COURSER

HORSE-COURSER

I have been all this day seeking one maister Fustian. Mass,
see where he is! God save you, maister doctor.   10

FAUSTUS

What, horse-courser, you are well met.

HORSE-COURSER

Do you hear sir, I have brought you forty dollars for your
horse.

FAUSTUS

I cannot sell him so. If thou likest him for fifty, take him.

HORSE-COURSER

Alas, sir, I have no more. [*To* MEPHOSTOPHILIS] I pray you   15
speak for me.

MEPHOSTOPHILIS

I pray you, let him have him; he is an honest fellow and he
has a great charge, neither wife nor child.

FAUSTUS

Well, come, give me your money; my boy will deliver him
to you. But I must tell you one thing before you have him: 20
ride him not into the water at any hand.

HORSE-COURSER

Why, sir, will he not drink of all waters?

FAUSTUS

O yes, he will drink of all waters, but ride him not into the
water; ride him over hedge or ditch or where thou wilt, but
not into the water.   25

HORSE-COURSER

Well, sir. Now am I a made man for ever. I'll not leave my
horse for forty: if he had but the quality of hey-ding-
ding, hey-ding-ding, I'd make a brave living on him; he has
a buttock as slick as an eel. Well, God b'wi'ye, sir, your boy
will deliver him me. But hark ye sir, if my horse be sick, or   30
ill at ease, if I bring his water to you, you'll tell me what is?

---

21 *at any hand* on any account
22 *drink of all waters* (see note on IV.v, 13–14)
27 *for forty* for anything; forty is often used to indicate a large and
imprecise number; *cf. Coriolanus*, III.i, 242
27–8 *the quality of hey-ding-ding* 'the Horse-courser must mean
something by this. I suspect he means a complete horse, not a
gelding' (Greg)

FAUSTUS

Away you villain! What, dost think I am a horse-doctor?

Exit HORSE-COURSER

What art thou, Faustus, but a man condemned to die?
Thy fatal time doth draw to final end;
Despair doth drive distrust unto my thoughts.   35
Confound these passions with a quiet sleep:
Tush, Christ did call the thief upon the cross;
Then rest thee, Faustus, quiet in conceit.

Sleep in his chair

Enter HORSE-COURSER *all wet, crying*

HORSE-COURSER

Alas, alas! Doctor Fustian, quotha? Mass, Doctor Lopus
was never such a doctor. Has given me a purgation, has   40
purged me of forty dollars; I shall never see them more. But
yet, like an ass as I was, I would not be ruled by him, for he
bade me I should ride him into no water. Now I, thinking
my horse had had some rare quality that he would not have
had me known of, I, like a venturous youth, rid him into the   45
deep pond at the town's end. I was no sooner in the middle
of the pond, but my horse vanished away, and I sat upon a
bottle of hay, never so near drowning in my life. But I'll
seek out my doctor, and have my forty dollars again, or I'll
make it the dearest horse. O, yonder is his snipper-snapper.   50
Do you hear? You, hey-pass, where's your maister?

MEPHOSTOPHILIS

Why sir, what would you? You cannot speak with him.

HORSE-COURSER

But I will speak with him.

MEPHOSTOPHILIS

Why, he's fast asleep. Come some other time.

HORSE-COURSER

I'll speak with him now, or I'll break his glass-windows   55
about his ears.

MEPHOSTOPHILIS

I tell thee he has not slept this eight nights.

---

50 *snipper-snapper* conceited young fellow
51 *hey-pass* mumbo-jumbo
55 *glass-windows* spectacles

---

39 *Doctor Lopus* Dr. Lopez, personal physician to Elizabeth, was executed
in 1594 for his supposed part in a plot to poison the Queen. This is
the most obvious instance of an actor's interpolation – Marlowe cannot
possibly have known about the Lopez scandal.

HORSE-COURSER
And he have not slept this eight weeks I'll speak with him.
MEPHOSTOPHILIS
See where he is fast asleep.
HORSE-COURSER
Ay, this is he. God save ye, maister doctor. Maister doctor, 60
maister Doctor Fustian! Forty dollars, forty dollars for a
bottle of hay!
MEPHOSTOPHILIS
Why, thou seest he hears thee not.
HORSE-COURSER
So, ho, ho: so, ho, ho.

Holloa in his ear

No, will you not wake? I'll make you wake ere I go. 65

Pull him by the leg, and pull it away

Alas, I am undone! What shall I do?
FAUSTUS
O my leg, my leg! Help Mephostophilis! Call the officers!
My leg, my leg!
MEPHOSTOPHILIS
Come, villain, to the constable.
HORSE-COURSER
O Lord, sir, let me go, and I'll give you forty dollars more. 70
MEPHOSTOPHILIS
Where be they?
HORSE-COURSER
I have none about me. Come to my hostry and I'll give
them you.
MEPHOSTOPHILIS
Be gone quickly. HORSE-COURSER *runs away*
FAUSTUS
What, is he gone? Farewell he! Faustus has his leg again, 75
and the horse-courser, I take it, a bottle of hay for his
labour. Well, this trick shall cost him forty dollars more.

Enter WAGNER

How now, Wagner, what's the news with thee?
WAGNER
Sir, the Duke of Vanholt doth earnestly entreat your
company. 80
FAUSTUS
The Duke of Vanholt! An honourable gentleman to whom

---

64 *So, ho, ho,* huntsman's cry to direct hounds to the hare

I must be no niggard of my cunning. Come Mephostophilis,
let's away to him. *Exeunt*

Act V, Scene i, 35–51

The Old Man's speech.

OLD MAN
    Ah, Doctor Faustus, that I might prevail
    To guide thy steps unto the way of life,
    By which sweet path thou may'st attain the goal
    That shall conduct thee to celestial rest.
    Break heart, drop blood, and mingle it with tears,   5
    Tears falling from repentant heaviness
    Of thy most vile and loathsome filthiness,
    The stench whereof corrupts the inward soul
    With such flagitious crimes of heinous sins,
    As no commiseration may expel,   10
    But mercy, Faustus, of thy saviour sweet,
    Whose blood alone must wash away thy guilt.

Sejanus his Fall

BEN JONSON

Edited by

W. F. BOLTON

SEIANVS

his

FALL.

A Tragœdie.

Acted, in the yeere 1 6 0 3.
By the K. MAIESTIES
SERVANTS.

The Author B. I.

MART.

*Non hic Centauros, non Gorgonas, Harpyiaſʠ,
Inuenies: Hominem pagina noſtra ſapit.*

LONDON,

Printed by WILLIAM STANSBY,

M. DC. XVI.

Motto. Not here will you find centaurs, not gorgons and harpies: my
page tells of man (Martial, X.iv, 9–10).

TO THE NO LESS
NOBLE, BY VIRTUE,
THAN BLOOD:
Esmé
LORD AUBIGNÉ.

MY LORD,

If ever any ruin were so great, as to survive; I think this be one
I send you: the *Fall of Sejanus*. It is a poem, that (if I well
remember) in your Lordship's sight, suffered no less violence
from our people here, than the subject of it did from the rage   10
of the people of Rome; but, with a different fate, as (I hope)
merit: for this hath outlived their malice, and begot itself a
greater favour than he lost, the love of good men. Amongst
whom, if I make your Lordship the first it thanks, it is not
without a just confession of the bond your benefits have, and   15
ever shall hold upon me.

      Your Lordship's most faithful honourer,

               BEN. JONSON.

Esmé Lord 'Aubigné. Esme Stuart, Seigneur d'Aubigné (1574–1624),
friend and benefactor of Jonson, who honoured him in *Epigram* 127.

To the Readers.

The following, and voluntary labours of my friends, pre-
fixed to my book, have relieved me in much, whereat (without them) I should necessarily have touched: now, I will only
use three or four short, and needful notes, and so rest.   5

First, if it be objected, that what I publish is no true poem;
in the strict laws of time. I confess it: as also in the want of a
proper chorus, whose habit, and moods are such, and so
difficult, as not any, whom I have seen since the ancients, (no
not they who have most presently affected laws) have yet come   10
in the way of. Nor is it needful, or almost possible, in these
our times, and to such auditors, as commonly things are
presented, to observe the old state, and splendour of dramatic
poems, with preservation of any popular delight. But of this
I shall take more seasonable cause to speak; in my *Observations*   15
upon Horace his Art of Poetry, which (with the text translated)
I intend, shortly to publish. In the meantime, if in truth of
argument, dignity of persons, gravity and height of elocution,
fulness and frequency of sentence, I have discharged the
other offices of a tragic writer, let not the absence of these   20
forms be imputed to me, wherein I shall give you occasion
hereafter (and without my boast) to think I could better prescribe, than omit the due use, for want of a convenient knowledge.

The next is, lest in some nice nostril, the quotations might   25
savour affected, I do let you know, that I abhor nothing more;
and have only done it to show my integrity in the story, and
save myself in those common torturers, that bring all wit
to the rack: whose noses are ever like swine spoiling, and
rooting up the Muses' gardens, and their whole bodies, like   30
moles, as blindly working under earth to cast any, the least,
hills upon virtue.

1f *To the Readers . . . reducit opimum* Q (F omits)
2 *following . . . labours* commendatory poems omitted in F
8 *habit, and moods* behaviour and manner (cf. I, 34–35)
23 *convenient* available   25 *nice* over fastidious (usual in Jonson)
26 *affected* assumed artificially   28 *in those* amongst those

7 *laws of time.* Unity of time, a rule of classical drama requiring the action
   to represent a passage of time no longer than the play takes to present.
   Even with its changes of historical chronology, *Sejanus* includes events
   which took place over eight years (A.D. 23 – A.D. 31).

247

Whereas, they are in Latin and the work in English, it was presupposed, none but the learned would take the pains to confer them, the authors themselves being all in the learned tongues, 35 save one, with whose English side I have had little to do: to which it may be required, since I have quoted the page, to name what edition I followed. Tacitus, *Works*, ed. Justus Lipsius, in quarto, Antwerp 1600. Dio Cassius, *History of the Romans*, ed. Henri Estienne, folio, 1592. For the rest, as 40 Suetonius, Seneca, etc. the chapter doth sufficiently direct, or the edition is not varied.

Lastly I would inform you, that this book, in all numbers, is not the same with that which was acted on the public stage, wherein a second pen had good share: in place of which I have 45 rather chosen, to put weaker (and no doubt less pleasing) of mine own, than to defraud so happy a genius of his right, by my loathed usurpation.

Fare you well. And if you read farther of me, and like, I shall not be afraid of it though you praise me out. 50

Neque enim mihi cornea fibra est.

But that I should plant my felicity, in your general saying *good*, or *well*, etc. were a weakness which the better sort of you might worthily contemn, if not absolutely hate me for.

BEN. JONSON. and no such. 55

Quem palma negata macrum, donata reducit opimum.

---

34 *confer* compare
43 *numbers* verses
50 *praise me out* judge me precisely

---

36 *save one*. Richard Greenway, whose 1598 translation of Tacitus' *Annals* Jonson called 'ignorantly done' (*Conversations*, 18), but seems to have followed at least in IV, 399.
51 *Neque enim . . . fibra est*. My heart is not of horn (Persius, *Sat*. I, 47).
56 *Quem palma . . . reducit opimum*. Whom the palm denied sends home lean; the palm bestowed, plump (adapted from Horace, *Ep*. II.i, 180–181).

The Argument.

Ælius Sejanus, son to Sejus Strabo, a gentleman of Rome, and born at Vulsinium, after his long service in court; first, under Augustus, afterward, Tiberius: grew into that favour with the latter, and won him by those arts, as there wanted nothing, but the name, to make him a copartner of the Empire. Which greatness of his, Drusus, the Emperor's son not brooking, after many smothered dislikes (it one day breaking out) the Prince struck him publicly on the face. To revenge which disgrace, Livia, the wife of Drusus (being before corrupted by him to her dishonour, and the discovery of her husband's counsels) Sejanus practiseth with, together with her physician, called Eudemus, and one Lygdus, an eunuch, to poison Drusus. This their inhumane act having successful, and unsuspected passage, it emboldeneth Sejanus to farther, and more insolent projects, even the ambition of the Empire: where finding the lets, he must encounter, to be many, and hard, in respect of the issue of Germanicus (who were next in hope for the succession) he deviseth to make Tiberius' self, his means: and instills into his ears many doubts, and suspicions, both against the Princes, and their mother Agrippina: which Cæsar jealously hearkening to, as covetously consenteth to their ruin, and their friends'. In this time, the better to mature and strengthen his design, Sejanus labours to marry Livia, and worketh (with all his engine) to remove Tiberius from the knowledge of public business, with allurements of a quiet and retired life: the latter of which, Tiberius (out of a proneness to lust, and a desire to hide those unnatural pleasures, which he could not so publicly practise) embraceth: the former enkindleth his fears, and there, gives him first cause of doubt, or suspect toward Sejanus. Against whom, he raiseth (in private) a new instrument, one Sertorius Macro, and by him underworketh, discovers the other's counsels, his means, his ends, sounds the affections of the Senators, divides,

5

10

15

20

25

30

---

12 *practiseth* plots (usual in Jonson)   17 *lets* hindrances
25 *engine* ingenuity, trickery (frequent)
33 *underworketh* works secretly

10f.(*being before . . . husband's counsels*). This feature of the historical narrative Jonson changed to put the blow before the seduction, but overlooked the change when he translated this sentence without alteration from Lipsius' commentary on Tacitus.

distracts them: at last, when Sejanus least looketh, and is most   35
secure (with pretext of doing him an unwonted honour in
the Senate) he trains him from his guards, and with a long
doubtful letter, in one day, hath him suspected, accused,
condemned, and torn in pieces, by the rage of the people.

This do we advance as a mark of terror to all traitors, and   40
treasons; to show how just the heavens are in pouring and
thundering down a weighty vengeance on their unnatural intents, even to the worst princes: much more to those, for
guard of whose piety and virtue, the angels are in continual
watch, and God himself miraculously working.   45

37 *trains* entices
38 *doubtful* ambiguous
40f. *This do . . . miraculously working* Q (F *omits*)

The Persons of the Play.

Tiberius.

Drusus senior.	Sejanus.
Nero.	Latiaris.
Drusus junior.	Varro.
Caligula.	Macro.
Arruntius.	Cotta.
Silius.	Afer.
Sabinus.	Haterius.
Lepidus.	Sanquinius.
Cordus.	Pomponius.
Gallus.	Posthumus.
Regulus.	Trio.
Terentius.	Minutius.
Laco.	Satrius.
Eudemus.	Natta.
Rufus.	Opsius.

Tribuni.

Agrippina. } Livia.
            } Sosia.

Præcones.	Lictores.
Flamen.	Ministri.
Tubicines.	Tibicines.
Nuntius.	Servus.

The Scene.
ROME.

SEJANUS HIS FALL

Act I, [Scene i]

[The Palace. Enter] SABINUS, SILIUS

SABINUS
Hail, Caius Silius.

SILIUS   Titius Sabinus, hail.
You're rarely met in court!

SABINUS   Therefore, well met.

SILIUS
'Tis true: indeed, this place is not our sphere.

SABINUS
No, Silius, we are no good enginers;
We want the fine arts, and their thriving use,   5
Should make us graced, or favoured of the times:
We have no shift of faces, no cleft tongues,
No soft, and glutinous bodies, that can stick,
Like snails, on painted walls; or, on our breasts,
Creep up, to fall, from that proud height, to which   10
We did by slavery, not by service, climb.
We are no guilty men, and then no great;
We have nor place in court, office in state,
That we can say, we owe unto our crimes:
We burn with no black secrets, which can make   15
Us dear to the pale authors; or live feared
Of their still waking jealousies, to raise
Ourselves a fortune, by subverting theirs.
We stand not in the lines, that do advance
To that so courted point.

[Enter SATRIUS, NATTA*]*

SILIUS   But yonder lean   20
A pair that do.

[Enter LATIARIS*]*

---

4 *enginers* schemers
5 *want* lack
6 *Should make* that should make (zero relative, frequent)
7 *shift of faces* duplicity
 cleft tongues for flattery
12 *then* therefore
15f. *which . . . authors* which will force wrongdoers to favour us, who
 know their secrets
17 *jealousies* suspicions (frequent)

253

(SABINUS   Good cousin Latiaris.)

SILIUS

    Satrius Secundus, and Pinnarius Natta,
    The great Sejanus' clients: there be two,
    Know more, than honest counsels: whose close breasts
    Were they ripped up to light, it would be found   25
    A poor, and idle sin, to which their trunks
    Had not been made fit organs. These can lie,
    Flatter, and swear, forswear, deprave, inform,
    Smile, and betray; make guilty men; then beg
    The forfeit lives, to get the livings; cut   30
    Men's throats with whisperings; sell to gaping suitors
    The empty smoke, that flies about the palace;
    Laugh, when their patron laughs; sweat, when he sweats;
    Be hot, and cold with him; change every mood,
    Habit, and garb, as often as he varies;   35
    Observe him, as his watch observes his clock;
    And true, as turquoise in the dear lord's ring,
    Look well, or ill with him: ready to praise
    His lordship, if he spit, or but piss fair,
    Have an indifferent stool, or break wind well,   40
    Nothing can 'scape their catch.

SABINUS   Alas! these things

    Deserve no note, conferred with other vile,
    And filthier flatteries, that corrupt the times:
    When, not alone our gentry's chief are fain
    To make their safety from such sordid acts,   45
    But all our Consuls, and no little part
    Of such as have been Prætors, yea, the most
    Of Senators (that else not use their voices)
    Start up in public Senate, and there strive
    Who shall propound most abject things, and base,   50
    So much, as oft Tiberius hath been heard,

---

23 *clients* men under another's patronage
29f. *beg . . . livings* plead for condemned men, to gain control of them
31 *suitors* suppliants for favours

---

36 Probably one of the rare anachronisms of the play, with reference to
    correcting an inaccurate pocket watch by the more reliable public
    clocks; but possibly 'as his guards observe the sundial or waterclock',
    i.e., closely and often.
37 Turquoise is a stone of changeable colour.
44 Punctuation, and therefore syntax, unclear in Q and F, but explained
    by the Latin source (*primores civitatis*) as 'the leaders of the State'.
48 F has the marginal note *Pedarii*, the Senators who had low office and
    consequently only a silent vote.

Leaving the court, to cry 'O race of men,
Prepared for servitude!' Which showed, that, he
Who least the public liberty could like,
As loathly brooked their flat servility.   55

SILIUS
Well, all is worthy of us, were it more,
Who with our riots, pride, and civil hate,
Have so provoked the justice of the gods.
We, that (within these fourscore years) were born
Free, equal lords of the triumphèd world,   60
And knew no masters, but affections,
To which betraying first our liberties,
We since became the slaves to one man's lusts;
And now to many: every ministering spy
That will accuse, and swear, is lord of you,   65
Of me, of all, our fortunes, and our lives.
Our looks are called to question and our words,
How innocent soever, are made crimes;
We shall not shortly dare to tell our dreams,
Or think, but 'twill be treason.

SABINUS   Tyrants' arts   70
Are to give flatterers, grace; accusers, power;
That those may seem to kill whom they devour.

[Enter CORDUS, ARRUNTIUS]

Now good Cremutius Cordus.

CORDUS   Hail, to your lordship.

They whisper

NATTA
Who's that salutes your cousin?

LATIARIS   'Tis one Cordus,
A gentleman of Rome: one, that has writ   75
Annals of late, they say, and very well.

NATTA
Annals? of what times?

LATIARIS   I think of Pompey's,
And Caius Cæsar's; and so down to these.

NATTA
How stands h'affected to the present state?
Is he or Drusian? or Germanican?   80
Or ours? or neutral?

LATIARIS   I know him not so far.

61 *affections* passions (as opposed to reason)
79 *affected* inclined

NATTA
Those times are somewhat queasy to be touched.
Have you or seen, or heard part of his work?
LATIARIS
Not I, he means they shall be public shortly.
NATTA
O. Cordus do you call him?
LATIARIS   Ay.

                     [*Exeunt* NATTA, SATRIUS]
SABINUS   But these our times   85
Are not the same, Arruntius.
ARRUNTIUS   Times? the men,
The men are not the same: 'tis we are base,
Poor, and degenerate from th'exalted strain
Of our great fathers. Where is now the soul
Of god-like Cato? he, that durst be good,   90
When Cæsar durst be evil; and had power,
As not to live his slave, to die his master.
Or where the constant Brutus, that (being proof
Against all charm of benefits) did strike
So brave a blow into the monster's heart   95
That sought unkindly to captive his country?
O, they are fled the light. Those mighty spirits
Lie raked up, with their ashes in their urns,
And not a spark of their eternal fire
Glows in a present bosom. All's but blaze,   100
Flashes, and smoke, wherewith we labour so,
There's nothing Roman in us; nothing good,
Gallant, or great: 'tis true, that Cordus says,
'Brave Cassius was the last of all that race'.

    DRUSUS *passeth by* [*with* HATERIUS *and a retinue*]

SABINUS
Stand by, lord Drusus.
HATERIUS   Th'Emperor's son, give place.   105
SILIUS
I like the Prince well.
ARRUNTIUS   A riotous youth,
There's little hope of him.
SABINUS   That fault his age
Will, as it grows, correct. Me thinks, he bears
Himself, each day, more nobly than other:
And wins no less on men's affections,   110

96 *unkindly* unnaturally (*kind* nature)
   captive enslave

Than doth his father lose. Believe me, I love him;
And chiefly for opposing to Sejanus.

SILIUS
And I, for gracing his young kinsmen so,
The sons of Prince Germanicus: it shows
A gallant clearness in him, a straight mind,   115
That envies not, in them, their father's name.

ARRUNTIUS
His name was, while he lived, above all envy;
And being dead, without it. O, that man!
If there were seeds of the old virtue left,
They lived in him.

SILIUS   He had the fruits, Arruntius,   120
More than the seeds: Sabinus, and myself
Had means to know him, within; and can report him.
We were his followers, (he would call us friends.)
He was a man most like to virtue; in all,
And every action, nearer to the gods,   125
Than men, in nature; of a body as fair
As was his mind; and no less reverend
In face, than fame: he could so use his state,
Tempering his greatness, with his gravity,
As it avoided all self-love in him,   130
And spite in others. What his funerals lacked
In images, and pomp, they had supplied
With honourable sorrow, soldiers' sadness,
A kind of silent mourning, such, as men
(Who know no tears, but from their captives) use   135
To show in so great losses.

CORDUS   I thought once,
Considering their forms, age, manner of deaths,
The nearness of the places, where they fell,
T'have paralleled him with great Alexander:
For both were of best feature, of high race,   140
Yeared but to thirty, and, in foreign lands,
By their own people, alike made away.

SABINUS
I know not, for his death, how you might wrest it:
But, for his life, it did as much disdain
Comparison, with that voluptuous, rash,   145
Giddy, and drunken Macedon's, as mine
Doth with my bond-man's. All the good, in him,
(His valour, and his fortune) he made his;

143 *wrest* twist, interpret artificially

But he had other touches of late Romans,
That more did speak him: Pompey's dignity,   150
The innocence of Cato, Cæsar's spirit,
Wise Brutus' temperance, and every virtue,
Which, parted unto others, gave them name,
Flowed mixed in him. He was the soul of goodness:
And all our praises of him are like streams   155
Drawn from a spring, that still rise full, and leave
The part remaining greatest.

ARRUNTIUS   I am sure
He was too great for us, and that they knew
Who did remove him hence.

SABINUS   When men grow fast
Honoured, and loved, there is a trick in state   160
(Which jealous princes never fail to use)
How to decline that growth, with fair pretext,
And honourable colours of employment,
Either by embassy, the war, or such,
To shift them forth into another air,   165
Where they may purge, and lessen; so was he:
And had his seconds there, sent by Tiberius,
And his more subtle dame, to discontent him;
To breed, and cherish mutinies; detract
His greatest actions; give audacious check   170
To his commands; and work to put him out
In open act of treason. All which snares
When his wise cares prevented, a fine poison
Was thought on, to mature their practices.

CORDUS
Here comes Sejanus.

SILIUS   Now observe the stoops,   175
The bendings, and the falls.

ARRUNTIUS   Most creeping base!

    [*Enter*] SEJANUS, SATRIUS, TERENTIUS, *etc.*

        They pass over the stage

SEJANUS
I note 'em well: no more. Say you.

SATRIUS   My lord,
There is a gentleman of Rome would buy—

SEJANUS
How call you him you talked with?

SATRIUS   Please your lordship,

150 *speak* describe
167 *seconds* seconders, who support another's plans

It is Eudemus, the physician   180
To Livia, Drusus' wife.

SEJANUS   On with your suit.
Would buy, you said—

SATRIUS   A Tribune's place, my lord.

SEJANUS
What will he give?

SATRIUS   Fifty sestertia.

SEJANUS
Livia's physician, say you, is that fellow?

SATRIUS
It is, my lord; your lordship's answer?

SEJANUS   To what?   185

SATRIUS
The place, my lord. 'Tis for a gentleman,
Your lordship will well like of, when you see him;
And one, you may make yours, by the grant.

SEJANUS
Well, let him bring his money, and his name.

SATRIUS
Thank your lordship. He shall, my lord.

SEJANUS   Come hither.   190
Know you this same Eudemus? Is he learned?

SATRIUS
Reputed so, my lord: and of deep practice.

SEJANUS
Bring him in, to me, in the gallery;
And take you cause, to leave us there, together:
I would confer with him, about a grief.—On.   195
          [*Exeunt* SEJANUS, SATRIUS, TERENTIUS, *etc.*]

ARRUNTIUS
So, yet! another? Yet? O desperate state
Of grovelling honour! Seest thou this, O sun,
And do we see thee after? Me thinks, day
Should lose his light, when men do lose their shames,
And, for the empty circumstance of life,   200
Betray their cause of living.

SILIUS   Nothing so.
Sejanus can repair, if Jove should ruin.
He is the now court-god; and well applied
With sacrifice of knees, of crooks, and cringe,
He will do more than all the house of heav'n   205
Can, for a thousand hecatombs. 'Tis he

195 *grief* ailment
204 *knees . . . cringe* kneeling, bending, bowing

Makes us our day, or night; Hell, and Elysium
Are in his look: we talk of Rhadamanth,
Furies, and fire-brands; but 'tis his frown
That is all these, where, on the adverse part,   210
His smile is more, than e're (yet) poets fained
Of bliss, and shades, nectar—

ARRUNTIUS   A serving boy?
I knew him, at Caius' trencher, when for hire,
He prostituted his abusèd body
To that great gourmand, fat Apicius;   215
And was the noted pathic of the time.

SABINUS
And, now, the second face of the whole world.
The partner of the Empire, hath his image
Reared equal with Tiberius', born in ensigns,
Commands, disposes every dignity,   220
Centurions, Tribunes, heads of provinces,
Prætors, and Consuls, all that heretofore
Rome's general suffrage gave, is now his sale.
The gain, or rather spoil, of all the earth,
One, and his house, receives.

SILIUS   He hath of late   225
Made him a strength too, strangely, by reducing
All the Prætorian bands into one camp,
Which he commands: pretending, that the soldier
By living loose, and scattered, fell to riot;
And that if any sudden enterprise   230
Should be attempted, their united strength
Would be far more, than severed; and their life
More strict, if from the city more removed.

SABINUS
Where, now, he builds, what kind of forts he please,
Is hard to court the soldier, by his name,   235
Woos, feasts the chiefest men of action,
Whose wants, not loves, compel them to be his.
And, though he ne're were liberal by kind,
Yet, to his own dark ends, he's most profuse,
Lavish, and letting fly, he cares not what   240
To his ambition.

ARRUNTIUS   Yet, hath he ambition?
Is there that step in state can make him higher?
Or more? or anything he is, but less?

SILIUS
Nothing, but Emperor.

216 *pathic* sodomite   235 *hard* persistent (or *heard?*)

ARRUNTIUS   The name Tiberius
   I hope, will keep; how e'er he hath foregone   245
   The dignity, and power.
SILIUS   Sure, while he lives.
ARRUNTIUS
   And dead, it comes to Drusus. Should he fail,
   To the brave issue of Germanicus;
   And they are three: too many (ha?) for him
   To have a plot upon?
SABINUS   I do not know   250
   The heart of his designs; but, sure, their face
   Looks farther than the present.
ARRUNTIUS   By the gods,
   If I could guess he had but such a thought,
   My sword should cleave him down from head to heart,
   But I would find it out: and with my hand   255
   I'd hurl his panting brain about the air,
   In mites, as small as atomi, to undo
   The knotted bed—
SABINUS   You are observed, Arruntius.
ARRUNTIUS
   Death! I dare tell him so; and all his spies:
   You, sir, I would, do you look? and you.
         He turns to Sejanus' clients
SABINUS   Forbear.   260

       [*Enter*] SATRIUS, EUDEMUS

SATRIUS
   Here, he will instant be; let's walk a turn.
   You're in a muse, Eudemus?
EUDEMUS   Not I, sir.
   I wonder he should mark me out so! well,
   Jove, and Apollo form it for the best.
SATRIUS
   Your fortune's made unto you now, Eudemus,   265
   If you can but lay hold upon the means;
   Do but observe his humour, and—believe it—
   He's the noblest Roman, where he takes—
   Here comes his lordship.

       [*Enter* SEJANUS]

257 *atomi* atoms

---

258 Arruntius likens Sejanus' brain to a tangled cluster of serpents; cf.
   Pericles IV.ii, 155, 'beds of eels', and *Othello* IV.ii, 64, 'for foul toads to
   knot . . . in'.

SEJANUS   Now, good Satrius.
SATRIUS
  This is the gentleman, my lord.
SEJANUS   Is this?   270
  Give me your hand, we must be more acquainted.
  Report, sir, hath spoke out your art, and learning:
  And I am glad I have so needful cause,
  (How ever in itself painful, and hard)
  To make me known to so great virtue. Look,   275
  Who's that? Satrius— [*Exit* SATRIUS] I have a grief, sir,
  That will desire your help. Your name's Eudemus?
EUDEMUS
  Yes.
SEJANUS   Sir?
EUDEMUS   It is, my lord.
SEJANUS   I hear, you are
  Physician to Livia, the Princess?
EUDEMUS
  I minister unto her, my good lord.   280
SEJANUS
  You minister to a royal lady, then.
EUDEMUS
  She is, my lord, and fair.
SEJANUS   That's understood
  Of all their sex, who are, or would be so;
  And those, that would be, physic soon can make 'em:
  For those that are, their beauties fear no colours.   285
EUDEMUS
  Your lordship is conceited.
SEJANUS   Sir, you know it.
  And can (if need be) read a learnèd lecture,
  On this, and other secrets. Pray you tell me,
  What more of ladies, besides Livia,
  Have you your patients?
EUDEMUS   Many, my good lord.   290
  The great Augusta, Urgulania,
  Mutilia Prisca, and Plancina, divers—
SEJANUS
  And, all these tell you the particulars
  Of every several grief? how first it grew,

---

272 *art* medical skill   275 *virtue* ability, power
284 *physic* (medical) treatment, especially cathartic
286 *conceited* witty

---

285 *colours* are cosmetics, with a pun on military colours.

And then increased, what action causèd that;   295
What passion that: and answer to each point
That you will put 'em.
EUDEMUS   Else, my lord, we know not
How to prescribe the remedies.
SEJANUS   Go to,
You're a subtle nation, you physicians!
And grown the only cabinets, in court,   300
To ladies' privacies. Faith which of these
Is the most pleasant lady, in her physic?
Come, you are modest now.
EUDEMUS   'Tis fit, my lord.
SEJANUS
Why, sir, I do not ask you of their urines,
Whose smells most violet? or whose siege is best?   305
Or who makes hardest faces on her stool?
Which lady sleeps with her own face, a' nights?
Which puts her teeth off, with her clothes, in court?
Or, which her hair? which her complexion?
And, in which box she puts it? These were questions   310
That might, perhaps, have put your gravity
To some defence of blush. But, I enquired,
Which was the wittiest? merriest? wantonest?
Harmless intergatories, but conceits.
Me thinks, Augusta should be most perverse,   315
And froward in her fit?
EUDEMUS   She's so, my lord.
SEJANUS
I knew it. And Mutilia the most jocund?
EUDEMUS
Tis very true, my lord.
SEJANUS   And why would you
Conceal this from me, now? Come, what's Livia?
I know, she's quick, and quaintly spirited,   320
And will have strange thoughts, when she's at leisure;
She tells 'em all to you?
EUDEMUS   My noblest lord,
He breathes not in the Empire, or on earth,
Whom I would be ambitious to serve
(In any act, that may preserve mine honour)   325
Before your lordship.

300 *cabinets* secret receptacles   305 *siege* stool
314 *intergatories* questions   *but* mere
316 *froward in her fit* difficult in temperament
320 *quaintly spirited* having unusual ideas

SEJANUS   Sir, you can lose no honour,
  By trusting ought to me. The coarsest act
  Done to my service, I can so requite,
  As all the world shall style it honourable:
  Your idle, virtuous definitions   330
  Keep honour poor, and are as scorned, as vain:
  Those deeds breathe honour, that do suck in gain.
EUDEMUS
  But, good my lord, if I should thus betray
  The counsels of my patient, and a lady's
  Of her high place, and worth; what might your lordship,   335
  (Who presently are to trust me with your own)
  Judge of my faith?
SEJANUS   Only the best, I swear.
  Say now, that I should utter you my grief;
  And with it, the true cause; that it were love;
  And love to Livia: you should tell her this?   340
  Should she suspect your faith? I would you could
  Tell me as much, from her; see, if my brain
  Could be turned jealous.
EUDEMUS   Happily, my lord,
  I could, in time, tell you as much, and more;
  So I might safely promise but the first,   345
  To her, from you.
SEJANUS   As safely, my Eudemus,
  (I now dare call thee so) as I have put
  The secret into thee.
EUDEMUS   My lord—
SEJANUS   Protest not.
  Thy looks are vows to me, use only speed,
  And but affect her with Sejanus' love,   350
  Thou art a man, made, to make Consuls. Go.
EUDEMUS
  My lord, I'll promise you a private meeting
  This day, together.
SEJANUS   Canst thou?
EUDEMUS   Yes.
SEJANUS   The place?
EUDEMUS
  My gardens, whither I shall fetch your lordship.
SEJANUS
  Let me adore my Æsculapius.   355
  Why, this indeed is physic! and outspeaks

343 *Happily* perhaps

The knowledge of cheap drugs, or any use
Can be made out of it! more comforting
Than all your opiates, juleps, apozemes,
Magistral syrups, or—Begone, my friend, 360
Not barely styled, but created so;
Expect things, greater than thy largest hopes,
To overtake thee: Fortune, shall be taught
To know how ill she hath deserved thus long,
To come behind thy wishes. Go, and speed. 365

[*Exit* EUDEMUS]

Ambition makes more trusty slaves, than need,
These fellows, by the favour of their art,
Have, still, the means to tempt, oft-times, the power.
If Livia will be now corrupted, then
Thou hast the way, Sejanus, to work out 370
His secrets, who (thou knowest) endures thee not,
Her husband Drusus: and to work against them.
Prosper it, Pallas, thou, that betterest wit;
For Venus hath the smallest share in it.

[*Enter*] TIBERIUS, DRUSUS, [*attended*]
One kneels to him

TIBERIUS
We not endure these flatteries, let him stand; 375
Our Empire, ensigns, axes, rods, and state
Take not away our human nature from us:
Look up, on us, and fall before the gods.
SEJANUS
How like a god, speaks Cæsar!
ARRUNTIUS　　　　　　　　There, observe!
He can endure that second, that's no flattery. 380
O, what is it, proud slime will not believe
Of his own worth, to hear it equal praised
Thus with the gods?
CORDUS　　　　　　He did not hear it, sir.
ARRUNTIUS
He did not? Tut, he must not, we think meanly.
'Tis your most courtly, known confederacy, 385
To have your private parasite redeem

359 *opiates ... apozemes.* Sweet medicine, infusions, concentrated potions.
376 *axes, rods.* The *fasces*, axes with rods tied about them, carried before the chief magistrates.
385f. *most courtly ... a name.* It is a most court-like, recognized arrangement, that a flatterer should restore the name that a prince declines.

What he, in public subtlety, will lose
To making him a name.

HATERIUS   Right mighty lord—

TIBERIUS
We must make up our ears, 'gainst these assaults
Of charming tongues; we pray you use, no more   390
These contumelies to us: style not us
Or lord, or mighty, who profess ourself
The servant of the Senate, and are proud
T'enjoy them our good, just, and favouring lords.

CORDUS
Rarely dissembled.

ARRUNTIUS   Prince-like, to the life.   395

SABINUS
When power, that may command, so much descends,
Their bondage, whom it stoops to, it intends.

TIBERIUS
Whence are these letters?

HATERIUS   From the Senate.

TIBERIUS   So.
Whence these?

LATIARIS   From thence too.

TIBERIUS   Are they sitting, now?

LATIARIS
They stay thy answer, Cæsar.

SILIUS   If this man   400
Had but a mind allied unto his words,
How blest a fate were it to us, and Rome?
We could not think that state, for which to change,
Although the aim were our old liberty:
The ghosts of those that fell for that, would grieve   405
Their bodies lived not, now, again to serve.
Men are deceived, who think there can be thrall
Beneath a virtuous prince. Wished liberty
Ne're lovelier looks, than under such a crown.
But, when his grace is merely but lip-good,   410
And, that no longer, than he airs himself
Abroad in public, there, to seem to shun
The strokes, and stripes of flatterers, which within
Are lechery unto him, and so feed
His brutish sense with their afflicting sound,   415
As (dead to virtue) he permits himself
Be carried like a pitcher, by the ears,

---

413 *strokes, and stripes.* Blows, as aids to carnal pleasure.

To every act of vice: this is a case
Deserves our fear, and doth presage the nigh,
And close approach of blood and tyranny.　　　　　　420
Flattery is midwife unto princes' rage:
And nothing sooner, doth help forth a tyrant,
Than that, and whisperers' grace, who have the time,
The place, the power, to make all men offenders.

ARRUNTIUS
He should be told this; and be bid dissemble　　　　425
With fools, and blind men: we that know the evil,
Should hunt the palace-rats, or give them bane;
Fright hence these worse than ravens, that devour
The quick, where they but prey upon the dead:
He shall be told it.

SABINUS　　　　　　　　Stay, Arruntius,　　　　　　430
We must abide our opportunity:
And practise what is fit, as what is needful.
It is not safe t'enforce a sovereign's ear:
Princes hear well, if they at all will hear.

ARRUNTIUS
Ha? Say you so? well. In the meantime, Jove,　　　435
(Say not, but I do call upon thee now.)
Of all wild beasts, preserve me from a tyrant;
And of all tame, a flatterer.

SILIUS　　　　　　　　　　　　'Tis well prayed.

TIBERIUS
Return the lords this voice, we are their creature:
And it is fit, a good, and honest prince,　　　　　　440
Whom they, out of their bounty, have instructed
With so dilate, and absolute a power,
Should owe the office of it, to their service;
And good of all, and every citizen.
Nor shall it e'er repent us, to have wished　　　　445
The Senate just, and favouring lords unto us,
Since their free loves do yield no less defence
T'a prince's state, than his own innocence.
Say then, there can be nothing in their thought
Shall want to please us, that hath pleasèd them;　　450
Our suffrage rather shall prevent, than stay

---

433 *enforce* approach by force
441 *instructed* provided (Latin *instructum*)
442 *dilate* enlarged　　　445 *repent* make regret
451 *prevent* anticipate (Latin *prævenio*)

436 *Say not.* Don't bring up my former complaints against you.

Behind their wills: 'tis empire, to obey
Where such, so great, so grave, so good determine.
Yet, for the suit of Spain, t'erect a temple
In honour of our mother, and ourself,   455
We must (with pardon of the Senate) not
Assent thereto. Their lordships may object
Our not denying the same late request
Unto the Asian cities: we desire
That our defence, for suffering that, be known   460
In these brief reasons, with our after purpose.
Since deified Augustus hindered not
A temple to be built, at Pergamum,
In honour of himself, and sacred Rome,
We, that have all his deeds, and words observed   465
Ever, in place of laws, the rather followed
That pleasing precedent, because, with ours,
The Senate's reverence also, there, was joined.
But, as, t'have once received it, may deserve
The gain of pardon, so, to be adored   470
With the continued style, and note of gods,
Through all the provinces, were wild ambition,
And no less pride: yea, ev'n Augustus' name
Would early vanish, should it be profaned
With such promiscuous flatteries. For our part,   475
We here protest it, and are covetous
Posterity should know it, we are mortal;
And can but deeds of men: 'twere glory enough,
Could we be truly a prince. And, they shall add
Abounding grace, unto our memory,   480
That shall report us worthy our forefathers,
Careful of your affairs, constant in dangers,
And not afraid of any private frown
For public good. These things shall be to us
Temples, and statues, reared in your minds,   485
The fairest, and most during imagery:
For those of stone, or brass, if they become
Odious in judgement of posterity,
Are more contemned, as dying sepulchres,
Than ta'en for living monuments. We then   490
Make here our suit, alike to gods, and men,
The one, until the period of our race,
T'inspire us with a free, and quiet mind,
Discerning both divine, and human laws;

460 *suffering* allowing   471 *note* ceremony
478 *can* can do   492 *period of our race* end of our life

The other, to vouchsafe us after death,   495
An honourable mention, and fair praise,
T'accompany our actions, and our name:
The rest of greatness princes may command,
And (therefore) may neglect, only, a long,
A lasting, high, and happy memory   500
They should, without being satisfied, pursue.
Contempt of fame begets contempt of virtue.

NATTA
Rare!

SATRIUS Most divine!

SEJANUS   The oracles are ceased,
That only Cæsar, with their tongue, might speak.

ARRUNTIUS
Let me be gone, most felt, and open this!   505

CORDUS
Stay.

ARRUNTIUS What? to hear more cunning, and fine words,
With their sound flattered, ere their sense be meant?

TIBERIUS
Their choice of Antium, there to place the gift
Vowed to the goddess, for our mother's health,
We will the Senate know, we fairly like;   510
As also, of their grant to Lepidus,
For his repairing the Æmilian place,
And restoration of those monuments:
Their grace too in confining of Silanus,
To th'other isle Cithera, at the suit   515
Of his religious sister, much commends
Their policy, so tempered with their mercy.
But, for the honours, which they have decreed
To our Sejanus, to advance his statue
In Pompey's theatre (whose ruining fire   520
His vigilance, and labour kept restrained

505 *felt* easily perceived
511 *grant* permission
517 *policy* wisdom

503 A reference to Plutarch *On the Cessation of Oracles* and to the tradition
that the oracles ceased upon the coming of Christ, because no one believed in them.
509 Jonson explains in a marginal note, *Fortuna equestris*, a statue given by
the Roman knights (at V, 179, 'Antium' for 'action' has been—probably
wrongly—suggested because of the association).
512 The family court of the Æmilii, to whom Lepidus belonged. Perhaps
'place' should be 'palace'.

In that one loss) they have, therein, outgone
Their own great wisdoms, by their skilful choice,
And placing of their bounties, on a man,
Whose merit more adorns the dignity,　　　　　　　　525
Than that can him: and gives a benefit,
In taking, greater, than it can receive.
Blush not, Sejanus, thou great aid of Rome,
Associate of our labours, our chief helper,
Let us not force thy simple modesty　　　　　　　　530
With offering at thy praise, for more we cannot,
Since there's no voice can take it. No man, here,
Receive our speeches, as hyperboles;
For we are far from flattering our friend,
(Let envy know) as from the need to flatter.　　　　535
Nor let them ask the causes of our praise;
Princes have still their grounds reared with themselves,
Above the poor low flats of common men,
And, who will search the reasons of their acts,
Must stand on equal bases. Lead, away.　　　　　　540
Our loves unto the Senate.

　　　　　　　　[*Exeunt* TIBERIUS, SEJANUS, *and retinue*]

ARRUNTIUS　　　　　　　Cæsar.
SABINUS　　　　　　　　　　　　Peace.
CORDUS
　　Great Pompey's theatre was never ruined
　　Till now, that proud Sejanus hath a statue
　　Reared on his ashes.
ARRUNTIUS　　　　　　Place the shame of soldiers,
　　Above the best of generals? crack the world!　　　545
　　And bruise the name of Romans into dust,
　　Ere we behold it!
SILIUS　　　　　　Check your passion;
　　Lord Drusus tarries.
DRUSUS　　　　　　Is my father mad?
　　Weary of life, and rule, lords? thus to heave
　　An idol up with praise! make him his mate!　　　550
　　His rival in the Empire!
ARRUNTIUS　　　　　　O, good prince!

533 *hyperboles* exaggerations
551 *rival* partner

530f. *Let us . . . take it.* Don't let me do violence to your unfeigned modesty
　　with attempting to praise you; more than attempt I cannot do, since no
　　voice can adequately perform the task.
537f. *Princes have . . . common men.* Princes stand on a firmament suitably
　　high, above the lower ground of the commonality.

DRUSUS

Allow him statues? titles? honours? such,
As he himself refuseth?

ARRUNTIUS　　　　　　　　　Brave, brave Drusus!

DRUSUS

The first ascents to sovereignty are hard
But, entered once, there never wants or means,　　　　555
Or ministers, to help th'aspirer on.

ARRUNTIUS

True, gallant Drusus.

DRUSUS　　　　　　　　We must shortly pray
To modesty, that he will rest contented—

ARRUNTIUS

Ay, where he is, and not write emperor.

　　　　　SEJANUS, [LATIARIS,] etc.

　　　　He enters, followed with clients

SEJANUS

There is your bill, and yours; bring you your man:　　　560
I have moved for you, too, Latiaris.

DRUSUS　　　　　　　　　What?
Is your vast greatness grown so blindly bold,
That you will over us?

SEJANUS　　　　　　Why, then give way.

DRUSUS

Give way, Colossus? Do you lift? Advance you?
Take that.

　　　　　Drusus strikes him

ARRUNTIUS

　　　　　Good! brave! excellent brave Prince!　　　565

DRUSUS

Nay, come, approach. What? stand you off? at gaze?
It looks too full of death, for thy cold spirits.
Avoid mine eye, dull camel, or my sword
Shall make thy bravery fitter for a grave,
Than for a triumph. I'll advance a statue,　　　　570
Of your own bulk; but 't shall be on the cross:
Where I will nail your pride, at breadth, and length,
And crack those sinews, which are yet but stretched
With your swoll'n fortune's rage.

ARRUNTIUS　　　　　　　　A noble prince!

561 *moved* interceded
563 *over* overmaster
564 *lift* rise (like a rearing horse)
566 *at gaze* in bewilderment (like a hunted animal)

ALL

A Castor, a Castor, a Castor, a Castor!   575

                 [*Exeunt, leaving* SEJANUS]

SEJANUS

He that, with such wrong moved, can bear it through
With patience, and an even mind, knows how
To turn it back. Wrath, covered, carries fate:
Revenge is lost, if I profess my hate.
What was my practice late, I'll now pursue   580
As my fell justice. This hath styled it new.   [*Exit*]

CHORUS—OF MUSICIANS

Act II, [Scene i]

[*Eudemus' garden. Enter*] SEJANUS, LIVIA, EUDEMUS

SEJANUS

Physician, thou art worthy of a province,
For the great favours done unto our loves;
And, but that greatest Livia bears a part
In the requital of thy services,
I should alone, despair of ought, like means,   5
To give them worthy satisfaction.

LIVIA

Eudemus, (I will see it) shall receive
A fit, and full reward, for his large merit.
But for this potion, we intend to Drusus,
(No more our husband, now) whom shall we choose   10
As the most apt, and abled instrument,
To minister it to him?

EUDEMUS   I say, Lygdus.

SEJANUS

Lygdus? what's he?

LIVIA   An eunuch Drusus loves.

EUDEMUS

Ay, and his cup-bearer.

SEJANUS   Name not a second.
If Drusus love him, and he have that place,   15
We cannot think a fitter.

EUDEMUS   True, my lord,
For free access, and trust, are two main aids.

    5 *like* equal, adequate

SEJANUS
  Skilful physician!
LIVIA   But he must be wrought
  To th'undertaking, with some laboured art.
SEJANUS
  Is he ambitious?
LIVIA   No.
SEJANUS   Or covetous?   20
LIVIA
  Neither.
EUDEMUS Yet, gold is a good general charm.
SEJANUS
  What is he then?
LIVIA   Faith, only wanton, light.
SEJANUS
  How! Is he young? and fair?
EUDEMUS   A delicate youth.
SEJANUS
  Send him to me, I'll work him. Royal lady,
  Though I have loved you long, and with that height   25
  Of zeal, and duty, (like the fire, which more
  It mounts, it trembles) thinking nought could add
  Unto the fervour, which your eye had kindled;
  Yet, now I see your wisdom, judgement, strength,
  Quickness, and will, to apprehend the means   30
  To your own good, and greatness, I protest
  Myself through rarefied, and turned all flame
  In your affection: such a spirit as yours,
  Was not created for the idle second
  To a poor flash, as Drusus; but to shine   35
  Bright, as the moon, among the lesser lights,
  And share the sovereignty of all the world.
  Then Livia triumphs in her proper sphere,
  When she, and her Sejanus shall divide
  The name of Cæsar; and Augusta's star   40
  Be dimmed with glory of a brighter beam:
  When Agrippina's fires are quite extinct,
  And the scarce-seen Tiberius borrows all
  His little light from us, whose folded arms
  Shall make one perfect orb. Who's that? Eudemus,   45
  Look, 'tis not Drusus? [*Exit* EUDEMUS] Lady, do not fear.
LIVIA
  Not I, my lord. My fear, and love of him
  Left me at once.

  32 *through rarefied* entirely refined, purified

SEJANUS   Illustrous lady! stay—

[*Enter* EUDEMUS]

EUDEMUS
I'll tell his lordship.
SEJANUS   Who is't, Eudemus?
EUDEMUS
One of your lordship's servants, brings you word   50
The Emperor hath sent for you.
SEJANUS   O! where is he?
With your fair leave, dear Princess. I'll but ask
A question, and return.
                He goes out
EUDEMUS   Fortunate Princess!
How you are blest in the fruition
Of this unequalled man, this soul of Rome,   55
The Empire's life, and voice of Cæsar's world!
LIVIA
So blessed, my Eudemus, as to know
The bliss I have, with what I ought to owe
The means that wrought it. How do I look today?
EUDEMUS
Excellent clear, believe it. This same fucus   60
Was well laid on.
LIVIA   Me thinks, 'tis here not white.
EUDEMUS
Lend me your scarlet, lady, 'Tis the sun
Hath giv'n some little taint unto the ceruse,
You should have used of the white oil I gave you.
Sejanus, for your love! his very name   65
Commandeth above Cupid, or his shafts—
(LIVIA
Nay, now you've made it worse.
EUDEMUS   I'll help it straight.)
And, but pronounced, is a sufficient charm
Against all rumour; and of absolute power
To satisfy for any lady's honour.   70
(LIVIA
What do you now, Eudemus?
EUDEMUS   Make a light fucus,
To touch you o'er withal.) Honoured Sejanus!
What act (though ne'er so strange, and insolent)

48 *Illustrous* illustrious   54 *fruition* enjoyment (Latin *fruor*)
60 *fucus* cosmetic, face-wash
63 *ceruse* cosmetic of white lead

But that addition will at least bear out,
If't do not expiate?
LIVIA   Here, good physician.   75
EUDEMUS
I like this study to preserve the love
Of such a man, that comes not every hour
To greet the world. ('Tis now well, lady, you should
Use of the dentifrice, I prescribed you, too,
To clear your teeth, and the prepared pomatum,   80
To smooth the skin:) A lady cannot be
Too curious of her form, that still would hold
The heart of such a person, made her captive,
As you have his: who, to endear him more
In your clear eye, hath put away his wife,   85
The trouble of his bed, and your delights,
Fair Apicata, and made spacious room
To your new pleasures.
LIVIA   Have not we returned
That, with our hate of Drusus, and discovery
Of all his counsels?
EUDEMUS   Yes, and wisely, lady,   90
The ages that succeed, and stand far off
To gaze at your high prudence, shall admire
And reckon it an act, without your sex:
It hath that rare appearance. Some will think
Your fortune could not yield a deeper sound,   95
Than mixed with Drusus'; but, when they shall hear
That, and the thunder of Sejanus meet,
Sejanus, whose high name doth strike the stars,
And rings about the concave, great Sejanus,
Whose glories, style, and titles are himself,   100
The often iterating of Sejanus:
They then will lose their thoughts, and be ashamed
To take acquaintance of them.

[*Enter* SEJANUS]

SEJANUS   I must make
A rude departure, lady. Cæsar sends
With all his haste both of command, and prayer.   105
Be resolute in our plot; you have my soul,

74 *addition* title   82 *curious* careful (Latin *cura*)
93 *without* outside   95 *sound* sounding, measure of depth
104 *rude* early (Latin *rudis*)

88f. *Have not . . . his counsels?* Have not you and I justified Sejanus' actions
in our favour by telling him Drusus' secrets?

As certain yours, as it is my body's.
And, wise physician, so prepare the poison
As you may lay the subtle operation
Upon some natural disease of his. 110
Your eunuch send to me. I kiss your hands,
Glory of ladies, and commend my love
To your best faith, and memory.
LIVIA   My lord,
I shall but change your words. Farewell. Yet, this
Remember for your heed, he loves you not; 115
You know, what I have told you: his designs
Are full of grudge, and danger: we must use
More than a common speed.
SEJANUS   Excellent lady,
How you do fire my blood!
LIVIA   Well, you must go?
The thoughts be best, are least set forth to show. 120
                                        [*Exit* SEJANUS]

EUDEMUS
When will you take some physic, lady?
LIVIA   When
I shall, Eudemus: but let Drusus' drug
Be first prepared.
EUDEMUS   Were Lygdus made, that's done;
I have it ready. And tomorrow morning,
I'll send you a perfume, first to resolve, 125
And procure sweat, and then prepare a bath
To cleanse, and clear the cutis; against when,
I'll have an excellent new fucus made,
Resistive 'gainst the sun, the rain, or wind,
Which you shall lay on with a breath, or oil, 130
As you best like, and last some fourteen hours.
This change came timely, lady, for your health;
And the restoring your complexion,
Which Drusus' choler had almost burnt up:
Wherein your fortune hath prescribed you better 135
Than art could do.
LIVIA   Thanks, good physician,
I'll use my fortune (you shall see) with reverence.
Is my coach ready?
EUDEMUS   It attends your highness.   [*Exeunt*]

109 *lay* blame, attribute
114 *change* exchange, repeat
123 *made* prepared
127 *cutis* skin

[Act II, Scene ii]

[An apartment in the palace. Enter] SEJANUS

SEJANUS
If this be not revenge, when I have done
And made it perfect, let Egyptian slaves,   140
Parthians, and bare-foot Hebrews brand my face,
And print my body full of injuries.
Thou lost thyself, child Drusus, when thou thought's
Thou could'st outskip my vengeance: or outstand
The power I had to crush thee into air.   145
Thy follies now shall taste what kind of man
They have provoked, and this thy father's house
Crack in the flame of my incensèd rage,
Whose fury shall admit no shame, or mean.
Adultery? it is the lightest ill,   150
I will commit. A race of wicked acts
Shall flow out of my anger, and o'erspread
The world's wide face, which no posterity
Shall e'er approve, nor yet keep silent: things,
That for their cunning, close, and cruel mark,   155
Thy father would wish his; and shall (perhaps)
Carry the empty name, but we the prize.
On then, my soul, and start not in thy course;
Though heav'n drop sulphur, and hell belch out fire,
Laugh at the idle terrors: tell proud Jove,   160
Between his power, and thine, there is no odds.
'Twas only fear, first, in the world made gods.

[Enter] TIBERIUS *[and retinue]*

TIBERIUS
Is yet Sejanus come?
SEJANUS   He's here, dread Cæsar.
TIBERIUS
Let all depart that chamber, and the next: *[Exit retinue]*
Sit down, my comfort. When the master-prince   165

---

143 *child* prince
144 *outstand* withstand
148 *incensèd* kindled (Latin *incendo*)
158 *start* leap aside

140f. *Egyptian . . . Hebrews.* Races which gave homage to Rome, and thus
    humiliating for a Roman to be wounded by.

Of all the world, Sejanus, saith, he fears;
Is it not fatal?
SEJANUS   Yes, to those are feared.
TIBERIUS
And not to him?
SEJANUS   Not, if he wisely turn
That part of fate he holdeth, first on them.
TIBERIUS
That nature, blood, and laws of kind forbid.   170
SEJANUS
Do policy, and state forbid it?
TIBERIUS   No.
SEJANUS
The rest of poor respects, then, let go by:
State is enough to make th'act just, them guilty.
TIBERIUS
Long hate pursues such acts.
SEJANUS   Whom hatred frights,
Let him not dream on sovereignty.
TIBERIUS   Are rites   175
Of faith, love, piety, to be trod down?
Forgotten? and made vain?
SEJANUS   All for a crown.
The prince, who shames a tyrant's name to bear,
Shall never dare do anything, but fear;
All the command of sceptres quite doth perish   180
If it begin religious thoughts to cherish:
Whole empires fall, swayed by those nice respects.
It is the licence of dark deeds protects
Ev'n states most hated: when no laws resist
The sword, but that it acteth what it list.   185
TIBERIUS
Yet so, we may do all things cruelly,
Not safely:
SEJANUS   Yes, and do them thoroughly.
TIBERIUS
Knows yet, Sejanus, whom we point at?
SEJANUS   Ay,
Or else my thought, my sense, or both do err:
'Tis Agrippina?
TIBERIUS   She; and her proud race.   190

171 *state* statecraft
172 *respects* scruples

---

188 *Ay* might be emended *sir* to preserve the rhyme.

SEJANUS
> Proud? dangerous, Cæsar. For in them apace
> The father's spirit shoots up. Germanicus
> Lives in their looks, their gait, their form, t'upbraid us
> With his close death, if not revenge the same.

TIBERIUS
> The act's not known.

SEJANUS   Not proved. But whispering fame   195
> Knowledge, and proof doth to the jealous give,
> Who, than to fail, would their own thought believe.
> It is not safe, the children draw long breath,
> That are provokèd by a parent's death.

TIBERIUS
> It is as dangerous, to make them hence,   200
> If nothing but their birth be their offence.

SEJANUS
> Stay, till they strike at Cæsar: then their crime
> Will be enough, but late, and out of time
> For him to punish.

TIBERIUS   Do they purpose it?

SEJANUS
> You know, sir, thunder speaks not till it hit.   205
> Be not secure: none swiftlier are oppressed,
> Than they, whom confidence betrays to rest.
> Let not your daring make your danger such:
> All power's to be feared, where 'tis too much.
> The youths are (of themselves) hot, violent,   210
> Full of great thought; and that male-spirited dame,
> Their mother, slacks no means to put them on,
> By large allowance, popular presentings,
> Increase of train, and state, suing for titles,
> Hath them commended with like prayers, like vows,   215
> To the same gods, with Cæsar: days and nights
> She spends in banquets, and ambitious feasts
> For the nobility; where Caius Silius,
> Titius Sabinus, old Arruntius,
> Asinius Gallus, Furnius, Regulus,   220
> And others, of that discontented list,
> Are the prime guests. There, and to these, she tells
> Whose niece she was, whose daughter, and whose wife,
> And then must they compare her with Augusta,

194 *close* secret   195 *fame* rumour (Latin *fama*)
197 *than to fail* rather than do without proof   212 *slacks* spares
213 *large allowance* 'free rein'
223 *niece* granddaughter (Latin *neptis*)

Ay, and prefer her too, commend her form, 225
Extol her fruitfulness; at which a show'r
Falls for the memory of Germanicus,
Which they blow over straight, with windy praise,
And puffing hopes of her aspiring sons:
Who, with these hourly ticklings, grow so pleased, 230
And wantonly conceited of themselves,
As now, they stick not to believe they're such,
As these do give 'em out: and would be thought
(More than competitors) immediate heirs.
Whilst to their thirst of rule they win the rout 235
(That's still the friend of novelty) with hope
Of future freedom, which on every change,
That greedily, though emptily, expects.
Cæsar, 'tis age in all things breeds neglects,
And princes that will keep old dignity, 240
Must not admit too youthful heirs stand by;
Not their own issue: but so darkly set
As shadows are in picture, to give height,
And lustre to themselves.

TIBERIUS   We will command
Their rank thoughts down, and with a stricter hand 245
Than we have yet put forth, their trains must bate,
Their titles, feasts and factions.

SEJANUS   Or your state.
But how sir, will you work?

TIBERIUS   Confine 'em,

SEJANUS   No.
They are too great, and that too faint a blow,
To give them now: it would have served at first, 250
When, with the weakest touch, their knot had burst.
But, now, your care must be, not to detect
The smallest cord, or line of your suspect,
For such, who know the weight of princes' fear,
Will, when they find themselves discovered, rear 255
Their forces, like seen snakes, that else would lie
Rolled in their circles, close: nought is more high,
Daring, or desperate, than offenders found;
Where guilt is, rage, and courage both abound.
The course must be, to let 'em still swell up, 260
Riot, and surfeit on blind Fortune's cup;
Give 'em more place, more dignities, more style,

246 *trains* ruses (frequent)   *bate* abate
252 *detect* reveal   253 *suspect* suspicion
259 *both* Q (F doth)

Call 'em to court, to Senate: in the while,
Take from their strength some one or twain, or more
Of the main fautors; (it will fright the store)   265
And, by some by-occasion. Thus, with slight
You shall disarm them first, and they (in night
Of their ambition) not perceive the train,
Till, in the engine, they are caught, and slain.

TIBERIUS
We would not kill, if we knew how to save;   270
Yet, than a throne, 'tis cheaper give a grave.
Is there no way to bind them by deserts?

SEJANUS
Sir, wolves do change their hair, but not their hearts.
While thus your thought unto a mean is tied,
You neither dare enough, nor do provide.   275
All modesty is fond; and chiefly where
The subject is no less compelled to bear,
Than praise his sovereign's acts.

TIBERIUS   We can no longer
Keep on our mask to thee, our dear Sejanus;
Thy thoughts are ours, in all, and we but proved   280
Their voice, in our designs, which by assenting
Hath more confirmed us, than if heartening Jove
Had, from his hundred statues, bid us strike,
And at the stroke clicked all his marble thumbs.
But, who shall first be struck?

SEJANUS   First, Caius Silius;   285
He is the most of mark, and most of danger:
In power, and reputation equal strong,
Having commanded an imperial army
Seven years together, vanquished Sacrovir
In Germany, and thence obtained to wear   290
The ornaments triumphal. His steep fall,
By how much it doth give the weightier crack,

265 *fautors* supporters   *store* largest part, remainder
266 *by-occasion* incidental opportunity   267 *them* Q (F *omits*)
272 *bind them by deserts* gain their loyalty by favours
275 *provide* use foresight (Latin *provideo*)
276 *modesty* holding to a middle way
     fond foolish
280 *proved* tested   292 *crack* sound

284 *clicked all his marble thumbs.* Gave the gesture that meant a defeated
     gladiator was to be condemned; approved the sentence of death.
291 *ornaments triumphal.* Devices and garments worn by victorious generals,
     in place of the traditional triumph or procession through Rome, at this
     time reserved to the royal family.

Will send more wounding terror to the rest,
Command them stand aloof, and give more way
To our surprising of the principal.   295
TIBERIUS
But what, Sabinus?
SEJANUS   Let him grow awhile,
His fate is not yet ripe: we must not pluck
At all together, lest we catch ourselves.
And there's Arruntius too, he only talks.
But Sosia, Silius' wife, would be wound in   300
Now, for she hath a fury in her breast
More, than hell ever knew; and would be sent
Thither in time. Then, is there one Cremutius
Cordus, a writing fellow, they have got
To gather notes of the precedent times,   305
And make them into annals; a most tart
And bitter spirit (I hear) who, under colour
Of praising those, doth tax the present state,
Censures the men, the actions, leaves no trick.
No practice unexamined, parallels   310
The times, the governments, a professed champion,
For the old liberty—
TIBERIUS   A perishing wretch.
As if there were that'chaos bred in things,
That laws, and liberty would not rather choose
To be quite broken, and ta'en hence by us,   315
Than have the stain to be preserved by such.
Have we the means, to make these guilty, first?
SEJANUS
Trust that to me: let Cæsar, by his power,
But cause a formal meeting of the Senate,
I will have matter, and accusers ready.   320
TIBERIUS
But how? let us consult.
SEJANUS   We shall misspend
The time of action. Counsels are unfit
In business, where all rest is more pernicious
Than rashness can be. Acts of this close kind
Thrive more by execution, than advice.   325
There is no lingering in that work begun,
Which cannot praisèd be, until through done.
TIBERIUS
Our edict shall, forthwith, command a court.

300 *wound in* ensnared

While I can live, I will prevent earth's fury:
Ἐμοῦ θανόντος γαῖα μιχθήτω πυρί.   [*Exit*]   330

[*Enter*] POSTHUMUS

POSTHUMUS
My lord Sejanus—
SEJANUS   Julius Posthumus,
Come with my wish! what news from Agrippina's?
POSTHUMUS
Faith none. They all lock up themselves a' late;
Or talk in character: I have not seen
A company so changed. Except they had   335
Intelligence by augury of our practice.
SEJANUS
When were you there?
POSTHUMUS   Last night.
SEJANUS   And what guests found you?
POSTHUMUS
Sabinus, Silius, (the old list,) Arruntius,
Furnius, and Gallus.
SEJANUS   Would not these talk?
POSTHUMUS   Little.
And yet we offered choice of argument.   340
Satrius was with me.
SEJANUS   Well: 'tis guilt enough
Their often meeting. You forgot t'extol
The hospitable lady?
POSTHUMUS   No, that trick
Was well put home, and had succeeded too,
But that Sabinus caught a caution out;   345
For she began to swell:
SEJANUS   And may she burst.
Julius, I would have you go instantly,
Unto the palace of the great Augusta,
And, (by your kindest friend,) get swift access;
Acquaint her, with these meetings: tell the words   350
You brought me, (th'other day) of Silius,
Add somewhat to 'em. Make her understand
The danger of Sabinus, and the times,

334 *character* secret code   340 *argument* topic
345 *caught a caution out* gave warning

330 Translated by Milton, *Reason of Church Government*, I, v, 'When I die,
    let the earth be rolled in flames'. The Greek was a favourite phrase of
    Tiberius, from a lost source.
349 *kindest friend.* Jonson's marginal note explains, *Mutilia Prisca.*

Out of his closeness. Give Arruntius words
Of malice against Cæsar; so, to Gallus: 355
But (above all) to Agrippina. Say,
(As you may truly) that her infinite pride,
Propped with the hopes of her too fruitful womb,
With popular studies gapes for sovereignty;
And threatens Cæsar. Pray Augusta then,   360
That for her own, great Cæsar's, and the pub-
Lic safety, she be pleased to urge these dangers.
Cæsar is too secure (he must be told,
And best he'll take it from a mother's tongue.)
Alas! what is't for us to sound, t'explore,   365
To watch, oppose, plot, practise, or prevent,
If he, for whom it is so strongly laboured,
Shall, out of greatness, and free spirit, be
Supinely negligent? Our city's now
Divided as in time o'th' civil war,   370
And men forbear not to declare themselves
Of Agrippina's party. Every day,
The faction multiplies; and will do more
If not resisted: you can best enlarge it
As you find audience. Noble Posthumus,   375
Commend me to your Prisca: and pray her,
She will solicit this great business
To earnest, and most present execution,
With all her utmost credit with Augusta.

POSTHUMUS

I shall not fail in my instructions.   [*Exit*]   380

SEJANUS

This second (from his mother) will well urge
Our late design, and spur on Cæsar's rage:
Which else might grow remiss. The way, to put
A prince in blood, is to present the shapes
Of dangers, greater than they are (like late,   385
Or early shadows) and, sometimes, to feign
Where there are none, only, to make him fear;

354 *Give* attribute to
359 *studies* support (Latin *popularibus studiis*)
    gapes for covets

---

361 *pub-/Lic*. Herford and Simpson cite parallels for this 'ugly enjambment'
    from Jonson and his contemporaries; but the device is actually an overt
    classicism (*synapheia*), and appropriate references should include, e.g.,
    Horace, *Odes* I, 2, 18–19; I, 25, 11–12; II, 16, 7–8, and Catullus, 11,
    11–12; 61, 82–83.
374f. *you can best . . . find audience.* You can best embroider the story accord-
    ing to your audience.

His fear will make him cruel: and once entered,
He doth not easily learn to stop, or spare
Where he may doubt. This have I made my rule, 390
To thrust Tiberius into tyranny,
And make him toil, to turn aside those blocks,
Which I alone, could not remove with safety.
Drusus once gone, Germanicus' three sons
Would clog my way; whose guards have too much faith 395
To be corrupted: and their mother known
Of too too unreproved a chastity,
To be attempted, as light Livia was.
Work then, my art, on Cæsar's fears, as they
On those they fear, till all my lets be cleared: 400
And he in ruins of his house, and hate
Of all his subjects, bury his own state:
When, with my peace, and safety, I will rise,
By making him the public sacrifice.   [*Exit*]

[Act II, Scene iii]

[Agrippina's house. Enter] SATRIUS, NATTA

SATRIUS
They're grown exceeding circumspect, and wary. 405
NATTA
They have us in the wind: and yet, Arruntius
Cannot contain himself.
SATRIUS   Tut, he's not yet
Looked after, there are others more desired,
That are more silent.
NATTA   Here he comes. Away.   [*Exeunt*]

[Enter] SABINUS, ARRUNTIUS, CORDUS

SABINUS
How is it, that these beagles haunt the house 410
Of Agrippina?
ARRUNTIUS   O, they hunt, they hunt.
There is some game here lodged, which they must rouse,
To make the great one's sport.
CORDUS   Did you observe
How they inveighed 'gainst Cæsar?
ARRUNTIUS   Ay, baits, baits,
For us to bite at: would I have my flesh 415

400 *lets* Q (F betts)
408 *Looked after* sought for

Torn by the public hook, these qualified hang-men
Should be my company.

CORDUS   Here comes another.

[AFER *passeth by*]

ARRUNTIUS
Ay, there's a man, Afer the orator!
One, that hath phrases, figures, and fine flowers,
To strew his rhetoric with, and doth make haste   420
To get him note, or name, by any offer
Where blood, or gain be objects; steeps his words,
When he would kill, in artificial tears:
The crocodile of Tiber! him I love,
That man is mine. He hath my heart, and voice,   425
When I would curse, he, he.

SABINUS   Contemn the slaves,
Their present lives will be their future graves.   [*Exeunt*]

[*Enter*] SILIUS, AGRIPPINA, NERO, SOSIA

SILIUS
May't please your highness not forget yourself,
I dare not, with my manners, to attempt
Your trouble farther.

AGRIPPINA   Farewell, noble Silius.   430

SILIUS
Most royal Princess.

AGRIPPINA   Sosia stays with us?

SILIUS
She is your servant, and doth owe your grace
An honest, but unprofitable love.

AGRIPPINA
How can that be, when there's no gain, but virtue's?

SILIUS
You take the moral, not the politic sense.   435
I meant, as she is bold, and free of speech,
Earnest to utter what her zealous thought
Travails withal, in honour of your house;
Which act, as it is simply born in her,
Partakes of love, and honesty, but may,   440
By th'over-often, and unseasoned use,
Turn to your loss, and danger: for your state

419 *figures . . . flowers* turns of rhetorical speech
429 *manners* usual behaviour   *attempt* vex with afflictions
434 *virtue's* Q (F vertuous)

---

416 *public hook*. Executed criminals were dragged to the Gemonies by the
executioner's hook, and thence three days after to the Tiber.

Is waited on by envies, as by eyes;
And every second guest your tables take,
Is a fee'd spy, t'observe who goes, who comes,   445
What conference you have, with whom. where, when,
What the discourse is, what the looks, the thoughts
Of every person there, they do extract,
And make into a substance.

AGRIPPINA   Hear me, Silius,
Were all Tiberius' body stuck with eyes,   450
And every wall, and hanging in my house
Transparent, as this lawn I wear, or air;
Yea, had Sejanus both his ears as long
As to my inmost closet: I would hate
To whisper any thought, or change an act,   455
To be made Juno's rival. Virtue's forces
Show ever noblest in conspicuous courses.

SILIUS
'Tis great, and bravely spoken, like the spirit
Of Agrippina: yet, your highness knows,
There is nor loss, nor shame in providence: 460
Few can, what all should do, beware enough.
You may perceive with what officious face,
Satrius, and Natta, Afer, and the rest
Visit your house, of late, t'enquire the secrets;
And with what bold, and privileged art, they rail   465
Against Augusta: yea, and at Tiberius,
Tell tricks of Livia, and Sejanus, all
T'excite, and call your indignation on,
That they might hear it at more liberty.

AGRIPPINA
You're too suspicious, Silius.

SILIUS   Pray the gods,   470
I be so Agrippina: but I fear
Some subtle practice. They, that durst to strike
At so exambled a life,
As, that of the renowned Germanicus,
Will not sit down, with that exploit alone: 475
He threatens many, that hath injured one.

NERO
'Twere best rip forth their tongues, sear out their eyes,
When next they come.

SOSIA   A fit reward for spies.

[Enter] DRUSUS JUNIOR

449 AGRIPPINA edd. (Q, F ARR.)   460 *providence* careful foresight

DRUSUS JUNIOR
  Hear you the rumour?
AGRIPPINA   What?
DRUSUS JUNIOR   Drusus is dying.
AGRIPPINA
  Dying?
NERO   That's strange!
AGRIPPINA   You were with him, yesternight.   480
DRUSUS JUNIOR
  One met Eudemus, the physician,
  Sent for, but now: who thinks he cannot live.
SILIUS
  Thinks? if't be arrived at that, he knows,
  Or none.
AGRIPPINA   This's quick! what should be his disease?
SILIUS
  Poison. Poison—
AGRIPPINA   How, Silius!
NERO   What's that?   485
SILIUS
  Nay, nothing. There was (late) a certain blow
  Giv'n on the face.
NERO   Ay, to Sejanus?
SILIUS   True.
DRUSUS JUNIOR
  And, what of that?
SILIUS   I'm glad I gave it not.
NERO
  But, there is somewhat else?
SILIUS   Yes, private meetings,
  With a great lady, at a physician's,   490
  And, a wife turned away—
NERO   Ha!
SILIUS   Toys, mere toys:
  What wisdom's now i'th' streets? i'th' common mouth?
DRUSUS JUNIOR
  Fears, whisperings, tumults, noise, I know not what:
  They say, the Senate sit.
SILIUS   I'll thither, straight;
  And see what's in the forge.
AGRIPPINA   Good Silius do.   495
  Sosia, and I will in.

479 *rumour* popular report
480 *You were* one syllable (F yo' were)
484 *should be* is said to be

SILIUS   Haste you, my lords,
  To visit the sick Prince: tender your loves,
  And sorrows to the people. This Sejanus
  (Trust my divining soul) hath plots on all:
  No tree, that stops his prospect, but must fall. [*Exeunt*]   500

CHORUS—OF MUSICIANS

[Act III, Scene i]

The Senate. [*Enter*] SEJANUS, VARRO, LATIARIS. COTTA,
  AFER. [SABINUS] GALLUS, LEPIDUS, ARRUNTIUS.
            PRÆCONES, LICTORES

SEJANUS
  'Tis only you must urge against him, Varro,
  Nor I, nor Cæsar may appear therein,
  Except in your defence, who are the Consul:
  And, under colour of late enmity
  Between your father, and his, may better do it,   5
  As free from all suspicion of a practice.
  Here be your notes, what points to touch at; read:
  Be cunning in them. Afer has them too.

VARRO
  But he is summoned?

SEJANUS   No. It was debated
  By Cæsar, and concluded as most fit   10
  To take him unprepared.

AFER   And prosecute
  All under name of treason.

VARRO   I conceive.

SABINUS
  Drusus being dead, Cæsar will not be here.

GALLUS
  What should the business of this Senate be?

ARRUNTIUS
  That can my subtle whisperers tell you: we,   15
  That are the good-dull-noble lookers on,

500 *prospect* view (Latin *prospectus*), with a pun on 'future oppor-
      tunities'
s.d. SABINUS edd. (F *omits*)
  11 *take him* Q (F him take)

---

  5 *and his*. Should be *and him*, for Silius superseded Varro's father in the
      war against Sacrovir. In the Roman view, this personal element would
      have guaranteed Varro's sincerity.

Are only called to keep the marble warm.
What should we do with those deep mysteries,
Proper to these fine heads? let them alone.
Our ignorance may, perchance, help us be saved   20
From whips, and furies.

GALLUS   See, see, see, their action!

ARRUNTIUS
Ay, now their heads do travail, now they work;
Their faces run like shuttles, they are weaving
Some curious cobweb to catch flies.

SABINUS   Observe,
They take their places.

ARRUNTIUS   What so low?

GALLUS   O yes,   25
They must be seen to flatter Cæsar's grief
Though but in sitting.

VARRO   Bid us silence.

PRÆCO   Silence.

VARRO
Fathers Conscript, may this our present meeting
Turn fair, and fortunate to the Commonwealth.

                    [*Enter*] SILIUS, SENATE

SEJANUS
See, Silius enters.

SILIUS   Hail grave Fathers.

LICTOR   Stand.   30
Silius, forbear thy place.

SENATORS   How!

PRÆCO   Silius stand forth,
The Consul hath to charge thee.

LICTOR   Room for Cæsar.

ARRUNTIUS
Is he come too? nay then expect a trick.

SABINUS
Silius accused? sure he will answer nobly.

                    [*Enter*] TIBERIUS, [*etc.*]

TIBERIUS
We stand amazed, Fathers, to behold   35
This general dejection. Wherefore sit
Rome's Consuls thus dissolved, as they had lost

30 SEJANUS Q (F *omits*)
   Stand stay where you are
37 *dissolved* neglectful (Latin *dissolutus*)

All the remembrance both of style, and place?
It not becomes. No woes are of fit weight,
To make the honour of the Empire stoop: 40
Though I, in my peculiar self, may meet
Just reprehension, that so suddenly,
And, in so fresh a grief, would greet the Senate,
When private tongues, of kinsmen, and allies,
(Inspired with comforts) loathly are endured,   45
The face of men not seen, and scarce the day,
To thousands, that communicate our loss.
Nor can I argue these of weakness; since
They take but natural ways: yet I must seek
For stronger aids, and those fair helps draw out   50
From warm embraces of the Commonwealth.
Our mother, great Augusta, is struck with time,
Ourself impressed with agèd characters,
Drusus is gone, his children young, and babes,
Our aims must now reflect on those, that may   55
Give timely succour to these present ills,
And are our only glad-surviving hopes,
The noble issue of Germanicus,
Nero, and Drusus: might it please the Consul
Honour them in, (they both attend without.)   60
I would present them to the Senate's care,
And raise those suns of joy, that should drink up
These floods of sorrow, in your drownèd eyes.

ARRUNTIUS
By Jove, I am not Œdipus enough,
To understand this Sphinx.

SABINUS   The Princes come.   65

[*Enter*] NERO, DRUSUS JUNIOR

TIBERIUS
Approach you noble Nero, noble Drusus,
These Princes, Fathers, when their parent died,
I gave unto their uncle, with this prayer,
That, though he'd proper issue of his own,
He would no less bring up, and foster these,   70
Than that self-blood; and by that act confirm
Their worths to him, and to posterity:
Drusus ta'en hence, I turn my prayers to you,
And, 'fore our country, and our gods, beseech

41 *peculiar* private (frequent)
47 *communicate* share (Latin *communico*)
68 *uncle* Drusus senior (not strictly their uncle)

You take, and rule Augustus' nephew's sons,   75
Sprung of the noblest ancestors; and so
Accomplish both my duty, and your own.
Nero, and Drusus, these shall be to you
In place of parents, these your fathers, these,
And not unfitly: for you are so born,   80
As all your good, or ill's the Commonwealth's.
Receive them, you strong guardians; and blest gods,
Make all their actions answer to their bloods:
Let their great titles find increase by them,
Not they by titles. Set them, as in place,   85
So in example, above all the Romans:
And may they know no rivals, but themselves.
Let Fortune give them nothing; but attend
Upon their virtue: and that still come forth
Greater than hope, and better than their fame.   90
Relieve me, Fathers, with your general voice.

SENATORS
May all the gods consent to Cæsar's wish,
And add to any honours, that may crown
The hopeful issue of Germanicus.

TIBERIUS
We thank you, reverend Fathers, in their right.   95

ARRUNTIUS
If this were true now! but the space, the space
Between the breast, and lips—Tiberius' heart
Lies a thought farther, than another man's.

TIBERIUS
My comforts are so flowing in my joys,
As, in them, all my streams of grief are lost,   100
No less than are land-waters in the sea,
Or showers in rivers; though their cause was such,
As might have sprinkled ev'n the gods with tears:
Yet since the greater doth embrace the less,
We covetously obey.

(ARRUNTIUS   Well acted, Cæsar.)   105

TIBERIUS
And, now I am the happy witness made
Of your so much desired affections,
To this great issue, I could wish, the fates
Would here set peaceful period to my days;

105 *covetously* eagerly

---

93 Jonson adds in the margin, *A form of speaking they had*, and after III,
142, *Another form.*

However, to my labours, I entreat   110
(And beg it of this Senate) some fit ease.
(ARRUNTIUS
  Laugh, Fathers, laugh: have you no spleens about you?)
TIBERIUS
  The burden is too heavy, I sustain
  On my unwilling shoulders; and I pray
  It may be taken off, and reconferred   115
  Upon the Consuls, or some other Roman,
  More able, and more worthy.
(ARRUNTIUS   Laugh on, still.)
SABINUS
  Why, this doth render all the rest suspected!
GALLUS
  It poisons all.
ARRUNTIUS   O, do you taste it then?
SABINUS
  It takes away my faith to any thing   120
  He shall hereafter speak.
ARRUNTIUS   Ay, to pray that,
  Which would be to his head as hot as thunder,
  ('Gainst which he wears that charm) should but the court
  Receive him at his word.
GALLUS   Hear.
TIBERIUS   For myself,
  I know my weakness, and so little covet   125
  (Like some gone past) the weight that will oppress me,
  As my ambition is the counter-point.
(ARRUNTIUS
  Finely maintained; good still.)
SEJANUS   But Rome, whose blood,
  Whose nerves, whose life, whose very frame relies
  On Cæsar's strength, no less than heav'n on Atlas,   130
  Cannot admit it but with general ruin.
(ARRUNTIUS
  Ah! are you there, to bring him off?)
SEJANUS   Let Cæsar
  No more than urge a point so contrary
  To Cæsar's greatness, the grieved Senate's vows,
  Or Rome's necessity.
(GALLUS   He comes about.   135

112 *spleens* thought to be the seat of laughter
127 *counter-point* opposite   132 *bring him off* aid him

_____

123 Jonson adds in the margin, *A wreath of laurel.*

ARRUNTIUS
  More nimbly than Vertumnus.)
TIBERIUS   For the public,
  I may be drawn, to show, I can neglect
  All private aims; though I affect my rest:
  But, if the Senate still command me serve,
  I must be glad to practise my obedience.   140
(ARRUNTIUS   .
  You must, and will, sir. We do know it.)
SENATORS   Cæsar,
  Live long, and happy, great, and royal Cæsar,
  The gods preserve thee, and thy modesty,
  Thy wisdom, and thy innocence.
(ARRUNTIUS   Where is't?
  The prayer's made before the subject.)
SENATORS   Guard   145
  His meekness, Jove, his piety, his care,
  His bounty—
ARRUNTIUS   And his subtlety, I'll put in:
  Yet he'll keep that himself, without the gods.
  All prayers are vain for him.
TIBERIUS   We will not hold
  Your patience, Fathers, with long answer; but   150
  Shall still contend to be, what you desire,
  And work to satisfy so great a hope:
  Proceed to your affairs.
ARRUNTIUS   Now, Silius, guard thee;
  The curtain's drawing. Afer advanceth.
PRÆCO   Silence.
AFER
  Cite Caius Silius.
PRÆCO   Caius Silius.
SILIUS   Here.   155
AFER
  The triumph that thou hadst in Germany
  For thy late victory on Sacrovir,
  Thou hast enjoyed so freely, Caius Silius,
  As no man it envied thee; nor would Cæsar,
  Or Rome admit, that thou wert then defrauded   160
  Of any honours, thy deserts could claim,
  In the fair service of the Commonwealth:
  But now, if, after all their loves, and graces,

160 *admit* allow, permit

(Thy actions, and their courses being discovered)
It shall appear to Cæsar, and this Senate,　　　　165
Thou hast defiled those glories, with thy crimes—

SILIUS
Crimes?

AFER　　　　Patience, Silius.

SILIUS　　　　　　　　　Tell thy mule of patience,
I am a Roman. What are my crimes? Proclaim them.
Am I too rich? too honest for the times?
Have I or treasure, jewels, land, or houses　　　　170
That some informer gapes for? Is my strength
Too much to be admitted? Or my knowledge?
These now are crimes.

AFER　　　　　　Nay, Silius, if the name
Of crime so touch thee, with what impotence
Wilt thou endure the matter to be searched?　　　　175

SILIUS
I tell thee, Afer, with more scorn, than fear:
Employ your mercenary tongue, and art.
Where's my accuser?

VARRO　　　　　Here.

ARRUNTIUS　　　　　　Varro? The Consul?
Is he thrust in?

VARRO　　　　　'Tis I accuse thee, Silius.
Against the majesty of Rome, and Cæsar,　　　　180
I do pronounce thee here a guilty cause,
First, of beginning, and occasioning,
Next, drawing out the war in Gallia,
For which thou late triumph'st; dissembling long
That Sacrovir to be an enemy,　　　　185
Only to make thy entertainment more,
Whilst thou, and thy wife Sosia polled the province;
Wherein, with sordid-base desire of gain,
Thou hast discredited thy actions' worth
And been a traitor to the state.

SILIUS　　　　　　　　Thou liest.　　　　190

ARRUNTIUS
I thank thee, Silius, speak so still, and often.

VARRO
If I not prove it, Cæsar, but injustly
Have called him into trial, here I bind

174 *impotence* lack of self-restraint
181 *pronounce . . . cause* declare . . . agent
186 *entertainment* employment
187 *polled* plundered

Myself to suffer, what I claim 'gainst him;
And yield, to have what I have spoke, confirmed   195
By judgement of the court, and all good men.

SILIUS

Cæsar, I crave to have my cause deferred,
Till this man's consulship be out.

TIBERIUS   We cannot,
Nor may we grant it.

SILIUS   Why? shall he design
My day of trial? is he my accuser?   200
And must he be my judge?

TIBERIUS   It hath been usual,
And is a right, that custom hath allowed
The magistrate, to call forth private men;
And to appoint their day: which privilege
We may not in the Consul see infringed,   205
By whose deep watches, and industrious care
It is so laboured, as the Commonwealth
Receive no loss, by any oblique course.

SILIUS

Cæsar, thy fraud is worse than violence.

TIBERIUS

Silius, mistake us not, we dare not use   210
The credit of the Consul, to thy wrong,
But only do preserve his place, and power,
So far as it concerns the dignity,
And honour of the state.

ARRUNTIUS   Believe him, Silius.

COTTA

Why, so he may, Arruntius.

ARRUNTIUS   I say so.   215
And he may choose to.

TIBERIUS   By the Capitol,
And all our gods, but that the dear Republic,
Our sacred laws, and just authority
Are interest'd therein, I should be silent.

AFER

Please Cæsar to give way unto his trial.   220
He shall have justice.

199f. (204) *design* (*appoint*) *day* prosecute (Latin *diem dico*)
207 *laboured* accomplished with labour
219 *interest'd* have a stake in

---

216 *choose to*. Q, F, edd. *too*, perhaps the correct reading, although Jonson
does spell the particle *too* as well; cf. IV, 46, for a similar problem.

SILIUS   Nay, I shall have law;
Shall I not Afer? speak.
AFER   Would you have more?
SILIUS
  No, my well-spoken man, I would no more;
  Nor less: might I enjoy it natural,
  Not taught to speak unto your present ends,   225
  Free from thine, his, and all your unkind handling,
  Furious enforcing, most unjust presuming,
  Malicious, and manifold applying,
  Foul wresting, and impossible construction.
AFER
  He raves, he raves.
SILIUS   Thou durst not tell me so,   230
  Had'st thou not Cæsar's warrant. I can see
  Whose power condemns me.
VARRO   This betrays his spirit.
  This doth enough declare him what he is.
SILIUS
  What am I? speak.
VARRO   An enemy to the State.
SILIUS
  Because I am an enemy to thee,   235
  And such corrupted ministers of the State,
  That here art made a present instrument
  To gratify it with thine own disgrace.
SEJANUS
  This, to the Consul, is most insolent!
  And impious!
SILIUS   Ay, take part. Reveal yourselves. 240
  Alas, I scent not your confederacies?
  Your plots, and combinations? I not know
  Minion Sejanus hates me; and that all
  This boast of law, and law, is but a form,
  A net of Vulcan's filing, a mere engine,   245
  To take that life by a pretext of justice,
  Which you pursue in malice? I want brain,
  Or nostril to persuade me, that your ends,
  And purposes are made to what they are,
  Before my answer? O, you equal gods,   250
  Whose justice not a world of wolf-turned men
  Shall make me to accuse (how e'er provoke)

222 *more?* edd. (F mo)
229 *construction* interpretation of the law   245 *filing* workmanship
250 *equal* impartial   252 *provoke* provoked

Have I for this so oft engaged myself?
Stood in the heat, and fervour of a fight,
When Phœbus sooner hath forsook the day   255
Than I the field? Against the blue-eyed Gauls?
And crispèd Germans? when our Roman eagles
Have fanned the fire, with their labouring wings,
And no blow dealt, that left not death behind it?
When I have charged, alone, into the troops   260
Of curled Sicambrians, routed them, and came
Not off, with backward ensigns of a slave,
But forward marks, wounds on my breast, and face,
Were meant to thee, O Cæsar, and thy Rome?
And have I this return? did I, for this,   265
Perform so noble, and so brave defeat,
On Sacrovir? (O Jove, let it become me
To boast my deeds, when he, whom they concern,
Shall thus forget them.)

AFER   Silius, Silius,
These are the common customs of thy blood,   270
When it is high with wine, as now with rage:
This well agrees, with that intemperate vaunt,
Thou lately made'st at Agrippina's table,
That when all other óf the troops were prone
To fall into rebellion, only yours   275
Remained in their obedience. You were he,
That saved the Empire; which had then been lost,
Had but your legions, there, rebelled, or mutined.
Your virtue met, and fronted every peril.
You gave to Cæsar, and to Rome their surety.   280
Their name, their strength, their spirit, and their state,
Their being was a donative from you.

ARRUNTIUS
Well worded, and most like an orator.

TIBERIUS
Is this true, Silius?

SILIUS   Save thy question, Cæsar.
Thy spy, of famous credit, hath affirmed it.   285

ARRUNTIUS
Excellent Roman!

257 *crispèd* with stiff curled hair
278 *mutined* mutinied
282 *donative* gift (Latin *donativum*, imperial largesse)

257 *Roman eagles*. The image of an eagle formed the legionary standard.
286 *Excellent Roman!* Cf. 347, where Arruntius' *Excellent wolf* is probably
    not simply intensive, but an ironic glance back at this line.

SABINUS   He doth answer stoutly.
SEJANUS
  If this be so, there needs no farther cause
  Of crime against him.
VARRO   What can more impeach
  The royal dignity, and state of Cæsar,
  Than to be urgèd with a benefit   290
  He cannot pay?
COTTA   In this, all Cæsar's fortune
  Is made unequal to the courtesy.
LATIARIS
  His means are clean destroyed, that should requite.
GALLUS
  Nothing is great enough for Silius' merit.
ARRUNTIUS
  Gallus on that side too?
SILIUS   Come, do not hunt,   295
  And labour so about for circumstance,
  To make him guilty, whom you have foredoomed:
  Take shorter ways, I'll meet your purposes.
  The words were mine, and more I now will say:
  Since I have done thee that great service, Cæsar,   300
  Thou still hast feared me; and, in place of grace,
  Returned me hatred: so soon, all best turns,
  With doubtful princes, turn deep injuries
  In estimation, when they greater rise,
  Than can be answered. Benefits, with you,   305
  Are of no longer pleasure, than you can
  With ease restore them; that transcended once,
  Your studies are not how to thank, but kill.
  It is your nature, to have all men slaves
  To you, but you acknowledging to none.   310
  The means that makes your greatness, must not come
  In mention of it; if it do, it takes
  So much away, you think: and that, which helped,
  Shall soonest perish, if it stand in eye,
  Where it may front, or but upbraid the high.   315
COTTA
  Suffer him speak no more.
VARRO   Note but his spirit.
AFER
  This shows him in the rest.
LATIARIS   Let him be censured.

288 *crime* accusation (Latin *crimen*)   297 *foredoomed* prejudged
302 *turns* services (cf. 'a good turn')   315 *front* affront

SEJANUS
  He hath spoke enough to prove him Cæsar's foe.

COTTA
  His thoughts look through his words.

SEJANUS   A censure.

SILIUS   Stay,
  Stay, most officious Senate, I shall straight   320
  Delude thy fury. Silius hath not placed
  His guards within him, against Fortune's spite,
  So weakly, but he can escape your grip
  That are but hands of Fortune: she herself
  When virtue doth oppose, must lose her threats.   325
  All that can happen in humanity,
  The frown of Cæsar, proud Sejanus' hatred,
  Base Varro's spleen, and Afer's bloodying tongue,
  The Senate's servile flattery, and these
  Mustered to kill, I am fortified against;   330
  And can look down upon: they are beneath me.
  It is not life whereof I stand enamoured:
  Nor shall my end make me accuse my fate.
  The coward, and the valiant man must fall,
  Only the cause, and manner how, discerns them: 335
  Which then are gladdest, when they cost us dearest.
  Romans, if any here be in this Senate,
  Would know to mock Tiberius' tyranny,
  Look upon Silius, and so learn to die.
                [Stabs himself]

VARRO
  O, desperate act!

ARRUNTIUS   An honourable hand!   340

TIBERIUS
  Look, is he dead?

SABINUS   'Twas nobly struck, and home.

ARRUNTIUS
  My thought did prompt him to it. Farewell, Silius.
  Be famous ever for thy great example.

TIBERIUS
  We are not pleased, in this sad accident,
  That thus hath stalled, and abused our mercy,   345
  Intended to preserve thee, noble Roman:
  And to prevent thy hopes.

---

342 *My thought . . . to it.* Arruntius later committed suicide when accused
    by Macro. Cf. also V, 750f.

ARRUNTIUS   Excellent wolf!
  Now he is full, he howls.
SEJANUS   Cæsar doth wrong
  His dignity, and safety, thus to mourn
  The deserved end of so professed a traitor,   350
  And doth, by this his lenity, instruct
  Others as factious, to the like offence.
TIBERIUS
  The confiscation merely of his state
  Had been enough.
ARRUNTIUS   O, that was gaped for then?
VARRO
  Remove the body.
SEJANUS   Let citation   355
  Go out for Sosia.
GALLUS   Let her be proscribed.
  And for the goods, I think it fit that half
  Go to the treasure, half unto the children.
LEPIDUS
  With leave of Cæsar, I would think, that fourth
  Part, which the law doth cast on the informers,   360
  Should be enough; the rest go to the children:
  Wherein the Prince shall show humanity,
  And bounty, not to force them by their want
  (Which in their parent's trespass they deserved)
  To take ill courses.
TIBERIUS   It shall please us.
ARRUNTIUS   Ay,   365
  Out of necessity. This Lepidus
  Is grave and honest, and I have observed
  A moderation still in all his censures.
SABINUS
  And bending to the better—stay, who's this?
  Cremutius Cordus? what? is he brought in?   370
ARRUNTIUS
  More blood unto the banquet? Noble Cordus,
  I wish thee good: be as thy writings, free,
  And honest.
TIBERIUS   What is he?
SEJANUS   For th'annals, Cæsar.

          [*Enter*] PRÆCO, CORDUS, SATRIUS, NATTA

PRÆCO
  Cremutius Cordus.

351 *lenity* lenience   358 *treasure* public treasury

CORDUS   Here.
PRÆCO   Satrius Secundus,
  Pinnarius Natta, you are his accusers.   375
ARRUNTIUS
  Two of Sejanus' blood-hounds, whom he breeds
  With human flesh, to bay at citizens.
AFER
  Stand forth before the Senate, and confront him.
SATRIUS
  I do accuse thee here, Cremutius Cordus,
  To be a man factious, and dangerous,   380
  A sower of sedition in the State,
  A turbulent, and discontented spirit,
  Which I will prove from thine own writings, here,
  The annals thou hast published; where thou bite'st
  The present age, and with a viper's tooth,   385
  Being a member of it, dare'st that ill
  Which never yet degenerous bastard did
  Upon his parent.
NATTA   To this, I subscribe;
  And, forth a world of more particulars,
  Instance in only one: comparing men,   390
  And times, thou praisest Brutus, and affirm'st
  That Cassius was the last of all the Romans.
COTTA
  How! what are we then?
VARRO   What is Cæsar? nothing?
AFER
  My lords, this strikes at every Roman's private,
  In whom reigns gentry, and estate of spirit,   395
  To have a Brutus brought in parallel,
  A parricide, an enemy of his country,
  Ranked, and preferred to any real worth
  That Rome now holds. This is most strangely invective.
  Most full of spite, and insolent upbraiding.   400
  Nor is't the time alone is here disprised,
  But the whole man of time, yea Cæsar's self
  Brought in disvalue; and he aimed at most
  By oblique glance of his licentious pen.
  Cæsar, if Cassius were the last of Romans,   405
  Thou hast no name.

385 *with a viper's tooth* ungratefully
387 *degenerous* unworthily of family (Latin *degener*)
389 *forth* out of   394 *private* personal concern
397 *parricide* traitor (Latin *parricida*)   401 *disprised* held in contempt

TIBERIUS   Let's hear him answer. Silence.
CORDUS
  So innocent I am of fact, my lords,
  As but my words are argued; yet those words
  Not reaching either prince, or prince's parent:
  The which your law of treason comprehends.   410
  Brutus, and Cassius, I am charged, t' have praised:
  Whose deeds, when many more, besides myself,
  Have writ, not one hath mentioned without honour.
  Great Titus Livius, great for eloquence,
  And faith, amongst us, in his history,   415
  With so great praises Pompey did extol,
  As oft Augustus called him a Pompeian:
  Yet this not hurt their friendship. In his book
  He often names Scipio, Afranius,
  Yea, the same Cassius, and this Brutus too,   420
  As worthi'st men; not thieves, and parricides,
  Which notes, upon their fames, are now imposed.
  Asinius Pollio's writings quite throughout
  Give them a noble memory; so Messalla
  Renowned his general Cassius: yet both these   425
  Lived with Augustus, full of wealth, and honours.
  To Cicero's book, where Cato was heaved up
  Equal with heav'n, what else did Cæsar answer,
  Being then Dictator, but with a penned oration,
  As if before the judges? Do but see   430
  Antonius' letters; read but Brutus' pleadings:
  What vile reproach they hold against Augustus,
  False I confess, but with much bitterness.
  The epigrams of Bibaculus, and Catullus,
  Are read, full stuffed with spite of both the Cæsars; 435
  Yet deified Julius, and no less Augustus!
  Both bore them, and contemned them: (I not know
  Promptly to speak it, whether done with more
  Temper, or wisdom) for such obloquies
  If they despisèd be, they die suppressed,   440
  But, if with rage acknowledged, they are confessed.
  The Greeks I slip, whose licence not alone,
  But also lust did 'scape unpunishèd:
  Or where someone (by chance) exception took,
  He words with words revenged. But, in my work,   445
  What could be aimed more free, or farther off
  From the time's scandal, than to write of those,

410 *comprehends* includes
422 *notes* titles

Whom death from grace, or hatred had exempted?
Did I, with Brutus, and with Cassius,
Armed, and possessed of the Philippi fields,   450
Incense the people in the civil cause,
With dangerous speeches? or do they, being slain
Seventy years since, as by their images
(Which not the conqueror hath defaced) appears,
Retain that guilty memory with writers?   455
Posterity pays every man his honour.
Nor shall there want, though I condemnèd am,
That will not only Cassius well approve,
And of great Brutus' honour mindful be,
But that will, also, mention make of me.   460

ARRUNTIUS
Freely, and nobly spoken.

SABINUS   With good temper,
I like him, that he is not moved with passion.

ARRUNTIUS
He puts 'em to their whisper.

TIBERIUS   Take him hence,
We shall determine of him at next sitting.

COTTA
Meantime, give order, that his books be burnt,   465
To the Ædiles.

SEJANUS   You have well advised.

AFER
It fits not such licentious things should live
T'upbraid the age.

ARRUNTIUS   If th'age were good, they might.

LATIARIS
Let 'em be burnt.

GALLUS   All sought, and burnt, today.

PRÆCO
The court is up, Lictors, resume the fasces.   470
          [*Exeunt, leaving*] ARRUNTIUS, SABINUS, LEPIDUS

ARRUNTIUS
Let 'em be burnt! O, how ridiculous
Appears the Senate's brainless diligence,
Who think they can, with present power, extinguish
The memory of all succeeding times!

SABINUS
'Tis true, when (contrary) the punishment   475
Of wit, doth make th'authority increase.
Nor do they aught, that use this cruelty

Of interdiction, and this rage of burning;
But purchase to themselves rebuke, and shame,
And to the writers an eternal name.   480

LEPIDUS
It is an argument the times are sore,
When virtue cannot safely be advanced;
Nor vice reproved.

ARRUNTIUS   Ay, noble Lepidus,
Augustus well foresaw, what we should suffer,
Under Tiberius, when he did pronounce   485
The Roman race most wretched, that should live
Between so slow jaws, and so long a-bruising.   [*Exeunt*]

[Act III, Scene ii]

[*A room in the Palace. Enter*] TIBERIUS, SEJANUS

TIBERIUS
This business hath succeeded well, Sejanus:
And quite removed all jealousy of practice
'Gainst Agrippina, and our nephews. Now,   490
We must bethink us how to plant our engines
For th'other pair, Sabinus, and Arruntius,
And Gallus too (how e'er he flatter us,)
His heart we know.

SEJANUS   Give it some respite, Cæsar.
Time shall mature, and bring to perfect crown,   495
What we, with so good vultures, have begun:
Sabinus shall be next.

TIBERIUS   Rather Arruntius.

SEJANUS
By any means, preserve him. His frank tongue
Being lent the reins, will take away all thought
Of malice, in your course against the rest.   500
We must keep him to stalk with.

TIBERIUS   Dearest head,
To thy most fortunate design I yield it.

SEJANUS
Sir—I have been so long trained up in grace,
First, with your father, great Augustus, since,

485 *pronounce* Q (F pronouuce)
502 *fortunate* Q (F forunate)

___

496 *vultures.* Birds of augury, with a further reference to the role played by
Afer and Varro. Cf. IV, 140.

With your most happy bounties so familiar,   505
As I not sooner would commit my hopes
Or wishes to the gods, than to your ears.
Nor have I ever, yet, been covetous
Of overbright, and dazzling honours: rather
To watch, and travail in great Cæsar's safety,   510
With the most common soldier.
TIBERIUS   'Tis confessed.
SEJANUS
The only gain, and which I count most fair
Of all my fortunes, is that mighty Cæsar
Hath thought me worthy his alliance. Hence
Begin my hopes.
TIBERIUS   H'mh?
SEJANUS   I have heard, Augustus   515
In the bestowing of his daughter, thought
But even of gentlemen of Rome: if so,
(I know not how to hope so great a favour)
But if a husband should be sought for Livia,
And I be had in mind, as Cæsar's friend,   520
I would but use the glory of the kindred.
It should not make me slothful, or less caring
For Cæsar's state; it were enough to me
It did confirm, and strengthen my weak house,
Against the now unequal opposition   525
Of Agrippina; and for dear regard
Unto my children, this I wish: myself
Have no ambition farther, than to end
My days in service of so dear a master.
TIBERIUS
We cannot but commend thy piety,   530
Most loved Sejanus, in acknowledging
Those bounties; which we, faintly, such remember.
But to thy suit. The rest of mortal men,
In all their drifts, and counsels, pursue profit:
Princes, alone, are of a different sort,   535
Directing their main actions still to fame.
We therefore will take time to think, and answer.
For Livia, she can best, herself, resolve

517 *But even* equal (to a nobleman)   520 *friend* Q (F freind)
521 *kindred* kinship   530 *piety* filial duty (Latin *pietas*)

515 Jonson explains in a marginal note, *His daughter was betrothed to Claudius, his son.* Julia was married to Claudius Marcellus before she married Tiberius. The note, in Latin in Q, is quoted from Lipsius.

If she will marry, after Drusus, or
Continue in the family; besides   540
She hath a mother, and a granddame yet,
Whose nearer counsels she may guide her by:
But I will simply deal. That enmity,
Thou fear'st in Agrippina, would burn more,
If Livia's marriage should (as 'twere in parts)   545
Divide th'imperial house; an emulation
Between the women might break forth: and discord
Ruin the sons, and nephews, on both hands.
What if it cause some present difference?
Thou art not safe, Sejanus, if thou prove it.   550
Canst thou believe, that Livia, first the wife
To Caius Cæsar, then my Drusus, now
Would be contented to grow old with thee,
Born but a private gentleman of Rome?
And raise thee with her loss, if not her shame?   555
Or say, that I should wish it, canst thou think
The Senate, or the people (who have seen
Her brother, father, and our ancestors,
In highest place of empire) will endure it?
The state thou hold'st already, is in talk;   560
Men murmur at thy greatness; and the nobles
Stick not, in public, to upbraid thy climbing
Above our father's favours, or thy scale:
And dare accuse me, from their hate to thee.
Be wise, dear friend. We would not hide these things   565
For friendship's dear respect. Nor will we stand
Adverse to thine, or Livia's designments.
What we had purposed to thee, in our thought,
And with what near degrees of love to bind thee,
And make thee equal to us; for the present,   570
We will forbear to speak. Only, thus much
Believe, our loved Sejanus, we not know
That height in blood, or honour, which thy virtue,
And mind to us, may not aspire with merit.
And this we'll publish, on all watched occasion   575
The Senate, or the people shall present.

SEJANUS

I am restored, and to my sense again,
Which I had lost in this so blinding suit.
Cæsar hath taught me better to refuse,
Than I knew how to ask. How pleaseth Cæsar   580

---

546 *emulation* rivalry   550 *prove* attempt, try
563 *scale* relative size, magnitude   575 *watched* public

T'embrace my late advice, for leaving Rome?

TIBERIUS

We are resolved.

SEJANUS   Here are some motives more
Which I have thought on since, may more confirm.

TIBERIUS

Careful Sejanus! we will straight peruse them:
Go forward in our main design, and prosper.   [*Exit*]   585

SEJANUS

If those but take, I shall: dull, heavy Cæsar!
Wouldst thou tell me, thy favours were made crimes?
And that my fortunes were esteemed thy faults?
That thou, for me, wert hated? and not think
I would with wingèd haste prevent that change,   590
When thou might'st win all to thyself again,
By forfeiture of me? Did those fond words
Fly swifter from thy lips, than this my brain,
This sparkling forge, created me an armour
T'encounter chance, and thee? Well, read my charms,   595
And may they lay that hold upon thy senses,
As thou had'st snuffed up hemlock, or ta'en down
The juice of poppy, and of mandrakes. Sleep,
Voluptuous Cæsar, and security
Seize on thy stupid powers, and leave them dead   600
To public cares, awake but to thy lusts.
The strength of which makes thy libidinous soul
Itch to leave Rome; and I have thrust it on:
With blaming of the city business,
The multitude of suits, the confluence   605
Of suitors, then their importunacies,
The manifold distractions he must suffer,
Besides ill rumours, envies, and reproaches,
All which, a quiet and retirèd life,
(Larded with ease, and pleasure) did avoid;   610
And yet, for any weighty, and great affair,
The fittest place to give the soundest counsels.
By this, shall I remove him both from thought,
And knowledge of his own most dear affairs;
Draw all dispatches through my private hands;   615
Know his designments, and pursue mine own;
Make mine own strengths, by giving suits, and places;
Conferring dignities, and offices:

597f. *hemlock . . . mandrakes* opiates.
606 *importunacies* requests

And these, that hate me now, wanting access
To him, will make their envy none, or less.   620
For when they see me arbiter of all,
They must observe: or else, with Cæsar fall.   [*Exit*]

[*Enter*] TIBERIUS

TIBERIUS
To marry Livia? will no less, Sejanus,
Content thy aims? no lower object? well!
Thou know'st how thou art wrought into our trust;   625
Woven in our design; and think'st, we must
Now use thee, whatsoe'er thy projects are:
'Tis true. But yet with caution, and fit care.
And, now we better think—who's there, within?

[*Enter* SERVUS]

SERVUS
Cæsar?
TIBERIUS To leave our journey off, were sin   630
'Gainst our decreed delights; and would appear
Doubt: or (what less becomes a prince) low fear.
Yet, doubt hath law, and fears have their excuse,
Where princes' states plead necessary use;
As ours doth now: more in Sejanus' pride,   635
Than all fell Agrippina's hates beside.
Those are the dreadful enemies, we raise
With favours, and make dangerous, with praise;
The injured by us may have will alike,
But 'tis the favourite hath the power, to strike: 640
And fury ever boils more high, and strong,
Heat with ambition, than revenge of wrong.
'Tis then a part of supreme skill, to grace
No man too much; but hold a certain space
Between th'ascender's rise, and thine own flat,   645
Lest, when all rounds be reached, his aim be that.
'Tis thought—is Macro in the palace? See:
If not, go, seek him, to come to us—He   [*Exit* SERVUS]
Must be the organ, we must work by now;
Though none less apt for trust: need doth allow   650
What choice would not. I have heard, that aconite

642 *Heat* heated
646 *rounds* rungs of a ladder
651 *aconite* a poisonous plant.

Being timely taken, hath a healing might
Against the scorpion's stroke; the proof we'll give:
That, while two poisons wrestle, we may live.
He hath a spirit too working, to be used   655
But to th'encounter of his like; excused
Are wiser sovereigns then, that raise one ill
Against another, and both safely kill:
The prince, that feeds great natures, they will sway him;
Who nourisheth a lion, must obey him.   660

[Enter] MACRO, [SERVUS]

Macro, we sent for you.
MACRO   I heard so, Cæsar.
TIBERIUS
(Leave us awhile.) [Exit SERVUS] When you shall know,
                                            good Macro,
The causes of our sending, and the ends;
You then will harken nearer: and be pleased
You stand so high, both in our choice, and trust.   665
MACRO
The humblest place in Cæsar's choice, or trust,
May make glad Macro proud; without ambition:
Save to do Cæsar service.
TIBERIUS   Leave our courtings.
We are in purpose, Macro, to depart
The city for a time, and see Campania;   670
Not for our pleasures, but to dedicate
A pair of temples, one, to Jupiter
At Capua, th'other at Nola, to Augustus:
In which great work, perhaps, our stay will be
Beyond our will produced. Now, since we are   675
Not ignorant what danger may be born
Out of our shortest absence, in a state
So subject unto envy, and embroiled
With hate, and faction; we have thought on thee,
(Amongst a field of Romans,) worthiest Macro,   680
To be our eye, and ear, to keep strict watch
On Agrippina, Nero, Drusus, ay,
And on Sejanus: not, that we distrust
His loyalty, or do repent one grace,
Of all that heap, we have conferred on him.   685
(For that were to disparage our election,
And call that judgement now in doubt, which then

668 *our* of us
675 *produced* extended

Seemed as unquestioned as an oracle,)
But, greatness hath his cankers. Worms, and moths
Breed out of too fit matter, in the things   690
Which after they consume, transferring quite
The substance of their makers, int' themselves.
Macro is sharp, and apprehends. Besides,
I know him subtle, close, wise, and well read
In man, and his large nature. He hath studied   695
Affections, passions, knows their springs, their ends,
Which way, and whether they will work: 'tis proof
Enough, of his great merit, that we trust him.
Then, to a point; (because our conference
Cannot be long without suspicion)   700
Here, Macro, we assign thee, both to spy,
Inform, and chastise; think, and use thy means,
Thy ministers, what, where, on whom thou wilt;
Explore, plot, practise: all thou dost in this,
Shall be, as if the Senate, or the laws   705
Had giv'n it privilege, and thou thence styled
The saviour both of Cæsar, and of Rome.
We will not take thy answer, but in act;
Whereto, as thou proceed'st, we hope to hear
By trusted messengers. If't be enquired,   710
Wherefore we called you, say, you have in charge
To see our chariots ready, and our horse:
Be still our loved, and (shortly) honoured Macro.   [*Exit*]

MACRO
I will not ask, why Cæsar bids do this:
But joy, that he bids me. It is the bliss   715
Of courts, to be employed; no matter, how:
A prince's power makes all his actions virtue.
We, whom he works by, are dumb instruments,
To do, but not enquire: his great intents
Are to be served, not searched. Yet, as that bow   720
Is most in hand, whose owner best doth know
T'affect his aims, so let that statesman hope
Most use, most price, can hit his prince's scope.
Nor must he look at what, or whom to strike,
But loose at all; each mark must be alike.   725
Were it to plot against the fame, the life
Of one, with whom I twinned; remove a wife

707 *saviour* Q (F savier, edd. saver)
722 *affect* obtain   723 *scope* target
725 *loose* Q (F lose) discharge arrow
     mark target

From my warm side, as loved, as is the air;
Practise away each parent; draw mine heir
In compass, though but one; work all my kin   730
To swift perdition; leave no untrained engine,
For friendship, or for innocence; nay, make
The gods all guilty: I would undertake
This, being imposed me, both with gain, and ease.
The way to rise, is to obey, and please.   735
He that will thrive in state, he must neglect
The trodden paths, that truth and right respect;
And prove new, wilder ways: for virtue, there,
Is not that narrow thing, she is elsewhere.
Men's fortune there is virtue; reason, their will: 740
Their licence, law; and their observance, skill.
Occasion, is their foil; conscience, their stain;
Profit, their lustre: and what else is, vain.
If then it be the lust of Cæsar's power,
T'have raised Sejanus up, and in an hour   745
O'erturn him, tumbling, down, from height of all;
We are his ready engine: and his fall
May be our rise. It is no uncouth thing
To see fresh buildings from old ruins spring.   [*Exit*]

CHORUS—OF MUSICIANS

[Act IV, Scene i]

[*Agrippina's house. Enter*] GALLUS, AGRIPPINA

GALLUS
You must have patience, royal Agrippina.
AGRIPPINA
I must have vengeance, first: and that were nectar
Unto my famished spirits. O, my fortune,
Let it be sudden thou prepare'st against me;
Strike all my powers of understanding blind,   5
And ignorant of destiny to come:
Let me not fear, that cannot hope.
GALLUS   Dear Princess,
These tyrannies, on yourself, are worse than Cæsar's.
AGRIPPINA
Is this the happiness of being born great?

729f. *draw . . . in compass* trap
742 *Occasion, is their foil* opportunity is the track they follow
748 *uncouth* unknown

Still to be aimed at? still to be suspected?   10
To live the subject of all jealousies?
At the least colour made, if not the ground
To every painted danger? who would not
Choose once to fall, than thus to hang forever?

GALLUS
You might be safe, if you would—

AGRIPPINA   What, my Gallus?   15
Be lewd Sejanus' strumpet? Or the bawd
To Cæsar's lusts, he now is gone to practise?
Not these are safe, where nothing is. Yourself,
While thus you stand but by me, are not safe.
Was Silius safe? or the good Sosia safe?   20
Or was my niece, dear Claudia Pulchra safe?
Or innocent Furnius? They, that latest have
(By being made guilty) added reputation
To Afer's eloquence? O, foolish friends,
Could not so fresh example warn your loves,   25
But you must buy my favours, with that loss
Unto yourselves: and, when you might perceive
That Cæsar's cause of raging must forsake him,
Before his will? Away, good Gallus, leave me.
Here to be seen, is danger; to speak, treason: 30
To do me least observance, is called faction.
You are unhappy in me, and I in all.
Where are my sons? Nero? and Drusus? We
Are they, be shot at; let us fall apart:
Not, in our ruins, sepulchre our friends.   35
Or shall we do some action, like offence,
To mock their studies, that would make us faulty?
And frustrate practice, by preventing it?
The danger's like: for, what they can contrive,
They will make good. No innocence is safe,   40
When power contests. Nor can they trespass more,
Whose only being was all crime, before.

[*Enter* NERO, DRUSUS JUNIOR, CALIGULA]

37 *studies* schemes
39 *like* the same

12f. *colour made . . . painted danger?* Said to be the particular hue, if not the
    very background colour, of every painted danger (alleged plot).
34 *Are they, be shot at.* To be shot at, i.e., we share their peril, and they
    ours.
    fall apart. Meet our doom separately.

NERO
　　You hear, Sejanus is come back from Cæsar?
GALLUS
　　No. How? Disgraced?
DRUSUS JUNIOR　　　　　　More gracèd now, than ever.
GALLUS
　　By what mischance?
CALIGULA　　　　　　A fortune, like enough   45
　　Once to be bad.
DRUSUS JUNIOR　　　　But turned too good, to both.
GALLUS
　　What was't?
NERO　　　　　　Tiberius sitting at his meat,
　　In a farmhouse, they call Spelunca, sited
　　By the seaside, among the Fundane hills,
　　Within a natural cave, part of the grot   50
　　(About the entry) fell, and overwhelmed
　　Some of the waiters; others ran away:
　　Only Sejanus, with his knees, hands, face,
　　O'erhanging Cæsar, did oppose himself
　　To the remaining ruins, and was found   55
　　In that so labouring posture, by the soldiers
　　That came to succour him. With which adventure,
　　He hath so fixed himself in Cæsar's trust,
　　As thunder cannot move him, and is come
　　With all the height of Cæsar's praise, to Rome.   60
AGRIPPINA
　　And power, to turn those ruins all on us;
　　And bury whole posterities beneath them.
　　Nero, and Drusus, and Caligula,
　　Your places are the next, and therefore most
　　In their offence. Think on your birth, and blood,   65
　　Awake your spirits, meet their violence,
　　'Tis princely, when a tyrant doth oppose;
　　And is a fortune sent to exercise
　　Your virtue, as the wind doth try strong trees:
　　Who by vexation grow more sound, and firm.   70
　　After your father's fall, and uncle's fate,
　　What can you hope, but all the change of stroke
　　That force, or slight can give? Then stand upright;
　　And though you do not act, yet suffer nobly:
　　Be worthy of my womb, and take strong cheer;   75
　　What we do know will come, we should not fear. [_Exeunt_]

47 _meat_ meal

[Act IV, Scene ii]

[*The Street. Enter*] MACRO

MACRO
    Returned so soon? renewed in trust, and grace?
    Is Cæsar then so weak? or hath the place
    But wrought this alteration, with the air;
    And he, on next remove, will all repair?   80
    Macro, thou art engaged: and what before
    Was public; now, must be thy private, more.
    The weal of Cæsar, fitness did imply;
    But thine own fate confers necessity
    On thy employment: and the thoughts born nearest   85
    Unto ourselves, move swiftest still, and dearest.
    If he recover, thou art lost: yea, all
    The weight of preparation to his fall
    Will turn on thee, and crush thee. Therefore, strike
    Before he settle, to prevent the like   90
    Upon thyself. He doth his vantage know,
    That makes it home, and gives the foremost blow.   [*Exit*]

[Act IV, Scene iii]

[*Agrippina's house. Enter*] LATIARIS, RUFUS, OPSIUS

LATIARIS
    It is a service, great Sejanus will
    See well requited, and accept of nobly.
    Here place yourselves, between the roof, and ceiling,   95
    And when I bring him to his words of danger,
    Reveal yourselves, and take him.
RUFUS   Is he come?
LATIARIS
    I'll now go fetch him.   [*Exit*]

---

92 *foremost* first

80 *on next . . . all repair?* At the next stage of his journey will make every-
    thing as it was before.
95 According to Tacitus, 'they put their ears to the cracks'; probably the
    actors playing the spies remained on the upper stage of the Jacobean
    playhouse from their entrance until IV, 217, following Tacitus' des-
    cription at IV, 114.

OPSIUS   With good speed. I long
    To merit from the State, in such an action.

RUFUS
    I hope, it will obtain the Consulship   100
    For one of us.

OPSIUS   We cannot think of less,
    To bring in one, so dangerous as Sabinus.

RUFUS
    He was a follower of Germanicus,
    And still is an observer of his wife,
    And children, though they be declined in grace;   105
    A daily visitant, keeps them company
    In private, and in public; and is noted
    To be the only client, of the house:
    Pray Jove, he will be free to Latiaris.

OPSIUS
    He's allied to him, and doth trust him well.   110

RUFUS
    And he'll requite his trust?

OPSIUS   To do an office
    So grateful to the State, I know no man
    But would strain nearer bands, than kindred—

RUFUS   List,
    I hear them come.

OPSIUS   Shift to our holes, with silence. [*Exeunt*]

[*Enter*] LATIARIS, SABINUS

LATIARIS
    It is a noble constancy you show   115
    To this afflicted house: that not like others,
    (The friends of season) you do follow fortune,
    And in the winter of their fate, forsake
    The place, whose glories warmed you. You are just,
    And worthy such a princely patron's love,   120
    As was the world's renowned Germanicus:
    Whose ample merit when I call to thought,
    And see his wife, and issue, objects made
    To so much envy, jealousy, and hate;
    It makes me ready to accuse the gods   125
    Of negligence, as men of tyranny.

SABINUS
    They must be patient, so must we.

104 *observer* partisan
110 *allied* related
117 *friends of season* 'fair weather friends'

LATIARIS   O Jove.
  What will become of us, or of the times,
  When, to be high, or noble, are made crimes?
  When land, and treasure are most dangerous faults?   130
SABINUS
  Nay, when our table, yea our bed assaults
  Our peace, and safety? when our writings are,
  By any envious instruments (that dare
  Apply them to the guilty) made to speak
  What they will have, to fit their tyrannous wreak?   135
  When ignorance is scarcely innocence:
  And knowledge made a capital offence?
  When not so much, but the bare empty shade
  Of liberty, is reft us? and we made,
  The prey to greedy vultures, and vile spies,   140
  That first, transfix us with their murdering eyes?
LATIARIS
  Me thinks, the genius of the Roman race
  Should not be so extinct, but that bright flame
  Of liberty might be revived again,
  (Which no good man but with his life, should lose)   145
  And we not sit like spent, and patient fools,
  Still puffing in the dark, at one poor coal,
  Held on by hope, till the last spark is out.
  The cause is public, and the honour, name,
  The immortality of every soul   150
  That is not bastard, or a slave in Rome,
  Therein concerned: whereto, if men would change
  The wearied arm, and for the weighty shield
  So long sustained, employ the ready sword,
  We might have some assurance of our vows.   155
  This ass's fortitude doth tire us all.
  It must be active valour must redeem
  Our loss, or none. The rock, and our hard steel
  Should meet, t'enforce those glorious fires again,
  Whose splendour cheered the world, and heat gave life   160
  No less than doth the sun's.
SABINUS   'Twere better stay,
  In lasting darkness, and despair of day.
  No ill should force the subject undertake
  Against the sovereign, more than hell should make
  The gods do wrong. A good man should, and must   165
  Sit rather down with loss, than rise unjust.

139 *reft* or 'left'?

Though, when the Romans first did yield themselves
To one man's power, they did not mean their lives,
Their fortunes, and their liberties, should be
His absolute spoil, as purchased by the sword.   170

LATIARIS
Why we are worse, if to be slaves, and bond
To Cæsar's slave, be such, the proud Sejanus!
He that is all, does all, gives Cæsar leave
To hide his ulcerous, and anointed face,
With his bald crown at Rhodes, while he here stalks   175
Upon the heads of Romans, and their princes,
Familiarly to empire.

SABINUS   Now you touch
A point indeed, wherein he shows his art,
As well as power.

LATIARIS   And villany in both.
Do you observe where Livia lodges? How   180
Drusus came dead? What men have been cut off?

SABINUS
Yes, those are things removed: I nearer looked,
Into his later practice, where he stands
Declared a master in his mystery.
First, ere Tiberius went, he wrought his fear   185
To think that Agrippina sought his death.
Then put those doubts in her; sent her oft word,
Under the show of friendship, to beware
Of Cæsar, for he laid to poison her:
Drove them to frowns, to mutual jealousies,   190
Which, now, in visible hatred are burst out.
Since, he hath had his hirèd instruments
To work on Nero, and to heave him up;
To tell him Cæsar's old; that all the people,
Yea, all the army have their eyes on him;   195
That both do long to have him undertake
Something of worth, to give the world a hope;
Bids him to court their grace: the easy youth,
Perhaps, gives ear, which straight he writes to Cæsar;
And with this comment; 'See yond dangerous boy;   200
Note but the practice of the mother, there;
She's tying him, for purposes at hand,

177 *Familiarly to empire* to rule unceremoniously   189 *laid* planned

---

175 *Rhodes*. A rare error of history in the play; Tiberius' exile in Rhodes
took place during the reign of Augustus.
202f. *tying him . . . of sword*. She is allying him with fighters, for a coming time of need.

With men of sword.' Here's Cæsar put in fright
'Gainst son, and mother. Yet, he leaves not thus.
The second brother Drusus (a fierce nature,   205
And fitter for his snares, because ambitious,
And full of envy) him he clasps, and hugs,
Poisons with praise, tells him what hearts he wears,
How bright he stands in popular expectance;
That Rome doth suffer with him, in the wrong   210
His mother does him, by preferring Nero:
Thus sets he them asunder, each 'gainst other,
Projects the course, that serves him to condemn,
Keeps in opinion of a friend to all,
And all drives on to ruin.

LATIARIS   Cæsar sleeps,   215
And nods at this?

SABINUS   Would he might ever sleep,
Bogged in his filthy lusts.

                [*Enter* OPSIUS *and* RUFUS]

OPSIUS   Treason to Cæsar.

RUFUS
Lay hands upon the traitor, Latiaris,
Or take the name thyself.

LATIARIS   I am for Cæsar.

SABINUS
Am I then catched?

RUFUS   How think you, sir? you are.   220

SABINUS
Spies of this head! so white! so full of years!
Well, my most reverend monsters, you may live
To see yourselves thus snared.

OPSIUS   Away with him.

LATIARIS
Hale him away.

RUFUS   To be a spy for traitors,
Is honourable vigilance.

SABINUS   You do well,   225
My most officious instruments of state;
Men of all uses: drag me hence, away.
The year is well begun, and I fall fit,
To be an offering to Sejanus. Go.

208 *what hearts he wears* what men are loyal to him

228f. Sabinus regards himself as a New Year's sacrifice to Sejanus, the new
deity of Rome. The irony is heightened because by custom no execu-
tions took place in the sacred first days of the year.

OPSIUS
    Cover him with his garments, hide his face.   230
SABINUS
    It shall not need. Forbear your rude assault,
    The fault's not shameful villany makes a fault.   [*Exeunt*]

[Act IV, Scene iv]

[*The Street. Enter*] MACRO, CALIGULA

MACRO
    Sir, but observe how thick your dangers meet
    In his clear drifts! Your mother, and your brothers,
    Now cited to the Senate! Their friend, Gallus,   235
    Feasted today by Cæsar, since committed!
    Sabinus, here we met, hurried to fetters!
    The Senators all struck with fear, and silence,
    Save those, whose hopes depend not on good means,
    But force their private prey, from public spoil!   240
    And you must know, if here you stay, your state
    Is sure to be the subject of his hate,
    As now the object.
CALIGULA   What would you advise me?
MACRO
    To go for Capreæ presently: and there
    Give up yourself, entirely, to your uncle.   245
    Tell Cæsar (since your mother is accused
    To fly for succours to Augustus' statue,
    And to the army, with your brethren) you
    Have rather chose, to place your aids in him,
    Than live suspected; or in hourly fear   250
    To be thrust out, by bold Sejanus' plots:
    Which, you shall confidently urge, to be
    Most full of peril to the state, and Cæsar,
    As being laid to his peculiar ends,
    And not to be let run, with common safety.   255
    All which (upon the second) I'll make plain,
    So both shall love, and trust with Cæsar gain.
CALIGULA
    Away then, let's prepare us for our journey.   [*Exeunt*]

[*Enter*] ARRUNTIUS

234 *drifts* plots
245 *uncle* Tiberius (really great-uncle, brother of Germanicus' father,
    Nero Drusus)
256 *upon the second* as a supporter

ARRUNTIUS
    Still, dost thou suffer heav'n? will no flame,
    Not heat of sin make thy just wrath to boil   260
    In thy distempered bosom, and o'erflow
    The pitchy blazes of impiety,
    Kindled beneath thy throne? Still canst thou sleep,
    Patient, while vice doth make an antic face
    At thy dread power, and blow dust, and smoke   265
    Into thy nostrils? Jove, will nothing wake thee?
    Must vile Sejanus pull thee by the beard,
    Ere thou wilt open thy black-lidded eye,
    And look him dead? Well! Snore on, dreaming gods:
    And let this last of that proud giant-race,   270
    Heave mountain upon mountain, 'gainst your state—
    Be good unto me, Fortune, and you powers,
    Whom I, expostulating, have profaned;
    I see (what's equal with a prodigy)
    A great, a noble Roman, and an honest,   275

                [Enter LEPIDUS]

    Live an old man! O, Marcus Lepidus,
    When is our turn to bleed? Thyself, and I
    (Without our boast) are almost all the few
    Left, to be honest, in these impious times.
LEPIDUS
    What we are left to be, we will be, Lucius,   280
    Though tyranny did stare, as wide as death,
    To fright us from it.
ARRUNTIUS   'T hath so, on Sabinus.
LEPIDUS
    I saw him now drawn from the Gemonies,
    And (what increased the direness of the fact)
    His faithful dog (upbraiding all us Romans)   285
    Never forsook the corpse, but, seeing it thrown
    Into the stream, leaped in, and drowned with it.
ARRUNTIUS
    O act! to be envied him, of us men!
    We are the next, the hook lays hold on, Marcus:
    What are thy arts (good patriot, teach them me)   290
    That have preserved thy hairs, to this white dye,

---

264 *antic* ed. (F antique, a common 17th-century spelling)

270 *giant-race.* The sons of earth who tried to scale and conquer heaven by
    piling mountain upon mountain.

And kept so reverend, and so dear a head,
Safe, on his comely shoulders?

LEPIDUS   Arts, Arruntius?
None, but the plain, and passive fortitude,
To suffer, and be silent; never stretch   295
These arms, against the torrent; live at home,
With my own thoughts, and innocence about me,
Not tempting the wolves' jaws: these are my arts.

ARRUNTIUS
I would begin to study 'em, if I thought
They would secure me. May I pray to Jove,   300
In secret, and be safe? Ay, or aloud?
With open wishes? so I do not mention
Tiberius, or Sejanus? Yes, I must,
If I speak out. 'Tis hard, that. May I think,
And not be racked? What danger is't to dream?   305
Talk in one's sleep? or cough? who knows the law?
May I shake my head, without a comment? say
It rains, or it holds up, and not be thrown
Upon the Gemonies? These now are things,
Whereon men's fortune, yea their fate depends.   310
Nothing hath privilege 'gainst the violent ear.
No place, no day, no hour (we see) is free
(Not our religious, and most sacred times)
From some one kind of cruelty: all matter,
Nay all occasion pleaseth. Madmen's rage,   315
The idleness of drunkards, women's nothing,
Jesters' simplicity, all, all is good
That can be catched at. Nor is now th'event
Of any person, or for any crime,
To be expected; for, 'tis always one: 320
Death, with some little difference of place,
Or time—what's this? Prince Nero? guarded?

[*Enter*] LACO, NERO, [LICTORS]

LACO
On, Lictors, keep your way: my lords, forbear.
On pain of Cæsar's wrath, no man attempt
Speech with the prisoner.

NERO   Noble friends, be safe: 325
To lose yourselves for words, were as vain hazard,
As unto me small comfort: fare you well.
Would all Rome's sufferings in my fate did dwell.

318 *event* consequence, outcome (Latin *eventus*)
320 *expected* in doubt   326 *lose* ed. (Q, F loose)

LACO
  Lictors, away.
LEPIDUS   Where goes he, Laco?
LACO   Sir,
  He's banished into Pontia, by the Senate.   330
ARRUNTIUS
  Do I see? and hear? and feel? May I trust sense?
  Or doth my fant'sy form it?
LEPIDUS   Where's his brother?
LACO
  Drusus is prisoner in the palace.
ARRUNTIUS   Ha?
  I smell it now: 'tis rank. Where's Agrippina?
LACO
  The Princess is confined, to Pandataria.   335
ARRUNTIUS
  Bolts, Vulcan; bolts, for Jove! Phœbus, thy bow;
  Stern Mars, thy sword; and blue-eyed maid, thy spear;
  Thy club, Alcides: all the armoury
  Of heaven is too little!—Ha? to guard
  The gods, I meant. Fine, rare dispatch! This same   340
  Was swiftly born! confined? imprisoned? banished?
  Most tripartite! The cause, sir?
LACO   Treason.
ARRUNTIUS   O?
  The complement of all accusings? that
  Will hit, when all else fails.
LEPIDUS   This turn is strange!
  But yesterday, the people would not hear   345
  Far less objected, but cried, Cæsar's letters
  Were false, and forged; that all these plots were malice:
  And that the ruin of the Prince's house
  Was practised 'gainst his knowledge. Where are now
  Their voices? now, that they behold his heirs   350
  Locked up, disgraced, led into exile?
ARRUNTIUS   Hushed.
  Drowned in their bellies. Wild Sejanus' breath
  Hath, like a whirlwind, scattered that poor dust,
  With this rude blast.
             He turns to Laco, and the rest
             We'll talk no treason, sir,
  If that be it you stand for? Fare you well.   355

---

337 *blue-eyed maid*. Pallas Athene, a warrior goddess; perhaps a misunder-
    standing of Homer's 'bright-eyed Athene'.

We have no need of horse-leeches. Good spy,
Now you are spied, be gone.
                              [*Exeunt* LACO, NERO, LICTORS]
LEPIDUS   I fear, you wrong him.
He has the voice to be an honest Roman.
ARRUNTIUS
    And trusted to this office? Lepidus,
    I'd sooner trust Greek Sinon, than a man   360
    Our State employs. He's gone: and being gone,
    I dare tell you (whom I dare better trust)
    That our night-eyed Tiberius doth not see
    His minion's drifts; or, if he do, he's not
    So arrant subtle, as we fools do take him: 365
    To breed a mongrel up, in his own house,
    With his own blood, and (if the good gods please)
    At his own throat, flesh him, to take a leap.
    I do not beg it, heav'n: but, if the fates
    Grant it these eyes, they must not wink.
LEPIDUS   They must   370
    Not see it, Lucius.
ARRUNTIUS   Who should let 'em?
LEPIDUS   Zeal,
    And duty; with the thought, he is our prince.
ARRUNTIUS
    He is our monster: forfeited to vice
    So far, as no racked virtue can redeem him.
    His loathèd person fouler than all crimes: 375
    An emperor, only in his lusts. Retired
    (From all regard of his own fame, or Rome's)
    Into an obscure island; where he lives
    (Acting his tragedies with a comic face)
    Amidst his rout of Chaldees: spending hours,   380
    Days, weeks, and months, in the unkind abuse
    Of grave astrology, to the bane of men,
    Casting the scope of men's nativities,
    And having found ought worthy in their fortune,
    Kill, or precipitate them in the sea,   385

---

356 *horse-leeches.* Especially large medicinal leeches, hence insatiably
     greedy people.
368 *flesh him, to take a leap.* Reward him with a bit of flesh, to encourage him;
     part of the extensive imagery of hunting in this act, which is antici-
     pated in II, 406.
379 Tiberius acts out the tragedy of Rome and her people wearing a face
     like the lewd masks of late Roman comedies, one of which satirized
     Tiberius' retirement to Capreæ.

And boast, he can mock fate. Nay, muse not: these
Are far from ends of evil, scarce degrees.
He hath his slaughter-house, at Capreæ;
Where he doth study murder, as an art:
And they are dearest in his grace, that can   390
Devise the deepest tortures. Thither, too,
He hath his boys, and beauteous girls ta'en up,
Out of our noblest houses, the best formed,
Best nurtured, and most modest: what's their good
Serves to provoke his bad. Some are allured,   395
Some threatened; others (by their friends detained)
Are ravished hence, like captives, and, in sight
Of their most grievèd parents, dealt away
Unto his spintries, sellaries, and slaves,
Masters of strange, and new-commented lusts,   400
For which wise nature hath not left a name.
To this (what most strikes us, and bleeding Rome,)
He is, with all his craft, become the ward
To his own vassal, a stale catamite:
Whom he (upon our low, and suffering necks)   405
Hath raised, from excrement, to side the gods,
And have his proper sacrifice in Rome:
Which Jove beholds, and yet will sooner rive
A senseless oak with thunder, than his trunk.

[*Enter*] LACO, POMPONIUS, MINUTIUS

To them

LACO
These letters make men doubtful what t'expect,   410
Whether his coming, or his death.
POMPONIUS   Troth, both:
And which comes soonest, thank the gods for.
(ARRUNTIUS   List,
Their talk is Cæsar, I would hear all voices.)
MINUTIUS
One day, he's well; and will return to Rome:
The next day, sick; and knows not when to hope it.   415

387 *degrees* steps toward it
400 *commented* invented (Latin *commentus*)
404 *catamite* sodomite
406 *to side* to stand alongside
407 *proper* own

___

399 *spintries, sellaries.* Male prostitutes and practitioners of unnatural vice;
    the words appear in Greenway's translation of Tacitus' *Annals.*

LACO

　True, and today, one of Sejanus' friends
　Honoured by special writ; and on the morrow
　Another punished—

POMPONIUS　　　　　　　By more special writ.

MINUTIUS

　This man receives his praises of Sejanus,
　A second, but slight mention: a third, none:　　　　　420
　A fourth, rebukes. And thus he leaves the Senate
　Divided, and suspended, all uncertain.

LACO

　These forkèd tricks, I understand 'em not,
　Would he would tell us whom he loves, or hates,
　That we might follow, without fear, or doubt.　　　425

(ARRUNTIUS

　Good Heliotrope! Is this your honest man?
　Let him be yours so still. He is my knave.)

POMPONIUS

　I cannot tell, Sejanus still goes on,
　And mounts, we see: new statues are advanced,
　Fresh leaves of titles, large inscriptions read,　　430
　His fortune sworn by, himself new gone out
　Cæsar's colleague, in the fifth Consulship,
　More altars smoke to him, than all the gods:
　What would we more?

(ARRUNTIUS　　　　　That the dear smoke would choke him,
　That would I more.

LEPIDUS　　　　　　Peace, good Arruntius.)　　　435

LACO

　But there are letters come (they say) ev'n now,
　Which do forbid that last.

MINUTIUS　　　　　　Do you hear so?

LACO　　　　　　　　　　　　　　Yes.

POMPONIUS

　By Pollux, that's the worst.

(ARRUNTIUS　　　　　By Hercules, best.)

MINUTIUS

　I did not like the sign, when Regulus,
　(Whom all we know no friend unto Sejanus)　　　440
　Did, by Tiberius' so precise command,

---

426 *Heliotrope.* A flower that follows the sun, therefore a symbol of oppor-
　tunism; but unusual in this sense. The more common association of the
　flower is, on the contrary, with the loyal follower, especially Christian,
　who shuts himself up in his master's absence.

Succeed a fellow in the Consulship:
It boded somewhat.
POMPONIUS   Not a mote. His partner,
Fulcinius Trio, is his own, and sure.
Here comes Terentius. He can give us more.   445

[*Enter* TERENTIUS]
They whisper with Terentius

LEPIDUS
I'll ne'er believe, but Cæsar hath some scent
Of bold Sejanus' footing. These cross points
Of varying letters, and opposing Consuls,
Mingling his honours, and his punishments,
Feigning now ill, now well, raising Sejanus,   450
And then depressing him, (as now of late
In all reports we have it) cannot be
Empty of practice: 'tis Tiberius' art.
For (having found his favourite grown too great,
And, with his greatness, strong; that all the soldiers   455
Are, with their leaders, made at his devotion;
That almost all the Senate are his creatures,
Or hold on him their main dependances,
Either for benefit, or hope, or fear;
And that himself hath lost much of his own,   460
By parting unto him; and by th'increase
Of his rank lusts, and rages, quite disarmed
Himself of love, or other public means,
To dare an open contestation)
His subtlety hath chose this doubling line,   465
To hold him even in: not so to fear him,

---

444 *his own* Sejanus'   447 *footing* established place
456 *made at his devotion* made devoted to him
461 *parting unto* sharing with
466 *even in* in check   *fear* frighten

---

438 In Q and the first state of F, this line read
   POMPONIUS
      By Castor, that's the worst.
   (ARRUNTIUS   By Pollux, best.)
In the same state, line 435 did not exist, and the parenthesis closed after
him. The addition of 435 in the corrected state merely clarifies the point
of Arruntius' remark, but the change in 438—the most substantial of all
the proof-corrections in F—is a classical nicety, for only women swore
by Castor, men by Hercules (Jonson made the same mistake in *Poetaster*
IV.i, 15, where in Q Cytheris swears by Hercules, but he corrected this
to Juno in the first state of F; in both places the hero's name must be
pronounced 'Herc'les'). The improvement in accuracy barely justifies
the loss of balance and wit.

As wholly put him out, and yet give check
Unto his farther boldness. In mean time,
By his employments, makes him odious
Unto the staggering rout, whose aid (in fine)   470
He hopes to use, as sure, who (when they sway)
Bear down, o'erturn all objects in their way.

ARRUNTIUS
You may be a Linceus, Lepidus: yet, I
See no such cause, but that a politic tyrant
(Who can so well disguise it) should have ta'en   475
A nearer way: fained honest, and come home
To cut his throat, by law.

LEPIDUS   Ay, but his fear
Would ne'er be masked, albe his vices were.

POMPONIUS
His lordship then is still in grace?

TERENTIUS   Assure you,
Never in more, either of grace, or power.   480

POMPONIUS
The gods are wise, and just.

(ARRUNTIUS   The fiends they are.
To suffer thee belie 'em?)

TERENTIUS   I have here
His last, and present letters, where he writes him
The 'partner of his cares', and 'his Sejanus'—

LACO
But is that true, it is prohibited,   485
To sacrifice unto him?

TERENTIUS   Some such thing
Cæsar makes scruple of, but forbids it not;
No more than to himself: says, he could wish
It were forborn to all.

LACO   Is it no other?

TERENTIUS
No other, on my trust. For your more surety,   490
Here is that letter too.

(ARRUNTIUS   How easily,
Do wretched men believe, what they would have!
Looks this like plot?

LEPIDUS   Noble Arruntius, stay.)

LACO
He names him here without his titles.

(LEPIDUS   Note.

478 *albe* although
485 *it is* edd. (Q, F it 'tis)

ARRUNTIUS
Yes, and come off your notable fool. I will.) 495
LACO
No other, than Sejanus.
POMPONIUS That's but haste
In him that writes. Here he gives large amends.
MINUTIUS
And with his own hand written?
POMPONIUS Yes.
LACO Indeed?
TERENTIUS
Believe it, gentlemen, Sejanus' breast
Never received more full contentments in, 500
Than at this present.
POMPONIUS Takes he well th'escape
Of young Caligula, with Macro?
TERENTIUS Faith,
At the first air, it somewhat troubled him.
(LEPIDUS
Observe you?
ARRUNTIUS Nothing. Riddles. Till I see
Sejanus struck, no sound thereof strikes me.) 505
POMPONIUS
I like it not. I muse he'd not attempt
Somewhat against him in the Consulship,
Seeing the people 'gin to favour him.
TERENTIUS
He doth repent it, now; but he's employed
Pagonianus after him: and he holds 510
That correspondence, there, with all that are
Near about Cæsar, as no thought can pass
Without his knowledge, thence, in act to front him.
POMPONIUS
I gratulate the news.
LACO But, how comes Macro
So in trust, and favour, with Caligula? 515
POMPONIUS
O sir, he has a wife; and the young Prince
An appetite: he can look up, and spy

495 *off* edd. (Q, F of) 498 MINUTIUS edd. (Q, F MAR.)
503 *air* news 506 *muse* imagine
514 *gratulate* welcome LACO edd. (Q, F MAC.)

517f. *look up . . . his sleeps.* He can turn a blind eye to things near him, and
has trained his senses to ignore what is going on.

Flies in the roof, when there are fleas in bed;
And hath a learnèd nose to assure his sleeps.
Who, to be favoured of the rising sun,　　　　　　　　520
Would not lend little of his waning moon?
'Tis the safe'st ambition. Noble Terentius.

TERENTIUS

The night grows fast upon us. At your service.　　　[*Exeunt*]

CHORUS—OF MUSICIANS

[Act V, Scene i]

[Sejanus' house. Enter] SEJANUS

SEJANUS

Swell, swell, my joys: and faint not to declare
Yourselves, as ample, as your causes are.
I did not live, till now; this my first hour:
Wherein I see my thoughts reached by my power.
But this, and grip my wishes. Great, and high,　　　　5
The world knows only two, that's Rome, and I.
My roof receives me not; 'tis air I tread:
And, at each step, I feel my advancèd head
Knock out a star in heav'n! Reared to this height,
All my desires seem modest, poor and slight,　　　　10
That did before sound impudent: 'tis place,
Not blood, discerns the noble, and the base.
Is there not something more, than to be Cæsar?
Must we rest there? It irks, t'have come so far,
To be so near a stay. Caligula,　　　　　　　　　　15
Would thou stood'st stiff, and many, in our way.
Winds lose their strength, when they do empty fly,
Unmet of woods or buildings; great fires die,
That want their matter to withstand them: so,
It is our grief, and will be our loss, to know　　　　20

15 *stay* enforced stop

5 *grip my wishes.* Only let my power reach my thoughts, and I shall obtain
　my desires.
7 *My roof receives me not.* Sejanus thinks of himself as risen above his
　'house'; the image continues and completes a sequence which began at
　I, 225 ('One, and his house, receives') and continued in Macro's speech,
　III, 748–749 ('It is no uncouth thing/To see fresh buildings from old
　ruins spring') and Agrippina's (IV, 35), who sees the relation of this
　image to Sejanus' deed at Spelunca (IV, 55, 61). It is another example
　of interplay of language and action.

Our power shall want opposites; unless
The gods, by mixing in the cause, would bless
Our fortune with their conquest. That were worth
Sejanus' strife: durst fates but bring it forth.

[*Enter*] TERENTIUS, [SERVUS]

TERENTIUS
  Safety, to great Sejanus.
SEJANUS   Now, Terentius?   25
TERENTIUS
  Hears not my lord the wonder?
SEJANUS   Speak it, no.
TERENTIUS
  I meet it violent in the people's mouths,
  Who run, in routs, to Pompey's theatre,
  To view your statue: which, they say, sends forth
  A smoke, as from a furnace, black, and dreadful.   30
SEJANUS
  Some traitor hath put fire in: (you, go see.)
  And let the head be taken off, to look
  What 'tis—[*Exit* SERVUS] some slave hath practised an
                                         imposture,
  To stir the people. How now? why return you?

[*Enter*] SATRIUS, NATTA, [SERVUS]
                To them

SATRIUS
  The head, my lord, already is ta'en off,   35
  I saw it: and, at opening, there leapt out
  A great, and monstrous serpent!
SEJANUS   Monstrous! why?
  Had it a beard? and horns? no heart? a tongue
  Forked as flattery? looked it of the hue,
  To such as live in great men's bosoms? was   40
  The spirit of it Macro's?
NATTA   May it please
  The most divine Sejanus, in my days,
  (And by his sacred fortune, I affirm it)
  I have not seen a more extended, grown
  Foul, spotted, venomous, ugly —

33 *imposture* deception

---

34 Such a quick return of the servant is unreasonable, but Satrius' knowledge of Sejanus' order is equally so. The present arrangement assumes
   that Satrius and Natta have met the servant as he left Sejanus' house,
   and told him what they have already learned.

SÉJANUS   O, the fates!   45
   What a wild muster's here of attributes,
   T'express a worm, a snake?
TERENTIUS   But how that should
   Come there, my lord!
SÉJANUS   What! and you too, Terentius?
   I think you mean to make't a prodigy
   In your reporting?
TERENTIUS   Can the wise Sejanus   50
   Think heav'n hath meant it less?
SÉJANUS   O, superstition!
   Why, then the falling of our bed, that broke
   This morning, burdened with the populous weight
   Of our expecting clients, to salute us;
   Or running of the cat, betwixt our legs,   55
   As we set forth unto the Capitol,
   Were prodigies.
TERENTIUS   I think them ominous!
   And, would they had not happened. As, today,
   The fate of some your servants! who, declining
   Their way, not able, for the throng, to follow,   60
   Slipped down the Gemonies, and broke their necks!
   Besides, in taking your last augury,
   No prosperous bird appeared, but croaking ravens
   Flagged up and down: and from the sacrifice
   Flew to the prison, where they sat, all night,   65
   Beating the air with their obstreperous beaks!
   I dare not counsel, but I could entreat
   That great Sejanus would attempt the gods,
   Once more, with sacrifice.
SÉJANUS   What excellent fools
   Religion makes of men? Believes Terentius   70
   (If these were dangers, as I shame to think them)
   The gods could change the certain course of fate?
   Of, if they could, they would (now, in a moment)
   For a beef's fat, or less, be bribed t'invert
   Those long decrees? Then think the gods, like flies,   75
   Are to be taken with the steam of flesh,
   Or blood, diffused about their altars: think
   Their power as cheap, as I esteem it small.
   Of all the throng, that fill th'Olympian hall,
   And (without pity) lade poor Atlas' back,   80

52 *bed* couch or sofa   54 *expecting* awaiting (Latin *expecto*)
59 *declining* departing from   64 *Flagged* flew unsteadily
75 *long* old

I know not that one deity, but Fortune;
To whom, I would throw up, in begging smoke,
One grain of incense: or whose ear I'd buy
With thus much oil. Her, I, indeed, adore;
And keep her grateful image in my house,   85
Sometimes belonging to a Roman king,
But, now called mine, as by the better style:
To her, I care not, if (for satisfying
Your scrupulous fant'sies) I go offer. Bid
Our priest prepare us honey, milk, and poppy,   90
His masculine odours, and night vestments: say,
Our rites are instant, which performed, you'll see
How vain, and worthy laughter, your fears be.   [*Exeunt*]

[Enter] COTTA, POMPONIUS

COTTA
Pomponius! whither in such speed?
POMPONIUS   I go
To give my lord Sejanus notice—
COTTA   What?   95
POMPONIUS
Of Macro.
COTTA   Is he come?
POMPONIUS   Entered but now
The house of Regulus.
COTTA   The opposite Consul?
POMPONIUS
Some half hour since.
COTTA   And, by night too! stay, sir;
I'll bear you company.
POMPONIUS   Along, then—   [*Exeunt*]

[Act V, Scene ii]

[Regulus' house. Enter] MACRO, REGULUS, [SERVUS]

MACRO
'Tis Cæsar's will, to have a frequent Senate.   100
And therefore must your edit lay deep mulct

85 *grateful* beneficent   86 *Sometimes* previously
100 *frequent* fully attended, frequented   101 *mulct* fine

---

91 *masculine odours*. 'A somewhat strange epithet in our tongue, but
proper to the thing: for they were only masculine odours, which were
offered to the altars' (Jonson, note to *Part of King James' Entertainment
in Passing to his Coronation*; he goes on to cite classical authorities).

On such, as shall be absent.
REGULUS   So it doth.
Bear it my fellow Consul to adscribe.
MACRO
And tell him it must early be proclaimed;
The place, Apollo's temple.   [*Exit* SERVUS]
REGULUS   That's remembered.   105
MACRO
And at what hour?
REGULUS   Yes.
MACRO   -   You do forget
To send one for the Provost of the watch?
REGULUS
I have not: here he comes.

[*Enter* LACO]

MACRO   Gracinus Laco,
You are a friend most welcome: by, and by,
I'll speak with you. (You must procure this list   110
Of the Prætorian cohorts, with the names
Of the Centurions, and their Tribunes.
REGULUS   Ay.)
MACRO
I bring you letters, and a health from Cæsar—
LACO
Sir, both come well.
MACRO   (And hear you, with your note,
Which are the eminent men, and most of action.   115
REGULUS
That shall be done you too.)
MACRO   Most worthy Laco,
          The Consul goes out
Cæsar salutes you. (Consul! death, and furies!
Gone now?) the argument will please you, sir.
(Hough! Regulus? The anger of the gods
Follow his diligent legs, and overtake 'em,   120
          Returns
In likeness of the gout.) O, good my lord,
We lacked you present; I would pray you send
Another to Fulcinius Trio, straight,
To tell him, you will come, and speak with him:
(The matter we'll devise) to stay him, there,   125
While I, with Laco, do survey the watch.

103 *adscribe* subscribe
116 s.d. *The Consul* Regulus

What are your strengths, Gracinus?
LACO   Seven cohorts.
                        Goes out again
MACRO
    You see, what Cæsar writes: and (— gone again?
    He's sure a vein of Mercury in his feet)
    Knew you, what store of the Prætorian soldiers   130
    Sejanus holds, about him, for his guard?
LACO
    I cannot the just number: but, I think,
    Three centuries.
MACRO   Three? good.
LACO   At most, not four.
MACRO
    And who be those Centurions?
LACO   That the Consul
    Can best deliver you.
MACRO   (When he's away: 135
    Spite, on his nimble industry.) Gracinus,
    You find what place you hold, there, in the trust
    Of royal Cæsar?
LACO   Ay, and I am—
MACRO   Sir,
    The honours, there proposed, are but beginnings
    Of his great favours.
LACO   They are more—
MACRO   I heard him   140
    When he did study, what to add—
LACO   My life,
    And all I hold—
MACRO   You were his own first choice;
    Which doth confirm as much, as you can speak:
    And will (if we succeed) make more—Your guards
    Are seven cohorts, you say?
LACO   Yes.
MACRO   Those we must   145
    Hold still in readiness, and undischarged.
LACO
    I understand so much. But how it can—
MACRO
    Be done without suspicion, you'll object?
                        Returns
REGULUS
    What's that?

132 *just* exact

LACO   The keeping of the watch in arms,
When morning comes.
MACRO   The Senate shall be met, and set   150
So early, in the temple, as all mark
Of that will be avoided.
REGULUS   If we need,
We have commission, to possess the palace;
Enlarge Prince Drusus, and make him our chief.
MACRO
(That secret would have burnt his reverend mouth,   155
Had he not spit it out, now:) by the gods,
You carry things too—let me borrow a man,
Or two, to bear these—that of freeing Drusus,
Cæsar projected as the last, and utmost;
Not else to be remembered.

                    [*Enter* SERVI]

REGULUS   Here are servants.   160
MACRO
These to Arruntius, these to Lepidus,
This bear to Cotta, this to Latiaris.
If they demand you of me: say, I have ta'en
Fresh horse, and am departed. You (my lord)
To your colleague, and be you sure, to hold him   165
With long narration, of the new fresh favours,
Meant to Sejanus, his great patron; I,
With trusted Laco, here, are for the guards:
Then, to divide. For, night hath many eyes,
Whereof, though most do sleep, yet some are spies. [*Exeunt*] 170

[Act V, Scene iii]

[*Sejanus' house. Enter*] PRÆCONES, FLAMEN, MINISTRI,
[TUBICINES, TIBICINES,] SEJANUS, TERENTIUS, SATRIUS,
[NATTA,] *etc*.

PRÆCO
Be all profane far hence; fly, fly far off:
Be absent far. Far hence be all profane.

Tubicines, Tibicines sound, while the Flamen washeth

FLAMEN
We have been faulty, but repent us now,
And bring pure hands, pure vestments, and pure minds.

154 *Enlarge* set free

1 MINISTER
Pure vessels.
2 MINISTER   And pure offerings.
3 MINISTER   Garlands pure.   175
FLAMEN
Bestow your garlands: and (with reverence) place
The vervin on the altar.
PRÆCO   Favour your tongues.
While they sound again, the Flamen takes of the honey,
with his finger, and tastes, then ministers to all the rest: so
of the milk, in an earthen vessel, he deals about; which done,
he sprinkleth, upon the altar, milk; then imposeth the honey,
and kindleth his gums, and after censing about the altar
placeth his censer thereon, into which they put several
branches of poppy, and the music ceasing, proceed
FLAMEN
Great mother Fortune, queen of human state,
Rectress of action, arbitress of fate,
To whom all sway, all power, all empire bows,   180
Be present, and propitious to our vows.
PRÆCO
Favour it with your tongues.
1 MINISTER
Be present, and propitious to our vows.
Accept our offering, and be pleased, great goddess.
TERENTIUS
See, see, the image stirs!
SATRIUS   And turns away!   185
NATTA
Fortune averts her face!
FLAMEN   Avert, you gods,
The prodigy. Still! still! Some pious rite
We have neglected. Yet! heav'n, be appeased.
And be all tokens false, or void, that speak
Thy present wrath.
SEJANUS   Be thou dumb, scrupulous priest: 190
And gather up thyself, with these thy wares,

177 *vervin* verbena, boughs used in sacrifices
190 *scrupulous* meticulous

177 *Favour your tongues.* Cf. V, 182, *Favour it with your tongues.* Jonson's
   note to Q explains the meaning of the phrase ('be silent') and the
   alternative translations of *favete linguis*, the first regarding the noun as
   dative, the second (correctly) as ablative. The note gives examples from
   Virgil and Ovid, and cites sixteenth-century scholarly authority.
   s.d. *gums.* Aromatics used in the censer.

Which I, in spite of thy blind mistress, or
Thy juggling mystery, religion, throw
Thus, scornèd on the earth. Nay, hold thy look
Averted, till I woo thee, turn again;   195
And thou shalt stand, to all posterity,
Th'eternal game, and laughter, with thy neck
Writhed to thy tail, like a ridiculous cat.
Avoid these fumes, these superstitious lights,
And all these cosening ceremonies: you,   200
Your pure, and spicèd conscience. [*Exeunt* FLAMEN,
                         ATTENDANTS] I, the slave,
And mock of fools, (scorn on my worthy head)
That have been titled, and adored a god,
Yea, sacrificed unto, myself, in Rome,
No less than Jove: and I be brought, to do   205
A peevish giglot rites? Perhaps, the thought,
And shame of that made Fortune turn her face,
Knowing herself the lesser deity,
And but my servant. Bashful queen, if so,
Sejanus thanks thy modesty. Who's that?   210

                [*Enter*] POMPONIUS, MINUTIUS

POMPONIUS
    His fortune suffers, till he hears my news:
    I have waited here too long. Macro, my lord—
SEJANUS
    Speak lower, and withdraw.
TERENTIUS   Are these things true?
MINUTIUS
    Thousands are gazing at it, in the streets.
SEJANUS
    What's that?
TERENTIUS   Minutius tells us here, my lord,   215
    That, a new head being set upon your statue,
    A rope is since found wreathed about it! and,
    But now, a fiery meteor, in the form
    Of a great ball, was seen to roll along
    The troubled air, where yet it hangs, unperfect,   220
    The amazing wonder of the multitude!

197 *game* object of scorn
198 *Writhed to thy tail* turned backwards
200 *cosening* duping
201 *spicèd* overdelicate
206 *giglot* a wanton woman (read 'to do rites unto a peevish giglot')
220 *unperfect* without having completed its flight

SEJANUS
    No more. That Macro's come, is more than all!
TERENTIUS
    Is Macro come?
POMPONIUS   I saw him.
TERENTIUS   Where? with whom?
POMPONIUS
    With Regulus.
SEJANUS   Terentius—
TERENTIUS   My lord?
SEJANUS
    Send for the Tribunes, we will straight have up   225
    More of the soldiers, for our guard. [*Exit* TERENTIUS]
                                            Minutius,
    We pray you, go for Cotta, Latiaris,
    Trio the Consul, or what Senators
    You know are sure, and ours. [*Exit* MINUTIUS] You, my
                                            good Natta,
    For Laco, Provost of the watch. [*Exit* NATTA] Now,
                                            Satrius,   230
    The time of proof comes on. Arm all our servants,
    And without tumult. [*Exit* SATRIUS] You, Pomponius,
    Hold some good correspondence, with the Consul,
    Attempt him, noble friend. [*Exit* POMPONIUS] These
                                            things begin
    To look like dangers, now, worthy my fates.   235
    Fortune, I see thy worst: let doubtful states,
    And things uncertain hang upon thy will:
    Me surest death shall render certain still.
    Yet, why is, now, my thought turned toward death,
    Whom fates have let go on, so far, in breath,   240
    Unchecked, or unreproved? I, that did help
    To fell the lofty cedar of the world,
    Germanicus; that, at one stroke, cut down
    Drusus, that upright elm; withered his vine;
    Laid Silius, and Sabinus, two strong oaks,   245
    Flat on the earth; besides, those other shrubs,
    Cordus, and Sosia, Claudia Pulchra,
    Furnius, and Gallus, which I have grubbed up;
    And since, have set my axe so strong, and deep
    Into the root of spreading Agrippine;   250
    Lopped off, and scattered her proud branches, Nero,

233 *correspondence* conversation
244 *vine* his wife Livia; the elm and vine was a marriage image

Drusus, and Caius too, although replanted;
If you will, destinies, that, after all,
I faint, now, ere I touch my period;
You are but cruel: and I already have done   255
Things great enough. All Rome hath been my slave;
The Senate sat an idle looker on,
And witness of my power; when I have blushed,
More, to command, than it to suffer; all
The Fathers have sat ready, and prepared,   260
To give me empire, temples, or their throats,
When I would ask 'em; and (what crowns the top)
Rome, Senate, people, all the world have seen
Jove, but my equal: Cæsar, but my second.
'Tis then your malice, fates, who (but your own)   265
Envy, and fear, t'have any power long known.   [*Exit*]

[*Enter*] TERENTIUS, TRIBUNES

TERENTIUS
Stay here: I'll give his lordship, you are come.

[*Enter*] MINUTIUS, COTTA, LATIARIS
They confer their letters

MINUTIUS
Marcus Terentius, pray you tell my lord,
Here's Cotta, and Latiaris.
TERENTIUS   Sir, I shall.
COTTA
My letter is the very same with yours;   270
Only requires me to be present there,
And give my voice, to strengthen his design.
LATIARIS
Names he not what it is?
COTTA   No, nor to you.
LATIARIS
'Tis strange, and singular doubtful!
COTTA   So it is?
It may be all is left to lord Sejanus.   275

[*Enter*] NATTA, LACO

To them

NATTA
Gentlemen, where's my lord?
TRIBUNE   We wait him here.

252 *Caius* Caligula
267 *give* tell

COTTA
  The Provost Laco? what's the news?
LATIARIS   My lord—

[Enter] SEJANUS
To them

SEJANUS
  Now, my right dear, noble, and trusted friends;
  How much I am a captive to your kindness!
  Most worthy Cotta, Latiaris; Laco,   280
  Your valiant hand; and gentlemen, your loves.
  I wish I could divide myself unto you;
  Or that it lay, within our narrow powers,
  To satisfy for so enlargèd bounty.
  Gracinus, we must pray you, hold your guards   285
  Unquit, when morning comes. Saw you the Consul?
MINUTIUS
  Trio will presently be here, my lord.
COTTA
  They are but giving order for the edict,
  To warn the Senate.
SEJANUS   How! the Senate?
LATIARIS   Yes.
  This morning, in Apollo's temple.
COTTA   We   290
  Are charged, by letter, to be there, my lord.
SEJANUS
  By letter? Pray you let's see!
LATIARIS   Knows not his lordship!
COTTA
  It seems so!
SEJANUS   A Senate warned? without my knowledge?
  And on this sudden? Senators by letters
  Required to be there! who brought these?
COTTA   Macro.   295
SEJANUS
  Mine enemy! And when?
COTTA   This midnight.
SEJANUS   Time,
  With every other circumstance, doth give
  It hath some strain of engine in't! *[Enter]* SATRIUS
                                                How now?
SATRIUS
  My lord, Sertorius Macro is without,

286 *Unquit* undischarged

Alone, and prays t'have private conference   300
In business, of high nature, with your lordship,
(He says to me) and which regards you much.
SEJANUS
Let him come here.
SATRIUS   Better, my lord, withdraw,
You will betray what store, and strength of friends
Are now about you; which he comes to spy.   305
SEJANUS
Is he not armed?
SATRIUS   We'll search him.
SEJANUS   No, but take,
And lead him to some room, where you, concealed,
May keep a guard upon us. [*Exit* SATRIUS] Noble Laco,
You are our trust: and, till our own cohorts
Can be brought up, your strengths must be our guard.   310
Now, good Minutius, honoured Latiaris,
                    He salutes them humbly
Most worthy, and my most unwearied friends:
I return instantly.   [*Exit* SEJANUS]
LACO   Most worthy lord!
COTTA
His lordship is turned instant kind, me thinks,
I have not observed it in him, heretofore.   315
1 TRIBUNE
'Tis true, and it becomes him nobly.
MINUTIUS   I
Am rapt withal.
2 TRIBUNE
                    By Mars, he has my lives,
(Were they a million) for this only grace.
LACO
Ay, and to name a man!
LATIARIS   As he did me!
MINUTIUS
And me!
LATIARIS   Who would not spend his life and fortunes,   320
To purchase but the look of such a lord?
LACO
He, that would nor be lord's fool, nor the world's.

318 *only* single

[Act V, Scene iv]

[*Another room in Sejanus' house. Enter*] SEJANUS, MACRO,
[SATRIUS]

SEJANUS
 Macro! most welcome, as most coveted friend!
 Let me enjoy my longings. When arrived you?
MACRO
 About the noon of night.
SEJANUS   Satrius, give leave.   [*Exit* SATRIUS] 325
MACRO
 I have been, since I came, with both the Consuls,
 On a particular design from Cæsar.
SEJANUS
 How fares it with our great, and royal master?
MACRO
 Right plentifully well; as, with a prince,
 That still holds out the great proportion   330
 Of his large favours, where his judgement hath
 Made once divine election: like the god,
 That wants not, nor is wearied to bestow
 Where merit meets his bounty, as it doth
 In you, already the most happy, and ere   335
 The sun shall climb the south, most high Sejanus.
 Let not my lord be amused. For, to this end
 Was I by Cæsar sent for, to the isle,
 With special caution to conceal my journey;
 And, thence, had my dispatch as privately   340
 Again to Rome; charged to come here by night;
 And, only to the Consuls, make narration
 Of his great purpose: that the benefit
 Might come more full, and striking, by how much
 It was less looked for, or aspired by you,   345
 Or least informèd to the common thought.

---

327 *particular design* private mission
337 *amused* amazed

---

325 *About the noon of night.* Herford and Simpson list contemporary
 imitators of this phrase, but Jonson was not the source, only an intermediary quoting Nonius' citation of Varro's *noctis circiter meridiem* (*De
 comp. doct.* 451, 9).
330f. *That still . . . his bounty.* That still extends the great quantity of his
 generous favours, to whom he formerly chose; like the god who lacks
 not bounty, and does not tire of giving it to the man who deserves it.

SEJANUS

    What may this be? part of my self, dear Macro!
    If good, speak out: and share with your Sejanus.

MACRO

    If bad, I should forever loathe myself,
    To be the messenger to so good a lord.   350
    I do exceed m'instructions, to acquaint
    Your lordship with thus much; but 'tis my venture
    On your retentive wisdom: and, because
    I would no jealous scruple should molest
    Or rack your peace of thought. For, I assure   355
    My noble lord, no Senator yet knows
    The business meant: though all, by several letters,
    Are warnèd to be there, and give their voices,
    Only to add unto the state, and grace
    Of what is purposed.

SEJANUS   You take pleasure, Macro,   360
    Like a coy wench, in torturing your lover.
    What can be worth this suffering?

MACRO   That which follows,
    The tribunicial dignity, and power:
    Both which Sejanus is to have this day
    Conferred upon him, and by public Senate.   365

SEJANUS

    Fortune, be mine again; thou hast satisfied
    For thy suspected loyalty.

MACRO   My lord,
    I have no longer time, the day approacheth,
    And I must back to Cæsar.

SEJANUS   Where's Caligula?

MACRO

    That I forgot to tell your lordship. Why,   370
    He lingers yonder, about Capreæ,
    Disgraced; Tiberius hath not seen him yet:
    He needs would thrust himself to go with me,
    Against my wish, or will, but I have quitted
    His forward trouble, with as tardy note   375
    As my neglect, or silence could afford him.
    Your lordship cannot now command me ought,
    Because, I take no knowledge that I saw you,
    But I shall boast to live to serve your lordship:
    And so take leave.

SEJANUS   Honest, and worthy Macro,   380

353 *retentive wisdom* wise secrecy
357 *several* separate

Your love, and friendship. Who's there? Satrius,
                              [*Exit* MACRO]

Attend my honourable friend forth. O!
How vain, and vile a passion is this fear?
What base, uncomely things it makes men do?
Suspect their noblest friends, (as I did this)   385
Flatter poor enemies, entreat their servants,
Stoop, court, and catch at the benevolence
Of creatures, unto whom (within this hour)
I would not have vouchsafed a quarter-look,
Or piece of face? By you, that fools call gods,   390
Hang all the sky with your prodigious signs,
Fill earth with monsters, drop the scorpion down,
Out of the zodiac, or the fiercer lion,
Shake off the loosened globe from her long hinge,
Roll all the world in darkness, and let loose   395
Th'enragèd winds to turn up groves and towns;
When I do fear again, let me be struck
With forkèd fire, and unpitied die:
Who fears, is worthy of calamity.   [*Exit*]

[Act V, Scene v]

[*Same as scene iii. Enter*] POMPONIUS, REGULUS, TRIO
To the rest

POMPONIUS
  Is not my lord here?
TERENTIUS   Sir, he will be straight.   400
COTTA
  What news, Fulcinius Trio?
TRIO   Good, good tidings.
  (But, keep it to yourself) my lord Sejanus
  Is to receive this day, in open Senate,
  The tribunicial dignity.
COTTA   Is't true?
TRIO
  No words; not to your thought: but, sir, believe it.   405
LATIARIS
  What says the Consul?
COTTA   (Speak it not again,)
  He tells me, that today my lord Sejanus—
(TRIO
  I must entreat you Cotta, on your honour
  Not to reveal it.

389 *quarter-look* face almost averted   394 *hinge* axis of the earth

COTTA On my life, sir.)
LATIARIS Say.
COTTA
  Is to receive the tribunicial power. 410
  But, as you are an honourable man,
  Let me conjure you, not to utter it:
  For it is trusted to me, with that bond.
LATIARIS
  I am Harpocrates.
TERENTIUS Can you assure it?
POMPONIUS
  The Consul told it me, but keep it close. 415
MINUTIUS
  Lord Latiaris, what's the news?
LATIARIS I'll tell you,
  But you must swear to keep it secret

[Enter] SEJANUS
To them

SEJANUS
  I knew the fates had on their distaff left
  More of our thread, than so.
REGULUS Hail, great Sejanus.
TRIO
  Hail, the most honoured.
COTTA Happy.
LATIARIS High Sejanus. 420
SEJANUS
  Do you bring prodigies too?
TRIO May all presage
  Turn to those fair effects, whereof we bring
  Your lordship news.
REGULUS May't please my lord withdraw.

To some that stand by

SEJANUS
  Yes (I will speak with you, anon.)
TERENTIUS My lord,
  What is your pleasure for the Tribunes?
SEJANUS Why, 425
  Let 'em be thanked, and sent away.
MINUTIUS My lord—
LACO
  Will't please your lordship to command me—
SEJANUS No.

418f. A reference to the goddesses that wind the thread of men's lives.

You are troublesome.
MINUTIUS   The mood is changed.
1 TRIBUNE   Not speak?
2 TRIBUNE
    Nor look?
LACO   Ay. He is wise, will make him friends
    Of such, who never love, but for their ends.   [*Exeunt*]   430

[Act V, Scene vi]

[*The temple of Apollo. Enter*] ARRUNTIUS, LEPIDUS, *divers
            other* SENATORS *passing by them*

ARRUNTIUS
    Ay, go, make haste; take heed you be not last
    To tender your 'All hail', in the wide hall
    Of huge Sejanus: run, a Lictor's pace;
    Stay not to put your robes on; but, away,
    With the pale troubled ensigns of great friendship   435
    Stamped in your face! Now, Marcus Lepidus,
    You still believe your former augury?
    Sejanus must go downward? you perceive
    His wane approaching fast?
LÉPIDUS   Believe me, Lucius,
    I wonder at this rising!
ARRUNTIUS   Ay, and that we   440
    Must give our suffrage to it? you will say,
    It is to make his fall more steep, and grievous?
    It may be so. But think it, they that can
    With idle wishes 'ssay to bring back time:
    In cases desperate, all hope is crime.   445
    See, see! what troops of his officious friends
    Flock to salute my lord! and start before
    My great, proud lord! to get a lordlike nod!
    Attend my lord, unto the Senate house!
    Bring back my lord! like servile ushers, make   450
    Way for my lord! proclaim his idol lordship,
    More than ten criers, or six noise of trumpets!
    Make legs, kiss hands, and take a scattered hair
    From my lord's eminent shoulder! See, Sanquinius!
    With his slow belly, and his dropsy! look,   455
    What toiling haste he makes! yet, here's another,

433 *Lictor's pace* rapidly
444 *'ssay* essay, attempt

Retarded with the gout, will be afore him!
Get thee Liburnian porters, thou gross fool,
To bear thy obsequious fatness, like thy peers.
They are met! The gout returns, and his great carriage.   460

LICTORS, CONSULS, SEJANUS, *etc., pass over the stage*

LICTOR
Give way, make place; room for the Consul.
SANQUINIUS   Hail,
Hail, great Sejanus.
HATERIUS   Hail, my honoured lord.
ARRUNTIUS
We shall be marked anon, for our not-hail.
LEPIDUS
That is already done.
ARRUNTIUS   It is a note
Of upstart greatness, to observe, and watch   465
For these poor trifles, which the noble mind
Neglects, and scorns.
LEPIDUS   Ay, and they think themselves
Deeply dishonoured, where they are omitted,
As if they were necessities, that helped
To the perfection of their dignities: 470
And hate the men, that but refrain 'em.
ARRUNTIUS   O!
There is a farther cause of hate. Their breasts
Are guilty, that we know their obscure springs,
And base beginnings: thence the anger grows. On. Follow.
                                                    [*Exeunt*]

[*Enter*] MACRO, LACO

MACRO
When all are entered, shut the temple doors;   475
And bring your guards up to the gate.
LACO   I will.
MACRO
If you shall hear commotion in the Senate,
Present yourself: and charge on any man
Shall offer to come forth.
LACO   I am instructed.   [*Exeunt*]

[*Enter*] THE SENATE. HATERIUS, TRIO, SANQUINIUS, COTTA,
REGULUS, SEJANUS, POMPONIUS, LATIARIS, LEPIDUS,
ARRUNTIUS, PRÆCONES, LICTORES, [PRÆTORS, SENATORS]

463 *marked* noticed (cf. V, 501)

HATERIUS
  How well his lordship looks today!
TRIO   As if   480
  He had been born, or made for this hour's state.
COTTA
  Your fellow Consul's come about, me thinks?
TRIO
  Ay, he is wise.
SANQUINIUS   Sejanus trusts him well.
TRIO
  Sejanus is a noble, bounteous lord.
HATERIUS
  He is so, and most valiant.
LATIARIS   And most wise.   485
1 SENATOR
  He's everything.
LATIARIS   Worthy of all, and more
  Than bounty can bestow.
TRIO   This dignity
  Will make him worthy.
POMPONIUS   Above Cæsar.
SANQUINIUS   Tut,
  Cæsar is but the rector of an isle,
  He of the Empire.
TRIO   Now he will have power   490
  More to reward, than ever.
COTTA   Let us look
  We be not slack in giving him our voices.
LATIARIS
  Not I.
SANQUINIUS Nor I.
COTTA   The readier we seem
  To propagate his honours, will more bind
  His thought, to ours.
HATERIUS   I think right, with your lordship.   495
  It is the way to have us hold our places.
SANQUINIUS
  Ay, and get more.
LATIARIS   More office, and more titles.
POMPONIUS
  I will not lose the part, I hope to share
  In these his fortunes, for my patrimony.

487f. *dignity . . . worthy* with a quibble on Latin *dignus*, 'worthy'
499 *patrimony* inheritance

LATIARIS
See, how Arruntius sits, and Lepidus.   500
TRIO
Let 'em alone, they will be marked anon.
1 SENATOR
I'll do with others.
2 SENATOR   So will I.
3 SENATOR   And I.
Men grow not in the State, but as they are planted
Warm in his favours.
COTTA   Noble Sejanus!
HATERIUS
Honoured Sejanus!
LATIARIS   Worthy, and great Sejanus!   505
ARRUNTIUS
Gods! how the sponges open, and take in!
And shut again! look, look! is not he blest
That gets a seat in eye-reach of him? more,
That comes in ear, or tongue-reach? O, but most,
Can claw his subtle elbow, or with a buzz   510
Fly-blow his ears.
PRÆTOR   Proclaim the Senate's peace;
And give last summons by the edict.
PRÆCO   Silence:
In name of Cæsar, and the Senate. Silence.
'Memmius Regulus, and Fulcinius Trio, Consuls, these
present kalends of June, with the first light, shall hold a   515
Senate, in the temple of Apollo Palatine, all that are Fathers,
and are registered Fathers, that have right of entering the
Senate, we warn, or command, you be frequently
present, take knowledge the business is the Common-
wealth's, whosoever is absent, his fine, or mulct, will be   520
taken, his excuse will not be taken.'
TRIO
Note, who are absent, and record their names.
REGULUS
Fathers Conscript. May, what I am to utter,
Turn good, and happy, for the Commonwealth.
And thou Apollo, in whose holy house   525
We here are met, inspire us all, with truth,
And liberty of censure, to our thought.
The majesty of great Tiberius Cæsar
Propounds to this grave Senate, the bestowing

527 *censure* judgment

Upon the man he loves, honoured Sejanus,   530
The tribunicial dignity, and power;
Here are his letters, signed with his signet:
What pleaseth now the Fathers to be done?

SENATORS
Read, read 'em, open, publicly, read 'em.

COTTA
Cæsar hath honoured his own greatness much,   535
In thinking of this act.

TRIO   It was a thought
Happy, and worthy Cæsar.

LATIARIS   And the lord,
As worthy it, on whom it is directed!

HATERIUS
Most worthy!

SANQUINIUS   Rome did never boast the virtue
That could give envy bounds, but his: Sejanus—   540

1 SENATOR
Honoured, and noble!

2 SENATOR   Good, and great Sejanus!

ARRUNTIUS
O, most tame slavery, and fierce flattery!

PRÆCO   Silence.

The Epistle is read

'Tiberius Cæsar to the Senate, greeting.
If you, Conscript Fathers, with your children, be in health,
it is abundantly well: we with our friends here, are so.   545
The care of the Commonwealth, howsoever we are removed
in person, cannot be absent to our thought; although, oftentimes, even to princes most present, the truth of their own
affairs is hid: than which, nothing falls out more miserable
to a state, or makes the art of governing more difficult. But 550
since it hath been our easeful happiness to enjoy both the
aids, and industry of so vigilant a Senate, we profess to have
been the more indulgent to our pleasures, not as being careless of our office, but rather secure of the necessity. Neither
do these common rumours of many, and infamous libels,   555
published against our retirement, at all afflict us; being born
more out of men's ignorance, than their malice: and will,
neglected, find their own grave quickly; whereas too sensibly
acknowledged, it would make their obloquy ours. Nor do
we desire their authors (though found) be censured, since   560

554 *necessity* the Senate's aid and industry

in a free state (as ours) all men ought to enjoy both their
minds, and tongues free.'
(ARRUNTIUS
The lapwing, the lapwing.)
'Yet, in things, which shall worthily, and more near concern
the majesty of a prince, we shall fear to be so unnaturally   565
cruel to our own fame, as to neglect them. True it is,
Conscript Fathers, that we have raised Sejanus, from
obscure, and almost unknown gentry,'
(SENATORS
How! how!)
'to the highest, and most conspicuous point of greatness,   570
and (we hope) deservingly; yet, not without danger: it
being a most bold hazard in that sovereign, who, by his
particular love to one, dares adventure the hatred of all his
other subjects.'
(ARRUNTIUS
This touches, the blood turns.)   575
'But we affy in your loves, and understandings, and do no
way suspect the merit of our Sejanus to make our favours
offensive to any.'
(SENATORS
O! good, good.)
'Though we could have wished his zeal had run a calmer course   580
against Agrippina, and our nephews, howsoever the open-
ness of their actions, declared them delinquents; and, that he
would have remembered, no innocence is so safe, but it
rejoiceth to stand in the sight of mercy: the use of which in
us, he hath so quite taken away, toward them, by his loyal   585
fury, as now our clemency would be thought but wearied
cruelty, if we should offer to exercise it.'
(ARRUNTIUS
I thank him, there I looked for't. A good fox!)
'Some there be, that would interpret this his public severity
to be particular ambition; and that, under a pretext of   590
service to us, he doth but remove his own lets: alleging the
strengths he hath made to himself, by the Prætorian soldiers,
by his faction in Court, and Senate, by the offices he holds
himself, and confers on others, his popularity, and dependants, his urging (and almost driving) us to this our   595
unwilling retirement, and lastly his aspiring to be our son-
in-law.'

563 *lapwing* said to divert predators from its nest by calling afar
576 *affy in* have trust in (cf. affidavit)

(SENATORS
    This's strange!
ARRUNTIUS
    I shall anon believe your vultures, Marcus.)
    'Your wisdoms, Conscript Fathers, are able to examine, and   600
    censure these suggestions. But, were they left to our ab-
    solving voice, we durst pronounce them, as we think them,
    most malicious.'
(SENATORS
    O, he has restored all, list.)
    'Yet, are they offered to be averred, and on the lives of the   605
    informers. What we should say, or rather what we should
    not say, lords of the Senate, if this be true, our gods, and
    goddesses confound us if we know! Only, we must think, we
    have placed our benefits ill: and conclude, that, in our
    choice, either we were wanting to the gods, or the gods to us.'   610
           The Senators shift their places.

(ARRUNTIUS
    The place grows hot, they shift.)
    'We have not been covetous, honourable Fathers, to change;
    neither is it now, any new lust that alters our affection, or
    old loathing: but those needful jealousies of state, that warn
    wiser princes, hourly, to provide their safety; and do teach   615
    them how learned a thing it is to beware of the humblest
    enemy; much more of those great ones, whom their own
    employed favours have made fit for their fears.'
(1 SENATOR
    Away.
2 SENATOR Sit farther.
COTTA   Let's remove—
ARRUNTIUS
    Gods! how the leaves drop off, this little wind!)   620
    'We therefore desire, that the offices he holds, be first seized
    by the Senate; and himself suspended from all exercise of
    place, or power —'
(SENATORS
    How!
SANQUINIUS By your leave.
ARRUNTIUS   Come, porpoise, (where's Haterius?
    His gout keeps him most miserably constant.)   625
    Your dancing shows a tempest.)
SEJANUS   Read no more.
REGULUS
    Lords of the Senate, hold your seats: read on.

624 *porpoise* its activity was said to warn of storm

SEJANUS
   These letters, they are forged.
REGULUS   A guard, sit still.
       Laco enters with the guards
ARRUNTIUS
   There's change.
REGULUS   Bid silence, and read forward.
PRÆCO   Silence —
   'and himself suspended from all exercise of place, or power,   630
   but till due and mature trial be made of his innocency,
   which yet we can faintly apprehend the necessity, to doubt.
   If, Conscript Fathers, to your more searching wisdoms,
   there shall appear farther cause (or of farther proceeding,
   either to seizure of lands, goods, or more —) it is not our   635
   power that shall limit your authority, or our favour, that
   must corrupt your justice: either were dishonourable in
   you, and both uncharitable to ourself. We would willingly
   be present with your counsels in this business, but the
   danger of so potent a faction (if it should prove so) forbids   640
   our attempting it: except one of the Consuls would be
   entreated for our safety, to undertake the guard of us home,
   then we should most readily adventure. In the meantime,
   it shall not be fit for us to importune so judicious a Senate,
   who know how much they hurt the innocent, that spare the   645
   guilty: and how grateful a sacrifice, to the gods, is the life
   of an ingrateful person. We reflect not, in this, on Sejanus
   (notwithstanding, if you keep an eye upon him — and there
   is Latiaris a Senator, and Pinnarius Natta, two of his most
   trusted ministers, and so professed, whom we desire not   650
   to have apprehended) but as the necessity of the cause
   exacts it.'
REGULUS
   A guard on Latiaris.
ARRUNTIUS   O, the spy!
   The reverend spy is caught, who pities him?
   Reward, sir, for your service: now, you've done   655
   Your property, you see what use is made?
   Hang up the instrument.
SEJANUS   Give leave.
LACO   Stand, stand,
   He comes upon his death, that doth advance
   And inch toward my point.

---

651 *apprehended* edd. (Q, F apprênded, after Latin *apprêndo*)
656 *property* function

SEJANUS   Have we no friends here?
ARRUNTIUS
Hushed. Where now are all the hails, and acclamations?   660

[Enter] MACRO

MACRO
Hail, to the Consuls, and this noble Senate.
SEJANUS
Is Macro here? O, thou art lost, Sejanus.
MACRO
Sit still, and unaffrighted, reverend Fathers.
Macro, by Cæsar's grace, the new-made Provost,
And now possessed of the Prætorian bands,   665
An honour late belonged to that proud man,
Bids you, be safe: and to your constant doom
Of his deservings, offers you the surety
Of all the soldiers, Tribunes, and Centurions,
Received in our command.
REGULUS   Sejanus, Sejanus,   670
Stand forth, Sejanus.
SEJANUS   Am I called?
MACRO   Ay, thou,
Thou insolent monster, art bid stand.
SEJANUS   Why, Macro,
It hath been otherwise, between you, and I?
This court that knows us both, hath seen a difference,
And can (if it be pleased to speak) confirm,   675
Whose insolence is most.
MACRO   Come down Typhœus,
If mine be most, lo, thus I make it more;
Kick up thy heels in air, tear off thy robe,
Play with thy beard, and nostrils. Thus 'tis fit,
(And no man take compassion of thy state)   680
To use th'ingrateful viper, tread his brains
Into the earth.
REGULUS   Forbear.
MACRO   If I could lose
All my humanity now, 'twere well to torture
So meriting a traitor. Wherefore, Fathers,
Sit you amazed, and silent? and not censure   685
This wretch, who in the hour he first rebelled
'Gainst Cæsar's bounty, did condemn himself?

667 *constant doom* loyal judgment

Phlegra, the field, where all the sons of earth
Mustered against the gods, did ne'er acknowledge
So proud, and huge a monster.

REGULUS   Take him hence.   690
And all the gods guard Cæsar.

TRIO   Take him hence.

HATERIUS
Hence.

COTTA
To the dungeon with him.

SANQUINIUS   He deserves it.

1 SENATOR
Crown all our doors with bays.

SANQUINIUS   And let an ox
With gilded horns, and garlands, straight be led
Unto the Capitol.

HATERIUS   And sacrificed   695
To Jove, for Cæsar's safety.

TRIO   All our gods
Be present still to Cæsar.

COTTA   Phœbus.

SANQUINIUS   Mars.

HATERIUS
Diana.

SANQUINIUS Pallas.

2 SENATOR   Juno, Mercury,
All guard him.

MACRO   Forth, thou prodigy of men. [*Exit* SEJANUS *guarded*]

COTTA
Let all the traitor's titles be defaced.   700

TRIO
His images, and statues be pulled down.

HATERIUS
His chariot wheels be broken.

ARRUNTIUS   And the legs

---

688 *Phlegra*. The form *P'hlegra* appears in both states of Q and of F. It may
    nevertheless be an error, perhaps caused by the movement of the in-
    verted comma from before aphetic *'Gainst* in the previous line, which
    lacks the mark in Q. More probably it is a hypercorrect spelling inven-
    ted by Jonson to show that the Greeks pronounced *ph* as an aspirated *p*
    (as in 'ha*ph*azard'), even though Macro, as a Roman, would have pro-
    nounced it *f*.

693, 698 In one or both of these lines the temptation to read *Senator* for
    Sanquinius (i.e., SEN. for F SAN.) is strong.

Of the poor horses, that deservèd naught,
Let them be broken too.
LEPIDUS   O, violent change,
And whirl of men's affections!
ARRUNTIUS   Like, as both   705
Their bulks and souls were bound on Fortune's wheel,
And must act only with her motion!
                    [Exeunt, leaving] LEPIDUS, ARRUNTIUS
LEPIDUS
Who would depend upon the popular air,
Or voice of men, that have today beheld
(That which if all the gods had foredeclared,   710
Would not have been believed) Sejanus' fall?
He, that this morn rose proudly, as the sun?
And, breaking through a mist of clients' breath,
Came on as gazed at, and admired, as he
When superstitious Moors salute his light!   715
That had our servile nobles waiting him
As common grooms; and hanging on his look,
No less than human life on destiny!
That had men's knees as frequent, as the gods;
And sacrifices, more, than Rome had altars: 720
And this man fall! fall? Ay, without a look,
That durst appear his friend; or lend so much
Of vain relief, to his changed state, as pity!
ARRUNTIUS
They, that before like gnats played in his beams,
And thronged to circumscribe him, now not seen!   725
Nor deign to hold a common seat with him!
Others, that waited him unto the Senate,
Now, inhumanly ravish him to prison!
Whom (but this morn) they followed as their lord,
Guard through the streets, bound like a fugitive!   730
Instead of wreaths, give fetters; strokes, for stoops:
Blind shame, for honours; and black taunts, for titles!
Who would trust slippery chance?
LEPIDUS   They, that would make
Themselves her spoil: and foolishly forget,
When she doth flatter, that she comes to prey.   735
Fortune, thou hadst no deity, if men
Had wisdom: we have placed thee so high,
By fond belief in thy felicity.
                    Shout within

715 *Moors.* The reference is to Roman belief that Libyans worshipped the
    sun.

SENATORS
    The gods guard Cæsar. All the gods guard Cæsar.

        [Enter] MACRO, REGULUS, SENATORS

MACRO
    Now great Sejanus, you that awed the State,   740
And sought to bring the nobles to your whip,
That would be Cæsar's tutor, and dispose
Of dignities, and offices! that had
The public head still bare to your designs,
And made the general voice to echo yours!   745
That looked for salutations, twelve score off,
And would have pyramids, yea, temples reared
To your huge greatness! now, you lie as flat,
As was your pride advanced.
REGULUS   Thanks, to the gods.
SENATORS
    And praise to Macro, that hath savèd Rome.   750
Liberty, liberty, liberty. Lead on,
And praise to Macro, that hath savèd Rome.
        [Exeunt leaving] ARRUNTIUS, LEPIDUS
ARRUNTIUS
    I prophesy, out of this Senate's flattery,
That this new fellow, Macro, will become
A greater prodigy in Rome, than he   755
That now is fall'n.

        [Enter] TERENTIUS

TERENTIUS   O you, whose minds are good,
And have not forced all mankind, from your breasts;
That yet have so much stock of virtue left,
To pity guilty states, when they are wretched:
Lend your soft ears to hear, and eyes to weep   760
Deeds done by men, beyond the acts of furies.
The eager multitude, (who never yet
Knew why to love, or hate, but only pleased
T'express their rage of power) no sooner heard
The murmur of Sejanus in decline,   765
But with that speed, and heat of appetite,
With which they greedily devour the way

---

757 *mankind* humanity   760 *soft* sympathetic

746 *twelve score off.* Two hundred forty yards, a common length for a shot
    in archery. Macro's taste for archery imagery (cf. III, 720f.) is an
    example of Jonson's 'poetic', as distinguished from 'dramatic' or
    'psychological', characterization.

To some great sports, or a new theatre,
They filled the Capitol, and Pompey's cirque;
Where, like so many mastiffs, biting stones,   770
As if his statues now were sensive grown
Of their wild fury, first, they tear them down:
Then fastening ropes, drag them along the streets,
Crying in scorn, 'this, this was that rich head
Was crowned with garlands, and with odours, this   775
That was in Rome so reverencèd! Now
The furnace, and the bellows shall to work
The great Sejanus crack, and piece, by piece,
Drop in the founder's pit!'
LEPIDUS   O, popular rage!
TERENTIUS
The whilst, the Senate, at the temple of Concord,   780
Make haste to meet again, and thronging cry,
'Let us condemn him, tread him down in water,
While he doth lie upon the bank; away:'
Where some, more tardy, cry unto their bearers,
'He will be censured ere we come, run knaves;'   785
And use that furious diligence, for fear
Their bondmen should inform against their slackness,
And bring their quaking flesh unto the hook:
The rout, they follow with confusèd voice,
Crying, they are glad, say they could ne'er abide him;   790
Enquire, what man he was? what kind of face?
What beard he had? what nose? what lips? protest,
They ever did presage he'd come to this:
They never thought him wise, nor valiant: ask
After his garments, when he dies? what death?   795
And not a beast of all the herd demands,
What was his crime? or, who were his accusers?
Under what proof, or testimony, he fell?
'There came' (says one) 'a huge, long, worded letter
From Capreæ against him.' 'Did there so?'   800
O, they are satisfied, no more.
LEPIDUS   Alas!
They follow fortune, and hate men condemned,
Guilty, or not.

769 *cirque* theatre
771 *sensive* capable of feeling sensation

779 *founder's pit.* Where broken pieces of metal were melted down to be re-
    cast; Sejanus' statue, which figured early in the play, embodies in the
    action the philosophical theme of mutability. (For the source, see
    Appendix A.)

ARRUNTIUS   But, had Sejanus thrived
In his design, and prosperously oppressed
The old Tiberius, then, in that same minute   805
These very rascals, that now rage like furies,
Would have proclaimed Sejanus Emperor.

LEPIDUS
But what hath followed?

TERENTIUS   Sentence, by the Senate;
To lose his head: which was no sooner off,
But that, and th'unfortunate trunk were seized   810
By the rude multitude; who not content
With what the forward justice of the State,
Officiously had done, with violent rage
Have rent it limb, from limb. A thousand heads,
A thousand hands, ten thousand tongues, and voices,   815
Employed at once in several acts of malice!
Old men not staid with age, virgins with shame,
Late wives with loss of husbands, mothers of children,
Losing all grief in joy of his sad fall,
Run quite transported with their cruelty!   820
These mounting at his head, these at his face,
These digging out his eyes, those with his brain,
Sprinkling themselves, their houses, and their friends;
Others are met, have ravished thence an arm,
And deal small pieces of the flesh for favours;   825
These with a thigh; this hath cut off his hands;
And this his feet; these fingers, and these toes;
That hath his liver; he his heart: there wants
Nothing but room for wrath, and the place for hatred!
What cannot oft be done, is now o'erdone.   830
The whole, and all of what was great Sejanus,
And next to Cæsar did possess the world,
Now torn, and scattered, as he needs no grave,
Each little dust covers a little part:

---

812 *forward* eager

821 *mounting*. Herford and Simpson believe this line corrupt and this word
'impossible'; Whalley quoted a suggested emendation to 'minting', i.e.,
'aiming', little improvement though it seems to make. The passage
follows fairly closely Claudius' description of the dismemberment of
another tyrant, Rufinus (who perished more than three centuries after
Sejanus; Jonson's employment of *In Rufinum* illustrates again his
artistic synchronization of history), but the Latin throws no light on
these words. Perhaps the line is to be understood 'some jumping at his
newly-removed head as it was hurled above the throng, some others
particularly at his face'.

So lies he nowhere, and yet often buried!   835

[*Enter*] NUNTIUS

ARRUNTIUS
  More of Sejanus?
NUNTIUS   Yes.
LEPIDUS   What can be added?
  We know him dead.
NUNTIUS   Then, there begin your pity.
  There is enough behind, to melt ev'n Rome,
  And Cæsar into tears: (since never slave
  Could yet so highly offend, but tyranny,   840
  In torturing him, would make him worth lamenting.)
  A son, and daughter, to the dead Sejanus,
  (Of whom there is not now so much remaining
  As would give fastening to the hangman's hook)
  Have they drawn forth for farther sacrifice;   845
  Whose tenderness of knowledge, unripe years,
  And childish silly innocence was such,
  As scarce would lend them feeling of their danger:
  The girl so simple, as she often asked,
  Where they would lead her? for what cause they dragged
                               her?   850
  Cried, she would do no more. That she could take
  Warning with beating. And because our laws
  Admit no virgin immature to die,
  The wittily, and strangely cruel Macro,
  Delivered her to be deflowered, and spoiled,   855
  By the rude lust of the licentious hangman,
  Then, to be strangled with her harmless brother.
LEPIDUS
  O, act, most worthy hell, and lasting night,
  To hide it from the world!
NUNTIUS   Their bodies thrown
  Into the Gemonies, (I know not how,   860
  Or by what accident returned) the mother,
  Th'expulsèd Apicata, finds them there;
  Whom when she saw lie spread on the degrees,
  After a world of fury in herself,
  Tearing her hair, defacing of her face,   865
  Beating her breasts, and womb, kneeling amazed,
  Crying to heaven, then to them; at last,
  Her drownèd voice got up above her woes:

854 *wittily* cleverly
862 *expulsèd* exiled
863 *degrees* steps

And with such black, and bitter execrations,
(As might affright the gods, and force the sun   870
Run backward to the east, nay, make the old
Deformèd chaos rise again, t'o'erwhelm
Them, us, and all the world) she fills the air;
Upbraids the heavens with their partial dooms,
Defies their tyrannous powers, and demands,   875
What she, and those poor innocents have transgressed,
That they must suffer such a share in vengeance,
Whilst Livia, Lygdus, and Eudemus live,
Who, (as she says, and firmly vows, to prove it
To Cæsar, and the Senate) poisoned Drusus?   880

LEPIDUS
Confederates with her husband?

NUNTIUS   Ay.

LEPIDUS   Strange act!

ARRUNTIUS
And strangely opened: what says now my monster,
The multitude? they reel now? do they not?

NUNTIUS
Their gall is gone, and now they 'gin to weep
The mischief they have done.

ARRUNTIUS   I thank 'em, rogues!   885

NUNTIUS
Part are so stupid, or so flexible,
As they believe him innocent; all grieve:
And some, whose hands yet reek with his warm blood,
And grip the part which they did tear of him,
Wish him collected, and created new.   890

LEPIDUS
How Fortune plies her sports, when she begins
To practise 'em! pursues, continues, adds!
Confounds, with varying her impassioned moods!

ARRUNTIUS
Dost thou hope Fortune to redeem thy crimes?
To make amends, for thy ill placèd favours,   895
With these strange punishments? Forbear, you things,
That stand upon the pinnacles of state,
To boast your slippery height; when you do fall,
You pash yourselves in pieces, ne'er to rise:
And he that lends you pity, is not wise.   900

874 *partial dooms* unjust judgements
899 *pash* smash

TERENTIUS

Let this example move th'insolent man,
Not to grow proud, and careless of the gods:
It is an odious wisdom, to blaspheme,
Much more to slighten, or deny their powers.
For, whom the morning saw so great, and high,　　905
Thus low, and little, 'fore the even doth lie.　　*[Exeunt]*

THE END

Appendix A

JUVENAL'S TENTH SATIRE

Jonson's many near and remote sources for *Sejanus* are listed and, in many cases, reprinted in the editions of W. D. Briggs, and Herford and Simpson. It would be pointless to reproduce them all here, but to afford some illustration of the kind of use he made of them, the relevant lines from Juvenal's tenth *Satire*, with references to the play, are given below in literal prose translation.

Jonson's method in assimilating Juvenal's poem, to which he turned for the end of Sejanus' life where Tacitus' *Annals* had an awkward gap, is very far from mere translation, *verbatim* and *seriatim*. Instead he breaks the material up so that it forms part of speeches by Sabinus, Arruntius, the Senators, Lepidus, and Terentius, drawing it into the dialogue of his dramatic poem. In Juvenal, the historical narrative is only one of several chosen to illustrate the moral of the last two lines; in Jonson the moral is the same, but the narrative is expanded from other sources to fill the entire poem.

(*Satire* X, 56–77)	(*Sejanus*)
Some men excessive power, a thing of great envy, hurls down; the long page, embellished with their honours, overwhelms them. Down come their statues, following the rope, the smashing axe breaks the wheels of their chariots and the legs of their innocent horses; now the flames hiss, now by the bellows and the forge the head adored by the populace is burnt and mighty Sejanus crackles, and from the face once second in the whole world, they make jugs, basins, frying pans and pots. Put laurel over your door, lead a bull covered with chalk to the Capitol. Sejanus is dragged by the hook, a spectacle, everyone rejoices: 'What lips he had, what a face!' 'Never, believe me, did I like the man.' 'But under what accusation did he fall? Who was the accuser? By what evidence, by what witness was he condemned?' 'Nothing of that kind; a long and wordy letter came from Capreæ.' 'Good enough, I ask no more.' And what does the mob of Remus say? They follow Fortune as always	V. 701 f. V. 776 f. I. 217 V. 779 V. 693 f. V. 792 f. V. 801 f.

and hate the condemned. The same crowd, if
Fortune had favoured her man, if a secret blow
had felled the Emperor, in the same hour would
have called Sejanus their Augustus.
(85–88)

'Let us run with haste and, as he lies on the   V. 781 f.
bank, let us trample Cæsar's enemy.' 'But let
the servants see, that none of them may bear
witness against his master, and drag him
trembling into court.'
(92–94)

'[If you were Sejanus, you would want] to be
thought the tutor of a prince, sitting on a   IV. 403
narrow ledge in Capreæ with his crowd of   IV. 380
Chaldees.'
(103–107)

Therefore you agree that Sejanus did not know   V. 896 f.
what things to seek; for he who sought too many
honours and had too much wealth, was building
the many stories of a high tower, whence the
fall would be greater, and horrible the crash   V. 442
of utter ruin.
(365–366)

You would have no deity, Fortune, if we had   V. 736 f.
but wisdom; it is we, we who make you a goddess
and put you in heaven.

Appendix B

GLOSSARY OF CLASSICAL NAMES

Names marked thus* are the subject of a separate entry.

Ædiles Administrative officials below Prætors*.

Æmilian Of the family of Manius Æmilius Lepidus*, who restored the 'Basilica Pauli', built by his grandfather.

Æsculapius God of healing.

Afer, Cnæus Domitius Orator who, in history, won the favour of Tiberius* by prosecuting Claudia Pulchra*.

Afranius, Lucius Consul* and legate under Pompey*, with whose party he was condemned for treachery.

Agrippina, Vipsania ('major') Widow of Germanicus*, granddaughter of Augustus*; starved to death in Pandataria* A.D. 33.

Alcides Hercules*.

Alexander 'The Great' of Macedon, adventurer and conqueror, died aged thirty-three, probably of fever.

Antium Modern Anzio, south of Rome; in classical times a fashionable resort known for its temples.

Antonius, Marcus Marc Anthony, soldier and follower of Julius Cæsar*. His letters are quoted by Suetonius.

Apicata Wife of Sejanus* whom he sent away during his intrigue with Livia*. After his death, Apicata revealed what she knew of the murder of Drusus senior*.

Apicius, Marcus Gavius Wealthy gourmet under Augustus* and Tiberius*.

Apollo God, especially of music, archery, prophecy, and medicine; his temple on the Palatine hill was erected by Augustus*.

Arruntius, Lucius Highly respected Senator*, committed suicide in A.D. 37 when accused by Macro*.

Atlas Mythological Titan, tricked into holding the world on his back.

Augusta, Livia Widow of Augustus* and mother of Tiberius*.

Augustus Cæsar, Caius Octavius Stepfather and adopted father of Tiberius*; Augusta* was his second wife. He died at Nola* and was declared a god of the State.

Bibaculus, Marcus Furius Author of a poem on Julius Cæsar's* wars in Gallia* which like his *Epigrams* has not survived.

Brutus, Marcus Junius Follower of Pompey*, pardoned by Julius Cæsar*, whom he conspired against with Cassius* and slew. He committed suicide after the battle of Philippi*. Nothing is known of his 'pleadings'.

Cæsar See under Augustus; Caius; Caligula.; Julius; Tiberius.

Caius Cæsar Grandson of Augustus*, first husband of Livia*.

Caligula, Caius Cæsar Youngest son of Germanicus*, joined Tiberius* on Capreæ* (historically, after Sejanus'* death); next in succession to the throne after Drusus senior* and his own brothers, he may have brought about the death of Tiberius* with the aid of Macro*. He died violently in A.D. 41.

Campania The region of middle Italy containing Capua*, Nola*, Naples and the island of Capreæ*.

Capitol One of the hills of Rome, the site of many temples.

Capreæ Modern Capri, an island near Naples whence Tiberius* retired and Caligula* fled.

Capua City in Campania* linked with Rome by the Via Appia, modern Santa Maria di Capua Vetere (not modern Capua).

Cassius Longinus, Caius Follower of Pompey* pardoned after the Civil War by Julius Cæsar*, whom he later conspired against with Brutus* and slew. He committed suicide at the battle of Philippi*.

Castor (i) A famous gladiator. (ii) Mythological son of Jupiter* and twin brother of Pollux*.

Cato Uticensis, Marcus Porcius Statesman who opposed Julius Cæsar* and followed Pompey* into exile, where he committed suicide.

Catullus Roman poet; his abuse of Julius Cæsar is in *Poems* 11, 29, 54, 57, 93.

Centurion Commander of a century*.

Century Division of troops made up of one hundred men.

Chaldees Astrologers; the science of predicting a person's destiny by the position of the stars at his birth was cultivated in Chaldea.

Cicero, Marcus Tullius Roman statesman who wrote, amongst many others, a work in favour of Cato*, answered by Julius Cæsar's* *Anticato*; both are lost.

Cithera An error, followed by Jonson, for Cythnos (modern Kythnos) in the Cyclades islands off Greece, near Gyaros (the 'other isle') where Silanus* was first exiled.

Claudia Pulchra Cousin (not niece) of Agrippina*, prosecuted by Afer* for adultery with Furnius* and for plotting to poison Tiberius*.

Cohort Division of troops containing six centuries*.

Colossus Vast statue of a man straddling the entrance to the harbour of Rhodes*.

Concord Goddess, personification of civil harmony.

Consul Supreme magistrate in Rome, of whom two were appointed by the Emperor to hold office for several months.

Cordus, Aulus Cremutius Historian; committed suicide in A.D. 25. His books were burnt, but some fragments were saved by his daughter.

Cotta, Maximus Messalinus Marcus Aurelius Senator* and Consul*, enemy of Lepidus*, later disgraced for remarks about Caligula*.

Cupid Mythological son of Venus*, he shot his victims with arrows which caused them to fall in love.

Diana Goddess, huntress.

Dictator Civil and military leader with authority not subject to veto or appeal.

Drusus (junior), Julius Cæsar Second son of Germanicus*, starved to death in the palace two years after Sejanus'* execution.

Drusus Cæsar (senior) Son of Tiberius* by his first wife, second husband of his own first cousin, Tiberius' niece Livia*.

Eudemus Physician, accomplice of Sejanus* and Livia* in the murder of Drusus senior*. He was accused by Apicata*, tortured and executed.

Fathers Conscript Really 'Fathers and Conscripts', Senators* of the usual sort and others 'enrolled' to make up the number to 600 after the exile of the Tarquin party.

Flamen Priest.

Fortune Goddess of chance in late Rome; her iconography for Jonson's age is discussed in the Introduction and in Shakespeare's *Henry V*, III.vi.

Fundane Relating to the area about modern Fondi, half way between Rome and Naples.

Furies Spirits of vengeance for wrong.

Furnius Put to death for adultery with Claudia Pulchra*.

Gallia The Roman province Gaul, about the same area as modern France.

Gallus, Caius Asinius Married the divorced first wife of Tiberius*, who sentenced him and starved him to death.

Gauls Natives of Gallia*.

Gemonies 'The Gemonian steps ... on which bodies were thrown to dishonour them, sometimes dragged by the hangman's hook' (Jonson's note to IV, 309).

Germanicus, Julius Cæsar Nephew of Tiberius*, who later adopted him; husband of Agrippina*. He may have died of poison.

Germany The Roman province of Germania, roughly equivalent to modern Germany and south central Europe.

Gracinus See Laco.

Harpocrates God of silence and secrecy.

Haterius, Quintus Senator* and orator, the object of Tiberius'* remark (also applied by Jonson to Shakespeare) 'Haterius needs a brake'.

Hecatomb Sacrifice of a hundred oxen.

Hell and Elysium Places of abode in the after-life: Hell an underworld not necessarily painful, Elysium the Isles of the Blessed.

Hercules Hero, sometimes worshipped as a god, noted for his great strength and ability to avert evil.

Horace (*Quintus Horatius Flaccus*) Roman poet, author of, amongst other things, *Satires* and a discussion of *The Art of Poetry*, including drama; for a time a follower of Brutus*.

Jove Jupiter, the supreme deity.

Julius See Cæsar; Posthumus.

Julius Cæsar, Caius Became Consul* in league with Pompey* and established the army with which he warred in Gallia*, returning across the Rubicon and driving Pompey into exile. The Pompeians conducted a peripheral war with him, but he was the subject of extraordinary honours in Rome. He was murdered in a conspiracy led by Brutus* and Cassius*.

Juno Wife of Jove* and supreme goddess.

Jupiter Jove*.

Kalends First day of the month.

Laco, Græcinus ('*Gracinus*') Provost* of the night-watch at the crisis of Sejanus'* career.

Latiaris, Latinius (*Lucanius*) Friend, not — historically — a relative, of Sabinus*, whom he betrayed; denounced in Tiberius'* letter to the Senate.

Lepidus, Manius Æmilius ('*Marcus*') A responsible elder statesman. (Jonson's error about his prænomen follows Lipsius.)

Liburnians Central European slaves who acted as court messengers.
Lictores Attendants on Roman magistrates who carried the fasces.
Linceus Argonaut, known for the power of his sight.
Livia (*Livilla*) Niece of Tiberius*, daughter of Nero Drusus, sister
of Germanicus*, married first to Caius Cæsar*, grandson of
Augustus*, and second to Drusus senior*. In history she died
before Sejanus*.
Lucius See Arruntius.
Lygdus Handsome young eunuch, cupbearer to Drusus senior*; as
such he would taste his master's wine to guard against poison.

Macedon See Alexander.
Macro, Nævius Sertorius Tiberius'* agent in the overthrow of
Sejanus*, whom he followed as Provost* of the Prætorian*
guard; died under persecution of Caligula*, whom he helped to
the throne.
Marcus See Lepidus.
Mars God of war.
Mercury Messenger of the gods, noted for swiftness.
Messalla Corvinus Next in command to Brutus* and Cassius* at
Philippi*; wrote a history of the civil war.
Ministri (singular *Minister*) Attendants.
Minutius Thermus Minor associate of Sejanus*, after whose death
he was condemned.

Natta, Pinnarius Client of Sejanus* who accused Cordus*.
Nero, Julius Cæsar Eldest son of Germanicus*, next in succession
to the throne after Drusus senior*; exiled to Pontia* and starved
to death there. (Not to be confused with C. Julius Cæsar* or with
Nero the arsonist.)
Nola Town in Campania* near Naples, still known by this name.
Nuntius Messenger.

Œdipus Greek who solved the riddle of the Sphinx*.
Olympia Mountain dwelling-place of the gods.
Opsius, Marcus Conspirator with Latiaris* and Rufus* in the
betrayal of Sabinus*.

Pagonianus (*Paconianus*), *Sextius* Helper of Sejanus* in the plot
against Caligula*; later strangled in prison.
Pallas Athene Goddess of wisdom, often shown armed.
Pandataria See Pontia.

Parthian Citizen of central Asia minor.

Pergamum Modern Bergama, Turkey.

Philippi Scene in northern Greece of the battle in which Antonius* defeated Brutus* and Cassius*.

Phlegra Pallene, in Macedonia, where the struggle between the giants, including Typhœus*, and the gods took place (cf. IV, 270, note).

Phœbus Personification of the sun. (See also Apollo.)

Plancina Wife of Piso, with him suspected of a hand in the death of Germanicus*.

Pollio, Asinius Poet, historian and statesman, of whose writing fragments only remain.

Pollux Twin brother of Castor*. The pair functioned as protective deities.

Pompey, Cnæus General, first associate and later opponent of Julius Cæsar*, by whom he was defeated at Pharsalus.

Pomponius Minor confederate of Sejanus*.

Pontia Modern Ponza, like Pandataria an island near Naples employed as a place of confinement.

Posthumus, Julius Lover of Augusta's* friend Mutilia Prisca*, through whom Sejanus* influenced Tiberius*.

Prœcones (singular *Prœco*) Heralds.

Prœtor State official below Consuls* and above Ædiles*, twelve in number at this time.

Prœtorian The imperial bodyguard, the garrison for Rome.

Prisca, Mutilia Mistress of Julius Posthumus* and intimate friend of Augusta*.

Provost Commander of the Prætorian* guard.

Regulus, Livineus Friend of Agrippina* mentioned II, 220; not the same as the next entry.

Regulus, Publius Memmius Consul* in the year of Sejanus'* death.

Rhadamanth Mythological judge of the dead.

Rhodes Island of Tiberius'* exile during Augustus'* reign; the Colossus* stood at the harbour entrance.

Rufus, Petilius Betrayer, with Opsius* and Latiaris*, of Sabinus*.

Sabinus, Titius Friend of Germanicus*, betrayed by Latiaris* and executed for treason.

Sacrovir Leader of a rebellion in Gallia* in A.D. 21.

Sanquinius Senator*, later accuser of Arruntius*.

Satrius Secundus Client of Sejanus* who accused Cordus*, but he may have been amongst those who divulged Sejanus' conspiracy.

Scipio, Metellus Father-in-law of Pompey*.

Sejanus, Lucius Ælius Son of Sejus Strabo*, became with his father commander of the Prætorian* guard and subsequently an influence on Tiberius*. He lost control of the guard when Tiberius became suspicious, and was condemned in A.D. 31.

Senate, Senators Chief council of state with a membership of 600, largely hereditary, partly by election and imperial nomination.

Servus (plural *Servi*) Servant, attendant.

Sestertia (singular *Sestertium*) A thousand *sestertii*. A Roman private soldier earned just under a *sestertium* a year, minus his keep.

Sicambrians (*Sugambrians*) A tribe in Germany*.

Silanus, Caius Exiled in A.D. 22 for plundering Asia.

Silius, Caius Served under Germanicus*, defeated Sacrovir*, killed himself (but not in the Senate*) when accused of treason and extortion.

Sinon Greek who duped the Trojans into accepting the wooden horse.

Sosia Galla Wife of Caius Silius* and friend of Agrippina*.

Spain Roman province of Hispania, roughly the Iberian peninsula.

Spelunca Modern Sperlonga, between Rome and Naples.

Sphinx Monster which kept Thebes under its power until Œdipus* solved its riddle.

Strabo, Sejus Lucius A knight from Vulsinii*, Provost* of the Prætorian* guard and father of Sejanus*.

Terentius, Marcus Friend of Sejanus*, but later acquitted of guilt. The last lines of the play are his.

Tiber The principal river of Rome.

Tiberius Cæsar Stepson and adopted son of Augustus*, father of Drusus senior*, uncle of Germanicus*. At the time of the play in his sixties.

Tibicines Flautists.

Titus Livius The Roman historian Livy; wrote under Augustus*.

Tribune One of the six commanding officers of a Roman legion; also, a civilian official with wide powers, including veto.

Trio, Lucius Fulcinius Conspirator with Sejanus*, whom he aided as Consul*; the association forced him to commit suicide in A.D. 35.

Tubicines Trumpeters.

Typhœus One of the giants who sought to overthrow Zeus (cf. IV, 270, note) and failed.

Urgulania Friend of Augusta.*

Varro, Lucius Visellius Consul* suborned by Sejanus* in the prosecution of Silius*.

Venus Goddess of love; wife of Vulcan*, mother of Cupid*, mistress of Mars*.

Vertumnus God of the changing year.

Vulcan Armourer of the gods. He trapped his wife Venus* with her lover Mars* in a net of wires.

Vulsinii Modern Bolsena, between Rome and Florence. Birthplace of Sejanus*, it paid particular honour to Nortia, the Etruscan equivalent of Fortune*.

Women Beware Women

THOMAS MIDDLETON

Edited by
ROMA GILL

ABBREVIATIONS

O	The first (octavo) edition of *Women Beware Women*.
Bullen	*The Works of Thomas Middleton*, ed. A. H. Bullen (1885–6).
Dyce	*The Works of Thomas Middleton*, ed. Alexander Dyce (1840).
Hipolito & *Isabella*	*The True History of the Tragicke Loves of Hipolito and Isabella* (1628).
Moryson 4	*Shakespeare's Europe* (Part IV of Fynes Moryson's *Itinerary*), ed. Charles Hughes (1903).
Mulryne	*Women Beware Women*, ed. J. R. Mulryne (unpublished thesis, Cambridge, 1962).
Simpson	'Thomas Middleton's *Women Beware Women*', by Percy Simpson, *Modern Language Review* XXXIII (1938).

WOMEN
BEWARE
WOMEN.

A
TRAGEDY,
BY
Tho. Middleton, Gent.

LONDON:
Printed for *Humphrey Moseley*, 1657.

TO THE READER

WHEN THESE[1] amongst others of Mr Thomas Middleton's excellent poems came to my hands, I was not a little confident but that his name would prove as great an inducement for thee to read, as me to print them, since those issues of his brain that have already seen the sun have by their worth gained themselves a free entertainment amongst all that are ingenious; and I am most certain that these will no way lessen his reputation, nor hinder his admission to any noble and recreative spirits. All that I require at thy hands, is to continue the author in his deserved esteem, and to accept of my endeavours which have ever been to please thee.

Farewell

Upon the Tragedy of My Familiar Acquaintance Tho. Middleton

> *Women beware Women:* 'tis a true text
> Never to be forgot. Drabs of state vexed
> Have plots, poisons, mischiefs that seldom miss
> To murther virtue with a venom kiss—
> Witness this worthy tragedy, expressed
> By him that well deserved amongst the best
> Of poets in his time. He knew the rage,
> Madness of women crossed; and for the stage
> Fitted their humours, hell-bred malice, strife
> Acted in state, presented to the life.
> I that have seen't can say, having just cause,
> Never came tragedy off with more applause.
>   Nath. Richards[2]

[1] *Women Beware Women* was printed along with *More Dissemblers Besides Women.*
[2] Nathaniel Richards (*fl* 1630–54) was author of *The Tragedy of Messallina.*

[DRAMATIS PERSONAE]

DUKE OF FLORENCE
LORD CARDINAL, *brother to the* DUKE
TWO CARDINALS *more*
A LORD
FABRITIO, *father to* ISABELLA
HIPPOLITO, *brother to* FABRITIO
GUARDIANO, *uncle to the foolish* WARD
THE WARD, *a rich young heir*
LEANTIO, *a factor, husband to* BIANCA
SORDIDO, *the* WARD'S *man*

LIVIA, *sister to* FABRITIO
ISABELLA, *niece to* LIVIA
BIANCA, LEANTIO'S *wife*
THE WIDOW, *his* [LEANTIO'S] *mother*
STATES OF FLORENCE, CITIZENS, A 'PRENTICE, BOYS, MESSENGER, SERVANTS
[TWO LADIES, *other* LORDS, PAGES, GUARD]

The Scene:
FLORENCE.

---

9 *factor* agent
15 *States* Nobility

---

13 BIANCA. O's *Brancha* (here and throughout the play) probably represents a misreading of MS's *i* as *r*.

Act I, Scene i

Enter LEANTIO *with* BIANCA *and* MOTHER

MOTHER

 Thy sight was never yet more precious to me;
 Welcome, with all the affection of a mother,
 That comfort can express from natural love:
 Since thy birth-joy—a mother's chiefest gladness
 After sh'as undergone her curse of sorrows—   5
 Thou wast not more dear to me, than this hour
 Presents thee to my heart. Welcome again.

LEANTIO

 'Las, poor affectionate soul, how her joys speak to me!
 I have observed it often, and I know it is
 The fortune commonly of knavish children   10
 To have the loving'st mothers.

MOTHER   What's this gentlewoman?

LEANTIO

 Oh you have named the most unvalued'st purchase,
 That youth of man had ever knowledge of.
 As often as I look upon that treasure,
 And know it to be mine—there lies the blessing—   15
 It joys me that I ever was ordained
 To have a being, and to live 'mongst men;
 Which is a fearful living, and a poor one,
 Let a man truly think on't,
 To have the toil and griefs of fourscore years   20
 Put up in a white sheet, tied with two knots.
 Methinks it should strike earthquakes in adúlterers,
 When ev'n the very sheets they commit sin in,
 May prove, for aught they know, all their last garments.
 Oh what a mark were there for women then!   25
 But beauty able to content a conqueror,

3 *express* distil
12 *unvalued'st* invaluable

---

21 *two knots.* The deathbed portrait of Donne shows how the shroud was
 fastened with a knot at head and feet.
26–7 *conqueror . . . content.* Alexander the Great is said to have wept because
 there were no new worlds for him to conquer.

Whom earth could scarce content, keeps me in compass;
I find no wish in me bent sinfully
To this man's sister, or to that man's wife:
In love's name let 'em keep their honesties, 30
And cleave to their own husbands, 'tis their duties.
Now when I go to church, I can pray handsomely;
Nor come like gallants only to see faces,
As if lust went to market still on Sundays.
I must confess I am guilty of one sin, mother, 35
More than I brought into the world with me;
But that I glory in: 'tis theft, but noble
As ever greatness yet shot up withal.

MOTHER
How's that?

LEANTIO   Never to be repented, mother,
Though sin be death! I had died, if I had not sinned, 40
And here's my masterpiece. Do you now behold her!
Look on her well, she's mine; look on her better—
Now say, if't be not the best piece of theft
That ever was committed. And I have my pardon for't:
'Tis sealed from Heaven by marriage.

MOTHER   Married to her! 45

LEANTIO
You must keep council mother, I am undone else;
If it be known, I have lost her. Do but think now
What that loss is—life's but a trifle to't.
From Venice her consent and I have brought her,
From parents great in wealth, more now in rage; 50
But let storms spend their furies. Now we have got
A shelter o'er our quiet innocent loves,
We are contented. Little money sh'as brought me:
View but her face, you may see all her dowry,
Save that which lies locked up in hidden virtues, 55
Like jewels kept in cabinets.

MOTHER   Y'are too blame,
If your obedience will give way to a check,
To wrong such a perfection.

LEANTIO   How?

---

27 *in compass* within limits

32–4 *Now ... Sundays.* '... come abroad where matter is frequent, to
court, to tiltings, publique showes, and feasts, and church sometimes . . .
In these places a man shall find whom to love, whom to play with,
whom to touch once, whom to hold ever' (Jonson, *Epicoene*, IV, i, 57–62).

MOTHER   Such a creature,
  To draw her from her fortune, which no doubt,
  At the full time, might have proved rich and noble: 60
  You know not what you have done. My life can give you
  But little helps, and my death lesser hopes;
  And hitherto your own means has but made shift
  To keep you single, and that hardly too.
  What ableness have you to do her right, then,   65
  In maintenance fitting her birth and virtues,
  Which ev'ry woman of necessity looks for,
  And most to go above it, not confined
  By their conditions, virtues, bloods, or births,
  But flowing to affections, wills and humours?   70

LEANTIO
  Speak low sweet mother; you are able to spoil as many
  As come within the hearing; if it be not
  Your fortune to mar all, I have much marvel.
  I pray do not you teach her to rebel,
  When she's in a good way to obedience;   75
  To rise with other women in commotion
  Against their husbands, for six gowns a year,
  And so maintain their cause, when they're once up,
  In all things else that require cost enough.
  They are all of 'em a kind of spirits—soon raised,   80
  But not so soon laid, mother. As for example,
  A woman's belly is got up in a trice:
  A simple charge ere it be laid down again:
  So ever in all their quarrels, and their courses.
  And I'm a proud man, I hear nothing of 'em;   85
  They're very still, I thank my happiness,
  And sound asleep; pray let not your tongue wake 'em.
  If you can but rest quiet, she's contented
  With all conditions that my fortunes bring her to:
  To keep close as a wife that loves her husband;   90
  To go after the rate of my ability,
  Not the licentious swindge of her own will,
  Like some of her old schoolfellows. She intends

84 *courses* actions

---

83 *A simple charge.* Either this must be spoken with a heavy irony (which
    to my mind is not appropriate here); or it must be allowed that Middle-
    ton is using *simple* in a sense not recorded by *O.E.D.* similar to his use
    of *simply* (= absolutely) at, for instance, IV, i, 43.
92 *swindge.* Sway: 'They give the full swindge to their bold and violent
    affections' (Beard, *Theatre of God's Judgements*, p. 272).

To take out other works in a new sampler,
And frame the fashion of an honest love,   95
Which knows no wants but, mocking poverty,
Brings forth more children, to make rich men wonder
At divine Providence, that feeds mouths of infants,
And sends them none to feed, but stuffs their rooms
With fruitful bags, their beds with barren wombs.   100
Good mother, make not you things worse than they are
Out of your too much openness—pray take heed on't—
Nor imitate the envy of old people,
That strive to mar good sport, because they are perfect.
I would have you more pitiful to youth,   105
Especially to your own flesh and blood.
I'll prove an excellent husband—here's my hand—
Lay in provision, follow my business roundly,
And make you a grandmother in forty weeks!
Go, pray salute her, bid her welcome cheerfully.   110

MOTHER
Gentlewoman, thus much is a debt of courtesy
                              [*she kisses* BIANCA]
Which fashionable strangers pay each other
At a kind meeting; then there's more than one,
Due to the knowledge I have of your nearness;
I am bold to come again, and now salute you   115
By th'name of daughter, which may challenge more
Than ordinary respect.

LEANTIO   Why, this is well now,
And I think few mothers of threescore will mend it.

MOTHER
What I can bid you welcome to, is mean;
But make it all your own: we are full of wants,   120
And cannot welcome worth.

LEANTIO   Now this is scurvy,
And spoke as if a woman lacked her teeth!
These old folks talk of nothing but defects,
Because they grow so full of 'em themselves.

BIANCA
Kind mother, there is nothing can be wanting   125
To her that does enjoy all her desires.

104 *perfect* contented (*O.E.D.* 7)
122 *spoke* ed (spake O)

---

100 *fruitful . . . wombs.* 'Where bags are fruitful'st there the womb's most
    barren' (Middleton, *Michaelmas Term*, Induction, line 25).
121-2 *scurvy . . . teeth.* One of the symptoms of scurvy is loss of teeth.

Heaven send a quiet peace with this man's love,
And I am as rich, as virtue can be poor—
Which were enough, after the rate of mind,
To erect temples for content placed here.   130
I have forsook friends, fortunes, and my country;
And hourly I rejoice in't. Here's my friends,
And few is the good number. Thy successes,
Howe'er they look, I will still name my fortunes;
Hopeful or spiteful, they shall all be welcome: 135
Who invites many guests, has of all sorts
As he that traffics much, drinks of all fortunes:
Yet they must all be welcome, and used well.
I'll call this place the place of my birth now—
And rightly too, for here my love was born,   140
And that's the birthday of a woman's joys.
You have not bid me welcome since I came.
LEANTIO
  That I did, questionless.
BIANCA   No sure, how was't?
  I have quite forgot it.
LEANTIO   Thus. [kisses her]
BIANCA   Oh sir, 'tis true,
  Now I remember well: I have done thee wrong,   145
  Pray take't again, sir. [kisses him]
LEANTIO   How many of these wrongs
  Could I put up in an hour? and turn up the glass
  For twice as many more.
MOTHER
  Will't please you to walk in, daughter?
BIANCA   Thanks, sweet
                                              mother;
  The voice of her that bare me is not more pleasing.   150
                        Exeunt [MOTHER and BIANCA]
LEANTIO
  Though my own care and my rich master's trust
  Lay their commands both on my factorship,
  This day and night I'll know no other business
  But her and her dear welcome. 'Tis a bitterness
  To think upon tomorrow, that I must leave her   155
  Still to the sweet hopes of the week's end.
  That pleasure should be so restrained and curbed
  After the course of a rich workmaster,
  That never pays till Saturday night!

147 *turn up the glass* reverse the hour-glass

Marry, it comes together in a round sum then,   160
And does more good, you'll say. Oh fair-eyed Florence!
Didst thou but know what a most matchless jewel
Thou now art mistress of, a pride would take thee
Able to shoot destruction through the bloods
Of all thy youthful sons! But 'tis great policy   165
To keep choice treasures in obscurest places:
Should we show thieves our wealth, 'twould make 'em bolder.
Temptation is a devil will not stick
To fasten upon a saint—take heed of that.
The jewel is cased up from all men's eyes: 170
Who could imagine now a gem were kept,
Of that great value, under this plain roof?
But how in times of absence—what assurance
Of this restraint then? yes, yes—there's one with her!
Old mothers know the world; and such as these,   175
When sons lock chests, are good to look to keys.   *Exit*

Act I, Scene ii

Enter GUARDIANO, FABRITIO, *and* LIVIA [*with* SERVANT]

GUARDIANO
What, has your daughter seen him yet? know you that?
FABRITIO
No matter—she shall love him.
GUARDIANO   Nay, let's have fair play!
He has been now my ward some fifteen year,
And 'tis my purpose, as time calls upon me,
By custom seconded, and such moral virtues,   5
To tender him a wife; now, sir, this wife
I'ld fain elect out of a daughter of yours.
You see my meaning's fair. If now this daughter,
So tendered—let me come to your own phrase, sir—
Should offer to refuse him, I were handselled.   10
—Thus am I fain to calculate all my words
For the meridian of a foolish old man,
To take his understanding! What do you answer, sir?

12 *meridian* point of highest development

175–6 *Old mothers . . . keys*. '. . . the poor wife sitts alone at home, locked
    upp and kept by old women' (Moryson 4, p. 151).
10 *handselled*. A *handsel*, literally, is a New Year's gift; the ironic use of the
    verb (as here) is not uncommon.

FABRITIO
    I say still, she shall love him.

GUARDIANO   Yet again?
    And shall she have no reason for this love?   15

FABRITIO
    Why, do you think that women love with reason?

GUARDIANO
    I perceive fools are not at all hours foolish,
    No more than wisemen wise.

FABRITIO   I had a wife;
    She ran mad for me; she had no reason for't
    For aught I could perceive. What think you,   20
    Lady sister?

GUARDIANO   —'Twas a fit match that,
    Being both out of their wits! A loving wife, 'seemed,
    She strove to come as near you as she could.

FABRITIO
    And if her daughter prove not mad for love too,
    She takes not after her—nor after me,   25
    If she prefer reason before my pleasure.
    You're an experienced widow, lady sister;
    I pray let your opinion come amongst us.

LIVIA
    I must offend you then, if truth will do't,
    And take my niece's part, and call't injustice   30
    To force her love to one she never saw.
    Maids should both see and like—all little enough:
    If they love truly after that, 'tis well.
    Counting the time, she takes one man till death,
    That's a hard task, I tell you; but one may   35
    Enquire at three years' end amongst young wives,
    And mark how the game goes.

FABRITIO   Why, is not man
    Tied to the same observance, lady sister,
    And in one woman?

LIVIA   'Tis enough for him;
    Besides, he tastes of many sundry dishes   40
    That we poor wretches never lay our lips to—
    As obedience, forsooth, subjection, duty, and such kickshaws,
    All of our making, but served in to them;

---

42 *kickshaws* fancy dishes

---

17 *fools . . . foolish.* Proverbial: 'Even a fool sometimes speaks a wise word'
    (Tilley, F 449).

And if we lick a finger then, sometimes,
We are not too blame; your best cooks use it. 45
FABRITIO
Th'art a sweet lady, sister, and a witty.
LIVIA
A witty! Oh, the bud of commendation,
Fit for a girl of sixteen! I am blown, man!
I should be wise by this time—and, for instance,
I have buried my two husbands in good fashion, 50
And never mean more to marry.
GUARDIANO   No, why so, lady?
LIVIA
Because the third shall never bury me:
I think I am more than witty. How think you, sir?
FABRITIO
I have paid often fees to a counsellor
Has had a weaker brain.
LIVIA   Then I must tell you, 55
Your money was soon parted.
GUARDIANO   Light her now, brother!
LIVIA
Where is my niece? let her be sent for straight.
                                        [*Exit* SERVANT]

---

45 *use* are in the habit of doing

---

45 *best cooks*. Proverbial: 'He is an ill cook that cannot lick his own fingers'
(Tilley, C 636).
48 *blown*. Fully blossomed—but with a sense of being past the best: 'Against
the blown rose may they stop their nose, That kneel'd unto the buds'
(*Antony and Cleopatra*, III, xiii, 39–40). Simpson suggests that *blown
woman* would be a more appropriate reading; but the jocular *man* is
characteristic of Middleton's experienced women (cf. Livia again at
II, i, 40, and *The Witch*, II, ii, 127: 'we're all flesh and blood, man').
56 *money . . . parted*. Proverbial: 'A fool and his money are soon parted'
(Tilley, F 452).
56 *Light her now, brother*. O. Bullen, also following O, suggests the emendation *Like enow* (giving *brother* to Livia in the next line) and reminds
that there is no great difference in pronunciation between *Light her
now* and *Like enow*. This reasoning can only be valid, however, if we
postulate some oral stage in the transmission of the text. Simpson (also
giving *brother* to Livia) recommends that Guardiano should say
Plight her now—i.e. 'settle the business on the spot'. But this reading
attributes an urgency to the character which is at odds with his earlier
wishes to wait some little time. In the absence of any convincing
alternative I have adhered to O; perhaps Guardiano is inciting Fabritio
to answer Livia, to bring her down, now she is in full, witty flight?

If you have any hope 'twill prove a wedding,
'Tis fit i'faith she should have one sight of him,
And stop upon't, and not be joined in haste,   60
As if they went to stock a new found land.

FABRITIO
Look out her uncle, and y'are sure of her,
Those two are nev'r asunder; they've been heard
In argument at midnight, moonshine nights
Are noondays with them; they walk out their sleeps—   65
Or rather at those hours appear like those
That walk in 'em, for so they did to me.
Look you, I told you truth: they're like a chain,
Draw but one link, all follows.

Enter HIPPOLITO *and* ISABELLA *the niece*

GUARDIANO   Oh affinity,
What piece of excellent workmanship art thou?   70
'Tis work clean wrought, for there's no lust, but love in't,
And that abundantly—when in stranger things,
There is no love at all, but what lust brings.

FABRITIO
On with your mask, for 'tis your part to see now,
And not be seen. Go to, make use of your time;   75
See what you mean to like—nay, and I charge you,
Like what you see. Do you hear me? there's no dallying.
The gentleman's almost twenty, and 'tis time
He were getting lawful heirs, and you a-breeding on 'em.

ISABELLA
Good father!

FABRITIO   Tell not me of tongues and rumours!   80
You'll say the gentleman is somewhat simple—
The better for a husband, were you wise:
For those that marry fools, live ladies' lives.
On with the mask, I'll hear no more; he's rich:
The fool's hid under bushels.

---

61 *stock . . . land.* Attempts were being made in the early 17th century to
people Newfoundland; but the reference here is most probably to
Virginia—as in Donne's Elegy: 'Oh my America, my new found lande'
('To his Mistris Going to Bed'). Middleton uses the same analogy in an
earlier play: 'Take deliberation, sir; never choose a wife as if you were
going to Virginia' (*The Roaring Girl*, II, ii, 71–2).

74–5 *On . . . seen.* In a contract like this, the man and woman might not
see each other (officially at least) until the day of betrothal (see note at
III, iii, 9–10).

LIVIA   Not so hid neither,   85
But here's a foul great piece of him, methinks:
What will he be, when he comes altogether?

Enter the WARD *with a trapstick, and* SORDIDO *his man*

WARD
Beat him?
I beat him out o'th'field with his own cat-stick,
Yet gave him the first hand.
SORDIDO   Oh strange!
WARD   I did it,   90
Then he set jacks on me.
SORDIDO   What, my lady's tailor?
WARD
Ay, and I beat him too.
SORDIDO   Nay, that's no wonder,
He's used to beating.
WARD   Nay, I tickled him
When I came once to my tippings.
SORDIDO   Now you talk on 'em,
there was a poulterer's wife made a great complaint of   95
you last night to your guardianer, that you struck a bump
in her child's head, as big as an egg.
WARD
An egg may prove a chicken, then in time the poulterer's
wife will get by't. When I am in game, I am furious; came
my mother's eyes in my way, I would not lose a fair end—   100
no, were she alive, but with one tooth in her head, I should
venture the striking out of that. I think of nobody, when
I am in play, I am so earnest. Coads me, my guardiner!
Prithee lay up my cat and cat-stick safe.

---

90 *first hand* first strike
91 *jacks* fellows

---

87 s.d. trapstick. A trapstick (or catstick) was used in the country game of
tip-cat to strike the wooden cat (a short piece of wood tapered at both
ends) so that it would fly in the air and then be struck again by the
same player. The game is still played by schoolchildren in the north
of England, who call it 'piggy'.
91 *my lady's tailor.* Tailors were popularly noted for their cowardice.
93 *beating.* Marlowe uses the same pun in *Dr Faustus*, where Wagner
promises the Clown a whipping: he shall go 'in beaten silk' (I, iv, 15).
Silk was embroidered by having gold and silver beaten into it.

SORDIDO
  Where sir, i'th'chimney-corner?   105
WARD
  Chimney-corner!
SORDIDO
  Yes sir, your cats are always safe i'th'chimney-corner,
  unless they burn their coats.
WARD
  Marry, that I am afraid on.
SORDIDO
  Why then, I will bestow your cat i'th'gutter, and there   110
  she's safe, I am sure.
WARD
  If I but live to keep a house, I'll make thee a great man—
  if meat and drink can do't. I can stoop gallantly, and pitch
  out when I list; I'm dog at a hole. I mar'l my guardiner
  does not seek a wife for me; I protest, I'll have a bout with   115
  the maids else, or contract myself at midnight to the
  larder-woman in presence of a fool or a sack-posset.
GUARDIANO
  Ward!
WARD
  I feel myself after any exercise horribly prone: let me but
  ride, I'm lusty—a cockhorse straight, i'faith.   120

105–30 *Where . . . cradle* (as verse O)
114 *mar'l* marvel
117 *sack-posset* beverage made with sack (dry wine), eggs and sugar
119 *prone* i.e. to lechery

105–8 *chimney-corner . . . coats.* Obscenity is to be expected from the Ward
    and Sordido, but here it is obscured either by age or by imprecision.
    Cat is a common term for 'whore'; and 'A young fellow falne in love
    with a Whore, is said to be falne asleepe in the Chimney corner'
    (Overbury, *Characters* (11th imp. 1623), V 1). *Burn* is the usual de-
    scription of the action of syphilis: 'Bawds and Atturneys are Andyrons
    that hold up their Clyents till they burne each other to ashes' (*ibid*, T 8ᵛ).
113 *stoop gallantly.* A dog picking up the scent is said to *stoop*, but Mulryne
    has found a mention of the 'stoop gallant' or 'sweating sickness' (i.e.
    venereal disease) in Nashe's *Pierce Peniless* (ed. McKerrow, iii, 114).
114 *dog at a hole.* A good hunter: 'I am dog at a catch' (*Twelfth Night*,
    II, iii, 62). The Ward's train of thought makes the obscenity clear
    enough.
117 *fool.* The fruit and cream dish may be meant, but 'fowl' could also be
    intended, both here and at III, ii, 121. The homophony of *fool* and *fowl*
    made a pun available: Daedalus 'taught his son the office of a fowl!
    And yet, for all his wings, the fool was drown'd' (*3 Henry VI*, V, vi,
    19–20).

GUARDIANO
  Why, ward I say.

WARD
  I'll forswear eating eggs in moon-shine nights; there's
  nev'r a one I eat, but turns into a cock in four-and-twenty
  hours; if my hot blood be not took down in time, sure
  'twill crow shortly.   125

GUARDIANO
  Do you hear, sir? follow me; I must new school you.

WARD
  School me? I scorn that now; I am past schooling. I am
  not so base to learn to write and read; I was born to better
  fortunes in my cradle.
                    Exit [WARD, SORDIDO *and* GUARDIANO]

FABRITIO
  How do you like him, girl? this is your husband.   130
  Like him or like him not, wench, you shall have him,
  And you shall love him.

LIVIA   Oh, soft there, brother!
  Though you be a justice,
  Your warrant cannot be served out of your liberty.
  You may compel, out of the power of father,   135
  Things merely harsh to a maid's flesh and blood;
  But when you come to love, there the soil alters;
  Y'are in another country, where your laws
  Are no more set by, than the cacklings of geese
  In Rome's great Capitol.

FABRITIO   Marry him she shall then;   140
  Let her agree upon love afterwards.   *Exit*

LIVIA
  You speak now, brother, like an honest mortal

134 *liberty* district with its own commission of peace

---

122 *eggs ... nights.* Eggs were said to be aphrodisiac: 'The very sight o
  this egg has made him cockish' (Fletcher, *Women Pleased*, I, ii, 21).
  Mulryne has suggested eggs-in-moonshine (poached eggs with onion
  sauce, *O.E.D.* 3) as the proper collocation; but Middleton's fondness
  for the phrase 'moonshine nights' (as at I, ii, 64) makes me prefer O's
  punctuation.
128–9 *base ... cradle.* '... he can scarce write and read. He's the better
  regarded for that amongst courtiers, for that's but a needy quality'
  (*Michaelmas Term*, I, i, 305–7).
139–40 *cacklings ... Capitol.* Geese sacred to Juno were kept on the Capito-
  line Hill, and on a famous occasion their cackling warned the Romans
  of a surprise invasion by the Gauls. The comparison does not seem
  particularly apt.

That walks upon th'earth with a staff;
You were up i'th'clouds before; you'ld command love—
And so do most old folks that go without it.　　145
My best and dearest brother, I could dwell here;
There is not such another seat on earth
Where all good parts better express themselves.

HIPPOLITO
You'll make me blush anon.

LIVIA
'Tis but like saying grace before a feast, then,　　150
And that's most comely; thou art all a feast,
And she that has thee, a most happy guest.
Prithee cheer up thy niece with special counsel.　　[Exit]

HIPPOLITO
I would 'twere fit to speak to her what I would, but
'Twas not a thing ordained; Heaven has forbid it,　　155
And 'tis most meet that I should rather perish
Than the decree divine receive least blemish.
Feed inward, you my sorrows, make no noise;
Consume me silent, let me be stark dead
Ere the world know I'm sick. You see my honesty,　　160
If you befriend me—so.

ISABELLA　　　　　　　Marry a fool!
Can there be greater misery to a woman
That means to keep her days true to her husband,
And know no other man, so virtue wills it!
Why, how can I obey and honour him,　　165
But I must needs commit idolatry?
A fool is but the image of a man,
And that but ill made neither. Oh the heartbreakings
Of miserable maids, where love's enforced!
The best condition is but bad enough:　　170
When women have their choices, commonly
They do but buy their thraldoms, and bring great portions
To men to keep 'em in subjection:
As if a fearful prisoner should bribe
The keeper to be good to him, yet lies in still,　　175
And glad of a good usage, a good look
Sometimes. By'r Lady, no misery surmounts a woman's!

153 *thy* ed (that O)
177 *Sometimes. By'r Lady, no* ed (Sometimes by'r Lady; no O)

---

146 *here.* Presumably Livia kisses Hippolito at this point.
166 *idolatry.* God created man in His own image; but a fool is the image of a
　　man; therefore in promising to honour a fool, a woman commits idolatry.

Men buy their slaves, but women buy their masters.
Yet honesty and love makes all this happy
And, next to angels', the most blest estate.   180
That Providence, that has made ev'ry poison
Good for some use, and sets four warring elements
At peace in man, can make a harmony
In things that are most strange to human reason.
Oh but this marriage! What, are you sad too, uncle?   185
'Faith, then there's a whole household down together:
Where shall I go to seek my comfort now
When my best friend's distressed? What is't afflicts you, sir?

HIPPOLITO
'Faith, nothing but one grief that will not leave me,
And now 'tis welcome; ev'ry man has something   190
To bring him to his end, and this will serve,
Joined with your father's cruelty to you—
That helps it forward.

ISABELLA   Oh be cheered, sweet uncle!
How long has't been upon you? I nev'r spied it;
What a dull sight have I! how long, I pray sir?   195

HIPPOLITO
Since I first saw you, niece, and left Bologna.

ISABELLA
And could you deal so unkindly with my heart,
To keep it up so long hid from my pity?
Alas, how shall I trust your love hereafter!
Have we passed through so many arguments,   200
And missed of that still, the most needful one?
Walked out whole nights together in discourses,
And the main point forgot? We are too blame both;
This is an obstinate wilful forgetfulness,
And faulty on both parts. Let's lose no time now.   205
Begin, good uncle, you that feel't; what is it?

HIPPOLITO
You of all creatures, niece, must never hear on't;
'Tis not a thing ordained for you to know.

ISABELLA
Not I, sir! all my joys that word cuts off;

181–2 *poison . . . use.* 'No poison, sir, but serves us for some use' (*The
    Roaring Girl*, IV, i, 151).
182 *four . . . elements.* Four elements made up the world (in the Ptolemaic
    system) and also the little world of man, in which they strove continually
    for dominance over the personality: 'Nature, that fram'd us of four
    elements Warring within our breasts for regiment' (Marlowe, *1 Tam-
    burlaine*, II, vii, 18–19).

You made profession once you loved me best—   210
'Twas but profession!

HIPPOLITO   Yes, I do't too truly,
And fear I shall be chid for't. Know the worst then:
I love thee dearlier than an uncle can.

ISABELLA
Why, so you ever said, and I believed it.

HIPPOLITO
So simple is the goodness of her thoughts   215
They understand not yet th'unhallowed language
Of a near sinner: I must yet be forced
(Though blushes be my venture) to come nearer.
As a man loves his wife, so love I thee.

ISABELLA   What's that?
Methought I heard ill news come toward me,   220
Which commonly we understand too soon,
Than over-quick at hearing. I'll prevent it,
Though my joys fare the harder; welcome it—
It shall nev'r come so near mine ear again.
Farewell all friendly solaces and discourses;   225
I'll learn to live without ye, for your dangers
Are greater than your comforts. What's become
Of truth in love, if such we cannot trust.
When blood that should be love is mixed with lust!   *Exit*

HIPPOLITO
The worst can be but death, and let it come;   230
He that lives joyless, every day's his doom.   *Exit*

Act I, Scene iii

Enter LEANTIO *alone*

LEANTIO
Methinks I'm ev'n as dull now at departure
As men observe great gallants the next day
After a revels; you shall see 'em look
Much of my fashion, if you mark 'em well.

217 *near.* The first of several uses of this word which bring into play multiple meanings—here 'almost a sinner' and 'a closely related sinner'.

220-24 *Methought . . . again.* The sense of this is difficult to make out. Isabella seems to be saying that trouble is more readily apprehended intuitively ('we understand') than intellectually (by 'hearing') and that, having grasped her uncle's meaning from his stammered phrases, she will not wait for a fuller explanation but will anticipate ('prevent') the bad news; in thus meeting it ('welcome it') she will stop him from speaking further.

'Tis ev'n a second hell to part from pleasure   5
When man has got a smack on't. As many holidays
Coming together makes your poor heads idle
A great while after, and are said to stick
Fast in their fingers' ends; ev'n so does game
In a new-married couple for the time;   10
It spoils all thrift, and indeed lies a-bed

[*Enter*] BIANCA *and* MOTHER *above*

To invent all the new ways for great expenses.
See, and she be not got on purpose now
Into the window to look after me!
I have no power to go now and I should be hanged.   15
Farewell all business! I desire no more
Than I see yonder. Let the goods at quay
Look to themselves; why should I toil my youth out?
It is but begging two or three year sooner,
And stay with her continually: is't a match?   20
Oh fie, what a religion have I leaped into!
Get out again, for shame! The man loves best
When his care's most—that shows his zeal to love.
Fondness is but the idiot to affection,
That plays at hot-cockles with rich merchants' wives;   25
Good to make sport withal when the chest's full,
And the long warehouse cracks. 'Tis time of day
For us to be more wise; 'tis early with us,
And if they lose the morning of their affairs
They commonly lose the best part of the day.   30
Those that are wealthy and have got enough,
'Tis after sunset with 'em; they may rest,
Grow fat with ease, banquet, and toy and play,
When such as I enter the heat o'th'day;
And I'll do't cheerfully.
BIANCA   I perceive, sir,   35
Y'are not gone yet; I have good hope you'll stay now.

---

6 *smack* taste   15 *and* if

8–9 *stick . . . ends.* This sounds proverbial; or it may be a variant on the
expression 'to have something at one's fingertips'.
24–5 *Fondness . . . wives.* Infatuation ('Fondness') is a fool ('idiot') compared to real love and serves only to titillate rich women.
25 *hot-cockles.* Literally, a country game similar to blind man's buff; by
frequent application it comes to refer also to sexual play.
29–30 *lose . . . day.* Proverbial: 'He who sleeps all the morning may go a
begging all the day after' (Tilley, M 1172).

LEANTIO
  Farewell, I must not.
BIANCA   Come, come; pray return.
  Tomorrow, adding but a little care more,
  Will dispatch all as well—believe me, 'twill sir.
LEANTIO
  I could well wish myself where you would have me;   40
  But love that's wanton must be ruled awhile
  By that that's careful, or all goes to ruin.
  As fitting is a government in love
  As in a kingdom; where 'tis all mere lust
  'Tis like an insurrection in the people   45
  That, raised in self-will, wars against all reason:
  But love that is respective of increase
  Is like a good king, that keeps all in peace.
  Once more, farewell.
BIANCA   But this one night, I prithee.
LEANTIO
  Alas, I'm in for twenty, if I stay,   50
  And then for forty more, I have such luck to flesh:
  I never bought a horse, but he bore double.
  If I stay any longer, I shall turn
  An everlasting spendthrift; as you love
  To be maintained well, do not call me again,   55
  For then I shall not care which end goes forward.
  Again, farewell to thee.   *Exit*
BIANCA   Since it must, farewell too.
MOTHER
  'Faith daughter, y'are too blame; you take the course
  To make him an ill husband, troth you do,
  And that disease is catching, I can tell you—   60
  Ay, and soon taken by a young man's blood,
  And that with little urging. Nay, fie, see now—

---

47 *respective of* careful for

43–5 *government ... people*. Leantio makes the stock Elizabethan comparison
    between the individual (here, the lovers) and the body politic: '. . . the
    state of man, Like to a little kingdom, suffers then The nature of an
    insurrection' (*Julius Caesar*, II, i, 67–9).
48 *good king . . . peace*. Jacobean dramatists were often careful to introduce
    flattery of James the peacemaker into their plays. Middleton shows
    more discrimination in this than the sometimes sycophantic Massinger
    (cf. the character of Roberto in *The Maid of Honour*).
56 *care . . . forward*. Proverbial: 'He cares not which end goes forward'
    (Tilley, E 130).

What cause have you to weep? would I had no more,
That have lived threescore years; there were a cause
And 'twere well thought on. Trust me, y'are too blame;   65
His absence cannot last five days at utmost.
Why should those tears be fetched forth? cannot love
Be ev'n as well expressed in a good look,
But it must see her face still in a fountain?
It shows like a country maid dressing her head   70
By a dish of water. Come, 'tis an old custom
To weep for love.

Enter two or three BOYS, *and a* CITIZEN *or two, with an*
APPRENTICE

BOYS
Now they come! now they come!
2 BOY   The duke!
3 BOY   The state!
CITIZEN
How near, boy?
1 BOY   I'th'next street sir, hard at hand.
CITIZEN
You sirra, get a standing for your mistress,   75
The best in all the city.
APPRENTICE   I have't for her, sir.
'Twas a thing I provided for her over-night,
'Tis ready at her pleasure.
CITIZEN
Fetch her to't then; away sir!
BIANCA
What's the meaning of this hurry,   80
Can you tell, mother?
MOTHER   What a memory
Have I! I see by that years come upon me.
Why, 'tis a yearly custom and solemnity,
Religiously observed by th'duke and state,
To St Mark's temple, the fifteenth of April.   85
See if my dull brains had not quite forgot it!
'Twas happily questioned of thee; I had gone down else,
Sat like a drone below, and never thought on't.

83 *solemnity* festival

---

85 *the fifteenth of April.* The Feast of St Mark, when this procession
(according to Moryson) took place, is 25 April. Perhaps Middleton,
neither chronologist nor hagiolater, arrived at his date simply by
subtracting the ten days by which the English (Julian) calendar was
behind the continental (Gregorian).

I would not to be ten years younger again
That you had lost the sight; now you shall see   90
Our duke, a goodly gentleman of his years.

BIANCA
Is he old then?

MOTHER   About some fifty-five.

BIANCA
That's no great age in man; he's then at best
For wisdom and for judgement.

MOTHER   The lord cardinal,
His noble brother—there's a comely gentleman,   95
And greater in devotion than in blood.

BIANCA
He's worthy to be marked.

MOTHER   You shall behold
All our chief states of Florence; you came fortunately
Against this solemn day.

BIANCA   I hope so always.   *Music*

MOTHER
I hear 'em near us now; do you stand easily?   100

BIANCA
Exceeding well, good mother.

MOTHER   Take this stool.

BIANCA
I need it not, I thank you.

MOTHER   Use your will, then.

Enter in great solemnity six KNIGHTS *bare-headed, then two*
CARDINALS, *and then the* LORD CARDINAL, *then the* DUKE; *after
him the* STATES *of* FLORENCE *by two and two, with variety of
music and song*

                                                  Exit

MOTHER
How like you, daughter?

BIANCA   'Tis a noble state.
Methinks my soul could dwell upon the reverence
Of such a solemn and most worthy custom.   105
Did not the duke look up? me-thought he saw us.

MOTHER
That's everyone's conceit that sees a duke:
If he look steadfastly, he looks straight at them—
When he perhaps, good careful gentleman,
Never minds any, but the look he casts   110
Is at his own intentions, and his object
Only the public good.

BIANCA   Most likely so.
MOTHER
Come, come, we'll end this argument below.   *Exeunt*

Act II, Scene i

Enter HIPPOLITO *and* LADY LIVIA *the widow*

LIVIA
A strange affection, brother, when I think on't!
I wonder how thou cam'st by't.
HIPPOLITO   Ev'n as easily
As man comes by destruction, which oft-times
He wears in his own bosom.
LIVIA   Is the world
So populous in women, and creation   5
So prodigal in beauty and so various,
Yet does love turn thy point to thine own blood?
'Tis somewhat too unkindly. Must thy eye
Dwell evilly on the fairness of thy kindred,
And seek not where it should? It is confined   10
Now in a narrower prison than was made for't:
It is allowed a stranger; and where bounty
Is made the great man's honour, 'tis ill husbandry
To spare, and servants shall have small thanks for't.
So he Heaven's bounty seems to scorn and mock,   15
That spares free means, and spends of his own stock.
HIPPOLITO
Never was man's misery so soon sewed up,
Counting how truly.
LIVIA   Nay, I love you so,
That I shall venture much to keep a change from you
So fearful as this grief will bring upon you—   20
'Faith, it even kills me, when I see you faint
Under a reprehension; and I'll leave it,
Though I know nothing can be better for you.

17 *sewed* ed (sow'd O; summ'd Bullen); *sow* is a regular variant for
    sew
19 *venture* hazard
22 *reprehension* reprimand

───────────────────────────────

2–4 *Ev'n . . . bosom.* 'See, sin needs No other destruction than [what] it
    breeds In its own bosom' (Middleton, *The Mayor of Queenborough*,
    V, ii, 76–8).
8 *unkindly.* With a pun (again, the first of many) on *kin/kind*: 'A little
    more than kin and less than kind' (*Hamlet*, I, ii, 65).

Prithee, sweet brother, let not passion waste
The goodness of thy time, and of thy fortune;   25
Thou keep'st the treasure of that life I love
As dearly as mine own; and if you think
My former words too bitter, which were ministered
By truth and zeal—'tis but a hazarding
Of grace and virtue, and I can bring forth   30
As pleasant fruits as sensuality wishes
In all her teeming longings. This I can do.

HIPPOLITO
Oh nothing that can make my wishes perfect!

LIVIA
I would that love of yours were pawned to't, brother,
And as soon lost that way as I could win.   35
Sir, I could give as shrewd a lift to chastity
As any she that wears a tongue in Florence:
Sh'ad need be a good horsewoman and sit fast
Whom my strong argument could not fling at last.
Prithee take courage, man; though I should counsel   40
Another to despair, yet I am pitiful
To thy afflictions, and will venture hard—
I will not name for what, 'tis not handsome;
Find you the proof, and praise me.

HIPPOLITO   Then I fear me,
I shall not praise you in haste.

LIVIA   This is the comfort,   45
You are not the first, brother, has attempted
Things more forbidden than this seems to be.
I'll minister all cordials now to you,
Because I'll cheer you up, sir.

HIPPOLITO   I am past hope.

LIVIA
Love, thou shalt see me do a strange cure then,   50

36 *give . . . a lift to* attack

26–7 *love . . . own.* In the source the nun tells Hipolito that what he needs
    'is the advice of a faithfull friend, and where can you expect it more
    faithfull, then from me, who you know have not onely loved you above
    my other Brothers, but even before my selfe' (*Hipolito & Isabella*,
    pp. 27–8).
37 *any . . . tongue.* Any articulate woman; but jewellery in the shape of
    tongues was popular at this time: the king in Marlowe's *Edward II*
    promises to 'hang a golden tongue' about his wife's neck (I, iv, 327).
46–7 *You . . . be.* The nun comforts Hipolito: 'You are not the first that
    have undertaken things as much forbidden, which have yet attained to a
    happie end' (*Hipolito & Isabella*, p. 33).

As e'er was wrought on a disease so mortal
And near akin to shame. When shall you see her?

HIPPOLITO
Never in comfort more.

LIVIA   Y'are so impatient too.

HIPPOLITO
Will you believe—'death, sh'as forsworn my company,
And sealed it with a blush.

LIVIA   So, I perceive   55
All lies upon my hands, then; well, the more glory
When the work's finished.

Enter SERVANT

                    How now, sir, the news?

SERVANT
Madam, your niece, the virtuous Isabella,
Is lighted now to see you.

LIVIA   That's great fortune.
Sir, your stars bless you simply. Lead her in.   60

                              Exit SERVANT

HIPPOLITO
What's this to me?

LIVIA   Your absence, gentle brother;
I must bestir my wits for you.

HIPPOLITO   Ay, to great purpose.

                              Exit HIPPOLITO

LIVIA
Beshrew you, would I loved you not so well!
I'll go to bed, and leave this deed undone;
I am the fondest where I once affect,   65
The carefull'st of their healths, and of their ease, forsooth,
That I look still but slenderly to mine own.
I take a course to pity him so much now,
That I have none left for modesty and myself.
This 'tis to grow so liberal—y'have few sisters   70
That love their brother's ease 'bove their own honesties:
But if you question my affections,
That will be found my fault.

---

54 *'death* by God's death   65 *fondest* most foolish

---

60 *bless you simply. Lead* Ed (bless, you simple, lead O; bless you.—Simple,
lead Dyce; bless you; you simple, lead Simpson). I am not happy about
the addressing of a servant as *Simple*, or even as *you simple*, and so have
emended to *simply* which I take to mean 'richly, abundantly' as at
IV, i, 43.

Enter ISABELLA *the niece*

                     Niece, your love's welcome.
Alas, what draws that paleness to thy cheeks?
This enforced marriage towards?
ISABELLA   It helps, good aunt,   75
Amongst some other griefs—but those I'll keep
Locked up in modest silence; for they're sorrows
Would shame the tongue more than they grieve the thought.
LIVIA
Indeed, the ward is simple.
ISABELLA   Simple! that were well:
Why, one might make good shift with such a husband.   80
But he's a fool entailed, he halts downright in't.
LIVIA
And knowing this, I hope 'tis at your choice
To take or refuse, niece.
ISABELLA   You see it is not.
I loathe him more than beauty can hate death,
Or age, her spiteful neighbour.
LIVIA   Let 't appear, then.   85
ISABELLA
How can I, being born with that obedience
That must submit unto a father's will?
If he command, I must of force consent.
LIVIA
Alas, poor soul! Be not offended, prithee,
If I set by the name of niece awhile,   90
And bring in pity in a stranger fashion.
It lies here in this breast, would cross this match.
ISABELLA
How, cross it, aunt?
LIVIA   Ay, and give thee more liberty
Than thou hast reason yet to apprehend.
ISABELLA
Sweet aunt, in goodness keep not hid from me   95
What may befriend my life.
LIVIA   Yes, yes, I must,
When I return to reputation,
And think upon the solemn vow I made
To your dead mother, my most loving sister . . .

---

75 *towards* approaching
81 *entailed* indissolubly
81 *halts . . . in't* stops completely at this   88 *of force* of necessity
94 *apprehend* understand   99 *sister* sister-in-law, to be exact

As long as I have her memory 'twixt mine eyelids,   100
Look for no pity, now.

ISABELLA   Kind, sweet, dear aunt—

LIVIA

No, 'twas a secret I have took special care of,
Delivered by your mother on her deathbed—
That's nine years now—and I'll not part from 't yet,
Though nev'r was fitter time nor greater cause for 't.   105

ISABELLA

As you desire the praises of a virgin—

LIVIA

Good sorrow! I would do thee any kindness,
Not wronging secrecy or reputation . . .

ISABELLA

Neither of which, as I have hope of fruit[ful]ness,
Shall receive wrong from me.

LIVIA   Nay, 'twould be your own
                                                    wrong   110
As much as any's, should it come to that once.

ISABELLA

I need no better means to work persuasion then.

LIVIA

Let it suffice, you may refuse this fool,
Or you may take him, as you see occasion
For your advantage: the best wits will do't.   115
Y'have liberty enough in your own will;
You cannot be enforced—there grows the flower,
If you could pick it out, makes whole life sweet to you.
That which you call your father's command's nothing:
Then your obedience must needs be as little.   120
If you can make shift here to taste your happiness,
Or pick out aught that likes you, much good do you.
You see your cheer, I'll make you no set dinner.

ISABELLA

And trust me, I may starve for all the good
I can find yet in this! Sweet aunt, deal plainlier.   125

LIVIA

Say I should trust you now upon an oath,
And give you in a secret that would start you;
How am I sure of you, in faith and silence?

ISABELLA

Equal assurance may I find in mercy,
As you for that in me.

---

109 *hope of fruit[ful]ness.* (fruitness O): 'By my hope of fruitfulness' (Middleton, *More Dissemblers Besides Women*, II, iii, 54).

LIVIA   It shall suffice.   130
　　Then know, however custom has made good,
　　For reputation's sake, the names of niece
　　And aunt 'twixt you and I, w'are nothing less.
ISABELLA
　　How's that!
LIVIA   I told you I should start your blood.
　　You are no more allied to any of us,   135
　　Save what the courtesy of opinion casts
　　Upon your mother's memory and your name,
　　Than the mer'st stranger is, or one begot
　　At Naples when the husband lies at Rome;
　　There's so much odds betwixt us. Since your knowledge   140
　　Wished more instruction, and I have your oath
　　In pledge for silence, it makes me talk the freelier.
　　Did never the report of that famed Spaniard,
　　Marquess of Coria, since your time was ripe
　　For understanding, fill your ear with wonder?   145
ISABELLA
　　Yes, what of him? I have heard his deeds of honour
　　Often related when we lived in Naples.
LIVIA
　　You heard the praises of your father then.
ISABELLA
　　My father!
LIVIA   That was he; but all the business
　　So carefully and so discreetly carried   150
　　That fame received no spot by't, not a blemish.
　　Your mother was so wary to her end;
　　None knew it but her conscience, and her friend,
　　Till penitent confession made it mine,
　　And now my pity, yours: it had been long else,   155
　　And I hope care and love alike in you,
　　Made good by oath, will see it take no wrong now.
　　How weak his commands now, whom you call father?
　　How vain all his enforcements, your obedience?
　　And what a largeness in your will and liberty   160
　　To take or to reject—or to do both?
　　For fools will serve to father wise men's children—
　　All this y'have time to think on. Oh my wench,
　　Nothing o'erthrows our sex but indiscretion!
　　We might do well else of a brittle people   165

164 *Nothing . . . indiscretion.* 'Neece (answered the Nunne) nothing undoth
　　us but indiscretion' (*Hipolito & Isabella*, p. 46).

As any under the great canopy.
I pray forget not but to call me aunt still—
Take heed of that, it may be marked in time else.
But keep your thoughts to yourself, from all the world,
Kindred or dearest friend—nay, I entreat you,   170
From him that all this while you have called uncle;
And though you love him dearly, as I know
His deserts claim as much ev'n from a stranger,
Yet let not him know this, I prithee do not;
As ever thou hast hope of second pity   175
If thou shouldst stand in need on't, do not do't.

ISABELLA
Believe my oath, I will not.

LIVIA   Why, well said.
—Who shows more craft t'undo a maidenhead,
I'll resign my part to her.

                    Enter HIPPOLITO

                              She's thine own, go.   *Exit*

HIPPOLITO
Alas, fair flattery cannot cure my sorrows!   180

ISABELLA
Have I passed so much time in ignorance,
And never had the means to know myself
Till this blest hour! Thanks to her virtuous pity
That brought it now to light—would I had known it
But one day sooner! he had then received   185
In favours what, poor gentleman, he took
In bitter words—a slight and harsh reward
For one of his deserts.

HIPPOLITO   There seems to me now
More anger and distraction in her looks.
I'm gone, I'll not endure a second storm;   190
The memory of the first is not past yet.

ISABELLA
Are you returned, you comforts of my life,
In this man's presence? I will keep you fast now,
And sooner part eternally from the world
Than my good joys in you. Prithee, forgive me.   195
I did but chide in jest; the best loves use it
Sometimes; it sets an edge upon affection.
When we invite our best friends to a feast
'Tis not all sweetmeats that we set before them,

166 *great canopy*. The firmament: 'This most excellent canopy the air, look
    you, this brave o'erhanging' (*Hamlet*, II, ii, 14).

There's somewhat sharp and salt, both to whet appetite,   200
And make 'em taste their wine well: so, methinks,
After a friendly, sharp, and savoury chiding,
A kiss tastes wondrous well and full o'th'grape—

                                                [*kisses him*]

—How think'st thou, does't not?

HIPPOLITO   'Tis so excellent,
I know not how to praise it, what to say to't!   205

ISABELLA

This marriage shall go forward.

HIPPOLITO   With the ward!
Are you in earnest?

ISABELLA   'Twould be ill for us else.

HIPPOLITO

For us! how means she that?

ISABELLA   Troth, I begin
To be so well, methinks, within this hour—
For all this match able to kill one's heart—   210
Nothing can pull me down now; should my father
Provide a worse fool yet (which I should think
Were a hard thing to compass) I'ld have him either:
The worse the better; none can come amiss now
If he want wit enough. So discretion love me,   215
Desert and judgement, I have content sufficient.
She that comes once to be a housekeeper
Must not look every day to fare well, sir,
Like a young waiting gentlewoman in service;
For she feeds commonly as her lady does,   220
No good bit passes her but she gets a taste on't;
But when she comes to keep house for herself,
She's glad of some choice cates then once a week,
Or twice at most, and glad if she can get 'em:
So must affection learn to fare with thankfulness.   225
Pray make your love no stranger, sir, that's all.
—Though you be one yourself, and know not on't,
And I have sworn you must not.   *Exit*

HIPPOLITO   This is beyond me!
Never came joys so unexpectedly
To meet desires in man. How came she thus?   230
What has she done to her, can any tell?
'Tis beyond sorcery, this, drugs or love-powders;
Some art that has no name, sure; strange to me
Of all the wonders I ere met withal

223 *cates* delicacies

Throughout my ten years' travels. But I'm thankful for't.   235
This marriage now must of necessity forward:
It is the only veil wit can devise
To keep our acts hid from sin-piercing eyes.   *Exit*

Act II, Scene ii

Enter GUARDIANO *and* LIVIA

LIVIA
How, sir, a gentlewoman so young, so fair,
As you set forth, spied from the widow's window?
GUARDIANO
She!
LIVIA
Our Sunday-dinner woman?
GUARDIANO
And Thursday-supper woman, the same still.   5
I know not how she came by her, but I'll swear
She's the prime gallant for a face in Florence,
And no doubt other parts follow their leader.
The duke himself first spied her at the window,
Then in a rapture, as if admiration   10
Were poor when it were single, beckoned me,
And pointed to the wonder warily,
As one that feared she would draw in her splendour
Too soon, if too much gazed at. I nev'r knew him
So infinitely taken with a woman;   15
Nor can I blame his appetite, or tax
His raptures of slight folly; she's a creature
Able to draw a state from serious business,
And make it their best piece to do her service.
What course shall we devise? h'as spoke twice now.   20
LIVIA
Twice?
GUARDIANO 'Tis beyond your apprehension
How strangely that one look has catched his heart!
'Twould prove but too much worth in wealth and favour
To those should work his peace.
LIVIA   And if I do't not,
Or at least come as near it (if your art   25
Will take a little pains and second me)
As any wench in Florence of my standing,
I'll quite give o'er, and shut up shop in cunning.

22 *strangely* ed (strangly O)

GUARDIANO
   'Tis for the duke; and if I fail your purpose,
   All means to come, by riches or advancement,   30
   Miss me and skip me over!
LIVIA   Let the old woman then
   Be sent for with all speed; then I'll begin.
GUARDIANO
   A good conclusion follow, and a sweet one,
   After this stale beginning with old ware.
   Within there!

Enter SERVANT

SERVANT   Sir, do you call?
GUARDIANO   Come near, list hither.   35
LIVIA
   I long myself to see this absolute creature
   That wins the heart of love and praise so much.
GUARDIANO
   Go sir, make haste.
LIVIA   Say I entreat her company;
   Do you hear, sir?
SERVANT   Yes, madam.   *Exit*
LIVIA   That brings her quickly.
GUARDIANO
   I would 'twere done; the duke waits the good hour,   40
   And I wait the good fortune that may spring from't:
   I have had a lucky hand these fifteen year
   At such court-passage with three dice in a dish.

Enter FABRITIO

   Signor Fabritio!
ABRITIO
   Oh sir, I bring an alteration in my mouth now.   45
GUARDIANO
   An alteration! no wise speech, I hope;
   He means not to talk wisely does he, trow?
   Good! what's the change, I pray sir?
FABRITIO   A new change.
GUARDIANO
   Another yet! 'faith, there's enough already.

---

43 *court-passage.* '*Passage* is a Game at Dice to be play'd at but by two, and
   it is performed with three Dice. The *Caster* throws continually till he
   hath thrown Doublets under ten, and then he is out and loseth; or
   doublets above ten, and then he *passeth* and wins' (Charles Cotton,
   The Compleat Gamester (1674), p. 167).

FABRITIO
My daughter loves him now.
GUARDIANO   What, does she, sir?   50
FABRITIO
Affects him beyond thought—who but the ward, forsooth!
No talk but of the ward; she would have him
To choose 'bove all the men she ever saw.
My will goes not so fast as her consent now;
Her duty gets before my command still.   55
GUARDIANO
Why then sir, if you'll have me speak my thoughts,
I smell 'twill be a match.
FABRITIO   Ay, and a sweet young couple,
If I have any judgement.
GUARDIANO   —'Faith, that's little.
Let her be sent tomorrow before noon,
And handsomely tricked up, for 'bout that time   60
I mean to bring her in and tender her to him.
FABRITIO
I warrant you for handsome; I will see
Her things laid ready, every one in order,
And have some part of her tricked up tonight.
GUARDIANO
Why, well said.
FABRITIO   'Twas a use her mother had   65
When she was invited to an early wedding;
She'ld dress her head o'ernight, sponge up herself,
And give her neck three lathers.
GUARDIANO   Ne'er a halter?
FABRITIO
On with her chain of pearl, her ruby bracelets,
Lay ready all her tricks and jiggambobs.   70
GUARDIANO
So must your daughter.
FABRITIO   I'll about it straight, sir.
                              Exit FABRITIO
LIVIA
How he sweats in the foolish zeal of fatherhood
After six ounces an hour, and seems
To toil as much as if his cares were wise ones!
GUARDIANO
Y'have let his folly blood in the right vein, lady.   75

---

68 *lathers . . . halter.* The *halter* would be made of leather—for which
  lather is a variant form.

LIVIA

And here comes his sweet son-in-law that shall be.
They're both allied in wit before the marriage;
What will they be hereafter, when they are nearer?
Yet they can go no further than the fool:
There's the word's end in both of 'em.

Enter WARD *and* SORDIDO, *one with a shuttlecock, the
other a battledore*

GUARDIANO　　　　　　　　　　　　　Now, young heir!　　80

WARD

What's the next business after shuttlecock, now?

GUARDIANO

Tomorrow you shall see the gentlewoman must be your
wife.

WARD

There's ev'n another thing too must be kept up with a
pair of battledores. My wife! what can she do?　　85

GUARDIANO

Nay, that's a question you should ask yourself, ward,
when y'are alone together.

WARD

That's as I list! A wife's to be asked anywhere, I hope;
I'll ask her in a congregation, if I have a mind to't, and
so save a licence.—My guardiner has no more wit than an　　90
herb-woman, that sells away all her sweet herbs and
nosegays, and keeps a stinking breath for her own pottage.

SORDIDO

Let me be at the choosing of your beloved, if you desire a
woman of good parts.

WARD

Thou shalt, sweet Sordido.　　95

SORDIDO

I have a plaguey guess; let me alone to see what she is.

---

80 *word's* ed (worlds O)
82-9 *Tomorrow . . . hope* (as verse O)　　　　88 *asked* ed (ask O)

84-5 *kept . . . battledores.* The Ward's intention is obscene—although
again obscurely so. Isabella for the banquet has 'a lusty sprouting sprig
in her hair' (III, ii, 14), and perhaps Middleton is thinking of her as one
of the harlots he describes in *Father Hubburd's Tales*: 'such shuttlecocks
as these, which, though they are tossed and played withal, go still like
maids, all white on top' (viii, 79).
89-90 *ask . . . licence.* Unless the banns of marriage were publicly proclaimed in church ('congregation') a special licence was necessary.

If I but look upon her—'way, I know all the faults to a
hair that you may refuse her for.

WARD

Dost thou? I prithee let me hear 'em Sordido.

SORDIDO

Well, mark 'em then; I have 'em all in rhyme.   100
    The wife your guardiner ought to tender,
    Should be pretty, straight and slender;
    Her hair not short, her foot not long,
    Her hand not huge, nor too too loud her tongue;
    No pearl in eye nor ruby in her nose,   105
    No burn or cut but what the catalogue shows.
    She must have teeth, and that no black ones,
    And kiss most sweet when she does smack once:
    Her skin must be both white and plumpt,
    Her body straight, not hopper-rumped,   110
    Or wriggle sideways like a crab.
    She must be neither slut nor drab,
    Nor go too splay-foot with her shoes
    To make her smock lick up the dews.
    And two things more which I forgot to tell ye: 115
    She neither must have bump in back nor belly.
These are the faults that will not make her pass.

WARD

    And if I spy not these I am a rank ass!

SORDIDO

Nay, more—by right, sir, you should see her naked,
For that's the ancient order.

WARD   See her naked?   120
That were good sport, i'faith. I'll have the books turned over,
And if I find her naked on record
She shall not have a rag on—but stay, stay!
How if she should desire to see me so too?
I were in a sweet case then; such a foul skin!   125

---

109 *plumpt* ed (plump O)

---

105 *pearl in eye.* The whitish spot in the eye left by certain diseases (such as
smallpox): 'A pearl in mine eye! I thank you for that; do you wish me
blind?' (Middleton, *The Spanish Gipsy*, II, i, 167–8).
110 *hopper-rumped.* The hopper of a mill is shaped like an inverted pyramid
and has a hopping or shaking movement.
119 *see her naked.* It was a Utopian custom: 'For a sad and honest matrone
sheweth the woman, be she mayde or widdowe, naked to the wower.
And lykewyse a sage and discrete man exhibyteth the wower naked to
the woman' (More, *Utopia* (ed. Arber, 1869), p. 123).

SORDIDO
But y'have a clean shirt, and that makes amends, sir.
WARD
I will not see her naked for that trick, though.   *Exit*
SORDIDO
Then take her with all faults with her clothes on,
And they may hide a number with a bum-roll.
'Faith, choosing of a wench in a huge farthingale   130
Is like the buying of ware under a great penthouse:
What with the deceit of one,
And the false light of th'other, mark my speeches,
He may have a diseased wench in's bed
And rotten stuff in's breeches.   *Exit* 135
GUARDIANO
It may take handsomely.
LIVIA   I see small hindrance.
How now, so soon returned?

Enter [SERVANT *with*] MOTHER

GUARDIANO   She's come.
LIVIA   That's well.
Widow, come, come; I have a great quarrel to you,
'Faith, I must chide you, that you must be sent for!
You make yourself so strange, never come at us,   140
And yet so near a neighbour, and so unkind!
Troth, y'are too blame; you cannot be more welcome
To any house in Florence, that I'll tell you.
MOTHER
My thanks must needs acknowledge so much, madam.
LIVIA
How can you be so strange then? I sit here   145
Sometime whole days together without company
When business draws this gentleman from home,
And should be happy in society
Which I so well affect as that of yours.
I know y'are alone too; why should not we,   150
Like two kind neighbours, then, supply the wants

---

129 *bum-roll* cushion to hold out the full skirt

130 *choosing . . . farthingale*. '. . . wires and tires, bents and bums, felts and
   falls, thou that shalt deceive the world, that gentlewomen indeed shall
   not be known from others' (*Michaelmas Term*, I, ii, 13–15).
133 *false light*. 'My shop is not altogether so dark as some of my neighbours',
   where a man may be made cuckold at one end, while he's measuring
   with his yard at t'other' (*Michaelmas Term*, II, iii, 34–7).

Of one another, having tongue-discourse,
Experience in the world, and such kind helps
To laugh down time, and meet age merrily?

MOTHER

Age, madam! you speak mirth; 'tis at my door,   155
But a long journey from your ladyship yet.

LIVIA

My faith, I'm nine-and-thirty, ev'ry stroke, wench;
And 'tis a general observation
'Mongst knights: wives or widows, we account
Ourselves then old, when young men's eyes leave looking at's: 160
'Tis a true rule amongst us, and ne'er failed yet
In any but in one that I remember;
Indeed, she had a friend at nine-and-forty!
—Marry, she paid well for him; and in th'end
He kept a quean or two with her own money,   165
That robbed her of her plate and cut her throat.

MOTHER

She had her punishment in this world, madam;
And a fair warning to all other women
That they live chaste at fifty.

LIVIA   Ay, or never, wench.
Come, now I have thy company I'll not part with't   170
Till after supper.

MOTHER   Yes, I must crave pardon, madam.

LIVIA

I swear you shall stay supper; we have no strangers, woman,
None but my sojourners and I—this gentleman
And the young heir, his ward. You know our company.

MOTHER

Some other time I will make bold with you, madam.   175

GUARDIANO

Nay, pray stay widow.

LIVIA   'Faith, she shall not go.
Do you think I'll be forsworn?   *Table and chess*

MOTHER   'Tis a great while
Till supper-time; I'll take my leave, then, now madam,
And come again i'th'evening, since your ladyship
Will have it so.

LIVIA   I'th'evening! By my troth, wench,   180

---

173 *sojourners* lodgers

---

177 s.d. Table and chess. O retains the prompt-book's warning of properties
that will be needed shortly.

I'll keep you while I have you; you have great business, sure,
To sit alone at home. I wonder strangely
What pleasure you take in't! were't to me now,
I should be ever at one neighbour's house
Or other all day long, having no charge,   185
Or none to chide you if you go or stay.
Who may live merrier—ay, or more at heart's ease?
Come, we'll to chess or draughts; there are an hundred tricks
To drive out time till supper, never fear't, wench.

MOTHER
I'll but make one step home and return straight, madam.   190

LIVIA
Come, I'll not trust you; you use more excuses
To your kind friends than ever I knew any.
What business can you have, if you be sure
Y'have locked the doors? and that being all you have,
I know y'are careful on't. One afternoon   195
So much to spend here! say I should entreat you now
To lie a night or two, or a week, with me,
Or leave your own house for a month together—
It were a kindness that long neighbourhood
And friendship might well hope to prevail in—   200
Would you deny such a request? i'faith,
Speak truth, and freely.

MOTHER   I were then uncivil, madam.

LIVIA
Go to then, set your men; we'll have whole nights
Of mirth together ere we be much older, wench.

MOTHER
As good now tell her, then, for she will know't;   205
I have always found her a most friendly lady.

LIVIA
Why widow, where's your mind?

MOTHER   Troth, ev'n at home,
                                                    madam.
To tell you truth, I left a gentlewoman
Ev'n sitting all alone, which is uncomfortable,
Especially to young bloods.

LIVIA   Another excuse!   210

MOTHER
No, as I hope for health madam, that's a truth.
Please you to send and see.

LIVIA   What gentlewoman? Pish!

199 *neighbourhood* being neighbours

MOTHER
Wife to my son, indeed, but not known, madam,
To any but yourself.
LIVIA   Now I beshrew you!
Could you be so unkind to her and me,   215
To come and not bring her? 'Faith, 'tis not friendly!
MOTHER
I feared to be too bold.
LIVIA   Too bold? Oh what's become
Of the true hearty love was wont to be
'Mongst neighbours in old time!
MOTHER   And she's a stranger,
                                                    madam.
LIVIA
The more should be her welcome. When is courtesy   220
In better practice, than when 'tis employed
In entertaining strangers? I could chide, i'faith.
Leave her behind, poor gentlewoman, alone too!
Make some amends, and send for her betimes; go.
MOTHER
Please you command one of your servants, madam.   225
LIVIA
Within there!

Enter SERVANT

SERVANT   Madam?
LIVIA   Attend the gentlewoman.
MOTHER
It must be carried wondrous privately
From my son's knowledge; he'll break out in storms else.
Hark you sir.   [*she gives instructions; exit* SERVANT]
LIVIA   Now comes in the heat of your part.
GUARDIANO
True, I know it, lady; and if I be out,   230
May the duke banish me from all employments,
Wanton or serious.
LIVIA   So, have you sent, widow?
MOTHER
Yes madam, he's almost at home by this.
LIVIA
And 'faith, let me entreat you, that henceforward
All such unkind faults may be swept from friendship,   235
Which does but dim the lustre. And think thus much:
It is a wrong to me, that have ability
To bid friends welcome, when you keep 'em from me;

You cannot set greater dishonour near me,
For bounty is the credit and the glory   240
Of those that have enough. I see y'are sorry,
And the good 'mends is made by't.
MOTHER   Here she'is, madam.

Enter BIANCA, *and* SERVANT [*who shows her in, then goes off*]

BIANCA
I wonder how she comes to send for me now?
LIVIA
Gentlewoman, y'are most welcome, trust me y'are,
As courtesy can make one, or respect   245
Due to the presence of you.
BIANCA   I give you thanks, lady.
LIVIA
I heard you were alone, and 't had appeared
An ill condition in me, though I knew you not,
Nor ever saw you (yet humanity
Thinks ev'ry case her own) to have kept your company   250
Here from you and left you all solitary.
I rather ventured upon boldness then
As the least fault, and wished your presence here—
A thing most happily motioned of that gentleman,
Whom I request you, for his care and pity,   255
To honour and reward with your acquaintance;
A gentleman that ladies' rights stands for:
That's his profession.
BIANCA   'Tis a noble one,
And honours my acquaintance.
GUARDIANO   All my intentions
Are servants to such mistresses.
BIANCA   'Tis your modesty,   260
It seems, that makes your deserts speak so low, sir.
LIVIA
Come widow—look you, lady, here's our business;
Are we not well employed, think you? an old quarrel
Between us, that will never be at an end.
BIANCA   No?
And methinks there's men enough to part you, lady.   265
LIVIA
Ho—but they set us on, let us come off
As well as we can, poor souls; men care no farther.

242 *'mends* amends
254 *motioned of* proposed by

I pray sit down, forsooth, if you have the patience
To look upon two weak and tedious gamesters.

GUARDIANO

'Faith madam, set these by till evening;   270
You'll have enough on't then. The gentlewoman,
Being a stranger, would take more delight
To see your rooms and pictures.

LIVIA   Marry, good sir,
And well remembered! I beseech you show 'em her,
That will beguile time well; pray heartily, do sir—   275
I'll do as much for you; here, take these keys,
Show her the monument too—and that's a thing
Everyone sees not; you can witness that, widow.

MOTHER

And that's worth sight indeed, madam.

BIANCA   Kind lady,
I fear I came to be a trouble to you.   280

LIVIA

Oh, nothing less, forsooth.

BIANCA

And to this courteous gentleman,
That wears a kindness in his breast so noble
And bounteous to the welcome of a stranger.

GUARDIANO

If you but give acceptance to my service,   285
You do the greatest grace and honour to me
That courtesy can merit.

BIANCA   I were too blame else,
And out of fashion much; I pray you lead, sir.

LIVIA

After a game or two we'are for you, gentlefolks.

GUARDIANO

We wish no better seconds in society   290
Than your discourses, madam, and your partner's there.

MOTHER

I thank your praise. I listened to you, sir,
Though when you spoke there came a paltry rook
Full in my way, and chokes up all my game.

                          Exit GUARDIANO *and* BIANCA

LIVIA

Alas, poor widow, I shall be too hard for thee.   295

MOTHER

Y'are cunning at the game, I'll be sworn, madam.

LIVIA

It will be found so, ere I give you over.

She that can place her man well—
MOTHER   As you do, madam—
LIVIA
As I shall wench—can never lose her game.
Nay, nay, the black king's mine.
MOTHER   Cry you mercy, madam.   300
LIVIA
And this my queen.
MOTHER   I see't now.
LIVIA   Here's a duke
Will strike a sure stroke for the game anon;
Your pawn cannot come back to relieve itself.
MOTHER
I know that, madam.
LIVIA   You play well the whilst;
How she belies her skill! I hold two ducats   305
I give you check and mate to your white king,
Simplicity itself, your saintish king there.
MOTHER
Well, ere now, lady,
I have seen the fall of subtlety. Jest on.
LIVIA
Ay, but simplicity receives two for one.   310
MOTHER
What remedy but patience!

Enter above GUARDIANO *and* BIANCA

BIANCA   Trust me, sir,
Mine eye nev'r met with fairer ornaments.

300 *Cry you mercy.* 'If you take up your Adversaries man, and after think
best to let it stand untaken, before you set your own piece in place
thereof, you must cry him mercy or lose the Game' (Cotton, p. 77).
301 *duke.* An alternative name for the rook; Livia's apparent identification
at this point of the duke of Florence with the chessman is confusing:
Bianca's seducer is the black king of line 300, and Guardiano is the rook:
IGNATIUS
    Dukes? they're called Rooks by some.
ERROR   Corruptively!
    Le Roc the word, *Custode de la Roche,*
    The Keeper of the Forts, in whom both Kings
    Repose much confidence
                                (*A Game at Chess*, Induction, 55–8).
303 *pawn . . . itself.* 'a Pawn is the soonest ensnared, because he cannot go
back for succour or relief' (Cotton, p. 67).

GUARDIANO
    Nay, livelier, I'm persuaded, neither Florence
    Nor Venice can produce.
BIANCA   Sir, my opinion
    Takes your part highly.
GUARDIANO   There's a better piece   315
    Yet than all these.   [*Enter*] DUKE *above*
BIANCA   Not possible, sir.
GUARDIANO   Believe it;
    You'll say so when you see't. Turn but your eye now,
    Y'are upon it presently.   *Exit*
BIANCA   Oh sir!
DUKE   He's gone, beauty!
    Pish, look not after him, he's but a vapour
    That when the sun appears is seen no more.   320
BIANCA
    Oh treachery to honour!
DUKE   Prithee tremble not.
    I feel thy breast shake like a turtle panting
    Under a loving hand that makes much on't.
    Why art so fearful? as I'm friend to brightness,
    There's nothing but respect and honour near thee.   325
    You know me, you have seen me; here's a heart
    Can witness I have seen thee.
BIANCA   The more's my danger.
DUKE
    The more's thy happiness. Pish, strive not, sweet!
    This strength were excellent employed in love, now,
    But here 'tis spent amiss. Strive not to seek   330
    Thy liberty and keep me still in prison.
    I'faith, you shall not out till I'm released now,
    We'll both be freed together, or stay still by't;
    So is captivity pleasant.
BIANCA   Oh my lord!
DUKE
    I am not here in vain: have but the leisure   335
    To think on that, and thou'lt be soon resolved.
    The lifting of thy voice is but like one
    That does exalt his enemy, who, proving high,
    Lays all the plots to confound him that raised him.
    Take warning, I beseech thee; thou seem'st to me   340

---

316 s.d. above. Bullen is probably correct in directing *Draws a curtain, and*
    discovers the DUKE. Guardiano and Bianca have already entered
    '*above*' (line 311), and there can hardly have been three acting levels.

A creature so composed of gentleness
And delicate meekness, such as bless the faces
Of figures that are drawn for goddesses
And make art proud to look upon her work,
I should be sorry the least force should lay   345
An unkind touch upon thee.
BIANCA   Oh my extremity!
My lord, what seek you?
DUKE   Love.
BIANCA   'Tis gone already;
I have a husband.
DUKE   That's a single comfort;
Take a friend to him.
BIANCA   That's a double mischief,
Or else there's no religion.
DUKE   Do not tremble   350
At fears of thine own making.
BIANCA   Nor, great lord,
Make me not bold with death and deeds of ruin
Because they fear not you; me they must fright,
Then am I best in health. Should thunder speak
And none regard it, it had lost the name,   355
And were as good be still. I'm not like those
That take their soundest sleeps in greatest tempests;
Then wake I most, the weather fearfullest,
And call for strength to virtue.
DUKE   Sure I think
Thou know'st the way to please me; I affect   360
A passionate pleading 'bove an easy yielding—
But never pitied any: they deserve none
That will not pity me. I can command:
Think upon that. Yet if thou truly knewest
The infinite pleasure my affection takes   365
In gentle, fair entreatings, when love's businesses
Are carried courteously 'twixt heart and heart,
You'ld make more haste to please me.
BIANCA   Why should you
                                    seek, sir,
To take away that you can never give?
DUKE
But I give better in exchange—wealth, honour.   370
She that is fortunate in a duke's favour

344 *make* ed (makes O)
353 *fear* frighten

Lights on a tree that bears all women's wishes:
If your own mother saw you pluck fruit there,
She would commend your wit, and praise the time
Of your nativity. Take hold of glory.   375
Do not I know y'have cast away your life
Upon necessities, means merely doubtful
To keep you in indifferent health and fashion
(A thing I heard too lately and soon pitied).
And can you be so much your beauty's enemy   380
To kiss away a month or two in wedlock,
And weep whole years in wants for ever after?
Come, play the wise wench, and provide for ever:
Let storms come when they list, they find thee sheltered;
Should any doubt arise, let nothing trouble thee.   385
Put trust in our love for the managing
Of all to thy heart's peace. We'll walk together,
And show a thankful joy for both our fortunes.

                                Exit [*both*] *above*

LIVIA
Did not I say my duke would fetch you over, widow?
MOTHER
I think you spoke in earnest when you said it, madam.   390
LIVIA
And my black king makes all the haste he can, too.
MOTHER
Well, madam, we may meet with him in time yet.
LIVIA
I have given thee blind mate twice.
MOTHER   You may see, madam,
My eyes begin to fail.
LIVIA   I'll swear they do, wench.

                        Enter GUARDIANO

GUARDIANO
I can but smile as often as I think on't!   395
How prettily the poor fool was beguiled,
How unexpectedly! It's a witty age;

383 *wise* ed (wife O)

372-3 *tree . . . fruit.* The duke seems to be advocating Eve's action in
        plucking the apple of knowledge.
393 *blind mate.* 'that is when your Adversary gives you a check that you
        cannot avoid by any means, and is indeed a *Mate absolute*; but he not
        seeing it to be a Mate, says only to you *check*, and it is therefore called a
        Blind-Mate: this should be both loss of Game and stake if you before
        agree not to the contrary' (Cotton, p. 75).

Never were finer snares for women's honesties
Than are devised in these days; no spider's web
Made of a daintier thread, than are now practised   400
To catch love's flesh-fly by the silver wing.
Yet to prepare her stomach by degrees
To Cupid's feast, because I saw 'twas queasy,
I showed her naked pictures by the way—
A bit to stay the appetite. Well, advancement,   405
I venture hard to find thee; if thou com'st
With a greater title set upon thy crest,
I'll take that first cross patiently, and wait
Until some other comes greater than that.
I'll endure all.   410

LIVIA
The game's ev'n at the best now; you may see, widow,
How all things draw to an end.

MOTHER   Ev'n so do I, madam.

LIVIA
I pray take some of your neighbours along with you.

MOTHER
They must be those are almost twice your years, then,
If they be chose fit matches for my time, madam.

LIVIA   415
Has not my duke bestirred himself?

MOTHER   Yes, 'faith madam,
H'as done me all the mischief in this game.

LIVIA
H'as showed himself in's kind.

MOTHER   In's kind, call you it?
I may swear that.

LIVIA   Yes 'faith, and keep your oath.

GUARDIANO
Hark, list! there's somebody coming down; 'tis she.   420

Enter BIANCA

BIANCA
Now bless me from a blasting! I saw that now
Fearful for any woman's eye to look on.
Infectious mists and mildews hang at's eyes,
The weather of a doomsday dwells upon him.

---

407 *a greater title* i.e. pander

---

404 *naked pictures.* Part of the penance imposed on the White Queen's
Pawn by the Black House was to kneel for twelve hours 'in a room
fill'd all with Aretine's pictures' (*A Game at Chess,* II, ii, 255).

Yet since mine honour's leprous, why should I   425
Preserve that fair that caused the leprosy?
Come, poison all at once! Thou in whose baseness
The bane of virtue broods, I'm bound in soul
Eternally to curse thy smooth-browed treachery
That wore the fair veil of a friendly welcome,   430
And I a stranger; think upon't, 'tis worth it.
Murders piled up upon a guilty spirit
At his last breath will not lie heavier
Than this betraying act upon thy conscience.
Beware of off'ring the first-fruits to sin: 435
His weight is deadly who commits with strumpets
After they have been abased and made for use;
If they offend to th'death, as wise men know,
How much more they, then, that first make 'em so?
I give thee that to feed on. I'm made bold now,   440
I thank thy treachery; sin and I'm acquainted,
No couple greater; and I'm like that great one
Who, making politic use of a base villain,
'He likes the treason well, but hates the traitor';
So I hate thee, slave.

GUARDIANO   Well, so the duke love me   445
I fare not much amiss then; two great feasts
Do seldom come together in one day,
We must not look for 'em.

BIANCA   What, at it still, mother?

MOTHER
You see we sit by't; are you so soon returned?

LIVIA
So lively and so cheerful! a good sign, that.   450

MOTHER
You have not seen all since, sure?

BIANCA   That have I, mother,
The monument and all: I'm so beholding
To this kind, honest, courteous gentleman.
You'ld little think it, mother—showed me all,
Had me from place to place so fashionably;   455
The kindness of some people, how't exceeds!
'Faith, I have seen that I little thought to see
I'th'morning when I rose.

425 *why* ed (who O)   436 *commits* fornicates

---

244 *that great one*. Machiavelli. The murder of Lightborn in *Edward II*
(Act V scene v) is a good example of loving the treason and hating the
traitor.

MOTHER   Nay, so I told you
  Before you saw't, it would prove worth your sight.
  I give you great thanks for my daughter, sir,   460
  And all your kindness towards her.
GUARDIANO   Oh good widow!
  —Much good may't do her—forty weeks hence, i'faith.

                    Enter SERVANT

LIVIA
  Now sir?
SERVANT   May't please you, madam, to walk in;
  Supper's upon the table.
LIVIA   Yes, we come.
  Will't please you, gentlewoman?
BIANCA   Thanks, virtuous lady   465
  —Y'are a damned bawd! I'll follow you, forsooth;
  Pray take my mother in—an old ass go with you—
  This gentleman and I vow not to part.
LIVIA
  Then get you both before.
BIANCA   There lies his art.
                    Exeunt [BIANCA *and* GUARDIANO]
LIVIA
  Widow, I'll follow you.   [*Exit* MOTHER]

                    Is't so, 'damned bawd'!   470
  Are you so bitter? 'Tis but want of use;
  Her tender modesty is sea-sick a little,
  Being not accustomed to the breaking billow
  Of woman's wavering faith, blown with temptations.
  'Tis but a qualm of honour, 'twill away;   475
  A little bitter for the time, but lasts not.
  Sin tastes at the first draught like wormwood water,
  But drunk again, 'tis nectar ever after.   *Exit*

                    Act III, Scene i

                    Enter MOTHER

MOTHER
  I would my son would either keep at home

462 *may't* ed (may O)

---

472 *sea-sick*. '. . . yet indeed 'tis the fashion of any courtesan to be sea-sick
  i'th'first voyage' (*Michaelmas Term*, I, ii, 10).

Or I were in my grave!
She was but one day abroad, but ever since
She's grown so cutted, there's no speaking to her.
Whether the sight of great cheer at my lady's,   5
And such mean fare at home, work discontent in her,
I know not; but I'm sure she's strangely altered.
I'll nev'r keep daughter-in-law i'th'house with me
Again, if I had a hundred. When read I of any
That agreed long together, but she and her mother   10
Fell out in the first quarter—nay, sometime
A grudging of a scolding the first week, by'r Lady.
So takes the new disease, methinks, in my house.
I'm weary of my part, there's nothing likes her;
I know not how to please her here o' late.   15
And here she comes.

Enter BIANCA

BIANCA   This is the strangest house
For all defects, as ever gentlewoman
Made shift withal, to pass away her love in!
Why is there not a cushion-cloth of drawn work,
Or some fair cut-work pinned up in my bed-chamber,   20
A silver-and-gilt casting-bottle hung by't?
Nay, since I am content to be so kind to you,
To spare you for a silver basin and ewer,
Which one of my fashion looks for of duty
She's never offered under, where she sleeps.   25
MOTHER
She talks of things here my whole state's not worth.
BIANCA
Never a green silk quilt is there i'th'house, mother,
To cast upon my bed?
MOTHER   No by troth is there,
Nor orange-tawny neither.

4 *cutted* querulous
20 *cut-work* lace   21 *casting-bottle* bottle for sprinkling scent

---

13 *the new disease.* Its symptoms are described by Jonson:
        A new disease? I know not, new, or old,
        But it may well be called poor mortals' plague:
        For, like a pestilence, it doth infect
        The houses of the brain. First, it begins
        Solely to work upon the fantasy,
        Filling her seat with such pestiferous air,
        As soon corrupts the judgement . . .
                        (*Every Man In His Humour*, II, i, 219–24).

BIANCA　　　　　　　　Here's a house
　　For a young gentlewoman to be got with child in!　　　30
MOTHER
　　Yes, simple though you make it, there has been three
　　Got in a year in't—since you move me to't—
　　And all as sweet-faced children and as lovely
　　As you'll be mother of: I will not spare you.
　　What, cannot children be begot, think you,　　　35
　　Without gilt casting-bottles? Yes, and as sweet ones:
　　The miller's daughter brings forth as white boys
　　As she that bathes herself with milk and bean-flour.
　　'Tis an old saying 'one may keep good cheer
　　In a mean house': so may true love affect　　　40
　　After the rate of princes, in a cottage.
BIANCA
　　Troth, you speak wondrous well for your old house here;
　　'Twill shortly fall down at your feet to thank you,
　　Or stoop when you go to bed, like a good child,
　　To ask you blessing. Must I live in want,　　　45
　　Because my fortune matched me with your son?
　　Wives do not give away themselves to husbands
　　To the end to be quite cast away; they look
　　To be the better used and tendered rather,
　　Highlier respected, and maintained the richer;　　　50
　　They're well rewarded else for the free gift
　　Of their whole life to a husband. I ask less now
　　Than what I had at home when I was a maid
　　And at my father's house; kept short of that
　　Which a wife knows she must have—nay, and will　　　55
　　—Will, mother, if she be not a fool born—
　　And report went of me that I could wrangle
　　For what I wanted when I was two hours old;
　　And by that copy, this land still I hold.
　　You hear me, mother.　　　　　　　　　　　*Exit*

37 *white boys* darlings　　　59 *copy* copyhold (legal)

---

38 *bathes . . . milk.* The epitome of wasteful luxury: the proud woman
　'grieve[s] her maker In sinful baths of milk, when many an infant
　starves' (Tourneur, *The Revenger's Tragedy*, III, v, 84–5).
38 *bean-flour.*
　　　I should be tumbling in cold baths now,
　　　Under each armpit a fine bean-flour bag,
　　　To screw out whiteness when I list
　　　　　　　　　(Middleton *et al.*, *The Old Law*, II, ii, 11–13).
39–40 *one . . . house.* The proverb has many variants: 'Content lodges
　oftener in cottages than palaces' (Tilley, C 626).

MOTHER   Ay, too plain, methinks;   60
    And were I somewhat deafer when you spake
    'Twere nev'r a whit the worse for my quietness.
    'Tis the most sudden'st, strangest alteration,
    And the most subtlest that ev'r wit at threescore
    Was puzzled to find out. I know no cause for't; but   65
    She's no more like the gentlewoman at first
    Than I am like her that nev'r lay with man yet,
    And she's a very young thing where'er she be.
    When she first lighted here, I told her then
    How mean she should find all things; she was pleased,
        forsooth,   70
    None better: I laid open all defects to her;
    She was contented still. But the devil's in her,
    Nothing contents her now. Tonight my son
    Promised to be at home; would he were come once,
    For I'm weary of my charge, and life too.   75
    She'ld be served all in silver, by her good will,
    By night and day; she hates the name of pewter
    More than sick men the noise, or diseased bones
    That quake at fall o'th'hammer, seeming to have
    A fellow-feeling with't at every blow.   80
    What course shall I think on? she frets me so.
                    [*Withdraws to back of stage*]

                    Enter LEANTIO

LEANTIO
    How near am I now to a happiness
    That earth exceeds not—not another like it!
    The treasures of the deep are not so precious
    As are the concealed comforts of a man,   85
    Locked up in woman's love. I scent the air
    Of blessings when I come but near the house.
    What a delicious breath marriage sends forth;
    The violet-bed's not sweeter. Honest wedlock
    Is like a banqueting-house built in a garden,   90

---

74 *once* once for all   77 *pewter* ed (pewterer O)   ⁊

---

78 *the noise*. 'Sounds supposed to have been heard before the death of any
    person' (*English Dialect Dictionary*).
90 *banqueting-house . . . garden*. Bacon's model garden was to be graced
    with such a banqueting-house: 'I wish also, in the very middle, a fair
    mount . . . and the whole mount to be thirty foot high; and some fine
    banqueting-house, with chimneys neatly cast, and without too much
    glass' (Essay 'Of Gardens').

On which the spring's chaste flowers take delight
To cast their modest odours—when base lust,
With all her powders, paintings and best pride,
Is but a fair house built by a ditch side.
When I behold a glorious dangerous strumpet,   95
Sparkling in beauty and destruction too,
Both at a twinkling, I do liken straight
Her beautified body to a goodly temple
That's built on vaults where carcasses lie rotting:
And so by little and little I shrink back again,   100
And quench desire with a cool meditation;
And I'm as well, methinks. Now for a welcome
Able to draw men's envies upon man:
A kiss now that will hang upon my lip
As sweet as morning dew upon a rose,   105
And full as long. After a five days' fast
She'll be so greedy now, and cling about me,
I take care how I shall be rid of her;
And here't begins.

          [*Enter* BIANCA; MOTHER *comes forward*]

BIANCA   Oh sir, y'are welcome home.
MOTHER
  Oh is he come? I am glad on't.
LEANTIO   Is that all?   110
  Why this? as dreadful now as sudden death
  To some rich man that flatters all his sins
  With promise of repentance when he's old,
  And dies in the midway before he comes to't.
  Sure y'are not well Bianca! How dost, prithee?   115
BIANCA
  I have been better than I am at this time.
LEANTIO
  Alas, I thought so.
BIANCA   Nay, I have been worse too
  Than now you see me sir.
LEANTIO   I'm glad thou mend'st yet;
  I feel my heart mend too. How came it to thee?
  Has anything disliked thee in my absence?   120

98-9 *goodly . . . rotting*. 'Woe unto you, scribes and Pharisees, hypocrites!
    for ye are like unto whited sepulchres, which indeed appear beautiful
    outward, but are within full of dead men's bones, and of all uncleanness'
    (*St Matthew*, xxiii, 27).

BIANCA

No, certain; I have had the best content
That Florence can afford.

LEANTIO   Thou makest the best on't;
Speak mother, what's the cause? you must needs know.

MOTHER

Troth, I know none, son; let her speak herself.
—Unless it be the same gave Lucifer   125
A tumbling-cast, that's pride.

BIANCA

Methinks this house stands nothing to my mind,
I'ld have some pleasant lodging i'th'high street, sir;
Or if 'twere near the court, sir, that were much better—
'Tis a sweet recreation for a gentlewoman   130
To stand in a bay-window and see gallants.

LEANTIO

Now I have another temper, a mere stranger
To that of yours, it seems; I should delight
To see none but yourself.

BIANCA   I praise not that:
Too fond is as unseemly as too churlish.   135
I would not have a husband of that proneness
To kiss me before company, for a world!
Beside, 'tis tedious to see one thing still, sir,
Be it the best that ever heart affected—
Nay, were't yourself, whose love had power, you know,   140
To bring me from my friends, I would not stand thus
And gaze upon you always; troth, I could not, sir.
As good be blind and have no use of sight
As look on one thing still: what's the eye's treasure
But change of objects? You are learned, sir,   145
And know I speak not ill. 'Tis full as virtuous

---

126 *tumbling-cast* wrestling throw   146 *'Tis* ed ('till O)

128–31 *I'ld . . . gallants.* 'the poore wife [has not] liberty to looke out of the
windowe, especially if it be towards the streete' (Moryson 4, p. 151).
Bianca is virtually proclaiming herself a whore—offering herself in the
window:
    I'll have that window next the street dammed up;
    It gives too full a prospect to temptation,
    And courts a gazer's glances. There's a lust
    Committed by the eye, that sweats and travails,
    Plots, wakes, contrives, till the deformed bear-whelp
    Adultery be licked into the act
                                    (Ford, *The Broken Heart*, II, i, 1–6).

For woman's eye to look on several men,
As for her heart, sir, to be fixed on one.

LEANTIO
Now thou com'st home to me; a kiss for that word.

BIANCA
No matter for a kiss, sir; let it pass;　　　　　　150
'Tis but a toy, we'll not so much as mind it.
Let's talk of other business and forget it.
What news now of the pirates; any stirring?
Prithee discourse a little.

MOTHER　　　　　　　　I am glad he's here yet
To see her tricks himself; I had lied monstrously　　155
If I had told 'em first.

LEANTIO　　　　　　Speak, what's the humour, sweet,
You make your lip so strange? this was not wont.

BIANCA
Is there no kindness betwixt man and wife
Unless they make a pigeon-house of friendship
And be still billing? 'tis the idlest fondness　　　160
That ever was invented, and 'tis pity
It's grown a fashion for poor gentlewomen;
There's many a disease kissed in a year by't,
And a French curtsy made to't. Alas, sir,
Think of the world, how we shall live, grow serious;　165
We have been married a whole fortnight now.

LEANTIO
How? a whole fortnight! why, is that so long?

BIANCA
'Tis time to leave off dalliance; 'tis a doctrine
Of your own teaching, if you be remembered,
And I was bound to obey it.

MOTHER　　　　　　　　Here's one fits him!　　170
This was well catched, i'faith son—like a fellow
That rids another country of a plague
And brings it home with him to his own house.
Who knocks?　　　　　　　　　　　*Knock within*

LEANTIO　　Who's there now? Withdraw you, Bianca;
Thou art a gem no stranger's eye must see,　　　175
Howev'r thou please now to look dull on me.

　　　　　　　　　　　　　　Exit [BIANCA]

176 *thou please* ed (thou pleas'd O; thou'rt pleas'd Bullen)

---

153 *news . . . pirates.* The duke of Florence kept a watch on the coasts 'for
　　feare of African pyrates, whome the Duke yearely provoked by the
　　Gallyes he sett out to spoyle the Turkes' (Moryson 4, p. 146).
164 *French curtsy.* An oblique reference to syphilis, the 'French disease'.

Enter MESSENGER

Y'are welcome sir; to whom your business, pray?

MESSENGER
To one I see not here now.

LEANTIO   Who should that be, sir?

MESSENGER
A young gentlewoman I was sent to.

LEANTIO
A young gentlewoman?

MESSENGER   Ay sir, about sixteen.   180
Why look you wildly sir?

LEANTIO   At your strange error;
Y'have mistook the house, sir, there's none such here,
I assure you.

MESSENGER   I assure you too:
The man that sent me cannot be mistook.

LEANTIO
Why, who is't sent you, sir?

MESSENGER   The duke.

LEANTIO   The duke!   185

MESSENGER
Yes, he entreats her company at a banquet
At Lady Livia's house.

LEANTIO   Troth, shall I tell you, sir,
It is the most erroneous business
That ere your honest pains was abused with.
I pray forgive me if I smile a little—   190
I cannot choose, i'faith sir, at an error
So comical as this (I mean no harm, though).
His grace has been most wondrous ill informed;
Pray so return it, sir. What should her name be?

MESSENGER
That I shall tell you straight too: Bianca Capello.   195

LEANTIO
How sir, Bianca? what do you call th'other?

MESSENGER
Capello. Sir, it seems you know no such, then?

LEANTIO
Who should this be? I never heard o'th'name.

MESSENGER
Then 'tis a sure mistake.

LEANTIO   What if you enquired
In the next street, sir? I saw gallants there   200

In the new houses that are built of late.
Ten to one, there you find her.

MESSENGER   Nay, no matter,
I will return the mistake and seek no further.

LEANTIO
Use your own will and pleasure sir; y'are welcome.

                                  Exit MESSENGER
What shall I think of first? Come forth Bianca.   205
Thou art betrayed, I fear me.

                [*Enter* BIANCA]

BIANCA   Betrayed—how sir?

LEANTIO
The duke knows thee.

BIANCA   Knows me! how know you that, sir?

LEANTIO
Has got thy name.

BIANCA   Ay, and my good name too,
That's worse o'th'twain.

LEANTIO   How comes this work about?

BIANCA
How should the duke know me? can you guess, mother?   210

MOTHER
Not I with all my wits; sure, we kept house close.

LEANTIO
Kept close! not all the locks in Italy
Can keep you women so. You have been gadding,
And ventured out at twilight to th'court-green yonder,
And met the gallant bowlers coming home,   215
Without your masks too, both of you; I'll be hanged else!
Thou hast been seen, Bianca, by some stranger;
Never excuse it.

BIANCA   I'll not seek the way, sir.
Do you think y'have married me to mew me up
Not to be seen; what would you make of me?   220

LEANTIO
A good wife, nothing else.

BIANCA   Why, so are some
That are seen ev'ry day, else the devil take 'em.

LEANTIO
No more then: I believe all virtuous in thee

213 *gadding.* 'A dishonest woman is hardly kept within her owne house, but
   shee must be a ramping and aroysting about to make herself knowne'
   (Barnaby Rich, *The Excellencie of Good Women* (1613), p. 24).
216 *Without your masks.* Young Italian wives were 'covered with vayles
   when they go abroade' (Moryson 4, p. 409).

Without an argument. 'Twas but thy hard chance
To be seen somewhere; there lies all the mischief, 225
But I have devised a riddance.

MOTHER   Now I can tell you, son,
The time and place.

LEANTIO   When? where?

MOTHER   What wits have I!
When you last took your leave, if you remember,
You left us both at window.

LEANTIO   Right, I know that.

MOTHER
And not the third part of an hour after 230
The duke passed by in a great solemnity
To St Mark's temple; and to my apprehension
He looked up twice to th'window.

LEANTIO   Oh, there quickened
The mischief of this hour.

BIANCA   If you call't mischief,
It is a thing I fear I am conceived with. 235

LEANTIO
Looked he up twice, and could you take no warning!

MOTHER
Why, once may do as much harm, son, as a thousand:
Do not you know one spark has fired an house
As well as a whole furnace?

LEANTIO   My heart flames for't!
Yet let's be wise and keep all smothered closely; 240
I have bethought a means. Is the door fast?

MOTHER
I locked it myself after him.

LEANTIO   You know, mother,
At the end of the dark parlour there's a place
So artificially contrived for a conveyance
No search could ever find it—when my father 245
Kept in for manslaughter, it was his sanctuary:
There will I lock my life's best treasure up.
Bianca!

BIANCA   Would you keep me closer yet?
Have you the conscience? Y'are best ev'n choke me up, sir!
You make me fearful of your health and wits, 250
You cleave to such wild courses. What's the matter?

LEANTIO
Why, are you so insensible of your danger

244 *artificially* artfully   244 *conveyance* secret passage (*O.E.D.* 12a)

To ask that now? The duke himself has sent for you
To Lady Livia's, to a banquet forsooth.

BIANCA

Now I beshrew you heartily. Has he so!   255
And you the man would never yet vouchsafe
To tell me on't till now! you show your loyalty
And honesty at once; and so farewell, sir.

LEANTIO

Bianca, whither now?

BIANCA   Why, to the duke, sir.
You say he sent for me.   260

LEANTIO   But thou dost not mean
To go, I hope.

BIANCA   No? I shall prove unmannerly,
Rude and uncivil, mad, and imitate you?
Come, mother, come; follow his humour no longer.
We shall be all executed for treason shortly.

MOTHER

Not I, i'faith; I'll first obey the duke,   265
And taste of a good banquet; I'm of thy mind.
I'll step but up and fetch two handkerchiefs
To pocket up some sweetmeats, and o'ertake thee.   *Exit*

BIANCA

Why, here's an old wench would trot into a bawd now
For some dry sucket or a colt in marchpane.   *Exit* 270

LEANTIO

Oh thou the ripe time of man's misery, wedlock,
When all his thoughts, like over-laden trees,

267–8 *handkerchiefs . . . sweetmeats.* 'I come not empty-pocketed from a
banquet, I learn'd that of my haberdasher's wife' (*The Witch*, I, ii, 217–8).
270 *dry . . . marchpane.* Gervase Markham gives instructions to the housewife about the kind and order of dishes to be served at a banquet:
. . . when they goe to the table, you shall first send forth a dish made
for shew onely, as Beast, bird, Fish, or Fowl, according to invention:
then your Marchpane, then preserved Fruite, then a Paste, then a
wet Sucket, then a dry Sucket, Marmelade, Cumfetts, Apples, Pears,
Wardens, Oranges and Lemmons sliced; and then Wafers, and another
dish of preserved Fruites, and so consequently all the rest before
(*Country Contentments* (1623), p. 125).
Sucket (wet and dry) was a kind of crystallised fruit. *Marchpane*
(= marzipan) could be moulded into the forms of bulls, rams, horses,
etc.: '*The banquet is brought in, six of* WEATHERWISE'S *Tenants carrying
the Twelve Signs . . . made of banqueting stuff*' (Middleton, *No Wit/
Help Like a Woman's*, II, i, 96 s.d.).

Crack with the fruits they bear, in cares, in jealousies—
Oh that's a fruit that ripens hastily
After 'tis knit to marriage: it begins   275
As soon as the sun shines upon the bride
A little to show colour. Blessed powers!
Whence comes this alteration? the distractions,
The fears and doubts it brings are numberless;
And yet the cause I know not. What a peace   280
Has he that never marries! if he knew
The benefit he enjoyed, or had the fortune
To come and speak with me, he should know then
The infinite wealth he had, and discern rightly
The greatness of his treasure by my loss.   285
Nay, what a quietness has he 'bove mine,
That wears his youth out in a strumpet's arms,
And never spends more care upon a woman
Than at the time of lust; but walks away,
And if he finds her dead at his return,   290
His pity is soon done: he breaks a sigh
In many parts, and gives her but a piece on't.
But all the fears, shames, jealousies, costs and troubles,
And still renewed cares of a marriage bed
Live in the issue when the wife is dead.   295

Enter MESSENGER

MESSENGER
A good perfection to your thoughts.
LEANTIO   The news, sir?
MESSENGER
Though you were pleased of late to pin an error on me,
You must not shift another in your stead too:
The duke has sent me for you.
LEANTIO   How, for me, sir?
I see then 'tis my theft; w'are both betrayed.   300
Well, I'm not the first has stol'n away a maid:
My countrymen have used it. I'll along with you, sir.

Exeunt

Act III, Scene ii

A banquet prepared:

Enter GUARDIANO *and* WARD

GUARDIANO
Take you especial note of such a gentlewoman,
She's here on purpose; I have invited her,
Her father and her uncle, to this banquet.

Mark her behaviour well, it does concern you;
And what her good parts are, as far as time   5
And place can modestly require a knowledge of,
Shall be laid open to your understanding.
You know I'm both your guardian and your uncle:
My care of you is double, ward and nephew,
And I'll express it here.
WARD   'Faith, I should know her   10
Now, by her mark, among a thousand women:
A little, pretty, deft and tidy thing, you say?
GUARDIANO
Right.
WARD
With a lusty sprouting sprig in her hair?
GUARDIANO
Thou goest the right way still; take one mark more: 15
Thou shalt nev'r find her hand out of her uncle's,
Or else his out of hers, if she be near him:
The love of kindred never yet stuck closer
Than their's to one another; he that weds her
Marries her uncle's heart too.   *Cornets*
WARD   Say you so, sir;   20
Then I'll be asked i'th'church to both of 'em.
GUARDIANO
Fall back, here comes the duke.
WARD
He brings a gentlewoman,
I should fall forward rather.

Enter DUKE, BIANCA, FABRITIO, HIPPOLITO, LIVIA, MOTHER,
        ISABELLA, *and Attendants*

DUKE
Come Bianca,   25
Of purpose sent into the world to show
Perfection once in woman; I'll believe
Henceforward they have ev'ry one a soul too,
14 *sprig* See note at II, ii, 84
_____

28 *ev'ry one a soul.* God breathed 'the breath of life' into Adam's nostrils, 'and
   man became a living soul' (*Genesis* ii, 7) but He did not do the same for Eve:
        Man to God's image, *Eve*, to mans was made,
        Nor finde wee that God breath'd a soul in her
                            (Donne, 'To the Countess of Huntingdon').
   By this time, however, a serious medieval debate had degenerated to
   just one more insult for the exasperated male to throw at women; and
   Donne can also write 'so we have given *women* soules onely to make
   them capable of damnation?' (*Paradoxes and Problemes*, Problem 6).

'Gainst all the uncourteous opinions
That man's uncivil rudeness ever held of 'em.   30
Glory of Florence, light into mine arms!

Enter LEANTIO

BIANCA
    Yon comes a grudging man will chide you, sir.
    The storm is now in's heart, and would get nearer
    And fall here if it durst; it pours down yonder.
DUKE
    If that be he, the weather shall soon clear;   35
    List and I'll tell thee how. [*Whispers to* BIANCA]
LEANTIO   A kissing too?
    I see 'tis plain lust now, adultery boldened.
    What will it prove anon, when 'tis stuffed full
    Of wine and sweetmeats, being so impudent fasting?
DUKE
    We have heard of your good parts, sir, which we honour   40
    With our embrace and love. Is not the captainship
    Of Rouens' citadel, since the late deceased,
    Supplied by any yet?
GENTLEMAN   By none, my lord.
DUKE
    Take it, the place is yours then;   [LEANTIO *kneels*]
                            and as faithfulness
    And desert grows, our favour shall grow with't: 45
    Rise now the captain of our fort at Rouens.
LEANTIO
    The service of whole life give your grace thanks.
DUKE
    Come, sit Bianca.
LEANTIO   This is some good yet,
    And more than ev'r I looked for—a fine bit
    To stay a cuckold's stomach! All preferment   50
    That springs from sin and lust, it shoots up quickly,
    As gardeners' crops do in the rotten'st grounds:

---

42 *Rouens.* The appointment is fictitious; and I can find no reason why
    Middleton should have seized on the name Rouens (Rouans O).
50–56 *All . . . mad.* Leantio, like Bosola in Webster's *The Duchess of Malfi*,
    takes on something of the traditional quality of the malcontent:
                    what's my place?
        The provisorship o'the'horse? say then my corruption
        Grew out of horse dung
                            (*The Duchess of Malfi*, I, ii, 206–7).

So is all means raised from base prostitution
Ev'n like a sallet growing upon a dunghill.
I'm like a thing that never was yet heard of,   55
Half merry and half mad—much like a fellow
That eats his meat with a good appetite,
And wears a plague-sore that would fright a country;
Or rather like the barren hardened ass,
That feeds on thistles till he bleeds again.   60
And such is the condition of my misery.

LIVIA
Is that your son, widow?

MOTHER   Yes, did your ladyship
Never know that till now?

LIVIA   No, trust me, did I.
—Nor ever truly felt the power of love
And pity to a man, till now I knew him.   65
I have enough to buy me my desires,
And yet to spare, that's one good comfort. Hark you?
Pray let me speak with you, sir, before you go.

LEANTIO
With me, lady? you shall; I am at your service.
—What will she say now, trow? more goodness yet?   70

WARD
I see her now, I'm sure; the ape's so little, I shall scarce
feel her! I have seen almost as tall as she sold in the fair
for tenpence. See how she simpers it—as if marmalade
would not melt in her mouth! She might have the kindness,
i'faith, to send me a gilded bull from her own trencher,   75
a ram, a goat, or somewhat to be nibbling; these women,
when they come to sweet things once, they forget all their
friends, they grow so greedy—nay, oftentimes their
husbands.

DUKE
Here's a health now, gallants,   80
To the best beauty at this day in Florence.

BIANCA
Whoe'er she be, she shall not go unpledged, sir.

---

54 *sallet* salad
59 *barren* stupid
71–9 *I see . . . husbands* (as verse O)
75 *gilded bull* See note at III, i, 270

73–4 *marmalade . . . mouth.* Proverbial: 'He looks as if butter would not
melt in his mouth' (Tilley, B 774).

DUKE
  Nay, you're excused for this.

BIANCA   Who, I my lord?

DUKE
  Yes, by the law of Bacchus; plead your benefit:
  You are not bound to pledge your own health, lady.   85

BIANCA
  That's a good way, my lord, to keep me dry.

DUKE
  Nay then, I will not offend Venus so much;
  Let Bacchus seek his 'mends in another court.
  Here's to thyself, Bianca.

BIANCA   Nothing comes
  More welcome to that name than your grace.

LEANTIO   So, so!   90
  Here stands the poor thief now that stole the treasure,
  And he's not thought on. Ours is near kin now
  To a twin misery born into the world:
  First the hard-conscienced worldling—he hoards wealth up:
  Then comes the next, and he feasts all upon't;   95
  One's damned for getting, th'other for spending on't.
  Oh equal justice, thou hast met my sin
  With a full weight; I'm rightly now oppressed:
  All her friends' heavy hearts lie in my breast.

DUKE
  Methinks there is no spirit amongst us, gallants,   100
  But what divinely sparkles from the eyes
  Of bright Bianca; we sat all in darkness
  But for that splendour. Who was't told us lately
  Of a match-making rite, a marriage-tender?

GUARDIANO
  'Twas I, my lord.

DUKE   'Twas you indeed. Where is she? 105

GUARDIANO
  This is the gentlewoman.

FABRITIO   My lord, my daughter.

DUKE
  Why, here's some stirring yet.

FABRITIO   She's a dear child to me.

DUKE
  That must needs be, you say she is your daughter.

FABRITIO
  Nay my good lord, dear to my purse, I mean,

---

84 *plead your benefit* claim exemption from the law

Beside my person; I nev'r reckoned that. 110
She has the full qualities of a gentlewoman;
I have brought her up to music, dancing, what not,
That may commend her sex and stir her husband.

DUKE
And which is he now?

GUARDIANO This young heir, my lord.

DUKE
What is he brought up to?

HIPPOLITO To cat and trap. 115

GUARDIANO
My lord, he's a great ward, wealthy but simple;
His parts consist in acres.

DUKE Oh, wise-acres!

GUARDIANO
Y'have spoke him in a word, sir.

BIANCA 'Las, poor gentlewoman,
She's ill bestead, unless sh'as dealt the wiselier
And laid in more provision for her youth: 120
Fools will not keep in summer.

LEANTIO No, nor such wives
From whores in winter.

DUKE Yea, the voice too, sir?

FABRITIO
Ay, and a sweet breast too, my lord, I hope,
Or I have cast away my money wisely;
She took her pricksong earlier, my lord, 125
Than any of her kindred ever did.
A rare child, though I say't—but I'ld not have
The baggage hear so much; 'twould make her swell straight,
And maids of all things must not be puffed up.

DUKE
Let's turn us to a better banquet, then; 130
For music bids the soul of man to a feast,
And that's indeed a noble entertainment

121 *Fools . . . summer* See note at I, ii, 117
131 *of man* ed (of a man O)

---

123 *breast.* Voice: 'the fool has an excellent breast' (*Twelfth Night*, II, iii, 19).
But from Bianca's comment at lines 159–62, it would seem that the
expression is old-fashioned.

125 *pricksong.* Written vocal music, the notes were 'pricked' on to the paper.
The term allows unlimited punning: '. . . your ladyship was the first
that brought up prick-song, being nothing else but the fatal notes of
your pitiful ravishment' (the ant to the nightingale in *Father Hubburd's
Tales*, viii, 88).

Worthy Bianca's self. You shall perceive, beauty,
Our Florentine damsels are not brought up idlely.

BIANCA

They'are wiser of themselves, it seems, my lord,　　135
And can take gifts, when goodness offers 'em.　　*Music*

LEANTIO

True; and damnation has taught you that wisdom,
You can take gifts too. Oh that music mocks me!

LIVIA

I am as dumb to any language now
But love's, as one that never learned to speak!　　140
I am not yet so old, but he may think of me.
My own fault—I have been idle a long time;
But I'll begin the week and paint tomorrow,
So follow my true labour day by day:
I never thrived so well as when I used it.　　145

ISABELLA

Song

What harder chance can fall to woman,
Who was born to cleave to some man,
Than to bestow her time, youth, beauty,
Life's observance, honour, duty,
On a thing for no use good,　　150
But to make physic work, or blood
Force fresh in an old lady's cheek?
She that would be
Mother of fools, let her compound with me.

WARD

Here's a tune indeed! Pish! I had rather hear one ballad　　155
sung i'th'nose now, of the lamentable drowning of fat
sheep and oxen, than all these simpering tunes played upon
cats-guts and sung by little kitlings.

---

143 *paint*. Middleton shared the Jacobean loathing of cosmetics:
　　　　　　　I'm a woman;
　　　Yet, I praise heaven, I never had th'ambition
　　　To go about to mend a better workman:
　　　She ever shames herself i'th'end that does it
　　　　　　　　　　　(Middleton, *The Widow*, II, i, 11–14).
146–58 Song . . . *kitlings*. O prints Isabella's song and the Ward's speech
　　　side by side, presumably to indicate that these take place simultaneously
　　　(and that the Ward does not hear the coarse insults).
151 *physic*. Laxative—which a gentle exercise would make more efficacious.
155–7 *ballad . . . oxen*. The Ward refers to the common material of the
　　　street ballad, the Jacobean newspaper (cf. *The Winter's Tale*, IV, iv,
　　　261–85).

FABRITIO
  How like you her breast now, my lord?
BIANCA   Her breast!
  He talks as if his daughter had given suck   160
  Before she were married, as her betters have;
  The next he praises sure will be her nipples.
DUKE
  Methinks now, such a voice to such a husband
  Is like a jewel of unvalued worth
  Hung at a fool's ear.
FABRITIO   May it please your grace   165
  To give her leave to show another quality?
DUKE
  Marry, as many good ones as you will, sir,
  The more the better welcome.
LEANTIO   But the less
  The better practised. That soul's black indeed
  That cannot commend virtue. But who keeps it?   170
  The extortioner will say to a sick beggar
  'Heaven comfort thee', though he give none himself.
  This good is common.
FABRITIO   Will it please you now, sir,
  To entreat your ward to take her by the hand
  And lead her in a dance before the duke?   175
GUARDIANO
  That will I, sir; 'tis needful. Hark you, nephew.
FABRITIO
  Nay you shall see, young heir, what y'have for your money,
  Without fraud or imposture.
WARD   Dance with her!
  Not I, sweet guardiner, do not urge my heart to't,
  'Tis clean against my blood; dance with a stranger!   180
  Let whos' will do't, I'll not begin first with her.
HIPPOLITO
  No, fear't not, fool; sh'as took a better order.
GUARDIANO
  Why, who shall take her, then?
WARD   Some other gentleman—

175–229 Middleton no doubt knew the mystical significance which the
    Elizabethans attached to dancing:
      by the joyning of a man and a woman in daunsynge may be signified
      matrimonye . . . In every daunse of a moste auncient custome, there
      daunseth to gyther a man and a woman, holdyng ech other by the
      hande or the arme, whych betokeneth concorde
          (Thomas Elyot, *The Boke named the Governour* (1534), p. 78).

Look, there's her uncle, a fine-timbered reveller;
Perhaps he knows the manner of her dancing too;   185
I'll have him do't before me. I have sworn, guardiner;
Then may I learn the better.

GUARDIANO   Thou'lt be an ass still.

WARD
Ay, all that 'uncle' shall not fool me out:
Pish, I stick closer to myself than so.

GUARDIANO
I must entreat you, sir, to take your niece   190
And dance with her; my ward's a little wilful,
He would have you show him the way.

HIPPOLITO   Me sir?
He shall command it at all hours; pray tell him so.

GUARDIANO
I thank you for him; he has not wit himself, sir.

HIPPOLITO
Come, my life's peace, I have a strange office on't here!   195
'Tis some man's luck to keep the joys he likes
Concealed for his own bosom; but my fortune
To set 'em out now for another's liking:
Like the mad misery of necessitous man,
That parts from his good horse with many praises,   200
And goes on foot himself. Need must be obeyed
In ev'ry action, it mars man and maid.

Music. A dance, making honours to the DUKE *and curtsy to
themselves, both before and after*

DUKE
Signor Fabritio, y'are a happy father;
Your cares and pains are fortunate; you see
Your cost bears noble fruits. Hippolito, thanks.   205

FABRITIO
Here's some amends for all my charges yet;
She wins both prick and praise where'er she comes.

DUKE
How lik'st, Bianca?

BIANCA   All things well, my lord,
But this poor gentlewoman's fortune, that's the worst.

---

184 *fine-timbered* well-built

---

207 *prick and praise.* The *prick* is the mark in the centre of an archery butt:
'. . . are you so ignorant in the rules of courtship, to think any one
man to bear all the prick and praise?' (Middleton, *The Family of Love*,
II, iv, 6–8).

DUKE
   There is no doubt, Bianca, she'll find leisure   210
   To make that good enough; he's rich and simple.
BIANCA
   She has the better hope o'th'upper hand, indeed,
   Which women strive for most.
GUARDIANO   Do't when I bid you, sir.
WARD
   I'll venture but a hornpipe with her, guardiner,
   Or some such married man's dance.
GUARDIANO   Well, venture
                                      something, sir.   215
WARD
   I have rhyme for what I do.
GUARDIANO   But little reason, I think.
WARD
   Plain men dance the measures, the cinquepace the gay;
   Cuckolds dance the hornpipe, and farmers dance the hay;
   Your soldiers dance the round, and maidens that grow big
   Your drunkards, the canaries; your whore and bawd, the jig. 220
   Here's your eight kind of dancers—he that finds the ninth,
   Let him pay the minstrels.
DUKE
   Oh, here he appears once in his own person!
   I thought he would have married her by attorney,
   And lain with her so too.
BIANCA   Nay, my kind lord,   225
   There's very seldom any found so foolish
   To give away his part there.
LEANTIO   Bitter scoff!
   Yet I must do't. With what a cruel pride
   The glory of her sin strikes by my afflictions!

   Music. WARD *and* ISABELLA *dance; he ridiculously imitates*
                     HIPPOLITO
DUKE
   This thing will make shift, sirs, to make a husband,   230
   For aught I see in him; how think'st, Bianca?

215 *Well* ed (We'll O)
217 *measures* a stately dance
217 *cinquepace* galliard (lively, French dance)
218 *hay* a rustic dance
219 *round* the watch kept by soldiers, also circling dance
220 *Your . . . your . . .* ed (you . . . you . . . O)
220 *canaries* a quick dance (thought to come from the Canary Islands)

BIANCA
  'Faith, an ill-favoured shift, my lord. Methinks
  If he would take some voyage when he's married,
  Dangerous or long enough, and scarce be seen
  Once in nine year together, a wife then   235
  Might make indifferent shift to be content with him.
DUKE
  A kiss! that wit deserves to be made much on.
  Come, our caroche!
GUARDIANO   Stands ready for your grace.
DUKE
  My thanks to all your loves. Come, fair Bianca;
  We have took special care of you, and provided   240
  Your lodging near us now.
BIANCA   Your love is great, my lord.
DUKE
  Once more, our thanks to all.
OMNES   All blest honours guard you.
                        Exeunt all but LEANTIO *and* LIVIA
                                    Cornets flourish

LEANTIO
  Oh, hast thou left me then, Bianca, utterly!
  Bianca! now I miss thee—Oh return,
  And save the faith of woman. I nev'r felt   245
  The loss of thee till now; 'tis an affliction
  Of greater weight than youth was made to bear—
  As if a punishment of after-life
  Were fallen upon man here, so new it is
  To flesh and blood; so strange, so insupportable   250
  A torment—ev'n mistook, as if a body
  Whose death were drowning, must needs therefore suffer it
  In scalding oil.
LIVIA   Sweet sir!
LEANTIO   As long as mine eye saw thee,
  I half enjoyed thee.
LIVIA   Sir?
LEANTIO   Canst thou forget
  The dear pains my love took, how it has watched   255
  Whole nights together in all weathers for thee,
  Yet stood in heart more merry than the tempests
  That sung about mine ears, like dangerous flatterers
  That can set all their mischiefs to sweet tunes;
  And then received thee from thy father's window   260
  Into these arms at midnight, when we embraced
  As if we had been statues only made for't,

To show art's life, so silent were our comforts;
And kissed as if our lips had grown together.

LIVIA
This makes me madder to enjoy him now.   265

LEANTIO
Canst thou forget all this? and better joys
That we met after this, which then new kisses
Took pride to praise?

LIVIA   I shall grow madder yet. Sir!

LEANTIO
This cannot be but of some close bawd's working.
Cry mercy, lady! what would you say to me?   270
My sorrow makes me so unmannerly,
So comfort bless me, I had quite forgot you.

LIVIA
Nothing, but ev'n in pity to that passion,
Would give your grief good counsel.

LEANTIO   Marry, and welcome,
                                                        lady;
It never could come better.

LIVIA   Then first, sir,   275
To make away all your good thoughts at once of her,
Know most assuredly she is a strumpet.

LEANTIO
Ha! most assuredly! Speak not a thing
So vilde so certainly; leave it more doubtful.

LIVIA
Then I must leave all truth, and spare my knowledge   280
A sin which I too lately found and wept for.

LEANTIO
Found you it?

LIVIA   Ay, with wet eyes.

LEANTIO   Oh perjurious friendship!

LIVIA
You missed your fortunes when you met with her, sir.
Young gentlemen that only love for beauty,
They love not wisely; such a marriage rather   285
Proves the destruction of affection:
It brings on want, and want's the key of whoredom.
I think y'had small means with her?

LEANTIO   Oh, not any, lady.

LIVIA
Alas, poor gentleman! What mean'st thou, sir,

279 *vilde* vile

Quite to undo thyself with thine own kind heart?   290
Thou art too good and pitiful to woman.
Marry sir, thank thy stars for this blest fortune
That rids the summer of thy youth so well
From many beggars, that had lain a-sunning
In thy beams only else, till thou hadst wasted   295
The whole days of thy life in heat and labour.
What would you say now to a creature found
As pitiful to you, and as it were
Ev'n sent on purpose from the whole sex general
To requite all that kindness you have shown to't?   300

LEANTIO
What's that, madam?

LIVIA   Nay, a gentlewoman,
And one able to reward good things; ay,
And bears a conscience to't. Couldst thou love such a one
That, blow all fortunes, would never see thee want?
Nay more, maintain thee to thine enemy's envy;   305
And shalt not spend a care for't, stir a thought,
Nor break a sleep—unless love's music waked thee,
No storm of fortune should. Look upon me,
And know that woman.

LEANTIO   Oh my life's wealth, Bianca!

LIVIA
Still with her name? will nothing wear it out?   310
That deep sigh went but for a strumpet, sir.

LEANTIO
It can go for no other that loves me.

LIVIA
He's vexed in mind. I came too soon to him;
Where's my discretion now, my skill, my judgement?
I'm cunning in all arts but my own love.   315
'Tis as unseasonable to tempt him now,
So soon, as a widow to be courted
Following her husband's corse, or to make bargain
By the grave-side, and take a young man there:
Her strange departure stands like a hearse yet   320
Before his eyes, which time will take down shortly.   *Exit*

---

304 *blow* hang (*O.E.D.* cites no such usage before 1835)

317–19 *widow . . . there.* As the Lady Anne was courted in *Richard III*
          (Act I scene ii).
320–21 *stands . . . shortly.* The hearse was originally a wooden structure
          erected over the coffin for a certain length of time. Before the Reforma-
          tion it carried candles; after, verses and epitaphs.

LEANTIO

Is she my wife till death, yet no more mine?
That's a hard measure. Then what's marriage good for?
Methinks by right I should not now be living,
And then 'twere all well. What a happiness   325
Had I been made of, had I never seen her!
For nothing makes man's loss grievous to him
But knowledge of the worth of what he loses:
For what he never had, he never misses.
She's gone for ever—utterly; there is   330
As much redemption of a soul from hell
As a fair woman's body from his palace.
Why should my love last longer than her truth?
What is there good in woman to be loved
When only that which makes her so has left her?   335
I cannot love her now, but I must like
Her sin and my own shame too, and be guilty
Of law's breach with her, and mine own abusing;
All which were monstrous. Then my safest course,
For health of mind and body, is to turn   340
My heart and hate her, most extremely hate her!
I have no other way. Those virtuous powers
Which were chaste witnesses of both our troths
Can witness she breaks first—and I'm rewarded
With captainship o'th'fort! a place of credit,   345
I must confess, but poor; my factorship
Shall not exchange means with't; he that died last in't,
He was no drunkard, yet he died a beggar
For all his thrift. Besides, the place not fits me:
It suits my resolution, not my breeding.   350

Enter LIVIA

LIVIA

I have tried all ways I can, and have not power
To keep from sight of him. How are you now, sir?

LEANTIO

I feel a better ease, madam.

LIVIA   Thanks to blessedness!
You will do well, I warrant you, fear it not, sir.
Join but your own good will to't; he's not wise   355
That loves his pain or sickness, or grows fond
Of a disease whose property is to vex him

330-31 *there . . . hell*. Proverbial: 'There is no redemption from hell'
    (Tilley, R 60).

And spitefully drink his blood up. Out upon't, sir,
Youth knows no greater loss. I pray let's walk, sir.
You never saw the beauty of my house yet,   360
Nor how abundantly fortune has blessed me
In worldly treasure; trust me, I have enough, sir,
To make my friend a rich man in my life,
A great man at my death—yourself will say so.
If you want anything and spare to speak,   365
Troth, I'll condemn you for a wilful man, sir.

LEANTIO
Why sure, this can be but the flattery of some dream.

LIVIA
Now by this kiss, my love, my soul and riches,
'Tis all true substance.
Come, you shall see my wealth, take what you list;   370
The gallanter you go, the more you please me.
I will allow you, too, your page and footman,
Your racehorses, or any various pleasure
Exercised youth delights in: but to me
Only, sir, wear your heart of constant stuff.   375
Do but you love enough, I'll give enough.

LEANTIO
Troth then, I'll love enough and take enough.

LIVIA
Then we are both pleased enough.   *Exeunt*

Act III, Scene iii

Enter GUARDIANO *and* ISABELLA *at one door, and the* WARD
and SORDIDO *at another*

GUARDIANO
Now nephew, here's the gentlewoman again.

WARD
Mass, here she's come again; mark her now, Sordido.

GUARDIANO
This is the maid my love and care has chose
Out for your wife, and so I tender her to you.
Yourself has been eye witness of some qualities   5
That speak a courtly breeding and are costly.
I bring you both to talk together now,
'Tis time you grew familiar in your tongues:

---

358 *drink ... up*. 'With sighs of love, that costs the fresh blood dear' (*A
Midsummer Night's Dream*, III, ii, 97).

Tomorrow you join hands, and one ring ties you,
And one bed holds you; if you like the choice.   10
Her father and her friends are i'th'next room
And stay to see the contract ere they part;
Therefore dispatch, good ward, be sweet and short.
Like her or like her not—there's but two ways;
And one your body, th'other your purse pays.   15

WARD
I warrant you guardiner, I'll not stand all day thrumming,
But quickly shoot my bolt at your next coming.

GUARDIANO
Well said! Good fortune to your birding then.   [*Exit*]

WARD
I never missed mark yet.

SORDIDO
Troth I think, master, if the truth were known, you never   20
shot at any but the kitchen-wench, and that was a she-
woodcock, a mere innocent, that was oft lost and cried at
eight-and-twenty.

WARD
No more of that meat, Sordido, here's eggs o'th'spit now;
we must turn gingerly. Draw out the catalogue of all the   25
faults of women.

SORDIDO
How, all the faults! have you so little reason to think so much
paper will lie in my breeches? Why, ten carts will not carry
it, if you set down but the bawds. All the faults! pray let's
be content with a few of 'em; and if they were less, you   30
would find 'em enough, I warrant you. Look you, sir.

ISABELLA
But that I have th'advantage of the fool
As much as woman's heart can wish and joy at,
What an infernal torment 'twere to be

---

16 *thrumming* trifling (from *thrum* = waste end of weaving thread)
19–26 *I never . . . women* (as verse O)
22 *woodcock* simpleton (the bird is easily snared)
22 *innocent* half-wit
22 *cried* i.e. by the town-crier

9–10 *Tomorrow . . . you*. 'Through all Italy ingenerall, the espousall or
betrothinge with the Ring, is made privately, the bride being never
seene by the Bridegrome before that day, and that performed, they
lye together in bedd' (Moryson 4, p. 453).
24 *eggs o'th'spit*. Delicate business in hand. Proverbial: 'I have eggs on the
spit' (Tilley, E 86).

Thus bought and sold and turned and pried into; when alas   35
The worst bit is too good for him! And the comfort is,
H'as but a cater's place on't, and provides
All for another's table—yet how curious
The ass is, like some nice professor on't,
That buys up all the daintiest food i'th'markets   40
And seldom licks his lips after a taste on't.

SORDIDO
Now to her, now y'have scanned all her parts over.

WARD
But at what end shall I begin now, Sordido?

SORDIDO
Oh, ever at a woman's lip, while you live, sir; do you ask
that question?   45

WARD
Methinks, Sordido, sh'as but a crabbed face to begin with.

SORDIDO
A crabbed face? that will save money.

WARD
How, save money, Sordido?

SORDIDO
Ay sir; for having a crabbed face of her own, she'll eat the
less verjuice with her mutton—'twill save verjuice at year's   50
end, sir.

WARD
Nay, and your jests begin to be saucy once, I'll make you
eat your meat without mustard.

SORDIDO
And that in some kind is a punishment.

WARD
Gentlewoman, they say 'tis your pleasure to be my wife; and   55
you shall know shortly whether it be mine or no to be your
husband. And thereupon thus I first enter upon you.
[*Kisses her*] Oh most delicious scent! methinks it tasted as if a
man had stepped into a comfit-maker's shop to let a cart go
by, all the while I kissed her. It is reported, gentlewoman,   60
you'll run mad for me, if you have me not.

ISABELLA
I should be in great danger of my wits, sir,
For being so forward—should this ass kick backward now!

37 *cater's* caterer's
38 *curious* fastidious
43 *at what end* ed (at end O)
50 *verjuice* sauce made from crab-apples

WARD

    Alas, poor soul. And is that hair your own?

ISABELLA

    Mine own? yes sure, sir; I owe nothing for't.   65

WARD

    'Tis a good hearing; I shall have the less to pay when I have
    married you. Look, does her eyes stand well?

SORDIDO

    They cannot stand better than in her head, I think; where
    would you have them? and for her nose, 'tis of a very good
    last.   70

WARD

    I have known as good as that has not lasted a year, though.

SORDIDO

    That's in the using of a thing; will not any strong bridge fall
    down in time, if we do nothing but beat at the bottom? A
    nose of buff would not last always, sir, especially if it came
    into th'camp once.   75

WARD

    But Sordido, how shall we do to make her laugh, that I may
    see what teeth she has—for I'll not bate her a tooth, nor
    take a black one into th'bargain.

SORDIDO

    Why, do but you fall in talk with her; you cannot choose
    but one time or other make her laugh, sir.   80

WARD

    It shall go hard, but I will. Pray what qualities have you
    beside singing and dancing? can you play at shuttlecock,
    forsooth?

ISABELLA

    Ay, and at stool-ball too, sir; I have great luck at it.

WARD

    Why, can you catch a ball well?   85

ISABELLA

    I have catched two in my lap at one game.

---

74 *buff* strong leather.

---

72 *strong bridge*. The bridge of the nose was affected in syphilis (to which
    camp-followers were particularly prone).

84 *stool-ball*. A game resembling cricket, in which the wicket was a stool.
    The mad maid in *The Two Noble Kinsmen*, obsessed with 'the *way of
    flesh*', invites her wooer to play at 'stoole ball' (Nonesuch Shakespeare,
    Act V scene ii).

WARD

What, have you, woman? I must have you learn to play at
trap too, then y'are full and whole.

ISABELLA

Anything that you please to bring me up to I shall take
pains to practise.   90

WARD

'Twill not do, Sordido; we shall never get her mouth
opened wide enough.

SORDIDO

No sir? that's strange; then here's a trick for your learning.
      He yawns [ISABELLA *yawns too, but covers her mouth*]
Look now, look now! quick, quick there.

WARD

Pox of that scurvy mannerly trick with handkerchief; it   95
hindered me a little, but I am satisfied. When a fair woman
gapes and stops her mouth so, it shows like a cloth stopple
in a cream-pot. I have fair hope of her teeth now, Sordido.

SORDIDO

Why, then y'have all well, sir, for aught I see. She's right
and straight enough now, as she stands—they'll commonly   100
lie crooked, that's no matter; wise gamesters never find
fault with that, let 'em lie still so.

WARD

I'ld fain mark how she goes, and then I have all—for of all
creatures I cannot abide a splay-footed woman: she's an
unlucky thing to meet in a morning; her heels keep together   105
so, as if she were beginning an Irish dance still, and the
wriggling of her bum playing the tune to't. But I have
bethought a cleanly shift to find it: dab down as you see me,
and peep of one side when her back's toward you; I'll
show you the way.   110

SORDIDO

And you shall find me apt enough to peeping!
I have been one of them has seen mad sights
Under your scaffolds.

WARD   Will it please you walk, forsooth,

87–102 *What . . . so* (as verse O)

104–5 *splay-footed . . . morning.* A splay foot was a mark to know a witch by:
      The doubles of a hare, or, in a morning,
      Salutes from a splay-footed witch . . .
      Are not so boding mischief

A turn or two by yourself? you are so pleasing to me,
I take delight to view you on both sides.   115

ISABELLA

I shall be glad to fetch a walk to your love, sir;
'Twill get affection a good stomach, sir
—Which I had need have, to fall to such coarse victuals.

[She walks about]

WARD

Now go thy ways for a clean-treading wench,
As ever man in modesty peeped under!   120

SORDIDO

I see the sweetest sight to please my master!
Never went Frenchman righter upon ropes
Than she on Florentine rushes.

WARD   'Tis enough, forsooth.

ISABELLA

And how do you like me now, sir?

WARD   'Faith, so well
I never mean to part with thee, sweetheart,   125
Under some sixteen children, and all boys.

ISABELLA

You'll be at simple pains, if you prove kind,
And breed 'em all in your teeth.

WARD   Nay, by my faith,
What serves your belly for? 'twould make my cheeks
Look like blown bagpipes.

Enter GUARDIANO

GUARDIANO   How now, ward and nephew,   130
Gentlewoman and niece! speak, is it so or not?

WARD

'Tis so; we are both agreed, sir.

GUARDIANO   In to your kindred, then;
There's friends, and wine and music, waits to welcome you.

122 *ropes* tightropes
123 *rushes* the (Jacobean) carpet
128–30 *Nay . . . bagpipes* (as prose O)

127–8 *simple . . . teeth.* A sympathetic toothache is one of the most common
psychosomatic ailments of husbands whose wives are pregnant:
>There beats not a more mutual pulse of passion
>In a kind husband when his wife breeds child
>Than in Martino; I ha' marked it ever:
>He breeds all my pains in's teeth still

(*The Widow*, III, iii, 142).

kind also carries its meaning of 'true to type'.

WARD
   Then I'll be drunk for joy.
SORDIDO   And I for company;
   I cannot break my nose in a better action.   *Exeunt* 135

Act IV, Scene i

Enter BIANCA *attended by two* LADIES

BIANCA
   How goes your watches, ladies; what's o'clock now?
1 LADY
   By mine, full nine.
2 LADY   By mine, a quarter past.
1 LADY
   I set mine by St Mark's.
2 LADY   St Antony's,
   They say, goes truer.
1 LADY   That's but your opinion, madam,
   Because you love a gentleman o'th'name.   5
2 LADY
   He's a true gentleman, then.
1 LADY   So may he be
   That comes to me tonight, for aught you know.
BIANCA
   I'll end this strife straight. I set mine by the sun;
   I love to set by th' best, one shall not then
   Be troubled to set often.
2 LADY   You do wisely in't.   10
BIANCA
   If I should set my watch as some girls do
   By ev'ry clock i'th'town, 'twould nev'r go true;

1–18 *How . . . parish.* Apparently inconsequential, this chatter about
watches serves to define the new Bianca. The clock/woman comparison
is a stock one: 'A woman that is like a German clock, Still a-repairing,
ever out of frame, And never going aright' (*Love's Labour's Lost*,
III, i, 186–9). In this interlude the implied comparison is extended to
become a comment on fidelity—just as it is in Dekker's *The Honest
Whore, Part the Second*, where Infælice suspects her husband, Hippolito:
   INFÆ   How works the day, my Lord (pray) by your watch?
   HIP   Lest you cuffe me, Ile tell you presently:
           I am neere two.
   INFÆ   How, two? I am scarce at one.
   HIP   One of us then goes false.
   INFÆ   Then sure 'tis you,
           Mine goes by heavens Diall (the Sunne) and it goes true
                                         (III, i, 109–13).

And too much turning of the dial's point,
Or tamp'ring with the spring, might in small time
Spoil the whole work too. Here it wants of nine now.   15

1 LADY
It does indeed, forsooth; mine's nearest truth yet.

2 LADY
Yet I have found her lying with an advocate, which showed
Like two false clocks together in one parish.

BIANCA
So now I thank you ladies. I desire
Awhile to be alone.

1 LADY   And I am nobody,   20
Methinks, unless I have one or other with me;
'Faith, my desire and hers will nev'r be sisters.
                                        Exeunt LADIES

BIANCA
How strangely woman's fortune comes about!
This was the farthest way to come to me,
All would have judged, that knew me born in Venice   25
And there with many jealous eyes brought up,
That never thought they had me sure enough
But when they were upon me; yet my hap
To meet it here, so far off from my birthplace,
My friends or kindred. 'Tis not good, in sadness,   30
To keep a maid so strict in her young days.
Restraint breeds wand'ring thoughts, as many fasting days
A great desire to see flesh stirring again.
I'll nev'r use any girl of mine so strictly;
Howev'r they're kept, their fortunes find 'em out—   35
I see't in me. If they be got in court
I'll never forbid 'em the country; nor the court,
Though they be born i'th'country. They will come to't,

---

30 *in sadness* seriously

32–3 *fasting . . . stirring*   since poor Fasting-Days
          Were not made reckoning on, the pampered flesh
          Has play'd the knave, maids have fuller bellies,
          Those meals that once were saved have stirr'd and leapt,
          And begot bastards, and they must be kept
                              (Middleton, *The Inner Temple Masque*, 135–9).
35 *their . . . out*   would a woman stray
          She need not gad abroad to seek her sin,
          It would be brought home one way or another
                              (Middleton, *The Changeling*, III, iii, 224–6).

And fetch their falls a thousand mile about,
Where one would little think on't.   40

Enter LEANTIO

LEANTIO
I long to see how my despiser looks
Now she's come here to court; these are her lodgings!
She's simply now advanced! I took her out
Of no such window, I remember, first;
That was a great deal lower, and less carved.   45
BIANCA
How now? what silkworm's this, i'th'name of pride;
What, is it he?
LEANTIO   A bow i'th'ham to your greatness;
You must have now three legs, I take it, must you not?
BIANCA
Then I must take another, I shall want else
The service I should have; you have but two there.   50
LEANTIO
Y'are richly placed.
BIANCA   Methinks y'are wondrous brave, sir.
LEANTIO
A sumptuous lodging!
BIANCA   Y'have an excellent suit there.
LEANTIO
A chair of velvet!
BIANCA   Is your cloak lined through, sir?
LEANTIO
Y'are very stately here.
BIANCA   'Faith, something proud, sir.
LEANTIO
Stay, stay; let's see your cloth-of-silver slippers.   55
BIANCA
Who's your shoemaker? h'as made you a neat boot.
LEANTIO
Will you have a pair? the duke will lend you spurs.
BIANCA
Yes, when I ride.
LEANTIO   'Tis a brave life you lead.
BIANCA
I could nev'r see you in such good clothes
In my time.

39 *fetch . . . about* take a roundabout course   43 *simply* absolutely
48 *legs* bows
51 *brave* well-dressed

LEANTIO   In your time?

BIANCA   Sure I think, sir,   60
We both thrive best asunder.

LEANTIO   Y'are a whore.

BIANCA
Fear nothing, sir.

LEANTIO   An impudent, spiteful strumpet.

BIANCA
Oh sir, you give me thanks for your captainship;
I thought you had forgot all your good manners.

LEANTIO
And to spite thee as much, look there, there read!   65
Vex! gnaw! thou shalt find there I am not love-starved.
The world was never yet so cold or pitiless
But there was ever still more charity found out
Than at one proud fool's door; and 'twere hard, 'faith,
If I could not pass that. Read to thy shame, there—   70
A cheerful and a beauteous benefactor too,
As ev'r erected the good works of love.

BIANCA   Lady Livia!
—Is't possible? Her worship was my pandress.
She dote and send and give, and all to him;
Why, here's a bawd plagued home! Y'are simply happy, sir,   75
Yet I'll not envy you.

LEANTIO   No, court-saint, not thou!
You keep some friend of a new fashion.
There's no harm in your devil, he's a suckling;
But he will breed teeth shortly, will he not?

BIANCA
Take heed you play not then too long with him.   80

LEANTIO
Yes, and the great one too. I shall find time
To play a hot religious bout with some of you,
And perhaps drive you and your course of sins
To their eternal kennels. I speak softly now—
'Tis manners in a noblewoman's lodgings,   85
And I well know all my degrees of duty—
But come I to your everlasting parting once,
Thunder shall seem soft music to that tempest.

79 *breed teeth* cut his teeth
83 *course* pack
84 *kennels* lairs (*O.E.D.* 1b)
86 *know* ed (knew O)

BIANCA
> 'Twas said last week there would be change of weather
> When the moon hung so; and belike you heard it.   90

LEANTIO
> Why, here's sin made, and nev'r a conscience put to't,
> A monster with all forehead and no eyes!
> Why do I talk to thee of sense or virtue,
> That art as dark as death? and as much madness
> To set light before thee, as to lead blind folks   95
> To see the monuments which they may smell as soon
> As they behold—marry, oft-times their heads,
> For want of light, may feel the hardness of 'em:
> So shall thy blind pride my revenge and anger,
> That canst not see it now; and it may fall   100
> At such an hour when thou least see'st of all.
> So to an ignorance darker than thy womb
> I leave thy perjured soul. A plague will come!   *Exit*

BIANCA
> Get you gone first, and then I fear no greater—
> Nor thee will I fear long! I'll have this sauciness   105
> Soon banished from these lodgings, and the rooms
> Perfumed well after the corrupt air it leaves.
> His breath has made me almost sick, in troth.
> A poor base start-up! 'Life—because h'as got
> Fair clothes by foul means, comes to rail and show 'em!   110

Enter the DUKE

DUKE
> Who's that?
BIANCA   Cry you mercy, sir.
DUKE   Prithee, who's that?
BIANCA
> The former thing, my lord, to whom you gave
> The captainship; he eats his meat with grudging still.
DUKE
> Still!
BIANCA He comes vaunting here of his new love
> And the new clothes she gave him—Lady Livia;   115
> Who but she now his mistress!
DUKE   Lady Livia?
> Be sure of what you say.
BIANCA   He showed me her name, sir,
> In perfumed paper—her vows, her letter—
> With an intent to spite me: so his heart said,

92 *forehead* front, impudence

And his threats made it good; they were as spiteful   120
As ever malice uttered; and as dangerous,
Should his hand follow the copy.
DUKE   But that must not.
Do not you vex your mind; prithee to bed, go.
All shall be well and quiet.
BIANCA   I love peace, sir.
DUKE
And so do all that love; take you no care for't,   125
It shall be still provided to your hand.   *Exit* [BIANCA]
Who's near us there?

                    Enter MESSENGER

MESSENGER   My lord?
DUKE   Seek out Hippolito,
Brother to Lady Livia, with all speed.
MESSENGER
He was the last man I saw, my lord.   *Exit*
DUKE   Make haste.
He is a blood soon stirred; and as he's quick   130
To apprehend a wrong, he's bold and sudden
In bringing forth a ruin. I know likewise
The reputation of his sister's honour's
As dear to him as life-blood to his heart;
Beside, I'll flatter him with a goodness to her   135
Which I now thought on—but nev'r meant to practise
Because I know her base; and that wind drives him.
The ulcerous reputation feels the poise
Of lightest wrongs, as sores are vexed with flies.
He comes. Hippolito, welcome.

                    Enter HIPPOLITO

HIPPOLITO   My loved lord.   140
DUKE
How does that lusty widow, thy kind sister?
Is she not sped yet of a second husband?
A bed-fellow she has, I ask not that;
I know she's sped of him.
HIPPOLITO   Of him, my lord?

122 *copy* example in a copybook
131 *sudden* impetuous
138 *poise* weight (*O.E.D.* 1b)
142 *sped . . . of* furnished with

DUKE
Yes, of a bed-fellow. Is the news so strange to you?   145
HIPPOLITO
I hope 'tis so to all.
DUKE   I wish it were, sir,
But 'tis confessed too fast. Her ignorant pleasures,
Only by lust instructed, have received
Into their services an impudent boaster,
One that does raise his glory from her shame,   150
And tells the midday sun what's done in darkness.
Yet blinded with her appetite, wastes her wealth;
Buys her disgraces at a dearer rate
Than bounteous housekeepers purchase their honour.
Nothing sads me so much, as that in love   155
To thee and to thy blood, I had picked out
A worthy match for her, the great Vincentio,
High in our favour and in all men's thoughts.
HIPPOLITO
Oh thou destruction of all happy fortunes,
Unsated blood! Know you the name, my lord,   160
Of her abuser?
DUKE   One Leantio.
HIPPOLITO
He's a factor!
DUKE   He nev'r made so brave a voyage
By his own talk.
HIPPOLITO   The poor old widow's son!
I humbly take my leave.
DUKE   —I see 'tis done.
Give her good counsel, make her see her error;   165
I know she'll harken to you.
HIPPOLITO   Yes, my lord,
I make no doubt—as I shall take the course
Which she shall never know till it be acted;
And when she wakes to honour, then she'll thank me for't.
I'll imitate the pities of old surgeons   170
To this lost limb, who ere they show their art
Cast one asleep, then cut the diseased part:
So out of love to her I pity most,
She shall not feel him going till he's lost;
Then she'll commend the cure.   *Exit*
DUKE   The great cure's past.   175
I count this done already; his wrath's sure,
And speaks an injury deep. Farewell, Leantio;
This place will never hear thee murmur more.

Enter LORD CARDINAL, *attended*

Our noble brother, welcome!
CARDINAL   Set those lights down.
　Depart till you be called.   [*Exit* ATTENDANT]
DUKE   There's serious business   180
　Fixed in his look—nay, it inclines a little
　To the dark colour of a discontentment.
　Brother, what is't commands your eye so powerfully?
　Speak, you seem lost.
CARDINAL   The thing I look on seems so,
　To my eyes lost for ever.
DUKE   You look on me.   185
CARDINAL
　What a grief 'tis to a religious feeling
　To think a man should have a friend so goodly,
　So wise, so noble—nay, a duke, a brother;
　And all this certainly damned!
DUKE   How!
CARDINAL   'Tis no wonder,
　If your great sin can do't. Dare you look up,   190
　For thinking of a vengeance? dare you sleep,
　For fear of never waking but to death?
　And dedicate unto a strumpet's love
　The strength of your affections, zeal and health?
　Here you stand now: can you assure your pleasures   195
　You shall once more enjoy her—but once more?
　Alas, you cannot! What a misery 'tis, then,
　To be more certain of eternal death
　Than of a next embrace. Nay, shall I show you
　How more unfortunate you stand in sin,   200
　Than the low private man: all his offences,
　Like enclosed grounds, keep but aboût himself
　And seldom stretch beyond his own soul's bounds;
　And when a man grows miserable, 'tis some comfort
　When he's no further charged than with himself: 205
　'Tis a sweet ease to wretchedness. But, great man,
　Ev'ry sin thou commit'st shows like a flame
　Upon a mountain; 'tis seen far about,
　And with a big wind made of popular breath
　The sparkles fly through cities; here one takes,   210
　Another catches there, and in short time
　Waste all to cinders: but remember still,
　What burnt the valleys, first came from the hill.

201 *low* ed (love O)

Ev'ry offence draws his particular pain;
But 'tis example proves the great man's bane. 215
The sins of mean men lie like scattered parcels
Of an unperfect bill; but when such fall,
Then comes example, and that sums up all.
And this your reason grants: if men of good lives,
Who by their virtuous actions stir up others 220
To noble and religious imitation,
Receive the greater glory after death—
As sin must needs confess—what may they feel
In height of torments and in weight of vengeance;
Not only they themselves not doing well, 225
But sets a light up to show men to hell?

DUKE

If you have done, I have. No more, sweet brother.

CARDINAL

I know time spent in goodness is too tedious;
This had not been a moment's space in lust, now.
How dare you venture on eternal pain, 230
That cannot bear a minute's reprehension?
Methinks you should endure to hear that talked of
Which you so strive to suffer. Oh my brother!
What were you, if you were taken now?
My heart weeps blood to think on't; 'tis a work 235
Of infinite mercy you can never merit,
That yet you are not death struck—no, not yet . . .
I dare not stay you long, for fear you should not
Have time enough allowed you to repent in.
There's but this wall betwixt you and destruction 240
When y'are at strongest; and but poor thin clay.
Think upon't, brother! Can you come so near it
For a fair strumpet's love, and fall into
A torment that knows neither end nor bottom
For beauty but the deepness of a skin, 245
And that not of their own neither? Is she a thing
Whom sickness dare not visit, or age look on,
Or death resist? does the worm shun her grave?
If not (as your soul knows it) why should lust
Bring man to lasting pain, for rotten dust? 250

DUKE

Brother of spotless honour, let me weep
The first of my repentance in thy bosom,
And show the blest fruits of a thankful spirit;
And if I ere keep woman more unlawfully,
May I want penitence at my greatest need: 255

And wise men know there is no barren place
Threatens more famine, than a dearth in grace.

CARDINAL
Why, here's a conversion is at this time, brother,
Sung for a hymn in Heaven; and at this instant,
The powers of darkness groan, makes all hell sorry.   260
First, I praise Heaven; then in my work I glory.
Who's there attends without?

Enter SERVANTS

SERVANT   My lord?
CARDINAL
Take up those lights; there was a thicker darkness
When they came first. The peace of a fair soul
Keep with my noble brother.   *Exit* CARDINAL, *etc.*
DUKE   Joys be with you, sir.   265
She lies alone tonight for't; and must still,
Though it be hard to conquer. But I have vowed
Never to know her as a strumpet more,
And I must save my oath. If fury fail not,
Her husband dies tonight, or at the most   270
Lives not to see the morning spent tomorrow;
Then will I make her lawfully mine own,
Without this sin and horror. Now I'm chidden
For what I shall enjoy then unforbidden,
And I'll not freeze in stoves; 'tis but a while   275
Live like a hopeful bridegroom, chaste from flesh,
And pleasure then will seem new, fair and fresh.   *Exit*

Act IV, Scene ii

Enter HIPPOLITO

HIPPOLITO
The morning so far wasted, yet his baseness
So impudent? See if the very sun do not blush at him!
Dare he do thus much, and know me alive!
Put case one must be vicious—as I know myself
Monstrously guilty—there's a blind time made for't;   5
He might use only that, 'twere conscionable;
Art, silence, closeness, subtlety and darkness

275 *stoves* heated rooms
  4 *Put case* Assuming

259 *Sung . . . Heaven.* 'There is joy in the presence of the angels of God over
    one sinner that repenteth' (*St Luke*, xv, 10).

Are fit for such a business: but there's no pity
To be bestowed on an apparent sinner,
An impudent daylight lecher! The great zeal   10
I bear to her advancement in this match
With Lord Vincentio, as the duke has wrought it,
To the perpetual honour of our house,
Puts fire into my blood, to purge the air
Of this corruption, fear it spread too far   15
And poison the whole hopes of this fair fortune.
I love her good so dearly, that no brother
Shall venture farther for a sister's glory
Than I for her preferment.

Enter LEANTIO *and a* PAGE

LEANTIO   Once again
I'll see that glist'ring whore shines like a serpent,   20
Now the court sun's upon her. Page!
PAGE   Anon sir!
LEANTIO
I'll go in state too; see the coach be ready.   [*Exit* PAGE]

I'll hurry away presently.
HIPPOLITO   Yes, you shall hurry,
And the devil after you; take that at setting forth!
                              [*Strikes him*]
Now, and you'll draw, we are upon equal terms, sir.   25
Thou took'st advantage of my name in honour
Upon my sister; I nev'r saw the stroke
Come, till I found my reputation bleeding;
And therefore count it I no sin to valour .
To serve thy lust so. Now we are of even hand,   30
Take your best course against me. You must die.
LEANTIO
How close sticks envy to man's happiness!
When I was poor, and little cared for life,
I had no such means offered me to die,
No man's wrath minded me. Slave, I turn this to thee, 35
To call thee to account for a wound lately
Of a base stamp upon me.
HIPPOLITO   'Twas most fit
For a base metal. Come and fetch one now,

---

9 *apparent* obvious
25 *and* if
38 *metal* with a pun on mettle

More noble, then; for I will use thee fairer
Than thou hast done thine own soul or our honour.   40
                              [*They fight*]
And there I think 'tis for thee.
VOICES *within*   Help, help! oh part 'em.
LEANTIO
False wife, I feel now th'hast paid heartily for me.
Rise, strumpet, by my fall! Thy lust may reign now;
My heart-string and the marriage-knot that tied thee
Breaks both together.
HIPPOLITO   There I heard the sound on't,   45
And never liked string better.

   Enter GUARDIANO, LIVIA, ISABELLA, WARD, *and* SORDIDO

LIVIA   'Tis my brother!
Are you hurt, sir?
HIPPOLITO   Not anything.
LIVIA   Blessed fortune!
Shift for thyself; what is he thou hast killed?
HIPPOLITO
Our honour's enemy.
GUARDIANO   Know you this man, lady?
LIVIA
Leantio! My love's joy! Wounds stick upon thee   50
As deadly as thy sins! art thou not hurt?
The devil take that fortune. And he dead!
Drop plagues into thy bowels without voice,
Secret and fearful. Run for officers!
Let him be apprehended with all speed,   55
For fear he 'scape away; lay hands on him,
We cannot be too sure. 'Tis wilful murder!
You do Heaven's vengeance and the law just service;
You know him not as I do—he's a villain,
As monstrous as a prodigy, and as dreadful.   60
HIPPOLITO
Will you but entertain a noble patience
Till you but hear the reason, worthy sister!
LIVIA
The reason! that's a jest hell falls a-laughing at!
Is there a reason found for the destruction
Of our more lawful loves? and was there none   65

40 *thine own soul* ed (thine soul O)
42 *paid* ed (praid O)
60 *prodigy* monster

To kill the black lust 'twixt thy niece and thee
That has kept close so long?

GUARDIANO   How's that, good madam?

LIVIA

Too true sir! There she stands, let her deny't;
The deed cries shortly in the midwife's arms,
Unless the parents' sins strike it still-born;   70
And if you be not deaf and ignorant,
You'll hear strange notes ere long. Look upon me, wench!
'Twas I betrayed thy honour subtilly to him
Under a false tale; it lights upon me now!
His arm has paid me home upon thy breast,   75
My sweet, beloved Leantio!

GUARDIANO   Was my judgement
And care in choice so dev'lishly abused,
So beyond-shamefully—all the world will grin at me!

WARD

Oh Sordido, Sordido, I'm damned, I'm damned!

SORDIDO

Damned! why, sir?

WARD   One of the wicked; dost not see't?   80
A cuckold, a plain reprobate cuckold!

SORDIDO

Nay, and you be damned for that, be of good cheer, sir—
y'have gallant company of all professions; I'll have a wife
next Sunday too, because I'll along with you myself.

WARD

That will be some comfort yet.   85

LIVIA

You, sir, that bear your load of injuries
As I of sorrows, lend me your grieved strength
To this sad burthen who, in life, wore actions
Flames were not nimbler. We will talk of things
May have the luck to break our hearts together.   90

GUARDIANO

I'll list to nothing but revenge and anger,
Whose counsels I will follow.

          Exeunt LIVIA *and* GUARDIANO [*carrying* LEANTIO'S *body*]

82–4 *Nay . . . myself* (as verse O)

83–4 *wife next Sunday*. When she would be wearing her best clothes and
looking deceptively virtuous. 'Who will have a handsome wife let him
choose her upon Saturday' and 'not upon Sunday' (Tilley, W 378).

SORDIDO

A wife, quoth'a! Here's a sweet plum-tree of your guardiner's
grafting!

WARD

Nay, there's a worse name belongs to this fruit yet, and you   95
could hit on't; a more open one! For he that marries a
whore looks like a fellow bound all his lifetime to a medlar-
tree; and that's good stuff—'tis no sooner ripe but it looks
rotten; and so do some queans at nineteen. A pox on't, I
thought there was some knavery abroach, for something   100
stirred in her belly the first night I lay with her.

SORDIDO

What, what sir!

WARD

This is she brought up so courtly! can sing and dance—and
tumble too, methinks. I'll never marry wife again that has
so many qualities.   105

SORDIDO

Indeed, they are seldom good, master. For likely when
they are taught so many, they will have one trick more of
their own finding out. Well, give me a wench but with one
good quality, to lie with none but her husband, and that's
bringing-up enough for any woman breathing.   110

WARD

This was the fault when she was tendered to me; you never
looked to this.

SORDIDO

Alas, how would you have me see through a great farthingale,

---

100 *abroach* flowing

93 *plum-tree.* 'Yea, Madam Gabriela, are you such an old jerker? then
   Hey ding a ding, up with your petticoats, have at your plum-tree'
   (Nashe, *Have with You to Saffron-Walden* (ed. McKerrow, iii, 113)).
97–8 *medlar-tree.* Eaten when decayed to a soft brownish pulp, the medlar
   (a species of pear) was often compared to the female genitals or,
   indirectly, to whores: 'You'll be rotten ere you be half ripe, and that's
   the right virtue of the medlar' (*As You Like It*, III, ii, 125).
103–4 *This . . . too.* Middleton seems to have mistrusted the 'extras' in a
   girl's education; he describes a 'delicate drab' kept at 'White-friar's
   nunnery':
       some unthrifty gentleman's daughter . . . for so much she seemed
       by her bringing up, though less by her casting down. Endued she
       was, as we heard, with some good qualities . . . she had likewise the
       gift of singing very deliciously . . .
                                   (*Father Hubburd's Tales*, viii, 81).

sir! I cannot peep through a millstone, or in the going, to
see what's done i'th'bottom.   115

WARD

Her father praised her breast! sh'ad the voice, forsooth!
I marvell'd she sung so small, indeed, being no maid; now
I perceive there's a young chorister in her breast—this
breeds a singing in my head, I'm sure.

SORDIDO

'Tis but the tune of your wives' cinquepace danced in a   120
featherbed. 'Faith, go lie down, master—but take heed
your horns do not make holes in the pillowberes!—I would
not batter brows with him for a hogshead of angels; he
would prick my skull as full of holes as a scrivener's sand-
box.   *Exeunt* WARD *and* SORDIDO   125

ISABELLA

Was ever maid so cruelly beguiled
To the confusion of life, soul and honour,
All of one woman's murd'ring! I'ld fain bring
Her name no nearer to my blood than woman,
And 'tis too much of that. Oh shame and horror!   130
In that small distance from yon man to me
Lies sin enough to make a whole world perish.
'Tis time we parted, sir, and left the sight
Of one another; nothing can be worse
To hurt repentance—for our very eyes   135
Are far more poisonous to religion
Than basilisks to them. If any goodness
Rest in you, hope of comforts, fear of judgements,
My request is, I nev'r may see you more;
And so I turn me from you everlastingly,   140
So is my hope to miss you. But for her,
That durst so dally with a sin so dangerous,
And lay a snare so spitefully for my youth—
If the least means but favour my revenge,
That I may practise the like cruel cunning   145

---

114 *going* passage
116–9 *Her . . . sure* (as verse O)
122 *pillowberes* pillowcases
123 *angels* gold coins (varying in value between 6/8d and 10/-)
124–5 *sand-box* perforated box filled with sand, used for blotting
137 *basilisks* fabulous reptiles with fatal glances

---

120 *your wives'*. O's *wives* could be a misprint for *wife's*, but I take the *your*
as a contemptuous generalisation applicable to all wives, and not to
Isabella in particular.

Upon her life, as she has on mine honour,
I'll act it without pity.
HIPPOLITO   Here's a care
Of reputation and a sister's fortune
Sweetly rewarded by her! Would a silence,
As great as that which keeps among the graves,   150
Had everlastingly chained up her tongue.
My love to her has made mine miserable.

Enter GUARDIANO *and* LIVIA

GUARDIANO
If you can but dissemble your heart's griefs now,
Be but a woman so far.
LIVIA   Peace! I'll strive, sir.
GUARDIANO
As I can wear my injuries in a smile.   155
Here's an occasion offered, that gives anger
Both liberty and safety to perform
Things worth the fire it holds, without the fear
Of danger or of law; for mischiefs acted
Under the privilege of a marriage-triumph   160
At the duke's hasty nuptials, will be thought
Things merely accidental, all's by chance,
Not got of their own natures.
LIVIA   I conceive you, sir,
Even to a longing for performance on't;
And here behold some fruits.
          [*Kneels before* HIPPOLITO *and* ISABELLA]
                    Forgive me both!   165
What I am now, returned to sense and judgement,
Is not the same rage and distraction
Presented lately to you; that rude form
Is gone for ever. I am now myself,
That speaks all peace and friendship; and these tears   170
Are the true springs of hearty, penitent sorrow
For those foul wrongs which my forgetful fury
Slandered your virtues with. This gentleman
Is well resolved now.
GUARDIANO   I was never otherways.
I knew, alas, 'twas but your anger spake it,   175
And I nev'r thought on't more.

162 *all's* all as

159–60 *mischiefs . . . triumph.* 'A mask is treason's licence: that build upon—
          'Tis murder's best face, when a vizard's on' (*The Revenger's Tragedy*,
          V, i, 176–7).

HIPPOLITO   Pray rise, good sister.
ISABELLA
    Here's ev'n as sweet amends made for a wrong now
    As one that gives a wound, and pays the surgeon—
    All the smart's nothing, the great loss of blood,
    Or time of hindrance! Well, I had a mother,   180
    I can dissemble too. What wrongs have slipped
    Through anger's ignorance, aunt, my heart forgives.
GUARDIANO
    Why, this is tuneful now.
HIPPOLITO   And what I did, sister,
    Was all for honour's cause, which time to come
    Will approve to you.
LIVIA   Being awaked to goodness,   185
    I understand so much, sir, and praise now
    The fortune of your arm and of your safety;
    For by his death y'have rid me of a sin
    As costly as ev'r woman doted on.
    'T has pleased the duke so well too that, behold sir,   190
    H'as sent you here your pardon, which I kissed
    With most affectionate comfort; when 'twas brought,
    Then was my fit just past—it came so well, methought,
    To glad my heart.
HIPPOLITO   I see his grace thinks on me.
LIVIA
    There's no talk now but of the preparation   195
    For the great marriage.
HIPPOLITO   Does he marry her, then?
LIVIA
    With all speed, suddenly, as fast as cost
    Can be laid on with many thousand hands.
    This gentleman and I had once a purpose
    To have honoured the first marriage of the duke   200
    With an invention of his own; 'twas ready,
    The pains well past, most of the charge bestowed on't—
    Then came the death of your good mother, niece,
    And turned the glory of it all to black.
    'Tis a device would fit these times so well, too,   205
    Art's treasury not better. If you'll join,
    It shall be done; the cost shall all be mine.

183 *this is* ed (thus O)

180–81 *mother . . . too.* 'O that a boy should so keep cut with his mother,
    and be given to dissembling' (*More Dissemblers Besides Women*, I, iv, 38–9).

HIPPOLITO
    Y'have my voice first: 'twill well approve my thankfulness
    For the duke's love and favour.
LIVIA   What say you, niece?
ISABELLA
    I am content to make one.
GUARDIANO   The plot's full, then;   210
    Your pages, madam, will make shift for cupids.
LIVIA
    That will they, sir.
GUARDIANO   You'll play your old part still?
LIVIA
    What is't? good troth, I have ev'n forgot it!
GUARDIANO
    Why, Juno Pronuba, the marriage goddess.
LIVIA
    'Tis right, indeed.
GUARDIANO   And you shall play the nymph   215
    That offers sacrifice to appease her wrath.
ISABELLA
    Sacrifice, good sir?
LIVIA   Must I be appeased, then?
GUARDIANO
    That's as you list yourself, as you see cause.
LIVIA
    Methinks 'twould show the more state in her deity
    To be incensed.
ISABELLA   'Twould—but my sacrifice   220
    Shall take a course to appease you, or I'll fail in't,
    And teach a sinful bawd to play a goddess.
GUARDIANO
    For our parts we'll not be ambitious, sir;
    Please you walk in and see the project drawn,
    Then take your choice.
HIPPOLITO   I weigh not, so I have one.   225
                         Exeunt [*all except* LIVIA]
LIVIA
    How much ado have I to restrain fury
    From breaking into curses! Oh how painful 'tis
    To keep great sorrow smothered! sure I think
    'Tis harder to dissemble grief than love.
    Leantio, here the weight of thy loss lies,   230
    Which nothing but destruction can suffice.   *Exit*

214 *Juno Pronuba*. In this one of her many aspects, Juno watched over the
    arrangement of marriages.

Act IV, Scene iii

Hoboys

Enter in great state the DUKE *and* BIANCA, *richly attired, with* LORDS, CARDINALS, LADIES, *and other* ATTENDANTS. *They pass solemnly over. Enter* LORD CARDINAL *in a rage, seeming to break off the ceremony*

CARDINAL

   Cease, cease! Religious honours done to sin
   Disparage virtue's reverence, and will pull
   Heaven's thunder upon Florence; holy ceremonies
   Were made for sacred uses, not for sinful.
   Are these the fruits of your repentance, brother?   5
   Better it had been you had never sorrowed
   Than to abuse the benefit, and return
   To worse than where sin left you.
   Vowed you then never to keep strumpet more,
   And are you now so swift in your desires   10
   To knit your honours and your life fast to her?
   Is not sin sure enough to wretched man
   But he must bind himself in chains to't?—Worse!
   Must marriage, that immaculate robe of honour
   That renders virtue glorious, fair and fruitful   15
   To her great Master, be now made the garment
   Of leprosy and foulness? is this penitence,
   To sanctify hot lust? What is it otherways
   Than worship done to devils? Is this the best
   Amends that sin can make after her riots: 20
   As if a drunkard, to appease Heaven's wrath,
   Should offer up his surfeit for a sacrifice!
   If that be comely, then lust's offerings are,
   On wedlock's sacred altar.

DUKE   Here y'are bitter
   Without cause, brother: what I vowed, I keep   25
   As safe as you your conscience; and this needs not.
   I taste more wrath in't than I do religion,
   And envy more than goodness. The path now
   I tread, is honest—leads to lawful love
   Which virtue in her strictness would not check.   30
   I vowed no more to keep a sensual woman:
   'Tis done; I mean to make a lawful wife of her.

s.d. Hoboys Oboes (French *hautbois*)
23 *comely* decent

CARDINAL

He that taught you that craft,
Call him not master long, he will undo you.
Grow not too cunning for your soul, good brother.   35
Is it enough to use adulterous thefts,
And then take sanctuary in marriage?
I grant, so long as an offender keeps
Close in a privileged temple, his life's safe;
But if he ever venture to come out,   40
And so be taken, then he surely dies for't:
So now y'are safe; but when you leave this body,
Man's only privileged temple upon earth
In which the guilty soul takes sanctuary,
Then you'll perceive what wrongs chaste vows endure   45
When lust usurps the bed that should be pure.

BIANCA

Sir, I have read you over all this while
In silence, and I find great knowledge in you,
And severe learning; yet 'mongst all your virtues   50
I see not charity written, which some call
The first-born of religion; and I wonder
I cannot see't in yours. Believe it, sir,
There is no virtue can be sooner missed
Or later welcomed; it begins the rest,
And sets 'em all in order. Heaven and angels   55
Take great delight in a converted sinner:
Why should you, then, a servant and professor,
Differ so much from them? If ev'ry woman
That commits evil should be therefore kept
Back in desires of goodness, how should virtue   60
Be known and honoured? From a man that's blind
To take a burning taper, 'tis no wrong,
He never misses it; but to take light
From one that sees, that's injury and spite.
Pray, whether is religion better served: 65
When lives that are licentious are made honest,
Than when they still run through a sinful blood?
'Tis nothing virtue's temple to deface:
But build the ruins, there's a work of grace.

DUKE

I kiss thee for that spirit; thou hast praised thy wit   70
A modest way. On, on there!   *Hoboys*

CARDINAL   Lust is bold,
And will have vengeance speak, ere't be controlled.

                                                  Exeunt

Act V, Scene i

Enter GUARDIANO *and* WARD

GUARDIANO
Speak, hast thou any sense of thy abuse? dost thou know
what wrong's done thee?

WARD
I were an ass else; I cannot wash my face but I am feeling
on't.

GUARDIANO
Here, take this caltrop, then; convey it secretly into the   5
place I showed you. Look you, sir, this is the trap-door to't.

WARD
I know't of old, uncle, since the last triumph—here rose up
a devil with one eye, I remember, with a company of
fireworks at's tail.

GUARDIANO
Prithee leave squibbing now; mark me and fail not—but   10
when thou hear'st me give a stamp, down with't; the villain's
caught then.

WARD
If I miss you, hang me; I love to catch a villain, and your
stamp shall go current, I warrant you. But how shall I rise
up and let him down too, all at one hole? That will be a   15
horrible puzzle. You know I have a part in't—I play
Slander.

GUARDIANO
True, but never make you ready for't.

WARD
No?—but my clothes are bought and all, and a foul fiend's
head with a long contumelious tongue i'th'chaps on't, a   20
very fit shape for Slander i'th'out-parishes.

GUARDIANO
It shall not come so far; thou understand'st it not.

WARD
Oh, oh?

1–6 *Speak . . . to't* (as verse O)
5 *caltrop* spiked instrument, used to stop horses
7 *triumph* pageant

---

21 *out-parishes.* Parishes outside the city boundaries (where the Morality
plays featuring such characters as Slander might still be acted).

GUARDIANO

    He shall lie deep enough ere that time, and stick first upon
    those.   25

WARD

    Now I conceive you, guardiner.

GUARDIANO

    Away; list to the privy stamp, that's all thy part.

WARD

    Stamp my horns in a mortar if I miss you, and give the
    powder in white wine to sick cuckolds—a very present
    remedy for the headache.   *Exit* WARD   30

GUARDIANO

    If this should any way miscarry now—
    As, if the fool be nimble enough, 'tis certain—
    The pages that present the swift-winged cupids
    Are taught to hit him with their shafts of love,
    Fitting his part, which I have cunningly poisoned.   35
    He cannot 'scape my fury; and those ills
    Will be laid all on fortune, not our wills—
    That's all the sport on't! for who will imagine
    That at the celebration of this night
    Any mischance that haps can flow from spite?   *Exit*   40

Act V, Scene ii

Flourish. Enter above DUKE, BIANCA, LORD CARDINAL, FABRITIO,
and other CARDINALS, LORDS *and* LADIES *in state*

DUKE

    Now our fair duchess, your delight shall witness
    How y'are beloved and honoured: all the glories
    Bestowed upon the gladness of this night
    Are done for your bright sake.

BIANCA   I am the more

    In debt, my lord, to loves and courtesies,   5
    That offer up themselves so bounteously
    To do me honoured grace, without my merit.

DUKE

    A goodness set in greatness! how it sparkles
    Afar off, like pure diamonds set in gold.
    How perfect my desires were, might I witness   10
    But a fair noble peace 'twixt your two spirits!
    The reconcilement would be more sweet to me
    Than longer life to him that fears to die.
    Good sir!

CARDINAL   I profess peace, and am content.

DUKE
I'll see the seal upon't, and then 'tis firm.   15

CARDINAL
You shall have all you wish.   [*Kisses* BIANCA]

DUKE   I have all indeed now.

BIANCA
But I have made surer work; this shall not blind me.
He that begins so early to reprove,
Quickly rid him, or look for little love:
Beware a brother's envy—he's next heir too.   20
Cardinal, you die this night; the plot's laid surely:
In time of sports death may steal in securely.
Then 'tis least thought on:
For he that's most religious, holy friend,
Does not at all hours think upon his end;   25
He has his times of frailty, and his thoughts
Their transportations too, through flesh and blood,
For all his zeal, his learning, and his light,
As well as we poor souls that sin by night.

DUKE
What's this, Fabritio?

FABRITIO   Marry, my lord, the model   30
Of what's presented.

DUKE   Oh, we thank their loves.
Sweet duchess, take your seat; list to the argument.

Reads:
There is a nymph that haunts the woods and springs
In love with two at once, and they with her;
Equal it runs; but to decide these things,   35
The cause to mighty Juno they refer,
She being the marriage-goddess. The two lovers,
They offer sighs; the nymph, a sacrifice;
All to please Juno, who by signs discovers
How the event shall be. So that strife dies.   40
Then springs a second; for the man refused
Grows discontent, and out of love abused
He raises Slander up, like a black fiend,
To disgrace th'other, which pays him i'th'end.

BIANCA
In troth, my lord, a pretty, pleasing argument,   45
And fits th'occasion well: envy and slander

29 *we poor souls that sin* ed (we, poor soul that sin O)

Are things soon raised against two faithful lovers;
But comfort is, they are not long unrewarded.   *Music*

DUKE
This music shows they're upon entrance now.

BIANCA
Then enter all my wishes!   50

Enter HYMEN *in yellow,* GANYMEDE *in a blue robe powdered with
stars, and* HEBE *in a white robe with golden stars, with covered
cups in their hands. They dance a short dance, then bowing to the
DUKE etc.,* HYMEN *speaks:*

HYMEN
     To thee, fair bride, Hymen offers up
     Of nuptial joys this the celestial cup;
     Taste it, and thou shalt ever find
     Love in thy bed, peace in thy mind.

BIANCA
We'll taste you, sure; 'twere pity to disgrace   55
So pretty a beginning.

DUKE   'Twas spoke nobly.

GANYMEDE
     Two cups of nectar have we begged from Jove:
     Hebe, give that to Innocence; I this to Love.

[HEBE *gives a cup to the* CARDINAL, GANYMEDE *one to the* DUKE;
                      both drink]

     Take heed of stumbling more, look to your way;
     Remember still the Via Lactea.   60

HEBE
     Well Ganymede, you have more faults, though not so
        known;
     I spilled one cup, but you have filched many a one.

---

50 s.d. *Hymen* in yellow. Hymen, the god of marriage, is traditionally
     represented in yellow robes.
57 *Two . . . Jove.* Ganymede was cup-bearer to Jupiter.
59–60 *Take . . . Lactea.* Mulryne has found an explanation for this unusual
     connexion of Hebe with the Milky Way (*Via Lactea*):
          . . . Hebe, one which was *Jupiters* Cupbearer, on a tyme, stombled
     at a starre, and shedde the wyne or mylke, that was in the cuppe,
     which colloured that part of heaven to this daye, wherefore she was
     pout out of her office
          (William Fulke, *A goodly gallerye with a most pleasaunt prospect
     into the garden of natural contemplation* (1563), E 6ᵛ).

HYMEN

> No more, forbear for Hymen's sake;
> In love we met, and so let's parting take.   *Exeunt*

DUKE

> But soft! here's no such persons in the argument   65
> As these three, Hymen, Hebe, Ganymede;
> The actors that this model here discovers
> Are only four—Juno, a nymph, two lovers.

BIANCA

> This is some antemasque belike, my lord,
> To entertain time;—now my peace is perfect.   70
> Let sports come on apace; now is their time, my lord,
>   *Music*
> Hark you, you hear from 'em.

DUKE   The nymph indeed!

Enter two dressed like nymphs, bearing two tapers lighted; then ISABELLA *dressed with flowers and garlands, bearing a censer with fire in it. They set the censer and tapers on Juno's altar with much reverence, this ditty being sung in parts*

Ditty

> Juno, nuptial goddess, thou that rul'st o'er coupled
>   bodies,
> Ti'st man to woman, never to forsake her; thou only
>   powerful marriage-maker;
>   Pity this amazed affection: 75
>   I love both and both love me;
>   Nor know I where to give rejection,
>   My heart likes so equally,
>   Till thou set'st right my peace of life,
>   And with thy power conclude this strife.   80

ISABELLA

> Now with my thanks depart, you to the springs,
> I to these wells of love.   [*Exeunt the two* NYMPHS]

---

64 *parting take* ed (part O); a rhyme seems to be called for

---

69 *antemasque.* A brief interlude (often comic) introduced before the masque proper; subsequent events show Bianca's responsibility for this one.

72 s.d. Enter ... ditty. Middleton's masque here is appropriate to the action of the play, but it also bears close resemblance to the masque in Act V of *The Two Noble Kinsmen.* The use of incense was common enough; it was recommended by Bacon in his essay 'Of Masques and Triumphs' as being especially pleasant in hot, steamy rooms.

> Thou sacred goddess,
And queen of nuptials, daughter to great Saturn,
Sister and wife to Jove, imperial Juno!
Pity this passionate conflict in my breast,   85
This tedious war 'twixt two affections;
Crown me with victory, and my heart's at peace.

Enter HIPPOLITO *and* GUARDIANO *like shepherds*

HIPPOLITO
> Make me that happy man, thou mighty goddess.
GUARDIANO
> But I live most in hope, if truest love
> Merit the greatest comfort.
ISABELLA   I love both   90
> With such an even and fair affection,
> I know not which to speak for, which to wish for,
> Till thou, great arbitress 'twixt lovers' hearts,
> By thy auspicious grace, design the man:
> Which pity I implore.
HIPPOLITO *and* GUARDIANO   We all implore it.   95
ISABELLA
> And after sighs, contrition's truest odours,

> > LIVIA *descends like Juno*

> I offer to thy powerful deity
> This precious incense; may it ascend peacefully.
> —And if it keep true touch, my good aunt Juno,
> 'Twill try your immortality ere't be long;   100
> I fear you'll never get so nigh Heaven again,
> When you're once down.
LIVIA   Though you and your affections
> Seem all as dark to our illustrious brightness
> As night's inheritance, hell, we pity you,
> And your requests are granted. You ask signs: 105
> They shall be given you; we'll be gracious to you.
> He of those twain which we determine for you,
> Love's arrows shall wound twice; the later wound
> Betokens love in age: for so are all
> Whose love continues firmly all their lifetime   110

90–92 *I love . . . wish for.*
> a husband I have pointed,
> But doe not know him, out of two, I should
> Choose one, and pray for his successe, but I
> Am guiltlesse of election of mine eyes. . . .
> > (*The Two Noble Kinsmen*, V, ii).

Twice wounded at their marriage, else affection
Dies when youth ends.—This savour overcomes me!
—Now for a sign of wealth and golden days,
Bright-eyed prosperity which all couples love,
Ay, and makes love—take that!
> [*Throws flaming gold upon* ISABELLA *who falls dead*]
                                        Our brother Jove   115
Never denies us of his burning treasure
T'express bounty.
DUKE   She falls down upon't;
What's the conceit of that?
FABRITIO   As over-joyed, belike:
Too much prosperity overjoys us all,
And she has her lapful, it seems, my lord.   120
DUKE
This swerves a little from the argument, though:
Look you, my lords.
GUARDIANO
All's fast; now comes my part to toll him hither;
Then, with a stamp given, he's dispatched as cunningly.

> [GUARDIANO *stamps on the floor; the trapdoor opens and he him-*
> *self falls through it.* HIPPOLITO *bends over* ISABELLA'S *body*]

HIPPOLITO
Stark dead! Oh treachery—cruelly made away! how's that?   125
FABRITIO
Look, there's one of the lovers dropped away too.
DUKE
Why sure, this plot's drawn false; here's no such thing.
LIVIA
Oh, I am sick to th'death! let me down quickly.
This fume is deadly. Oh, 't has poisoned me!
My subtilty is sped; her art has quitted me.   130
My own ambition pulls me down to ruin.   [*dies*]
HIPPOLITO
Nay, then I kiss thy cold lips, and applaud
This thy revenge in death.
> *Cupids shoot* [*at* HIPPOLITO]
FABRITIO   Look, Juno's down too!
What makes she there? her pride should keep aloft.

112 *savour* ed (favor O)
123 *toll* entice

She was wont to scorn the earth in other shows.   135
Methinks her peacocks' feathers are much pulled.

HIPPOLITO
Oh, death runs through my blood in a wild flame too!
Plague of those cupids! some lay hold on 'em.
Let 'em not 'scape, they have spoiled me; the shaft's deadly.

DUKE
I have lost myself in this quite.   140

HIPPOLITO
My great lords, we are all confounded.

DUKE   How!

HIPPOLITO
Dead; and, ay, worse.

FABRITIO   Dead? my girl dead? I hope
My sister Juno has not served me so.

HIPPOLITO
Lust and forgetfulness has been amongst us,
And we are brought to nothing. Some blest charity   145
Lend me the speeding pity of his sword
To quench this fire in blood! Leantio's death
Has brought all this upon us—now I taste it—
And made us lay plots to confound each other:
The event so proves it; and man's understanding   150
Is riper at his fall than all his lifetime.
She, in a madness for her lover's death,
Revealed a fearful lust in our near bloods,
For which I am punished dreadfully and unlooked for;
Proved her own ruin too: vengeance met vengeance   155
Like a set match: as if the plagues of sin
Had been agreed to meet here altogether.
But how her fawning partner fell, I reach not,
Unless caught by some springe of his own setting—
For on my pain, he never dreamed of dying;   160
The plot was all his own, and he had cunning
Enough to save himself: but 'tis the property
Of guilty deeds to draw your wise men downward.
Therefore the wonder ceases.—Oh this torment!

---

156 *plagues* ed (plague O)

136 *peacocks' feathers.* Juno is often represented as accompanied by peacocks.
151 *riper . . . fall.* Perhaps Middleton learned this from Webster, many of
     whose characters, in dying, look back upon their lives and comment
     on the 'shadow, or deep pit of darkness' that they lived in (*The Duchess
     of Malfi*, V, v, 100).

DUKE
  Our guard below there!

Enter a LORD *with a* GUARD

LORD   My lord?
HIPPOLITO   Run and meet death then,   165
  And cut off time and pain.   [*Runs on* GUARD'S *sword*]
LORD   Behold, my lord,
  H'as run his breast upon a weapon's point.
DUKE
  Upon the first night of our nuptial honours
  Destruction play her triumph, and great mischiefs
  Mask in expected pleasures! 'tis prodigious!   170
  They're things most fearfully ominous: I like 'em not.
  Remove these ruined bodies from our eyes.
                    [*The bodies are taken away*]
BIANCA
  Not yet? no change? when falls he to the earth?
LORD
  Please but your excellence to peruse that paper,
  Which is a brief confession from the heart   175
  Of him that fell first, ere his soul departed;
  And there the darkness of these deeds speaks plainly:
  'Tis the full scope, the manner and intent.
  His ward, that ignorantly let him down,
  Fear put to present flight at the voice of him.   180
BIANCA
  Nor yet?
DUKE   Read, read; for I am lost in sight and strength.
CARDINAL
  My noble brother!
BIANCA   Oh the curse of wretchedness!
  My deadly hand is fal'n upon my lord.
  Destruction take me to thee, give me way—
  The pains and plagues of a lost soul upon him   185
  That hinders me a moment!
DUKE
  My heart swells bigger yet; help here, break't ope!
  My breast flies open next.   [*dies*]
BIANCA   Oh, with the poison
  That was prepared for thee—thee, Cardinal!
  'Twas meant for thee!
CARDINAL   Poor prince!
BIANCA   Accursed error!   190
  Give me thy last breath, thou infected bosom,

And wrap two spirits in one poisoned vapour.
Thus, thus, reward thy murderer, and turn death
Into a parting kiss! My soul stands ready at my lips,
Ev'n vexed to stay one minute after thee.   195

CARDINAL
The greatest sorrow and astonishment
That ever struck the general peace of Florence
Dwells in this hour.

BIANCA   So ... my desires are satisfied,
I feel death's power within me!
Thou hast prevailed in something, cursed poison,   200
Though thy chief force was spent in my lord's bosom.
But my deformity in spirit's more foul:
A blemished face best fits a leprous soul.
What make I here? these are all strangers to me,
Not known but by their malice, now th'art gone,   205
Nor do I seek their pities.

CARDINAL   Oh restrain
Her ignorant, wilful hand.

[BIANCA *seizes the poisoned cup and drinks from it*]

BIANCA   Now do; 'tis done.
Leantio, now I feel the breach of marriage
At my heart-breaking! Oh the deadly snares
That women set for women—without pity   210
Either to soul or honour! Learn by me
To know your foes. In this belief I die:
Like our own sex, we have no enemy.

LORD
See, my lord,
What shift sh'as made to be her own destruction.   215

BIANCA
Pride, greatness, honours, beauty, youth, ambition—
You must all down together; there's no help for't.
Yet this my gladness is, that I remove,
Tasting the same death in a cup of love.   [*dies*]

---

213 *no enemy* ed (no Enemy, no Enemy O)

---

203 *blemished face*. Possibly the poison she has kissed from the Duke's lips
    has burned into Bianca's own; with this her first impulse after the
    seduction is achieved (cf. II, ii, 425–7).

CARDINAL

Sin, what thou art, these ruins show too piteously!   220
Two kings on one throne cannot sit together
But one must needs down, for his title's wrong:
So where lust reigns, that prince cannot reign long.

Exeunt

FINIS

The White Devil

JOHN WEBSTER

Edited by
ELIZABETH M. BRENNAN

ABBREVIATIONS

Q1–the edition of 1612 (British Museum copies: Ashley 2205; C.34. e.18. [the Garrick copy]; 840.c.37).

Q1a–uncorrected state of Q1.

Q1b–corrected state of Q1.

Q1c–second corrected state of Q1, found only in sheet M inner forme (in this edition V, vi, 205–78). Variant readings of Q1 are taken from the list given by Dr. J. R. Brown in 'The Printing of John Webster's Plays (II)', *Studies in Bibliography*, VIII (1956), 113–7.

Q2–the edition of 1631 (British Museum copy 644.a.7).

Q3–the edition of 1665 (British Museum copy 644.f.76).

Q4–the edition of 1672 (British Museum copy 644.f.77).

Qq–all four quarto editions.

Dodsley ii–R. Dodsley, *A Select Collection of Old Plays* (1780), vi.

Scott–Walter Scott, *Ancient British Drama* (1810), iii.

Dodsley iii–R. Dodsley, I. Reed, O. Gilchrist and J. P. Collier, *A Select Collection of Old Plays* (1825), vi.

Dyce–Alexander Dyce, *The Works of John Webster* (1857) [a revision of his edition of 1830].

Hazlitt–W. C. Hazlitt, *The Dramatic Works of John Webster* (1857), ii.

Sampson–Martin W. Sampson, *The White Devil* and *The Duchess of Malfi*, The Belles Lettres Series (1904).

Brereton–J. le Gay Brereton, 'Webster's Twin Masterpieces', *Elizabethan Drama: Notes and Studies* (Sydney, 1909) [an expanded version of his review, published in *Hermes* (1905), of Sampson's edition, with notes on readings and verse arrangement].

Wheeler–C. B. Wheeler, *Six Plays by Contemporaries of Shakespeare* (1915).

Lucas–F. L. Lucas, *The Complete Works of John Webster* (1927), i.

Harrison–G. B. Harrison, *The White Devil*, The Temple Dramatists (1933).

Brown–J. R. Brown, *The White Devil*, The Revels Plays (1960).

Dent–R. W. Dent, *John Webster's Borrowing* (Berkeley and Los Angeles, 1960).

THE
WHITE DIVEL,

OR,

The Tragedy of *Paulo Giordano Ursini*, Duke of *Brachiano*,

With

The Life and Death of Vittoria Corombona the famous Venetian Curtizan.

Acted by the Queenes Maiesties Seruants.

Written by IOHN WEBSTER.

Non inferiora secutus.

LONDON,
Printed by N.O. for *Thomas Archer*, and are to be sold
at his Shop in Popes head Pallace, neere the
Royall Exchange. 1612.

[DRAMATIS PERSONÆ]

[MONTICELSO, a Cardinal; afterwards Pope PAUL IV.

FRANCISCO DE MEDICIS, Duke of Florence; in the fifth act disguised for a Moor, under the name of MULINASSAR

BRACHIANO, otherwise PAULO GIORDANO URSINI, Duke of Brachiano; husband to Isabella and in love with Vittoria

GIOVANNI, his son, by Isabella

LODOVICO or LODOWICK, an Italian Count, but decayed

ANTONELLI ⎫
GASPARO ⎭ his friends, and dependants of the Duke of Florence

CAMILLO, husband to Vittoria

HORTENSIO, one of Brachiano's officers

MARCELLO, an attendant of the Duke of Florence, and brother to Vittoria

FLAMINEO, his brother; secretary to Brachiano

CARDINAL OF ARRAGON

DOCTOR JULIO, a conjuror

*CHRISTOPHERO, his assistant

*GUID-ANTONIO

*FERNEZE

*JACQUES, a Moor, servant to Giovanni

ISABELLA, sister to Francisco de Medicis, and wife to Brachiano

VITTORIA COROMBONA, a Venetian lady, first married to Camillo, afterwards to Brachiano

CORNELIA, mother to Vittoria, Flamineo and Marcello

ZANCHE, a Moor; servant to Vittoria

MATRONA of the House of Convertites

AMBASSADORS	PHYSICIANS
COURTIERS	LAWYERS
OFFICERS	ATTENDANTS
CHANCELLOR	REGISTER
PAGE	ARMOURER
CONJUROR]	

* non-speaking parts or 'ghost characters'
   [DRAMATIS PERSONÆ]: see Additional Notes

MONTICELSO. Some stage directions give the form 'Montcelso'. The real Cardinal Montalto, uncle of Vittoria's husband, Francesco Peretti, took the title of Sixtus V when he succeeded Pope Gregory XIII.

TO THE READER

IN publishing this tragedy, I do but challenge to myself that
liberty, which other men have tane before me; not that I affect
praise by it, for *nos haec novimus esse nihil*, only since it was
acted, in so dull a time of winter, presented in so open and
black a theatre, that it wanted (that which is the only grace and   5
setting out of a tragedy) a full and understanding auditory:
and that since that time I have noted, most of the people that
come to that playhouse, resemble those ignorant asses (who
visiting stationers' shops, their use is not to inquire for good
books, but new books) I present it to the general view with   10
this confidence:

> *Nec rhoncos metues, maligniorum,*
> *Nec scombris tunicas, dabis molestas.*

If it be objected this is no true dramatic poem, I shall easily
confess it, – *non potes in nugas dicere plura meas: ipse ego quam*   15
dixi, – willingly, and not ignorantly, in this kind have I faulted:
for should a man present to such an auditory, the most sententious tragedy that ever was written, observing all the
critical laws, as height of style, and gravity of person; enrich
it with the sententious *Chorus*, and as it were lifen death, in the   20
passionate and weighty *Nuntius:* yet after all this divine
rapture, *O dura messorum ilia*, the breath that comes from the

1 *challenge* claim; demand as a right
3 *nos haec novimus esse nihil* 'we know these things are nothing'
   (Martial, XIII, 2)
4 *in so . . . presented* Q1 (Q2, Q3, Q4 [omit])
4–6 see Introduction, p. viii above.
6 *auditory* audience
15–16 'You are unable to say more against my trifles than I have
   said myself.' (Martial, XIII, 2)
16 *have I faulted* have I been deficient; come short of a desired
   standard
20 *lifen* ed. (Q1, Q2 life'n; Q3, Q4 enliven)
22 *O dura messorum ilia* 'O strong stomachs of harvesters!'
   (Horace, *Epodes*, III, 4)

12–13 'You [i.e. the poet's book] shall not fear the turned-up noses of the
malicious
Nor give robes of torture to mackerel.' (Martial, IV, 86).
A *tunica molesta* was 'the inflammable garment smeared with pitch
which was put on criminals destined to be burnt alive in the Amphi-
theatre or to illuminate the Imperial Gardens.' (Lucas). Brown renders
these lines: 'You [the poet's book] will not fear the sneers of the malicious, nor be used for wrapping mackerel.'

uncapable multitude is able to poison it, and ere it be acted, let
the author resolve to fix to every scene, this of Horace,

    – – – – *Haec hodie porcis comedenda relinques.*   25

To those who report I was a long time in finishing this
tragedy, I confess I do not write with a goose-quill, winged
with two feathers, and if they will needs make it my fault, I
must answer them with that of Euripides to Alcestides, a
tragic writer: Alcestides objecting that Euripides had only in   30
three days composed three verses, whereas himself had written
three hundred: 'Thou tell'st truth', quoth he, 'but here's the
difference: thine shall only be read for three days, whereas
mine shall continue three ages.'

Detraction is the sworn friend to ignorance. For mine own   35
part I have ever truly cherish'd my good opinion of other
men's worthy labours, especially of that full and height'ned
style of Master Chapman, the labour'd and understanding
works of Master Jonson: the no less worthy composures of
the both worthily excellent Master Beaumont, and Master   40
Fletcher: and lastly (without wrong last to be named) the
right happy and copious industry of Master Shakespeare,
Master Dekker, and Master Heywood, wishing what I write
may be read by their light: protesting, that, in the strength of
mine own judgement, I know them so worthy, that though I   45
rest silent in my own work, yet to most of theirs I dare
(without flattery) fix that of Martial:

    – – – *non norunt, haec monumenta mori.*

25 'What you leave will go today to feed the pigs.' (Horace, *Epistles*,
   I.vii, 19)
31 *verses* i.e. lines
32 *hundred* Q2, Q3, Q4 (Q1 hundreth)
42–43 *Master* Q3 (Q1, Q2 M.; Q4 Mr.)
48 'These monuments do not know how to die.' (Martial, XII, 2.)

29–34 In the original version of this story, told by Valerius Maximus (*De
  Dictus, III, 7) 'Alcestis' writes a hundred verses in three days. Erasmus,
  Manutius and Lycosthenes say '*Alcestidi glorianti quod ipse perfacile
  centum absoluisset uno die.*' Webster probably found the story, with the
  change of the poet's name to Alcestides (caused by the use of the dative
  form) and the reference to three hundred verses in three days, in
  Lodowick Lloyd's *Linceus Spectacles* (1607).
38–43 George Chapman (*c.* 1560–1634); Ben Jonson (1572–1637); Francis
  Beaumont (1584–1616) and John Fletcher (1575–1625); William
  Shakespeare (1564–1616) and Thomas Heywood (?1573–1641) had all
  written tragedies before 1611–12. Thomas Dekker (*c.* 1572–1632) col-
  laborated with Webster in the citizen comedies *Westward Ho!* and
  Northward Ho!. He is not now known as a tragic writer, but some of the
  lost collaborative plays, written during the period of his dramatic
  apprenticeship in the employment of Philip Henslowe (1598–1604)
  were tragedies.

THE TRAGEDY
OF PAVLO GIORDANO
Vrſini Duke of Brachiano, and Vittoria Corombona.

[Act I, Scene i]

Enter Count LODOVICO, ANTONELLI *and* GASPARO

LODOVICO
Banish'd?
ANTONELLI   It griev'd me much to hear the sentence.
LODOVICO
Ha, ha, O Democritus thy gods
That govern the whole world! Courtly reward,
And punishment! Fortune's a right whore.
If she gives ought, she deals it in small parcels,   5
That she may take away all at one swoop.
This 'tis to have great enemies, God quite them:
Your wolf no longer seems to be a wolf
Than when she's hungry.
GASPARO   You term those enemies
Are men of princely rank.   10
LODOVICO   Oh I pray for them.

---

5 *in small parcels* in small portions, piecemeal
6 *at one swoop* at one stroke or blow; *swoop* Q4 (Q1, Q2 swope;
   Q3 swop)
7 *quite* Q1 (Q2, Q3, Q4 quit) requite, reward
10 *rank.* Q1 (Q2, Q3, Q4 rank?)

Act I, Scene i. The action, up to the end of Act IV, takes place in Rome.
   An interesting and detailed analysis of the opening scene is given by
   James Smith in 'The Tragedy of Blood', *Scrutiny*, VIII (Cambridge,
   1939), 266–72.
1 *Banish'd?* ed. (Qq Banisht?) W. W. Greg thought the scene could possibly be located in a gallery or anteroom to a judgement-hall. '. . . More
   probably, however, a street, since at the opening of the play the quartos
   read 'Banished?' (query, not exclamation), as if Lodovico had not heard
   his own sentence, but had just received the news from his friends.'
   'Webster's "White Devil"', *Modern Language Quarterly*, III (London,
   1900), 122–123.
2–3 In fact, Democritus did not hold these views, but they were attributed
   to him by Pliny and, specifically, in Webster's probable source for these
   lines, North's translation of Guevara's *Diall of Princes* (1557).

493

The violent thunder is adored by those
Are pash'd in pieces by it.

ANTONELLI   Come my lord,
You are justly doom'd; look but a little back
Into your former life: you have in three years
Ruin'd the noblest earldom —

GASPARO   Your followers   15
Have swallowed you like mummia, and being sick
With such unnatural and horrid physic
Vomit you up i'th' kennel —

ANTONELLI   All the damnable degrees
Of drinkings have you stagger'd through; one citizen
Is lord of two fair manors, call'd you master   20
Only for caviare.

GASPARO   Those noblemen
Which were invited to your prodigal feasts,
Wherein the phoenix scarce could scape your throats,
Laugh at your misery, as fore-deeming you
An idle meteor which drawn forth the earth   25
Would be soon lost i'th' air.

ANTONELLI   Jest upon you,
And say you were begotten in an earthquake,
You have ruin'd such fair lordships.

---

12 *pash'd* ed. (Q1, Q2 pasht; Q3, Q4 dasht) dashed.
16 *mummia* a medicinal preparation made from Egyptian mummies;
   cf. *The Duchess of Malfi*, IV.ii, 124.
18 *kennel* channel, i.e. gutter
19 *you* Q3, Q4 (Q1 you, Q2 you,)
20 *call'd* ed. (Q1 cald; Q2, Q3, Q4 call)
20–21 i.e. 'he had sold his estates to purchase dainties' (Wheeler)
22 *prodigal* extravagant
24 *fore-deeming* prejudging

---

21 *caviare* was extremely rare in the early seventeenth century. The first
   use of the name recorded by *O.E.D.* is in Giles Fletcher's *Of the Russe
   Common Wealth* (1591).
23 *the phoenix.* This legendary bird was supposed to live about a hundred
   years. Only one bird, and that a male, lived at any time, and the young
   phoenix was said to rise from the ashes of the old bird, which died in a
   conflagration of its nest. Thus, if it were possible to have the phoenix
   as an edible delicacy, it would be the rarest dish in the world.
25 *meteor.* 'In Elizabethan cosmology . . . meteors belonged to the sub-
   lunary world of change and decay, and were transitory, of evil omen,
   and the result, or indication, of corruption . . .' N. W. Bawcutt, Ed.
   The Changeling (Revels Plays, 1958), p. 109.

LODOVICO   Very good,
  This well goes with two buckets, I must tend
  The pouring out of either.
GASPARO   Worse than these,   30
  You have acted certain murders here in Rome,
  Bloody and full of horror.
LODOVICO   'Las they were flea-bitings:
  Why took they not my head then?
GASPARO   O my lord
  The law doth sometimes mediate, thinks it good
  Not ever to steep violent sins in blood;   35
  This gentle penance may both end your crimes,
  And in the example better these bad times.
LODOVICO
  So; but I wonder then some great men scape
  This banishment; there's Paulo Giordano Orsini,
  The Duke of Brachiano, now lives in Rome,   40
  And by close panderism seeks to prostitute
  The honour of Vittoria Corombona:
  Vittoria, she that might have got my pardon
  For one kiss to the Duke.
ANTONELLI   Have a full man within you.
  We see that trees bear no such pleasant fruit   45
  There where they grew first, as where they are new set.
  Perfumes the more they are chaf'd the more they render
  Their pleasing scents, and so affliction
  Expresseth virtue, fully, whether true,
  Or else adulterate.

---

29 *This well goes with two buckets* i.e. 'the full content of this speech
    is shared between you two.'; *tend* attend, wait for
31 *acted* Q4 (Q1, Q2, Q3 acted,) brought about; performed
38 *scape* escape
39 *Orsini* Q1 (Q2 Vrsini; Q3, Q4 Ursini)
41 *close* secret, private
44 *Have a full man within you.* i.e. 'Be complete in yourself; self-
    reliant.'
45 *such* Q1b (Q1a   sweet)
46 *they are* Q2, Q3, Q4 (Q1 the are)
47 *render* give out, emit, yield
49 *Expresseth* presses out

29–30 Cf. *The Duchess of Malfi*, I.ii, 213–49 where Ferdinand and the
    Cardinal use a similar technique in criticizing the Duchess.
43–44 These lines imply that Lodovico's banishment, decreed by the Pope,
    was at Duke Brachiano's instigation. Thus Lodovico is seen as an enemy
    of Brachiano from the start. See W. W. Greg, *op. cit.*, p. 115.

LODOVICO   Leave your painted comforts.   50
    I'll make Italian cut-works in their guts
    If ever I return.
GASPARO   O sir.
LODOVICO   I am patient.
    I have seen some ready to be executed
    Give pleasant looks, and money, and grown familiar
    With the knave hangman; so do I, I thank them,   55
    And would account them nobly merciful
    Would they dispatch me quickly.
ANTONELLI   Fare you well,
    We shall find time I doubt not, to repeal
    Your banishment.   [*A sennet sounds.*]
LODOVICO   I am ever bound to you:
    This is the world's alms; pray make use of it: 60
    Great men sell sheep, thus to be cut in pieces,
    When first they have shorn them bare and sold their fleeces.
                               Exeunt

[Act I, Scene ii]

Enter BRACHIANO, CAMILLO, FLAMINEO, VITTORIA
COROMBONA [*and* ATTENDANTS]

BRACHIANO
    Your best of rest.
VITTORIA   Unto my lord the Duke,
    The best of welcome. More lights, attend the Duke.
                [*Exeunt* VITTORIA *and* CAMILLO]
BRACHIANO
    Flamineo.
FLAMINEO   My lord.
BRACHIANO   Quite lost Flamineo.

---

50 *painted* artificial, unreal
51 *Italian cut-works* a kind of open-work made by cutting out or
    stamping, worn in Italy in the late sixteenth and the seventeenth
    centuries.
60 *This* i.e. the following
61 *sell sheep, thus* Qq (Dodsley iii, Dyce, Wheeler and Harrison:
    sell sheep thus   ; Lucas: sell sheep thus,)
 1 *Your best of rest.* 'Apparently a normal idiom for "good night".'
    (Dent)

    Act I, Scene ii. This scene would appear to take place in Camillo's house.
    As Brown points out (p. 11 n.) the sennet 'gives force to Monticelso's
    charge that Vittoria "did counterfeit a prince's court." '

FLAMINEO

    Pursue your noble wishes, I am prompt
    As lightning to your service, O my lord!   5
    (*whispers*) The fair Vittoria, my happy sister
    Shall give you present audience. Gentlemen
    Let the caroche go on, and 'tis his pleasure
    You put out all your torches and depart.

                           [*Exeunt* ATTENDANTS]

BRACHIANO

    Are we so happy?

FLAMINEO   Can't be otherwise?   10
    Observ'd you not tonight my honour'd lord,
    Which way so e'er you went she threw her eyes?
    I have dealt already with her chamber-maid
    Zanche the Moor, and she is wondrous proud
    To be the agent for so high a spirit.   15

BRACHIANO

    We are happy above thought, because 'bove merit.

FLAMINEO

    'Bove merit! We may now talk freely: 'bove merit; what is't
you doubt? her coyness? That's but the superficies of lust
most women have; yet why should ladies blush to hear that
nam'd, which they do not fear to handle? O they are politic!   20
They know our desire is increas'd by the difficulty of
enjoying; whereas satiety is a blunt, weary and drowsy
passion; if the buttery-hatch at court stood continually
open there would be nothing so passionate crowding, nor
hot suit after the beverage, —   25

BRACHIANO

    O but her jealous husband.

FLAMINEO

    Hang him, a gilder that hath his brains perish'd with

---

  6 (*whispers*) ed. (Q1 (*whisper* in the margin, opposite l. 7)
  7 *present* immediate
  8 *caroche* large coach
 10 *Can't* can it
 18 *superficies* outside covering
 22 *whereas* ed. (Qq where a); *satiety* Q1b (Q1a sotiety)
 23 *buttery-hatch* half-door over which provisions, especially, drinks
    are served from the buttery (the room where they are stored)

27–28 In gilding, through the application of heat, mercury was drawn off
    an object covered with mercury and gold. The mercury vapour was
    poisonous and thus gilders, by inhaling it, became subject to tremors
    and insanity.
27–33. For an analysis of these lines see J. R. Brown, *The White Devil*,
    Introduction, p. xlviii.

quicksilver is not more cold in the liver. The great barriers
moulted not more feathers than he hath shed hairs, by the
confession of his doctor. An Irish gamester that will play   30
himself naked, and then wage all downward, at hazard, is
not more venturous. So unable to please a woman that
like a Dutch doublet all his back is shrunk into his breeches.
Shroud you within this closet, good my lord;
Some trick now must be thought on to divide   35
My brother-in-law from his fair bed-fellow.

BRACHIANO

O should she fail to come, —

FLAMINEO

I must not have your lordship thus unwisely amorous; I
myself have loved a lady and pursued her with a great deal
of under-age protestation, whom some 3 or 4 gallants that   40
have enjoyed would with all their hearts have been glad to
have been rid of. 'Tis just like a summer bird-cage in a
garden: the birds that are without, despair to get in, and
the birds that are within despair and are in a consumption
for fear they shall never get out. Away, away my lord,   45

Enter CAMILLO

See, here he comes.

[*Exit* BRACHIANO; FLAMINEO *speaks aside*]
          This fellow by his apparel
Some men would judge a politician,
But call his wit in question you shall find it
Merely an ass in's foot-cloth. [*To* CAMILLO] How now,
                                        brother,

28 *the liver* the supposed seat of the passions; *great barriers* waist
    high barriers which prevented dangerous close fighting during
    duels which were performed for entertainment
29 *moulted* i.e. caused the plumes of the combatants' helmets to fall
31 *wage all downward* Q1 (Q2, Q3, Q4 wage all downwards): see
    Additional Notes
33 *Dutch doublet:* a Dutch doublet was close-fitting, its accompany-
    ing breeches were wide; *back* virility (*cf. The Duchess of Malfi*, II.
    iv, 53–56.)
40 *under-age protestation* immature wooing
44 *consumption* a wasting disease
47 *politician* crafty person   49 *in's* in his

29 *shed hairs.* F. L. Lucas says that this implies the shedding of hairs
    through the treatment of venereal disease (*Webster*, i, 202) but Brown
    thinks that possibly it here merely implies lack of virility (p. 13 n.).
49 *foot-cloth* an ornamental cloth which covered the horse's back and hung
    down to the ground. It was considered a sign of diginity. Thus Camillo's
    long gown, also worn as a sign of dignity, resembles the foot-cloth. His
    mind is like the dull ass under the dignified trappings.

What, travelling to bed to your kind wife?   50
CAMILLO
I assure you brother, no. My voyage lies
More northerly, in a far colder clime;
I do not well remember, I protest,
When I last lay with her.
FLAMINEO   Strange you should lose your count.
CAMILLO
We never lay together but ere morning   55
There grew a flaw between us.
FLAMINEO   'T had been your part
To have made up that flaw.
CAMILLO   True, but she loathes
I should be seen in't.
FLAMINEO   Why sir, what's the matter?
CAMILLO
The Duke your master visits me, I thank him,
And I perceive how like an earnest bowler   60
He very passionately leans that way,
He should have his bowl run.
FLAMINEO   I hope you do not think —
CAMILLO
That noblemen bowl booty? 'Faith his cheek
Hath a most excellent bias; it would fain
Jump with my mistress.
FLAMINEO   Will you be an ass   65
Despite your Aristotle or a cuckold
Contrary to your ephemerides

---

50 *travelling* Q3, Q4 (Q1, Q2 travailing). Webster may have intended
  a pun on the two meanings implicit in the spelling of Q1: travelling; working hard.
54 *lose* Q4 (Q1, Q2, Q3 loose); *count* a double entendre
56–57 *flaw* storm, squall; crack, imperfection
61–62 *that way,* / *He* i.e. that way, that he . . .
66 *your* Q3, Q4 (Q1, Q2 you); *Despite your Aristotle* illogically
  (Sampson); 'despite your knowledge of Aristotle' (Lucas)
67 *ephemerides* almanac or calendar containing astrological or
  meteorological predictions for each day of a specific period

---

63–65 Camillo's quibbles refer to the game of bowls. In bowling booty two
  players combined together against a third. 'Booty' also carries the usual
  connotations of plunder. The 'cheek' is the round surface of the bowl;
  the 'bias' is a weight in its side; the mistress is the 'jack' at which the
  bowls are aimed. To 'jump with' is to run up against; also to lie with.

Which shows you under what a smiling planet
You were first swaddled?

CAMILLO   Pew wew, sir tell not me
Of planets nor of ephemerides.   70
A man may be made cuckold in the day-time
When the stars' eyes are out.

FLAMINEO   Sir God boy you,
I do commit you to your pitiful pillow
Stuff'd with horn-shavings.

CAMILLO   Brother?

FLAMINEO   God refuse me,
Might I advise you now your only course   75
Were to lock up your wife.

CAMILLO   'Twere very good.

FLAMINEO
Bar her the sight of revels.

CAMILLO   Excellent.

FLAMINEO
Let her not go to church, but like a hound
In leon at your heels.

CAMILLO   'Twere for her honour.

FLAMINEO
And so you should be certain in one fortnight,   80
Despite her chastity or innocence
To be cuckolded, which yet is in suspense:
This is my counsel and I ask no fee for't.

CAMILLO
Come, you know not where my nightcap wrings me.

FLAMINEO
Wear it o'th' old fashion, let your large ears come through,   85
it will be more easy; nay, I will be bitter: bar your wife of
her entertainment: women are more willingly and more
gloriously chaste, when they are least restrained of their
liberty. It seems you would be a fine capricious mathematically jealous coxcomb, take the height of your own   90

71 *God boy you* God buy you, i.e. 'God be with you'
74 *horn-shavings* shavings from the horns which were supposed to
   grow on the foreheads of men cuckolded by their wives' adultery;
   God refuse me 'May God cast me off' (an oath)
78 *but* except
79 *leon* leash:
84 *wrings* pinches. (The nightcap would be tight if there were
   cuckold's horns on Camillo's forehead.)
89–90 *mathematically* with mathematical accuracy

horns with a Jacob's staff afore they are up. These politic
enclosures for paltry mutton makes more rebellion in the
flesh than all the provocative electuaries doctors have
uttered since last Jubilee.

CAMILLO

This does not physic me.   95

FLAMINEO

It seems you are jealous. I'll show you the error of it by a
familiar example: I have seen a pair of spectacles fashion'd
with such perspective art, that lay down but one twelve
pence o'th' board, 'twill appear as if there were twenty;
now should you wear a pair of these spectacles, and see   100
your wife tying her shoe, you would imagine twenty hands
were taking up of your wife's clothes, and this would put
you into a horrible causeless fury.

CAMILLO

The fault there sir is not in the eyesight—

FLAMINEO

True, but they that have the yellow jaundice, think all   105
objects they look on to be yellow. Jealousy is worser, her
fits present to a man, like so many bubbles in a basin of
water, twenty several crabbed faces; many times makes his
own shadow his cuckold-maker.

Enter [VITTORIA] COROMBONA

See she comes; what reason have you to be jealous of this   110
creature? What an ignorant ass or flattering knave might

91 *Jacob's staff* an instrument for measuring heights and distances;
    politic cunning
92 makes Q1, Q2, Q3 (Q4 make)
93 *provocative electuaries* aphrodisiacs which excite to lust
94 *uttered* put forth for sale; *last* Q1, Q2 (Q3, Q4 the last)
106 *worser* Q1 (Q2, Q3, Q4 worse)   107 *fits* Q3, Q4 (Q1, Q2 fit's)
108 *several* different

---

92 *mutton* ed. (Qq mutton,) loose women (slang). The passage also refers
    to the enclosure of land for sheepfarming by rich landowners. This
    caused great hardship and provoked minor peasants' risings in the early
    seventeenth century.
94 *Jubilee.* Since the institution of the year of Jubilee in 1300 by Pope
    Boniface VIII as a time when plenary indulgence could be obtained by
    certain acts of piety, the period between recurrences of the year had
    been reduced from a hundred years to fifty, and in 1450, to twenty-five
    years. The 'last Jubilee' before the performance of the play would
    therefore have been in 1600.
97–99: these spectacles were made from glass cut into facets by optical skill
    so that one image was made to seem a hundred.

he be counted, that should write sonnets to her eyes, or call
her brow the snow of Ida, or ivory of Corinth, or compare
her hair to the blackbird's bill, when 'tis liker the blackbird's feather. This is all. Be wise; I will make you friends   115
and you shall go to bed together; marry look you, it shall
not be your seeking, do you stand upon that by any means;
walk you aloof, I would not have you seen in't. Sister,
[aside to VITTORIA] my lord attends you in the banqueting-
house–your husband is wondrous discontented.   120

VITTORIA

I did nothing to displease him, I carved to him at supper-
time.

FLAMINEO [aside to VITTORIA]

You need not have carved him in faith, they say he is a capon
already. I must now seemingly fall out with you.–Shall a
gentleman so well descended as Camillo–a lousy slave that   125
within this twenty years rode with the black-guard in the
Duke's carriage 'mongst spits and dripping-pans,—

CAMILLO

Now he begins to tickle her.

FLAMINEO

An excellent scholar,–one that hath a head fill'd with
calves' brains without any sage in them,–come crouching   130
in the hams to you for a night's lodging–that hath an itch
in's hams, which like the fire at the glass-house hath not

---

117 *stand upon* be urgent or insistent about   118 *aloof* at a distance
119 *attends* waits for.
121 *carved* served at table; made advances to ('a sort of digitary ogle'
Lucas)
123 *carved* castrated; *capon* a castrated cock.
126 *black-guard* meanest drudges; scullions and turnspits
127 *carriage* baggage train   128 *tickle* excite, arouse.
130 *calves' brains* usual meaning; fools' brains; *sage* the herb; wisdom
130–31 *crouching in the hams* squatting down in a position of humility
or pleading
131 *itch* irritating desire; disease
132 *hams* thighs and buttocks; *glass-house* glass factory. There was a famous
one near the Blackfriars theatre: *cf. The Duchess of Malfi*, II. ii, 6; IV.
ii, 78.

---

113 *Ida* was the sacred mountain, rising above Troy. Brown thinks the
reference here may be ironic, for Ida was usually associated with the
green groves where Paris lived as a shepherd; or, possibly, Ida is the
mountain in Crete.
113 *ivory of Corinth.* Corinth was a trading centre famous for its expensive
wares, including marble and beautiful prostitutes. Perhaps Flamineo
is thinking of the latter.
114–15: the blackbird's bill was yellow; his feathers black.

gone out this seven years. – Is he not a courtly gentleman? –
When he wears white satin one would take him by his black
muzzle to be no other creature than a maggot. – You are a   135
goodly foil, I confess, well set out – but cover'd with a false
stone yon counterfeit diamond.

CAMILLO
He will make her know what is in me.

FLAMINEO
Come, my lord attends you; thou shalt go to bed to my lord.

CAMILLO
Now he comes to't.   140

FLAMINEO
With a relish as curious as a vintner going to taste new wine.
[To CAMILLO] I am opening your case hard.

CAMILLO
A virtuous brother, o' my credit.

FLAMINEO
He will give thee a ring with a philosopher's stone in it.

CAMILLO
Indeed I am studying alchemy.   145

FLAMINEO
Thou shalt lie in a bed stuff'd with turtles' feathers, swoon
in perfumed linen like the fellow was smothered in roses;
so perfect shall be thy happiness, that as men at sea think
land and trees and ships go that way they go, so both heaven
and earth shall seem to go your voyage. Shalt meet him,   150
'tis fix'd, with nails of diamonds to inevitable necessity.

---

136 *foil* thin metal foil placed under a gem to enhance its brilliance;
setting for a jewel; *cover'd* Q3, Q4 (Q1a couer; Q1b couerd; Q2
couer'd): a double entendre
137 *yon* Q1b, Q3 (Q1a your; Q2, Q4 you)
139 Flamineo refers to Brachiano; Camillo thinks Flamineo speaks of
him.
142 *case* usual (legal) meaning; a case of wine; also a double entendre.
146 *turtles'* i.e. turtle doves'; turtle doves were proverbially renowned
for devotion to their mates.

---

144 The *philosopher's stone*, sought after by the experiments of the alchemist, would turn base metals to gold; prolong life; and cure disease.
Flamineo uses the phrase as a double entendre.
147 *smothered in roses*: cf. *The Duchess of Malfi*, IV.ii, 213–14.
151 *nails of diamond*. Dent (p. 83) points out that Webster is here merely
repeating an idea found in de Serres-Matthieu, *General Inventorie*,
'. . . that which was yesterday voluntarie, is this day fastened with
nayles of Diamonds to an ineuitable necessity.'

VITTORIA [*aside to* FLAMINEO]
How shall's rid him hence?

FLAMINEO
I will put breese in's tail, set him gadding presently. [*To*
CAMILLO] I have almost wrought her to it, I find her coming,
but might I advise you now for this night I would not lie   155
with her; I would cross her humour to make her more
humble.

CAMILLO
Shall I? Shall I?

FLAMINEO
It will show in you a supremacy of judgement.

CAMILLO
True, and a mind differing from the tumultuary opinion,   160
for *quae negata grata*.

FLAMINEO
Right: you are the adamant shall draw her to you, though
you keep distance off.

CAMILLO
A philosophical reason.

FLAMINEO
Walk by her o' the nobleman's fashion, and tell her you   165
will lie with her at the end of the progress.

CAMILLO
Vittoria, I cannot be induc'd or as a man would say incited —

VITTORIA
To do what sir?

CAMILLO
To lie with you tonight; your silkworm useth to fast every
third day, and the next following spins the better. Tomorrow   170
at night I am for you.

152 *shall's* shall us
153 *breese* gadflies; *presently* immediately
154 *coming* forward
156 *humour* mood, inclination
160 *tumultuary* irregular, hastily formed
161 *quae negata grata* 'what is denied is desired'
162 *adamant* loadstone, magnet and (by confused etymology) the
    hardest metal or stone
166 *progress* state journey
169 *useth to* is accustomed to

169–70 *every third day*. Brown notes that 'silkworms fast two days before they
spin, and then spin for not more than nine days consecutively without
food.' (p. 22 n.) There was considerable interest in the possibility of
founding a silk industry in England at this time.

VITTORIA
You'll spin a fair thread, trust to't.

FLAMINEO
But do you hear, I shall have you steal to her chamber
about midnight.

CAMILLO
Do you think so? Why look you brother, because you shall   175
not think I'll gull you, take the key, lock me into the chamber, and say you shall be sure of me.

FLAMINEO
In troth I will, I'll be your jailer once;
But have you ne'er a false door?

CAMILLO
A pox on't, as I am a Christian tell me tomorrow how   180
scurvily she takes my unkind parting.

FLAMINEO
I will.

CAMILLO
Didst thou not mark the jest of the silkworm?
Good night: in faith I will use this trick often,—

FLAMINEO
Do, do, do.   *Exit* CAMILLO   185
So now you are safe. Ha ha ha, thou entanglest thyself
in thine own work like a silkworm.   *Enter* BRACHIANO
Come sister, darkness hides your blush; women are like
curs'd dogs, civility keeps them tied all daytime, but they
are let loose at midnight; then they do most good or most   190
mischief. My lord, my lord.

BRACHIANO
Give credit: I could wish time would stand still
And never end this interview, this hour,
But all delight doth itself soon'st devour.

ZANCHE *brings out a carpet, spreads it and lays on it two fair*
cushions. Enter CORNELIA [*listening, behind*].

---

181 *scurvily* sourly
183 *mark* Q4 (Q1, Q2, Q3 make; Wheeler ?take)
189 *curs'd* fierce, savage; *civility* Q1 (Q2, Q3, Q4 cruelty) civil order

---

172 *You'll spin a fair thread.* This proverbial phrase was usually applied
ironically to a badly performed action. Brown calls attention to a close
parallel to Vittoria's usage in Sharpham's *Cupid's Whirligig* (1607):
'. . . haue not I spun a faire thred . . . to be a verry Baude, and arrant
wittall.' (p. 22 n.)
173–4 Flamineo is, perhaps, suggesting that Camillo set a wife trap, to
catch Vittoria with a lover; but Camillo thinks that he is advocating
spending the night with Vittoria after all.

Let me into your bosom happy lady,   195
Pour out instead of eloquence my vows;
Loose me not madam, for if you forgo me
I am lost eternally.
VITTORIA   Sir in the way of pity
I wish you heart-whole.
BRACHIANO   You are a sweet physician.
VITTORIA
Sure sir a loathed cruelty in ladies   200
Is as to doctors many funerals.
It takes away their credit.
BRACHIANO   Excellent creature.
We call the cruel fair, what name for you
That are so merciful?
                        [*Embraces her*]
ZANCHE   See now they close.
FLAMINEO
Most happy union.   205
CORNELIA [*aside*]
My fears are fall'n upon me, oh my heart!
My son the pander: now I find our house
Sinking to ruin. Earthquakes leave behind,
Where they have tyrannized, iron or lead, or stone,
But, woe to ruin! violent lust leaves none.   210
BRACHIANO
What value is this jewel?
VITTORIA   'Tis the ornament
Of a weak fortune.
BRACHIANO
In sooth I'll have it; nay I will but change
My jewel for your jewel.
FLAMINEO   Excellent,
His jewel for her jewel; well put in Duke.   215
BRACHIANO
Nay let me see you wear it.
VITTORIA   Here sir.
BRACHIANO
Nay lower, you shall wear my jewel lower.
FLAMINEO
That's better; she must wear his jewel lower.
VITTORIA
To pass away the time I'll tell your Grace

209 *or lead*, Q1 (Q2, Q3, Q4 lead,)
211–18: a series of double entendres connected with 'jewel'
216 *Here* Q2, Q3, Q4 (Q1 Heare)

A dream I had last night.

BRACHIANO   Most wishedly.   220

VITTORIA

A foolish idle dream:
Methought I walk'd about the mid of night,
Into a church-yard, where a goodly yew-tree
Spread her large root in ground; under that yew,
As I sat sadly leaning on a grave,   225
Checkered with cross-sticks, there came stealing in
Your Duchess and my husband; one of them
A pick-axe bore, th'other a rusty spade,
And in rough terms they gan to challenge me,
About this yew.

BRACHIANO   That tree.

VITTORIA   This harmless yew.   230
They told me my intent was to root up
That well-grown yew, and plant i'th' stead of it
A withered blackthorn, and for that they vow'd
To bury me alive: my husband straight
With pick-axe gan to dig, and your fell Duchess   235
With shovel, like a fury, voided out
The earth and scattered bones. Lord how methought
I trembled, and yet for all this terror
I could not pray.

223–30 In Q1 'yew' is written *Eu*, the italics emphasizing the punning
meaning of Vittoria's words.
229 *gan* began
232 *stead of* Q3, Q4 (Q1, Q2 steed of) in the place of; in succession
to (one who has died)
234 *straight* immediately
235 *fell* cruel, ruthless
236 *a fury* Q1 (Q2 a Furie; Q3, Q4 a Fury) see IV.iii, 125, 151 note;
voided out emptied out; cleared out

221–39 For comments on and interpretations of Vittoria's dream see P.
Haworth, *English Hymns and Ballads* ... (Oxford, 1927), pp. 80–81;
F. L. Lucas, *Webster*, i, 213; Lord David Cecil, *Poets and Storytellers*
(1949), pp. 41–43; Gabriele Baldini, *John Webster e il linguaggio della
tragedia* (Rome, 1953), pp. 79–80; Henri Fluchère, *Shakespeare and the
Elizabethans* [translated by Guy Hamilton] (New York, 1956), pp.
112–13; J. R. Brown ed. *The White Devil* (1960), p. 25; R. W. Dent,
John Webster's Borrowing (Berkeley and Los Angeles, 1960), pp. 87–88;
Harold Jenkins, 'The White Devil, edited by J. R. Brown', *Review of
English Studies*, N.S. XII (1961), 292–4.
226 *cross-sticks*. No satisfactory explanation has been given for this. The
cross-sticks may be either wooden crosses stuck in a grave or osiers
which are criss-crossed to protect or bind a grave together. Dent (p. 87)
records a reference in Ben Jonson's *Masque of Queenes* to cross sticks
as one of the devices used by witches to raise storm and tempest.

FLAMINEO   No the devil was in your dream.

VITTORIA

When to my rescue there arose methought   240
A whirlwind, which let fall a massy arm
From that strong plant,
And both were struck dead by that sacred yew
In that base shallow grave that was their due.

FLAMINEO

Excellent devil.   245
She hath taught him in a dream
To make away his Duchess and her husband.

BRACHIANO

Sweetly shall I interpret this your dream:
You are lodged within his arms who shall protect you,
From all the fevers of a jealous husband,   250
From the poor envy of our phlegmatic Duchess;
I'll seat you above law and above scandal,
Give to your thoughts the invention of delight
And the fruition; nor shall government
Divide me from you longer than a care   255
To keep you great: you shall to me at once
Be dukedom, health, wife, children friends and all.

CORNELIA [approaching them]

Woe to light hearts, they still forerun our fall.

FLAMINEO

What fury rais'd thee up? Away, away!   Exit ZANCHE

CORNELIA

What make you here my lord this dead of night?   260
Never dropp'd mildew on a flower here,
Till now.

FLAMINEO   I pray will you go to bed then,
Lest you be blasted?

---

251 *envy* usual meaning; ill-will, malice
254-6 i.e. 'Governing my dukedom shall keep me from you only as
   long as it takes to maintain your great position.'
259 *fury* see IV.iii, 125, 151 note.
263 *blasted* blighted; stricken by a supernatural agency; cursed

---

251 *phlegmatic*. Of the four humours, each characterized by its association
   with one of the four elements, the phlegmatic or watery humour was
   thought to be obvious in a cold temperament. Thus Brachiano may
   here refer to Isabella's 'cold' chastity as well as to her cold personality.
   In either sense she is obviously contrasted with Vittoria.
258ff: see Travis Bogard, *The Tragic Satire of John Webster*, pp. 103–4.

CORNELIA   O that this fair garden,
Had with all poison'd herbs of Thessaly,
At first been planted, made a nursery   265
For witchcraft; rather than a burial plot
For both your honours.
VITTORIA   Dearest mother hear me.
CORNELIA
O thou dost make my brow bend to the earth,
Sooner than nature; see the curse of children:
In life they keep us frequently in tears,   270
And in the cold grave leave us in pale fears.
BRACHIANO
Come, come, I will not hear you.
VITTORIA   Dear my lord.
CORNELIA
Where is thy Duchess now adulterous Duke?
Thou little dream'd'st this night she is come to Rome.
FLAMINEO
How? Come to Rome,—
VITTORIA   The Duchess,—
BRACHIANO   She had been better,—   275
CORNELIA
The lives of princes should like dials move,
Whose regular example is so strong,
They make the times by them go right or wrong.
FLAMINEO
So, have you done?
CORNELIA   Unfortunate Camillo.
VITTORIA
I do protest if any chaste denial,   280
If anything but blood could have allayed
His long suit to me—
CORNELIA   I will join with thee,
To the most woeful end e'er mother kneel'd,
If thou dishonour thus thy husband's bed,
Be thy life short as are the funeral tears   285
In great men's.

264 *with all* Q3, Q4 (Q1, Q2 all)
266 *rather than* Q3, Q4 (Q1, Q2 rather)
270 *frequently* incessantly; repeatedly
271 *leave* Q4 (Q1, Q2, Q3 leaues)
276 *dials* sundials
281 *blood* life-blood; bloodshed; sensual desire: *cf.* V.vi, 237–8.
286 *In great men's.* i.e. 'In great men's lives'

264 *herbs of Thessaly.* Thessaly, a district of Northern Greece, was renowned for poisonous herbs.

BRACHIANO   Fie, fie, the woman's mad.

CORNELIA

Be thy act Judas-like, betray in kissing;
May'st thou be envied during his short breath,
And pitied like a wretch after his death.

VITTORIA

O me accurs'd.   *Exit* VITTORIA   290

FLAMINEO

Are you out of your wits, my lord?
I'll fetch her back again.

BRACHIANO   No I'll to bed.

Send Doctor Julio to me presently.
Uncharitable woman, thy rash tongue
Hath rais'd a fearful and prodigious storm,   295
Be thou the cause of all ensuing harm.   *Exit* BRACHIANO

FLAMINEO

Now, you that stand so much upon your honour,
Is this a fitting time o' night think you,
To send a duke home without e'er a man?
I would fain know where lies the mass of wealth   300
Which you have hoarded for my maintenance,
That I may bear my beard out of the level
Of my lord's stirrup.

CORNELIA   What? Because we are poor
Shall we be vicious?

FLAMINEO   Pray what means have you
To keep me from the galleys, or the gallows?   305
My father prov'd himself a gentleman,
Sold all's land, and like a fortunate fellow,
Died ere the money was spent. You brought me up,
At Padua I confess, where, I protest,
For want of means, (the university judge me,)   310

289 *his death* Q2, Q3, Q4 (Q1 this death)
293 *presently* immediately
295 *prodigious* ominous; monstrous
302–303 i.e. 'that I may become one of his mounted attendants instead
    of one who has to walk on foot beside his horse.'
304 *means* methods; financial means
307 *all's* all his
308 *brought me up* educated me

282–9 For the significance of this curse, see M. C. Bradbrook, 'Two
    Notes upon Webster', *Modern Language Review*, XLII (1947), 282–3.
    Cornelia later prays for Brachiano's forgiveness: V.ii, 52–55.
298–9 In the real story, Vittoria's husband Francesco Peretti set out with
    only a single torchbearer to keep the assignation which proved to be
    for his death.

I have been fain to heel my tutor's stockings
At least seven years. Conspiring with a beard
Made me a graduate, then to this Duke's service;
I visited the court, whence I return'd —
More courteous, more lecherous by far,   315
But not a suit the richer; and shall I,
Having a path so open and so free
To my preferment, still retain your milk
In my pale forehead? No, this face of mine
I'll arm and fortify with lusty wine   320
'Gainst shame and blushing.

CORNELIA
O that I ne'er had borne thee, —
FLAMINEO   So would I.
I would the common'st courtezan in Rome
Had been my mother rather than thyself.
Nature is very pitiful to whores   325
To give them but few children, yet those children
Plurality of fathers; they are sure
They shall not want. Go, go,
Complain unto my great lord cardinal,
Yet may be he will justify the act.   330
Lycurgus wond'red much men would provide
Good stallions for their mares, and yet would suffer
Their fair wives to be barren, —
CORNELIA   Misery of miseries.

                                         Exit CORNELIA

FLAMINEO
The Duchess come to court? I like not that;
We are engag'd to mischief and must on.   335
As rivers to find out the ocean
Flow with crook bendings beneath forced banks,

315 *courteous* polite; like a courtier (i.e. in expensive habits)
325–7: see Additional Notes
330 *Yet may* Q1 (Q2, Q3, Q4 It may)
337 *crook* ed. (Q1, Q2 crooke; Q3, Q4 crookt) crooked; *forced*
    artificial

312–13 The source of these lines is Plutarch's *Lycurgus*, 15. Dent comments
       that 'the argument is highly appropriate to both speaker and dramatic
       situation. Flamineo has repeatedly stressed the impotence of Camillo,
       has frequently equated man with the beasts, and is now bitterly attempt-
       ing to "justifie" serving as pander.' (p. 89)
331–3 Flamineo may mean either that the passing of his youth towards
       maturity rather than academic study or attainment, made him a grad-
       uate; or that his degree was obtained by corrupt conspiracy with an
       older member of the university.

Or as we see, to aspire some mountain's top
The way ascends not straight, but imitates
The subtle foldings of a winter's snake,   340
So who knows policy and her true aspect,
Shall find her ways winding and indirect.   *Exit*

[Act II, Scene i]

Enter FRANCISCO DE MEDICI, *Cardinal* MONTICELSO,
MARCELLO, ISABELLA, *young* GIOVANNI, *with little* JAQUES
the Moor

FRANCISCO
Have you not seen your husband since you arrived?
ISABELLA
Not yet sir.
FRANCISCO   Surely he is wondrous kind.
If I had such a dove house as Camillo's
I would set fire on't, were't but to destroy
The pole-cats that haunt to't, – – – my sweet cousin.   5
GIOVANNI
Lord uncle you did promise me a horse
And armour.
FRANCISCO   That I did my pretty cousin.
Marcello see it fitted.
MARCELLO   My lord, the Duke is here.
FRANCISCO
Sister away, you must not yet be seen.
ISABELLA
I do beseech you   10
Entreat him mildly, let not your rough tongue
Set us at louder variance; all my wrongs
Are freely pardoned, and I do not doubt
As men to try the precious unicorn's horn
Make of the powder a preservative circle   15
And in it put a spider, so these arms

338 *aspire* attain to
340 *winter's snake* ed. (Q1, Q4 Winters snake; Q2, Q3 Winter snake)
S.D. MEDICI ed. (Qq *Medicis*); MONTICELSO Q4 (Q1, Q2 *Mountcelso*;
      Q3 Monu'celso); *little* JAQUES *the Moor* Qq.
  2 *wondrous* Q1 (Q2 wonderfull; Q3, Q4 wonderful)
  3 *such a* Q2, Q4 (Q1 a such; Q3 Iuch a)
  5 *pole-cats* fetid smelling animals, like ferrets; prostitutes; *haunt to't*
      resort to it; *cousin* a term used generally of kinsfolk and often
      applied to nephew or niece

14–18 see Additional Notes

Shall charm his poison, force it to obeying
And keep him chaste from an infected straying.

FRANCISCO
I wish it may. Be gone.   *Exit* [ISABELLA]

Enter BRACHIANO *and* FLAMINEO

Void the chamber.
[*Exeunt* FLAMINEO, MARCELLO, GIOVANNI *and* JAQUES]
You are welcome, will you sit? I pray my lord   20
Be you my orator, my heart's too full;
I'll second you anon.

MONTICELSO   Ere I begin
Let me entreat your Grace forgo all passion
Which may be raised by my free discourse.

BRACHIANO
As silent as i'th' church – you may proceed.   25

MONTICELSO
It is a wonder to your noble friends,
That you that have as 'twere ent'red the world,
With a free sceptre in your able hand,
And have to th'use of nature well applied
High gifts of learning, should in your prime age   30
Neglect your awful throne, for the soft down
Of an insatiate bed. Oh my lord,
The drunkard after all his lavish cups,
Is dry, and then is sober; so at length,
When you awake from this lascivious dream,   35
Repentance then will follow; like the sting
Plac'd in the adder's tail: wretched are princes
When fortune blasteth but a petty flower
Of their unwieldy crowns; or ravisheth
But one pearl from their sceptre: but alas!   40
When they to wilful shipwreck loose good fame

---

18 *infected* poisoned; diseased; immoral
19 *Void* empty, clear
25 *church–you* Lucas, Brown (Q1, Q2, Q3, Sampson: church you;
Q4 church, you)
27 *you that have* ed. (Q1 you have; Q2, Q3, Q4 you having)
29 *And have to* Qq
29–30 i.e. 'And have [previously] well applied high gifts of learning
to the ability to use your natural capacity . . .'
31 *awful* commanding profound respect

36–37 Adders were supposed to be able to sting with both mouth and tail.

All princely titles perish with their name.

BRACHIANO

You have said my lord, —

MONTICELSO   Enough to give you taste
How far I am from flattering your greatness?

BRACHIANO

Now you that are his second, what say you?   45
Do not like young hawks fetch a course about;
Your game flies fair and for you, —

FRANCISCO   Do not fear it:
I'll answer you in your own hawking phrase.
Some eagles that should gaze upon the sun
Seldom soar high, but take their lustful ease   50
Since they from dunghill birds their prey can seize.
You know Vittoria?

BRACHIANO   Yes.

FRANCISCO   You shift your shirt there
When you retire from tennis.

BRACHIANO   Happily.

FRANCISCO

Her husband is lord of a poor fortune
Yet she wears cloth of tissue, —

BRACHIANO   What of this?   55
Will you urge that my good lord cardinal
As part of her confession at next shrift,
And know from whence it sails?

FRANCISCO   She is your strumpet, —

BRACHIANO

Uncivil sir there's hemlock in thy breath
And that black slander; were she a whore of mine   60
All thy loud cannons, and thy borrowed Switzers
Thy galleys, nor thy sworn confederates
Durst not supplant her.

FRANCISCO   Let's not talk on thunder.

42 *name* i.e. good name, reputation
46 *fetch a course about* turn tail, refusing to fly to the mark; *about*;
     Q4 (Q1, Q2 about   ; Q3 about,)
52 *shift* change
53 *Happily* Q3 (Q1, Q2 Happely; Q4 Haply) haply, perhaps
54 *lord of* Qq
55 *cloth of tissue* expensive material into which gold or silver was
     often woven
56 *urge* press by inquiry or statement   57 *shrift* confession
61 *Switzers* Swiss mercenary soldiers: cf. *The Duchess of Malfi*, II.
     ii, 35–58.
63 *supplant her* trip her up, cause her to fall from her position
     talk on Q1, Q2, Q3 (Q4 talk of) talk about

Thou hast a wife, our sister; would I had given
Both her white hands to death, bound and lock'd fast   65
In her last winding-sheet, when I gave thee
But one.

BRACHIANO Thou hadst given a soul to God then.

FRANCISCO   True:
Thy ghostly father with all's absolution,
Shall ne'er do so by thee.

BRACHIANO   Spit thy poison,—

FRANCISCO
I shall not need, lust carries her sharp whip   70
At her own girdle; look to't for our anger
Is making thunder-bolts.

BRACHIANO   Thunder? in faith,
They are but crackers.

FRANCISCO   We'll end this with the cannon.

BRACHIANO
Thou'lt get nought by it but iron in thy wounds,
And gunpowder in thy nostrils.

FRANCISCO   Better that   75
Than change perfumes for plasters,—

BRACHIANO   Pity on thee,
'Twere good you'ld show your slaves or men condemn'd
Your new-plough'd forehead. Defiance!—and I'll meet thee,
Even in a thicket of thy ablest men.

MONTICELSO
My lords, you shall not word it any further   80
Without a milder limit.

FRANCISCO   Willingly.

BRACHIANO
Have you proclaimed a triumph that you bait
A lion thus?

68 *ghostly* spiritual
73 *crackers* fireworks that explode with a sharp report; ?boasts or
   lies (Brown)
76 *change perfumes for plasters* change indulgence for its results:
   disease
79 *thicket* closely packed group
80 *lords* Q1 (Q2, Q3, Q4 lord); *word it* talk excessively or violently

---

67 *Thou hadst given a soul to God then.* Lucas wondered if this were a
   momentary admission of Isabella's goodness or a sneer at the saintliness
   of one who would have made a fitter bride for Christ (i.e. as a nun) than
   for Brachiano. In support of the latter suggestion Lucas compares the
   sentiment with Gloucester's gibe at the expense of the dead Henry VI
   in Shakespeare's *Richard III*, I.ii, 105. See Lucas, *Webster*, i, 215–16.

MONTICELSO   My lord.
BRACHIANO   I am tame, I am tame sir.
FRANCISCO
We send unto the Duke for conference
'Bout levies 'gainst the pirates; my lord Duke   85
Is not at home; we come ourself in person,
Still my lord Duke is busied; but we fear
When Tiber to each prowling passenger
Discovers flocks of wild ducks, then my lord
('Bout moulting time I mean,) we shall be certain   90
To find you sure enough and speak with you.
BRACHIANO   Ha?
FRANCISCO
A mere tale of a tub, my words are idle,
But to express the sonnet by natural reason,
When stags grow melancholic you'll find the season—

Enter GIOVANNI

MONTICELSO
No more my lord; here comes a champion,   95
Shall end the difference between you both,
Your son the prince Giovanni. See my lords
What hopes you store in him; this is a casket
For both your crowns, and should be held like dear:
Now is he apt for knowledge; therefore know   100
It is a more direct and even way
To train to virtue those of princely blood
By examples than by precepts: if by examples
Whom should he rather strive to imitate
Than his own father? Be his pattern then,   105
Leave him a stock of virtue that may last,
Should fortune rend his sails, and split his mast.
BRACHIANO
Your hand boy—growing to a soldier?

88 *prowling* ed. (Qq, Sampson, Lucas: proling; Dodsley ii, Scott:
      prouling)
89 *wild ducks* prostitutes (Lucas)
90 *moulting time* i.e. when the mating season is over; when hair is
      falling through disease: *cf.* I.ii, 29.
92 *tale of a tub* cock-and-bull story; a story that refers to the use of
      the sweating-tub in the treatment of venereal disease
93 Lucas suggests 'to give a commonsense explanation to my rhyme'
95 *champion* i.e. Giovanni, in his new suit of armour
101 *even* straightforward
106 *stock* line of ancestors (i.e. to be proud of); supply
108 *boy—growing . . . soldier?* Q3, Q4 (Q1, Q2 boy growing . . .
      soldier.) *a soldier* Q2, Q3, Q4 (Q1 soldier)

GIOVANNI
Give me a pike.
FRANCISCO
What, practising your pike so young, fair coz?   110
GIOVANNI
Suppose me one of Homer's frogs, my lord,
Tossing my bullrush thus. Pray sir tell me
Might not a child of good discretion
Be leader to an army?
FRANCISCO   Yes cousin, a young prince
Of good discretion might.
GIOVANNI   Say you so?   115
Indeed I have heard 'tis fit a general
Should not endanger his own person oft,
So that he make a noise, when he's a horseback
Like a Dansk drummer. O 'tis excellent!
He need not fight; methinks his horse as well   120
Might lead an army for him; if I live
I'll charge the French foe, in the very front
Of all my troops, the foremost man.
FRANCISCO   What, what,—
GIOVANNI
And will not bid my soldiers up and follow
But bid them follow me.
BRACHIANO   Forward lapwing.   125
He flies with the shell on's head.

113 *discretion* good judgement
115 *discretion* prudence; ability to distinguish what is advisable with
    regard to one's own conduct, i.e. when to lead the army and when
    to follow
119 *Dansk* ed. (Q1 danske; Q2 Danske; Q3 Dantzicke; Q4 Dantzick)
    Danish

---

110 Francisco's question is a double entendre. *Cf.* Eric Partridge, *Shakes-
    peare's Bawdy* (1947), p. 164.
111 *Homer's frogs.* Giovanni is here thinking of *The Battle of Frogs and Mice*
    which was a burlesque epic, attributed to Homer. Brown, p. 38 n.
    indicates that Webster's source seems to have been W. Fowldes' trans-
    lation of 1603 which mentions the tossing of the bulrush 'for a pike or
    spear.'
125 *lapwing* the type of precocity. In 'John Webster: Playwright and
    Naturalist', *Nineteenth Century*, CIII (January, 1928) E. W. Hendy
    pointed out that the lapwing's young are incapable of flying until some
    weeks after they are hatched. Horatio's comment on the lapwing that
    runs away with the shell on his head (*Hamlet*, V.ii, 177) shows Shakes-
    peare's greater ornithological accuracy. 'But Webster's phrase is the
    more telling because of its conscious exaggeration.' Such exaggeration
    was, in fact, part of the Elizabethan view of the precocity of the lapwing.

FRANCISCO   Pretty cousin.
GIOVANNI
 The first year uncle that I go to war
 All prisoners that I take I will set free
 Without their ransome.
FRANCISCO   Ha, without their ransome?
 How then will you reward your soldiers   130
 That took those prisoners for you?
GIOVANNI   Thus my lord:
 I'll marry them to all the wealthy widows
 That falls that year.
FRANCISCO   Why then the next year following
 You'll have no men to go with you to war.
GIOVANNI
 Why then I'll press the women to the war,   135
 And then the men will follow.
MONTICELSO   Witty prince.
FRANCISCO
 See a good habit makes a child a man,
 Whereas a bad one makes a man a beast:
 Come, you and I are friends.
BRACHIANO   Most wishedly;
 Like bones which broke in sunder and well set 140
 Knit the more strongly.
FRANCISCO [calls offstage] Call Camillo hither.
 You have received the rumour, how Count Lodowick
 Is turn'd a pirate?
BRACHIANO   Yes.
FRANCISCO   We are now preparing
 Some ships to fetch him in.

[Enter ISABELLA]

      Behold your Duchess;
We now will leave you and expect from you   145
Nothing but kind entreaty.
BRACHIANO   You have charm'd me.

---

141 *Camillo* Q1, Q2, Q3 (Q4, Sampson: Isabella)
144 S.D. Q4 adds to end of 146 S.D.; (Q1, Q2, Q3 [omit])

142–3 Although the Italian coast was marauded by pirates at the time of the
 action of the play, none of the documents referring to Count Lodovico
 describe him as one. Before his execution at the age of thirty-four he is
 supposed to have admitted that he personally murdered forty people,
 but the exact details of his life between his banishment and his execution
 are unknown. See Gunnar Boklund, *The Sources of 'The White Devil'*,
 pp. 66–68; 79–80.

Exeunt FR[ANCISCO], MON[TICELSO], GIOV[ANNI]

You are in health we see.

ISABELLA   And above health
To see my lord well.

BRACHIANO   So I wonder much,
What amorous whirlwind hurried you to Rome—

ISABELLA
Devotion my lord.

BRACHIANO   Devotion?   150
Is your soul charg'd with any grievous sin?

ISABELLA
'Tis burdened with too many, and I think
The oft'ner that we cast our reck'nings up,
Our sleeps will be the sounder.

BRACHIANO   Take your chamber.

ISABELLA
Nay my dear lord, I will not have you angry;   155
Doth not my absence from you two months
Merit one kiss?

BRACHIANO   I do not use to kiss.
If that will dispossess your jealousy,
I'll swear it to you.

ISABELLA   O my loved lord,
I do not come to chide; my jealousy?   160
I am to learn what that Italian means;
You are as welcome to these longing arms,
As I to you a virgin.

                    [*She tries to embrace him; he turns away*]

BRACHIANO   O your breath!
Out upon sweetmeats, and continued physic!
The plague is in them.

ISABELLA   You have oft for these two lips   165
Neglected cassia or the natural sweets
Of the spring violet; they are not yet much withered.
My lord I should be merry; these your frowns
Show in a helmet lovely, but on me,
In such a peaceful interview methinks   170
They are too too roughly knit.

156 *two* Q1, Q2 (Q3, Q4 now two)
      months ed. (Qq moneths)
157 *I do not use to* I am not accustomed to
160 *jealousy?* Q2, Q3, Q4 (Q1 jealousy,)
161 *I am to learn* i.e. I am yet to learn; *am to* Q1b (Q1a come to);
      Italian i.e. because Italians were proverbially jealous
166 *cassia* a kind of cinnamon; but also used to refer to a fragrant or
      expensive perfume. *Cf. The Duchess of Malfi*, IV.ii, 212–214.

BRACHIANO   O dissemblance!
Do you bandy factions 'gainst me? Have you learnt
The trick of impudent baseness to complain
Unto your kindred?

-ISABELLA   Never my dear lord.

BRACHIANO
Must I be haunted out, or was't your trick   175
To meet some amorous gallant here in Rome
That must supply our discontinuance?

ISABELLA
I pray sir burst my heart, and in my death
Turn to your ancient pity, though not love.

BRACHIANO
Because your brother is the corpulent Duke,   180
That is the great Duke,—'Sdeath I shall not shortly
Racket away five hundred crowns at tennis,
But it shall rest upon record. I scorn him
Like a shav'd Polack; all his reverent wit
Lies in his wardrobe; he's a discreet fellow   185
When he's made up in his robes of state,—
Your brother the great Duke, because h'as galleys,
And now and then ransacks a Turkish fly-boat,
(Now all the hellish Furies take his soul,)
First made this match,—accursed be the priest   190
That sang the wedding mass, and even my issue.

ISABELLA
O too too far you have curs'd.

BRACHIANO   Your hand I'll kiss:

172 *bandy factions* form leagues (Lucas); *learnt* Q4 (Q1, Q2, Q3 learn't)
175 *was't* Q3, Q4 (Q1, Q2 wast)
177 *supply our discontinuance* make up for [my] absence
179 *ancient* former
181 *great Duke*: Francisco was Grand Duke of Tuscany; *'Sdeath* [By] God's death!
187 *h'as* he has
188 *fly-boat* a pinnace or small fast boat used in the coasting trade
189 *Furies* Q2, Q3, Q4 (Q1 furies): see IV.iii, 125, 151 note.

---

175 *haunted out* Q1, Q2, (Q4 hunted out). Brown points out (p. 42 n.) that though 'to haunt' could mean 'to frequent' or 'to visit' the closest parallel to the meaning here is not found earlier than *c.* 1679, according to *O.E.D.*: 'My ghost shall haunt thee out in every place.' Q4's 'hunted out' may be correct. 'Or, possibly, Webster intended to combine the meanings of both verbs.'
183–4 *I scorn . . . Polack* I scorn him as worthless. In his *Itinerary* (1617) Fynes Moryson reported that the Poles shaved all their heads, except for the hair of the forehead, very close.

This is the latest ceremony of my love,
Henceforth I'll never lie with thee, by this,
This wedding ring: I'll ne'er more lie with thee.   195
And this divorce shall be as truly kept,
As if the judge had doom'd it: fare you well,
Our sleeps are sever'd.
ISABELLA   Forbid it the sweet union
Of all things blessed; why the saints in heaven
Will knit their brows at that.
BRACHIANO   Let not thy love   200
Make thee an unbeliever; this my vow
Shall never on my soul be satisfied
With my repentance: let thy brother rage
Beyond a horrid tempest or sea-fight,
My vow is fixed.
ISABELLA   O my winding sheet,   205
Now shall I need thee shortly. Dear my lord,
Let me hear once more what I would not hear:
Never?
BRACHIANO Never!
ISABELLA
O my unkind lord may your sins find mercy,
As I upon a woeful widowed bed   210
Shall pray for you, if not to turn your eyes
Upon your wretched wife, and hopeful son,
Yet that in time you'll fix them upon heaven.
BRACHIANO
No more; go, go, complain to the great Duke.
ISABELLA
No my dear lord, you shall have present witness   215
How I'll work peace between you; I will make
Myself the author of your cursed vow.
I have some cause to do it, you have none;
Conceal it I beseech you, for the weal
Of both your dukedoms, that you wrought the means   220
Of such a separation; let the fault
Remain with my supposed jealousy,
And think with what a piteous and rent heart
I shall perform this sad ensuing part.

    Enter FRANCISCO, FLAMINEO, MONTICELSO, MARCELLO

193 *latest* last, final
202–3 *satisfied / With* fully discharged by
204 *horrid* frightful   215 *present* immediate
224–5 S.D. MONTICELSO Q4 (Q1, Q2, Q3 *Montcelso*). Qq add *Camillo:*
    an unnecessary duplication.

BRACHIANO
    Well, take your course; my honourable brother!   225
FRANCISCO
    Sister!–this is not well my lord,–why sister!
    She merits not this welcome.
BRACHIANO   Welcome, say?
    She hath given a sharp welcome.
FRANCISCO   Are you foolish?
    Come dry your tears; is this a modest course?
    To better what is nought, to rail, and weep?   230
    Grow to a reconcilement, or by heaven,
    I'll ne'er more deal between you.
ISABELLA   Sir you shall not,
    No though Vittoria upon that condition
    Would become honest.
FRANCISCO   Was your husband loud,
    Since we departed?
ISABELLA   By my life sir no.   235
    I swear by that I do not care to lose.
    Are all these ruins of my former beauty
    Laid out for a whore's triumph?
FRANCISCO   Do you hear?
    Look upon other women, with what patience
    They suffer these slight wrongs, with what justice   240
    They study to requite them; take that course.
ISABELLA
    O that I were a man, or that I had power
    To execute my apprehended wishes,
    I would whip some with scorpions.
FRANCISCO   What? turn'd fury?
ISABELLA
    To dig the strumpet's eyes out, let her lie   245

225 *course*; Q4 (Q1, Q2, Q3 course)
227 *say?* say you?
229 *course?* Q2, Q3, Q4 (Q1 course.)
230 *weep?* ed. (Q1 weepe,   ; Q2 weepe: ; Q3, Q4 weep:)
234 *honest* chaste, virtuous
236 *lose* Q4 (Q1, Q2, Q3 loose)
243 *my apprehended wishes* 'the desires of which I feel the force'
244 *fury* Q1 (Q2, Q3, Q4 Fury): see IV.iii, 225, 251 note.

244 *I would whip some with scorpions*. Isabella here echoes–with the kind of
    slight variation that is typical of Webster's borrowing–the young men's
    advice to Rehoboam in I Kings xii, 11: '. . . my father chastised you
    with whips, but I will chastise you with scorpions.' Webster repeated
    the idea in *The Duchess of Malfi*, II.v, 79–80.

Some twenty months a-dying, to cut off
Her nose and lips, pull out her rotten teeth,
Preserve her flesh like mummia, for trophies
Of my just anger. Hell to my affliction
Is mere snow-water: by your favour sir, —   250
Brother draw near, and my lord cardinal, —
Sir let me borrow of you but one kiss,
Henceforth I'll never lie with you, by this,
This wedding-ring.

FRANCISCO   How? ne'er more lie with him?

ISABELLA
And this divorce shall be as truly kept,   255
As if in thronged court, a thousand ears
Had heard it, and a thousand lawyers' hands
Seal'd to the separation.

BRACHIANO
Ne'er lie with me?

ISABELLA   Let not my former dotage
Make thee an unbeliever; this my vow   260
Shall never on my soul be satisfied
With my repentance: *manet alta mente repostum.*

FRANCISCO
Now by my birth you are a foolish, mad,
And jealous woman.

BRACHIANO   You see 'tis not my seeking.

FRANCISCO
Was this your circle of pure unicorn's horn,   265
You said should charm your lord? Now horns upon thee,
For jealousy deserves them; keep your vow,
And take your chamber.

ISABELLA
No sir I'll presently to Padua,
I will not stay a minute.

MONTICELSO   O good madam.   270

---

248 *mummia* Q1 (Q2 Mummie: Q3, Q4 Mummy): see I.i, 16 note.
253–63: see Additional Notes
262 *manet alta mente repostum* Q2, Q3, Q4 (Q1 *manet . . . repositum*):
     'It is treasured up deep in my mind'. Virgil, *Aeneid*, I, 26.

---

266 *horns* i.e. the horns supposedly acquired by the cuckold, the man whose
     wife is unfaithful. Although the cuckold's horns belong to the husband
     Francisco here wishes them on his sister, and thus expresses the hope
     that she may be cursed with the mental agony that they bring with
     them: the misery of jealousy.

BRACHIANO
'Twere best to let her have her humour,
Some half-day's journey will bring down her stomach,
And then she'll turn in post.

FRANCISCO   To see her come
To my lord cardinal for a dispensation
Of her rash vow will beget excellent laughter.   275

ISABELLA
Unkindness do thy office, poor heart break,
Those are the killing griefs which dare not speak.   *Exit*

                    Enter CAMILLO

MARCELLO
Camillo's come my lord.

FRANCISCO   Where's the commission?

MARCELLO
'Tis here.   280

FRANCISCO Give me the signet.

FLAMINEO [*to* BRACHIANO]
My lord do you mark their whispering; I will compound a
medicine out of their two heads, stronger than garlic, deadlier
than stibium; the cantharides which are scarce seen to stick
upon the flesh when they work to the heart, shall not do it   285
with more silence or invisible cunning.

                    Enter Doctor [JULIO]

BRACHIANO
About the murder.

271 *humour* strange disposition, unaccountable frame of mind
272 *bring down her stomach* reduce the swelling caused by hysterical
    passion (the mother): *cf. The Duchess of Malfi*, II.i, 119–20.
273 *turn in post* return in post-haste.
282 [*to* BRACHIANO] ed. i.e. Flamineo and Brachiano walk apart,
    claiming the audience's attention till II.i, 319; *do you mark* pay
    attention to; *whispering*; Q2, Q3 (Q1, Lucas: whispering,   ;
    Q4, Dyce, Sampson, Brown *et al.*: whispering?)
284 *stibium* metallic antimony, used especially as a poison;
    cantharides i.e. cantharis vesicatoria or Spanish fly: see Additional
    Notes

277: *Cf.* the words of Seneca's Phaedra in *Hippolytus*, 607: 'Curae leves
    locuntur, ingentes stupent.' This was frequently repeated as a common
    proverb in the sixteenth and seventeenth centuries.

FLAMINEO

They are sending him to Naples, but I'll send him to Candy;
here's another property too.

BRACHIANO

O the doctor, —   290

FLAMINEO

A poor quack-salving knave, my lord, one that should have
been lash'd for's lechery, but that he confess'd a judgement,
had an execution laid upon him, and so put the whip to a
non plus.

DOCTOR

And was cozen'd, my lord, by an arranter knave than myself,   295
and made pay all the colourable execution.

FLAMINEO

He will shoot pills into a man's guts, shall make them have
more ventages than a cornet or a lamprey; he will poison a
kiss, and was once minded, for his masterpiece, because
Ireland breeds no poison, to have prepared a deadly vapour   300
in a Spaniard's fart that should have poison'd all Dublin.

BRACHIANO

O Saint Anthony's fire!

DOCTOR

Your secretary is merry my lord.

FLAMINEO

O thou cursed antipathy to nature! Look his eye's bloodshed
like a needle a chirurgeon stitcheth a wound with. Let me   305
embrace thee toad, and love thee, O thou abhominable

---

288 *him* i.e. Camillo, commissioned to fight the pirates; *Candy* (literally) Crete; to his death
289 *here's* Q3, Q4 (Q1, Q2 her's); *property* tool; means to an end
291 *quack-salving knave* rascal acting like a quack doctor
295 *cozen'd* cheated; *arranter* more rascally; more good-for-nothing
296 *colourable* pretended, feigned
298 *cornet* musical instrument like an oboe; *lamprey* see Additional
   Notes
299–301: see Additional Notes
303 *secretary*: this meant confidant as well as amanuensis.
304 *eye's* ed. (Qq eyes); *bloodshed* bloodshot   305 *chirurgeon* surgeon
306 *abhominable* Q1, Q2 (Q3, Q4 abominable)

291–4 When convicted and sentenced to whipping for his lechery the doctor
   pretended that he had already been sentenced for debt. He was taken
   into custody, but though he escaped the whipping, another rogue,
   pretending to be the creditor, made him pay according to the supposed
   judgment.
302 *O Saint Anthony's fire!* Dent (p. 96) thinks that this may be slang for
   breaking wind.

loathsome gargarism, that will fetch up lungs, lights, heart,
and liver by scruples.

BRACHIANO
No more; I must employ thee honest doctor,
You must to Padua and by the way,   310
Use some of your skill for us.

DOCTOR   Sir I shall.

BRACHIANO
But for Camillo?

FLAMINEO
He dies this night by such a politic strain,
Men shall suppose him by's own engine slain.
But for your Duchess' death?

DOCTOR   I'll make her sure.   315

BRACHIANO
Small mischiefs are by greater made secure.

FLAMINEO
Remember this you slave; when knaves come to preferment
they rise as gallowses are raised i'th' Low Countries: one
upon another's shoulders.
            Exeunt [BRACHIANO, FLAMINEO *and Doctor* JULIO]

MONTICELSO
Here is an emblem nephew, pray peruse it.   320
'Twas thrown in at your window,—

CAMILLO   At my window?
Here is a stag my lord hath shed his horns,
And for the loss of them the poor beast weeps.
The word *Inopem me copia fecit.*

MONTICELSO   That is:
Plenty of horns hath made him poor of horns.   325

307 *gargarism* gargle
308 *by scruples* in small quantities
311b Q1b (Q1a [omits])
313 *politic strain* cunning compulsion; spraining of a muscle
314 *by's own engine* by his own ingenuity, contrivance
318 *gallowses* gallows-birds
319 *another's* ed. (Q1, Q2 another; Q3, Q4 anothers)
320 *emblem* emblematic picture
324 *word* motto; *Inopem me copia fecit* 'Abundance has left me desti-
      tute': see Additional Notes. *That is*: Q2, Q3 (Q1 That is. ;
      Q4 That is;)

318–19 *they rise . . . shoulders.* Flamineo refers here to improvised gallows
      made by 'placing the condemned man on the shoulders of another man,
      who then steps aside, leaving the person hanging.' (Sampson). *Cf. The
      Duchess of Malfi*, I.i, 66–68.

CAMILLO
  What should this mean?
MONTICELSO   I'll tell you: 'tis given out
  You are a cuckold.
CAMILLO   Is it given out so?
  I had rather such report as that my lord,
  Should keep within doors.
FRANCISCO   Have you any children?
CAMILLO
  None my lord.
FRANCISCO   You are the happier: 330
  I'll tell you a tale.
CAMILLO   Pray my lord.
FRANCISCO   An old tale.
  Upon a time Phoebus the god of light,
  Or him we call the sun, would need be married.
  The gods gave their consent, and Mercury
  Was sent to voice it to the general world.   335
  But what a piteous cry there straight arose
  Amongst smiths, and feltmakers, brewers and cooks,
  Reapers and butter-women, amongst fishmongers
  And thousand other trades, which are annoyed
  By his excessive heat; 'twas lamentable.   340
  They came to Jupiter all in a sweat
  And do forbid the bans; a great fat cook
  Was made their speaker, who entreats of Jove
  That Phoebus might be gelded, for if now
  When there was but one sun, so many men   345
  Were like to perish by his violent heat,
  What should they do if he were married
  And should beget more, and those children
  Make fireworks like their father? So say I,
  Only I will apply it to your wife: 350
  Her issue, should not providence prevent it,
  Would make both nature, time, and man repent it.
MONTICELSO
  Look you cousin,
  Go change the air for shame; see if your absence

327 *Is it* Q1 (Q2, Q3, Q4 It is); *given out* published abroad; sent forth
331 *Pray* i.e. pray do
335 *the general world* the whole world
342 *bans* i.e. of marriage, called in church
343 *speaker* spokesman
349 *fireworks* sparks of fire; created works (i.e. children) of fire
354 *Go change the air* go [and] leave this place

Will blast your cornucopia; Marcello   355
Is chosen with you joint commissioner
For the relieving our Italian coast
From pirates.

MARCELLO   I am much honour'd in't.

CAMILLO   But sir
Ere I return the stag's horns may be sprouted,
Greater than these are shed.

MONTICELSO   Do not fear it,   360
I'll be your ranger.

CAMILLO   You must watch i'th' nights,
Then's the most danger.

FRANCISCO   Farewell good Marcello.
All the best fortunes of a soldier's wish
Bring you o' ship-board.

CAMILLO
Were I not best now I am turn'd soldier,   365
Ere that I leave my wife, sell all she hath
And then take leave of her.

MONTICELSO   I expect good from you,
Your parting is so merry.

CAMILLO
Merry my lord, o'th' captain's humour right;
I am resolved to be drunk this night.   370
                    Exit [CAMILLO; *with* MARCELLO]

FRANCISCO
So, 'twas well fitted: now shall we discern
How his wish'd absence will give violent way
To Duke Brachiano's lust,—

MONTICELSO   Why that was it;
To what scorn'd purpose else should we make choice
Of him for a sea-captain, and besides,   375
Count Lodowick which was rumour'd for a pirate,
Is now in Padua.

FRANCISCO   Is't true?

MONTICELSO   Most certain.
I have letters from him, which are suppliant
To work his quick repeal from banishment;
He means to address himself for pension   380

---

355 *blast* blow on perniciously; destroy; *cornucopia* 'horn of plenty',
    i.e. the cuckold's horn: *cf.* II.i, 325.
360 *these are* Q1 (Q2, Q3, Q4 those are) i.e. these [that] are
361 *ranger* game-keeper
365 *turn'd* Qq
369 *lord,* ed. (Q1 Lord,   ; Q2, Q3, Q4 Lord?); *right* exactly

Unto our sister Duchess.

FRANCISCO　　　　　　　　　O 'twas well.
　We shall not want his absence past six days;
　I fain would have the Duke Brachiano run
　Into notorious scandal, for there's nought
　In such curs'd dotage, to repair his name,　　　　　385
　Only the deep sense of some deathless shame.

MONTICELSO
　It may be objected I am dishonourable,
　To play thus with my kinsman, but I answer,
　For my revenge I'd stake a brother's life,
　That being wrong'd durst not avenge himself.　　　　390

FRANCISCO
　Come to observe this strumpet.

MONTICELSO　　　　　　　　Curse of greatness,
　Sure he'll not leave her.

FRANCISCO　　　　　　　　There's small pity in't.
　Like mistletoe on sere elms spent by weather,
　Let him cleave to her and both rot together.　　　　*Exeunt*

[Act II, Scene ii]

Enter BRACHIANO *with one in the habit of a Conjuror*

BRACHIANO
　Now sir I claim your promise; 'tis dead midnight,
　The time prefix'd to show me by your art
　How the intended murder of Camillo,
　And our loathed Duchess grow to action.

CONJUROR
　You have won me by your bounty to a deed　　　　5
　I do not often practise; some there are,
　Which by sophistic tricks, aspire that name

---

392 *pity* cause for pity (Brown)
7 *sophistic* of the nature of sophistry or specious reasoning

---

381 *our sister Duchess.* In *Modern Language Quarterly*, III (1900), 115,
　　W. W. Greg suggested that Webster had confused his Monticelso–the
　　real Cardinal Montalto–with Isabella's brother, the Cardinal de Medici;
　　but Lucas indicated that '*sister* need be no more than a courtesy title.'
　　(*Webster*, i, 222)
383–6 The code of honour taught that, among gentlemen, honour was to
　　be preferred before life. Public dishonour was the thing most feared by
　　gentlemen of the sixteenth and seventeenth centuries. The sense that
　　his dishonour was publicly known should, therefore, make Brachiano
　　return to honourable behaviour and thus repair his reputation.
Act II, Scene ii. This scene takes place in Camillo's house.

Which I would gladly lose, of nigromancer;
As some that use to juggle upon cards,
Seeming to conjure, when indeed they cheat;   10
Others that raise up their confederate spirits,
'Bout windmills, and endanger their own necks,
For making of a squib; and some there are
Will keep a curtal to show juggling tricks
And give out 'tis a spirit: besides these   15
Such a whole ream of almanac-makers, figure-flingers,
Fellows indeed that only live by stealth,
Since they do merely lie about stol'n goods,
They'd make men think the devil were fast and loose,
With speaking fustian Latin. Pray sit down,   20
Put on this night-cap sir, 'tis charm'd, and now
I'll show you by my strong-commanding art
The circumstance that breaks your Duchess' heart.

A DUMB SHOW

Enter suspiciously, JULIO *and* CHRISTOPHERO; *they draw a curtain where* BRACHIANO's *picture is, they put on spectacles of glass which cover their eyes and noses, and then burn perfumes afore the picture, and wash the lips of the picture; that done, quenching the fire, and putting off their spectacles they depart laughing.*

---

8 *lose* Q4 (Q1, Q2, Q3 loose)   12 *windmills* fanciful schemes or projects
16 *ream* ream of paper; realm; *figure-flingers* those who cast figures or
    horoscopes
20 *fustian* gibberish, bombastic: *cf.* III.ii, 46 note.
DUMB SHOW: see Additional Notes; BRACHIANO's Q4 (Q1, Q2, Q3
    Brachian's); *spectacles of glass* Q1b (Q1a *spectacles*); *cover* Q1b
    (Q1a *covers*); *noses* Q1b (Q1a *noses, of glass*)

---

8 *nigromancer* necromancer, i.e. one who claims to foretell events by
   communicating with the dead; more generally, a wizard or conjuror.
   The spelling Webster uses here associates the word with the 'black art'
   (Latin *niger*).
14 *curtal* a docked horse. This is a reference to Morocco, a docked bay
   gelding belonging to a travelling showman called Banks and exhibited
   by him from 1595 onwards. Banks had previously trained a white horse
   to perform tricks, but Morocco was famed for the variety of his,
   which ranged from dancing and counting money to showing appropriate
   reactions to the names of Queen Elizabeth and the King of Spain. It
   was commonly believed that Banks possessed magic powers and that
   Morocco was his familiar.
18 On the casting of horoscopes to find stolen goods, see Johnstone Parr,
   *Tamburlaine's Malady and Other Essays on Astrology in Elizabethan
   Drama* (Alabama, 1953), pp. 101–6.
19 Originally *fast and loose* was the name of a cheating game in which the
   person being gulled was invited to say whether a belt, handkerchief or
   string was knotted (i.e. fast) or loose. Either answer would be the
   wrong one.

Enter ISABELLA *in her nightgown as to bedward, with lights
after her, Count* LODOVICO, GIOVANNI, GUID-ANTONIO *and
others waiting on her; she kneels down as to prayers, then draws
the curtain of the picture, does three reverences to it, and kisses it
thrice, she faints and will not suffer them to come near it, dies;
sorrow express'd in* GIOVANNI *and in Count* LODOVICO; *she's
convey'd out solemnly.*

BRACHIANO
Excellent, then she's dead,—
CONJUROR   She's poisoned,
By the fum'd picture: 'twas her custom nightly,   25
Before she went to bed, to go and visit
Your picture, and to feed her eyes and lips
On the dead shadow; Doctor Julio
Observing this, infects it with an oil   30
And other poison'd stuff, which presently
Did suffocate her spirits.
BRACHIANO   Methought I saw
Count Lodowick there.
CONJUROR   He was, and by my art
I find he did most passionately dote
Upon your Duchess. Now turn another way,
And view Camillo's far more politic fate: 35
Strike louder music from this charmed ground,
To yield, as fits the act, a tragic sound.

THE SECOND DUMB SHOW

Enter FLAMINEO, MARCELLO, CAMILLO *with four more as Captains,
they drink healths and dance; a vaulting-horse is brought into the
room,* MARCELLO *and two more whisper'd out of the room, while*
FLAMINEO *and* CAMILLO *strip themselves into their shirts, as to
vault; compliment who shall begin, as* CAMILLO *is about to vault,*
FLAMINEO *pitcheth him upon his neck, and with the help of the*

    with lights Q1b (Q1a *lighs*)
35 *politic* cunning, contrived; *fate* Q4 (Q1, Q2, Q3 face)
SECOND DUMB SHOW: *whisper'd out of* signalled to leave, by whispers;
    compliment Q1 (Q2, Q3, Q4 *they compliment*)

DUMB SHOW: *sorrow express'd.* This 'probably meant that they tore their
    hair and wrung their hands'. (M. C. Bradbrook, *Themes and Conventions
    of Elizabethan Tragedy*, p. 28.)
SECOND DUMB SHOW: *a vaulting-horse.* In *John Webster e il linguaggio della
    tragedia* (Rome, 1953), pp. 291–2 Gabriele Baldini suggested that
    Webster might have misunderstood the original story and turned the
    place of Francesco Peretti's assassination, Montecavallo, into the means
    of his death. Brown points out that a 'curious and cumbersome means
    of murder was just what Webster required.' (p. 57 n.) He may have
    altered his source wittingly.

rest, writhes his neck about, seems to see if it be broke, and lays
him folded double as 'twere under the horse, makes shows to call
for help, MARCELLO *comes in, laments, sends for the Cardinal and*
Duke, who comes forth with armed men, wonder at the act;
commands the body to be carried home, apprehends FLAMINEO,
MARCELLO, *and the rest, and go as 'twere to apprehend* VITTORIA.

BRACHIANO
  'Twas quaintly done, but yet each circumstance
  I taste not fully.
CONJUROR   O 'twas most apparent,
  You saw them enter charged with their deep healths   40
  To their boon voyage, and to second that,
  Flamineo calls to have a vaulting-horse
  Maintain their sport. The virtuous Marcello
  Is innocently plotted forth the room,
  Whilst your eye saw the rest, and can inform you   45
  The engine of all.
BRACHIANO
  It seems Marcello, and Flamineo
  Are both committed.
CONJUROR   Yes, you saw them guarded,
  And now they are come with purpose to apprehend
  Your mistress, fair Vittoria; we are now   50
  Beneath her roof: 'twere fit we instantly
  Make out by some back postern.
BRACHIANO   Noble friend,
  You bind me ever to you; this shall stand
  As the firm seal annexed to my hand
  It shall enforce a payment.
CONJUROR   Sir I thank you.   *Exit* BRACHIANO   55
  Both flowers and weeds spring when the sun is warm,
  As great men do great good, or else great harm.
                         Exit CONJUROR

SECOND DUMB SHOW: *the Cardinal* i.e. Monticelso; *Duke* i.e. Francisco;
  commands . . . go i.e. Francisco commands and they go
38 *quaintly* ingeniously   40 *charged* loaded, filled
41 *boon voyage* 'bon voyage'   44 *plotted forth* sent out by contrivance
46 *engine* skill in contriving
47 speech-prefix: Q4 *Bra.* (Q1, Q2, Q3 *Mar.*)
53 *this* i.e. this that you have done
54 *annexed to my hand* attached to my signature
55 s.d. Q4 (Q1, Q2, Q3 *Exit Brac.* opposite 1.54)
57 s.d. Q4 (Q1, Q2, Q3 *Exit Con.*)

[Act III, Scene i]

Enter FRANCISCO, *and* MONTICELSO, *their* CHANCELLOR *and*
REGISTER

FRANCISCO
> You have dealt discreetly to obtain the presence
> Of all the grave lieger ambassadors
> To hear Vittoria's trial.
MONTICELSO   'Twas not ill,
> For sir you know we have nought but circumstances
> To charge her with, about her husband's death;   5
> Their approbation therefore to the proofs
> Of her black lust, shall make her infamous
> To all our neighbouring kingdoms. I wonder
> If Brachiano will be here.
FRANCISCO   O fie,
> 'Twere impudence too palpable.   [*Exeunt*]   10

Enter FLAMINEO *and* MARCELLO *guarded, and a* LAWYER

LAWYER
> What, are you in by the week? So—I will try now whether
> thy wit be close prisoner: methinks none should sit upon
> thy sister but old whore-masters,—
FLAMINEO
> Or cuckolds, for your cuckold is your most terrible tickler
> of lechery: whore-masters would serve, for none are judges   15
> at tilting, but those that have been old tilters.
LAWYER
> My lord Duke and she have been very private.
FLAMINEO
> You are a dull ass; 'tis threat'ned they have been very
> public.

---

2 *lieger ambassadors* 'resident ambassadors as contrasted with
  special envoys' (Lucas)
11 *in by the week?* thoroughly caught, ensnared; *week? So—* ed. (Q1
  week, so   ; Q2, Q3 week, so,   ; Q4 week? so,)
12 *sit upon* i.e. in judgement
14 *tickler* castigator; exciter
16 *tilting . . . tilters*: a double entendre
17 *private* intimate; secret
19 *public* unchaste; unconcealed

Act III, Scene i. This scene takes place in a court-room in Rome or in some
  room adjoining the papal consistory.

LAWYER
    If it can be proved they have but kiss'd one another.   20

FLAMINEO
    What then?

LAWYER
    My lord cardinal will ferret them,—

FLAMINEO
    A cardinal I hope will not catch conies.

LAWYER
    For to sow kisses (mark what I say), to sow kisses, is to reap
    lechery, and I am sure a woman that will endure kissing is   25
    half won.

FLAMINEO
    True, her upper part by that rule; if you will win her nether
    part too, you know what follows.

LAWYER
    Hark, the ambassadors are lighted,—

FLAMINEO [*aside*]
    I do put on this feigned garb of mirth   30
    To gull suspicion.

MARCELLO   O my unfortunate sister!
    I would my dagger's point had cleft her heart
    When she first saw Brachiano. You 'tis said,
    Were made his engine, and his stalking-horse
    To undo my sister.

FLAMINEO   I made a kind of path   35
    To her and mine own preferment.

MARCELLO   Your ruin.

FLAMINEO
    Hum! thou art a soldier,
    Followest the great Duke, feedest his victories,
    As witches do their serviceable spirits,
    Even with thy prodigal blood; what hast got?   40

22 *ferret* (literally) to catch rabbits with ferrets; to hunt out; to
    question searchingly
23 *catch conies* (literally) catch rabbits; to cozen fools (usually of
    money)
29 *lighted* alighted from their carriages
31 *gull* Q1, Q4 (Q2, Q3 gall) cheat deceive
32 *dagger's point* ed. (Q1 daggers point; Q2, Q3, Q4 dagger-point).
34 *engine* tool, instrument; *stalking-horse* a person whose agency or
    participation in an action is made use of to prevent suspicion of
    its real design
35 *I made* Q1 (Q2, Q3, Q4 I am)
39 *serviceable* ministering
40 *prodigal* wastefully lavish

But, like the wealth of captains, a poor handful,
Which in thy palm thou bear'st, as men hold water;
Seeking to gripe it fast, the frail reward
Steals through thy fingers.

MARCELLO   Sir,—
FLAMINEO   Thou hast scarce maintenance
To keep thee in fresh chamois.

MARCELLO   Brother!
FLAMINEO   Hear me,—   45
And thus when we have even poured ourselves
Into great fights, for their ambition
Or idle spleen, how shall we find reward,
But as we seldom find the mistletoe
Sacred to physic on the builder oak   50
Without a mandrake by it, so in our quest of gain.
Alas the poorest of their forc'd dislikes
At a limb proffers, but at heart it strikes:
This is lamented doctrine.

MARCELLO   Come, come.
FLAMINEO
When age shall turn thee   55
White as a blooming hawthorn,—

MARCELLO   I'll interrupt you.
For love of virtue bear an honest heart,
And stride over every politic respect,
Which where they most advance they most infect.
Were I your father, as I am your brother,   60
I should not be ambitious to leave you
A better patrimony.

Enter Savoy [Ambassador]

45 *chamois* i.e. the jerkins of chamois which were worn under
   armour
49–51: 'Good is often accompanied by evil, the beneficial mistletoe
   by the deadly mandrake; so too ambition finds poisonous flies in
   its ointment.'
50 *physic on* ed.; *builder* used for building
58 *politic respect* consideration of policy

49 *mistletoe.* According to Pliny, the Druids thought mistletoe would heal
   anything. (See Holland's translation of the *Natural History*, Book XVI,
   chapter xliv.)
51 *mandrake* a plant of the genus Mandragora. It has a forked root and thus
   resembles the human form. It was supposed to grow under the gallows,
   to feed on blood (*cf.* III.iii, 110–11) and to shriek when pulled from the
   ground (*cf.* V.vi, 65). Moreover, plucking it would lead to madness.
   (*Cf. The Duchess of Malfi*, II.v, 1–2.)

FLAMINEO   I'll think on't,—
The lord ambassadors.

Here there is a passage of the lieger Ambassadors over the stage
severally. Enter French Ambassador.

LAWYER
O my sprightly Frenchman, do you know him?
He's an admirable tilter.   65

FLAMINEO
I saw him at last tilting; he showed like a pewter candle-
stick fashioned like a man in armour, holding a tilting staff
in his hand, little bigger than a candle of twelve i'th' pound.

LAWYER
O but he's an excellent horseman.

FLAMINEO
A lame one in his lofty tricks; he sleeps o' horseback like a   70
poulter,—

Enter English and Spanish [Ambassadors]

LAWYER
Lo you my Spaniard.

FLAMINEO
He carries his face in's ruff, as I have seen a serving-man
carry glasses in a cypress hat-band, monstrous steady for
fear of breaking. He looks like the claw of a blackbird, first   75
salted and then broiled in a candle.   *Exeunt*

---

63 s.d. *French Ambassador* ed. (Q1, Q2 *French Embassadours;* Q3
     French Embassadors; Q4 *French Embassador*)
65 *tilter: cf.* III.i, 16 note.
66 *showed like* looked like
74 *cypress* cobweb fine lawn or crêpe
76 *broiled* grilled

---

71 *poulter* poulterer. Poulterers went to market so early that they often fell
     asleep on horseback, leaning over the baskets which they carried in front
     of them.

[Act III, Scene ii]

THE ARRAIGNMENT OF VITTORIA

Enter FRANCISCO, MONTICELSO, *the six lieger Ambassadors,*
BRACHIANO, VITTORIA, [ZANCHE, FLAMINEO, MARCELLO,]
LAWYER, *and a guard*

MONTICELSO
    Forbear my lord, here is no place assign'd you,
    The business by his holiness is left
    To our examination.
BRACHIANO   May it thrive with you!
           Lays a rich gown under him
FRANCISCO
    A chair there for his lordship.
BRACHIANO
    Forbear your kindness; an unbidden guest   5
    Should travel as Dutch women go to church:
    Bear their stools with them.
MONTICELSO   At your pleasure sir.
    Stand to the table gentlewomen. Now signior
    Fall to your plea.
LAWYER
    Domine Judex converte oculos in hanc pestem mulierum   10
    corruptissimam.
VITTORIA
    What's he?
FRANCISCO   A lawyer, that pleads against you.
VITTORIA
    Pray my lord, let him speak his usual tongue.
    I'll make no answer else.
FRANCISCO   Why you understand Latin.
VITTORIA
    I do sir, but amongst this auditory   15

S.D. MONTICELSO Q2, Q3, Q4 (Q1 *Montcelso*); VITTORIA, Q4 (Q1,
    Q2, Q3 *Vittoria, Isabella*)
1 *assign'd* Q3, Q4 (Q1, Q2 assing'd)   3 *our* Q1, Q4 (Q2, Q3 your)
6 *travel* Q3, Q4 (Q1, Q2 trauaile)
8 *gentlewomen* Q1, Q2, Q3 (Q4 gentlewoman) i.e. Vittoria and
    Zanche:
10 speech-prefix: Q2, Q3, Q4 *Law.* (Q1 [omits])
10–11: 'Lord Judge, turn your eyes to this plague, the most corrupt
    of women.'

Act III, Scene ii: see Additional Notes.

Which come to hear my cause, the half or more
May be ignorant in't.
MONTICELSO   Go on sir.
VITTORIA   By your favour,
I will not have my accusation clouded
In a strange tongue: all this assembly
Shall hear what you can charge me with.
FRANCISCO   Signior,   20
You need not stand on't much; pray change your language.
MONTICELSO
Oh for God sake: gentlewoman, your credit
Shall be more famous by it.
LAWYER   Well then have at you.
VITTORIA
I am at the mark sir, I'll give aim to you,
And tell you how near you shoot.   25
LAWYER
Most literated judges, please your lordships,
So to connive your judgements to the view
Of this debauch'd and diversivolent woman
Who such a black concatenation
Of mischief hath effected, that to extirp   30
The memory of't, must be the consummation
Of her and her projections—
VITTORIA   What's all this?—
LAWYER
Hold your peace.
Exorbitant sins must have exulceration.
VITTORIA
Surely my lords this lawyer here hath swallowed   35

18 *clouded* made obscure   21 *stand on't* insist on it
22 *credit* reputation
23 *have at you* 'here goes', an expression indicating desire to attack
24 *the mark* i.e. archery; *give aim to* to act as marker at the butts to
    signal where each shot strikes
26 *literated* learned
27 *connive your judgements:* 'This jargon, did it possess any meaning,
    would have exactly the wrong one—"shut your eyes towards".'
    (Lucas)
28 *diversivolent* desiring strife
29 *black concatenation* Q1 (Q2, Q3, Q4 concatenation)
30 *extirp* root out, exterminate
32 *projections* projects
34 *Exorbitant* anomalous, not coming within the intended scope of a
    law; *exculceration* (literally) ulceration; exasperation
35 *lawyer here* Q1 (Q2, Q3, Q4 lawyer)

Some pothecary's bills, or proclamations.
And now the hard and undigestible words
Come up like stones we use give hawks for physic.
Why this is Welsh to Latin.

LAWYER   My lords, the woman
Knows not her tropes nor figures, nor is perfect   40
In the academic derivation
Of grammatical elocution.

FRANCISCO   Sir your pains
Shall be well spared, and your deep eloquence
Be worthily applauded amongst those
Which understand you.

LAWYER   My good lord.

FRANCISCO *speaks this as in scorn*   Sir,   45
Put up your papers in your fustian bag,—
Cry mercy sir, 'tis buckram,—and accept
My notion of your learn'd verbosity.

LAWYER
I most graduatically thank your lordship.
I shall have use for them elsewhere.   50

                                                    [*Exit*]

MONTICELSO
I shall be plainer with you, and paint out
Your follies in more natural red and white
Than that upon your cheek.

VITTORIA   O you mistake.
You raise a blood as noble in this cheek

---

36 *pothecary's* ed.
39 *to Latin* in comparison to Latin
40 *tropes nor figures* Q1 (Q2, Q3, Q4 tropes)
42 *elocution* expression
45 S.D. opposite 46–47 in Qq.
46 *fustian* coarse cloth; bombastic language
47 *Cry mercy* I cry you mercy; *buckram* ed. (Q1, Q2, Q3 buckeram;
   Q4 Buck'ram) coarse linen traditionally used for lawyers' bags
49 *graduatically* in the manner of a graduate

---

36 *Pothecaries' bills* or prescriptions were written in polysyllabic medical
   Latin; *proclamations* i.e. official notices, of which there were many in
   James I's reign, were also 'full of tortuous sentences and long unnecessary words.' (G. B. Harrison).
38 Gervase Markham's *Cheape and Good Husbandry* (1614) tells how to
   dose hawks with stones, 'seven to fifteen fine white pebbles from a
   river.' (Sampson).
40 In rhetoric, *tropes* are figures of speech in which words are used out of
   their literal meaning; *figures* are any of the various 'forms' of expression
   in which words are used out of their ordinary construction.

 As ever was your mother's.   55

MONTICELSO

 I must spare you till proof cry whore to that;
 Observe this creature here my honoured lords,
 A woman of a most prodigious spirit
 In her effected.

VITTORIA Honourable my lord,
 It doth not suit a reverend cardinal   60
 To play the lawyer thus—

MONTICELSO

 Oh your trade instructs your language!
 You see my lords what goodly fruit she seems,
 Yet like those apples travellers report
 To grow where Sodom and Gomorrah stood   65
 I will but touch her and you straight shall see
 She'll fall to soot and ashes.

VITTORIA   Your envenom'd
 Pothecary should do't—

MONTICELSO   I am resolved
 Were there a second paradise to lose
 This devil would betray it.

VITTORIA   O poor charity!   70
 Thou art seldom found in scarlet.

MONTICELSO

 Who knows not how, when several night by night
 Her gates were chok'd with coaches, and her rooms
 Outbrav'd the stars with several kind of lights
 When she did counterfeit a prince's court?   75

---

58 *prodigious* unnatural, monstrous
59 *In her effected* Q1, Q2 (Q3, Q4 [omit]); *Honourable my lord* Q1
 (Q2, Q3 My honourable lord; Q4 My honourable lords)
67-68 *envenom'd / Pothecary* i.e. the lawyer
68 *resolved* convinced
69 *lose* Q4 (Q1, Q2, Q3 loose)
71 *scarlet:* the colour both of the cardinal's vestments and of the
 lawyer's robes
75 *court?* ed.

---

59 *In her effected.* If this reading is correct, 'effected' must mean 'put into
 effect, fulfilled', though there is no evidence in *O.E.D.* to support this.
 If it is wrong, 'In her affected,' as Brown points out (p. 68 n.) offers the
 simplest palaeographical explanation and, moreover, makes good sense
 in its meanings of 'desired' or 'cherished, beloved', which were common
 in the sixteenth and seventeenth centuries.
64-7 Sir John Mandeville was one traveller who elaborated this legend
 which is, apparently, based on Deuteronomy xxxii, 32: 'For their vine
 is of the vine of Sodom, and of the fields of Gomorrah: their grapes are
 grapes of gall, their clusters are bitter: . . .'

In music, banquets and most riotous surfeits
This whore, forsooth, was holy.

VITTORIA   Ha? whore? what's that?

MONTICELSO

Shall I expound whore to you? Sure I shall;
I'll give their perfect character. They are first
Sweetmeats which rot the eater: in man's nostril   80
Poison'd perfumes. They are coz'ning alchemy,
Shipwracks in calmest weather! What are whores?
Cold Russian winters, that appear so barren,
As if that nature had forgot the spring.
They are the true material fire of hell,   85
Worse than those tributes i'th' Low Countries paid,
Exactions upon meat, drink, garments, sleep;
Ay even on man's perdition, his sin.
They are those brittle evidences of law
Which forfeit all a wretched man's estate   90
For leaving out one syllable. What are whores?
They are those flattering bells have all one tune,
At weddings, and at funerals: your rich whores
Are only treasuries by extortion fill'd,
And emptied by curs'd riot. They are worse,   95
Worse than dead bodies, which are begg'd at gallows
And wrought upon by surgeons, to teach man
Wherein he is imperfect. What's a whore?
She's like the guilty counterfeited coin

77 *whore?* Q2, Q3, Q4 (Q1 whore   )
79 *character* character sketch: see Additional Notes
81 *coz'ning alchemy* see Additional Notes
82 *weather!* ed. (Q1, Q2, weather?; Q3 whether?; Q4 weather.)
85 *material fire* fire formed of matter: *cf. The Duchess of Malfi,* V.v. 2
88 *man's perdition* i.e. prostitution   89–91 see Additional Notes,
96 *at gallows* Q1 (Q2, Q3, Q4 at th'gallows)
99 *guilty* Q1 (Q2, Q3, Q4 gilt): 'perhaps with a play on "gilt" '
    (Lucas)

---

77 *what's that?* Lucas (*Webster,* i, 230) supposes that Vittoria means 'what
    is a whore?', rather than 'what's that you say?', her question being 'an
    audacious climax of assumed innocence.' Dent (p. 103) thinks that
    'Vittoria may be shocked, or may be pretending to be shocked, that
    Monticelso actually dares call her "whore".'
86–88 At this time the taxes imposed on commodities 'for belly and back'
    in the Low Countries, and especially the tax on wine, either equalled or
    exceeded the original value of the commodity.
95–99 The reference here is to bodies used by surgeons for instructing
    students in anatomy. Lucas notes that 'the 1540 charter of the Barber-
    Surgeons allowed them four executed felons a year; but doubtless
    others were commonly begged for, by them or by private practitioners.'
    (*Webster,* i, 231)

Which whosoe'er first stamps it brings in trouble   100
All that receive it—

VITTORIA   This character scapes me.

MONTICELSO
You gentlewoman?
Take from all beasts, and from all minerals
Their deadly poison.

VITTORIA   Well what then?

MONTICELSO   I'll tell thee.
I'll find in thee a pothecary's shop   105
To sample them all.

FRENCH AMBASSADOR   She hath liv'd ill.

ENGLISH AMBASSADOR
True, but the cardinal's too bitter.

MONTICELSO
You know what whore is; next the devil, Adult'ry,
Enters the devil, Murder.

FRANCISCO   Your unhappy
Husband is dead.

VITTORIA   O he's a happy husband   110
Now he owes nature nothing.

FRANCISCO
And by a vaulting engine.

MONTICELSO   An active plot.
He jump'd into his grave.

FRANCISCO   What a prodigy was't,
That from some two yards' height a slender man
Should break his neck?

MONTICELSO   I'th'rushes.

FRANCISCO   And what's more,   115
Upon the instant lose all use of speech,
All vital motion, like a man had lain
Wound up three days. Now mark each circumstance.

MONTICELSO
And look upon this creature was his wife.

100 *brings* Q2, Q3, Q4 (Q1 bring)
101 *scapes* escapes, eludes
111: i.e. 'He has paid his debt to nature.'
112 *vaulting-engine* instrument for vaulting, i.e. vaulting-horse.
114 *height* Q1 (Q2, Q3, Q4 high)
116 *lose* Q4 (Q1, Q2, Q3 loose)
118 *Wound up* i.e. in his shroud

---

115 Monticelso's words imply that the rushes, commonly used as floor
covering at this time, must have been thickly strewn.

She comes not like a widow: she comes arm'd   120
With scorn and impudence. Is this a mourning habit?
VITTORIA
Had I foreknown his death as you suggest,   *according to the*
I would have bespoke my mourning.   *custom in*
MONTICELSO   O you are cunning.   *corrupted society*
VITTORIA
You shame your wit and judgement
To call it so. What, is my just defence   125
By him that is my judge call'd impudence?
Let me appeal then from this Christian court
To the uncivil Tartar.
MONTICELSO   See my lords,
She scandals our proceedings.
VITTORIA   Humbly thus,
Thus low, to the most worthy and respected   130
Lieger ambassadors, my modesty
And womanhood I tender; but withal
So entangled in a cursed accusation
That my defence of force like Perseus,
Must personate masculine virtue to the point.   135
Find me but guilty, sever head from body: *quick*
We'll part good friends: I scorn to hold my life   *death*
At yours or any man's entreaty, sir.   *without*
ENGLISH AMBASSADOR   *spiritual*
She hath a brave spirit—   *agony*
MONTICELSO   Well, well, such counterfeit jewels
Make true ones oft suspected.
VITTORIA   You are deceived.   140
For know that all your strict-combined heads,
Which strike against this mine of diamonds,
Shall prove but glassen hammers, they shall break;
These are but feigned shadows of my evils.

129 *scandals* disgraces
134 *of force* perforce, of necessity
135 *to the point* in every detail
141 *strict-combined* i.e. closely (possibly secretly) allied; *heads* military
     forces; hammer-heads (Brown)
143 *glassen* glazen; made of glass

128 *the uncivil Tartar.* For an account of the popular Elizabethan image of
     Tartars, see R. R. Cawley, *The Voyagers and Elizabethan Drama* (Boston
     and London, 1938), pp. 188–207.
134 *Perseus* Qq. (Hazlitt, Sampson, Wheeler: Portia's) In Jonson's *Masque
     of Queenes* (1609) Perseus was presented as expressing heroic and mas-
     culine virtue. There is no need to amend the reading of Qq.

Terrify babes, my lord, with painted devils,   145
I am past such needless palsy; for your names
Of whore and murd'ress, they proceed from you,
As if a man should spit against the wind,
The filth returns in's face.

MONTICELSO
Pray you mistress satisfy me one question: 150
Who lodg'd beneath your roof that fatal night
Your husband brake his neck?

BRACHIANO   That question
Enforceth me break silence: I was there.

MONTICELSO
Your business?

BRACHIANO   Why I came to comfort her,
And take some course for sett'ling her estate,   155
Because I heard her husband was in debt
To you my lord.

MONTICELSO   He was.

BRACHIANO   And 'twas strangely fear'd
That you would cozen her.

MONTICELSO   Who made you overseer?

BRACHIANO
Why my charity, my charity, which should flow
From every generous and noble spirit,   160
To orphans and to widows.

MONTICELSO   Your lust.

BRACHIANO
Cowardly dogs bark loudest. Sirrah priest,
I'll talk with you hereafter,——Do you hear?
The sword you frame of such an excellent temper,
I'll sheathe in your own bowels: 165
There are a number of thy coat resemble
Your common post-boys.

MONTICELSO   Ha?

BRACHIANO   Your mercenary post-boys;
Your letters carry truth, but 'tis your guise

146 *needless palsy* unnecessary, useless shaking
150 *satisfy me one question* answer one question fully for me
164 *sword* i.e. of justice; *temper* peculiar degree of hardness and
      elasticity or resiliency imparted to steel by tempering
166 *of thy coat* of thy profession
168 *guise* custom, habit

154–8. F. L. Lucas thinks Brachiano's accusation of Monticelso as de-
      frauding Vittoria and her husband 'is clearly an echo of the grievances
      of the Accoramboni family over her portion.' (*Webster*, i, 87.) *Cf*.
      III.ii, 171–2.

To fill your mouths with gross and impudent lies.
                    [*He makes for the door*]

SERVANT
    My lord your gown.
BRACHIANO   Thou liest, 'twas my stool.   170
    Bestow't upon thy master that will challenge
    The rest o'th' household stuff; for Brachiano
    Was ne'er so beggarly, to take a stool
    Out of another's lodging: let him make
    Valence for his bed on't, or a demi-foot-cloth,   175
    For his most reverent moil; Monticelso,
    Nemo me impune lacessit.   *Exit* BRACHIANO
MONTICELSO
    Your champion's gone.
VITTORIA   The wolf may prey the better.
FRANCISCO
    My lord there's great suspicion of the murder,
    But no sound proof who did it: for my part   180
    I do not think she hath a soul so black
    To act a deed so bloody; if she have,
    As in cold countries husbandmen plant vines,
    And with warm blood manure them, even so
    One summer she will bear unsavoury fruit,   185
    And ere next spring wither both branch and root.
    The act of blood let pass, only descend
    To matter of incontinence.
VITTORIA   I discern poison
    Under your gilded pills.
MONTICELSO
    Now the Duke's gone, I will produce a letter,   190
    Wherein 'twas plotted he and you should meet,
    At an apothecary's summer-house,

171 *challenge* lay claim to
175 *valence* bed curtains; drapes around the canopy; *demi-foot-cloth*
    half-length covering for a horse: *cf.* I.ii, 49 note.
176 *moil* mule
177: 'No one injures me with impunity.'; *lacessit* Q2, Q3, Q4 (Q1
    lacescit)
178 *prey*: 'perhaps with a pun on "pray" ' (Lucas)
189 *gilded*: 'the ordinary medical term, not a metaphor' (Dent); but
    cf. The Duchess of Malfi, IV.i, 19–20.
191 *he* Q3, Q4 (Q1, Q2 her)
192 *summer-house* garden house; arbour

___

183–5 Lucas compared these lines with John Marston's *Sophonisba* (1606),
    II. iii, 35–36:
        Through the rotten'st dung best plants both sprout and live;
        By blood vines grow.   (*Webster*, i, 232.)

Down by the river Tiber:—view't my lords:—
Where after wanton bathing and the heat
Of a lascivious banquet.—I pray read it,   195
I shame to speak the rest.
VITTORIA   Grant I was tempted,
Temptation to lust proves not the act,
Casta est quam nemo rogavit,
You read his hot love to me, but you want
My frosty answer.
MONTICELSO   Frost i'th' dog-days! strange!   200
VITTORIA
Condemn you me for that the Duke did love me?
So may you blame some fair and crystal river
For that some melancholic distracted man,
Hath drown'd himself in't.
MONTICELSO   Truly drown'd indeed.
VITTORIA
Sum up my faults I pray, and you shall find,   205
That beauty and gay clothes, a merry heart,
And a good stomach to a feast, are all,
All the poor crimes that you can charge me with:
In faith my lord you might go pistol flies,
The sport would be more noble.
MONTICELSO   Very good.   210
VITTORIA
But take you your course, it seems you have beggar'd me
                                        first
And now would fain undo me; I have houses,
Jewels, and a poor remnant of crusadoes,
Would those would make you charitable.
MONTICELSO   If the devil
Did ever take good shape behold his picture.   215
VITTORIA
You have one virtue left,
You will not flatter me.
FRANCISCO   Who brought this letter?
VITTORIA
I am not compell'd to tell you.

198: 'She is chaste whom no one has solicited.'
207 *a feast* ed. (Qq feast)
211 *you your* Qq
213 *crusadoes* gold or silver Portuguese coins

---

200 *dog-days* evil or unhealthy times, associated with hot weather when
Sirius, the dog-star, is high in the sky. They were also traditionally
associated with lust.

MONTICELSO
My lord Duke sent to you a thousand ducats,
The twelfth of August.
VITTORIA   'Twas to keep your cousin   220
From prison; I paid use for't.
MONTICELSO   I rather think
'Twas interest for his lust.
VITTORIA
Who says so but yourself? If you be my accuser
Pray cease to be my judge, come from the bench,
Give in your evidence 'gainst me, and let these   225
Be moderators. My lord cardinal,
Were your intelligencing ears as long
As to my thoughts, had you an honest tongue
I would not care though you proclaim'd them all.
MONTICELSO
Go to, go to.   230
After your goodly and vain-glorious banquet,
I'll give you a choke-pear.
VITTORIA   O' your own grafting?
MONTICELSO
You were born in Venice, honourably descended
From the Vitelli; 'twas my cousin's fate,—
Ill may I name the hour—to marry you;   235
He bought you of your father.
VITTORIA   Ha?
MONTICELSO
He spent there in six months

220 *cousin* kinsman, i.e. nephew
221 *use* interest
226 *moderators* arbitrators, judges
227 *intelligencing* for finding out secret information; *long* ed. (Qq
   loving)
228 *As to* i.e. as to reach to
230 *Go to, go to.* i.e. 'Come on, come on.'
232 *choke-pear* rough and unpalatable kind of pear; something difficult to swallow; *grafting*: a double entendre; *cf. The Duchess of
   Malfi*, II.i, 148–9.

223–9 'The fact that Vittoria is given speeches of the wronged Agrippina
   and of Silius is perhaps an indication of Webster's attitude to her at this
   point.' (M. C. Bradbrook, *Themes and Conventions of Elizabethan
   Tragedy*, p. 93). The borrowings are from *Sejanus*, III, 200–201 and II,
   453–7.
233–4. The Vitelli were a famous Roman family, having no connection with
   the Accoramboni. Lucas suggested that, since Lodovico Orsini was
   banished for the murder of Vincenzo Vitelli, Webster may have remembered the name from that. (*Webster*, i, 80, 233)

Twelve thousand ducats, and to my acquaintance
Receiv'd in dowry with you not one julio:
'Twas a hard penny-worth, the ware being so light.   240
I yet but draw the curtain, now to your picture:
You came from thence a most notorious strumpet,
And so you have continued.

VITTORIA   My lord.

MONTICELSO   Nay hear me,
You shall have time to prate. My lord Brachiano,—
Alas I make but repetition,   245
Of what is ordinary and Rialto talk,
And ballated, and would be play'd o'th' stage,
But that vice many times finds such loud friends
That preachers are charm'd silent.
You gentlemen Flamineo and Marcello,   250
The court hath nothing now to charge you with,
Only you must remain upon your sureties
For your appearance.

FRANCISCO   I stand for Marcello.

FLAMINEO
And my lord Duke for me.

MONTICELSO
For you Vittoria, your public fault,   255
Join'd to th' condition of the present time,
Takes from you all the fruits of noble pity.
Such a corrupted trial have you made
Both of your life and beauty, and been styl'd
No less in ominous fate than blazing stars   260
To princes; here's your sentence: you are confin'd

238 *acquaintance* Q1, Q2 (Q3, Q4 knowledge)
239 *julio* coin of Pope Julius II (1503–13), worth about sixpence
240 *light* usual meaning; unchaste
246 *Rialto talk* common gossip
247 *ballated* balladed
252–3 *remain . . . appearance* remain pledged to appear (your sponsors
being liable in the event of your non-appearance)
255 *public* cf. III.i, 19 note.
260 *in* Q1 (Q2, Q3, Q4 an)

247 *play'd o'th' stage. The Late Murder of the Son upon the Mother, or Keep
the Widow Waking* written by Webster, Dekker, Ford and Rowley, which
was performed at the Red Bull theatre in September, 1624 presented on
the stage a notorious murder and the story of fortune-hunters in pursuit
of an intemperate and wealthy old widow. In the second plot actual
incidents which had taken place were repeated on the stage. See C. J.
Sisson, *Lost Plays of Shakespeare's Age* (Cambridge, 1936), pp. 80–124.

Unto a house of convertites and your bawd—
FLAMINEO [*aside*]
Who I?
MONTICELSO The Moor.
FLAMINEO [*aside*]   O I am a sound man again.
VITTORIA
A house of convertites, what's that?
MONTICELSO   A house
Of penitent whores.
VITTORIA   Do the noblemen in Rome   265
Erect it for their wives, that I am sent
To lodge there?
FRANCISCO
You must have patience.
VITTORIA   I must first have vengeance.
I fain would know if you have your salvation
By patent, that you proceed thus.
MONTICELSO   Away with her.   270
Take her hence.
VITTORIA
A rape, a rape!
MONTICELSO   How?
VITTORIA   Yes, you have ravish'd justice,
Forc'd her to do your pleasure.
MONTICELSO   Fie, she's mad—
VITTORIA
Die with those pills in your most cursed maw,
Should bring you health, or while you sit o'th' bench,   275
Let your own spittle choke you.
MONTICELSO   She's turn'd fury.
VITTORIA
That the last day of judgement may so find you,
And leave you the same devil you were before.
Instruct me some good horse-leech to speak treason,
For since you cannot take my life for deeds,   280

262 *Unto a* Q3, Q4 (Q1, Q2 VIT. Unto a); *convertites* Q1 (Q2, Q3,
     Q4 converts); *bawd*— ed. (Q1a, Q2, Q3 baud. ; Q1b baud ; Q4
     bawd.)
264 *convertites* Q1b (Q1a couertites; Q2, Q3, Q4 converts) reformed
     prostitutes
270 *patent* special licence, or title (Brown)
274 *those* Q4 (Q1, Q2, Q3 these); *maw* Q3, Q4 (Q1 mawes; Q2 mawe)
276 *fury* Q1 (Q2, Q3, Q4 Fury)
279 *horse-leech* blood-sucker

267: another borrowing from *Sejanus* (IV. i, 1–2.)

Take it for words. O woman's poor revenge
Which dwells but in the tongue! I will not weep,
No I do scorn to call up one poor tear
To fawn on your injustice; bear me hence,
Unto this house of—what's your mitigating title?   285
MONTICELSO
Of convertites.
VITTORIA
It shall not be a house of convertites.
My mind shall make it honester to me
Than the Pope's palace, and more peaceable
Than thy soul, though thou art a cardinal,   290
Know this, and let it somewhat raise your spite,
Through darkness diamonds spread their richest light.
                    Exit VITTORIA [*with* ZANCHE, *guarded*]

                    Enter BRACHIANO

BRACHIANO
Now you and I are friends sir, we'll shake hands,
In a friend's grave, together: a fit place,
Being the emblem of soft peace t'atone our hatred.   295
FRANCISCO
Sir, what's the matter?
BRACHIANO
I will not chase more blood from that lov'd cheek,
You have lost too much already; fare you well.

                                                         [*Exit*]
FRANCISCO
How strange these words sound? What's the interpretation?
FLAMINEO [*aside*]
Good, this is a preface to the discovery of the Duchess'   300
death. He carries it well. Because now I cannot counterfeit
a whining passion for the death of my lady, I will feign a
mad humour for the disgrace of my sister, and that will
keep off idle questions. Treason's tongue hath a villainous
palsy in't; I will talk to any man, hear no man, and for a   305
time appear a politic madman.

                                                         [*Exit*]

                    Enter GIOVANNI, *Count* LODOVICO

286;287: *convertites* Q1 (Q2, Q3, Q4 converts)
295 *atone* reconcile   304 *hath a* Q1 (Q2, Q3, Q4 with a)
305 *palsy* nervous disease, sometimes characterized by involuntary tremors
306 *politic* cunning

FRANCISCO
  How now my noble cousin; what, in black?

GIOVANNI
  Yes uncle, I was taught to imitate you
  In virtue, and you must imitate me
  In colours for your garments; my sweet mother   310
  Is, —

FRANCISCO How? Where?

GIOVANNI
  Is there, no yonder; indeed sir I'll not tell you,
  For I shall make you weep.

FRANCISCO
  Is dead.

GIOVANNI Do not blame me now,   315
  I did not tell you so.

LODOVICO   She's dead my lord.

FRANCISCO
  Dead?

MONTICELSO
  Blessed lady; thou art now above thy woes.
  Wilt please your lordships to withdraw a little?

                              [*Exeunt* AMBASSADORS]

GIOVANNI
  What do the dead do, uncle? Do they eat,   320
  Hear music, go a-hunting, and be merry,
  As we that live?

FRANCISCO
  No coz; they sleep.

GIOVANNI   Lord, Lord, that I were dead, —
  I have not slept these six nights. When do they wake?

FRANCISCO
  When God shall please.

GIOVANNI   Good God let her sleep ever. 325
  For I have known her wake an hundred nights,
  When all the pillow, where she laid her head,
  Was brine-wet with her tears. I am to complain to you sir.
  I'll tell you how they have used her now she's dead:
  They wrapp'd her in a cruel fold of lead,   330
  And would not let me kiss her.

FRANCISCO   Thou didst love her.

---

325 speech-prefix: Q3, Q4 (Q1, Q2 [misplace at 326])
326 *hundred* Q4 (Q1, Q2, Q3 hundreth)
330 *fold* wrapping; layer
331 *love her.* Qq (Lucas: love her?)

GIOVANNI
   I have often heard her say she gave me suck,
   And it should seem by that she dearly lov'd me,
   Since princes seldom do it.

FRANCISCO
   O, all of my poor sister that remains!   335
   Take him away for God's sake.

                       [*Exit* GIOVANNI, *attended*]

MONTICELSO   How now my lord?

FRANCISCO
   Believe me I am nothing but her grave,
   And I shall keep her blessed memory
   Longer than thousand epitaphs.

                            [*Exeunt*]

[Act III, Scene iii]

Enter FLAMINEO *as distracted* [, MARCELLO *and* LODOVICO]

FLAMINEO
   We endure the strokes like anvils or hard steel,
   Till pain itself make us no pain to feel.
   Who shall do me right now? Is this the end of service?
   I'd rather go weed garlic; travel through France, and
   be mine own ostler; wear sheep-skin linings; or shoes that   5
   stink of blacking; be ent'red into the list of the forty
   thousand pedlars in Poland.   *Enter Savoy* [*Ambassador*]
   Would I had rotted in some surgeon's house at Venice,
   built upon the pox as well as on piles, ere I had serv'd
   Brachiano.   10

SAVOY AMBASSADOR
   You must have comfort.

FLAMINEO
   Your comfortable words are like honey. They relish well in
   your mouth that's whole; but in mine that's wounded they

---

  4 *travel* Q3, Q4 (Q1, Q2 trauaile)
  5 *linings* drawers; leather breeches; *shoes* Q4 (Q1, Q2, Q3 shoos)
  6 *list* roll
  9 *built upon the pox* financially established on fees taken for curing
     venereal disease; *piles* wooden supports; haemorrhoids

Act III, Scene iii. This scene is located in the ante-chamber of the Pope's
    palace, adjoining the court room.
  7 *pedlars in Poland.* In the seventeenth century the Poles were, apparently,
    proverbially poor and there were many pedlars in the country.

go down as if the sting of the bee were in them. Oh they
have wrought their purpose cunningly, as if they would not   15
seem to do it of malice. In this a politician imitates the
devil, as the devil imitates a cannon. Wheresoever he comes
to do mischief, he comes with his backside towards you.

Enter the French [Ambassador]

FRENCH AMBASSADOR

The proofs are evident.

FLAMINEO

Proof! 'twas corruption. O gold, what a god art thou! and   20
O man, what a devil art thou to be tempted by that cursed
mineral! Yon diversivolent lawyer; mark him; knaves turn
informers, as maggots turn to flies; you may catch gudgeons
with either. A cardinal;–I would he would hear me,–there's
nothing so holy but money will corrupt and putrify it, like   25
victual under the line.   *Enter English Ambassador*
You are happy in England, my lord; here they sell justice
with those weights they press men to death with. O horrible
salary!

ENGLISH AMBASSADOR

Fie, fie, Flamineo.   30

FLAMINEO

Bells ne'er ring well, till they are at their full pitch, and I
hope yon cardinal shall never have the grace to pray well,
till he come to the scaffold.   *[Exeunt Ambassadors]*
If they were rack'd now to know the confederacy! But your
noblemen are privileged from the rack; and well may. For   35
a little thing would pull some of them a' pieces afore they
came to their arraignment. Religion; oh how it is commeddled with policy. The first bloodshed in the world
happened about religion. Would I were a Jew.

16 *politician* crafty and intriguing schemer
22 *Yon* ed.; *diversivolent cf.* III.ii, 28 and note.
23 *gudgeons* small fish; simpletons
26 *victual* ed. (Q1 vittell; Q2, Q3, Q4 victuals); *under the line* at the
   equator
28 see Additional Notes, p. 147.
29 *salary* recompense; reward for services rendered
31 *pitch* height; *and* ed. (Qq And)   32 *grace* God's help
35 *well may* i.e. well they may (should) be
36 *pull . . . a' pieces* i.e. on the rack; in argument
37–38 *commeddled* mixed or mingled together; *policy* intrigue; dissimulation

38–39 *bloodshed . . . religion* i.e. Cain's murder of Abel: see Genesis iv, 3–8.

MARCELLO

O, there are too many.   40

FLAMINEO

You are deceiv'd. There are not Jews enough; priests
enough, nor gentlemen enough.

MARCELLO

How?

FLAMINEO

I'll prove it. For if there were Jews enough, so many
Christians would not turn usurers; if priests enough, one   45
should not have six benefices; and if gentlemen enough, so
many early mushrooms, whose best growth sprang from a
dunghill, should not aspire to gentility. Farewell. Let
others live by begging. Be thou one of them; practise the
art of Wolner in England to swallow all's given thee; and   50
let one purgation make thee as hungry again as fellows that
work in a sawpit. I'll go hear the screech-owl.   *Exit*

LODOVICO [*aside*]

This was Brachiano's pander, and 'tis strange
That in such open and apparent guilt
Of his adulterous sister, he dare utter   55
So scandalous a passion. I must wind him.

Enter FLAMINEO

FLAMINEO [*aside*]

How dares this banish'd count return to Rome,
His pardon not yet purchas'd? I have heard
The deceas'd Duchess gave him pension,
And that he came along from Padua   60
I'th' train of the young prince. There's somewhat in't.
Physicians, that cure poisons, still do work
With counterpoisons.

MARCELLO   Mark this strange encounter.

47 *mushrooms* upstarts
52 *in a* Q2, Q3, Q4 (Q1 in)
56 *wind him* i.e. get wind of his purposes
58 *purchas'd* obtained (not necessarily 'bought')

---

50 *Wolner*, a singing-man of Windsor, was a famous Elizabethan glutton,
renowned for his ability to digest iron, glass, oyster-shells, raw meat and
raw fish, who nevertheless died from eating a raw eel.
51-2 *as hungry again . . . sawpit.* I have been unable to trace the origin of
this phrase; it is not recorded in Tilley's *A Dictionary of the Proverbs in
England in the Sixteenth and Seventeenth Centuries.*

FLAMINEO
  The god of melancholy turn thy gall to poison,
  And let the stigmatic wrinkles in thy face,   65
  Like to the boisterous waves in a rough tide
  One still overtake another.
LODOVICO   I do thank thee
  And I do wish ingeniously for thy sake
  The dog-days all year long.
FLAMINEO   How croaks the raven?
  Is our good Duchess dead?
LODOVICO   Dead.
FLAMINEO   O fate!   70
  Misfortune comes like the crowner's business,
  Huddle upon huddle.
LODOVICO
  Shalt thou and I join housekeeping?
FLAMINEO   Yes, content.
  Let's be unsociably sociable.
LODOVICO
  Sit some three days together, and discourse.   75
FLAMINEO
  Only with making faces;
  Lie in our clothes.
LODOVICO
  With faggots for our pillows.
FLAMINEO   And be lousy.
LODOVICO
  In taffeta linings; that's gentle melancholy;
  Sleep all day.
FLAMINEO   Yes: and like your melancholic hare   80
  Feed after midnight.

      Enter ANTONELLI [*and* GASPARO, *laughing*]

  We are observed: see how yon couple grieve.
LODOVICO
  What a strange creature is a laughing fool,
  As if a man were created to no use
  But only to show his teeth.

---

65 *stigmatic* marked with a 'stigma' or brand; deformed; ill-favoured
68 *ingeniously* usual meaning; also, ingenuously: thus equivocal here.
68–70: i.e. I wish thee 'an eternal season of heat and lust, best
    weather for panders.' (Dent); *cf*. III.ii, 200; *raven* bird of ill omen
72 *Huddle upon huddle* in heaps, piling up
79 *taffata linings* drawers or underclothes made of taffeta, which was
    supposed to be louse-proof

FLAMINEO   I'll tell thee what,   85
 It would do well instead of looking-glasses
 To set one's face each morning by a saucer
 Of a witch's congealed blood.
LODOVICO   Precious girn, rogue.
 We'll never part.
FLAMINEO   Never: till the beggary of courtiers,
 The discontent of churchmen, want of soldiers,   90
 And all the creatures that hang manacled,
 Worse than strappado'd, on the lowest felly
 Of Fortune's wheel be taught in our two lives
 To scorn that world which life of means deprives.
ANTONELLI
 My lord I bring good news. The Pope on's death-bed,   95
 At th'earnest suit of the great Duke of Florence,
 Hath sign'd your pardon, and restor'd unto you—
LODOVICO
 I thank you for your news. Look up again
 Flamineo, see my pardon.
FLAMINEO   Why do you laugh?
 There was no such condition in our covenant.
LODOVICO   Why?   100
FLAMINEO
 You shall not seem a happier man than I;
 You know our vow sir, if you will be merry,
 Do it i'th' like posture, as if some great man
 Sat while his enemy were executed:
 Though it be very lechery unto thee,   105
 Do't with a crabbed politician's face.
LODOVICO
 Your sister is a damnable whore.
FLAMINEO   Ha?
LODOVICO
 Look you; I spake that laughing.

---

87 *saucer* a technical term in surgery (Lucas)
88 *girn, rogue* ed.; *girn* a snarl, growl, the act of showing the teeth
 in a disagreeable way (Wright, *English Dialect Dictionary*)
92 *strappado'd* hung up by the hands, which have been tied across
 the back; *felly* felloe or section of the rim of a wheel
106 *crabbed* Q1 (Q2, Q3, Q4 sabby)

---

93 *Fortune's wheel.* The goddess Fortune was supposed to turn a wheel
 upon which men would be raised to the highest 'felly' and then allowed
 to sink again to the lowest. Flamineo here also refers to the torturing
 wheel: *cf.* V.vi, 292.

FLAMINEO
  Dost ever think to speak again?
LODOVICO   Do you hear?
  Wilt sell me forty ounces of her blood,   110
  To water a mandrake?
FLAMINEO   Poor lord, you did vow
  To live a lousy creature.
LODOVICO   Yes;—
FLAMINEO   Like one
  That had for ever forfeited the daylight,
  By being in debt,—
LODOVICO   Ha, ha!
FLAMINEO
  I do not greatly wonder you do break: 115
  Your lordship learn't long since. But I'll tell you,—
LODOVICO
  What?
FLAMINEO And't shall stick by you.
LODOVICO   I long for it.
FLAMINEO
  This laughter scurvily becomes your face;
  If you will not be melancholy, be angry.   *Strikes him*
  See, now I laugh too.   120
MARCELLO
  You are to blame, I'll force you hence.
LODOVICO   Unhand me.
                         Exit MAR[CELLO] & FLAM[INEO]
  That e'er I should be forc'd to right myself,
  Upon a pander!
ANTONELLI   My lord.
LODOVICO
  H'had been as good meet with his fist a thunderbolt.
GASPARO
  How this shows!
LODOVICO   Ud's death, how did my sword miss him?   125
  These rogues that are most weary of their lives,
  Still scape the greatest dangers.
  A pox upon him: all his reputation;—
  Nay all the goodness of his family;—
  Is not worth half this earthquake.   130

111 *mandrake*: cf. III.i, 51 note.
115 *break* break your oath; go bankrupt
116 *learn't* Q1, Q2, Q3 (Q4 learnt) i.e. learnt it
124 *H'had* he had
127 *dangers.* Q2, Q3, Q4 (Q1 dangers,)

I learnt it of no fencer to shake thus;
Come, I'll forget him, and go drink some wine.   *Exeunt*

[Act IV, Scene i]

Enter FRANCISCO *and* MONTICELSO

MONTICELSO
Come, come my lord, untie your folded thoughts,
And let them dangle loose as a bride's hair.
Your sister's poisoned.
FRANCISCO   Far be it from my thoughts
To seek revenge.
MONTICELSO   What, are you turn'd all marble?
FRANCISCO
Shall I defy him, and impose a war   5
Most burthensome on my poor subjects' necks,
Which at my will I have not power to end?
You know; for all the murders, rapes, and thefts,
Committed in the horrid lust of war,
He that unjustly caus'd it first proceed,   10
Shall find it in his grave and in his seed.
MONTICELSO
That's not the course I'd wish you: pray, observe me.
We see that undermining more prevails
Than doth the cannon. Bear your wrongs conceal'd,
And, patient as the tortoise, let this camel   15
Stalk o'er your back unbruis'd: sleep with the lion,
And let this brood of secure foolish mice
Play with your nostrils; till the time be ripe
For th' bloody audit, and the fatal gripe:
Aim like a cunning fowler, close one eye,   20
That you the better may your game espy.
FRANCISCO
Free me my innocence, from treacherous acts:
I know there's thunder yonder: and I'll stand,
Like a safe valley, which low bends the knee
To some aspiring mountain: since I know   25

131 *learnt* Q1, Q4 (Q2, Q3 learn't)
  2 Jacobean brides wore their hair loose.
 12 *observe me* Q1, Q2 (Q3, Q4 observe)
 16 *your back unbruis'd* i.e. 'your back being unbruised'
 19 *audit* day when accounts are presented for inspection
 20 *fowler* one who hunts birds, especially for food

Act IV, *Scene i*. The scene takes place in another room of the pope's palace.

Treason, like spiders weaving nets for flies,
By her foul work is found, and in it dies.
To pass away these thoughts, my honour'd lord,
It is reported you possess a book
Wherein you have quoted, by intelligence,   30
The names of all notorious offenders
Lurking about the city.
MONTICELSO   Sir I do;
And some there are which call it my black book:
Well may the title hold: for though it teach not
The art of conjuring, yet in it lurk   35
The names of many devils.
FRANCISCO   Pray let's see it.
MONTICELSO
I'll fetch it to your lordship.   *Exit* MONTICELSO
FRANCISCO   Monticelso,
I will not trust thee, but in all my plots
I'll rest as jealous as a town besieg'd.
Thou canst not reach what I intend to act;   40
Your flax soon kindles, soon is out again,
But gold slow heats, and long will hot remain.

Enter MONT[ICELSO,] *presents* FRAN[CISCO] *with a book*

MONTICELSO
'Tis here my lord.
FRANCISCO
First your intelligencers, pray let's see.
MONTICELSO
Their number rises strangely,   45
And some of them
You'd take for honest men.
Next are panders.
These are your pirates: and these following leaves,
For base rogues that undo young gentlemen   50
By taking up commodities: for politic bankrupts:
For fellows that are bawds to their own wives,
Only to put off horses and slight jewels,
Clocks, defac'd plate, and such commodities,

30 *by intelligence* by secret information
33 *black book:* originally the term for certain black-bound official
    registers, this came to mean a list of rogues and villians.
35 *The art of conjuring* i.e. the black art: *cf.* II, ii, 8 note.
39 *jealous* vigilant; apprehensive of evil
40 *reach* i.e. mentally
53 *put off* sell away fraudulently

At birth of their first children.

FRANCISCO   Are there such?   55

MONTICELSO
These are for impudent bawds,
That go in men's apparel; for usurers
That share with scriveners for their good reportage:
For lawyers that will antedate their writs:
And some divines you might find folded there,   60
But that I slip them o'er for conscience' sake.
Here is a general catalogue of knaves.
A man might study all the prisons o'er,
Yet never attain this knowledge.

FRANCISCO   Murderers.
Fold down the leaf I pray.   65
Good my lord let me borrow this strange doctrine.

MONTICELSO
Pray us't my lord.

FRANCISCO   I do assure your lordship,
You are a worthy member of the state,
And have done infinite good in your discovery
Of these offenders.

MONTICELSO   Somewhat sir.

FRANCISCO   O God!   70
Better than tribute of wolves paid in England,
'Twill hang their skins o'th' hedge.

MONTICELSO   I must make bold

---

57 *go in* go about in
58 *reportage* repute; recommendation
59 *writs* Q1, Q2 (Q3, Q4 Deeds)
60 *folded* included in the fold; the allusion is to divines as themselves
   spiritual shepherds of the fold
66 *doctrine* collection of information (with punning reference to the
   cardinal's doctrine in the sense of 'religious tenets')

50–55. By *taking up commodities* swindlers would demand a cash repayment
   for goods which they had given the young gentlemen who had asked for
   the loan of money, the goods being grossly exaggerated in value in the
   first instance; *politic bankrupts* were men who cunningly hid their assets
   and then absconded, thus making money out of their pretended 'bank-
   ruptcy'; the third kind of swindlers mentioned would act as bawds to
   their own wives, giving goods – again their value being exaggerated – in
   return for the high price really paid for their services and their silence
   when their wives had borne bastards.
57–58. These usurers would pay scriveners to recommend them to the
   clients who would probably have to borrow money to pay the scriveners
   for writing out lengthy and complicated legal documents.

To leave your lordship.
FRANCISCO   Dearly sir, I thank you;
  If any ask for me at court, report
  You have left me in the company of knaves.   75
                              Exit MONT[ICELSO]
  I gather now by this, some cunning fellow
  That's my lord's officer, one that lately skipp'd
  From a clerk's desk up to a justice' chair,
  Hath made this knavish summons; and intends,
  As th'Irish rebels wont were to sell heads,   80
  So to make prize of these. And thus it happens,
  Your poor rogues pay for't, which have not the means
  To present bribe in fist: the rest o'th' band
  Are raz'd out of the knaves' record; or else
  My lord he winks at them with easy will,   85
  His man grows rich, the knaves are the knaves still.
  But to the use I'll make of it; it shall serve
  To point me out a list of murderers,
  Agents for any villainy. Did I want
  Ten leash of courtezans, it would furnish me;   90
  Nay laundress three armies. That in so little paper
  Should lie th'undoing of so many men!
  'Tis not so big as twenty declarations.
  See the corrupted use some make of books:
  Divinity, wrested by some factious blood,   95
  Draws swords, swells battles, and o'erthrows all good.
  To fashion my revenge more seriously,

77 *one* Q1b (Q1a and)
80 *wont were* Q1 (Q2, Q3, Q4 were wont)
81–82: i.e. 'Thus it happens [that] your poor . . .'
82 *the means* Q1 (Q2, Q3, Q4 means)
88 *list* Q1b (Q1a life)
90 *leash* sporting term for a set of three; *furnish* supply
91 *Nay* Q1, Q2 (Q3, Q4 [omit]); *laundress* supply with laundresses,
   who were reputedly of easy virtue; *in so* Q2, Q3, Q4 (Q1a so;
   Q1b so in)
92 *lie* Q1b (Q1a be)
93 *declarations* official proclamations

---

71 *tribute of wolves.* King Edgar (944–975) is supposed to have exacted
   from the Welsh a tribute of three hundred wolves a year to rid the
   land of ravenous animals. Webster may have found the story in Drayton's
   Polyolbion (1612). The *Dictionary of National Biography* thinks it is
   highly improbable that such a tribute was exacted, but gives its supposed
   date as ?968.
80. On 9th April, 1600 Mountjoy wrote to Cecil: 'I have heard you complain that you could not hear of one head brought in for all the Queen's
   money; but I assure you now the kennels of the streets are full of them.'
   (Quoted by Lucas, *Webster*, i, 238.)

Let me remember my dead sister's face:
Call for her picture: no; I'll close mine eyes,
And in a melancholic thought I'll frame   100

Enter ISABEL[L]A'S *Ghost*

Her figure 'fore me. Now I ha't – – – how strong
Imagination works! How she can frame
Things which are not! Methinks she stands afore me;
And by the quick idea of my mind,
Were my skill pregnant, I could draw her picture.   105
Thought, as a subtle juggler, makes us deem
Things supernatural, which have cause
Common as sickness. 'Tis my melancholy.
How cam'st thou by thy death?——How idle am I
To question my own idleness – – – Did éver   110
Man dream awake till now? – – – Remove this object,
Out of my brain with't: what have I to do
With tombs, or death-beds, funerals, or tears,
That have to meditate upon revenge?

                                             [*Exit Ghost*]
So now 'tis ended, like an old wives' story.   115
Statesmen think often they see stranger sights
Than madmen. Come, to this weighty business.
My tragedy must have some idle mirth in't,
Else it will never pass. I am in love,
In love with Corombona, and my suit   120
Thus halts to her in verse.—   *He writes.*
I have done it rarely: O the fate of princes!
I am so us'd to frequent flattery,

99   *Call* Q1b (Q1a Looke)
101 *I ha't* – – – ed.
104 *quick* living; active; *idea* mental image
105 *pregnant* resourceful, inventive
106 *juggler* magician
107 *which* Q1, Q2 (Q3, Q4 which yet).
121 *halts* limps; s.d. opposite 123 in Q1

---

108 *melancholy.* Francisco treats the apparition as an hallucination, which
     was one of the recognised symptoms of melancholy. See Burton's
     Anatomy of Melancholy (Oxford, 1621), Part I, Section III, Member 3,
     Subsection I, where 'hearing and seeing strange noyses, visions' are
     included in a list of symptoms of melancholy which are expounded on
     later in the same subsection. See also J. B. Bamborough, *The Little
     World of Man* (1952), pp. 99–100.
117ff. See J. R. Mulryne, '*The White Devil* and *The Duchess of Malfi*',
     Stratford-upon-Avon Studies: I: Jacobean Theatre (1960), p. 211.

That being alone I now flatter myself;
But it will serve; 'tis scal'd. [*calls offstage*] Bear this   125

Enter SERVANT

To th'house of convertites; and watch your leisure
To give it to the hands of Corombona,
Or to the matron, when some followers
Of Brachiano may be by. Away!   *Exit* SERVANT
He that deals all by strength, his wit is shallow: 130
When a man's head goes through, each limb will follow.
The engine for my business, bold Count Lodowick;
'Tis gold must such an instrument procure,
With empty fist no man doth falcons lure.
Brachiano, I am now fit for thy encounter.   135
Like the wild Irish I'll ne'er think thee dead,
Till I can play at football with thy head.
Flectere si nequeo superos, Acheronta movebo.   *Exit*

[Act IV, Scene ii]

Enter the MATRON, *and* FLAMINEO

MATRON
  Should it be known the Duke hath such recourse
  To your imprison'd sister, I were like
  T'incur much damage by it.
FLAMINEO   Not a scruple.
  The Pope lies on his death-bed, and their heads

126 *convertites* Q1 (Q2, Q3, Q4 converts)
132 *engine* tool, instrument
134 *man doth* Q1, Q4 (Q2, Q3 man do)
  3 *damage* discredit; disapprobation; *scruple* a minute quantity
  4 Gregory XIII died on 10th April, 1585

---

131 This was a proverbial phrase, consistently applied to politic villians,
    though the image usually involved the head of a fox or snake rather
    than that of a man. (Dent, p. 121.)
134 The *lure* was a bunch of feathers or some other object resembling their
    prey with which falcons were recalled to the falconer. As a verb, *lure*
    came to mean, figuratively, 'to entice, tempt'.
136–7 It was commonly reported of the 'wild Irish' of Webster's day that
    they would not believe an enemy dead till they had cut off his head.
    The practice of playing football with heads or skulls was not uncommon.
    See Dent, pp. 121–2.
138 'If I cannot prevail upon the gods above, I will move the gods of the
    infernal regions.' (Virgil, *Æneid*, VII, 312). This 'was perhaps the most
    standard tag of all for villians. . . . Though often used soberly by in-
    dignant authors, it had become popular even within comic contexts.'
    (Dent, p. 122)
Act IV, Scene ii. This scene is set in the house of convertites, in Rome.

Are troubled now with other business   5
Than guarding of a lady.   *Enter* SERVANT

SERVANT [*aside*]
  Yonder's Flamineo in conference
  With the Matrona. [*To the* MATRON] Let me speak with you.
  I would entreat you to deliver for me
  This letter to the fair Vittoria.   10

MATRON
  I shall sir.

                 Enter BRACHIANO

SERVANT   With all care and secrecy;
  Hereafter you shall know me, and receive
  Thanks for this courtesy.

                                        [*Exit*]

FLAMINEO   How now? What's that?
MATRON
  A letter.
FLAMINEO To my sister: I'll see't delivered.

                              [*Exit* MATRON]
BRACHIANO
  What's that you read Flamineo?
FLAMINEO   Look.   15
BRACHIANO
  Ha? [*reads*] *To the most unfortunate his best respected*
  Vittoria—
  Who was the messenger?
FLAMINEO   I know not.
BRACHIANO
  No! Who sent it?
FLAMINEO   Ud's foot you speak, as if a man
  Should know what fowl is coffin'd in a bak'd meat   20
  Afore you cut it up.
BRACHIANO
  I'll open't, were't her heart. What's here subscribed—
  Florence? This juggling is gross and palpable.
  I have found out the conveyance; read it, read it.

16–17; 23: Italics are used here to conform with the printing of other
  quotations from the letter
20 *coffin'd* enclosed in a coffin i.e. pie-crust (*cf. Titus Andronicus*, V.
  ii, 189)
24 *conveyance* means of communication: *cf. The Duchess of Malfi*, II.v,
  8–11. There is also a play on the legal sense of a document by
  which property (i.e. Vittoria) is transferred from one person to
  another: *cf.* V.vi, 12

FLAMINEO (*Reads the letter*)

 Your tears I'll turn to triumphs, be but mine. 25
 Your prop is fall'n; I pity that a vine
 Which princes heretofore have long'd to gather,
 Wanting supporters, now should fade and wither.
Wine i'faith, my lord, with lees would serve his turn.
 Your sad imprisonment I'll soon uncharm, 30
 And with a princely uncontrolled arm
 Lead you to Florence, where my love and care
 Shall hang your wishes in my silver hair.
A halter on his strange equivocation.
 Nor for my years return me the sad willow: 35
 Who prefer blossoms before fruit that's mellow?
Rotten on my knowledge with lying too long i'th' bed-straw.
 And all the lines of age this line convinces:
 The gods never wax old, no more do princes.
A pox on't, rear it, let's have no more atheists for God's
           sake. 40

BRACHIANO

 Ud's death, I'll cut her into atomies
 And let th'irregular north-wind sweep her up
 And blow her int' his nostrils. Where's this whore?

FLAMINEO

 That—? what do you call her?

BRACHIANO   O, I could be mad,
 Prevent the curs'd disease she'll bring me to, 45

---

25 S.D. opposite 25–26 in Q1; brackets ed.
29 *lees* sediment deposited at the bottom of wine; dregs
34 *equivocation* use of words with double meaning with intent to
 deceive; Flamineo puns on the equivocation of 'hang' with his
 reference to 'halter' i.e. noose.
35 *willow* sign of a rejected lover
37 *bed-straw* was used instead of mattresses; straw was used to help
 ripen fruit
40 *atheists* unbelievers (here referring to the confusion of gods and
 princes); wicked or infamous people
41 *atomies* Q1 (Q2 Atomes; Q3, Q4 Atoms) pieces as small as motes
 of dust   42 *irregular* wild, uncontrolled
44 *That—? what do* ed.
45 *prevent* act in anticipation of
45–46: see notes on I, ii, 29; II. i, 90

25–40. Webster repeats the device of a character's commenting on the
 equivocations of a letter in *The Duchess of Malfi*, III. v, 26–40.
38 *convinces* overcomes; demonstrates or proves any quality: 'a quibble:
 this maxim (1) "confutes all old maxims to the contrary", and (2) "is of
 more force than the wrinkles which suggest old age".' (Brown, p. 101 n.)

And tear my hair off. Where's this changeable stuff?

FLAMINEO
O'er head and ears in water, I assure you,
She is not for your wearing.

BRACHIANO   In you pander!

FLAMINEO
What me, my lord, am I your dog?

BRACHIANO
A blood-hound: do you brave? do you stand me?   50

FLAMINEO
Stand you? Let those that have diseases run;
I need no plasters.

BRACHIANO   Would you be kick'd?

FLAMINEO
Would you have your neck broke?
I tell you Duke, I am not in Russia;
My shins must be kept whole.

BRACHIANO   Do you know me?   55

FLAMINEO
O my lord! methodically.
As in this world there are degrees of evils:
So in this world there are degrees of devils.
You're a great Duke; I your poor secretary.
I look now for a Spanish fig, or an Italian sallet daily.   60

BRACHIANO
Pander, ply your convoy, and leave your prating.

FLAMINEO
All your kindness to me is like that miserable courtesy of
Polyphemus to Ulysses; you reserve me to be devour'd
last; you would dig turves out of my grave to feed your
larks: that would be music to you. Come, I'll lead you to her.   65

---

46 *changeable stuff* material that shows different colours under
   different aspects (e.g. shot or watered silk); fickle women
48 *In you* Q1b (Q1a No you; Q2 ee'n you; Q3, Q4 You!)
50 *brave* defy; *stand* withstand
51 *run* is used here with reference to a 'running' sore
52 *plasters* ed. (Q1 plaisters; Q2, Q3, Q4 plaister)
54–55 see Additional Notes
56 *methodically* with scientific accuracy
60 *a Spanish fig, or an Italian sallet* i.e. poisoned food. A Spanish
   fig was also an expression of contempt, accompanied by an indecent gesture.
61 *ply your convoy* get on with [the conduct of] your business, i.e.
   bring us together
63 *Polyphemus* one of the Cyclops: see *Odyssey*, IX, 369–70

BRACHIANO
  Do you face me?

FLAMINEO
  O sir I would not go before a politic enemy with my back
  towards him, though there were behind me a whirlpool.

Enter VITTORIA *to* BRACHIANO *and* FLAMINEO

BRACHIANO
  Can you read mistress? Look upon that letter;
  There are no characters nor hieroglyphics.   70
  You need no comment, I am grown your receiver;
  God's precious, you shall be a brave great lady,
  A stately and advanced whore.

VITTORIA   Say sir?

BRACHIANO
  Come, come, let's see your cabinet, discover
  Your treasury of love-letters. Death and furies,   75
  I'll see them all.

VITTORIA   Sir, upon my soul,
  I have not any. Whence was this directed?

BRACHIANO
  Confusion on your politic ignorance!
          [*Gives her the letter*]
  You are reclaimed, are you? I'll give you the bells
  And let you fly to the devil.

FLAMINEO   Ware hawk, my lord.   80

67 *O sir* Q1b (Q1a Sir)
70 *characters* emblematic signs; ciphers
71 *comment* commentary, exposition; *receiver* pimp who receives
  love-letters
72 *God's precious* i.e. blood or body
73 *sir?* ed. (Q1 Sir. ; Q2 Sir, ; Q3, Q4 S Sir?); *cf.* II.i, 227 note.
74 *cabinet* often a piece of furniture fitted with compartments for
  jewels, letters etc.; a case for valuables
75 *furies* Q1 (Q2, Q3, Q4 Furies)   78 *politic* cunning, scheming
79 *reclaimed* reformed; called back or tamed (a technical term in
  falconry); *bells* i.e. those worn by the hawk to direct one to her
  and her quarry and to frighten the prey

69–70. Hazlitt marked Scene ii here; Sampson Scene iii. Lucas points out
  that a scene division here destroys the tension. He suggests that Flamineo
  merely draws the traverse to reveal Vittoria in her room. (*Webster*, i,
  240)

80 *hawk* the bird; slang for swindler. *Ware hawk, my lord.* Vittoria is the
  hawk, or swindler and cheat. In the first sense, which is related to
  Brachiano's use of the terms of falconry in the previous lines, 'It is not
  clear whether Flamineo is being cynical and means "Let her fly to feast
  on her prey", or is warning Brachiano against ungenerous impatience.'
  (Dent, p. 125)

VITTORIA [*reads*]
    Florence! This is some treacherous plot, my lord.
    To me, he ne'er was lovely I protest,
    So much as in my sleep.
BRACHIANO   Right: they are plots.
    Your beauty! O, ten thousand curses on't.
    How long have I beheld the devil in crystal?   85
    Thou hast led me, like an heathen sacrifice,
    With music, and with fatal yokes of flowers
    To my eternal ruin. Woman to man
    Is either a god or a wolf.
VITTORIA   My lord.
BRACHIANO   Away.
    We'll be as differing as two adamants;   90
    The one shall shun the other. What? dost weep?
    Procure but ten of thy dissembling trade,
    Ye'ld furnish all the Irish funerals
    With howling, past wild Irish.
FLAMINEO   Fie, my lord.
BRACHIANO
    That hand, that cursed hand, which I have wearied   95
    With doting kisses! O my sweetest Duchess
    How lovely art thou now! [*to* VITTORIA] Thy loose thoughts
    Scatter like quicksilver; I was bewitch'd;
    For all the world speaks ill of thee.
VITTORIA   No matter.
    I'll live so now I'll make that world recant   100
    And change her speeches. You did name your Duchess.
BRACHIANO
    Whose death God pardon.
VITTORIA   Whose death God revenge
    On thee most godless Duke.
FLAMINEO   Now for two whirlwinds.

---

 81 *Florence:* Q4 italics; Q1, Q2, Q3 roman type
 82 *lovely* Q1b (Q1a thought on)
 90 *adamants* loadstones
 93 *Ye'ld* ed. (Q1a ee'ld; Q1b Yee'ld; Q2 Wee'l; Q3 Weel; Q4 We'l)
 97 *Thy* Q1, Q2, Q3 (Q4, Sampson My); *loose* unconfined; unchaste
103 *two* ed. (Q1a ten; Q1b tow; Q2, Q3, Q4 the)

---

 85 *the devil in crystal*: see Additional Notes
93-4 Webster here refers to the 'keening' lamentation still heard, as in the
    sixteenth century, particularly from women who lament at wakes and
    funerals in Ireland. Brown notes that Barnabe Riche's *A New Descrip-*
    tion (1610) relates how, for the wealthy dead, women were hired who
    'will furnish the cry, with greater shriking & howling, then those that
    are grieued indeede, . . .' (p. 105 n.)

VITTORIA

What have I gain'd by thee but infamy?
Thou hast stain'd the spotless honour of my house,   105
And frighted thence noble society:
Like those, which sick o'th' palsy, and retain
Ill-scenting foxes 'bout them, are still shunn'd
By those of choicer nostrils. What do you call this house?
Is this your palace? Did not the judge style it   110
A house of penitent whores? Who sent me to it?
Who hath the honour to advance Vittoria
To this incontinent college? Is't not you?
Is't not your high preferment? Go, go brag
How many ladies you have undone, like me.   115
Fare you well sir; let me hear no more of you.
I had a limb corrupted to an ulcer,
But I have cut it off: and now I'll go
Weeping to heaven on crutches. For your gifts,
I will return them all; and I do wish   120
That I could make you full executor
To all my sins. O that I could toss myself
Into a grave as quickly: for all thou art worth
I'll not shed one tear more;——I'll burst first.
          She throws herself upon a bed

BRACHIANO

I have drunk Lethe. Vittoria?   125
My dearest happiness! Vittoria!
What do you ail my love? Why do you weep?

VITTORIA

Yes, I now weep poniards, do you see.

BRACHIANO

Are not those matchless eyes mine?

---

107 *sick* are sick
114 *preferment* advancement or promotion in condition, status or
     position in life; often used with reference to the raising of social
     status through marriage   125 *Lethe* waters of oblivion

---

107–8 Lucas (*Webster*, i, 242) states that the use of the fox in the treatment
     of paralysis, or the palsy, seems to have been quite regular. Ben Jonson
     used one, which had been sent to him as a present, when he was stricken
     with the palsy in 1628.
119–20. *Cf.* St. Mark ix, i, 45: 'And if thy foot offend thee, cut it off: it is
     better for thee to enter halt into life, than having two feet to be cast into
     hell, into the fire that never shall be quenched:' One wonders if, per-
     haps, the words 'a limb corrupted to an ulcer' might imply, on Webster's
     part, not only a reference to the malignant ulcer on the real Duke of
     Bracciano's leg, but the idea that this physical corruption was a reflec-
     tion of spiritual corruption also.

VITTORIA   I had rather
They were not matches.
BRACHIANO   Is not this lip mine?   130
VITTORIA
Yes: thus to bite it off, rather than give it thee.
FLAMINEO
Turn to my lord, good sister.
VITTORIA   Hence you pander.
FLAMINEO
Pander! Am I the author of your sin?
VITTORIA
Yes. He's a base thief that a thief lets in.
FLAMINEO
We're blown up, my lord,—
BRACHIANO   Wilt thou hear me?   135
Once to be jealous of thee is t'express
That I will love thee everlastingly,
And never more be jealous.
VITTORIA   O thou fool,
Whose greatness hath by much o'ergrown thy wit!
What dar'st thou do, that I not dare to suffer,   140
Excepting to be still thy whore? For that,
In the sea's bottom sooner thou shalt make
A bonfire.
FLAMINEO   O, no oaths for God's sake.
BRACHIANO
Will you hear me?
VITTORIA   Never.
FLAMINEO
What a damn'd imposthume is a woman's will?   145
Can nothing break it? [to BRACHIANO, aside] Fie, fie, my
                                                                lord.
Women are caught as you take tortoises,
She must be turn'd on her back.—Sister, by this hand
I am on your side.—Come, come, you have wrong'd her.
What a strange credulous man were you, my lord,   150
To think the Duke of Florence would love her?
Will any mercer take another's ware
When once 'tis tows'd and sullied? And, yet sister,

129–30 i.e. 'I had rather that they were ugly, or squinted.'
130 *matches* Q1 (Q2 matchles; Q3, Q4 matchless)
135 *blown up* i.e. by a mine   142 *sea's* ed. (Qq seas)
145 *imposthume* ulcer   151 *would* Q1b (Q1a could)
153 *tows'd* toused, dishevelled; also used of a woman who has been
     pulled about indelicately

How scurvily this frowardness becomes you!
Young leverets stand not long; and women's anger   155
Should, like their flight, procure a little sport;
A full cry for a quarter of an hour;
And then be put to th' dead quat.
BRACHIANO   Shall these eyes,
Which have so long time dwelt upon your face,
Be now put out?
FLAMINEO   No cruel landlady i'th' world,   160
Which lends forth groats to broom-men, and takes use for
                                                    them
Would do't.
Hand her, my lord, and kiss her: be not like
A ferret to let go your hold with blowing.
BRACHIANO
Let us renew right hands.
VITTORIA   Hence.   165
BRACHIANO
Never shall rage, or the forgetful wine,
Make me commit like fault.
FLAMINEO
Now you are i'th' way on't, follow't hard.
BRACHIANO
Be thou at peace with me; let all the world
Threaten the cannon.
FLAMINEO   Mark his penitence.   170
Best natures do commit the grossest faults,
When they're giv'n o'er to jealousy; as best wine
Dying makes strongest vinegar. I'll tell you;

---

154 *frowardness* perversity
155 *leverets* young hares; *stand* hunting term, usually 'stand up',
  meaning hold out
156 *their* i.e. the leverets'
157 *full cry* full pursuit; full weeping
158 *quat* squat (a hunting term)
161 *broom-men* street-sweepers; *use* usury, interest
163 *hand* grasp, fondle
170 *Threaten the cannon* Q1, Q2 (Q3, Q4 Threaten, I care not) i.e.
  'Threaten us with their cannon.'

163–4 It is apparently a superstition, not a fact, that blowing on a ferret will
  make it let go of something in which its teeth are fixed. (Lucas, *Webster*,
  i, 242–3)
166 *the forgetful wine*. Though in fact referring to the oblivion induced by
  alcohol, Brachiano may also be echoing his sentiment of IV.ii, 125:
  'I have drunk Lethe.'

The sea's more rough and raging than calm rivers,
But nor so sweet nor wholesome. A quiet woman   175
Is a still water under a great bridge.
A man may shoot her safely.

VITTORIA
O ye dissembling men!

FLAMINEO   We suck'd that, sister,
From women's breasts, in our first infancy.

VITTORIA
To add misery to misery.

BRACHIANO   Sweetest.   180

VITTORIA
Am I not low enough?
Ay, ay, your good heart gathers like a snowball
Now your affection's cold.

BRACHIANO   Ud's foot, it shall melt
To a heart again, or all the wine in Rome
Shall run o'th' lees for't.   185

VITTORIA
Your hawk or dog should be rewarded better
Than I have been. I'll speak not one word more.

FLAMINEO
Stop her mouth,
With a sweet kiss, my lord.
So now the tide's turn'd the vessel's come about.   190
He's a sweet armful. O we curl'd-hair'd men
Are still most kind to women. This is well.

BRACHIANO
That you should chide thus!

FLAMINEO   O, sir, your little chimneys
Do ever cast most smoke. I sweat for you.
Couple together with as deep a silence   195
As did the Grecians in their wooden horse.
My lord, supply your promises with deeds.
You know that painted meat no hunger feeds.

BRACHIANO
Stay—ingrateful Rome!

175 *But nor* Q1 (Q2, Q3, Q4 But not)
176 *a great bridge* Q1, Q2 (Q3, Q4 *London-Bridge*)
186 *rewarded:* a technical term for giving part of the hunting prey to
   dogs or hounds who have helped to bring it down; cf. *The Duchess
   of Malfi,* I.i, 58–59.
190 *come about* returned to port
192 *still* always
199 *Stay—ingrateful Rome* ed.

FLAMINEO   Rome! it deserves
  To be call'd Barbary, for our villainous usage.   200

BRACHIANO
  Soft; the same project which the Duke of Florence,
  (Whether in love or gullery I know not)
  Laid down for her escape, will I pursue.

FLAMINEO
  And no time fitter than this night, my lord;
  The Pope being dead; and all the cardinals ent'red   205
  The conclave for th'electing a new Pope;
  The city in a great confusion;
  We may attire her in a page's suit,
  Lay her post-horse, take shipping, and amain
  For Padua.   210

BRACHIANO
  I'll instantly steal forth the Prince Giovanni,
  And make for Padua. You two with your old mother
  And young Marcello that attends on Florence,
  If you can work him to it, follow me.
  I will advance you all: for you Vittoria,   215
  Think of a duchess' title.

FLAMINEO   Lo you sister.
  Stay, my lord; I'll tell you a tale. The crocodile, which lives
  in the river Nilus, hath a worm breeds i'th' teeth of't, which
  puts it to extreme anguish: a little bird, no bigger than a
  wren, is barber-surgeon to this crocodile; flies into the   220
  jaws of't; picks out the worm; and brings present remedy.
  The fish, glad of ease but ingrateful to her that did it, that

202 *gullery* trickery, deception
209 *Lay her post-horse* provide her with relays of post-horses;
    amain at main (i.e. full) speed; without delay
211 *I'll instantly* Q1 (Q2, Q3, Q4 Instantly)

---

200 *Barbary* literally 'was a term of convenience as used by the Elizabethans
    because it could be made to cover practically the whole of Africa's north
    coast west of Egypt.' Barbary pirates were 'a sore spot in the side of
    English traders.' (R. R. Cawley, *The Voyagers and Elizabethan Drama*,
    pp. 92; 93.) The reference here could be to pirates, but probably to the
    country of the Barbarians, i.e. cruel savages. From 1564 onwards
    (according to *O.E.D.*) Barbary was a term used to equal 'barbarity,
    barbarism' and 'barbarousness'.
217–29 This fable is not one of Webster's inventions. For notes on Webster's
    probable sources, e.g. Topsell's *Historie of Serpents* (1608) see Dent,
    pp. 129–30 and Brown, p. 112 n. For comment on its dramatic sig-
    nificance see: F. L. Lucas, *Webster*, i, 244–5; Clifford Leech, *John
    Webster: A Critical Study* (1951), p. 115 and Travis Bogard, *The
    Tragic Satire of John Webster* (Berkeley and Los Angeles, 1955), p.
    104.

the bird may not talk largely of her abroad for non-payment,
closeth her chaps intending to swallow her, and so put her
to perpetual silence. But nature loathing such ingratitude,   225
hath arm'd this bird with a quill or prick on the head, top
o'th' which wounds the crocodile i'th' mouth; forceth her
open her bloody prison; and away flies the pretty tooth-
picker from her cruel patient.

BRACHIANO
Your application is, I have not rewarded   230
The service you have done me.

FLAMINEO   No my lord;
You sister are the crocodile: you are blemish'd in your
fame, my lord cures it. And though the comparison hold
not in every particle; yet observe, remember, what good
the bird with the prick i'th' head hath done you; and   235
scorn ingratitude.
[*aside*] It may appear to some ridiculous
Thus to talk knave and madman; and sometimes
Come in with a dried sentence, stuff'd with sage.
But this allows my varying of shapes,   240
Knaves do grow great by being great men's apes.   *Exeunt*

[Act IV, Scene iii]

Enter LODOVICO, GASPARO, *and six Ambassadors.*
At another door [FRANCISCO] *the Duke of Florence.*

FRANCISCO
So, my lord, I commend your diligence.
Guard well the conclave, and, as the order is,
Let none have conference with the cardinals.

LODOVICO
I shall, my lord. Room for the ambassadors!

GASPARO
They're wondrous brave today: why do they wear   5
These several habits?

---

224 *chaps* jaws
239 *sentence* aphorism; maxim; *sage* the herb; wisdom (*cf.* I.ii, 130)
   5 *brave* finely or splendidly dressed
   6 and 15 *several* various, diverse

Act IV, Scene iii. The action of this scene takes place near the Sistine chapel,
   outside the pope's palace. For Webster's use of sources in the scene, see:
   J. R. Brown, 'The Papal Election in John Webster's "The White Devil"'
   (1612), *Notes and Queries*, N.S. IV (1957), 490–94; Gunnar Boklund,
   The Sources of 'The White Devil', pp. 30–32; Dent, pp. 130–33.

LODOVICO   O sir, they're knights
Of several orders.
That lord i'th' black cloak with the silver cross
Is Knight of Rhodes; the next Knight of S. Michael;
That of the Golden Fleece; the Frenchman there   10
Knight of the Holy Ghost; my lord of Savoy
Knight of th'Annunciation; the Englishman
Is Knight of th'honoured Garter, dedicated
Unto their saint, S. George. I could describe to you
Their several institutions, with the laws   15
Annexed to their orders; but that time
Permits not such discovery.
FRANCISCO   Where's Count Lodowick?
LODOVICO
Here my lord.
FRANCISCO   'Tis o'th' point of dinner time;
Marshal the cardinals' service.
LODOVICO   Sir, I shall.

Enter SERVANTS *with several dishes covered*

Stand, let me search your dish; who's this for?   20
SERVANT
For my lord Cardinal Monticelso.
LODOVICO
Who's this?
SERVANT   For my Lord Cardinal of Bourbon.
FRENCH AMBASSADOR
Why doth he search the dishes? to observe
What meat is dress'd?
ENGLISH AMBASSADOR   No sir, but to prevent
Lest any letters should be convey'd in   25
To bribe or to solicit the advancement

---

18 *Here* Q1, Q2 (Q3, Q4 [omit])
22 *Who's* ed. (Qq Whose)
24 *dress'd* prepared

9–14 The *Knight of Rhodes* belongs to the order of the Knights of St. John
    of Jerusalem which moved first from Jerusalem to Rhodes. The order
    was founded during the First Crusade. Malta was granted to them by
    the Emperor Charles V in 1530. The order of *St. Michael* was founded
    in 1469 by Louis XI. The order of the *Golden Fleece* was founded by
    Philip the Good, Duke of Burgundy in 1430. Henri III founded the
    order of the *Holy Ghost* in 1578. The order of the *Annunciation*, the
    highest order of Knights in Italy, was founded in 1362 by Amadeus VI
    of Savoy. The order of the *Garter*, the highest order in England, was
    apparently founded 1346–8. Its origin is obscure.

Of any cardinal. When first they enter
'Tis lawful for the ambassadors of princes
To enter with them, and to make their suit
For any man their prince affecteth best;   30
But after, till a general election,
No man may speak with them.

LODOVICO
You that attend on the lord cardinals
Open the window, and receive their viands.

A CARDINAL
You must return the service; the lord cardinals   35
Are busied 'bout electing of the Pope;
They have given o'er scrutiny, and are fallen
To admiration.

LODOVICO   Away, away.

                    [*Exeunt* SERVANTS *with dishes*]

FRANCISCO
I'll lay a thousand ducats you hear news
Of a Pope presently. Hark; sure he's elected,—   40

       [*The*] *Cardinal* [*of* ARRAGON *appears*] *on the terrace*

Behold! my lord of Arragon appears
On the church battlements.

ARRAGON
Denuntio vobis gaudium magnum. Reverendissimus Cardinalis
LORENZO *de* MONTICELSO *electus est in sedem apostolicam, et*
eligit sibi nomen PAULUM *quartum.*   45

OMNES
Vivat Sanctus Pater Paulus Quartus.

                    [*Enter* SERVANT]

35 *the service* the dishes   37 *scrutiny* counting the votes
39 *ducats* were worth 4/8d in 1608.
40 s.d. Brown (Qq *A Cardinal on the Tarras.*)
43 *Denuntio* Q1 (Q2, Q3, Q4 *Annuntio*)
43–45: 'I announce to you tidings of great joy. The Most Reverend
    Cardinal Lorenzo di Monticelso has been elected to the Apostolic
    See, and has chosen for himself the name of Paul IV.'
46 *Everybody.* 'Long live the Holy Father, Paul IV.'
46 s.d. Q4 (Q1, Q2, Q3 [omit])

---

38 *admiration.* The technical term 'adoration', which Webster should have
    used, described the method of electing a pope, an alternative to voting
    (i.e. scrutiny), whereby a pope was elected if two-thirds of the cardinals
    present turned towards and made reverence to the one whom they
    wished to be made pope.
43–45. The historical Cardinal Montalto became Pope Sixtus V.

SERVANT
  Vittoria my lord—
FRANCISCO Well: what of her?
SERVANT
  Is fled the city—
FRANCISCO Ha?
SERVANT With Duke Brachiano.
FRANCISCO
  Fled? Where's the Prince Giovanni?
SERVANT Gone with his father.
FRANCISCO
  Let the Matrona of the convertites 50
  Be apprehended. Fled? O damnable!

                   [*Exit* SERVANT]
  [*aside*] How fortunate are my wishes. Why? 'Twas this
  I only labour'd. I did send the letter
  T'instruct him what to do. Thy fame, fond Duke,
  I first have poison'd; directed thee the way 55
  To marry a whore; what can be worse? This follows:
  The hand must act to drown the passionate tongue,
  I scorn to wear a sword and prate of wrong.

       Enter MONTICELSO *in state*

MONTICELSO
  Concedimus vobis apostolicam benedictionem et remissionem
  peccatorum. 60
           [FRANCISCO *whispers to him*]
  My lord reports Vittoria Corombona
  Is stol'n from forth the house of convertites
  By Brachiano, and they're fled the city.
  Now, though this be the first day of our seat,
  We cannot better please the divine power, 65
  That to sequester from the holy church
  These cursed persons. Make it therefore known,

---

50 *Matrona* Q1 (Q2, Q3 Matrone; Q4 Matron); *convertites* Q1 (Q2,
   Q3, Q4 converts)
51 *Fled?* Q4 (Q1 fled ; Q2, Q3, fled?)
54 *fond* foolish
59–60: Q1b (Q1a [omits]) 'We grant you the apostolic blessing and
   remission of sins.'; *et* ed. (Qq &); *peccatorum* Q2, Q3, Q4 (Q1b
   peccatorem)
62 *convertites* Q1 (Q2, Q3, Q4 converts)
64 *seat* Q3, Q4 (Q1b, Q2 seate; Q1a state): 'the technical term for
   the throne or office of a Pope' (Brown)

plot

We do denounce excommunication
Against them both: all that are theirs in Rome
We likewise banish. Set on.   70

          Exeunt [all except FRANCISCO *and* LODOVICO]

FRANCISCO
Come dear Lodovico
You have tane the sacrament to prosecute
Th'intended murder.
LODOVICO   With all constancy.
But, sir, I wonder you'll engage yourself
In person, being a great prince.
FRANCISCO   Divert me not.   75
Most of this court are of my faction,
And some are of my counsel. Noble friend,
Our danger shall be 'like in this design;
Give leave, part of the glory may be mine.

        Exit FRAN[CISCO]   *Enter* MONTICELSO

MONTICELSO
Why did the Duke of Florence with such care   80
Labour your pardon? Say.
LODOVICO
Italian beggars will resolve you that
Who, begging of an alms, bid those they beg of
Do good for their own sakes; or't may be
He spreads his bounty with a sowing hand,   85
Like kings, who many times give out of measure;
Not for desert so much as for their pleasure.
MONTICELSO
I know you're cunning. Come, what devil was that
That you were raising?
LODOVICO   Devil, my lord?
MONTICELSO   I ask you
How doth the Duke employ you, that his bonnet   90
Fell with such compliment unto his knee,
When he departed from you?
LODOVICO   Why, my lord,
He told me of a resty Barbary horse

---

78 *'like* Q1 (Q2, Q3, Q4 like) alike   79 s.d. Q1b (Q1a [omits])
80 speech-prefix: Q1b MON. (Q1a [omits])
81 *Labour* labour for
86 *out of measure* excessively
88 *was that* Q1, Q2 (Q3, Q4 is that)
93 *resty* restive; *Barbary horse* a small, swift and hot-tempered
    horse from Barbary (*cf.* IV.ii, 200 note.)

Which he would fain have brought to the career,
The 'sault, and the ring-galliard. Now, my lord,   95
I have a rare French rider.
MONTICELSO   Take you heed:
Lest the jade break your neck. Do you put me off
With your wild horse-tricks? Sirrah you do lie.
O, thou'rt a foul black cloud, and thou dost threat
A violent storm.
LODOVICO   Storms are i'th' air, my lord;   100
I am too low to storm.
MONTICELSO   Wretched creature!
I know that thou art fashion'd for all ill,
Like dogs, that once get blood, they'll ever kill.
About some murder? Was't not?
LODOVICO   I'll not tell you;
And yet I care not greatly if I do;   105
Marry with this preparation. Holy Father,
I come not to you as an intelligencer,
But as a penitent sinner. What I utter
Is in confession merely; which you know
Must never be reveal'd.
MONTICELSO   You have o'ertane me.   110
LODOVICO
Sir I did love Brachiano's Duchess dearly;
Or rather I pursued her with hot lust,
Though she ne'er knew on't. She was poison'd;
Upon my soul she was: for which I have sworn
T'avenge her murder.
MONTICELSO   To the Duke of Florence?   115

97 *jade* horse; woman (i.e. Vittoria)
98 *horse-tricks* tricks taught to horses; horse-play; *you do* Q1, Q2
    (Q3, Q4 you)
104 *murder* Q1, Q2 (Q3, Q4 murther)
107 *intelligencer* spy, informer
110 *o'ertane* overreached

94–95 *the career* / *The 'sault and the ring-galliard:* technical terms for the
    different exercises in the 'manage' of a horse. The *career* consisted in
    running a horse at full speed and then making him stop quickly and
    firmly; *the 'sault* was the name given to various leaps which the horse
    was trained to do; *the ring-galliard* was 'a mixture of bounding forward,
    curvetting, and yerking' i.e. lashing out with the heels. (Lucas, *Webster*,
    i, 247)
96 *French rider.* The French were famous for their horsemanship: cf. *The
    Duchess of Malfi* I.ii, 60–63.
111–15 P. Haworth comments: 'The illicit passion of Vittoria and Brachiano
    is thus punished by means of an equally criminal lust.' (*English Hymns
    and Ballads* . . . p. 92)

LODOVICO
  To him I have.

MONTICELSO   Miserable creature!
If thou persist in this, 'tis damnable.
Dost thou imagine thou canst slide on blood
And not be tainted with a shameful fall?
Or, like the black and melancholic yew-tree,   120
Dost think to root thyself in dead men's graves,
And yet to prosper? Instruction to thee
Comes like sweet showers to over-hard'ned ground:
They wet, but pierce not deep. And so I leave thee
With all the Furies hanging 'bout thy neck,   125
Till by thy penitence thou remove this evil,
In conjuring from thy breast that cruel devil.

                              Exit MON[TICELSO]

LODOVICO
  I'll give it o'er. He says 'tis damnable:
Besides I did expect his suffrage,
By reason of Camillo's death.   130

              Enter SERVANT *and* FRANCISCO

FRANCISCO
  Do you know that count?
SERVANT   Yes, my lord.
FRANCISCO
  Bear him these thousand ducats to his lodging;
Tell him the Pope hath sent them. Happily
That will confirm more than all the rest.   [*Exit*]
SERVANT   Sir.
        [SERVANT *delivers purse of money to* LODOVICO]

128 *give it o'er* give it up
129 *suffrage* support, assistance
133 *Happily* Q1, Q2, Q3 (Q4 Haply) haply, perhaps
134 *confirm* Qq

125; 151 *Furies* the three avenging goddesses, with snakes in their hair—
      Tisiphone, Megæra and Alecto—who were sent from Tartarus to avenge
      wrong and punish crime. Reference to them was a common feature of
      Senecan revenge plays in the 1590's. For example, in George Peele's
      Battle of Alcazar (1594), written *circa* 1588–89
              Alecto with her brand and bloudie torch
              Megæra with her whip and snakie haire,
              Tysiphone with her fatall murthering yron   (Sig. B₃)
      are described as conspiring to avenge the wrongs and murders committed
      by the villain hero, Muly Mahamet. By transference *fury* was used for
      likening anyone—but especially a ferociously angry or malignant woman
      —to an infernal spirit or minister of vengeance. In transcribing *Fury* of
      Q1 I have distinguished between *Fury*—a direct reference to one of the
      goddesses—and *fury*—the metaphorical use of the word—by the use of
      the capital. In each case the collation is given.

LODOVICO
    To me sir?   135
SERVANT
    His Holiness hath sent you a thousand crowns,
    And wills you, if you travel, to make him
    Your patron for intelligence.
LODOVICO   His creature
    Ever to be commanded.   [*Exit* SERVANT]
    Why now 'tis come about. He rail'd upon me;   140
    And yet these crowns were told out and laid ready,
    Before he knew my voyage. O the art,
    The modest form of greatness! that do sit
    Like brides at wedding dinners, with their looks turn'd
    From the least wanton jests, their puling stomach   145
    Sick of the modesty, when their thoughts are loose,
    Even acting of those hot and lustful sports
    Are to ensue about midnight: such his cunning!
    He sounds my depth thus with a golden plummet;
    I am doubly arm'd now. Now to th'act of blood;   150
    There's but three Furies found in spacious hell;
    But in a great man's breast three thousand dwell.
                     [*Exit*]

[Act V, Scene i]

A passage over the stage of BRACHIANO, FLAMINEO, MARCELLO,
HORTENSIO, [VITTORIA] COROMBONA, CORNELIA, ZANCHE
and others

[*Enter* FLAMINEO *and* HORTENSIO]

137 *wills* Q3, Q4 (Q1 will; Q2 wils); *travel* Q4 (Q1, Q2 trauaile;
    Q3 travail)
138 *intelligence* supplying with secret information
141 *told out* counted out
145 *jests* Q1 (Q2, Q3, Q4 jest); *puling* sickly, weak
150 *arm'd now. Now* Qq:

---

136 *crowns.* Since a ducat was worth 4/8d (see IV.iii, 39 note) the term
    crown–i.e. 5/––used here is rather a translation of the sum into English
    than a mistake or confusion between the names of coins.
Act V, Scene i et seq. The whole of the fifth act takes place in Brachiano's
    palace in Padua.
  s.D. *and others.* Brown (p. 123 n.) comments that these probably include the
    ambassadors whose 'mere presence on the stage would enforce Webster's
    often-repeated comments on the power of great men and the sycophancy
    of court society.' Moreover, since there would hardly have been time
    for the actors to change their costumes, they would still be dressed in
    the habits of their various orders, worn at the papal election, 'tokens of
    holiness, virtue, and honour–an ironical display for the marriage of a
    proclaimed whore and an excommunicate duke.'

FLAMINEO

In all the weary minutes of my life,
Day ne'er broke up till now. This marriage
Confirms me happy.

HORTENSIO   'Tis a good assurance.
Saw you not yet the Moor that's come to court?

FLAMINEO

Yes, and conferr'd with him i'th' Duke's closet;   5
I have not seen a goodlier personage,
Nor ever talk'd with man better experienc'd
In state affairs or rudiments of war.
He hath by report serv'd the Venetian
In Candy these twice seven years, and been chief   10
In many a bold design.

HORTENSIO   What are those two
That bear him company?

FLAMINEO

Two noblemen of Hungary, that living in the emperor's
service as commanders, eight years since, contrary to the
expectation of all the court ent'red into religion, into the   15
strict order of Capuchins: but being not well settled in
their undertaking they left their order and returned to
court: for which being after troubled in conscience, they
vowed their service against the enemies of Christ; went to
Malta; were there knighted; and in their return back, at   20
this great solemnity, they are resolved for ever to forsake
the world, and settle themselves here in a house of Capuchins
in Padua.

HORTENSIO

'Tis strange.

FLAMINEO

One thing makes it so. They have vowed for ever to wear   25
next their bare bodies those coats of mail they served in.

HORTENSIO

Hard penance. Is the Moor a Christian?

8 *rudiments* principles (*not* fundamentals)
10 *Candy* Crete
20 *knighted* i.e. in the order of St. John of Jerusalem

1–3 With the dramatic irony of these confident lines of Flamineo's Dent
    (pp. 135–6) compares Jonson's *Sejanus*, V, 3–4.
16 *Capuchins*. This order had originally separated itself from the main body
    of the Franciscans about 1528 so that it might return to the strict
    austerity of St. Francis. It was not established as an independent order
    till 1619.

FLAMINEO
  He is.
HORTENSIO
  Why proffers he his service to our Duke?
FLAMINEO
  Because he understands there's like to grow   30
  Some wars between us and the Duke of Florence,
  In which he hopes employment.
  I never saw one in a stern bold look
  Wear more command, nor in a lofty phrase
  Express more knowing, or more deep contempt   35
  Of our slight airy courtiers. He talks
  As if he had travell'd all the princes' courts
  Of Christendom; in all things strives t'express
  That all that should dispute with him may know,
  Glories, like glow-worms, afar off shine bright   40
  But look'd to near, have neither heat nor light.
  The Duke!

  Enter BRACHIANO, [FRANCISCO, *Duke of*] *Florence disguised*
  like Mulinassar; LODOVICO, ANTONELLI, GASPARO, FERNESE
           having their swords and helmets.

BRACHIANO
  You are nobly welcome. We have heard at full
  Your honourable service 'gainst the Turk.
  To you, brave Mulinassar, we assign   45
  A competent pension: and are inly sorrow,
  The vows of those two worthy gentlemen
  Make them incapable of our proffer'd bounty.
  Your wish is you may leave your warlike swords
  For monuments in our chapel. I accept it   50
  As a great honour done me, and must crave
  Your leave to furnish out our Duchess' revels.

32 Q1, Q2 have duplicate entry for Brachiano here.
37 *travell'd* Q4 (Q1, Q2 trauail'd; Q3 travail'd)
42 *The Duke!* ed. (Q1, Q2, Q3 The Duke. ; Q4 *The Duke.—*)
42 S.D. LODOVICO, i.e. disguised as Carlo; GASPARO Q4 (Q1, Q2,
    Q3 *Gaspar*) i.e. disguised as Pedro; FARNESE *bearing* Q1 (Q2
    Farnese, bearing; Q3, Q4 *bearing*): see V.vi, 164 S.D. note
46 *competent* sufficient in means for comfortable living; *sorrow* Q1
    (Q2 sorrie; Q3, Q4 sorry) sorry
48 *incapable of* i.e. incapable of accepting
50 *monuments* evidence, or tokens [of the fact of a change in a man's
    way of life]
52 *leave* permission for absence

40–41 Webster repeated these lines in *The Duchess of Malfi*, IV.ii, 141–2.

Only one thing, as the last vanity
You e'er shall view, deny me not to stay
To see a barriers prepar'd tonight;   55
You shall have private standings. It hath pleas'd
The great ambassadors of several princes
In their return from Rome to their own countries
To grace our marriage, and to honour me
With such a kind of sport.

FRANCISCO   I shall persuade them   60
To stay, my lord.

BRACHIANO   Set on there to the presence.
            Exeunt BRACHIANO, FLAMINEO *and* [HORTENSIO]

LODOVICO
Noble my lord, most fortunately welcome,
                        The conspirators here embrace
You have our vows seal'd with the sacrament
To second your attempts.

GASPARO   And all things ready.
He could not have invented his own ruin,   65
Had he despair'd, with more propriety.

LODOVICO
You would not take my way.

FRANCISCO   'Tis better ordered.

LODOVICO
T'have poison'd his prayer book, or a pair of beads,
The pommel of his saddle, his looking-glass,
Or th'handle of his racket. O that, that!   70
That while he had been bandying at tennis,
He might have sworn himself to hell, and struck
His soul into the hazard! O my lord!
I would have our plot be ingenious,
And have it hereafter recorded for example   75

---

55 *barriers*: cf. I.ii, 28 note.   56 *standings* standing-places
61 speech-prefix: Dyce *et al.* (Qq continue as Francisco's speech);
presence presence or audience chamber
61 S.D. [HORTENSIO] ed. (Qq *Marcello*)
62 speech-prefix: Q3, Q4 *Lod.* (Q1, Q2 *Car.*); *Noble my* Q1, Q2 (Q3,
Q4 My noble); S.D. opposite 62–64 in Q1.
64 speech-prefix: Q3, Q4 *Gas.* (Q1, Q2 *Ped.*)
66 *propriety* Q1, Q2 (Q3, Q4 dexterity)
68 *pair of beads* set or string of beads
59 *our* Q1, Q4 (Q2 ,Q3 your)
68–70; 71–73: See Additional Notes
71 *bandying* knocking the ball about

68–76 This speech brands Lodovico as a real Machiavellian villain, comparable with Marlowe's Guise or Barabas.

Rather than borrow example.

FRANCISCO   There's no way
More speeding than this thought on.

LODOVICO   On then.

FRANCISCO
And yet methinks that this revenge is poor,
Because it steals upon him like a thief;
To have tane him by the cask in a pitch'd field,   80
Led him to Florence!

LODOVICO   It had been rare.—And there
Have crown'd him with a wreath of stinking garlic,
T'have shown the sharpness of his government,
And rankness of his lust. Flamineo comes.

       Exeunt LODOVICO, ANTONELLI [*and* GASPARO]

    Enter FLAMINEO, MARCELLO *and* ZANCHE

MARCELLO
Why doth this devil haunt you? Say.

FLAMINEO   I know not.   85
For by this light I do not conjure for her.
'Tis not so great a cunning as men think
To raise the devil: for here's one up already;
The greatest cunning were to lay him down.

MARCELLO
She is your shame.

FLAMINEO   I prithee pardon her.   90
In faith you see, women are like to burs;
Where their affection throws them, there they'll stick.

ZANCHE
That is my countryman, a goodly person;
When he's at leisure I'll discourse with him
In our own language.

FLAMINEO   I beseech you do.   *Exit* ZANCHE   95

---

76 *example* Q1, Q2 (Q3, Q4 from it)
77 *speeding* effective, decisive
80 *cask* casque, i.e. helmet or head-piece
84 (Q1, Q2 divide: *lust. / Flamineo;* Q3, Q4 *lust—But, peace: /*
    Flamineo)
87 *cunning* magical knowledge or skill

---

85 *this devil* i.e. Zanche, because she is dark-skinned
88–89 Lucas thinks that this is a double entendre comparable with *Romeo*
    and Juliet, II.i, 23–9, but Dent (p. 137) says that this seems far-fetched
    and comments that 'Flamineo is simply complaining that he cannot now
    get rid of his old mistress Zanche.'

How is't brave soldier? O that I had seen
Some of your iron days! I pray relate
Some of your service to us.

FRANCISCO

'Tis a ridiculous thing for a man to be his own chronicle;
I did never wash my mouth with mine own praise for fear of   100
getting a stinking breath.

MARCELLO

You're too stoical. The Duke will expect other discourse
from you.

FRANCISCO

I shall never flatter him, I have studied man too much to do
that. What difference is between the Duke and I? No more   105
than between two bricks; all made of one clay. Only 't may
be one is plac'd on the top of a turret; the other in the
bottom of a well by mere chance; if I were plac'd as high
as the Duke, I should stick as fast; make as fair a show;
and bear out weather equally.   110

FLAMINEO

If this soldier had a patent to beg in churches, then he
would tell them stories.

MARCELLO

I have been a soldier too.

FRANCISCO

How have you thriv'd?

MARCELLO

Faith, poorly.   115

FRANCISCO

That's the misery of peace. Only outsides are then respected.
As ships seem very great upon the river, which show very
little upon the seas: so some men i'th' court seem Colossuses
in a chamber, who if they came into the field would appear
pitiful pigmies.   120

FLAMINEO

Give me a fair room yet hung with arras, and some great

98 *service* military operations
109 *fair*. 'There may be a quibbling allusion to his disguise as the
   dark-skinned Mulinassar.' (Brown)
111 *patent* licence, obtained from a justice of the peace, without which
   beggars were not allowed to beg, on pain of whipping
118 *Colossuses* enormous statues (from the Colossus at Rhodes, a
   bronze statue of the sun-god Helios: one of the seven wonders of
   the ancient world)
121 *arras* a tapestry, often suspended a little distance from the walls:
   thus a spy could hide behind it. *Cf. Hamlet*, II.ii, 161–2; III.iv,
   1–33.

cardinal to lug me by th'ears as his endeared minion.

FRANCISCO

And thou may'st do,–the devil knows what villainy.

FLAMINEO

And safely.

FRANCISCO

Right; you shall see in the country in harvest time, pigeons,   125
though they destroy never so much corn, the farmer dare
not present the fowling-piece to them! Why? Because
they belong to the lord of the manor; whilst your poor
sparrows that belong to the Lord of heaven, they go to
the pot for't.   130

FLAMINEO

I will now give you some politic instruction. The Duke
says he will give you pension; that's but bare promise: get
it under his hand. For I have known men that have come
from serving against the Turk; for three or four months
they have had pension to buy them new wooden legs and   135
fresh plasters; but after 'twas not to be had. And this
miserable courtesy shows, as if a tormentor should give
hot cordial drinks to one three-quarters dead o'th' rack,
only to fetch the miserable soul again to endure more
dog-days.   140

Enter HORTENSIO, *a* YOUNG LORD, ZANCHE *and two more*

How now, gallants; what, are they ready for the barriers?
                                                    [*Exit* FRANCISCO]

YOUNG LORD

Yes: the lords are putting on their armour.

HORTENSIO

What's he?

FLAMINEO

A new upstart: one that swears like a falc'ner, and will lie
in the Duke's ear day by day like a maker of almanacs; and   145
yet I knew him since he came to th'court smell worse of
sweat than an under-tennis-court-keeper.

123 *do,–the* ed. (Q1, Q2 doe, the; Q3, Q4 do the; Lucas: doe–the)
127 *fowling-piece* light gun for shooting wild fowl
131 *instruction* Q1 (Q2, Q3, Q4 instructions)
132 *you* Q1 (Q2, Q3, Q4 you a)
133 *under his hand* i.e. a signed statement
137 *miserable* miserly, mean; compassionate
138 *cordial* for the heart; strengthening and restorative
140 *dog-days* see III.ii, 200 note.
141 *what,* Q4 (Q1, Q2, Q3 what)
144 *falc'ner* falconer

HORTENSIO

Look you, yonder's your sweet mistress.

FLAMINEO

Thou art my sworn brother; I'll tell thee, I do love that
Moor, that witch, very constrainedly: she knows some of   150
my villainy; I do love her, just as a man holds a wolf by the
ears. But for fear of turning upon me, and pulling out my
throat, I would let her go to the devil.

HORTENSIO

I hear she claims marriage of thee.

FLAMINEO

'Faith, I made to her some such dark promise, and in   155
seeking to fly from't I run on, like a frighted dog with a
bottle at's tail, that fain would bite it off and yet dares not
look behind him. [*to* ZANCHE] Now my precious gipsy!

ZANCHE

Ay, your love to me rather cools than heats.

FLAMINEO

Marry, I am the sounder lover; we have many wenches   160
about the town heat too fast.

HORTENSIO

What do you think of these perfum'd gallants then?

FLAMINEO

Their satin cannot save them. I am confident
They have a certain spice of the disease.
For they that sleep with dogs, shall rise with fleas.   165

ZANCHE

Believe it! A little painting and gay clothes
Make you loathe me.

FLAMINEO

How? Love a lady for painting or gay apparel? I'll unkennel
one example more for thee. Æsop had a foolish dog that let
go the flesh to catch the shadow. I would have courtiers be   170
better diners.

ZANCHE

You remember your oaths.

FLAMINEO

Lovers' oaths are like mariners' prayers, uttered in extremity; but when the tempest is o'er, and that the vessel

150 *constrainedly* in a constrained manner, without spontaneity
158 *gipsy:* an allusion to Zanche's dark skin and passionate nature
159 *cools . . . heats:* both verbs are used transitively and intransitively
160 *sounder lover* Q2, Q3, Q4 (Q1 sounder, lover)
171 *diners* ed. (Q1, Q2 *Diuers* [i.e. turned *n*]; Q3, Q4 *Divers*)

leaves tumbling, they fall from protesting to drinking. And 175
yet amongst gentlemen protesting and drinking go together,
and agree as well as shoemakers and Westphalia bacon. They
are both drawers on: for drink draws on protestation; and
protestation draws on more drink. Is not this discourse
better now than the morality of your sunburnt gentleman? 180

Enter CORNELIA

CORNELIA
Is this your perch, you haggard? Fly to th'stews.
                                        [*Strikes* ZANCHE]

FLAMINEO
You should be clapp'd by th'heels now: strike i'th'court?
                                        [*Exit* CORNELIA]

ZANCHE
She's good for nothing but to make her maids
Catch cold o'nights; they dare not use a bedstaff,
For fear of her light fingers.

MARCELLO   You're a strumpet.   185
An impudent one.

FLAMINEO   Why do you kick her? Say,
Do you think that she's like a walnut-tree?
Must she be cudgell'd ere she bear good fruit?

MARCELLO
She brags that you shall marry her.

FLAMINEO   What then?

177-8 i.e. 'The shoemaker draws on shoes and salt things induce
       thirstiness.' (Sampson)
180 *morality* Q4 (Q1, Q2, Q3 mortality); *sunburnt gentleman* i.e.
       Francisco, disguised as Mulinassar: see Additional Notes
181 *haggard* wild hawk; wanton woman
`^2 *clapp'd by th' heels* fasten by the ankles in stocks or irons
184 *a bedstaff* Q1, Q2 (Q3 bed-staff; Q4 bed-staves): see Addditional
       Notes

173-5 Webster's simile is an imaginatively extended form of an expression
       found in George Pettie's translation of Guazzo's *Civil Conversation*
       (1581): 'The othes of lovers, carry as much credite as the vowes of
       Mariners.' Other dramatic references to mariners' oaths and their
       drinking habits will be found in R. R. Cawley, *The Voyagers and
       Elizabethan Drama*, pp. 194-200.
182 *strike i'th' court?* Lucas (*Webster*, i, 250) quotes from Stephen's *Com-
       mentaries on the Laws of England* (ed. 1914), IV, 156: 'By 33 Hen. VIII
       (1541), c. 12, malicious striking in the palace, which drew blood, was
       punishable with perpetual imprisonment and fine at the King's pleasure,
       and the loss of the striker's right hand.'

MARCELLO
I had rather she were pitch'd upon a stake   190
In some new-seeded garden, to affright
Her fellow crows thence.
FLAMINEO   You're a boy, a fool,
Be guardian to your hound, I am of age.
MARCELLO
If I take her near you I'll cut her throat.
FLAMINEO
With a fan of feathers?
MARCELLO   And for you, I'll whip   195
This folly from you.
FLAMINEO   Are you choleric?
I'll purge't with rhubarb.
HORTENSIO   O your brother!
FLAMINEO   Hang him.
He wrongs me most that ought t'offend me least.
[to MARCELLO] I do suspect my mother play'd foul play
When she conceiv'd thee.
MARCELLO   Now by all my hopes,   200
Like the two slaught'red sons of Œdipus,
The very flames of our affection
Shall turn two ways. Those words I'll make thee answer
With thy heart blood.
FLAMINEO   Do; like the gesses in the progress,
You know where you shall find me,—
MARCELLO   Very good.   205
                                   [*Exit* FLAMINEO]
And thou beest a noble friend, bear him my sword,
And bid him fit the length on't.
YOUNG LORD   Sir I shall.
                                   [*Exeunt all but* ZANCHE]

190 *pitch'd* stuck, fastened
192 *You're* Q3, Q4 (Q1 Your; Q2 you'r)
196–7 Rhubarb, considered to be choleric itself, was a recognised
    antidote for an excess of the choleric humour. *Cf. The Duchess of
    Malfi*, II.v, 12–13.
197 *brother!* ed. (Qq brother.)   203 *two* Q1b (Q1a 10)
204 *Do:* Q4 (Q1 Doe ; Q2 Doe,   ; Q3 Do,); *gesses* ed. stopping-places
    on a royal progress
206 *noble friend* Q2, Q3, Q4 (Q1 noble, friend)

201–203 After Œdipus' sons Eteocles and Polynices had killed each other in
    single combat for the throne of Thebes, their bodies were burnt to-
    gether, but the flames were seen miraculously to part from one another.
    Webster may have found a reference to the legend in Pettie's translation
    of Guazzo's *Civil Conversation* (1581), Book II, p. 84.

Enter FRANCISCO *the Duke of Florence*

ZANCHE [*aside*]
　He comes. Hence petty thought of my disgrace!
　I ne'er lov'd my complexion till now,
　Cause I may boldly say without a blush,   210
　I love you.
FRANCISCO　　Your love is untimely sown;
　There's a Spring at Michaelmas, but 'tis but a faint one.
　I am sunk in years, and I have vowed never to marry.
ZANCHE
　Alas! poor maids get more lovers than husbands. Yet you
　may mistake my wealth. For, as when ambassadors are sent   215
　to congratulate princes, there's commonly sent along with
　them a rich present; so that though the prince like not the
　ambassador's person nor words, yet he likes well of the
　presentment. So I may come to you in the same manner,
　and be better loved for my dowry than my virtue.   220
FRANCISCO
　I'll think on the motion.
ZANCHE
　Do, I'll now detain you no longer. At your better leisure
　I'll tell you things shall startle your blood.
　Nor blame me that this passion I reveal;
　Lovers die inward that their flames conceal.   225
FRANCISCO [*aside*]
　Of all intelligence this may prove the best,
　Sure I shall draw strange fowl, from this foul nest. *Exeunt.*

[Act V, Scene ii]

Enter MARCELLO *and* CORNELIA [*and a* PAGE, *who remains in
the background*]

CORNELIA
　I hear a whispering all about the court,
　You are to fight; who is your opposite?
　What is the quarrel?

207　S.D. FRANCISCO i.e. disguised as Mulinassar
211　speech-prefix: Q3, Q4 *Fra.* (Q1, Q2 FLA.)
212　*but 'tis but* Qq (Sampson conjectured 'but 'tis'.)
221　speech-prefix: Q3, Q4 *Fra.* (Q1, Q2 FLA.); *motion* proposal;
　　　(sudden) impulse
226　speech-prefix: Q3, Q4 *Fra.* (Q1, Q2 FLA.)
　2　*You are* Q2, Q3, Q4 (Q1 Your are)

MARCELLO   'Tis an idle rumour.
CORNELIA
Will you dissemble? Sure you do not well
To fright me thus; you never look thus pale,   5
But when you are most angry. I do charge you
Upon my blessing;——nay I'll call the Duke,
And he shall school you.
MARCELLO   Publish not a fear
Which would convert to laughter; 'tis not so.
Was not this crucifix my father's?
CORNELIA   Yes.   10
MARCELLO
I have heard you say, giving my brother suck,
He took the crucifix between his hands,   *Enter* FLAMINEO
And broke a limb off.
CORNELIA   Yes: but 'tis mended.
FLAMINEO
I have brought your weapon back.
          FLAMINEO *runs* MARCELLO *through*
CORNELIA   Ha, O my horror!
MARCELLO
You have brought it home indeed.
CORNELIA   Help! oh he's murdered.   15
FLAMINEO
Do you turn your gall up? I'll to sanctuary,
And send a surgeon to you.   [*Exit*]

          Enter CARL[O,] HORT[ENSIO,] PEDRO

8 *school* teach, punish (Harrison)
10 *this crucifix:* It must hang round Cornelia's neck
16 *gall* Q2, Q3 (Q1 gaule; Q4 gill): *sanctuary* a place, such as a church,
     where, according to medieval ecclesiastical law, a fugitive from
     justice was entitled to immunity from arrest: *cf. The Duchess of
     Malfi*, IV.ii, 269

16 *gall.* 'It is . . . not quite clear whether the phrase here is figurative, of
     dying; or literal, because Marcello is vomiting from his wound. Probably
     the former.' (Lucas, *Webster*, i, 252). Gall was used to denote bitterness
     of spirit.
17 s.d. CAR[LO] i.e. Lodovico; PEDRO i.e. Gasparo: the presence of
     CARLO and PEDRO here confirms their identity as Lodovico and Gasparo
     since they, the human revengers of Brachiano's crimes, are thus per-
     mitted to witness the beginning of the great punishment of Brachiano,
     Vittoria and Vittoria's brothers. Marcello here interprets his own death
     as divine vengeance for his family's sin. This pattern of the presence of
     revengers at the death of one of their enemies and a man's acceptance
     of his death as part of a scheme of divine vengeance was common in
     Elizabethan and Jacobean revenge plays.

HORTENSIO   How? o'th' ground?

MARCELLO

O mother now remember what I told
Of breaking off the crucifix: farewell.
There are some sins which heaven doth duly punish   20
In a whole family. This it is to rise
By all dishonest means. Let all men know
That tree shall long time keep a steady foot
Whose branches spread no wider than the root.

CORNELIA

O my perpetual sorrow!

HORTENSIO   Virtuous Marcello.   25
He's dead: pray leave him lady; come, you shall.

CORNELIA

Alas he is not dead: he's in a trance.
Why here's nobody shall get anything by his death. Let me
call him again for God's sake.

LODOVICO

I would you were deceiv'd.   30

CORNELIA

O you abuse me, you abuse, me, you abuse me. How many
have gone away thus for lack of tendance; rear up's head,
rear up's head. His bleeding inward will kill him.

HORTENSIO

You see he is departed.

CORNELIA

Let me come to him; give me him as he is; if he be turn'd   35
to earth; let me but give him one hearty kiss, and you shall
put us both into one coffin; fetch a looking-glass, see if his
breath will not stain it; or pull out some feathers from my
pillow, and lay them to his lips,—will you lose him for a
little pains-taking?   40

HORTENSIO

Your kindest office is to pray for him.

CORNELIA

Alas! I would not pray for him yet. He may live to lay me
i'th' ground, and pray for me, if you'll let me come to him.

Enter BRACHIANO *all armed, save the beaver, with* FLAMINEO
[and FRANCISCO]

19 *breaking off* Q1 (Q2, Q3, Q4 breaking of)
24 *wider* Q4 (Q1, Q2, Q3 wilder)
30 speech-prefix: *Lodovico* ed. (Q1 CAR.; Q2, Q3 *Cor.*; Q4 *Hor.*)
39 *lose* Q4 (Q1, Q2, Q3 loose)
43 S.D. FRANCISCO i.e. disguised as Mulinassar

35–40 *cf. King Lear*, V.iii, 261–5.

BRACHIANO
    Was this your handiwork?
FLAMINEO
    It was my misfortune.   45
CORNELIA
    He lies, he lies, he did not kill him: these have kill'd him,
    that would not let him be better look'd to.
BRACHIANO
    Have comfort my griev'd mother.
CORNELIA
    O you screech-owl.
HORTENSIO
    Forbear, good madam.   50
CORNELIA
    Let me go, let me go.
        She runs to FLAMINEO *with her knife drawn and coming to him
                                    lets it fall*
    The God of heaven forgive thee. Dost not wonder
    I pray for thee? I'll tell thee what's the reason:
    I have scarce breath to number twenty minutes;
    I'd not spend that in cursing. Fare thee well—   55
    Half of thyself lies there: and may'st thou live
    To fill an hour-glass with his mould'red ashes,
    To tell how thou shouldst spend the time to come
    In blest repentance.
BRACHIANO   Mother, pray tell me
    How came he by his death? What was the quarrel?   60
CORNELIA
    Indeed my younger boy presum'd too much
    Upon his manhood; gave him bitter words;
    Drew his sword first; and so I know not how,
    For I was out of my wits, he fell with's head
    Just in my bosom.
PAGE   This is not true madam.   65
CORNELIA
    I pray thee peace.
    One arrow's graz'd already; it were vain
    T'lose this: for that will nere be found again.
BRACHIANO
    Go, bear the body to Cornelia's lodging:
    And we command that none acquaint our Duchess   70
    With this sad accident: for you Flamineo,

---

51 s.d. opposite 52–56 in Qq.
67 *graz'd* grassed i.e. lost in the grass

Hark you, I will not grant your pardon.
FLAMINEO   No?
BRACHIANO
  Only a lease of your life. And that shall last
  But for one day. Thou shalt be forc'd each evening
  To renew it, or be hang'd.
FLAMINEO   At your pleasure.   75

      LODOVICO *sprinkles* BRACHIANO'S *beaver with a poison*

  Your will is law now, I'll not meddle with it.
BRACHIANO
  You once did brave me in your sister's lodging;
  I'll now keep you in awe for't. Where's our beaver?
FRANCISCO [*aside*]
  He calls for his destruction. Noble youth,
  I pity thy sad fate. Now to the barriers.   80
  This shall his passage to the black lake further,
  The last good deed he did, he pardon'd murther.   *Exeunt*

[Act V, Scene iii]

*Charges and shouts. They fight at barriers; first single
pairs, then three to three.*

Enter BRACHIANO *and* FLAMINEO *with others* [*including*
GIOVANNI, VITTORIA, *and* FRANCISCO]

BRACHIANO
  An armourer! Ud's death, an armourer!
FLAMINEO
  Armourer; where's the armourer?
BRACHIANO
  Tear off my beaver.
FLAMINEO   Are you hurt, my lord?
BRACHIANO
  O my brain's on fire,   *Enter* ARMOURER
  The helmet is poison'd.
ARMOURER   My lord upon my soul —   5
BRACHIANO
  Away with him to torture.   [*Exit* ARMOURER, *guarded*]
  There are some great ones that have hand in this,
  And near about me.

75 S.D. *beaver* lower part of the face-guard of a helmet
81 *black lake* i.e. the Styx (thought of as a lake or river)
  S.D. *shouts* Q1, Q2 (Q3, Q4 *shoots*); FRANCISCO i.e. disguised as
    Mulinassar

VITTORIA   O my loved lord; poison'd?

FLAMINEO
Remove the bar: here's unfortunate revels,
Call the physicians; a plague upon you; Ent[er] 2 PHYSICIANS   10
We have too much of your cunning here already.
I fear the ambassadors are likewise poisoned.

BRACHIANO
Oh I am gone already: the infection
Flies to the brain and heart. O thou strong heart!
There's such a covenant 'tween the world and it,   15
They're loth to break.

GIOVANNI   O my most loved father!

BRACHIANO
Remove the boy away.
Where's this good woman? Had I infinite worlds
They were too little for thee. Must I leave thee?
What say yon screech-owls, is the venom mortal?   20

PHYSICIANS
Most deadly.

BRACHIANO   Most corrupted politic hangman!
You kill without book; but your art to save
Fails you as oft as great men's needy friends.
I that have given life to offending slaves
And wretched murderers, have I not power   25
To lengthen mine own a twelvemonth?
[to VITTORIA] Do not kiss me, for I shall poison thee.
This unction is sent from the great Duke of Florence.

FRANCISCO
Sir be of comfort.

BRACHIANO
O thou soft natural death, that art joint-twin   30

---

8 Q4 has 'Enter Vittoria' to right of this line.
9 bar: either the barriers or some fastening of the beaver
15 'tween Q1, Q2, Q3 (Q4 'twixt)
16 Q4 has 'Enter Giovanni' to right of this line
20 yon screech-owls ed.
22 without book by heart
23 men's Qq
28 unction unguent, ointment (the poison); extreme unction: cf. V.
   iii, 38.
30 art Q1, Q4 (Q2, Q? are)
31 rough-bearded comet: rough-bearded refers to the comet's shape;
   comets were supposed to presage disasters and evil

---

27 In Soliman and Perseda (circa 1589–92) Soliman is killed by kissing the
   poisoned lips of Perseda who lies dying from the mortal wounds he has
   given her in single combat.

To sweetest slumber: no rough-bearded comet
Stares on thy mild departure: the dull owl
Beats not against thy casement: the hoarse wolf
Scents not thy carrion. Pity winds thy corse,
Whilst horror waits on princes.

VITTORIA   I am lost for ever.   35

BRACHIANO

How miserable a thing it is to die
'Mongst women howling!

    [*Enter* LODOVICO *and* GASPARO *disguised as Capuchins*]

                What are those?

FLAMINEO   Franciscans.

They have brought the extreme unction.

BRACHIANO

On pain of death, let no man name death to me,
It is a word infinitely terrible.   40
Withdraw into our cabinet.

          Exeunt omnes praeter FRANCISCO *and* FLAMINEO

FLAMINEO

To see what solitariness is about dying princes. As heretofore they have unpeopled towns; divorc'd friends, and made
great houses unhospitable: so now, O justice! where are their
flatterers now? Flatterers are but the shadows of princes'   45
bodies, the least thick cloud makes them invisible.

FRANCISCO

There's great moan made for him.

FLAMINEO

'Faith, for some few hours salt water will run most plentifully in every office o'th'court. But believe it; most of them
do but weep over their stepmothers' graves.   50

FRANCISCO

How mean you?

---

34 *Scents* Q4 (Q1, Q2, Q3 Sents); *corse* ed. (Q1, Q2, Q4 coarse; Q3
    course) corpse
35 *waits* Q3, Q4 (Q1 waights; Q2 waites); *princes* Qq (Hazlitt:
    princes')
37 *Franciscans:* see V, i, 16 note; members of the order of St. Francis;
    servants of Francisco (the pun is unknown to Flamineo)
37 s.d. *Capuchins* i.e. the Hungarians Carlo and Pedro
41 s.d. *Exeunt omnes praeter* Q4 (Q1, Q2, Q3 *Exeunt but*) 'All leave
    except'
46 *bodies, the* Q2, Q3, Q4 (Q1 bodies the)
50 *graves* Q1 (Q2, Q3, Q4 grave)

FLAMINEO

Why? They dissemble, as some men do that live within
compass o'th' verge.

FRANCISCO

Come you have thriv'd well under him.

FLAMINEO

'Faith, like a wolf in a woman's breast; I have been fed   55
with poultry: but for money, understand me, I had as good
a will to cozen him, as e'er an officer of them all. But I had
not cunning enough to do it.

FRANCISCO

What did'st thou think of him? 'Faith speak freely.

FLAMINEO

He was a kind of statesman, that would sooner have reckon'd   60
how many cannon-bullets he had discharged against a town,
to count his expense that way, than how many of his valiant
and deserving subjects he lost before it.

FRANCISCO

O speak well of the Duke.

FLAMINEO

I have done. Wilt hear some of my court wisdom?   65

Enter LODOVICO

To reprehend princes is dangerous: and to over-commend
some of them is palpable lying.

FRANCISCO

How is it with the Duke?

LODOVICO   Most deadly ill.
He's fall'n into a strange distraction.
He talks of battles and monopolies,   70
Levying of taxes, and from that descends
To the most brain-sick language. His mind fastens
On twenty several objects, which confound
Deep sense with folly. Such a fearful end
May teach some men that bear too lofty crest,   75

52 *some men* an ironic understatement (Lucas)
55 *wolf* = lupus (ulcer)
62 *expense* ed. (Q1, Q2, Q3 expence; Q4 expences)
65 S.D. LODOVICO i.e. disguised as the Capuchin, Carlo

52–53 *within compass o'th' verge.* 'The *verge* was an area extending to a
      distance of twelve miles round the King's Court, which lay under the
      jurisdiction of the Lord High Steward (from Lat. *virga*, the steward's
      rod of office).' (Lucas, *Webster*, i, 253)
55–56. Ulcers were regularly treated by the application of the raw flesh of
      poultry or with raw meat to prevent them from feeding on the sick
      person's flesh. The historical Bracciano had raw meat applied to the
      malignant ulcer in his leg.

Though they live happiest, yet they die not best.
He hath conferr'd the whole state of the dukedom
Upon your sister, till the Prince arrive
At mature age.

FLAMINEO   There's some good luck in that yet.

FRANCISCO
See here he comes.

Enter BRACHIANO, *presented in a bed,* VITTORIA *and others*
[*including* GASPARO].

                    There's death in's face already.   80

VITTORIA
O my good lord!

These speeches are several kinds of distractions and in the action
should appear so

BRACHIANO   Away, you have abus'd me.
You have convey'd coin forth our territories;
Bought and sold offices; oppress'd the poor,
And I ne'er dreamt on't. Make up your accounts;
I'll now be mine own steward.

FLAMINEO   Sir, have patience.   85

BRACHIANO
Indeed I am too blame.
For did you ever hear the dusky raven
Chide blackness? Or was't ever known the devil
Rail'd against cloven creatures?

VITTORIA   O my lord!

BRACHIANO
Let me have some quails to supper.

FLAMINEO   Sir, you shall.   90

---

77 *state* estate; power   81 S.D. opposite 82–88 in Q1
86 *too blame* Q1, Q2, Q4 (Q3 to blame) too blameworthy
90 *quails* the birds (a delicacy); loose women

---

80 S.D. *presented in a bed* i.e. the traverse is drawn to discover Brachiano
and the others on the inner stage; GASPARO i.e. disguised as the Capuchin
Pedro

81ff. For critical comment on Brachiano's death scene, see: William Hazlitt,
Lectures on the Dramatic Literature of the Age of Elizabeth (1821),
pp. 129–32; W. W. Greg, 'Webster's "White Devil" ', *Modern Language*
Quarterly, III (1900), p. 118; J. R. Mulryne, '*The White Devil and The*
Duchess of Malfi', *Stratford-upon-Avon Studies 1: Jacobean Theatre*,
p. 213; Irving Ribner, *Jacobean Tragedy: The Quest for Moral Order*
(1962), pp. 104–5.

BRACHIANO
No: some fried dog-fish. Your quails feed on poison;—
That old dog-fox, that politician Florence,—
I'll forswear hunting and turn dog-killer;
Rare! I'll be friends with him: for mark you, sir, one dog
Still sets another a-barking: peace, peace,   95
Yonder's a fine slave come in now.

FLAMINEO   Where?

BRACHIANO
Why there.
In a blue bonnet, and a pair of breeches
With a great codpiece. Ha, ha, ha,
Look you his codpiece is stuck full of pins   100
With pearls o'th' head of them. Do not you know him?

FLAMINEO
No my lord.

BRACHIANO   Why 'tis the devil.
I know him by a great rose he wears on's shoe
To hide his cloven foot. I'll dispute with him.
He's a rare linguist.

VITTORIA   My lord here's nothing.   105

BRACHIANO
Nothing? rare! nothing! When I want money
Our treasury is empty; there is nothing.
I'll not be used thus.

VITTORIA   O! lie still my lord—

BRACHIANO
See, see, Flamineo that kill'd his brother
Is dancing on the ropes there: and he carries   110
A money-bag in each hand, to keep him even,
For fear of breaking's neck. And there's a lawyer
In a gown whipt with velvet, stares and gapes
When the money will fall. How the rogue cuts capers!

91 *dog-fish* 'technically the name of a kind of small shark, but com-
    mon as a term of abuse' (Dent)
92 *politician* secretive, cunning person
99 *cod-piece* an appendage, often ornamented, to the close-fitting hose
    or breeches of the 15th–17th centuries
103 *rose* silk rosette or knot of ribbons
105 *linguist* master of language, eloquent disputant (Lucas)
113 *whipt* edged, trimmed; ornamented

91 *feed on poison.* The idea that quails fed on poison was an Elizabethan
    commonplace which has been traced back through Erasmus to Pliny.
    Dent comments: 'Surely the audience would think of Vittoria, advanced
    through the poisoning of Isabella, and now advanced again through
    that of Brachiano.' (p. 148)

It should have been in a halter.   115
'Tis there; what's she?
FLAMINEO   Vittoria, my lord.
BRACHIANO
Ha, ha, ha. Her hair is sprinkled with arras powder,
That makes her look as if she had sinn'd in the pastry.
What's he?
FLAMINEO
A divine my lord.   120
BRACHIANO
He will be drunk. Avoid him: th'argument is fearful when
churchmen stagger in't.
Look you; six gray rats that have lost their tails,
Crawl up the pillow; send for a rat-catcher.
I'll do a miracle: I'll free the court   125
From all foul vermin. Where's Flamineo?
FLAMINEO
I do not like that he names me so often,
Especially on's death-bed: 'tis a sign
I shall not live long: see he's near his end.
          BRACHIANO *seems here near his end.*
LODOVICO *and* GASPARO *in the habit of Capuchins present him in*
          his bed with a crucifix and hallowed candle.

LODOVICO
Pray give us leave: *Attende Domine Brachiane.*   130
FLAMINEO
See, see, how firmly he doth fix his eye
Upon the crucifix.
VITTORIA   O hold it constant.
It settles his wild spirits; and so his eyes
Melt into tears.
LODOVICO (*By the crucifix*)
Domine Brachiane, solebas in bello tutus esse tuo clypeo,   135
nùnc hanc clypeum hosti tuo opponas infernali.

118 *the pastry* place where pastry is made
122 *rats* Q1 (Q2, Q3, Q4 cats)   129 S.D. opposite 121–132 in Q1
130 'Listen Lord Brachiano.' *Brachiane* Q1, Q3, Q4 (Q2 *Brachiano*)
135–6. 'Lord Brachiano, you were accustomed in battle to be guarded
    by your shield, now you shall oppose *this* shield against your
    infernal enemy.'

───────────────────────────────────

117 *arras powder* or orris powder, made from orris root, smelt of violets. *Cf.*
    The Duchess of Malfi, II.ii, 59–60. Vittoria's hair has been sprinkled with
    the powder for her marriage earlier in the day. Dent (p. 150) remarks
    that the following comment by Brachiano is therefore doubly shocking,
    'though perfectly consistent with the implications of his speeches above.
    Throughout this episode . . . he associates her with falsehood and
    wantonness.'

GASPARO *(By the hallowed taper)*
> *Olim hastâ valuisti in bello; nùnc hanc sacram hastam vibrabis*
> *contra hostem animarum.*

LODOVICO
> *Attende Domine Brachiane si nunc quòque probas ea quæ acta*
> *sunt inter nos, flecte caput in dextrum.*   140

GASPARO
> *Esto securus. Domine Brachiane: cogita quantum habeas*
> *meritorum—denique memineris meam animam pro tua oppig-*
> *noratam si quid esse periculi.*

LODOVICO
> *Si nùnc quoque probas ea quæ acta sunt inter nos, flecte caput*
> *in lævum.*   145
> He is departing: pray stand all apart,
> And let us only whisper in his ears
> Some private meditations, which our order
> Permits you not to hear.

> *Here the rest being departed* LODOVICO *and* GASPARO
> *discover themselves*

GASPARO   Brachiano.
LODOVICO
> Devil Brachiano. Thou art damn'd.
GASPARO   Perpetually.   150
LODOVICO
> A slave condemn'd, and given up to the gallows
> Is thy great lord and master.
GASPARO   True: for thou
> Art given up to the devil.

137–8: 'Once you did prevail with your spear in battle; now you shall
    wield *this* sacred spear against the enemy of souls.'
139–40: 'Listen Lord Brachiano, if you now also approve what has
    been done between us, turn your head to the right.'
141–3: 'Be assured, Lord Brachiano: consider how many good deeds
    you have done – lastly remember that my soul is pledged for
    yours, should there be any peril.'
144–5: 'If you now also approve what has been done between us, turn
    your head to the left.'
149 s.d. opposite 148–150 in Q1

135–45 This passage, as A. W. Reed pointed out in *The Times Literary
Supplement* (14th June, 1947) p. 295, is borrowed from Erasmus'
Colloquy *Funus* in which the elaborate business of the death and burial
of Georgius Balearicus who, trusting to his wealth, sought by purchase
to retain his standing beyond the grave, is contrasted with the moving
description of that of Cornelius Montius 'qui Christianeri more se ad
mortem composuit.'

LODOVICO   O you slave!
  You that were held the famous politician;
  Whose art was poison.
GASPARO   And whose conscience murder.   155
LODOVICO
  That would have broke your wife's neck down the stairs
  Ere she was poison'd.
GASPARO   That had your villainous sallets—
LODOVICO
  And fine embroidered bottles, and perfumes
  Equally mortal with a winter plague—
GASPARO
  Now there's mercury—
LODOVICO   And copperas—
GASPARO   And quicksilver—   160
LODOVICO
  With other devilish pothecary stuff
  A-melting in your politic brains: dost hear?
GASPARO
  This is Count Lodovico.
LODOVICO   This Gasparo.
  And thou shalt die like a poor rogue.
GASPARO   And stink
  Like a dead fly-blown dog.
LODOVICO
  And be forgotten before thy funeral sermon.
BRACHIANO
  Vittoria! Vittoria!
LODOVICO   O the cursed devil,
  Come to himself again! We are undone.

Enter VITTORIA *and the* ATTEND[ANTS]

GASPARO [*aside to* LODOVICO]
  Strangle him in private. [*to* VITTORIA] What? Will you call
                            him again

157 *villainous sallets* see IV.ii, 60 note.
160 *copperas* sulphate of copper
168 *Come* Q1 (Q2, Q3, Q4 Comes)

---

158 *fine embroidered bottles.* One assumes that these were bottles made of
    patterned silver or glass bottles covered in decorated material or jewels.
160 *mercury:* 'corrosive sublimate, mercuric chloride; not the metal itself',
    since quicksilver is also mentioned (Lucas, *Webster*, i, 258), but Brown
    suggests that 'Gasparo repeats himself in trying to terrify Brachiano
    with words.' (p. 152 n.)

To live in treble torments? For charity,   170
For Christian charity, avoid the chamber.
                              Exeunt [VITTORIA *and* ATTENDANTS]

LODOVICO
You would prate, sir. This is a true-love knot
Sent from the Duke of Florence.   BRACHIANO *is strangled*

GASPARO   What, is it done?

LODOVICO
The snuff is out. No woman-keeper i'th' world,
Though she had practis'd seven year at the pest-house,   175
Could have done't quaintlier.
[*Enter* VITTORIA, FRANCISCO, FLAMINEO, *and* ATTENDANTS]
                              My lords he's dead.

OMNES
Rest to his soul.

VITTORIA   O me! this place is hell.   *Exit* VITTORIA
                              [*with* ATTENDANTS *and* GASPARO]

FRANCISCO
How heavily she takes it.

FLAMINEO   O yes, yes;
Had women navigable rivers in their eyes
They would dispend them all; surely I wonder   180
Why we should wish more rivers to the city
When they sell water so good cheap. I'll tell thee,
These are but moonish shades of griefs or fears,
There's nothing sooner dry than women's tears.
Why here's an end of all my harvest, he has given me nothing.   185
Court promises! Let wise men count them curs'd
For while you live he that scores best pays worst.

FRANCISCO
Sure, this was Florence' doing.

---

171 *avoid* empty, clear
171 s.d.: Q3, Q4 *Exeunt.* (Q1, Q2 [omit])
176 *done't* Q1 (Q2, Q3, Q4 don't); *quaintlier* more skilfully
176 s.d. ed. (Q3, Q4 *They return;* Q1, Q2 [omit])
178, 188, 198, 205, 217 speech-prefixes: Q3, Q4 *Fra.* (Q1, Q2 FLO.)
182 *cheap* bargain price
183 *moonish* like the moon, changeable

---

174 *woman-keeper* female nurse. At this time nurses were frequently sus-
     pected of strangling or smothering patients who were sick of the plague.
181 *more rivers to the city:* 'Certainly a reference to the New River project of
     Sir Hugh Myddleton to supply London with fresh water. The scheme
     was sanctioned in 1606 and after serious interruptions was completed
     in 1613.' (Sampson, p. 202)

FLAMINEO   Very likely.
Those are found weighty strokes which come from th'hand,
But those are killing strokes which come from th'head.   190
O the rare tricks of a Machivillian!
He doth not come like a gross plodding slave
And buffet you to death. No, my quaint knave,
He tickles you to death; makes you die laughing;
As if you had swallow'd down a pound of saffron.   195
You see the feat, 'tis practis'd in a tricc:
To teach court-honesty, it jumps on ice.

FRANCISCO
Now have the people liberty to talk
And descant on his vices.

FLAMINEO   Misery of princes,
That must of force be censur'd by their slaves!   200
Not only blam'd for doing things are ill,
But for not doing all that all men will.
One were better be a thresher.
Ud's death, I would fain speak with this Duke yet.

FRANCISCO
Now he's dead?   205

FLAMINEO
I cannot conjure; but if prayers or oaths
Will get to th'speech of him: though forty devils
Wait on him in his livery of flames,
I'll speak to him, and shake him by the hand,
Though I be blasted.   *Exit* FLAMINEO

FRANCISCO   Excellent Lodovico!   210
What? Did you terrify him at the last gasp?

LODOVICO
Yes; and so idly, that the Duke had like
T'have terrified us.

FRANCISCO   How?

Enter [ZANCHE] *the Moor*

---

191 *a Machivillian* i.e. a Machiavellian, since Machiavelli was wrongly
    supposed to be the type of scheming villains
196 *feat* Q2, Q3, Q4 (Q1 seat)
199 *descant* comment on, criticize
200 *of force* of necessity   212 *idly* carelessly

194–5. This idea about the effects of immoderate taking of saffron was a
    commonplace of Elizabethan herbals.
196–207: 'You see, this feat, accomplished in such a short time, is to teach
    the kind of honesty found at court [i.e. that of the scheming 'politician']
    how dangerously insecure its footing is.' Cf. *The Duchess of Malfi*, V.
    ii, 327–9.

LODOVICO   You shall hear that hereafter.
See! yon's the infernal that would make us sport.
Now to the revelation of that secret   215
She promis'd when she fell in love with you.

FRANCISCO
You're passionately met in this sad world.

ZANCHE
I would have you look up, sir; these court tears
Claim not your tribute to them. Let those weep
That guiltily partake in the sad cause.   220
I knew last night by a sad dream I had
Some mischief would ensue; yet to say truth
My dream most concern'd you.

LODOVICO   Shall's fall a-dreaming?

FRANCISCO
Yes, and for fashion sake I'll dream with her.

ZANCHE
Methought sir, you came stealing to my bed.   225

FRANCISCO
Wilt thou believe me sweeting? By this light
I was a-dreamt on thee too: for methought
I saw thee naked.

ZANCHE   Fie sir! as I told you,
Methought you lay down by me.

FRANCISCO   So dreamt I:
And lest thou shouldst take cold, I cover'd thee   230
With this Irish mantle.

ZANCHE   Verily I did dream,
You were somewhat bold with me; but to come to't.

LODOVICO
How? how? I hope you will not go to't here.

FRANCISCO
Nay: you must hear my dream out.

ZANCHE   Well, sir, forth.

FRANCISCO
When I threw the mantle o'er thee, thou didst laugh   235
Exceedingly methought.

ZANCHE   Laugh?

214 *the infernal* i.e. spirit; *us* Q4, Lucas (Q1, Q2, Q3, Sampson and
    Brown: up)
218 *et seq.*: speech-prefixes for Zanche: Q3, Q4 *Zan.* Q1, Q2 Moo.
    or MOORE.
231 *Irish mantle* kind of blanket or plaid worn by Irish peasants till the
    17th century, often (as implied here) with nothing underneath it
233 *go to't here* Q1b [go to.t here] (Q1a go to it here; Q2 go to there;
    Q3, Q4 go to't there)

FRANCISCO   And cried'st out,
  The hair did tickle thee.
ZANCHE   There was a dream indeed.
LODOVICO
  Mark her I prithee, she simpers like the suds
  A collier hath been wash'd in.
ZANCHE
  Come, sir; good fortune tends you; I did tell you   240
  I would reveal a secret: Isabella
  The Duke of Florence' sister was empoison'd,
  By a fum'd picture: and Camillo's neck
  Was broke by damn'd Flamineo; the mischance
  Laid on a vaulting-horse.
FRANCISCO   Most strange!
ZANCHE   Most true.   245
LODOVICO
  The bed of snakes is broke.
ZANCHE
  I sadly do confess I had a hand
  In the black deed.
FRANCISCO   Thou kept'st their counsel, —
ZANCHE   Right.
  For which, urg'd with contrition, I intend
  This night to rob Vittoria.
LODOVICO   Excellent penitence!   250
  Usurers dream on't while they sleep out sermons.
ZANCHE
  To further our escape, I have entreated
  Leave to retire me, till the funeral
  Unto a friend i'th' country. That excuse
  Will further our escape. In coin and jewels   255
  I shall, at least, make good unto your use
  A hundred thousand crowns.
FRANCISCO   O noble wench!
LODOVICO
  Those crowns we'll share.
ZANCHE   It is a dowry,
  Methinks, should make that sunburnt proverb false,

---

238 *simpers:* ' "Simper" being an old alternate form of "simmer",
    play on the word was common.' (Dent)
243 *fum'd* perfumed
246 *bed* nest, thick entanglement
248 *kept'st* Q3, Q4 (Q1 kepts; Q2 keps't)
259 *sunburnt* dark-skinned; see V.i, 180

And wash the Ethiop white.
FRANCISCO   It shall, away!   260
ZANCHE
  Be ready for our flight.
FRANCISCO   An hour 'fore day.
                              Exit [ZANCHE] *the Moor*
  O strange discovery! Why till now we knew not
  The circumstance of either of their deaths.

                 Enter [ZANCHE *the*] *Moor*

ZANCHE
  You'll wait about midnight in the chapel?
FRANCISCO   There.
LODOVICO
  Why now our action's justified,—
FRANCISCO   Tush for justice.   265
  What harms it justice? We now, like the partridge
  Purge the disease with laurel: for the fame
  Shall crown the enterprise and quit the shame.   *Exeunt*

                    [Act V, Scene iv]

       Enter FLAM[INEO] *and* GASP[ARO] *at one door, another*
                    way GIOVANNI *attended*

GASPARO
  The young Duke. Did you e'er see a sweeter prince?
FLAMINEO
  I have known a poor woman's bastard better favour'd. This

---

264 *chapel?* ed. (Qq Chappel.)
267 *laurel* (literally) laurel leaves; laurel wreath betokening a famous
       achievement; *fame* Q1 (Q2, Q3, Q4 same)
268 *quit* clear, rid, absolve [one] of
S.D. GASP[ARO] being still disguised as Pedro, here establishes his separate
       identity just as Lodovico, disguised as Carlo, had established his in the
       previous scene

---

260 *And wash the Ethiop white.* This is probably derived from Jeremiah xiii,
       23: 'Can the Ethiopian change his skin, or the leopard his spots?' The
       phrase was used to express impossibility in Lucian, *Adversus Indoctum*,
       28. As a proverb it was particularly popular in the Elizabethan Age. (See
       R. R. Cawley, *The Voyagers and Elizabethan Drama*, pp. 37–38.)
266–7. The source of this statement is Pliny's *Natural History*, Book VIII,
       chapter xxvii: 'palumbes, graculi, merulae, perdices lauri folio annuum
       fastidium purgent.' Holland's translation (1601) reads: 'The Stock-
       doves, the Iaies, Merles, Blackbirds, Ousels, recover their appetite,
       which once in a year they loose, with eating Bay-leaves that purge their
       stomacke.' Partridges, omitted from this list, are included in the list
       which follows of birds which purge themselves with the herb pellitory.

is behind him. Now, to his face: all comparisons were hateful. Wise was the courtly peacock, that being a great minion,
and being compar'd for beauty, by some dottrels that   5
stood by, to the kingly eagle, said the eagle was a far fairer
bird than herself, not in respect of her feathers, but in respect
of her long tallants. His will grow out in time.
My gracious lord.

GIOVANNI
I pray leave me sir.   10

FLAMINEO
Your Grace must be merry: 'tis I have cause to mourn; for
wot you what said the little boy that rode behind his father
on horseback?

GIOVANNI
Why, what said he?

FLAMINEO
'When you are dead father,' said he, 'I hope then I shall ride   15
in the saddle.' O 'tis a brave thing for a man to sit by himself: he may stretch himself in the stirrups, look about, and
see the whole compass of the hemisphere; you're now, my
lord, i'th'saddle.

GIOVANNI
Study your prayers sir, and be penitent;   20
'Twere fit you'd think on what hath former bin,
I have heard grief nam'd the eldest child of sin.

Exit GIOV[ANNI]

FLAMINEO
Study my prayers? He threatens me divinely; I am falling
to pieces already; I care not, though, like Anacharsis I
were pounded to death in a mortar. And yet that death were   25
fitter for usurers' gold and themselves to be beaten together,
to make a most cordial cullis for the devil.

---

5 *dottrels* Q1b (Q1a dottrles) species of plover; fools, simpletons
8 *tallants* talons; talents   15–16 inverted commas ed.; (Qq (said he))
15 *I hope then I* Q1 (Q2, Q3, Q4 I hope that I)
21 *bin* Q1 (Q2, Q3, Q4 been): cf. *The Duchess of Malfi*, V.v, 53–4
24 *to* Q1, Q2, Q3 (Q4 in)
26 *usurers'* ed.
27 *cordial* see V.i, 138 note; *cullis* ed. (Q1a chullice; Q1b cullice)
    strengthening broth made by bruising meat

---

24 *Anarcharsis* was a Thracian prince of the 6th century B.C. It was, in
fact, Anaxarchus who, by order of Nicocreon, was pounded to death in
a mortar. The confusion of names belongs not to Webster, but his
source, Nicholas de Montreux, *Honours Academie*, translated by R.
Tofte (1610: '. . . *Anacharsis*, being pounded to death in a morter,
iested at death.' (Dent, p. 156)

He hath his uncle's villainous look already,
In *decimo-sexto*. Now sir, what are you?   *Enter* COURTIER

COURTIER
It is the pleasure sir, of the young Duke   30
That you forbear the presence, and all rooms
That owe him reverence.

FLAMINEO   So, the wolf and the raven
Are very pretty fools when they are young.
Is it your office, sir, to keep me out?

COURTIER
So the Duke wills.   35

FLAMINEO
Verily, master courtier, extremity is not to be used in all
offices. Say that a gentlewoman were taken out of her bed
about midnight, and committed to Castle Angelo, to the
tower yonder, with nothing about her, but her smock:
would it not show a cruel part in the gentleman porter to   40
lay claim to her upper garment, pull it o'er her head and
ears; and put her in naked?

COURTIER
Very good: you are merry.   [*Exit*]

FLAMINEO
Doth he make a court ejectment of me? A flaming firebrand
casts more smoke without a chimney, than within 't. I'll   45
smoor some of them.

            Enter [FRANCISCO, *Duke of*] *Florence*

How now? Thou art sad.

FRANCISCO
I met even now with the most piteous sight.

FLAMINEO
Thou met'st another here, a pitiful
Degraded courtier.

29 *decimo-sexto* a book of very small pages, each being only $\frac{1}{16}$th of a
   full sheet of paper
31 *presence* presence or audience chamber
39 *nothing about* no money on; no clothes around
42 *naked* Q2, Q3, Q4 (Q1 nak'd)
44 *flaming firebrand:* 'with a play on his own name, Flamineo?'
   (Lucas)
46 *smoor* smother, suffocate
   S.D. FRANCISCO i.e. disguised as Mulinassar
   ────────────────────────────────
38 *Castle Angelo.* Vittoria was herself imprisoned in Castle Sant Angelo in
   Rome, 1581–2.

FRANCISCO   Your reverend mother   50
  Is grown a very old woman in two hours.
  I found them winding of Marcello's corse;
  And there is such a solemn melody
  'Tween doleful songs, tears, and sad elegies:
  Such as old grandames, watching by the dead,   55
  Were wont t'outwear the nights with; that believe me
  I had no eyes to guide me forth the room,
  They were so o'ercharg'd with water.
FLAMINEO   I will see them.
FRANCISCO
  'Twere much uncharity in you: for your sight
  Will add unto their tears.
FLAMINEO   I will see them.   60
FRANCISCO
  They are behind the traverse. I'll discover
  Their superstitious howling. [*Draws the traverse*]

    CORNELIA, [ZANCHE] *the Moor and 3. other Ladies*
    discovered, winding MARCELLO'S *corse.   A song.*

CORNELIA
  This rosemary is wither'd, pray get fresh;
  I would have these herbs grow up in his grave
  When I am dead and rotten. Reach the bays,   65
  I'll tie a garland here about his head:
  'Twill keep my boy from lightning. This sheet
  I have kept this twenty year, and every day
  Hallow'd it with my prayers; I did not think
  He should have wore it.

65 *the bays* a garland of bay (or bay laurel) leaves such as was used
    to crown a poet or conqueror
67 *This sheet* i.e. her own winding-sheet
68 *year* ed. (Q1 yere; Q2 yeeres; Q3, Q4 years)

63ff. 'Partially because she was depicted without a real trace of melodrama,
    [Cornelia] remains . . . one of the most authentic pathological studies in
    the Jacobean drama.' (R. R. Reed, *Bedlam on the Jacobean Stage*
    (Cambridge, Mass., 1952), pp. 91–92). See also J. R. Mulryne, *op. cit.*,
    pp. 213–14. Cornelia's distribution of flowers recalls Ophelia's in
    Hamlet, IV.v, 175–83, but Dent (pp. 157–58) thinks that it hardly parallels
    Ophelia's in significance and suggests that it makes most sense if all
    three flowers are given to Flamineo.
67 *'Twill keep . . . lightning.* Holland's translation of Pliny's *Natural History*
    (1601), Book II, chapter lv reads: 'Of all those things which growe out of
    the earth, Lightning blasteth not the Laurell tree; . . .' and Book XV,
    chapter xxx: 'It is reported, that *Tiberius Caesar* the Emperor ever
    used to weare a chaplet thereof when it thundered, for feare of being
    strucken with lightning.'

ZANCHE   Look you; who are yonder?   70

CORNELIA
O reach me the flowers.

ZANCHE
Her ladyship's foolish.

WOMAN   Alas her grief
Hath turn'd her child again.

CORNELIA *to* FLAMINEO   You're very welcome.
There's rosemary for you, and rue for you,
Heart's-ease for you. I pray make much of it.   75
I have left more for myself.

FRANCISCO   Lady, who's this?

CORNELIA
You are, I take it, the grave-maker.

FLAMINEO   So.

ZANCHE
'Tis Flamineo.

[CORNELIA *takes his hand*]

CORNELIA
Will you make me such a fool? Here's a white hand:
Can blood so soon be wash'd out? Let me see: 80
When screech-owls croak upon the chimney tops,
And the strange cricket i'th' oven sings and hops,
When yellow spots do on your hands appear,
Be certain then you of a corse shall hear.
Out upon't, how 'tis speckled! H'as handled a toad sure.   85
Cowslip-water is good for the memory:
Pray buy me 3. ounces of't.

FLAMINEO
I would I were from hence.

CORNELIA   Do you hear, sir?
I'll give you a saying which my grandmother
Was wont, when she heard the bell toll, to sing o'er   90
Unto her lute—

FLAMINEO   Do and you will, do.

CORNELIA *doth this in several forms of distraction*

CORNELIA
Call for the robin red breast and the wren,

70, 72, 78 speech-prefixes for Zanche: Qq. MOO. or MOOR.
70 *yonder?* Q2, Q3, Q4 (Q1 yonder.)
84 *corse* ed. (Q1 Course; Q2, Q3, Q4 Coarse)
85 *H'as* ed. (Qq h'as) he has
91 S.D. opposite 93–95 in Q1

92–101 'No direct source has been suggested for any part of this beautiful
   song.' (Dent, p. 159)

Since o'er shady groves they hover,
And with leaves and flow'rs do cover
The friendless bodies of unburied men.   95
Call unto his funeral dole
The ant, the field-mouse, and the mole
To rear him hillocks, that shall keep him warm
And (when gay tombs are robb'd) sustain no harm,
But keep the wolf far thence: that's foe to men,   100
For with his nails he'll dig them up again.
They would not bury him 'cause he died in a quarrel
But I have an answer for them.
Let holy church receive him duly
Since he paid the church tithes truly.   105
His wealth is summ'd, and this is all his store:
This poor men get; and great men get no more.
Now the wares are gone, we may shut up shop.
Bless you all good people.

　　　　　　　　　Exeunt CORNELIA [,ZANCHE] *and Ladies*

FLAMINEO
I have a strange thing in me, to the which   110
I cannot give a name, without it be
Compassion; I pray leave me.　　　　　　*Exit* FRANCISCO
This night I'll know the utmost of my fate,
I'll be resolv'd what my rich sister means
T'assign me for my service. I have liv'd   115
Riotously ill, like some that live in court.
And sometimes, when my face was full of smiles
Have felt the maze of conscience in my breast.
Oft gay and honour'd robes those tortures try,
We think cag'd birds sing, when indeed they cry.   120

　96 *funeral dole* funeral rites
110 *to the* ed. (Qq to th')
114 *resolv'd* settled in my own mind; satisfied
117 *my* Q1 (Q2, Q3, Q4 his)
118 *maze* Q2, Q3, Q4 (Q1 mase) bewilderment
120 italics: ed. (Qq mark the line with inverted commas)

　92–5. The belief that the robin would cover the face or whole body of a
　　dead person was common in Europe in the sixteenth century. It is found
　　in the 'babe in the wood' story of the murder of the orphan Pertillo by
　　ruffians hired by his uncle Fallerio in Robert Yarington's *Two Lamen-*
　　table Tragedies (1594-*circa* 1598). 'The wren appears here as well
　　because she is, in popular belief, the robin's wife.' (Lucas, *Webster*, i,
　　263)
100–101 *cf. The Duchess of Malfi*, IV.ii, 303–305.

Enter BRACHIA[NO'S] *Ghost. In his leather cassock and
breeches, boots, a cowl [and in his hand] a pot of lily-
flowers with a skull in't.*

Ha! I can stand thee. Nearer, nearer yet.
What a mockery hath death made of thee? Thou look'st sad.
In what place art thou? in yon starry gallery,
Or in the cursed dungeon? No? not speak?
Pray, sir, resolve me, what religion's best   125
For a man to die in? or is it in your knowledge
To answer me how long I have to live?
That's the most necessary question.
Not answer? Are you still like some great men
That only walk like shadows up and down,   130
And to no purpose: say:———
    The ghost throws earth upon him and shows him the skull
What's that? O fatal! He throws earth upon me.
A dead man's skull beneath the roots of flowers.
I pray speak sir; our Italian churchmen
Make us believe, dead men hold conference   135
With their familiars, and many times
Will come to bed to them, and eat with them.   *Exit Ghost*
He's gone; and see, the skull and earth are vanish'd.
This is beyond melancholy. I do dare my fate
To do its worst. Now to my sister's lodging,   140
And sum up all these horrors; the disgrace
The Prince threw on me; next the piteous sight
Of my dead brother; and my mother's dotage;
And last this terrible vision. All these
Shall with Vittoria's bounty turn to good,   145
Or I will drown this weapon in her blood.   *Exit*

120 S.D. *cassock* long cloak; *cowl* ed. (Q1 coole; Q2 coule; Q3, Q4
    coul); *lily* ed. (Q1 *lilly*; Q2, Q3, Q4 *lilly*)
121 *stand* withstand: a word which recalls IV.ii, 50 'whether inten-
    tionally or no.' (Lucas)
122 *of thee* Q1 (Q2, Q3, Q4 thee)   132 *earth* Q1, Q2, Q3 (Q4 dirt)
136 *familiars* familiar spirits; close friends or relations

---

120 S.D. It was a common superstition that if a wicked man were buried in
    a Friar's *cowl* he would obtain remission for some part of his sins. A *pot
    of lily-flowers* was frequently used as a religious emblem to denote life in
    pictures of the Annunciation. The *skull* denoted death. 'Webster evi-
    dently intended a grotesque, though perhaps common, juxtaposition of
    symbols, . . .' (Dent, p. 161).
142-3 It was not unknown for villainous revengers, summing up the list of
    their wrongs before the final execution of vengeance, to include afflic-
    tions that they had brought upon themselves. Thus, in *Soliman and
    Perseda* the death of Erastus, carried out by Soliman's own command,
    is included in the final enumeration of his wrongs.

[Act V, Scene v]

Enter FRANCISCO, LODOVICO, *and* HORTENSIO [*over-*
hearing them]

LODOVICO
My lord upon my soul you shall no further:
You have most ridiculously engag'd yourself
Too far already. For my part, I have paid
All my debts, so if I should chance to fall
My creditors fall not with me; and I vow   5
To quite all in this bold assembly
To the meanest follower. My lord leave the city,
Or I'll forswear the murder.
FRANCISCO   Farewell Lodovico.
If thou dost perish in this glorious act,
I'll rear unto thy memory that fame   10
Shall in the ashes keep alive thy name.
                    [*Exeunt* FRANCISCO *and* LODOVICO]
HORTENSIO
There's some black deed on foot. I'll presently
Down to the citadel, and raise some force.
These strong court factions that do brook no checks,
In the career oft break the riders' necks.   [*Exit*] 15

[Act V, Scene vi]

Enter VITTORIA *with a book in her hand*, ZANCHE;
FLAMINEO *following them*

FLAMINEO
What, are you at your prayers? Give o'er.
VITTORIA   How ruffin?
FLAMINEO
I come to you 'bout worldly business:

  6 *quite* Q1, Q2 (Q3, Q4 quit) requite, repay
  7 *To the* i.e. down to and including
  8 *forswear* deny, repudiate
 15 *career* see IV.iii, 94–95 note; *Exit*. Q3, Q4 (Q1, Q2 [omit])
  1 *ruffin* cant term for the devil

Act V, Scene v: 'This brief scene is dramatically necessary, in order to account
    for the entrance of Giovanni and the English ambassador after the triple
    murder in the following scene.' (Sampson, p. 204)

Sit down, sit down. Nay, stay blouze, you may hear it,
The doors are fast enough.

VITTORIA   Ha, are you drunk?

FLAMINEO

Yes, yes, with wormwood water; you shall taste   5
Some of it presently.

VITTORIA   What intends the fury?

FLAMINEO

You are my lord's executrix, and I claim
Reward, for my long service.

VITTORIA   For your service?

FLAMINEO

Come therefore, here is pen and ink, set down
What you will give me.   10

VITTORIA

There.   *She writes*

FLAMINEO Ha! have you done already?
'Tis a most short conveyance.

VITTORIA   I will read it.
[*reads*] *I give that portion to thee, and no other*
Which Cain groan'd under having slain his brother.

FLAMINEO

A most courtly patent to beg by.

VITTORIA   You are a villain.   15

FLAMINEO

Is't come to this? They say affrights cure agues:
Thou hast a devil in thee; I will try
If I can scare him from thee. Nay sit still:
My lord hath left me yet two case of jewels

---

3 *blouze* beggar's trull; a fat, red-faced, slatternly wench
4 *fast* secure
5 *wormwood water* medicine made of the leaves and tips of artemisia
    absinthium, a plant proverbial for its very bitter taste; an emblem
    or type of what is bitter and grievous to the soul
6 *fury?* Q1 (Q2, Q3, Q4 Fury?): see IV.iii, 125 and 151 note
8 *your service?* Q2, Q4 (Q1 your seruice   ; Q3 you service?)
12 *conveyance* document by which property is transferred
13 *portion* part or share of an estate given by law to an heir
14 *which Cain groan'd under* i.e. God's curse: see Genesis iv, 11–15
15 *patent* see V.i, 111 note
18 *scare* Q3, Q4 (Q1, Q2 scarre)

18ff. An excellent analysis of the relationship between Flamineo and
    Vittoria as it is found in this scene, especially in the imagery, is given by
    B. J. Layman, 'The Equilibrium of Opposites in *The White Devil:*
    A Reinterpretation', *PMLA*, LXXIV (1959), 344–7.

Shall make me scorn your bounty; you shall see them. [*Exit*]　20
VITTORIA
Sure he's distracted.
ZANCHE　　　　　　　　O he's desperate!
For your own safety give him gentle language.

He enters with two case of pistols

FLAMINEO
Look, these are better far at a dead lift,
Than all your jewel house.
VITTORIA　　　　　　　And yet methinks,
These stones have no fair lustre, they are ill set.　　25
FLAMINEO
I'll turn the right side towards you: you shall see
How they will sparkle.
VITTORIA　　　　　Turn this horror from me:
What do you want? What would you have me do?
Is not all mine, yours? Have I any children?
FLAMINEO
Pray thee good woman do not trouble me　　30
With this vain worldly business; say your prayers;
I made a vow to my deceased lord,
Neither yourself, nor I should outlive him,
The numb'ring of four hours.
VITTORIA　　　　　Did he enjoin it?
FLAMINEO
He did, and 'twas a deadly jealousy,　　35
Lest any should enjoy thee after him,
That urg'd him vow me to it. For my death,
I did propound it voluntarily, knowing
If he could not be safe in his own court
Being a great Duke, what hope then for us?　　40
VITTORIA
This is your melancholy and despair.
FLAMINEO　　　　　　　　Away;
Fool that thou art to think that politicians
Do use to kill the effects of injuries
And let the cause live: shall we groan in irons,

21 *desperate!* Q2, Q3, Q4 (Q1 *desperate*)
22 S.D. Q1, Q2 (Q3, Q4 *And returns . . .*)
31 *worldly* Q2, Q3, Q4 (Q1 *wordly*)
32–33 *lord, / Neither* i.e. lord, [that] neither
42 *Fool that* ed.

23 *at a dead lift* in a tight corner. This phrase was originally applied to a
　horse which had to drag a dead weight that was too heavy for it. Here
　Flamineo is punning on *dead*.

Or be a shameful and a weighty burthen————   45
To a public scaffold? This is my resolve:
I would not live at any man's entreaty
Nor die at any's bidding.
VITTORIA   Will you hear me?
FLAMINEO
My life hath done service to other men,
My death shall serve mine own turn; make you ready.   50
VITTORIA
Do you mean to die indeed?
FLAMINEO   With as much pleasure
As e'er my father gat me.
VITTORIA [*aside to* ZANCHE]   Are the doors lock'd?
ZANCHE
Yes madam.
VITTORIA
Are you grown an atheist? Will you turn your body,
Which is the goodly palace of the soul   55
To the soul's slaughter house? O the cursed devil
Which doth present us with all other sins
Thrice candied o'er; despair with gall and stibium,
Yet we carouse it off; [*aside to* ZANCHE] Cry out for help.
Makes us forsake that which was made for man,   60
The world, to sink to that was made for devils,
Eternal darkness.
ZANCHE   Help, help!
FLAMINEO   I'll stop your throat
With winter plums,—
VITTORIA   I prithee yet remember,
Millions are now in graves, which at last day
Like mandrakes shall rise shrieking.
FLAMINEO   Leave your prating,   65
For these are but grammatical laments,

48 *hear me* i.e. give me a hearing (with connotation of legal or judicial
hearing): *cf. The Duchess of Malfi*, III.ii, 83
54 *atheist* see IV.ii, 40 note
58 *candied o'er* sugared over; *gall* bile; venom, poison; bitterness of
spirit; *stibium* the poison antimony
65 *Like mandrakes* see III.i, 51 note
66 *grammatical laments* laments made according to formal rules

56–58 i.e. 'O the cursed devil that presents all others sins to us under a
sugar cover, [but] despair covered with bitterness and poison.' *Cf. The
Duchess of Malfi*, I.ii, 196–8; IV.i, 19–20. *Despair* was considered one
of the greatest sins because it meant denying the grace of God: *cf. The
Duchess of Malfi*, IV.ii, 74–75.

Feminine arguments, and they move me
As some in pulpits move their auditory
More with their exclamation than sense
Of reason, or sound doctrine.

ZANCHE [aside]   Gentle madam   70
Seem to consent, only persuade him teach
The way to death; let him die first.

VITTORIA [aside]
'Tis good, I apprehend it.—
To kill oneself is meat that we must take
Like pills, not chew't, but quickly swallow it;   75
The smart o'th' wound, or weakness of the hand
May else bring treble torments.

FLAMINEO   I have held it
A wretched and most miserable life,
Which is not able to die.

VITTORIA   O but frailty!
Yet I am now resolv'd; farewell affliction.   80
Behold Brachiano, I that while you liv'd
Did make a flaming altar of my heart
To sacrifice unto you; now am ready
To sacrifice heart and all. Farewell Zanche.

ZANCHE
How madam! Do you think that I'll outlive you?   85
Expecially when my best self Flamineo
Goes the same voyage.

FLAMINEO   O most loved Moor!

ZANCHE
Only, by all my love let me entreat you;
Since it is most necessary none of us
Do violence on ourselves; let you or I   90
Be her sad taster, teach her how to die.

FLAMINEO
Thou dost instruct me nobly; take these pistols,
Because my hand is stain'd with blood already:
Two of these you shall level at my breast,
The other 'gainst your own, and so we'll die,   95
Most equally contented. But first swear
Not to outlive me.

VITTORIA and ZANCHE Most religiously.

69 *exclamation* formal declamation; emphatic or vehement speech
73 *apprehend* understand, feel the force of: *cf.* II.i, 243.
75 *chew't* chew it
89 *none* Q1 (Q2, Q3, Q4 one)
95 *The other* ed. (Qq Th'other) i.e. the other pair (case) of pistols

FLAMINEO

Then here's an end of me: farewell daylight;
And O contemptible physic! that dost take
So long a study, only to preserve   100
So short a life, I take my leave of thee.

Showing the pistols

These are two cupping-glasses, that shall draw
All my infected blood out.
Are you ready?

VITTORIA and ZANCHE   Ready.

FLAMINEO

Whither shall I go now? O Lucian thy ridiculous purgatory!   105
to find Alexander the Great cobbling shoes, Pompey tagging
points, and Julius Caesar making hair buttons, Hannibal
selling blacking, and Augustus crying garlic, Charlemagne
selling lists by the dozen, and King Pippin crying apples in
a cart drawn with one horse.   110
Whether I resolve to fire, earth, water, air,
Or all the elements by scruples, I know not
Nor greatly care.—Shoot, shoot,
Of all deaths the violent death is best,
For from ourselves it steals ourselves so fast   115
The pain once apprehended is quite past.

They shoot and run to him and tread upon him

VITTORIA

What, are you dropp'd?

FLAMINEO

I am mix'd with earth already. As you are noble
Perform your vows, and bravely follow me.

VITTORIA

Whither? to hell?

ZANCHE   To most assured damnation.   120

---

104 speech-prefix ed. (Qq *Both*)
105–110: see Additional Notes
107 *tagging points* 'fixing metal tags on the laces or points which
    largely did the work of buttons in Elizabethan dress' (Lucas)
108 *crying garlic* i.e. calling out the price of his garlic, like a street-
    vendor
109 *lists* strips of cloth   109–110: see Additional Notes
112 *by scruples* by small degrees or amounts
116 S.D. opposite 115–118 in Q1.

101–2 *Cupping-glasses* are surgical vessels used to draw off blood through
    the creation of a vacuum in them by means of heat. It was assumed that
    only *infected blood* would be drawn off, leaving the body healthy. *Cf.*
    The Duchess of Malfi, II.v, 23–6; Middleton and Rowley, *The Changeling*,
    ed. Patricia Thomson (The New Mermaids, 1964) V.iii, 149–53.

VITTORIA
O thou most cursed devil.
ZANCHE Thou art caught—
VITTORIA
In thine own engine; I tread the fire out
That would have been my ruin.
FLAMINEO
Will you be perjur'd? What a religious oath was Styx that
the gods never durst swear by and violate? O that we had 125
such an oath to minister, and to be so well kept in our
courts of justice.
VITTORIA
Think whither thou art going.
ZANCHE And remember
What villanies thou hast acted.
VITTORIA This thy death
Shall make me like a blazing ominous star,— 130
Look up and tremble.
FLAMINEO O I am caught with a springe!
VITTORIA
You see the fox comes many times short home,
'Tis here prov'd true.
FLAMINEO Kill'd with a couple of braches
VITTORIA
No fitter offcring for the infernal Furies
Than one in whom they reign'd while he was living. 135
FLAMINEO
O the way's dark and horrid! I cannot see,
Shall I have no company?
VITTORIA O yes thy sins
Do run before thee to fetch fire from hell,
To light thee thither.
FLAMINEO O I smell soot,
Most stinking soot, the chimney is a-fire, 140
My liver's parboil'd like Scotch holy-bread;

122 *engine* contrivance
130 *star,—* ed. (Q1, Q2 starre,   ; Q3, Q4 star,)
131 *springe* snare for catching small game
132 *short home* i.e. without his tail, i.e. dead; *or* quickly home
133 *braches* bitches 134 *Furies* Q2, Q3, Q4 (Q1 furies)
140 *stinking* Q2, Q3, Q4 (Q1 sinking)
141 *parboil'd* Q2, Q3, Q4 (Q1 purboil'd) boiled through and through;
holy bread Q4 (Q1, Q2, Q3 holly-bread)

141 *Scotch holy bread.* Cotgrave's *Dictionarie of the French and English
Tongues* (1611) [quoted by Sampson, p. 205]: '*Pain benist d'Escosse—A*
sodden sheepes liver.'

There's a plumber, laying pipes in my guts, it scalds;
Wilt thou outlive me?
ZANCHE   Yes, and drive a stake
Through thy body; for we'll give it out,
Thou didst this violence upon thyself.   145
FLAMINEO
O cunning devils! now I have try'd your love,
And doubled all your reaches. I am not wounded:

                                        FLAMINEO *riseth*

The pistols held no bullets: 'Twas a plot
To prove your kindness to me; and I live
To punish your ingratitude; I knew
One time or other you would find a way   150
To give me a strong potion. O men
That lie upon your death-beds, and are haunted
With howling wives, ne'er trust them; they'll remarry
Ere the worm pierce your winding sheet; ere the spider
Make a thin curtain for your epitaphs.   155
How cunning you were to discharge! Do you practise at the
Artillery Yard? Trust a woman? Never, never; Brachiano
be my president: we lay our souls to pawn to the devil for
a little pleasure, and a woman makes the bill of sale. That
ever man should marry! For one Hypermnestra that sav'd   160
her lord and husband, forty-nine of her sisters cut their
throats all in one night. There was a shoal of virtuous horse-
leeches.
Here are two other instruments.

    Enter LOD[OVICO], GASP[ARO, *disguised as*] CARLO, PEDRO
                    [*with others*]

147 *doubled all your reaches* i.e. 'matched, or been equal to, all your
    contrivances' (Brown)
149 *knew* Q1 (Q2, Q3, Q4 know)   156 *cunning* skilful
158 *president* precedent; (also with connotation 'president')
162–3 *horse-leeches* blood-suckers; *cf.* III.ii, 279.
164 s.d. Q1, Q2 *Enter Lod. Gasp. Pedro, Carlo*; Q3 *Enter Lod., Gasp.*;
    Q4 *Enter Lodovico and Gasparo*

144–5 'the traditional treatment of suicides, who were thus buried at cross-
    roads' (Lucas)
157 *Artillery Yard:* or Artillery Gardens, in Bishopsgate, was where,
    according to Stowe, *Annals* (1631), pp. 995–6, weekly exercise of arms
    and military discipline were revived in 1610. (Brown, p. 178 n.)
160 *Hypermnestra*, one of the fifty daughters of Danus who were forced to
    marry their uncle's fifty sons. Their father, having been warned by an
    oracle that one of his nephews would kill him, asked his daughters to
    kill their husbands on their wedding night. Forty-nine of them did as he
    wished. Hypermnestra alone spared her husband.

VITTORIA   Help, help!
FLAMINEO
  What noise is that? hah? false keys i'th' court.   165
LODOVICO
  We have brought you a masque.
FLAMINEO   A matachin it seems,
  By your drawn swords. Churchmen turn'd revellers.
CONSPIRATORS
  Isabella, Isabella!
               [*They throw off their disguises*]
LODOVICO
  Do you know us now?
FLAMINEO   Lodovico and Gasparo.
LODOVICO
  Yes, and that Moor the Duke gave pension to   170
  Was the great Duke of Florence.
VITTORIA   O we are lost.
FLAMINEO
  You shall not take justice from forth my hands;
  O let me kill her.———I'll cut my safety
  Through your coats of steel. Fate's a spaniel,
  We cannot beat it from us. What remains now?   175
  Let all that do ill take this president:
  Man may his fate foresee, but not prevent.
  And of all axioms this shall win the prize,
  'Tis better to be fortunate than wise.
GASPARO
  Bind him to the pillar.
VITTORIA   O your gentle pity!   180
  I have seen a blackbird that would sooner fly
  To a man's bosom, than to stay the gripe
  Of the fierce sparrow-hawk.
GASPARO   Your hope deceives you.
VITTORIA
  If Florence be i'th' court, would he would kill me.
GASPARO
  Fool! Princes give rewards with their own hands,   185
  But death or punishment by the hands of others.

166 *matachin* a sword dance performed by masked dancers wearing
    fantastic costumes
168 speech-prefix: *Conspirators* Wheeler (Q1, Q2 con.; Q3, Q4
    Gas.)
177, 179: italicized in Qq
182 *stay* wait for
184 *would he would* Q1, Q2 (Q3, Q4 he would not)

LODOVICO
  Sirrah you once did strike me; I'll strike you
  Into the centre.

FLAMINEO
  Thou'lt do it like a hangman; a base hangman;
  Not like a noble fellow, for thou seest   190
  I cannot strike again.

LODOVICO   Dost laugh?

FLAMINEO
  Wouldst have me die, as I was born, in whining?

GASPARO
  Recommend yourself to heaven.

FLAMINEO
  No I will carry mine own commendations thither.

LODOVICO
  Oh could I kill you forty times a day   195
  And use't four year together; 'twere too little:
  Nought grieve's but that you are too few to feed
  The famine of our vengeance. What dost think on?

FLAMINEO
  Nothing; of nothing: leave thy idle questions;
  I am i'th'way to study a long silence   200
  To prate were idle; I remember nothing.
  There's nothing of so infinite vexation
  As man's own thoughts.

LODOVICO   O thou glorious strumpet,
  Could I divide thy breath from this pure air
  When't leaves thy body, I would suck it up   205
  And breathe't upon some dunghill.

VITTORIA   You, my death's-man;
  Methinks thou dost not look horrid enough,
  Thou hast too good a face to be a hangman;
  If thou be, do thy office in right form;
  Fall down upon thy knees and ask forgiveness.   210

188 *Into* Q1 (Q2, Q3, Q4 Unto); *the centre* i.e. the heart
189 *hangman* i.e. executioner, whose prisoner is unable to resist him: cf. V.vi, 208 below.
196 *four year* Q3 (Q1, Q2 foure yeere; Q4 for years)
197 *grieve's* ed. (Q1, Q2 greeu's; Q3, Q4 griev's) grieves us
201 *idle* foolish, useless
206 *death's-man;* ed. (Q1, Q2 Deaths man; Q3 Deaths-man;   Q4 deaths-man?)

199 cf. *The Duchess of Malfi*, IV.ii, 15–17.

LODOVICO
  O thou hast been a most prodigious comet,
  But I'll cut off your train: kill the Moor first.

VITTORIA
  You shall not kill her first. Behold my breast,
  I will be waited on in death; my servant
  Shall never go before me.   215

GASPARO
  Are you so brave?

VITTORIA   Yes I shall welcome death
  As princes do some great ambassadors;
  I'll meet thy weapon half way.

LODOVICO   Thou dost tremble,
  Methinks fear should dissolve thee into air.

VITTORIA
  O thou art deceiv'd, I am too true a woman: 220
  Conceit can never kill me: I'll tell thee what;
  I will not in my death shed one base tear,
  Or if look pale, for want of blood, not fear.

GASPARO
  Thou art my task, black fury.

ZANCHE   I have blood
  As red as either of theirs: wilt drink some?   225
  'Tis good for the falling sickness. I am proud
  Death cannot alter my complexion,
  For I shall ne'er look pale.

LODOVICO   Strike, strike,
  With a joint motion.   [They strike]

VITTORIA   'Twas a manly blow.
  The next thou giv'st, murder some sucking infant,   230
  And then thou wilt be famous.

FLAMINEO   O what blade is't?
  A toledo, or an English fox?
  I ever thought a cutler should distinguish
  The cause of my death, rather than a doctor.

212 *train* comet's tail; train of servants, i.e. Zanche
220 *true* Q1c (Q1a treue; Q1b treu)
221 *Conceit* imagination; vanity; conception
224 speech-prefix: Q3, Q4 *Gas.* (Q1 CAR.; Q2 *Cor.*); see note on
    164 S.D. above; *fury* Q1 (Q2, Q3, Q4 Fury)
226 *falling sickness* epilepsy

216ff. On the deaths of Vittoria and Flamineo see: J. R. Mulryne, *op. cit*
    pp. 212–13; Dent, p. 169; B. J. Layman, *op. cit.*, pp. 246–7.
232 *fox*: a common name for a sword in Elizabethan England, either because
    of the brown colour of the steel, or because the figure of a wolf on some
    blades was taken to be that of a fox.

Search my wound deeper: tent it with the steel   235
That made it.

VITTORIA
O my greatest sin lay in my blood.
Now my blood pays for't.

FLAMINEO   Th'art a noble sister,
I love thee now; if woman do breed man
She ought to teach him manhood. Fare thee well.   240
Know many glorious women that are fam'd
For masculine virtue, have been vicious
Only a happier silence did betide them.
She hath no faults, who hath the art to hide them.

VITTORIA
My soul, like to a ship in a black storm,   245
Is driven I know not whither.

FLAMINEO   Then cast anchor.
Prosperity doth bewitch men seeming clear,
But seas do laugh, show white, when rocks are near.
We cease to grieve, cease to be Fortune's slaves,
Nay cease to die by dying. [*to* ZANCHE] Art thou gone?   250
[*to* VITTORIA] And thou so near the bottom? False report
Which says that women vie with the nine Muses
For nine tough durable lives. I do not look
Who went before, nor who shall follow me;
No, at myself I will begin and end.   255
While we look up to heaven we confound
Knowledge with knowledge. O I am in a mist.

VITTORIA
O happy they that never saw the court,
Nor ever knew great man but by report.   VITTORIA *dies*

FLAMINEO
I recover like a spent taper, for a flash   260
And instantly go out.
Let all that belong to great men remember th'old wives'
tradition, to be like the lions i'th' Tower on Candlemas day,

---

235 *tent* probe; apply a tent to it (A tent was a plug of soft material
used for searching, cleaning or distending a wound.)
246 *anchor* Q4 (Q1 ancor; Q2, Q3 anclior)
247–50: These lines are preceded by inverted commas in Qq.
256–7; 259; 270–271: preceded by inverted commas in Qq.
259 *man* ed. (Q1 Man; Q2, Q3, Q4 Men)

---

263 *lions i'th' Tower*. Lions and, according to Stowe, other animals were
kept in the Tower of London. There are records of lion-baiting for the
amusement of the nobility in 1609 and 1610. The animals continued to
be kept in the Tower till 1834 when they were removed to the Zoo.
Candlemas day 2nd February: according to an old proverb, a fair and
sunny Candlemas day foretold the coming of further severe wintry
weather.

to mourn if the sun shine, for fear of the pitiful remainder of
winter to come.   265
'Tis well yet there's some goodness in my death,
My life was a black charnel. I have cought
An everlasting cold. I have lost my voice
Most irrecoverably. Farewell glorious villains,
This busy trade of life appears most vain,   270
Since rest breeds rest, where all seek pain by pain.
Let no harsh flattering bells resound my knell,
Strike thunder, and strike loud to my farewell.   *Dies*

    Enter [AMBASSADORS] *and* GIOVANNI. [GUARDS *follow.*]

ENGLISH AMBASSADOR
This way, this way, break ope the doors, this way.
LODOVICO
Ha, are we betray'd?   275
Why then let's constantly die all together,
And having finish'd this most noble deed,
Defy the worst of fate; not fear to bleed.
ENGLISH AMBASSADOR
Keep back the Prince: shoot, shoot—
       [GUARDS *shoot at conspirators*]
LODOVICO   O I am wounded.
I fear I shall be tane.
GIOVANNI   You bloody villains,   280
By what authority have you commited
This massacre?
LODOVICO   By thine.
GIOVANNI   Mine?
LODOVICO   Yes, thy uncle,
Which is a part of thee enjoin'd us to't:
Thou know'st me I am sure, I am Count Lodowick,
And thy most noble uncle in disguise   285
Was last night in thy court.
GIOVANNI   Ha!
GASPARO   Yes, that Moor
Thy father chose his pensioner.
GIOVANNI   He turn'd murderer?
Away with them to prison, and to torture;

---

267 *cought* Q1 (Q2, Q3, Q4 caught): possibly a pun is intended:
    coughed / caught
273 S.D. [AMBASSADORS] ed. (Q1, Q2 *Embassad:* Q3, Q4 *Embassador*)
282 *is a* Q1 (Q2, Q3, Q4 is)
286 speech-prefix: Q1, Q2 CAR.; Q3, Q4 *Gas.*

All that have hands in this, shall taste our justice,
As I hope heaven.

LODOVICO   I do glory yet   290
That I can call this act mine own. For my part,
The rack, the gallows, and the torturing wheel
Shall be but sound sleeps to me; here's my rest:
I limb'd this night-piece and it was my best.

GIOVANNI
Remove the bodies; see my honoured lord,   295
What use you ought make of their punishment.
Let guilty men remember their black deeds
Do lean on crutches, made of slender reeds.   [*Exeunt*]

Instead of an Epilogue only this of Martial supplies me:
            Haec fuerint nobis praemia si placui.   300

For the action of the play, 'twas generally well, and I dare
affirm, with the joint testimony of some of their own quality,
(for the true imitation of life, without striving to make nature
a monster) the best that ever became them: whereof as I make
a general acknowledgement, so in particular I must remem-   305
ber the well approved industry of my friend Master Perkins,
and confess the worth of his action did crown both the
beginning and end.

FINIS

292 *torturing* Q1, Q2 (Q3, Q4 torturious)
294 italics: ed. (Qq mark the line with inverted commas.); *limb'd* Q1,
      Q2, Q4 (Q3 limm'd) limned, i.e. painted; *night-piece* painting of
      a night scene
295 *lord* Qq
296 *you ought make* Q1, Q2, Q3 (Q4 we ought to make)
300: 'These things will be our reward, if I have pleased.' (Martial II.
      xci, 8.)
302 *quality* profession

---

306 *Master Perkins* i.e. Richard Perkins, was the most famous 'straight' actor
      in the Queen's Men. In 'The Red Bull Company and the Importunate
      Widow', *Shakespeare Survey* 7 (Cambridge, 1954), p. 59 Professor C. J.
      Sisson comments '. . . Richard Perkins, at the peak of his career, when
      he gave his great performance in *The White Devil* at the Red Bull, was
      barely 30 years of age. A professional actor of that age would probably
      have had 14 years of experience on the public boards.' We know, in fact,
      that Perkins had belonged to Worcester's Men in 1602. Since Webster
      refers to his action as having crowned 'both the beginning and end' of
      the play, we assume that he took the part of Flamineo. For further
      details of Perkins' career, see G. E. Bentley, *The Jacobean and Caroline
      Stage*, ii (1941), pp. 525–6.

489   *the famous Venetian Curtizan:* The real Vittoria Accoramboni,
      born in Gubbio, came of a noble Roman family. It has been
      suggested that Webster may have confused her with the
      Venetian born Bianca Capello, the heroine of Thomas
      Middleton's *Women Beware Women* (*c.* 1620–27) who, after
      the murder of the husband with whom she eloped to
      Florence, became the mistress and then the wife of Francisco
      de Medicis, Bracciano's brother-in-law. (See F. L. Lucas,
      Webster, i, 89, 194.) Venice was famous for its courtesans,
      and many English readers would be familiar with the per-
      sonal account of them given by Thomas Coryate in *Coryat's
      Crudities* (1611). Thus, as Dr. Gunnar Boklund points out,
      once Webster had decided to present Vittoria as a famous
      courtesan—which neither she nor Bianca Capello really was
      —'the transfer from Rome to Venice would follow naturally
      . . .' (*The Sources of 'The White Devil'*, (Uppsala, 1957),
      p. 138.)

490   [DRAMATIS PERSONÆ] Q1 and Q2 omit the names of the
      characters. Q3 and Q4 supply a list of 'The Persons' which
      is reproduced here with the addition of characters omitted
      by that list but included in the action of the play (e.g. the
      Cardinal of Arragon, Doctor Julio, the Matrona and such
      'extras' as Lawyers). The 'ghost characters' Christophero,
      Guid-Antonio, Ferneze and Jaques the Moor are each
      mentioned once in the stage directions (see II. i; II. ii [first
      dumb show] and V. i, 42) but have no speaking parts. It may
      be supposed that either Webster intended to make these small
      parts and then changed his mind, or that each originally had
      something to say which was later removed from the play (see
      Brown, p. 31); or it may be that these parts gave importance
      as well as 'something to do' to minor members of an acting
      company. Their presence or absence in a production of the
      play today will depend on the producer's ideas for the dis-
      position of 'Attendants' and on his resources in the cast.

498   I. ii, 31 *wage all downward.* According to R. Stanyhurst's Des-
      cription of Ireland, given in Holinshed's *Chronicles* (1577),
      some of the wild Irish would play away their clothes, truss
      themselves in straw or leaves and then, for lack of other stuff,
      would pawn the locks of hair on their foreheads, their finger
      or toe nails and their testicles, which they would lose or

redeem at the courtesy of the winner. Thus F. L. Lucas explains the allusion here as meaning that Camillo would be as ready as an Irish gambler to stake his virility (having none) but Dent (p. 79) finds this interpretation far-fetched and suggests that Flamineo 'probably means that Camillo has ventured all his amourousness, has lost brains, beard, "back", etc.'

511 I. ii, 325–7. Thomas Coryate's description of Venice, published in *Coryat's Crudities* (1611), was the most detailed account of the city that had hitherto been given in English. Coryate's personal investigation into the courtesans' way of life contained an idea similar to Flamineo's here: 'There is one most notable thing more to be mentioned concerning these Venetian Cortezans, with the relation whereof I will end this discourse of them. If any of them happen to haue any children (as indeede they haue but few, for according to the old prouerbe the best carpenters make the fewest chips) they are brought vp either at their owne charge, or in a certaine house of the citie appointed for no other vse but onely for the bringing vp of the Cortezans bastards, which I saw Eastward aboue Saint *Markes* streete neare to the sea side.'

512 II. i, 14–18. Isabella here refers to a test to prove the genuineness of powdered unicorn's horn by its ability to prevent the spider—supposedly poisonous—from leaving the circle. The belief in the efficacy of the unicorn's horn as an antidote to poison is as old as the legend of the unicorn itself. In the sixteenth century the supposed horn, both whole and powdered, was more expensive than gold. In his *Historie of Foure-Footed Beastes* (1607) Edward Topsell declared that there were only twenty whole horns in Europe. Sir Thomas Browne, in *Pseudodoxia Epidemica* (1646) Book III, chapter xxiii declared that 'many in common use and high esteeme are no hornes at all', but Birch's *History of the Royal Society*, i (1756) records how on 24th July, 1661 the test to which Isabella refers was actually made with powdered horn and a spider. See Brown, p. 32 n.

523 II. i, 253–63. Isabella deliberately repeats Brachiano's own cruelly ironic method of swearing divorce by a wedding ring in II. i, 194–205. It is a measure of Brachiano's callousness that he, in turn, is prepared to echo the sentiment, though not the words, of his wife's former pleas to him. The quotation from Virgil that she makes—*manet alta mente repostum* (l. 262)—is cited by two sixteenth-century accounts of the capture and trial of Count Lodovico as part of his

reply to the question of the *rettori* whether he can throw any
light on the murders of Vittoria and Flamineo. See Gunnar
Boklund, *op. cit.*, pp. 50–51; 63; 83–84; 128 ff. and *cf.* Introduction, p. xii above.

524 II. i, 284. Spanish flies were used medicinally. They were
applied externally, to raise blisters and thus act as a counter-
irritant; and a drug prepared of their wings was taken
internally, but was dangerous if taken in any but the smallest
quantities. Some of their poison might be absorbed through
the skin, but Webster's image of their secret working is an
exaggeration, perhaps 'suggested by the fact that they were
both medicinal *and* poisonous.' (Brown, p. 47 n.)

525 II. i, 298. *lamprey*. Observation of the row of seven branchial
openings found on each side, behind the lamprey's head,
and which convey water to and from its gills, gave rise to the
idea, discussed by Sir Thomas Browne in *Pseudodoxia
Epidemica*, Book III, chapter xix, that the lamprey had nine
eyes. Webster also refers to this fish in *The Duchess of Malfi*,
I.ii, 255. The notion that lampreys are full of eyes on both
sides is mentioned in John Marston's *The Malcontent*, I, i,
335.

II. i, 300–301. Ireland was said to breed no poison because St.
Patrick collected all the venomous beasts in the island and
cast them into the sea at Clew Bay, Co. Mayo. A Spaniard,
Don Diego, was notorious for having broken wind in St.
Paul's, sometime before 1598. According to Thomas Nashe,
'The Irishman will drawe his dagger, and bee ready to kill
and slay, if one breake winde in his company.' (*Pierce
Pennilesse his Supplication to the Devil* (1592))

526 II. i, 324. *Inopem me copia fecit:* 'Abundance has made me
destitute.' This is Narcissus' complaint to his own reflection in Ovid's *Metamorphoses*, III, 466. Lucas suggests that
this means that Camillo's having so fair a wife has left him
worse off than having no wife at all. Brown paraphrases
Monticelso's comment as 'the plentiful sexual satisfaction
others have received has meant that he has received none at
all.' Dent (p. 97) thinks that Brachiano is the stag, behaving
traditionally after satisfying his lust; his loss of horns signi-
fies the consequences of his hours with Vittoria. 'Thus *copia*
in the tag may refer to the virile activity of Brachiano, and
at the same time glance at the plenty of horns thereby transferred to the cuckolded Camillo.'

530 II. ii, A DUMB SHOW. The earliest use of the dumb show in
sixteenth-century drama was that of preparing an audience
for the significance or the main action of the following play.

(See *Gorboduc* and *cf. Hamlet*, III. ii.) Later, in such plays as Peele's *Battle of Alcazar* and Greene's *Friar Bacon and Friar Bungay*, dumb shows provided the dramatist with a means of cramming more action into the play without producing more dialogue and of providing variety of action by showing the audience, as well as characters on the stage, something that is happening elsewhere. Webster's use of the dumb show here is closely parallel to Greene's use of it in *Friar Bacon and Friar Bungay* (*circa* 1589) II.iii and IV.iii. In the latter scene two young men see in Bacon's magic glass, how their fathers meet and kill each other. For comment on the effect of Webster's two dumb shows in this scene, see H. Fluchère, *Shakespeare and the Elizabethans* (New York, 1956), pp. 112–13 and J. R. Mulryne, '*The White Devil* and *The Duchess of Malfi*', *Stratford-upon-Avon Studies I: Jacobean Theatre*, pp. 203–204.

537 III. ii. Vittoria's arraignment takes place in the papal consistory. The most famous scene in the play, it has attracted the attention of many critics whose comments examine both the total effect of the scene and the light it throws on the character of Vittoria. See Charles Lamb, *Specimens of English Dramatic Poets . . .* (1808), pp. 229–30; William Hazlitt, *Lectures on the Dramatic Literature of the Age of Elizabeth* (1821), pp. 126–7; J. A. Symonds, 'Vittoria Accoramboni, and the Tragedy of Webster', *Italian Byways* (1883), p. 177; W. W. Greg, 'Webster's *White Devil*', *Modern Language Quarterly*, III (1900), 118–19; P. Haworth, 'Prelude to the Study of Webster's Plays', *English Hymns and Ballads . . .* (Oxford, 1927), pp. 82–84; M. C. Bradbrook, *Themes and Conventions of Elizabethan Tragedy* (Cambridge, 1935), pp. 93 (on the borrowings from Jonson's *Sejanus* in the trial scene); 119; W. Farnham, *Shakespeare's Tragic Frontier* (Berkeley and Los Angeles, 1950), p. 29; Clifford Leech, *John Webster: A Critical Study* (1951), pp. 36–39; G. Baldini, *John Webster e il linguaggio della tragedia* (Rome, 1953), pp. 80–95; Hereward T. Price, 'The Function of Imagery in John Webster', *PMLA*, LXX (1955), 724–5; B. J. Layman, 'The Equilibrium of Opposites in *The White Devil*: A Reinterpretation', *PMLA*, LXXIV (1959), 339–40; H. Bruce Franklin, 'The Trial Scene of Webster's *The White Devil* examined in terms of Renaissance Rhetoric', *Studies in English Literature*, I, 2 (1961), 35–51.

541 III. ii, 79 *character*. This kind of analysis, based on the classical models of Theophrastus, was found in many literary forms in the seventeenth century. Among collections of 'characters'

the most celebrated is that of Sir Thomas Overbury and it is
of particular interest here because Webster almost certainly
contributed to the second edition.

Webster used the analytical technique to give several
different types of 'character' in his work. For example, in
The Duchess of Malfi Antonio gives a full-length portrait in
his idealized 'character' of the Duchess (I. ii, 109–31); Delio
gives a brief, humorous 'character' of Bosola to Silvio (III.
iii, 40–46) while Delio and Silvio combine to produce an
amusing 'character' of Malateste for Ferdinand (III.iii,
12–33). Dent (p. 104) has pointed out that Monticelso's description of a whore, composed wholly of metaphors and
similes and without any direct description of the whore's
activities, 'has little in common with the prose characters of
Hall, Overbury or Webster himself.' Its rhetoric is intended
to impress the audience on stage and in the theatre. For
comment on Webster's affinities with the mannered prose of
the character writers, see W. A. Edwards, 'John Webster',
Determinations, ed. F. R. Leavis (1934), pp. 158–65 and M. C.
Bradbrook, *Themes and Conventions of Elizabethan Tragedy*,
pp. 108–109.

III. ii, 81. *coz'ning alchemy*. From the Middle Ages onwards
cheats had extracted money from their avaricious victims by
claiming the ability to produce the philosopher's stone
which would turn base metals into gold. The methods by
which these alchemists propagated their fraud seem to have
varied little down the centuries, as a comparison of Chaucer's
Canon's Yeoman's Tale, John Lyly's *Gallathea* and Ben
Jonson's *The Alchemist* will show.

III. ii, 89–91. This may have been an allusion to Sir Walter
Raleigh's loss of his estate of Sherborne through a clerk's
omission of ten words from an early transfer to his wife.
The judgment taking the estate from Lady Raleigh was
made in 1609. (See G. V. P. Akrigg, 'Webster and Raleigh',
Notes and Queries, CXCIII (1948), 427–8.) Brown (pp.
69–70 n.) quotes from Florio and from *The Atheist's
Tragedy* to show that the idea was quite a common one.

553 III. iii. 28. *Those weights ... death with.* This is 'the *peine
forte et dure* inflicted by English law up to 1772 on those
who refused to plead guilty or not guilty, when charged
with felonies other than treason.' (Lucas) If the victim remained silent and was pressed to death, his goods could
not be confiscated, because he had not been convicted.
Cf. Richard II, III.iv,72—*Queen.* O I am pressed to
death through want of speaking.—and see Clifford Dobb,

'London's Prisons', *Shakespeare Survey* 17 (1964), p. 89 and Plate XIII.

566 IV. ii, 54–55. R. R. Cawley, *The Voyagers and Elizabethan Drama* (Boston and London, 1938), p. 262 cites three English travellers who described the punishment of debtors in Russia by beating on the shins: Richard Chancellor, whose account of his accompanying Sir Hugh Willoughby to Russia in 1553 was published by Richard Hakluyt (1589); Edward Webbe, who published a 'newly enlarged' description of the 'Rare and wonderfull' things he had seen and passed 'in his troublesome trauailes' in 1590; and Giles Fletcher whose work *Of the Russe Common Wealth* appeared in 1591.

568 IV. ii, 85. *the devil in crystal.* More than one meaning may be suggested for this phrase which probably alludes to the title of the play. Witches were supposed to be able to make devils appear in their crystals. According to Dent (p. 125) 'To behold the devil in crystal appears to have meant, generally, simply to be deceived, as by the apparent reality of an illusion.' G. V. P. Akrigg, 'John Webster's "Devil in Crystal"', *Notes and Queries*, N.S. I, (1954), p. 52 suggested that the image might well refer to a type of small shrine of rock crystal in which the figure of a saint was enclosed. 'If we take it that Webster had these Renaissance crystal shrines in mind, his metaphor gains in effect. Not only is Brachiano repeating the "white devil" theme, he is saying that he has given to the devil Vittoria the worship one gives to a saint set in her crystal shrine.'

584 V. i, 68–70. The anonymous play *Arden of Feversham* (*circa* 1585–92), based on a true murder story of the reign of Edward VI demonstrates a genuine belief in the efficacy of strange methods of poison. In 1598 Edward Squire, employed in Queen Elizabeth's stable, was executed for having attempted to poison the pommel of her saddle in the previous year with a drug which he had received from the Spanish Jesuits.

V. i, 71–73. The original game of tennis was played indoors (lawn tennis dates only from 1873) on a court whose two sides were called the service side and the hazard side. The *hazard* is one of the openings, of which there are two on the hazard side and one on the service side, on the inner wall of the court into which a winning stroke may be played. The game, which originated in France and is known to have been played in Canterbury in 1396, is still played on the Royal Tennis Court built by Henry VIII at Hampton Court in

1530. Used metaphorically, *hazard* means peril or jeopardy. Both senses are implicit here.

589 V. i, 180. *ṣunburnt gentleman*. It was assumed, on the basis of the Song of Solomon i, 6——'I am black, because the sun hath looked upon me'——for instance, that dark skin was the result of excessive exposure to the sun. Bishop Hall expressed this theory in his *Contemplations*, ii (1614), Book V, pp. 121–2: 'A man may passe through Æthiopia vnchaunged: but he cannot dwell there, and not be discoloured.' *Cf.* V.iii, 259.

V. i, 184. *a bedstaff*. C. B. Wheeler notes, 'According to Johnson, "a wooden pin stuck anciently on sides of the bedstead to hold the clothes from slipping"; it would be a handy weapon.' *O.E.D.* says that there is no corroborative evidence for Dr. Johnson's definition. Lucas (*Webster*, i, 250) defines it as either one of the staves which supported the bedding, or a staff used for making a bed, especially when it stood in a recess. As well as meaning a staff with which Cornelia might beat her maids, the phrase here also refers to a lover who might keep the maids warm at night.

620 V. vi, 105–10. Lucian's purgatory, described in his *Menippos*, in fact included different examples of the ridiculous fates of the famous, e.g. Philip, King of Macedon 'sitting in a little corner, cobbling old shoes to get somewhat towards his living' (Hickes' version, published in Oxford in 1634, as quoted by Sampson, p. 204). Rabelais used the same idea in the thirtieth chapter of *Pantagruel*, where he sees 'Alexander as a clothes patcher, Hannibal a kettle maker and seller of eggshells.' (Dent, p. 165). H. Dugdale Sykes pointed out a parallel with *Love's Labour's Lost*, IV.iii, 166–9 where the listing of notables and their activities is again different from Webster's.

V. vi, 109. *King Pippin* i.e. Pepin III, king of the Franks, known as 'The Short' who was the most famous monarch of that name. His coronation, performed by St. Boniface, was a ceremony new to France. By wresting the exarchate of Ravenna from Aistulf, King of the Lombards and conferring it on the Pope, Pepin became the veritable creator of the Papal state. Upon his death in 768 his Kingdom was divided between his sons Charles (Charlemagne) and Carloman. Webster is also punning on the name pippin as a type of apple.

622 V. vi, 164 s.d. Q1, Q2 *Enter Lod. Gasp. Pedro, Carlo*. The confusion of this entry and in the use of the disguise names of the conspirators in the speech-prefix at l. 224 below which is found in Q1 and Q2 is eliminated in Q3 and Q4, and all previous editors, except Brown, have followed the assumption of Q3 and Q4 that, in the fifth act, Lodovico is disguised as Carlo and Gasparo as Pedro, the supposed Hungarians who have entered the strict order of Capuchins. Dr. Brown feels that this confusion, with the facts that at V. i, 62 Lodovico welcomes Francisco and Gasparo who are supposed to have travelled to Padua with him, that more than two conspirators are necessary to execute the murders of the last scene and that more than two remain alive at the end, means that Carlo and Pedro are separate conspirators, not to be identified with Lodovico and Gasparo. (p. 126 n.) Yet, Brown is prepared to consider the entry of Isabella at III.ii (she was murdered in II.ii) as an irrational slip: 'anyone familiar with the *dramatis personæ* might have made it, but it is easier to imagine the author doing so (correcting his manuscript confidently and, perhaps, in haste), than an 'editor' (reconstructing the action as he worked from scene to scene.)' (p. lxvii n.) It seems to me equally possible to accept that, sure in his own mind of the separate identity of Lodovico and Gasparo, Webster was quite capable of confusing their disguise names. If he did make some hasty additions to his manuscript before sending it to the printer, as Dr. Brown suggests, he may well have added the duplicate names (though in the reverse of the proper order) to identify them for the printer. The variation between real and disguise names in speech-prefixes is comparable with the variation between *Zan.* and *Moo.* for Zanche in V.iv.

'Tis Pity She's a Whore

JOHN FORD

Edited by
BRIAN MORRIS

ABBREVIATIONS

Q	Quarto, 1633.
Q *a.c.*	Quarto after correction.
Q *b.c.*	Quarto before correction.
Bawcutt	N. W. Bawcutt ed., *'Tis Pity She's a Whore* (Regents Renaissance Drama Series), London, 1966.
Gifford-Dyce	W. Gifford and A. Dyce ed., *The Works of John Ford*, 1869.
Sherman	S. P. Sherman ed., *'Tis Pity She's a Whore* and *The Broken Heart*, Boston, 1915.

'TIS
Pitty Shee s a Whore

Acted by the *Queenes* Maiesties Seruants, at *The Phænix* in
Drury-Lane.

LONDON.
Printed by *Nicholas Okes* for *Richard*
Collins, and are to be sold at his shop
in *Pauls* Church-yard, at the signe
of the three Kings. 1633.

TO MY FRIEND THE AUTHOR

With admiration I beheld this Whore
Adorned with beauty such as might restore
(If ever being as thy muse hath famed)
Her Giovanni, in his love unblamed:
The ready Graces lent their willing aid,
Pallas herself now played the chambermaid,
And helped to put her dressings on. Secure
Rest thou that thy name herein shall endure
To th' end of age; and Annabella be
Gloriously fair, even in her infamy.

THOMAS ELLICE

Thomas Ellice. Nothing is known of him, but it seems likely that he was related to Robert Ellice of Gray's Inn, to whom Ford dedicated *The Lover's Melancholy.* The leaf on which the above lines appear is missing from many copies of Q.

TO THE TRULY NOBLE
JOHN, EARL OF PETERBOROUGH, LORD
MORDAUNT, BARON OF TURVEY

MY LORD,

Where a truth of merit hath a general warrant, there love is but a debt, acknowledgment a justice. Greatness cannot often claim virtue by inheritance; yet in this, yours appears most eminent, for that you are not more rightly heir to your fortunes than glory shall be to your memory. Sweetness of disposition ennobles a freedom of birth; in both, your lawful interest adds honour to your own name and mercy to my presumption. Your noble allowance of these first fruits of my leisure in the action emboldens my confidence of your as noble construction in this presentment; especially since my service must ever owe particular duty to your favours by a particular engagement. The gravity of the subject may easily excuse the lightness of the title, otherwise I had been a severe judge against mine own guilt. Princes have vouchsafed grace to trifles offered from a purity of devotion; your lordship may likewise please to admit into your good opinion, with these weak endeavours, the constancy of affection from the sincere lover of your deserts in honour,

JOHN FORD

8 *allowance* approval
8–9 *in the action* on stage
9 *construction* interpretation
10 *in this presentment* in print

John Mordaunt (1599–1642) had been a courtier since boyhood, when James I was struck with his intelligence and beauty. He was created first Earl of Peterborough on 9 March 1627/8 by Charles I. On the outbreak of the civil war he adhered to Parliament and was general of ordnance under the Earl of Essex, but died of consumption on 18 June 1642. Nothing is known about the relationship between playwright and patron.

The Actors' Names

BONAVENTURA, a friar.
A CARDINAL, nuncio to the Pope.
SORANZO, a nobleman.
FLORIO, a citizen of Parma.
DONADO, another citizen.
GRIMALDI, a Roman gentleman.
GIOVANNI, son to Florio.
BERGETTO, nephew to Donado.
RICHARDETTO, a supposed physician.
VASQUES, servant to Soranzo.
POGGIO, servant to Bergetto.
BANDITTI, [OFFICERS, SERVANTS etc.].

Women

ANNABELLA, daughter to Florio.
HIPPOLITA, wife to Richardetto.
PHILOTIS, his niece.
PUTANA, tut'ress to Annabella.

The Scene:
PARMA

'TIS PITY SHE'S A WHORE

[Act I, Scene i]

Enter FRIAR *and* GIOVANNI

FRIAR
Dispute no more in this, for know, young man,
These are no school-points; nice philosophy
May tolerate unlikely arguments,
But Heaven admits no jest: wits that presumed
On wit too much, by striving how to prove   5
There was no God, with foolish grounds of art,
Discovered first the nearest way to hell,
And filled the world with devilish atheism.
Such questions, youth, are fond; for better 'tis
To bless the sun than reason why it shines;   10
Yet He thou talk'st of is above the sun.
No more; I may not hear it.
GIOVANNI   Gentle father,
To you I have unclasped my burdened soul,
Emptied the storehouse of my thoughts and heart,
Made myself poor of secrets; have not left   15
Another word untold, which hath not spoke
All what I ever durst, or think, or know;
And yet is here the comfort I shall have,
Must I not do what all men else may, love?
FRIAR
Yes, you may love, fair son.
GIOVANNI   Must I not praise   20
That beauty which, if framed anew, the gods
Would make a god of, if they had it there,
And kneel to it, as I do kneel to them?
FRIAR
Why, foolish madman!

---

2 *school-points* matters for academic discussion or debate
6 *art* knowledge
9 *fond* foolish

This scene is very similar in dramatic function and tone to the scene
between Orgilus and Tecnicus in *The Broken Heart*, I.iii, 1–32.

GIOVANNI   Shall a peevish sound,
  A customary form, from man to man,   25
  Of brother and of sister, be a bar
  'Twixt my perpetual happiness and me?
  Say that we had one father, say one womb
  (Curse to my joys) gave both us life and birth;
  Are we not therefore each to other bound   30
  So much the more by nature? by the links
  Of blood, of reason? nay, if you will have't,
  Even of religion, to be ever one,
  One soul, one flesh, one love, one heart, one all?

FRIAR
  Have done, unhappy youth, for thou art lost.   35

GIOVANNI
  Shall then, for that I am her brother born,
  My joys be ever banished from her bed?
  No, father; in your eyes I see the change
  Of pity and compassion; from your age,
  As from a sacred oracle, distils   40
  The life of counsel: tell me, holy man,
  What cure shall give me ease in these extremes.

FRIAR
  Repentance, son, and sorrow for this sin:
  For thou hast moved a Majesty above
  With thy unranged (almost) blasphemy.   45

GIOVANNI
  O do not speak of that, dear confessor.

FRIAR
  Art thou, my son, that miracle of wit
  Who once, within these three months, wert esteemed
  A wonder of thine age, throughout Bononia?
  How did the University applaud   50
  Thy government, behaviour, learning, speech,
  Sweetness, and all that could make up a man!

24 *peevish* trifling (see V.iii, 40)
25 *customary form* conventional formality
45 *unranged* disordered, deranged
46 *confessor* accented on first syllable
49 *Bononia* Bologna, famous for its university
51 *government* way of life

28–34 *Say that . . . all.* Cf. Giovanni's use of the same argument at I.ii,
  235ff.

I was proud of my tutelage, and chose
Rather to leave my books than part with thee.
I did so: but the fruits of all my hopes 55
Are lost in thee, as thou art in thyself.
O, Giovanni, hast thou left the schools
Of knowledge to converse with lust and death?
For death waits on thy lust. Look through the world,
And thou shalt see a thousand faces shine 60
More glorious than this idol thou ador'st:
Leave her, and take thy choice, 'tis much less sin,
Though in such games as those they lose that win.

GIOVANNI
It were more ease to stop the ocean
From floats and ebbs than to dissuade my vows. 65

FRIAR
Then I have done, and in thy wilful flames
Already see thy ruin; Heaven is just.
Yet hear my counsel.

GIOVANNI   As a voice of life.

FRIAR
Hie to thy father's house, there lock thee fast
Alone within thy chamber, then fall down 70
On both thy knees, and grovel on the ground:
Cry to thy heart, wash every word thou utter'st
In tears (and if't be possible) of blood:

57 *Giovanni* four syllables
65 *vows* wishes, prayers (Latin *vota*)

53–4 *I was . . . thee.* Despite its European reputation throughout the
Middle Ages the University of Bologna does not seem to have had any
fixed residence before 1562. Until then professors lectured in their own
houses, or later in rooms hired or lent by the civic authorities.

62 *'tis much less sin.* The view that fornication is a lesser sin than incest is
probably based on the argument exemplified by Montaigne, *Of Moderation* (Florio's translation, 1603): 'The love we beare to women is very
lawful; yet doth Divinitie bridle and restraine the same. I remember to
have read in Saint Thomas, in a place where he condemneth marriages
of kinsfolkes in forbidden degrees, this one reason amongst others; that
the love a man beareth to such a woman may be immoderate; for, if the
wedlocke, or husband-like affection be sound and perfect, as it ought to
be, and also surcharged with that a man oweth to alliance and kindred;
there is no doubt but that surcease may easily transport a husband
beyond the bounds of reason.'

65 *floats.* The flux or flood of a tide. Cf. *Love's Sacrifice*, II.iii, 'though the
float/of infinite desires swell to a tide/Too high so soon to ebb . . .'

Beg Heaven to cleanse the leprosy of lust
That rots thy soul, acknowledge what thou art,   75
A wretch, a worm, a nothing: weep, sigh, pray
Three times a day, and three times every night.
For seven days' space do this, then if thou find'st
No change in thy desires, return to me:
I'll think on remedy. Pray for thyself   80
At home, whilst I pray for thee here.—Away,
My blessing with thee, we have need to pray.

GIOVANNI
All this I'll do, to free me from the rod
Of vengeance; else I'll swear my fate's my god.   *Exeunt*

[Act I, Scene ii]

Enter GRIMALDI *and* VASQUES *ready to fight*

VASQUES
Come sir, stand to your tackling; if you prove craven, I'll
make you run quickly.

GRIMALDI
Thou art no equal match for me.

VASQUES
Indeed I never went to the wars to bring home news, nor
cannot play the mountebank for a meal's meat, and swear   5
I got my wounds in the field. See you these grey hairs?
They'll not flinch for a bloody nose. Wilt thou to this gear?

GRIMALDI
Why, slave, think'st thou I'll balance my reputation with
a cast-suit? Call thy master, he shall know that I dare—

VASQUES
Scold like a cot-quean, that's your profession. Thou poor   10
shadow of a soldier, I will make thee know my master keeps
servants thy betters in quality and performance. Com'st thou
to fight or prate?

---

1 *tackling* weapons
7 *gear* business (i.e. of fighting)
9 *cast-suit* dependent (wearing his master's old clothes)
10 *cot-quean* shrew, vulgar woman (*O.E.D.* 2)

---

84 *my fate's my god.* This is the first of Giovanni's references to being
governed by destiny. The progress of this fatalism can be traced, with
its various modulations, through the play: see I.ii, 139, I.ii, 224–5,
III.ii, 20, V.v, 11–12, V.vi, 11, 72.

GRIMALDI

    Neither, with thee. I am a Roman and a gentleman; one that
    have got mine honour with expense of blood.   15

VASQUES

    You are a lying coward and a fool. Fight, or by these hilts
    I'll kill thee—brave my lord!—you'll fight?

GRIMALDI

    Provoke me not, for if thou dost—

VASQUES

    Have at you!   *They fight;* GRIMALDI *hath the worst*

Enter FLORIO, DONADO, SORANZO

FLORIO

    What mean these sudden broils so near my doors?   20
    Have you not other places but my house
    To vent the spleen of your disordered bloods?
    Must I be haunted still with such unrest
    As not to eat or sleep in peace at home?
    Is this your love, Grimaldi? Fie, 'tis naught.   25

DONADO

    And Vasques, I may tell thee 'tis not well
    To broach these quarrels; you are ever forward
    In seconding contentions.

Enter above ANNABELLA *and* PUTANA

FLORIO   What's the ground?

SORANZO

    That, with your patience, signors, I'll resolve:
    This gentleman, whom fame reports a soldier,   30
    (For else I know not) rivals me in love
    To Signor Florio's daughter, to whose ears
    He still prefers his suit, to my disgrace,
    Thinking the way to recommend himself
    Is to disparage me in his report.   35
    But know, Grimaldi, though, may be, thou art
    My equal in thy blood, yet this bewrays
    A lowness in thy mind which, wert thou noble,

20 *mean* Q *a.c.*; meaned Q *b.c.*
37 *bewrays* reveals

---

28 s.d. *Enter above.* i.e. on the upper stage, in order to hear the ensuing
    dialogue unobserved. They then overhear Bergetto and Poggio (103–
    16), and when Giovanni enters below they descend from the upper to
    the main stage during his soliloquy (139–58). Some editors un-
    necessarily begin a new scene after line 138.

Thou wouldst as much disdain as I do thee
For this unworthiness; and on this ground   40
I willed my servant to correct his tongue,
Holding a man so base no match for me.

VASQUES
And had not your sudden coming prevented us, I had let my
gentleman blood under the gills; I should have wormed
you, sir, for running mad.   45

GRIMALDI
I'll be revenged, Soranzo.

VASQUES
On a dish of warm broth to stay your stomach—do, honest
innocence, do; spoon-meat is a wholesomer diet than a
Spanish blade.

GRIMALDI
Remember this.   50

SORANZO
I fear thee not, Grimaldi.   *Exit* GRIMALDI

FLORIO
My Lord Soranzo, this is strange to me,
Why you should storm, having my word engaged:
Owing her heart, what need you doubt her ear?
Losers may talk by law of any game.   55

VASQUES
Yet the villainy of words, Signor Florio, may be such as
would make any unspleened dove choleric. Blame not my
lord in this.

FLORIO
Be you more silent.
I would not for my wealth my daughter's love   60

41 *his* ed. this Q
43 *had not* ed. had Q
45 *for* to prevent
48 *innocence* fool
54 *Owing* Owning
56 *villainy* ed. villaine Q

---

44 *wormed.* The small vermiform ligament in a dog's tongue was often cut
out in puppyhood, as a supposed safeguard against rabies. Vasques'
anger moves easily from fish (line 44) to dog.

57 *unspleened dove.* The idea that the dove has no gall is an ancient fallacy.
It is discussed and rejected by Sir Thomas Browne, *Pseudodoxia
Epidemica*, III.iii, though he allows a metaphoric sense: 'If therefore
any affirm a Pigeon hath no gall, implying no more thereby then the
lenity of the Animal, we shall not controvert his affirmation.'

Should cause the spilling of one drop of blood.
Vasques, put up, let's end this fray in wine.
        Exeunt [FLORIO, DONADO, SORANZO *and* VASQUES]

PUTANA

How like you this, child? Here's threatening, challenging,
quarrelling, and fighting, on every side, and all is for your
sake; you had need look to yourself, charge, you'll be stolen 65
away sleeping else shortly.

ANNABELLA

But, tut'ress, such a life gives no content
To me, my thoughts are fixed on other ends;
Would you would leave me.

PUTANA

Leave you? No marvel else. Leave me no leaving, charge; 70
this is love outright. Indeed I blame you not, you have choice
fit for the best lady in Italy.

ANNABELLA

Pray do not talk so much.

PUTANA

Take the worst with the best, there's Grimaldi the soldier,
a very well-timbered fellow. They say he is a Roman, 75
nephew to the Duke Montferrato, they say he did good
service in the wars against the Milanese, but 'faith, charge,
I do not like him, an't be for nothing but for being a soldier;
not one amongst twenty of your skirmishing captains but
have some privy maim or other that mars their standing 80
upright. I like him the worse, he crinkles so much in the
hams; though he might serve if there were no more men,
yet he's not the man I would choose.

ANNABELLA

Fie, how thou prat'st.

PUTANA

As I am a very woman, I like Signor Soranzo well; he is 85
wise, and what is more, rich; and what is more than that,
kind, and what is more than all this, a nobleman; such a
one, were I the fair Annabella myself, I would wish and
pray for. Then he is bountiful; besides, he is handsome, and
by my troth, I think wholesome (and that's news in a gallant 90
of three and twenty); liberal, that I know; loving, that you

62 *put up* sheathe your sword
78 *an't* ed. and Q
79 *not one* ed. one Q
80-1 *mars . . . upright* makes them impotent
90 *wholesome* not diseased

know; and a man sure, else he could never ha' purchased
such a good name with Hippolita, the lusty widow, in her
husband's lifetime: and 'twere but for that report, sweetheart, would 'a were thine. Commend a man for his qualities,   95
but take a husband as he is a plain-sufficient, naked man:
such a one is for your bed, and such a one is Signor Soranzo,
my life for't.

ANNABELLA
Sure the woman took her morning's draught too soon.

Enter BERGETTO *and* POGGIO

PUTANA
But look, sweetheart, look what thing comes now: here's   100
another of your ciphers to fill up the number. O brave old
ape in a silken coat. Observe.

BERGETTO
Didst thou think, Poggio, that I would spoil my new clothes,
and leave my dinner, to fight?

POGGIO
No, sir, I did not take you for so arrant a baby.   105

BERGETTO
I am wiser than so: for I hope, Poggio, thou never heardst
of an elder brother that was a coxcomb. Didst, Poggio?

POGGIO
Never indeed, sir, as long as they had either land or money
left them to inherit.

BERGETTO
Is it possible, Poggio? O monstrous! Why, I'll undertake   110
with a handful of silver to buy a headful of wit at any time;
but sirrah, I have another purchase in hand, I shall have the
wench, mine uncle says. I will but wash my face, and shift
socks, and then have at her i'faith. Mark my pace, Poggio.

POGGIO
Sir—[*Aside*] I have seen an ass and a mule trot the Spanish   115
pavin with a better grace, I know not how often.

                    Exeunt [BERGETTO *and* POGGIO]

ANNABELLA
This idiot haunts me too.

PUTANA
Ay, ay, he needs no description; the rich magnifico that is

116 *pavin* pavan, a grave, stately dance

101–2 *O brave old ape* etc. Proverbial: An ape is an ape though clad in
    scarlet (Tilley, A263).

below with your father, charge, Signor Donado his uncle,
for that he means to make this his cousin a golden calf,   120
thinks that you will be a right Israelite and fall down to him
presently: but I hope I have tutored you better. They say a
fool's bauble is a lady's playfellow, yet you having wealth
enough, you need not cast upon the dearth of flesh at any
rate: hang him, innocent.   125

Enter GIOVANNI

ANNABELLA
  But see, Putana, see: what blessed shape
  Of some celestial creature now appears?
  What man is he, that with such sad aspect
  Walks careless of himself?
PUTANA   Where?
ANNABELLA   Look below.
PUTANA
  O, 'tis your brother, sweet.
ANNABELLA   Ha!
PUTANA   'Tis your brother.   130
ANNABELLA
  Sure 'tis not he; this is some woeful thing
  Wrapped up in grief, some shadow of a man.
  Alas, he beats his breast, and wipes his eyes
  Drowned all in tears: methinks I hear him sigh.
  Let's down, Putana, and partake the cause;   135
  I know my brother, in the love he bears me,
  Will not deny me partage in his sadness.
  My soul is full of heaviness and fear.   *Exit* [*with* PUTANA]
GIOVANNI
  Lost. I am lost. My fates have doomed my death.
  The more I strive, I love; the more I love,   140
  The less I hope: I see my ruin, certain.
  What judgment or endeavours could apply
  To my incurable and restless wounds
  I throughly have examined, but in vain.

120 *cousin* kinsman, here nephew
120 *golden calf* see Exodus, 32
123 *bauble* baton or stick (with an indecent pun)
137 *partage* a part or share
144 *throughly* thoroughly

123–5 *yet you . . . rate.* i.e. you are rich enough; you need not wager
    recklessly and accept Bergetto for fear you will have no other suitors.

O that it were not in religion sin 145
To make our love a god, and worship it.
I have even wearied Heaven with prayers, dried up
The spring of my continual tears, even starved
My veins with daily fasts: what wit or art
Could counsel, I have practised; but alas, 150
I find all these but dreams and old men's tales
To fright unsteady youth; I'm still the same.
Or I must speak, or burst. 'Tis not, I know,
My lust, but 'tis my fate that leads me on.
Keep fear and low faint-hearted shame with slaves; 155
I'll tell her that I love her, though my heart
Were rated at the price of that attempt.
O me! She comes.

Enter ANNABELLA *and* PUTANA

ANNABELLA   Brother.
GIOVANNI [*Aside*]   If such a thing
As courage dwell in men, ye heavenly powers,
Now double all that virtue in my tongue. 160
ANNABELLA
Why, brother, will you not speak to me?
GIOVANNI
Yes; how d'ee, sister?
ANNABELLA
Howsoever I am, methinks you are not well.
PUTANA
Bless us, why are you so sad, sir?
GIOVANNI
Let me entreat you, leave us a while, Putana. Sister, 165
I would be private with you.
ANNABELLA
Withdraw, Putana.
PUTANA
I will. [*Aside*] If this were any other company for her, I

---

155 *Keep fear* Let fear dwell

145-6 *sin To make our love a god.* This is precisely Adam's sin in Paradise:
          . . . he scrupl'd not to eat
          Against his better knowledge, not deceav'd,
          But fondly overcome with Femal charm.
                    (*Paradise Lost*, IX, 997-9)
Adam sinned deliberately, preferring the love of Eve to the love of
God, as St Paul recognises (1 Timothy 2. 14).

should think my absence an office of some credit; but I
will leave them together.   *Exit* PUTANA   170

GIOVANNI
  Come, sister, lend your hand, let's walk together.
  I hope you need not blush to walk with me;
  Here's none but you and I.

ANNABELLA
  How's this?

GIOVANNI
  Faith, I mean no harm.   175

ANNABELLA
  Harm?

GIOVANNI
  No, good faith; how is't with 'ee?

ANNABELLA
  [*Aside*] I trust he be not frantic.—I am very well, brother.

GIOVANNI
  Trust me, but I am sick, I fear so sick
  'Twill cost my life.   180

ANNABELLA
  Mercy forbid it. 'Tis not so, I hope.

GIOVANNI
  I think you love me, sister.

ANNABELLA
  Yes, you know I do.

GIOVANNI
  I know't indeed.—Y'are very fair.

ANNABELLA
  Nay then, I see you have a merry sickness.   185

GIOVANNI
  That's as it proves. The poets feign, I read,
  That Juno for her forehead did exceed
  All other goddesses: but I durst swear
  Your forehead exceeds hers, as hers did theirs.

ANNABELLA
  Troth, this is pretty.

169 *of some credit* deserving reward
186 *The* ed. They Q

187–8 *That Juno . . . goddesses.* Apart from her beauty, Juno is an apt
    choice for Giovanni to make at this point, since she was not only the
    wife of Jupiter, but his sister as well. See Ovid, *Fasti*, 6, 29, and
    Homer, *Iliad*, xvi.

GIOVANNI   Such a pair of stars   190
  As are thine eyes would, like Promethean fire,
  If gently glanced, give life to senseless stones.
ANNABELLA
  Fie upon 'ee.
GIOVANNI
  The lily and the rose, most sweetly strange,
  Upon your dimpled cheeks do strive for change.   195
  Such lips would tempt a saint; such hands as those
  Would make an anchorite lascivious.
ANNABELLA
  D'ee mock me, or flatter me?
GIOVANNI
  If you would see a beauty more exact
  Than art can counterfeit or nature frame,   200
  Look in your glass and there behold your own.
ANNABELLA
  O you are a trim youth.
GIOVANNI
  Here.   *Offers his dagger to her*
ANNABELLA
  What to do?
GIOVANNI
  And here's my breast, strike home.   205
  Rip up my bosom, there thou shalt behold
  A heart in which is writ the truth I speak.
  Why stand 'ee?
ANNABELLA   Are you earnest?
GIOVANNI   Yes, most earnest.
  You cannot love?
ANNABELLA   Whom?
GIOVANNI   Me. My tortured soul
  Hath felt affliction in the heat of death.   210
  O Annabella, I am quite undone.
  The love of thee, my sister, and the view
  Of thy immortal beauty hath untuned
  All harmony both of my rest and life.
  Why d'ee not strike?

205 *strike* ed. strick Q

191–2 *Promethean . . . stones.* One of Ford's typically suggestive phrases,
  recalling both *Othello*, V.ii, 12 'I know not where is that Promethean
  heat', and Chapman's *Bussy D'Ambois*, V.iii, 191–2 'like a falling star
  Silently glanc'd.'

ANNABELLA   Forbid it, my just fears.   215
  If this be true, 'twere fitter I were dead.
GIOVANNI
  True, Annabella; 'tis no time to jest.
  I have too long suppressed the hidden flames
  That almost have consumed me; I have spent
  Many a silent night in sighs and groans,   220
  Ran over all my thoughts, despised my fate,
  Reasoned against the reasons of my love,
  Done all that smoothed-cheek virtue could advise,
  But found all bootless: 'tis my destiny
  That you must either love, or I must die.   225
ANNABELLA
  Comes this in sadness from you?
GIOVANNI   Let some mischief
  Befall me soon, if I dissemble aught.
ANNABELLA
  You are my brother Giovanni.
GIOVANNI   You
  My sister Annabella; I know this:
  And could afford you instance why to love   230
  So much the more for this; to which intent
  Wise nature first in your creation meant
  To make you mine; else't had been sin and foul
  To share one beauty to a double soul.
  Nearness in birth or blood doth but persuade   235
  A nearer nearness in affection.
  I have asked counsel of the holy church,
  Who tells me I may love you, and 'tis just
  That since I may, I should; and will, yes, will.
  Must I now live, or die?
ANNABELLA   Live. Thou hast won   240
  The field, and never fought; what thou hast urged
  My captive heart had long ago resolved.
  I blush to tell thee—but I'll tell thee now—
  For every sigh that thou hast spent for me
  I have sighed ten; for every tear shed twenty: 245
  And not so much for that I loved, as that
  I durst not say I loved, nor scarcely think it.

224 *bootless* useless
226 *sadness* earnest   246 *for that* because

232–4 *Wise nature . . . soul.* Cf. Spenser, *An Hymne in Honour of Beautie*,
    204–10.

GIOVANNI

Let not this music be a dream, ye gods,
For pity's sake, I beg 'ee.

ANNABELLA   On my knees,   *She kneels*

Brother, even by our mother's dust, I charge you,   250
Do not betray me to your mirth or hate,
Love me, or kill me, brother.

GIOVANNI   On my knees,   *He kneels*

Sister, even by my mother's dust, I charge you,
Do not betray me to your mirth or hate,
Love me, or kill me, sister.   255

ANNABELLA

You mean good sooth then?

GIOVANNI   In good troth I do,

And so do you, I hope: say, I'm in earnest.

ANNABELLA

I'll swear't, I.

GIOVANNI   And I, and by this kiss,   *Kisses her*

(Once more, yet once more; now let's rise by this)
                                                  [They rise]

I would not change this minute for Elysium.   260
What must we now do?

ANNABELLA   What you will.

GIOVANNI   Come then,

After so many tears as we have wept,
Let's learn to court in smiles, to kiss, and sleep.   *Exeunt*

[Act I, Scene iii]

Enter FLORIO *and* DONADO

FLORIO

Signor Donado, you have said enough,
I understand you; but would have you know
I will not force my daughter 'gainst her will.
You see I have but two, a son and her;
And he is so devoted to his book,   5
As I must tell you true, I doubt his health:
Should he miscarry, all my hopes rely
Upon my girl; as for worldly fortune,
I am, I thank my stars, blest with enough.

256 *sooth* truth
258 *swear't, I* ed. swear't and I Q
  6 *doubt* fear for
  8 *girl* pronounced as two syllables throughout

My care is how to match her to her liking: 10
I would not have her marry wealth, but love,
And if she like your nephew, let him have her.
Here's all that I can say.

DONADO   Sir, you say well,
Like a true father, and for my part I,
If the young folks can like ('twixt you and me),   15
Will promise to assure my nephew presently
Three thousand florins yearly during life,
And after I am dead, my whole estate.

FLORIO
'Tis a fair proffer, sir; meantime your nephew
Shall have free passage to commence his suit.   20
If he can thrive, he shall have my consent.
So for this time I'll leave you, signor.   *Exit*

DONADO   Well,
Here's hope yet, if my nephew would have wit;
But he is such another dunce, I fear
He'll never win the wench. When I was young   25
I could have done't, i'faith, and so shall he
If he will learn of me; and in good time
He comes himself.

                  Enter BERGETTO *and* POGGIO

How now, Bergetto, whither away so fast?

BERGETTO
O uncle, I have heard the strangest news that ever came   30
out of the mint, have I not, Poggio?

POGGIO
Yes indeed, sir.

DONADO
What news, Bergetto?

BERGETTO
Why, look ye, uncle, my barber told me just now that
there is a fellow come to town who undertakes to make a   35
mill go without the mortal help of any water or wind, only
with sand-bags: and this fellow hath a strange horse, a most
excellent beast, I'll assure you, uncle (my barber says),

29 *How . . . fast* Assigned to Donado since Weber's edition (1811);
    to Poggio in Q

30–1 *that ever came out of the mint.* Proverbial: New out of the Mint
    (Tilley M985). Cf. *Twelfth Night*, III.ii, 22 '. . . some excellent jests,
    fire-new from the mint.'

whose head, to the wonder of all Christian people, stands
just behind where his tail is. Is't not true, Poggio?   40

POGGIO

So the barber swore, forsooth.

DONADO

And you are running thither?

BERGETTO

Ay forsooth, uncle.

DONADO

Wilt thou be a fool still? Come sir, you shall not go: you
have more mind of a puppet-play than on the business I   45
told ye; why, thou great baby, wilt never have wit, wilt
make thyself a may-game to all the world?

POGGIO

Answer for yourself, master.

BERGETTO

Why, uncle, should I sit at home still, and not go abroad to
see fashions like other gallants?   50

DONADO

To see hobby-horses! What wise talk, I pray, had you with
Annabella, when you were at Signor Florio's house?

BERGETTO

O, the wench! Uds sa' me, uncle, I tickled her with a rare
speech, that I made her almost burst her belly with laughing.

DONADO

Nay, I think so; and what speech was't?   55

BERGETTO

What did I say, Poggio?

POGGIO

Forsooth, my master said that he loved her almost as well
as he loved parmasent, and swore (I'll be sworn for him)
that she wanted but such a nose as his was to be as pretty a
young woman as any was in Parma.   60

DONADO

O gross.

BERGETTO

Nay, uncle, then she asked me whether my father had any

---

42 *thither* ed. hither Q
53 *Uds sa' me* God save me
58 *parmasent* parmesan, the cheese of Parma

---

47 *may-game.* Laughing-stock. Cf. *The Lover's Melancholy*, I.ii, 10
'Why should not I, a May-game, scorn the weight/Of my sunk fortunes?'

more children than myself: and I said 'No, 'twere better
he should have had his brains knocked out first.'

DONADO

This is intolerable.   65

BERGETTO

Then said she 'Will Signor Donado your uncle leave you
all his wealth?'

DONADO

Ha! that was good; did she harp upon that string?

BERGETTO

Did she harp upon that string? Ay, that she did. I answered
'Leave me all his wealth? Why, woman, he hath no other wit;   70
if he had, he should hear on't to his everlasting glory and
confusion: I know,' quoth I, 'I am his white boy, and will
not be gulled'; and with that she fell into a great smile and
went away. Nay, I did fit her.

DONADO

Ah, sirrah, then I see there is no changing of nature. Well,   75
Bergetto, I fear thou wilt be a very ass still.

BERGETTO

I should be sorry for that, uncle.

DONADO

Come, come you home with me. Since you are no better a
speaker, I'll have you write to her after some courtly manner,
and enclose some rich jewel in the letter.   80

BERGETTO

Ay marry, that will be excellent.

DONADO

Peace, innocent.
Once in my time I'll set my wits to school,
If all fail, 'tis but the fortune of a fool.

BERGETTO

Poggio, 'twill do, Poggio.   *Exeunt*   85

Act II, [Scene i]

Enter GIOVANNI *and* ANNABELLA, *as from their chamber*

GIOVANNI

Come Annabella: no more sister now,
But love, a name more gracious; do not blush,

74 *fit her* answer her aptly   82 *innocent* simpleton

---

72 *white boy.* Favourite, pet. For this use of 'white' in the sense of 'highly
prized, precious' see *O.E.D.* White, a 9.

Beauty's sweet wonder, but be proud to know
That yielding thou hast conquered, and inflamed
A heart whose tribute is thy brother's life.   5

ANNABELLA
And mine is his. O, how these stol'n contents
Would print a modest crimson on my cheeks,
Had any but my heart's delight prevailed.

GIOVANNI
I marvel why the chaster of your sex
Should think this pretty toy called maidenhead   10
So strange a loss, when, being lost, 'tis nothing,
And you are still the same.

ANNABELLA   'Tis well for you;
Now you can talk.

GIOVANNI   Music as well consists
In th' ear as in the playing.

ANNABELLA   O, y'are wanton.
Tell on't, y'are best: do.

GIOVANNI   Thou wilt chide me then.   15
Kiss me:—so. Thus hung Jove on Leda's neck,
And sucked divine ambrosia from her lips.
I envy not the mightiest man alive,
But hold myself in being king of thee
More great than were I king of all the world.   20
But I shall lose you, sweetheart.

ANNABELLA   But you shall not.

GIOVANNI
You must be married, mistress.

ANNABELLA   Yes? To whom?

GIOVANNI
Someone must have you.

ANNABELLA   You must.

GIOVANNI   Nay, some other.

---

16 *Thus hung Jove.* Leda was seduced by Jove in the form of a swan. See
Ovid, *Metamorphoses*, 6, 109. The myth is aptly used by Giovanni as the
example of an unnatural union the sensationalism of which has been
dignified by art.

22 *Yes? To whom?* Q reads 'Yes, to whom?' and it is difficult in a modern-
ised text to suggest the tone of Annabella's reply. Her three speeches
(21-3) are probably playful repartee, unconscious of Giovanni's
serious intent. Perhaps the closest tonal analogue to this moment is in
As You Like It, IV.i, 90ff. The contrast makes her realisation ('Now
prithee do not speak so') an intensely dramatic point.

ANNABELLA
Now prithee do not speak so: without jesting,
You'll make me weep in earnest.
GIOVANNI   What, you will not?   25
But tell me, sweet, canst thou be dared to swear
That thou wilt live to me, and to no other?
ANNABELLA
By both our loves I dare, for didst thou know,
My Giovanni, how all suitors seem
To my eyes hateful, thou wouldst trust me then.   30
GIOVANNI
Enough, I take thy word. Sweet, we must part.
Remember what thou vowst; keep well my heart.
ANNABELLA
Will you be gone?
GIOVANNI   I must.
ANNABELLA   When to return?
GIOVANNI
Soon.
ANNABELLA   Look you do.
GIOVANNI   Farewell.   *Exit*
ANNABELLA
Go where thou wilt, in mind I'll keep thee here,   35
And where thou art, I know I shall be there.
Guardian!

Enter PUTANA

PUTANA
Child, how is't, child? Well, thank Heaven, ha?
ANNABELLA
O guardian, what a paradise of joy
Have I passed over!   40
PUTANA
Nay, what a paradise of joy have you passed under! Why,
now I commend thee, charge; fear nothing, sweetheart;
what though he be your brother? Your brother's a man,
I hope, and I say still, if a young wench feel the fit upon her,
let her take anybody, father or brother, all is one.   45
ANNABELLA
I would not have it known for all the world.
PUTANA
Nor I, indeed, for the speech of the people; else 'twere
nothing.
FLORIO *within*
Daughter Annabella.

ANNABELLA
O me, my father!—Here, sir!—Reach my work.   50
FLORIO *within*
What are you doing?
ANNABELLA   So: let him come now.

Enter FLORIO, RICHARDETTO *like a doctor of physic, and*
PHILOTIS *with a lute in her hand*

FLORIO
So hard at work? That's well; you lose no time.
Look, I have brought you company; here's one,
A learned doctor lately come from Padua,
Much skilled in physic, and for that I see   55
You have of late been sickly, I entreated
This reverend man to visit you some time.
ANNABELLA
Y'are very welcome, sir.
RICHARDETTO   I thank you, mistress.
Loud fame in large report hath spoke your praise
As well for virtue as perfection: .   60
For which I have been bold to bring with me
A kinswoman of mine, a maid, for song
And music one perhaps will give content;
Please you to know her.
ANNABELLA   They are parts I love,
And she for them most welcome.
PHILOTIS   Thank you, lady.   65
FLORIO
Sir, now you know my house, pray make not strange,
And if you find my daughter need your art,
I'll be your paymaster.
RICHARDETTO   Sir, what I am
She shall command.
FLORIO   You shall bind me to you.
Daughter, I must have conference with you   70
About some matters that concerns us both.
Good master doctor, please you but walk in,
We'll crave a little of your cousin's cunning.
I think my girl hath not quite forgot
To touch an instrument: she could have done't.   75
We'll hear them both.
RICHARDETTO   I'll wait upon you, sir.   *Exeunt*

54 *Padua* famous for its university's medical school
55 *for that* because   64 *parts* abilities   73 *cunning* skill

[Act II, Scene ii]

Enter SORANZO *in his study reading a book*

SORANZO
'Love's measure is extreme, the comfort, pain,
The life unrest, and the reward disdain.'
What's here? Look't o'er again: 'tis so, so writes
This smooth licentious poet in his rhymes.
But Sannazar, thou liest, for had thy bosom   5
Felt such oppression as is laid on mine,
Thou wouldst have kissed the rod that made thee smart.
To work then, happy muse, and contradict
What Sannazar hath in his envy writ.
'Love's measure is the mean, sweet his annoys,   10
His pleasure's life, and his reward all joys.'
Had Annabella lived when Sannazar
Did in his brief encomium celebrate
Venice, that queen of cities, he had left
That verse which gained him such a sum of gold,   15
And for one only look from Annabel
Had writ of her and her diviner cheeks.
O how my thoughts are—
VASQUES *within*
Pray forbear; in rules of civility, let me give notice
on't: I shall be taxed of my neglect of duty and service.   20
SORANZO
What rude intrusion interrupts my peace?
Can I be nowhere private?
VASQUES *within*
Troth you wrong your modesty.
SORANZO
What's the matter, Vasques? Who is't?

7 *thee* ed. the Q
20 *taxed of* blamed for

---

5 *Sannazar*. Jacopo Sannazaro, an Italian poet, was born in Naples circa
1456 and died there in 1530. His best known work, the *Arcadia*, was
well known in England.

13 *brief encomium*. A short Latin poem in praise of Venice, for which the
city lavishly rewarded him. It is quoted by Thomas Coryat in *Coryat's
Crudities* (1611), and Sherman points out (p. 128) that it appears with
an English translation in a letter from James Howell to Robert Brown
of the Middle Temple from Venice, 12 August 1621. Ford, as well as
Brown, was a member of the Middle Temple.

Enter HIPPOLITA *and* VASQUES

HIPPOLITA
  'Tis I: 25
  Do you know me now? Look, perjured man, on her
  Whom thou and thy distracted lust have wronged.
  Thy sensual rage of blood hath made my youth
  A scorn to men and angels, and shall I
  Be now a foil to thy unsated change?   30
  Thou knowst, false wanton, when my modest fame
  Stood free from stain or scandal, all the charms
  Of hell or sorcery could not prevail
  Against the honour of my chaster bosom.
  Thine eyes did plead in tears, thy tongue in oaths   35
  Such and so many, that a heart of steel
  Would have been wrought to pity, as was mine:
  And shall the conquest of my lawful bed,
  My husband's death urged on by his disgrace,
  My loss of womanhood, be ill rewarded   40
  With hatred and contempt? No; know, Soranzo,
  I have a spirit doth as much distaste
  The slavery of fearing thee, as thou
  Dost loathe the memory of what hath passed.

SORANZO
  Nay, dear Hippolita—

HIPPOLITA   Call me not dear,   45
  Nor think with supple words to smooth the grossness
  Of my abuses; 'tis not your new mistress,
  Your goodly Madam Merchant, shall triumph
  On my dejection: tell her thus from me,
  My birth was nobler and by much more free.   50

SORANZO
  You are too violent.

HIPPOLITA   You are too double
  In your dissimulation. Seest thou this,

---

30 *foil . . . change* background for your promiscuity
42 *distaste* dislike
48 *triumph* accented on second syllable

---

48 *Madam Merchant.* Q prints *Madam Merchant* as if to emphasise the
  phrase (though Q's use of italic is by no means regular). *O.E.D.* quotes
  the line (Madam sb 2d) as an example of 'playful or derisive uses', and
  compares *Measure for Measure*, I.ii, 43 'Behold, behold, where Madam
  Mitigation comes'. Hippolita is disparaging Annabella's family, and
  pointing out that her own birth 'was nobler and by much more free.'

This habit, these black mourning weeds of care?
'Tis thou art cause of this, and hast divorced
My husband from his life and me from him,   55
And made me widow in my widowhood.

SORANZO
Will you yet hear?

HIPPOLITA   More of thy perjuries?
Thy soul is drowned too deeply in those sins;
Thou need'st not add to th' number.

SORANZO   Then I'll leave you;
You are past all rules of sense.

HIPPOLITA   And thou of grace.   60

VASQUES
Fie, mistress, you are not near the limits of reason: if my lord
had a resolution as noble as virtue itself, you take the course
to unedge it all. Sir, I beseech you, do not perplex her;
griefs, alas, will have a vent. I dare undertake Madam
Hippolita will now freely hear you.   65

SORANZO
Talk to a woman frantic! Are these the fruits of your love?

HIPPOLITA
They are the fruits of thy untruth, false man.
Didst thou not swear, whilst yet my husband lived,
That thou wouldst wish no happiness on earth
More than to call me wife? Didst thou not vow,   70
When he should die, to marry me? For which,
The devil in my blood, and thy protests,
Caused me to counsel him to undertake
A voyage to Ligorn, for that we heard
His brother there was dead, and left a daughter   75
Young and unfriended, who, with much ado,
I wished him to bring hither: he did so,
And went; and as thou know'st died on the way.
Unhappy man, to buy his death so dear
With my advice. Yet thou for whom I did it   80
Forget'st thy vows, and leav'st me to my shame.

SORANZO
Who could help this?

HIPPOLITA   Who? Perjured man, thou couldst,

---

57 *thy* Q *a.c.*; *the* Q *b.c.*
61 *not near* i.e. beyond (but carefully ambiguous)
63 *unedge* blunt
74 *Ligorn* Leghorn (Italian *Livorno*)

If thou hadst faith or love.

SORANZO   You are deceived.
The vows I made, if you remember well,
Were wicked and unlawful: 'twere more sin   85
To keep them than to break them. As for me,
I cannot mask my penitence. Think thou
How much thou hast digressed from honest shame
In bringing of a gentleman to death
Who was thy husband; such a one as he,   90
So noble in his quality, condition,
Learning, behaviour, entertainment, love,
As Parma could not show a braver man.

VASQUES
You do not well; this was not your promise.

SORANZO
I care not; let her know her monstrous life.   95
Ere I'll be servile to so black a sin,
I'll be accursed. Woman, come here no more.
Learn to repent and die, for by my honour
I hate thee and thy lust: you have been too foul.   [*Exit*]

VASQUES
[*Aside*] This part has been scurvily played.   100

HIPPOLITA
How foolishly this beast contemns his fate,
And shuns the use of that which I more scorn
Than I once loved, his love. But let him go;
My vengeance shall give comfort to this woe.
                              She offers to go away

VASQUES
Mistress, mistress, Madam Hippolita, pray, a word or two!   105

---

100 *scurvily played* badly acted
101 *contemns* despises
104 *this* ed. his Q

84–6 *The vows . . . break them.* St Augustine, in *De bono coniugali* (Corpus
   Scriptorum Ecclesiasticorum Latinorum, Vienna, 1866ff., XLI,
   187ff.), argues that breaking a contract made in sin to return to virtue
   was no sin at all. But this was not everyone's view. See Alan T. Gaylord,
   'The Promises in the Franklin's Tale', *ELH*, XXXI, 4 (1964), 331–65.
97 *accursed.* a Curse Q *b.c.*; a Coarse Q *a.c.* Bawcutt's emendation,
   'accurs'd', has everything to commend it. The three forms could be
   very similar in seventeenth-century handwriting, and 'accursed' gives
   the best sense. It does suggest, however, that Q's press corrections are
   not authorial. Cf. note to IV.iii, 63.

HIPPOLITA
   With me, sir?
VASQUES
   With you, if you please.
HIPPOLITA
   What is't?
VASQUES
   I know you are infinitely moved now, and you think you
   have cause; some I confess you have, but sure not so much as   110
   you imagine.
HIPPOLITA
   Indeed.
VASQUES
   O, you were miserably bitter, which you followed even to
   the last syllable. Faith, you were somewhat too shrewd;
   by my life you could not have took my lord in a worse   115
   time, since I first knew him: tomorrow you shall find him
   a new man.
HIPPOLITA
   Well, I shall wait his leisure.
VASQUES
   Fie, this is not a hearty patience, it comes sourly from you;
   troth, let me persuade you for once.   120
HIPPOLITA
   [*Aside*] I have it, and it shall be so; thanks, opportunity!—
   Persuade me to what?
VASQUES
   Visit him in some milder temper. O if you could but master
   a little your female spleen, how might you win him.
HIPPOLITA
   He will never love me. Vasques, thou hast been a too   125
   trusty servant to such a master, and I believe thy reward
   in the end will fall out like mine.
VASQUES
   So perhaps too.
HIPPOLITA
   Resolve thyself it will. Had I one so true, so truly honest,
   so secret to my counsels, as thou hast been to him and his,   130
   I should think it a slight acquittance, not only to make him
   master of all I have, but even of myself.

114 *shrewd* scolding
129 *Resolve* Assure
131 *acquittance* discharge of debt

VASQUES
O you are a noble gentlewoman.

HIPPOLITA
Wilt thou feed always upon hopes? Well, I know thou art
wise, and seest the reward of an old servant daily, what it is.   135

VASQUES
Beggary and neglect.

HIPPOLITA
True: but Vasques, wert thou mine, and wouldst be
private to me and my designs, I here protest myself and all
what I can else call mine should be at thy dispose.

VASQUES
[*Aside*] Work you that way, old mole? Then I have the wind   140
of you.—I were not worthy of it by any desert that could lie
within my compass; if I could—

HIPPOLITA
What then?

VASQUES
I should then hope to live in these my old years with rest
and security.   145

HIPPOLITA
Give me thy hand: now promise but thy silence,
And help to bring to pass a plot I have,
And here in sight of Heaven, that being done,
I make thee lord of me and mine estate.

VASQUES
Come, you are merry; this is such a happiness that I can   150
neither think or believe.

HIPPOLITA
Promise thy secrecy, and 'tis confirmed.

VASQUES
Then here I call our good genii for witnesses, whatsoever
your designs are, or against whomsoever, I will not only be
a special actor therein, but never disclose it till it be effected.   155

HIPPOLITA
I take thy word, and with that, thee for mine;
Come then, let's more confer of this anon.
On this delicious bane my thoughts shall banquet:
Revenge shall sweeten what my griefs have tasted.   *Exeunt*

140 *have the wind* understand your intention
153 *for witnesses* ed. foe-witnesses Q
158 *bane* poison

[Act II, Scene iii]

Enter RICHARDETTO *and* PHILOTIS

RICHARDETTO
  Thou seest, my lovely niece, these strange mishaps,
  How all my fortunes turn to my disgrace,
  Wherein I am but as a looker-on,
  Whiles others act my shame, and I am silent.
PHILOTIS
  But uncle, wherein can this borrowed shape   5
  Give you content?
RICHARDETTO   I'll tell thee, gentle niece:
  Thy wanton aunt in her lascivious riots
  Lives now secure, thinks I am surely dead
  In my late journey to Ligorn for you
  (As I have caused it to be rumoured out).   10
  Now would I see with what an impudence
  She gives scope to her loose adultery,
  And how the common voice allows hereof:
  Thus far I have prevailed.
PHILOTIS   Alas, I fear
  You mean some strange revenge.
RICHARDETTO   O, be not troubled;   15
  Your ignorance shall plead for you in all.
  But to our business: what, you learned for certain
  How Signor Florio means to give his daughter
  In marriage to Soranzo?
PHILOTIS   Yes, for certain.
RICHARDETTO
  But how find you young Annabella's love   20
  Inclined to him?
PHILOTIS   For aught I could perceive,
  She neither fancies him or any else.
RICHARDETTO
  There's mystery in that which time must show.
  She used you kindly?
PHILOTIS   Yes.
RICHARDETTO   And craved your company?
PHILOTIS
  Often.

   5 *borrowed shape* disguise
  13 *how . . . hereof* what people say about it
  16 *Your . . . all* The less you know the better

RICHARDETTO   'Tis well; it goes as I could wish.   25
  I am the doctor now, and as for you,
  None knows you; if all fail not, we shall thrive.
  But who comes here?

Enter GRIMALDI

          I know him: 'tis Grimaldi,
  A Roman and a soldier, near allied
  Unto the duke of Montferrato, one   30
  Attending on the nuncio of the Pope
  That now resides in Parma, by which means
  He hopes to get the love of Annabella.

GRIMALDI
  Save you, sir.

RICHARDETTO   And you, sir.

GRIMALDI   I have heard
  Of your approved skill, which through the city   35
  Is freely talked of, and would crave your aid.

RICHARDETTO
  For what, sir?

GRIMALDI   Marry, sir, for this—
  But I would speak in private.

RICHARDETTO   Leave us, cousin.

Exit PHILOTIS

GRIMALDI
  I love fair Annabella, and would know
  Whether in art there may not be receipts   40
  To move affection.

RICHARDETTO   Sir, perhaps there may,
  But these will nothing profit you.

GRIMALDI   Not me?

RICHARDETTO
  Unless I be mistook, you are a man
  Greatly in favour with the cardinal.

GRIMALDI
  What of that?

RICHARDETTO   In duty to his grace,   45
  I will be bold to tell you, if you seek
  To marry Florio's daughter, you must first
  Remove a bar 'twixt you and her.

GRIMALDI   Who's that?

35 *through* pronounced 'thorough'
40 *art* ed. Arts Q
40 *receipts* recipes (love-potions)

RICHARDETTO
　　Soranzo is the man that hath her heart;
　　And while he lives, be sure you cannot speed.   50
GRIMALDI
　　Soranzo! What, mine enemy! Is't he?
RICHARDETTO
　　Is he your enemy?
GRIMALDI　　　　　　　The man I hate
　　Worse than confusion;
　　I'll kill him straight.
RICHARDETTO　　　　　　　Nay then, take mine advice
　　(Even for his grace's sake, the cardinal):   55
　　I'll find a time when he and she do meet,
　　Of which I'll give you notice, and to be sure
　　He shall not 'scape you, I'll provide a poison
　　To dip your rapier's point in; if he had
　　As many heads as Hydra had, he dies.   60
GRIMALDI
　　But shall I trust thee, doctor?
RICHARDETTO　　　　　　　As yourself;
　　Doubt not in aught. [*Aside*] Thus shall the fates decree:
　　By me Soranzo falls, that ruined me.   *Exeunt*

[Act II, Scene iv]

Enter DONADO, BERGETTO *and* POGGIO

DONADO
　　Well, sir, I must be content to be both your secretary and
　　your messenger myself. I cannot tell what this letter may
　　work, but as sure as I am alive, if thou come once to talk
　　with her, I fear thou wilt mar whatsoever I make.
BERGETTO
　　You make, uncle? Why, am not I big enough to carry mine   5
　　own letter, I pray?
DONADO
　　Ay, ay, carry a fool's head o' thy own. Why, thou dunce,
　　wouldst thou write a letter and carry it thyself?
BERGETTO
　　Yes, that I would, and read it to her with my own mouth;
　　for you must think, if she will not believe me myself when   10
　　she hears me speak, she will not believe another's hand-

50 *speed* succeed
54 *kill* Q *a.c.*; tell Q *b.c.*
63 *ruined* ruin'd Q *a.c.*; min'd Q *b.c.*

writing. O, you think I am a blockhead, uncle. No, sir,
Poggio knows I have indited a letter myself, so I have.

POGGIO

Yes truly, sir; I have it in my pocket.

DONADO

A sweet one, no doubt; pray let's see't.   15

BERGETTO

I cannot read my own hand very well, Poggio; read it,
Poggio.

DONADO

Begin.

POGGIO *reads*

'Most dainty and honey-sweet mistress, I could call
you fair, and lie as fast as any that loves you, but my uncle   20
being the elder man, I leave it to him, as more fit for his age
and the colour of his beard. I am wise enough to tell you I
can bourd where I see occasion; or if you like my uncle's
wit better than mine, you shall marry me; if you like mine
better than his, I will marry you in spite of your teeth. So   25
commending my best parts to you, I rest—Yours upwards
and downwards, or you may choose, Bergetto.'

BERGETTO

Aha, here's stuff, uncle.

DONADO

Here's stuff indeed to shame us all. Pray whose advice did
you take in this learned letter?   30

POGGIO

None, upon my word, but mine own.

BERGETTO

And mine, uncle, believe it, nobody's else; 'twas mine own
brain, I thank a good wit for't.

DONADO

Get you home, sir, and look you keep within doors till I
return.   35

BERGETTO

How! That were a jest indeed; I scorn it i'faith.

DONADO

What! You do not?

BERGETTO

Judge me, but I do now.

POGGIO

Indeed, sir, 'tis very unhealthy.

23 *bourd* jest

DONADO

Well, sir, if I hear any of your apish running to motions   40
and fopperies, till I come back, you were as good no; look
to't.   *Exit* DONADO

BERGETTO

Poggio, shall's steal to see this horse with the head in's tail?

POGGIO

Ay, but you must take heed of whipping.

BERGETTO

Dost take me for a child, Poggio? Come, honest Poggio.   45
                                        Exeunt

[Act II, Scene v]

Enter FRIAR *and* GIOVANNI

FRIAR

Peace. Thou hast told a tale, whose every word
Threatens eternal slaughter to the soul.
I'm sorry I have heard it; would mine ears
Had been one minute deaf, before the hour
That thou cam'st to me. O young man castaway,   5
By the religious number of mine order,
I day and night have waked my aged eyes,
Above my strength, to weep on thy behalf:
But Heaven is angry, and be thou resolved,
Thou art a man remarked to taste a mischief.   10
Look for't; though it come late, it will come sure.

GIOVANNI

Father, in this you are uncharitable;
What I have done I'll prove both fit and good.

---

40 *motions* puppet shows
8 *my* ed. thy Q
9 *resolved* assured
10 *remarked* marked out
10 *mischief* disaster

---

6 *By the religious* etc. The text may well be corrupt here. 'Number' has
been explained as 'group' or 'company', but the subdued oath would be
an odd one, and even odder in Gifford's emendation of 'number' to
'founder'. I would tentatively suggest moving the comma after 'castaway' (line 5) and placing it after 'man', thus emphasising the point
that the Friar makes (I.i, 53–5) that he has left all to follow Giovanni.

It is a principle (which you have taught
When I was yet your scholar), that the frame 15
And composition of the mind doth follow
The frame and composition of the body:
So where the body's furniture is beauty,
The mind's must needs be virtue; which allowed,
Virtue itself is reason but refined, 20
And love the quintessence of that. This proves
My sister's beauty being rarely fair
Is rarely virtuous; chiefly in her love,
And chiefly in that love, her love to me.
If hers to me, then so is mine to her; 25
Since in like causes are effects alike.

FRIAR

O ignorance in knowledge. Long ago,
How often have I warned thee this before?
Indeed, if we were sure there were no deity,
Nor Heaven nor hell, then to be led alone 30
By nature's light (as were philosophers
Of elder times), might instance some defence.
But 'tis not so; then, madman, thou wilt find
That nature is in Heaven's positions blind.

GIOVANNI

Your age o'errules you; had you youth like mine, 35
You'd make her love your Heaven, and her divine.

FRIAR

Nay then, I see th'art too far sold to hell,
It lies not in the compass of my prayers

15 *frame* ed. Fame Q
17 *the body* ed. Body Q
34 *positions* propositions, doctrines

14–19 *It is a principle* etc. Cf. Spenser, *An Hymne in Honour of Beautie*,
132–3:

> For of the soule the bodie forme doth take:
> For soule is forme, and doth the bodie make.

Giovanni's argument brings together a number of vaguely neoplatonic
ideas about the relationship of the good to the beautiful, but forms no
proper links between them. Cf. Ford's *Honour Triumphant*, Third
Position (*Works*, ed. Gifford—Dyce, iii, 359), and Tilley F1.
31–2 *philosophers Of elder times.* Pre-Christian philosophers. Cf. Donne,
Satire III, 11–15. It was sometimes argued by theologians that pagan
philosophers, who followed the light of nature, would thus come to
salvation by 'imputed' grace.
34 *That nature* etc. i.e. to study nature teaches us nothing about God.

To call thee back; yet let me counsel thee:
Persuade thy sister to some marriage.   40
GIOVANNI
Marriage? Why, that's to damn her. That's to prove
Her greedy of variety of lust.
FRIAR
O fearful! If thou wilt not, give me leave
To shrive her, lest she should die unabsolved.
GIOVANNI
At your best leisure, father; then she'll tell you   45
How dearly she doth prize my matchless love.
Then you will know what pity 'twere we two
Should have been sundered from each other's arms.
View well her face, and in that little round
You may observe a world of variety: 50
For colour, lips; for sweet perfumes, her breath;
For jewels, eyes; for threads of purest gold,
Hair; for delicious choice of flowers, cheeks;
Wonder in every portion of that throne.
Hear her but speak, and you will swear the spheres   55
Make music to the citizens in Heaven.
But, father, what is else for pleasure framed,
Lest I offend your ears, shall go unnamed.
FRIAR
The more I hear, I pity thee the more,
That one so excellent should give those parts   60
All to a second death; what I can do
Is but to pray: and yet I could advise thee,
Wouldst thou be ruled.
GIOVANNI   In what?
FRIAR   Why, leave her yet;
The throne of mercy is above your trespass;
Yet time is left you both—
GIOVANNI   To embrace each other,   65
Else let all time be struck quite out of number.
She is like me, and I like her, resolved.
FRIAR
No more! I'll visit her. This grieves me most,
Things being thus, a pair of souls are lost.   *Exeunt*

61 *second death* damnation

[Act II, Scene vi]

Enter FLORIO, DONADO, ANNABELLA, PUTANA

FLORIO
  Where's Giovanni?
ANNABELLA   Newly walked abroad,
  And, as I heard him say, gone to the friar,
  His reverend tutor.
FLORIO   That's a blessed man,
  A man made up of holiness; I hope
  He'll teach him how to gain another world.   5
DONADO
  Fair gentlewoman, here's a letter sent
  To you from my young cousin; I dare swear
  He loves you in his soul: would you could hear
  Sometimes what I see daily, sighs and tears,
  As if his breast were prison to his heart.   10
FLORIO
  Receive it, Annabella.
ANNABELLA
  Alas, good man.
DONADO
  What's that she said?
PUTANA
  An't please you, sir, she said, 'Alas, good man.' Truly I
  do commend him to her every night before her first sleep,   15
  because I would have her dream of him, and she hearkens
  to that most religiously.
DONADO
  Say'st so? God-a-mercy, Putana, there's something for thee,
  and prithee do what thou canst on his behalf; sha' not be
  lost labour, take my word for't.   20
PUTANA
  Thank you most heartily, sir; now I have a feeling of your
  mind, let me alone to work.
ANNABELLA
  Guardian!
PUTANA
  Did you call?
ANNABELLA
  Keep this letter.   25

14 *An't* ed. And Q

DONADO
  Signor Florio, in any case bid her read it instantly.
FLORIO
  Keep it for what? Pray read it me hereright.
ANNABELLA
  I shall, sir.   *She reads*
DONADO
  How d'ee find her inclined, signor?
FLORIO
  Troth, sir, I know not how; not all so well   30
  As I could wish.
ANNABELLA
  Sir, I am bound to rest your cousin's debtor.
  The jewel I'll return; for if he love,
  I'll count that love a jewel.
DONADO   Mark you that?
  Nay, keep them both, sweet maid.
ANNABELLA   You must excuse me,   35
  Indeed I will not keep it.
FLORIO   Where's the ring,
  That which your mother in her will bequeathed,
  And charged you on her blessing not to give't
  To any but your husband? Send back that.
ANNABELLA
  I have it not.
FLORIO   Ha, have it not! Where is't?   40
ANNABELLA
  My brother in the morning took it from me,
  Said he would wear't today.
FLORIO   Well, what do you say
  To young Bergetto's love? Are you content
  To match with him? Speak.
DONADO   There's the point indeed.
ANNABELLA
  [*Aside*] What shall I do? I must say something now.   45

27 *hereright* straightaway

---

39 *Send back that.* Florio's conduct has been sharply judged: 'Florio
  juggles strangely with his daughter's suitors. He tells Soranzo in Act I
  that he had "his word engaged;" and yet here he endeavours to force
  her upon another! His subsequent conduct is not calculated to increase
  our respect for his character, or our sympathy for his overwhelming
  afflictions.' (Gifford). But perhaps Florio's hypocrisy is no more than
  tact.

FLORIO
    What say? Why d'ee not speak?
ANNABELLA   Sir, with your leave,
    Please you to give me freedom?
FLORIO   Yes, you have it.
ANNABELLA
    Signor Donado, if your nephew mean
    To raise his better fortunes in his match,
    The hope of me will hinder such a hope;   50
    Sir, if you love him, as I know you do,
    Find one more worthy of his choice than me.
    In short, I'm sure I sha' not be his wife.
DONADO
    Why, here's plain dealing; I commend thee for't,
    And all the worst I wish thee is, Heaven bless thee!   55
    Your father yet and I will still be friends,
    Shall we not, Signor Florio?
FLORIO   Yes, why not?
    Look, here your cousin comes.

            Enter BERGETTO *and* POGGIO

DONADO
    [*Aside*] O coxcomb, what doth he make here?
BERGETTO
    Where's my uncle, sirs?   60
DONADO
    What's the news now?
BERGETTO
    Save you, uncle, save you. You must not think I come for
    nothing, masters; and how, and how is't? What, you have
    read my letter? Ah, there I—tickled you i'faith.
POGGIO
    But 'twere better you had tickled her in another place.   65
BERGETTO
    Sirrah sweetheart, I'll tell thee a good jest; and riddle what
    'tis.
ANNABELLA
    You say you'd tell me.
BERGETTO
    As I was walking just now in the street, I met a swaggering
    fellow would needs take the wall of me, and because he   70

    47 *have it* ed. have Q
    70 *take the wall* jostle off the pavement

did thrust me, I very valiantly called him rogue. He hereupon bade me draw; I told him I had more wit than so, but when he saw that I would not, he did so maul me with the hilts of his rapier that my head sung whilst my feet capered in the kennel.   75

DONADO

[*Aside*] Was ever the like ass seen?

ANNABELLA

And what did you all this while?

BERGETTO

Laugh at him for a gull, till I see the blood run about mine ears, and then I could not choose but find in my heart to cry; till a fellow with a broad beard (they say he   80 is a new-come doctor) called me into his house, and gave me a plaster—look you, here 'tis—and, sir, there was a young wench washed my face and hands most excellently, i'faith, I shall love her as long as I live for't, did she not, Poggio?   85

POGGIO

Yes, and kissed him too.

BERGETTO

Why, la now, you think I tell a lie, uncle, I warrant.

DONADO

Would he that beat thy blood out of thy head had beaten some wit into it; for I fear thou never wilt have any.

BERGETTO

O, uncle, but there was a wench would have done a man's   90 heart good to have looked on her—by this light she had a face methinks worth twenty of you, Mistress Annabella.

DONADO

Was ever such a fool born?

ANNABELLA

I am glad she liked you, sir.

BERGETTO

Are you so? By my troth I thank you, forsooth.   95

FLORIO

Sure 'twas the doctor's niece, that was last day with us here.

BERGETTO

'Twas she, 'twas she.

---

75 *kennel* gutter
78 *gull* dupe, simpleton
81 *his* ed. this Q
94 *liked* pleased

DONADO
  How do you know that, simplicity?
BERGETTO
  Why, does not he say so? If I should have said no, I should
  have given him the lie, uncle, and so have deserved a dry   100
  beating again; I'll none of that.
FLORIO
  A very modest well-behaved young maid
  As I have seen.
DONADO   Is she indeed?
FLORIO   Indeed
  She is, if I have any judgment.
DONADO
  Well, sir, now you are free, you need not care for sending   105
  letters: now you are dismissed, your mistress here will none
  of you.
BERGETTO
  No. Why, what care I for that? I can have wenches enough
  in Parma for half-a-crown apiece, cannot I, Poggio?
POGGIO
  I'll warrant you, sir.   110
DONADO
  Signor Florio,
  I thank you for your free recourse you gave
  For my admittance; and to you, fair maid,
  That jewel I will give you 'gainst your marriage.
  Come, will you go, sir?   115
BERGETTO
  Ay, marry will I. Mistress, farewell, mistress. I'll come
  again tomorrow. Farewell, mistress.
                    Exit DONADO, BERGETTO, *and* POGGIO

                    Enter GIOVANNI

FLORIO
  Son, where have you been? What, alone, alone still?
  I would not have it so, you must forsake
  This over-bookish humour. Well, your sister   120
  Hath shook the fool off.
GIOVANNI   'Twas no match for her.
FLORIO
  'Twas not indeed, I meant it nothing less;

100 *dry* severe, bruising (not drawing blood)
114 *'gainst* in anticipation of
118 *still* ed. still, still Q

Soranzo is the man I only like—
Look on him, Annabella. Come, 'tis supper-time,
And it grows late.   *Exit* FLORIO   125
GIOVANNI
Whose jewel's that?
ANNABELLA   Some sweetheart's.
GIOVANNI   So I think.
ANNABELLA
A lusty youth,
Signor Donado, gave it me to wear
Against my marriage.
GIOVANNI   But you shall not wear it.
Send it him back again.
ANNABELLA   What, you are jealous?   130
GIOVANNI
That you shall know anon, at better leisure.
Welcome, sweet night! The evening crowns the day.
                                              Exeunt

Act III, [Scene i]

Enter BERGETTO *and* POGGIO

BERGETTO
Does my uncle think to make me a baby still? No, Poggio,
he shall know I have a sconce now.
POGGIO
Ay, let him not bob you off like an ape with an apple.
BERGETTO
'Sfoot, I will have the wench if he were ten uncles, in despite
of his nose, Poggio.   5
POGGIO
Hold him to the grindstone and give not a jot of ground.
She hath in a manner promised you already.
BERGETTO
True, Poggio, and her uncle the doctor swore I should
marry her.
POGGIO
He swore, I remember.   10

123 *only* specially, singularly
  2 *sconce* brain
  3 *bob* fob
  8 s.p. BERGETTO ed. Poggio Q

132 *The evening crowns the day.* Proverbial. Tilley E190.

BERGETTO

And I will have her, that's more; didst see the codpiece-
point she gave me and the box of marmalade?

POGGIO

Very well; and kissed you, that my chops watered at the
sight on't. There's no way but to clap up a marriage in
hugger-mugger.   15

BERGETTO

I will do't; for I tell thee, Poggio, I begin to grow valiant
methinks, and my courage begins to rise.

POGGIO

Should you be afraid of your uncle?

BERGETTO

Hang him, old doting rascal. No, I say I will have her.

POGGIO

Lose no time then.   20

BERGETTO

I will beget a race of wise men and constables, that shall
cart whores at their own charges, and break the duke's
peace ere I have done myself.—Come away.   *Exeunt*

[Act III, Scene ii]

Enter FLORIO, GIOVANNI, SORANZO, ANNABELLA, PUTANA
and VASQUES

FLORIO

My Lord Soranzo, though I must confess
The proffers that are made me have been great
In marriage of my daughter, yet the hope
Of your still rising honours have prevailed
Above all other jointures. Here she is;   5
She knows my mind, speak for yourself to her,
And hear you, daughter, see you use him nobly;
For any private speech I'll give you time.
Come, son, and you the rest, let them alone:
Agree they as they may.

SORANZO   I thank you, sir.   10

GIOVANNI

[*Aside*] Sister, be not all woman, think on me.

11–12 *codpiece-point* ornamental lace for tying codpiece
14 *clap up* make or settle hastily
15 *in hugger-mugger* secretly, clandestinely
22 *cart whores* exhibit them in streets, as part of punishment
10 *Agree they* ed. Agree Q

SORANZO
  Vasques.
VASQUES
  My lord?
SORANZO
  Attend me without.
                    Exeunt omnes, manet SORANZO *and* ANNABELLA
ANNABELLA
  Sir, what's your will with me?
SORANZO   Do you not know   15
  What I should tell you?
ANNABELLA   Yes, you'll say you love me.
SORANZO
  And I'll swear it too; will you believe it?
ANNABELLA
  'Tis no point of faith.

                    Enter GIOVANNI *above*

SORANZO   Have you not will to love?
ANNABELLA
  Not you.
SORANZO   Whom then?
ANNABELLA   That's as the fates infer.
GIOVANNI
  [*Aside*] Of those I'm regent now.
SORANZO   What mean you, sweet?   20
ANNABELLA
  To live and die a maid.
SORANZO   O, that's unfit.
GIOVANNI
  [*Aside*] Here's one can say that's but a woman's note.
SORANZO
  Did you but see my heart, then would you swear—
ANNABELLA
  That you were dead.
GIOVANNI [*Aside*]   That's true, or somewhat near it.
SORANZO
  See you these true love's tears?
ANNABELLA   No.
GIOVANNI [*Aside*]   Now she winks.   25
SORANZO
  They plead to you for grace.
ANNABELLA   Yet nothing speak.

  18 *no* ed. not Q   18 *point of faith* dogma necessary to salvation

SORANZO
  O grant my suit.
ANNABELLA   What is't?
SORANZO   To let me live—
ANNABELLA
  Take it.
SORANZO —Still yours.
ANNABELLA   That is not mine to give.
GIOVANNI
  [*Aside*] One such another word would kill his hopes.
SORANZO
  Mistress, to leave those fruitless strifes of wit,   30
  Know I have loved you long and loved you truly;
  Not hope of what you have, but what you are,
  Have drawn me on; then let me not in vain
  Still feel the rigour of your chaste disdain.
  I'm sick, and sick to th' heart.
ANNABELLA   Help, aqua-vitae.   35
SORANZO
  What mean you?
ANNABELLA   Why, I thought you had been sick.
SORANZO
  Do you mock my love?
GIOVANNI [*Aside*]   There, sir, she was too nimble.
SORANZO
  [*Aside*] 'Tis plain, she laughs at me.—These scornful taunts
  Neither become your modesty or years.
ANNABELLA
  You are no looking glass; or if you were,   40
  I'd dress my language by you.
GIOVANNI [*Aside*]   I'm confirmed.
ANNABELLA
  To put you out of doubt, my lord, methinks
  Your common sense should make you understand
  That if I loved you, or desired your love,
  Some way I should have given you better taste: 45
  But since you are a nobleman, and one
  I would not wish should spend his youth in hopes,
  Let me advise you here to forbear your suit,
  And think I wish you well, I tell you this.
SORANZO
  Is't you speak this?

 31 *Know* ed. I know Q
 35 *aqua-vitae* spirits, used here as a restorative

ANNABELLA   Yes, I myself; yet know—   50
  Thus far I give you comfort—if mine eyes
  Could have picked out a man (amongst all those
  That sued to me) to make a husband of,
  You should have been that man. Let this suffice;
  Be noble in your secrecy and wise.   55

GIOVANNI
  [*Aside*] Why, now I see she loves me.

ANNABELLA   One word more:
  As ever virtue lived within your mind,
  As ever noble courses were your guide,
  As ever you would have me know you loved me,
  Let not my father know hereof by you;   60
  If I hereafter find that I must marry,
  It shall be you or none.

SORANZO   I take that promise.

ANNABELLA
  O, O, my head.

SORANZO
  What's the matter? Not well?

ANNABELLA
  O, I begin to sicken.   65

GIOVANNI
  [*Aside*] Heaven forbid.   *Exit from above*

SORANZO
  Help, help within there, ho!

Enter FLORIO, GIOVANNI, PUTANA

  Look to your daughter, Signor Florio.

FLORIO
  Hold her up, she swoons.

GIOVANNI
  Sister, how d'ee?   70

ANNABELLA
  Sick—brother, are you there?

FLORIO
  Convey her to her bed instantly, whilst I send for a physician;
  quickly, I say.

PUTANA
  Alas, poor child!   *Exeunt, manet* SORANZO

Enter VASQUES

67 s.d. ed.; after line 68 in Q
68 assigned to Soranzo since Gifford's ed.; to Giovanni in Q

VASQUES
> My lord.   75
SORANZO
> O Vasques, now I doubly am undone
> Both in my present and my future hopes.
> She plainly told me that she could not love,
> And thereupon soon sickened, and I fear
> Her life's in danger.   80
VASQUES
> [*Aside*] By'r lady, sir, and so is yours, if you knew all.—
> 'Las, sir, I am sorry for that; may be 'tis but the maid's-
> sickness, an over-flux of youth, and then, sir, there is no such
> present remedy as present marriage. But hath she given you
> an absolute denial?   85
SORANZO
> She hath and she hath not; I'm full of grief,
> But what she said I'll tell thee as we go.   *Exeunt*

[Act III, Scene iii]

Enter GIOVANNI *and* PUTANA

PUTANA
> O sir, we are all undone, quite undone, utterly undone, and
> shamed forever; your sister, O your sister.
GIOVANNI
> What of her? For Heaven's sake, speak; how does she?
PUTANA
> O that ever I was born to see this day.
GIOVANNI
> She is not dead, ha? Is she?   5
PUTANA
> Dead? No, she is quick; 'tis worse, she is with child. You
> know what you have done; Heaven forgive 'ee. 'Tis too late
> to repent now, Heaven help us.
GIOVANNI
> With child? How dost thou know't?
PUTANA
> How do I know't? Am I at these years ignorant what the   10
> meanings of qualms and water-pangs be? Of changing of
> colours, queasiness of stomachs, pukings, and another
> thing that I could name? Do not, for her and your credit's

82–3 *maid's-sickness* green-sickness, chlorosis, a form of anaemia
83 *over-flux* overflow
 6 *quick* both 'alive' and 'pregnant'

sake, spend the time in asking how, and which way, 'tis so;
she is quick, upon my word: if you let a physician see her   15
water, y'are undone.

GIOVANNI
But in what case is she?

PUTANA
Prettily amended; 'twas but a fit which I soon espied, and
she must look for often henceforward.

GIOVANNI
Commend me to her, bid her take no care;   20
Let not the doctor visit her, I charge you,
Make some excuse, till I return.—O me!
I have a world of business in my head.—
Do not discomfort her.—
How does this news perplex me!—If my father   25
Come to her, tell him she's recovered well,
Say 'twas but some ill diet; d'ee hear, woman?
Look you to't.

PUTANA
I will, sir.   *Exeunt*

[Act II, Scene iv]

Enter FLORIO *and* RICHARDETTO

FLORIO
And how d'ee find her, sir?

RICHARDETTO   Indifferent well;
I see no danger, scarce perceive she's sick,
But that she told me she had lately eaten
Melons, and, as she thought, those disagreed
With her young stomach.

FLORIO   Did you give her aught?   5

RICHARDETTO
An easy surfeit-water, nothing else.
You need not doubt her health; I rather think
Her sickness is a fulness of her blood—
You understand me?

FLORIO   I do; you counsel well,

17 *case* state
20 *take no care* not worry
25 *does* ed. doe Q
 1 *Indifferent* Fairly
 6 *surfeit-water* cure for indigestion

And once, within these few days, will so order't   10
She shall be married ere she know the time.
RICHARDETTO
Yet let not haste, sir, make unworthy choice;
That were dishonour.
FLORIO   Master Doctor, no;
I will not do so neither; in plain words,
My Lord Soranzo is the man I mean.   15
RICHARDETTO
A noble and a virtuous gentleman.
FLORIO
As any is in Parma. Not far hence
Dwells Father Bonaventure, a grave friar,
Once tutor to my son; now at his cell
I'll have 'em married.
RICHARDETTO   You have plotted wisely.   20
FLORIO
I'll send one straight to speak with him tonight.
RICHARDETTO
Soranzo's wise, he will delay no time.
FLORIO
It shall be so.

                 Enter FRIAR *and* GIOVANNI

FRIAR   Good peace be here and love.
FLORIO
Welcome, religious friar; you are one
That still bring blessing to the place you come to.   25
GIOVANNI
Sir, with what speed I could, I did my best
To draw this holy man from forth his cell
To visit my sick sister, that with words
Of ghostly comfort, in this time of need,
He might absolve her, whether she live or die.   30
FLORIO
'Twas well done, Giovanni; thou herein
Hast showed a Christian's care, a brother's love.
Come, father, I'll conduct you to her chamber,
And one thing would entreat you.
FRIAR   Say on, sir.

25 *still* always
29 *ghostly* spiritual

FLORIO
    I have a father's dear impression,   35
    And wish, before I fall into my grave,
    That I might see her married, as 'tis fit;
    A word from you, grave man, will win her more
    Than all our best persuasions.
FRIAR   Gentle sir,
    All this I'll say, that Heaven may prosper her.   *Exeunt*   40

[Act III, Scene v]

Enter GRIMALDI

GRIMALDI
    Now if the doctor keep his word, Soranzo,
    Twenty to one you miss your bride; I know
    'Tis an unnoble act, and not becomes
    A soldier's valour, but in terms of love,
    Where merit cannot sway, policy must.   5
    I am resolved; if this physician
    Play not on both hands, then Soranzo falls.

Enter RICHARDETTO

RICHARDETTO
    You are come as I could wish; this very night
    Soranzo, 'tis ordained, must be affied
    To Annabella, and, for aught I know,   10
    Married.
GRIMALDI How!
RICHARDETTO   Yet your patience:—
    The place, 'tis Friar Bonaventure's cell.
    Now I would wish you to bestow this night
    In watching thereabouts; 'tis but a night:
    If you miss now, tomorrow I'll know all.   15

---

  5 *policy* cunning
  7 *Play . . . hands* Does not double cross me
  9 *affied* betrothed
 12 *Friar* ed. Fryars Q

---

35 *impression.* Notion, idea, belief impressed on the mind—*O.E.D.* 7,
    quoting 1613 PURCHAS *Pilgrimage* (1614) 2 'That there is a God;
    . . . This is a common notion, and impression, sealed up in the minde
    of every man.' Bawcutt says 'The meaning is not clear.'
14–15 *'tis but . . . all.* i.e. you only risk wasting a night: if nothing happens
    I shall learn the full details tomorrow, and instruct you accordingly.

GRIMALDI
  Have you the poison?
RICHARDETTO   Here 'tis in this box.
  Doubt nothing, this will do't; in any case,
  As you respect your life, be quick and sure.
GRIMALDI
  I'll speed him.
RICHARDETTO   Do. Away; for 'tis not safe
  You should be seen much here.—Ever my love!   20
GRIMALDI
  And mine to you.   *Exit* GRIMALDI
RICHARDETTO
  So. If this hit, I'll laugh and hug revenge;
  And they that now dream of a wedding-feast
  May chance to mourn the lusty bridegroom's ruin.
  But to my other business.—Niece Philotis!   25

                    Enter PHILOTIS
PHILOTIS
  Uncle?
RICHARDETTO
  My lovely niece,
  You have bethought 'ee?
PHILOTIS   Yes, and, as you counselled,
  Fashioned my heart to love him; but he swears
  He will tonight be married, for he fears   30
  His uncle else, if he should know the drift,
  Will hinder all, and call his coz to shrift.
RICHARDETTO
  'Tonight? Why, best of all;—but let me see,
  I—ha—yes—so it shall be; in disguise
  We'll early to the friar's, I have thought on't.   35

                Enter BERGETTO *and* POGGIO
PHILOTIS
  Uncle, he comes.
RICHARDETTO   Welcome, my worthy coz.
BERGETTO
  Lass, pretty lass, come buss, lass!—Aha, Poggio!
                              [*Kisses her*]

  22 *hit* succeed
  37 *buss* kiss

POGGIO
    There's hope of this yet.

RICHARDETTO
    You shall have time enough; withdraw a little,
    We must confer at large.   40

BERGETTO
    Have you not sweetmeats or dainty devices for me?

PHILOTIS
    You shall have enough, sweetheart.

BERGETTO
    Sweetheart! Mark that, Poggio. By my troth, I cannot
    choose but kiss thee once more for that word 'sweetheart.'—
    Poggio, I have a monstrous swelling about my stomach,   45
    whatsoever the matter be.

POGGIO
    You shall have physic for't, sir.

RICHARDETTO
    Time runs apace.

BERGETTO
    Time's a blockhead.

RICHARDETTO
    Be ruled; when we have done what's fit to do,   50
    Then you may kiss your fill, and bed her too.   *Exeunt*

[Act III, Scene vi]

Enter the FRIAR *sitting in a chair,* ANNABELLA *kneeling and
whispering to him; a table before them and wax-lights; she
weeps and wrings her hands*

FRIAR
    I am glad to see this penance; for, believe me,
    You have unripped a soul so foul and guilty
    As I must tell you true, I marvel how
    The earth hath borne you up; but weep, weep on,

40 *at large* at length, fully
42 *shall have* ed. shall Q
s.d. FRIAR ed. Fryar in his study Q (see III.iv, 33)
  2 *unripped* exposed

---

38 s.p. POGGIO. Assigned to Poggio by Bawcutt; Q (obviously wrongly)
     assigns it to Philotis, and earlier editors to Richardetto.
s.d. Ford frequently sets a scene with considerable exactness, and an eye for
     significant stage-detail. Cf. *Love's Sacrifice*, III.iv, and V.iii, or *The
     Broken Heart*, V.iii.

These tears may do you good; weep faster yet,   5
Whiles I do read a lecture.

ANNABELLA   Wretched creature!

FRIAR
Ay, you are wretched, miserably wretched,
Almost condemned alive. There is a place—
List, daughter—in a black and hollow vault,
Where day is never seen; there shines no sun,   10
But flaming horror of consuming fires,
A lightless sulphur, choked with smoky fogs
Of an infected darkness; in this place
Dwell many thousand thousand sundry sorts
Of never-dying deaths; there damned souls   15
Roar without pity; there are gluttons fed
With toads and adders; there is burning oil
Poured down the drunkard's throat; the usurer
Is forced to sup whole draughts of molten gold;
There is the murderer forever stabbed,   20
Yet can he never die; there lies the wanton
On racks of burning steel, whiles in his soul
He feels the torment of his raging lust.

ANNABELLA
Mercy, O mercy!

FRIAR   There stands these wretched things
Who have dreamed out whole years in lawless sheets   25
And secret incests, cursing one another.
Then you will wish each kiss your brother gave
Had been a dagger's point; then you shall hear
How he will cry, 'O would my wicked sister
Had first been damned, when she did yield to lust!'—   30
But soft, methinks I see repentance work
New motions in your heart; say, how is't with you?

ANNABELLA
Is there no way left to redeem my miseries?

FRIAR
There is, despair not; Heaven is merciful,
And offers grace even now. 'Tis thus agreed,   35

6 *read a lecture* deliver a reprimand (*O.E.D.* 6)

---

24 *There stands* etc. The Friar seems unable to depict a punishment
appropriate to incest. The usurer drinking gold is a common subject in
art and literature, but I know of no such image for the incestuous.
Dante would presumably have considered incest among the Sins against
Nature, but the incestuous have no place in the *Inferno*.

First, for your honour's safety, that you marry
The Lord Soranzo; next, to save your soul,
Leave off this life, and henceforth live to him.

ANNABELLA
Ay me!

FRIAR   Sigh not; I know the baits of sin
Are hard to leave. O, 'tis a death to do't.   40
Remember what must come. Are you content?

ANNABELLA
I am.

FRIAR   I like it well; we'll take the time.
Who's near us there?

                    Enter FLORIO *and* GIOVANNI

FLORIO
Did you call, father?

FRIAR
Is Lord Soranzo come?

FLORIO   He stays below.   45

FRIAR
Have you acquainted him at full?

FLORIO   _   I have,
And he is overjoyed.

FRIAR   And so are we.
Bid him come near.

GIOVANNI [*Aside*]   My sister weeping, ha?
I fear this friar's falsehood.—I will call him.   *Exit*

FLORIO
Daughter, are you resolved?

ANNABELLA   Father, I am.   50

                    Enter GIOVANNI, SORANZO, *and* VASQUES

FLORIO
My Lord Soranzo, here
Give me your hand; for that I give you this.
                              [*Joins their hands*]

SORANZO
Lady, say you so too?

---

42 *take the time* seize the opportunity

51–6 *My Lord* etc. This is, strictly speaking, a betrothal not a marriage
(see Ernest Schanzer, *The Problem Plays of Shakespeare*, 1963, 75–9).
But such a betrothal would be legally binding, and would normally be
followed by a church service as soon as possible. There is perhaps some
slight discrepancy between III.vi, 55–6 and III.viii, 3–4.

ANNABELLA   I do, and vow
To live with you and yours.
FRIAR   Timely resolved:
My blessing rest on both; more to be done,   55
You may perform it on the morning sun.   *Exeunt*

[Act III, Scene vii]

Enter GRIMALDI *with his rapier drawn and a dark lantern*

GRIMALDI
'Tis early night as yet, and yet too soon
To finish such a work; here I will lie
To listen who comes next.   *He lies down*

Enter BERGETTO *and* PHILOTIS *disguised, and after*
RICHARDETTO *and* POGGIO

BERGETTO
We are almost at the place, I hope, sweetheart.
GRIMALDI
[*Aside*] I hear them near, and heard one say 'sweetheart'.   5
'Tis he; now guide my hand, some angry justice,
Home to his bosom.—Now have at you, sir!
                        Strikes BERGETTO *and exit*
BERGETTO
O help, help! Here's a stitch fallen in my guts. O for a
flesh-tailor quickly!—Poggio!
PHILOTIS
What ails my love?   10
BERGETTO
I am sure I cannot piss forward and backward, and yet I
am wet before and behind.—Lights, lights! ho, lights!
PHILOTIS
Alas, some villain here has slain my love.
RICHARDETTO
O Heaven forbid it.—Raise up the next neighbours
Instantly, Poggio, and bring lights.   *Exit* POGGIO   15
How is't, Bergetto? Slain? It cannot be;
Are you sure y'are hurt?

---

9 *flesh-tailor* surgeon

---

1 s.d. *dark lantern.* A lantern with a slide or arrangement by which the light
can be concealed.

BERGETTO
O my belly seethes like a porridge-pot; some cold water,
I shall boil over else; my whole body is in a sweat, that you
may wring my shirt; feel here—Why, Poggio!   20

Enter POGGIO *with* OFFICERS *and lights and halberts*

POGGIO
Here. Alas, how do you?
RICHARDETTO
Give me a light. What's here? All blood! O sirs,
Signor Donado's nephew now is slain.
Follow the murderer with all despatch
Up to the city, he cannot be far hence;   25
Follow, I beseech you.
OFFICERS
Follow, follow, follow.   *Exeunt* OFFICERS
RICHARDETTO
Tear off thy linen, coz, to stop his wounds.—
Be of good comfort, man.
BERGETTO
Is all this mine own blood? Nay then, good night with me.   30
Poggio, commend me to my uncle, dost hear? Bid him for
my sake make much of this wench. O!—I am going the
wrong way sure, my belly aches so.—O, farewell, Poggio!—
O!—O!—   *Dies*
PHILOTIS
O, he is dead.
POGGIO   How! Dead!
RICHARDETTO   He's dead indeed.   35
'Tis now too late to weep; let's have him home,
And with what speed we may, find out the murderer.
POGGIO
O my master, my master, my master!   *Exeunt*

[Act III, Scene viii]

Enter VASQUES *and* HIPPOLITA

HIPPOLITA
Betrothed?
VASQUES
I saw it.

24 *with all despatch.* Q reads 'with all the haste' but I cannot believe Ford
wrote it. The two forms, written down, could look alike.

HIPPOLITA
  And when's the marriage-day?

VASQUES
  Some two days hence.

HIPPOLITA
  Two days? Why, man, I would but wish two hours   5
  To send him to his last, and lasting sleep.
  And, Vasques, thou shalt see I'll do it bravely.

VASQUES
  I do not doubt your wisdom, nor, I trust, you my secrecy;
  I am infinitely yours.

HIPPOLITA
  I will be thine in spite of my disgrace.   10
  So soon? O, wicked man, I durst be sworn,
  He'd laugh to see me weep.

VASQUES
  And that's a villainous fault in him.

HIPPOLITA
  No, let him laugh, I'm armed in my resolves;
  Be thou still true.   15

VASQUES
  I should get little by treachery against so hopeful a preferment as I am like to climb to.

HIPPOLITA
  Even to my bosom, Vasques. Let my youth
  Revel in these new pleasures; if we thrive,
  He now hath but a pair of days to live.   *Exeunt* 20

[Act III, Scene ix]

Enter FLORIO, DONADO, RICHARDETTO, POGGIO *and*
OFFICERS

FLORIO
  'Tis bootless now to show yourself a child,
  Signor Donado; what is done, is done.
  Spend not the time in tears, but seek for justice.

RICHARDETTO
  I must confess, somewhat I was in fault
  That had not first acquainted you what love   5
  Passed 'twixt him and my niece; but, as I live,
  His fortune grieves me as it were mine own.

18 *my youth* Soranzo
1 *bootless* pointless

DONADO

Alas, poor creature, he meant no man harm,
That I am sure of.

FLORIO   I believe that too.
But stay, my masters, are you sure you saw   10
The murderer pass here?

OFFICER

And it please you, sir, we are sure we saw a ruffian, with a
naked weapon in his hand all bloody, get into my lord
cardinal's grace's gate, that we are sure of; but for fear of
his grace (bless us) we durst go no further.   15

DONADO

Know you what manner of man he was?

OFFICER

Yes, sure, I know the man; they say 'a is a soldier; he that
loved your daughter, sir, an't please ye; 'twas he for certain.

FLORIO

Grimaldi, on my life.

OFFICER   Ay, ay, the same.

RICHARDETTO

The cardinal is noble; he no doubt   20
Will give true justice.

DONADO

Knock someone at the gate.

POGGIO

I'll knock, sir.   POGGIO knocks

SERVANT within

What would 'ee?

FLORIO

We require speech with the lord cardinal   25
About some present business; pray inform
His grace that we are here.

Enter CARDINAL *and* GRIMALDI

CARDINAL

Why, how now, friends! What saucy mates are you
That know nor duty nor civility?
Are we a person fit to be your host,   30
Or is our house become your common inn,
To beat our doors at pleasure? What such haste
Is yours as that it cannot wait fit times?
Are you the masters of this commonwealth,

17 *'a* he
26 *present* urgent

And know no more discretion? O, your news   35
Is here before you; you have lost a nephew,
Donado, last night by Grimaldi slain:
Is that your business? Well, sir, we have knowledge on't.
Let that suffice.

GRIMALDI   In presence of your grace,
In thought I never meant Bergetto harm.   40
But Florio, you can tell, with how much scorn
Soranzo, backed with his confederates,
Hath often wronged me; I, to be revenged,
(For that I could not win him else to fight)
Had thought by way of ambush to have killed him,   45
But was unluckily therein mistook;
Else he had felt what late Bergetto did:
And though my fault to him were merely chance,
Yet humbly I submit me to your grace,
To do with me as you please.

CARDINAL   Rise up, Grimaldi.   50
You citizens of Parma, if you seek
For justice, know, as nuncio from the Pope,
For this offence I here receive Grimaldi
Into his holiness' protection.
He is no common man, but nobly born;   55
Of princes' blood, though you, Sir Florio,
Thought him too mean a husband for your daughter.
If more you seek for, you must go to Rome,
For he shall thither; learn more wit, for shame.
Bury your dead.—Away, Grimaldi; leave 'em.   60
                    Exeunt CARDINAL *and* GRIMALDI

DONADO
Is this a churchman's voice? Dwells justice here?

FLORIO
Justice is fled to Heaven and comes no nearer.
Soranzo. Was't for him? O impudence.
Had he the face to speak it, and not blush?
Come, come, Donado, there's no help in this,   65
When cardinals think murder's not amiss.
Great men may do their wills, we must obey;
But Heaven will judge them for't another day.   *Exeunt*

---

62 *fled to Heaven.* Astraea, goddess of Justice, fled to Heaven at the end of
the Golden Age on earth. See Ovid, *Metamorphoses,* I, 149.

Act IV, [Scene i]

A Banquet. Hautboys. Enter the FRIAR, GIOVANNI, ANNABELLA,
PHILOTIS, SORANZO, DONADO, FLORIO, RICHARDETTO, PUTANA,
and VASQUES

FRIAR
  These holy rites performed, now take your times
  To spend the remnant of the day in feast;
  Such fit repasts are pleasing to the saints,
  Who are your guests, though not with mortal eyes
  To be beheld.—Long prosper in this day,   5
  You happy couple, to each other's joy.

SORANZO
  Father, your prayer is heard; the hand of goodness
  Hath been a shield for me against my death;
  And, more to bless me, hath enriched my life
  With this most precious jewel; such a prize   10
  As earth hath not another like to this.
  Cheer up, my love, and gentlemen, my friends,
  Rejoice with me in mirth; this day we'll crown
  With lusty cups to Annabella's health.

GIOVANNI
  [*Aside*] O torture. Were the marriage yet undone,   15
  Ere I'd endure this sight, to see my love
  Clipped by another, I would dare confusion,
  And stand the horror of ten thousand deaths.

VASQUES
  Are you not well, sir?
GIOVANNI   Prithee, fellow, wait;
  I need not thy officious diligence.   20

FLORIO
  Signor Donado, come, you must forget
  Your late mishaps, and drown your cares in wine.

SORANZO
  Vasques.
VASQUES   My lord?

s.d. *Hautboys* Oboes
17 *Clipped* Embraced
19 *wait* wait on the guests

---

s.d. *A Banquet.* Bawcutt glosses 'a dessert of confectionery, fruit, wine, etc.'
    This is possible (*O.E.D.* 3), but the Friar's words (1–6) and Soranzo's
    reply suggest a more formal feast (*O.E.D.* 1). The question is important
    in staging the play; cf. V.iii, 42–3, and V.vi, 1–6.

SORANZO   Reach me that weighty bowl.
  Here, brother Giovanni, here's to you;
  Your turn comes next, though now a bachelor.   25
  Here's to your sister's happiness and mine.
GIOVANNI
  I cannot drink.
SORANZO   What?
GIOVANNI   'Twill indeed offend me.
ANNABELLA
  Pray do not urge him, if he be not willing.   *Hautboys*
FLORIO
  How now, what noise is this?
VASQUES
  O, sir, I had forgot to tell you; certain young maidens of   30
  Parma, in honour to Madam Annabella's marriage, have
  sent their loves to her in a masque, for which they humbly
  crave your patience and silence.
SORANZO
  We are much bound to them, so much the more
  As it comes unexpected; guide them in.   35

        Enter HIPPOLITA *and Ladies in* [*masks and*] *white robes,*
              with garlands of willows. Music and a dance

  Thanks, lovely virgins; now might we but know
  To whom we have been beholding for this love,
  We shall acknowledge it.
HIPPOLITA   Yes, you shall know;   [*Unmasks*]
  What think you now?
OMNES   Hippolita!
HIPPOLITA   'Tis she,
  Be not amazed; nor blush, young lovely bride,   40
  I come not to defraud you of your man.
  'Tis now no time to reckon up the talk
  What Parma long hath rumoured of us both:
  Let rash report run on; the breath that vents it
  Will, like a bubble, break itself at last.   45

28 s.d. *Hautboys* ed.; after line 35 in Q
29 *noise* music (*O.E.D.* 5)
34 *bound* obliged
35 s.d. *a dance* ed.; a Daunce. Dance Q
37 *this* Q *a.c.*; thy Q *b.c.*

35 s.d. *willows.* Symbol of disappointed love. Cf. *The Merchant of Venice*,
    V.i, 10 and *Othello*, IV.iii.

But now to you, sweet creature: lend's your hand;
Perhaps it hath been said that I would claim
Some interest in Soranzo, now your lord.
What I have right to do, his soul knows best;
But in my duty to your noble worth,   50
Sweet Annabella, and my care of you,
Here take, Soranzo, take this hand from me:
I'll once more join what by the holy church
Is finished and allowed. Have I done well?

SORANZO
You have too much engaged us.

HIPPOLITA   One thing more.   55
That you may know my single charity,
Freely I here remit all interest
I e'er could claim, and give you back your vows;
And to confirm't—reach me a cup of wine—
My Lord Soranzo, in this draught I drink   60
Long rest t'ee.—Look to it, Vasques.

VASQUES
Fear nothing.   *He gives her a poisoned cup: she drinks*

SORANZO
Hippolita, I thank you, and will pledge
This happy union as another life;
Wine, there!   65

VASQUES
You shall have none, neither shall you pledge her.

HIPPOLITA
How!

VASQUES
Know now, Mistress She-Devil, your own mischievous
treachery hath killed you; I must not marry you.

HIPPOLITA
Villain.   70

OMNES
What's the matter?

VASQUES
Foolish woman, thou art now like a firebrand that hath
kindled others and burnt thyself; *troppo sperar, inganna,*

55 *engaged* placed under obligation
56 *single* signal, outstanding
56 *charity* love
73 *inganna* ed. niganna Q

---

73 *troppo . . . inganna.* Too much hope deceives.

thy vain hope hath deceived thee, thou art but dead; if
thou hast any grace, pray.   75

HIPPOLITA

Monster.

VASQUES

Die in charity, for shame.—This thing of malice, this
woman, had privately corrupted me with promise of
marriage, under this politic reconciliation, to poison my
lord, whiles she might laugh at his confusion on his marriage   80
day. I promised her fair, but I knew what my reward
should have been; and would willingly have spared her
life, but that I was acquainted with the danger of her
disposition, and now have fitted her a just payment in her
own coin. There she is, she hath yet—and end thy days in   85
peace, vile woman; as for life there's no hope, think not on't.

OMNES

Wonderful justice!

RICHARDETTO   Heaven, thou art righteous.

HIPPOLITA

O, 'tis true;
I feel my minute coming. Had that slave
Kept promise (O, my torment) thou this hour   90
Hadst died, Soranzo—heat above hell fire—
Yet ere I pass away—cruel, cruel flames—
Take here my curse amongst you: may thy bed
Of marriage be a rack unto thy heart,
Burn blood and boil in vengeance—O my heart,   95
My flame's intolerable—Mayst thou live
To father bastards, may her womb bring forth
Monsters, and die together in your sins,
Hated, scorned, and unpitied—O!—O!—   *Dies*

FLORIO

Was e'er so vile a creature?

RICHARDETTO   Here's the end   100
Of lust and pride.

ANNABELLA   It is a fearful sight.

---

79 *marriage* ed. malice Q
79 *politic reconciliation* cunning agreement

---

85 *yet—and.* The manuscript was either incomplete or illegible at this
point, and some words are missing. The hiatus need be no longer than a
line; to bridge the sense we need only phrases like 'a moment to live.
Pray, then'.

SCENE II]   'TIS PITY SHE'S A WHORE   703

SORANZO
  Vasques, I know thee now a trusty servant,
  And never will forget thee.—Come, my love,
  We'll home, and thank the Heavens for this escape.
  Father and friends, we must break up this mirth;   105
  It is too sad a feast.
DONADO   Bear hence the body.
FRIAR
  Here's an ominous change;
  Mark this, my Giovanni, and take heed.
  I fear the event; that marriage seldom's good,
  Where the bride-banquet so begins in blood.   *Exeunt* 110

[Act IV, Scene ii]

Enter RICHARDETTO *and* PHILOTIS

RICHARDETTO
  My wretched wife, more wretched in her shame
  Than in her wrongs to me, hath paid too soon
  The forfeit of her modesty and life;
  And I am sure, my niece, though vengeance hover,
  Keeping aloof yet from Soranzo's fall,   5
  Yet he will fall, and sink with his own weight.
  I need not now—my heart persuades me so—
  To further his confusion; there is One
  Above begins to work, for, as I hear,
  Debates already 'twixt his wife and him   10
  Thicken and run to head; she, as 'tis said,
  Slightens his love, and he abandons hers.
  Much talk I hear. Since things go thus, my niece,
  In tender love and pity of your youth,
  My counsel is, that you should free your years   15
  From hazard of these woes by flying hence
  To fair Cremona, there to vow your soul
  In holiness a holy votaress:

109 *event* outcome
  2 *hath* Q *a.c.*; hath hath Q *b.c.*
10 *Debates* Quarrels, arguments
12 *Slightens* Disdains

---

11 *Thicken and run to head.* Come to maturation point, like a ripe boil
    ready to burst.
18 *In holiness* etc. The repetition in this line is weak, and unlike Ford's
    style. He may have written 'a godly votaress', the two forms being
    similar in seventeenth-century handwriting.

Leave me to see the end of these extremes.
All human worldly courses are uneven;   20
No life is blessed but the way to Heaven.

PHILOTIS
Uncle, shall I resolve to be a nun?

RICHARDETTO
Ay, gentle niece, and in your hourly prayers
Remember me, your poor unhappy uncle.
Hie to Cremona now, as fortune leads,   25
Your home your cloister, your best friends your beads.
Your chaste and single life shall crown your birth;
Who dies a virgin lives a saint on earth.

PHILOTIS
Then farewell, world, and worldly thoughts, adieu.
Welcome, chaste vows; myself I yield to you.   *Exeunt*   30

[Act IV, Scene iii]

Enter SORANZO *unbraced, and* ANNABELLA *dragged in*

SORANZO
Come, strumpet, famous whore! Were every drop
Of blood that runs in thy adulterous veins
A life, this sword (dost see't?) should in one blow
Confound them all. Harlot, rare, notable harlot,
That with thy brazen face maintainst thy sin,   5
Was there no man in Parma to be bawd
To your loose cunning whoredom else but I?
Must your hot itch and pleurisy of lust,
The heyday of your luxury, be fed
Up to a surfeit, and could none but I   10
Be picked out to be cloak to your close tricks,
Your belly-sports? Now I must be the dad
To all that gallimaufry that's stuffed
In thy corrupted bastard-bearing womb,
Say, must I?

ANNABELLA   Beastly man! Why, 'tis thy fate.   15
I sued not to thee; for, but that I thought

28 *lives* ed. live Q
s.d. *unbraced* cf. *Hamlet*, II.i, 78
 8 *pleurisy* superabundance, excess (*O.E.D.* 2)
 9 *heyday of your luxury* height of your lechery
11 *close* secret
13 *gallimaufry* mixture, hodge-podge
15 *Say* ed. Shey Q

Your over-loving lordship would have run
Mad on denial, had ye lent me time,
I would have told 'ee in what case I was.
But you would needs be doing.
SORANZO   Whore of whores!   20
Dar'st thou tell me this?
ANNABELLA   O yes, why not?
You were deceived in me; 'twas not for love
I chose you, but for honour; yet know this,
Would you be patient yet, and hide your shame,
I'd see whether I could love you.
SORANZO   Excellent quean!   25
Why, art thou not with child?
ANNABELLA   What needs all this
When 'tis superfluous? I confess I am.
SORANZO
Tell me by whom.
ANNABELLA   Soft, sir, 'twas not in my bargain.
Yet somewhat, sir, to stay your longing stomach,
I am content t'acquaint you with; the man,   30
The more than man, that got this sprightly boy—
For 'tis a boy, and therefore glory, sir,
Your heir shall be a son—
SORANZO   Damnable monster!
ANNABELLA
Nay, and you will not hear, I'll speak no more.
SORANZO
Yes, speak, and speak thy last.
ANNABELLA   A match, a match!   35
This noble creature was in every part
So angel-like, so glorious, that a woman
Who had not been but human, as was I,
Would have kneeled to him, and have begged for love.
You! Why, you are not worthy once to name   40
His name without true worship, or, indeed,
Unless you kneeled, to hear another name him.
SORANZO
What was he called?
ANNABELLA   We are not come to that.
Let it suffice that you shall have the glory
To father what so brave a father got.   45

25 *quean* whore
30 *I am* ed. I'me Q
32 *and therefore* ed. that for Q

In brief, had not this chance fallen out as't doth,
I never had been troubled with a thought
That you had been a creature; but for marriage,
I scarce dream yet of that.

SORANZO
Tell me his name.

ANNABELLA   Alas, alas, there's all.   50
Will you believe?

SORANZO   What?

ANNABELLA   You shall never know.

SORANZO
How!

ANNABELLA   Never; if you do, let me be cursed.

SORANZO
Not know it, strumpet? I'll rip up thy heart,
And find it there.

ANNABELLA   Do, do.

SORANZO   And with my teeth
Tear the prodigious lecher joint by joint.   55

ANNABELLA
Ha, ha, ha, the man's merry!

SORANZO   Dost thou laugh?
Come, whore, tell me your lover, or, by truth,
I'll hew thy flesh to shreds; who is't?

ANNABELLA *sings*
Che morte piu dolce che morire per amore?

SORANZO
Thus will I pull thy hair, and thus I'll drag   60
Thy lust-be-lepered body through the dust.
Yet tell his name.

ANNABELLA *sings*
Morendo in gratia Dei, morirei senza dolore.

SORANZO
Dost thou triumph? The treasure of the earth

---

59 *piu* ed. pluis Q   63 *Dei* ed. Lei Q
63 *morirei* ed. morirere Q *a.c.*; *morire* Q *b.c.*

---

59 *Che morte* etc. 'What death is sweeter than to die for love.'
63 *Morendo in gratia* etc. 'Dying in the grace of God, I should die without
    sorrow.' Bawcutt's emendation 'morirei' for the corrected Q reading
    'Morirere' is admirable; a compositor ignorant of Italian might easily
    misread this word twice—in an italic or mixed hand it is little more than
    a row of minims. No editor has identified Annabella's songs; nothing
    like them is listed in Einstein's *The Italian Madrigal*, Princeton, 1949.

Shall not redeem thee; were there kneeling kings   65
Did beg thy life, or angels did come down
To plead in tears, yet should not all prevail
Against my rage. Dost thou not tremble yet?

ANNABELLA
At what? To die? No, be a gallant hangman.
I dare thee to the worst: strike, and strike home;   70
I leave revenge behind, and thou shalt feel't.

SORANZO
Yet tell me ere thou diest, and tell me truly,
Knows thy old father this?

ANNABELLA   No, by my life.

SORANZO
Wilt thou confess, and I will spare thy life?

ANNABELLA
My life? I will not buy my life so dear.   75

SORANZO
I will not slack my vengeance.

Enter VASQUES

VASQUES
What d'ee mean, sir?

SORANZO
Forbear, Vasques; such a damned whore
Deserves no pity.

VASQUES
Now the gods forfend! And would you be her executioner,   80
and kill her in your rage too? O, 'twere most unmanlike.
She is your wife: what faults hath been done by her before
she married you, were not against you; alas, poor lady, what
hath she committed which any lady in Italy in the like case
would not? Sir, you must be ruled by your reason and not   85
by your fury; that were unhuman and beastly.

SORANZO
She shall not live.

VASQUES
Come, she must. You would have her confess the author
of her present misfortunes, I warrant 'ee; 'tis an unconscion-
able demand, and she should lose the estimation that I,   90

69 *hangman* general term for executioner
71 *I leave* Q *a.c.*; *leave* Q *b.c.*
76 *slack* reduce, mitigate
80 *forfend* forbid
88 *author* ed. Authors Q

for my part, hold of her worth, if she had done it. Why,
sir, you ought not of all men living to know it. Good sir,
be reconciled; alas, good gentlewoman.

ANNABELLA

Pish, do not beg for me; I prize my life
As nothing; if the man will needs be mad,   95
Why, let him take it.

SORANZO   Vasques, hear'st thou this?

VASQUES

Yes, and commend her for it; in this she shows the nobleness
of a gallant spirit, and beshrew my heart, but it becomes her
rarely. [*Aside*] Sir, in any case smother your revenge;
leave the scenting-out your wrongs to me; be ruled, as you   100
respect your honour, or you mar all. [*Aloud*] Sir, if ever
my service were of any credit with you, be not so violent
in your distractions. You are married now; what a triumph
might the report of this give to other neglected suitors. 'Tis
as manlike to bear extremities as godlike to forgive.   105

SORANZO

O Vasques, Vasques, in this piece of flesh,
This faithless face of hers, had I laid up
The treasure of my heart.—Hadst thou been virtuous,
Fair, wicked woman, not the matchless joys
Of life itself had made me wish to live   110
With any saint but thee; deceitful creature,
How hast thou mocked my hopes, and in the shame
Of thy lewd womb even buried me alive.
I did too dearly love thee.

VASQUES

[*Aside*] This is well; follow this temper with some passion. 115
Be brief and moving; 'tis for the purpose.

SORANZO

Be witness to my words thy soul and thoughts,
And tell me, didst not think that in my heart
I did too superstitiously adore thee?

ANNABELLA

I must confess I know you loved me well.   120

SORANZO

And wouldst thou use me thus? O, Annabella,
Be thou assured, whatsoe'er the villain was

 99 *in any case* by any means (*O.E.D.* 13)
101 *your* ed. hour Q
115 *temper* state of mind
122 *thou* ed. thus Q

That thus hath tempted thee to this disgrace,
Well he might lust, but never loved like me.
He doted on the picture that hung out   125
Upon thy cheeks, to please his humorous eye;
Not on the part I loved, which was thy heart,
And, as I thought, thy virtues.

ANNABELLA   O my lord!
These words wound deeper than your sword could do.

VASQUES

Let me not ever take comfort, but I begin to weep myself,   130
so much I pity him; why, madam, I knew when his rage was
over-past, what it would come to.

SORANZO

Forgive me, Annabella. Though thy youth
Hath tempted thee above thy strength to folly,
Yet will not I forget what I should be,   135
And what I am, a husband; in that name
Is hid divinity; if I do find
That thou wilt yet be true, here I remit
All former faults, and take thee to my bosom.

VASQUES

By my troth, and that's a point of noble charity.   140

ANNABELLA

Sir, on my knees—

SORANZO   Rise up, you shall not kneel.
Get you to your chamber, see you make no show
Of alteration; I'll be with you straight.
My reason tells me now that 'tis as common
To err in frailty as to be a woman.   145
Go to your chamber.   *Exit* ANNABELLA

VASQUES

So, this was somewhat to the matter; what do you think
of your heaven of happiness now, sir?

SORANZO

I carry hell about me; all my blood
Is fired in swift revenge.   150

VASQUES

That may be, but know you how, or on whom? Alas, to
marry a great woman, being made great in the stock to
your hand, is a usual sport in these days; but to know what

126 *humorous* whimsical
152 *great* pregnant
152 *stock* trunk, body
152-3 *to your hand* ready for you

ferret it was that haunted your cony-berry, there's the
cunning.   155

SORANZO
I'll make her tell herself, or—

VASQUES
Or what? You must not do so. Let me yet persuade your
sufferance a little while; go to her, use her mildly, win her
if it be possible to a voluntary, to a weeping tune; for the
rest, if all hit, I will not miss my mark. Pray, sir, go in; the   160
next news I tell you shall be wonders.

SORANZO
Delay in vengeance gives a heavier blow.   *Exit*

VASQUES
Ah, sirrah, here's work for the nonce. I had a suspicion of
a bad matter in my head a pretty whiles ago; but after my
madam's scurvy looks here at home, her waspish perver-   165
seness and loud fault-finding, then I remembered the
proverb, that where hens crow and cocks hold their peace
there are sorry houses. 'Sfoot, if the lower parts of a she-
tailor's cunning can cover such a swelling in the stomach,
I'll never blame a false stitch in a shoe whiles I live again.   170
Up and up so quick? And so quickly too? 'Twere a fine
policy to learn by whom; this must be known; and I have
thought on't—

Enter PUTANA

Here's the way, or none—What, crying, old mistress! Alas,
alas, I cannot blame 'ee, we have a lord, Heaven help us, is so   175
mad as the devil himself, the more shame for him.

PUTANA
O Vasques, that ever I was born to see this day. Doth he
use thee so too, sometimes, Vasques?

VASQUES
Me? Why, he makes a dog of me. But if some were of my
mind, I know what we would do; as sure as I am an honest   180
man, he will go near to kill my lady with unkindness. Say

---

154 *ferret* ed. secret Q
154 *cony-berry* rabbit-warren
155 *cunning* skill
173 s.d. ed.; after line 176 in Q

---

159 *voluntary*. Meaning, here, both 'an improvised piece of music' and 'a
     spontaneous confession'.
167–8 *where . . . houses*. Proverbial. See Tilley, H778.

she be with child, is that such a matter for a young woman
of her years to be blamed for?

PUTANA

Alas, good heart, it is against her will full sore.

VASQUES

I durst be sworn, all his madness is for that she will not   185
confess whose 'tis, which he will know, and when he doth
know it, I am so well acquainted with his humour, that he
will forget all straight. Well, I could wish she would in plain
terms tell all, for that's the way indeed.

PUTANA

Do you think so?   190

VASQUES

Foh, I know't; provided that he did not win her to't by
force. He was once in a mind that you could tell, and meant
to have wrung it out of you, but I somewhat pacified him
for that; yet sure you know a great deal.

PUTANA

Heaven forgive us all! I know a little, Vasques.   195

VASQUES

Why should you not? Who else should? Upon my conscience, she loves you dearly, and you would not betray her
to any affliction for the world.

PUTANA

Not for all the world, by my faith and troth, Vasques.

VASQUES

'Twere pity of your life if you should; but in this you should   200
both relieve her present discomforts, pacify my lord, and
gain yourself everlasting love and preferment.

PUTANA

Dost think so, Vasques?

VASQUES

Nay, I know't; sure 'twas some near and entire friend.

PUTANA

'Twas a dear friend indeed; but—   205

VASQUES

But what? Fear not to name him; my life between you and
danger. Faith, I think 'twas no base fellow.

PUTANA

Thou wilt stand between me and harm?

VASQUES

'Ud's pity, what else? You shall be rewarded too, trust me.

209 *'Ud's* God's

PUTANA

'Twas even no worse than her own brother.   210

VASQUES

Her brother Giovanni, I warrant 'ee!

PUTANA

Even he, Vasques; as brave a gentleman as ever kissed fair
lady. O, they love most perpetually.

VASQUES

A brave gentleman indeed; why, therein I commend her
choice.—Better and better!—You are sure 'twas he?   215

PUTANA

Sure; and you shall see he will not be long from her too.

VASQUES

He were to blame if he would: but may I believe thee?

PUTANA

Believe me! Why, dost think I am a Turk or a Jew? No,
Vasques, I have known their dealings too long to belie them
now.   220

VASQUES

Where are you? There within, sirs.

                    Enter BANDITTI

PUTANA

How now, what are these?

VASQUES

You shall know presently. Come, sirs, take me this old
damnable hag, gag her instantly, and put out her eyes.
Quickly, quickly!   225

PUTANA

Vasques, Vasques!

VASQUES

Gag her, I say. 'Sfoot, d'ee suffer her to prate? What d'ee
fumble about? Let me come to her; I'll help your old
gums, you toad-bellied bitch. Sirs, carry her closely into the
coalhouse, and put out her eyes instantly; if she roars, slit   230
her nose: d'ee hear, be speedy and sure. Why, this is
excellent and above expectation.

                    Exeunt [BANDITTI] *with* PUTANA

Her own brother! O horrible! To what a height of liberty
in damnation hath the devil trained our age. Her brother!

223 *presently* at once
232 s.d. *Exeunt* ed. Exit Q
233 *liberty* licence
234 *trained* lured

Well, there's yet but a beginning: I must to my lord, and   235
tutor him better in his points of vengeance; now I see
how a smooth tale goes beyond a smooth tail. But soft—
What thing comes next?

Enter GIOVANNI

Giovanni! As I would wish; my belief is strengthened,
'tis as firm as winter and summer.   240

GIOVANNI
Where's my sister?

VASQUES
Troubled with a new sickness, my lord; she's somewhat
ill.

GIOVANNI
Took too much of the flesh, I believe.

VASQUES
Troth, sir, and you, I think, have e'en hit it. But my virtuous   245
lady—

GIOVANNI
Where's she?

VASQUES
In her chamber; please you visit her; she is alone. [GIOVANNI
gives him money] Your liberality hath doubly made me
your servant, and ever shall, ever.   *Exit* GIOVANNI   250

Enter SORANZO

Sir, I am made a man, I have plied my cue with cunning
and success; I beseech you let's be private.

SORANZO
My lady's brother's come; now he'll know all.

VASQUES
Let him know't; I have made some of them fast enough.
How have you dealt with my lady?   255

SORANZO
Gently, as thou hast counselled. O, my soul
Runs circular in sorrow for revenge.
But, Vasques, thou shalt know—

VASQUES
Nay, I will know no more, for now comes your turn to
know; I would not talk so openly with you. Let my young   260

---

244 *Took . . . flesh.* Meaning both 'eaten too much meat' and 'had too much
   sexual experience'.
249 *liberality.* Both 'generosity' and 'sexual licence'.

master take time enough, and go at pleasure; he is sold to
death, and the devil shall not ransom him. Sir, I beseech
you, your privacy.

SORANZO

No conquest can gain glory of my fear.   *Exeunt*

Act V, [Scene i]

Enter ANNABELLA *above*

ANNABELLA

Pleasures, farewell, and all ye thriftless minutes
Wherein false joys have spun a weary life.
To these my fortunes now I take my leave.
Thou, precious Time, that swiftly rid'st in post
Over the world, to finish up the race   5
Of my last fate, here stay thy restless course,
And bear to ages that are yet unborn
A wretched, woeful woman's tragedy.
My conscience now stands up against my lust
With depositions charactered in guilt,   10

Enter FRIAR [*below*]

And tells me I am lost: now I confess
Beauty that clothes the outside of the face
Is cursèd if it be not clothed with grace.
Here like a turtle (mewed up in a cage)
Unmated, I converse with air and walls,   15
And descant on my vile unhappiness.
O Giovanni, that hast had the spoil
Of thine own virtues and my modest fame,
Would thou hadst been less subject to those stars
That luckless reigned at my nativity: 20

264 s.d. *Exeunt* ed. Exit Q
  9 *against* to witness against
 10 *depositions* ed. dispositions Q
 14 *turtle* turtle-dove
 14 *mewed up* imprisoned

---

  4 *rid'st in post.* With post horses, express, with haste (*O.E.D.*, adv.). The
     phrase may also carry something of the meaning 'in stages.'
 10 *charactered in guilt.* Bawcutt points out the pun: (1) with gilt lettering;
     (2) written so as to expose Annabella's guilt. Unlike the puns at the end
     of IV.iii, this one would not be easy to make on stage.
12-13 *Beauty . . . grace.* Cf. II.v, 15ff., and see Tilley, B175.

O would the scourge due to my black offence
Might pass from thee, that I alone might feel
The torment of an uncontrolled flame.

FRIAR
[*Aside*] What's this I hear?

ANNABELLA   That man, that blessed friar,
Who joined in ceremonial knot my hand   25
To him whose wife I now am, told me oft
I trod the path to death, and showed me how.
But they who sleep in lethargies of lust
Hug their confusion, making Heaven unjust,
And so did I.

FRIAR [*Aside*]   Here's music to the soul.   30

ANNABELLA
Forgive me, my good genius, and this once
Be helpful to my ends. Let some good man
Pass this way, to whose trust I may commit
This paper double-lined with tears and blood:
Which being granted, here I sadly vow   35
Repentance, and a leaving of that life
I long have died in.

FRIAR   Lady, Heaven hath heard you,
And hath by providence ordained that I
Should be his minister for your behoof.

ANNABELLA
Ha, what are you?

FRIAR   Your brother's friend, the friar;   40
Glad in my soul that I have lived to hear
This free confession 'twixt your peace and you.
What would you, or to whom? Fear not to speak.

ANNABELLA
Is Heaven so bountiful? Then I have found
More favour than I hoped. Here, holy man—   45
                    Throws a letter
Commend me to my brother; give him that,
That letter; bid him read it and repent.
Tell him that I (imprisoned in my chamber,
Barred of all company, even of my guardian,
Who gives me cause of much suspect) have time   50
To blush at what hath passed; bid him be wise,
And not believe the friendship of my lord.

35 *sadly* solemnly
39 *behoof* advantage
50 *suspect* suspicion

I fear much more than I can speak: good father,
The place is dangerous, and spies are busy;
I must break off—you'll do't?

FRIAR   Be sure I will;   55
And fly with speed—my blessing ever rest
With thee, my daughter; live, to die more blessed.

            Exit FRIAR

ANNABELLA
Thanks to the Heavens, who have prolonged my breath
To this good use: now I can welcome death. *Exit*

[Act V, Scene ii]

Enter SORANZO *and* VASQUES

VASQUES
Am I to be believed now? First marry a strumpet that cast
herself away upon you but to laugh at your horns, to feast
on your disgrace, riot in your vexations, cuckold you in your
bride-bed, waste your estate upon panders and bawds!

SORANZO
No more, I say, no more.   5

VASQUES
A cuckold is a goodly tame beast, my lord.

SORANZO
I am resolved; urge not another word.
My thoughts are great, and all as resolute
As thunder; in mean time I'll cause our lady
To deck herself in all her bridal robes,   10
Kiss her, and fold her gently in my arms.
Begone—yet hear you, are the banditti ready
To wait in ambush?

VASQUES
Good sir, trouble not yourself about other business than
your own resolution; remember that time lost cannot be   15
recalled.

SORANZO
With all the cunning words thou canst, invite
The states of Parma to my birthday's feast;
Haste to my brother-rival and his father,
Entreat them gently, bid them not to fail.   20
Be speedy, and return.

18 *states* nobles

15–16 *time lost* etc. Tilley, T332.

VASQUES
Let not your pity betray you till my coming back; think upon
incest and cuckoldry.

SORANZO
Revenge is all the ambition I aspire:
To that I'll climb or fall; my blood's on fire.   *Exeunt*   25

[Act V, Scene iii]

Enter GIOVANNI

GIOVANNI
Busy opinion is an idle fool,
That, as a school-rod keeps a child in awe,
Frights the unexperienced temper of the mind:
So did it me; who, ere my precious sister
Was married, thought all taste of love would die   5
In such a contract; but I find no change
Of pleasure in this formal law of sports.
She is still one to me, and every kiss
As sweet and as delicious as the first
I reaped, when yet the privilege of youth   10
Entitled her a virgin. O the glory
Of two united hearts like hers and mine!
Let poring book-men dream of other worlds,
My world, and all of happiness, is here,
And I'd not change it for the best to come: 15
A life of pleasure is Elysium.

Enter FRIAR

Father, you enter on the jubilee
Of my retired delights; now I can tell you,
The hell you oft have prompted is nought else
But slavish and fond superstitious fear;   20
And I could prove it too—

FRIAR   Thy blindness slays thee.
Look there, 'tis writ to thee.   *Gives the letter*

GIOVANNI
From whom?

19 *prompted* put forward in argument
20 *fond* foolish

___

17 *jubilee.* Meaning not clear. It usually means 'a time of celebration' > ·
'the fiftieth anniversary.'

FRIAR
 Unrip the seals and see;
 The blood's yet seething hot, that will anon   25
 Be frozen harder than congealed coral.
 Why d'ee change colour, son?
GIOVANNI   'Fore Heaven, you make
 Some petty devil factor 'twixt my love
 And your religion-masked sorceries.
 Where had you this?
FRIAR   Thy conscience, youth, is seared, 30
 Else thou wouldst stoop to warning.
GIOVANNI   'Tis her hand,
 I know't; and 'tis all written in her blood.
 She writes I know not what. Death? I'll not fear
 An armèd thunderbolt aimed at my heart.
 She writes, we are discovered—pox on dreams 35
 Of low faint-hearted cowardice! Discovered?
 The devil we are; which way is't possible?
 Are we grown traitors to our own delights?
 Confusion take such dotage, 'tis but forged;
 This is your peevish chattering, weak old man. 40

      Enter VASQUES

 Now, sir, what news bring you?
VASQUES
 My lord, according to his yearly custom keeping this day a
 feast in honour of his birthday, by me invites you thither.
 Your worthy father, with the Pope's reverend nuncio, and
 other magnificoes of Parma, have promised their presence; 45
 will't please you to be of the number?
GIOVANNI
 Yes, tell him I dare come.
VASQUES
 'Dare come'?
GIOVANNI
 So I said; and tell him more, I will come.
VASQUES
 These words are strange to me.   50
GIOVANNI
 Say I will come.

 30 *seared* dried up
 40 s.d. ed.; after line 41 in Q
 47 *him* ed. them Q

VASQUES
  You will not miss?
GIOVANNI
  Yet more? I'll come! Sir, are you answered?
VASQUES
  So I'll say.—My service to you.   *Exit* VASQUES
FRIAR
  You will not go, I trust.
GIOVANNI   Not go? For what?   55
FRIAR
  O, do not go. This feast, I'll gage my life,
  Is but a plot to train you to your ruin.
  Be ruled, you sha' not go.
GIOVANNI   Not go? Stood Death
  Threatening his armies of confounding plagues,
  With hosts of dangers hot as blazing stars,   60
  I would be there. Not go? Yes, and resolve
  To strike as deep in slaughter as they all.
  For I will go.
FRIAR   Go where thou wilt; I see
  The wildness of thy fate draws to an end,
  To a bad fearful end. I must not stay   65
  To know thy fall; back to Bononia I
  With speed will haste, and shun this coming blow.
  Parma, farewell; would I had never known thee,
  Or aught of thine. Well, young man, since no prayer
  Can make thee safe, I leave thee to despair.   *Exit* FRIAR 70
GIOVANNI
  Despair, or tortures of a thousand hells,
  All's one to me; I have set up my rest.
  Now, now, work serious thoughts on baneful plots,
  Be all a man, my soul; let not the curse

56 *gage* wager   57 *train* lure
71 s.p. GIOVANNI ed.; omitted by Q

---

66 *back to Bononia.* Cf. *The Broken Heart* IV.i, where, as the tension
   increases, Tecnicus abandons Sparta for Delphos. In each play, when
   the hero is finally fixed in his course of action, the 'adviser' withdraws
   from the impending disaster.
72 *set up my rest.* Made up my mind. In the card-game Primero the
   player 'sets up his rest' when he 'stands' on the cards he has, and so
   ventures his all on them (*O.E.D.* Rest sb²7c).
74–5 *the curse . . . prescription.* The curse pronounced, in the Old
   Testament, upon him who lay with his sister. See Deuteronomy, xxvii,
   22, and Leviticus, xx, 17.

Of old prescription rend from me the gall   75
Of courage, which enrols a glorious death.
If I must totter like a well-grown oak,
Some under-shrubs shall in my weighty fall
Be crushed to splits: with me they all shall perish.   *Exit*

[Act V, Scene iv]

Enter SORANZO, VASQUES, *and* BANDITTI

SORANZO
You will not fail, or shrink in the attempt?

VASQUES
I will undertake for their parts. Be sure, my masters, to be
bloody enough, and as unmerciful as if you were preying
upon a rich booty on the very mountains of Liguria; for
your pardons, trust to my lord, but for reward you shall   5
trust none but your own pockets.

BANDITTI OMNES
We'll make a murder.

SORANZO
Here's gold, here's more; want nothing; what you do
Is noble, and an act of brave revenge.
I'll make ye rich banditti, and all free.   10

OMNES
Liberty, liberty!

VASQUES
Hold, take every man a vizard; when ye are withdrawn,
keep as much silence as you can possibly. You know the
watchword; till which be spoken, move not, but when you
hear that, rush in like a stormy flood; I need not instruct 15
ye in your own profession.

OMNES
No, no, no.

VASQUES
In, then; your ends are profit and preferment.—Away!
                                        Exeunt BANDITTI

SORANZO
The guests will all come, Vasques?

VASQUES
Yes, sir. And now let me a little edge your resolution. You 20
see nothing is unready to this great work, but a great mind

75 *rend* ed. rent Q
79 *splits* splinters
18 s.d. *Exeunt* ed. Exit Q

in you: call to your remembrance your disgraces, your
loss of honour, Hippolita's blood, and arm your courage in
your own wrongs; so shall you best right those wrongs in
vengeance, which you may truly call your own.   25

SORANZO
'Tis well; the less I speak, the more I burn,
And blood shall quench that flame.

VASQUES
Now you begin to turn Italian. This beside—when my
young incest-monger comes, he will be sharp set on his old
bit: give him time enough, let him have your chamber and   30
bed at liberty; let my hot hare have law ere he be hunted
to his death, that if it be possible, he may post to hell in
the very act of his damnation.

Enter GIOVANNI

SORANZO
It shall be so; and see, as we would wish,
He comes himself first. Welcome, my much-loved brother,   35
Now I perceive you honour me; y'are welcome.
But where's my father?

GIOVANNI   With the other states,
Attending on the nuncio of the Pope,
To wait upon him hither. How's my sister?

SORANZO
Like a good housewife, scarcely ready yet;   40
Y'are best walk to her chamber.

GIOVANNI   If you will.

SORANZO
I must expect my honourable friends;
Good brother, get her forth.

GIOVANNI   You are busy, sir.

Exit GIOVANNI

VASQUES
Even as the great devil himself would have it; let him go
and glut himself in his own destruction.   *Flourish*   45

42 *expect* wait for

29–30 *sharp set on his old bit*. Meaning 'eager', 'hungry for', but I have not
been able to trace the metaphor further.
31 *law*. The 'start' which a hare is given before the chase begins.
32 *post to hell* etc. If he is killed while committing a sin his soul will go
straight to hell. Cf. *Hamlet*, III.iii.
45 s.d. *Flourish*. The corrector of Q mistakenly placed this direction after
line 47.

Hark, the nuncio is at hand; good sir, be ready to receive
him.

Enter CARDINAL, FLORIO, DONADO, RICHARDETTO, *and Attendants*

SORANZO
    Most reverend lord, this grace hath made me proud,
    That you vouchsafe my house; I ever rest
    Your humble servant for this noble favour.   50
CARDINAL
    You are our friend, my lord; his holiness
    Shall understand how zealously you honour
    Saint Peter's vicar in his substitute:
    Our special love to you.
SORANZO   Signors, to you
    My welcome, and my ever best of thanks   55
    For this so memorable courtesy.
    Pleaseth your grace to walk near?
CARDINAL   My lord, we come
    To celebrate your feast with civil mirth,
    As ancient custom teacheth: we will go.
SORANZO
    Attend his grace there!—Signors, keep your way.   *Exeunt*   60

[Act V, Scene v]

Enter GIOVANNI *and* ANNABELLA *lying on a bed*

GIOVANNI
    What, changed so soon? Hath your new sprightly lord
    Found out a trick in night-games more than we
    Could know in our simplicity? Ha! Is't so?
    Or does the fit come on you, to prove treacherous
    To your past vows and oaths?
ANNABELLA   Why should you jest   5
    At my calamity, without all sense
    Of the approaching dangers you are in?
GIOVANNI
    What danger's half so great as thy revolt?
    Thou art a faithless sister, else thou know'st

49 *vouchsafe* deign (to visit)

---

1 s.d. They may have been 'discovered' in bed, by moving a curtain on the
main stage, or, as Bawcutt suggests, the bed may have been pushed out
on to the stage, as in Middleton's *A Chaste Maid in Cheapside*, III.ii:
'A bed thrust out upon the stage; Allwit's wife in it.'

Malice, or any treachery beside, 10
Would stoop to my bent brows; why, I hold fate
Clasped in my fist, and could command the course
Of time's eternal motion, hadst thou been
One thought more steady than an ebbing sea.
And what? You'll now be honest, that's resolved? 15

ANNABELLA
Brother, dear brother, know what I have been,
And know that now there's but a dining-time
'Twixt us and our confusion: let's not waste
These precious hours in vain and useless speech.
Alas, these gay attires were not put on 20
But to some end; this sudden solemn feast
Was not ordained to riot in expense;
I, that have now been chambered here alone,
Barred of my guardian, or of any else,
Am not for nothing at an instant freed 25
To fresh access. Be not deceived, my brother,
This banquet is an harbinger of death
To you and me; resolve yourself it is,
And be prepared to welcome it.

GIOVANNI   Well, then;
The schoolmen teach that all this globe of earth 30
Shall be consumed to ashes in a minute.

ANNABELLA
So I have read too.

GIOVANNI   But 'twere somewhat strange
To see the waters burn; could I believe
This might be true, I could believe as well
There might be hell or Heaven.

ANNABELLA   That's most certain. 35

GIOVANNI
A dream, a dream! Else in this other world
We should know one another.

ANNABELLA   So we shall.

GIOVANNI
Have you heard so?

ANNABELLA   For certain.

17 *dining* Q *a.c.*; dying Q *b.c.*
30 *schoolmen* mediaeval theologians

11–12 *I hold fate* etc. Cf. Marlowe, *Tamburlaine*, Part I, 369–70:
    I hold the Fates bound fast in yron chaines,
    And with my hand turne Fortunes wheel about . . .

GIOVANNI But d'ee think
That I shall see you there?—You look on me?
May we kiss one another, prate or laugh, 40
Or do as we do here?

ANNABELLA I know not that.
But good, for the present, what d'ee mean
To free yourself from danger? Some way think
How to escape; I'm sure the guests are come.

GIOVANNI
Look up, look here; what see you in my face? 45

ANNABELLA
Distraction and a troubled countenance.

GIOVANNI
Death, and a swift repining wrath—yet look,
What see you in mine eyes?

ANNABELLA Methinks you weep.

GIOVANNI
I do indeed; these are the funeral tears
Shed on your grave; these furrowed up my cheeks 50
When first I loved and knew not how to woo.
Fair Annabella, should I here repeat
The story of my life, we might lose time.
Be record all the spirits of the air,
And all things else that are, that day and night, 55
Early and late, the tribute which my heart
Hath paid to Annabella's sacred love
Hath been these tears, which are her mourners now.
Never till now did Nature do her best
To show a matchless beauty to the world, 60
Which in an instant, ere it scarce was seen,
The jealous Destinies required again.
Pray, Annabella, pray; since we must part,
Go thou, white in thy soul, to fill a throne
Of innocence and sanctity in Heaven. 65
Pray, pray, my sister.

ANNABELLA Then I see your drift—
Ye blessed angels, guard me.

GIOVANNI So say I.
Kiss me. If ever after-times should hear
Of our fast-knit affections, though perhaps
The laws of conscience and of civil use 70

42 *good* i.e. good brother
51 *woo* Q *a.c.*; woe Q *b.c.*
62 *required* Q *a.c.*; require Q *b.c.*

May justly blame us, yet when they but know
Our loves, that love will wipe away that rigour
Which would in other incests be abhorred.
Give me your hand; how sweetly life doth run
In these well-coloured veins. How constantly   75
These palms do promise health. But I could chide
With Nature for this cunning flattery.
Kiss me again—forgive me.

ANNABELLA   With my heart.

GIOVANNI
Farewell.

ANNABELLA Will you be gone?

GIOVANNI   Be dark, bright sun,
And make this midday night, that thy gilt rays   80
May not behold a deed will turn their splendour
More sooty than the poets feign their Styx.
One other kiss, my sister.

ANNABELLA   What means this?

GIOVANNI
To save thy fame, and kill thee in a kiss.   *Stabs her*
Thus die, and die by me, and by my hand.   85
Revenge is mine; honour doth love command.

ANNABELLA
O brother, by your hand?

GIOVANNI   When thou art dead
I'll give my reasons for't; for to dispute
With thy (even in thy death) most lovely beauty,
Would make me stagger to perform this act,   90
Which I most glory in.

ANNABELLA
Forgive him, Heaven—and me my sins; farewell.
Brother unkind, unkind!—Mercy, great Heaven—O!—O!—
                                        Dies

GIOVANNI
She's dead, alas, good soul. The hapless fruit
That in her womb received its life from me   95
Hath had from me a cradle and a grave.
I must not dally. This sad marriage-bed,
In all her best, bore her alive and dead.
Soranzo, thou hast missed thy aim in this;
I have prevented now thy reaching plots,   100

93 unkind both 'cruel' and 'unnatural'   _94 hapless_ luckless
100 prevented forestalled   _100 reaching_ cunning

And killed a love, for whose each drop of blood
I would have pawned my heart. Fair Annabella,
How over-glorious art thou in thy wounds,
Triumphing over infamy and hate!
Shrink not, courageous hand, stand up, my heart,   105
And boldly act my last and greater part.

Exit with the body

[Act V, Scene vi]

A Banquet. Enter CARDINAL, FLORIO, DONADO, SORANZO,
RICHARDETTO, VASQUES, *and Attendants; they take their places*

VASQUES
Remember, sir, what you have to do; be wise and resolute.
SORANZO
Enough—my heart is fixed.—Pleaseth your grace
To taste these coarse confections; though the use
Of such set entertainments more consists
In custom than in cause, yet, reverend sir,   5
I am still made your servant by your presence.
CARDINAL
And we your friend.
SORANZO
But where's my brother Giovanni?

Enter GIOVANNI *with a heart upon his dagger*

GIOVANNI
Here, here, Soranzo; trimmed in reeking blood,
That triumphs over death; proud in the spoil   10
Of love and vengeance! Fate or all the powers
That guide the motions of immortal souls
Could not prevent me.
CARDINAL
What means this?
FLORIO
Son Giovanni!   15
SORANZO
Shall I be forestalled?
GIOVANNI
Be not amazed; if your misgiving hearts
Shrink at an idle sight, what bloodless fear
Of coward passion would have seized your senses,
Had you beheld the rape of life and beauty   20
Which I have acted? My sister, O my sister!

FLORIO
　　Ha! What of her?

GIOVANNI　　　　　　The glory of my deed
　　Darkened the midday sun, made noon as night.
　　You came to feast, my lords, with dainty fare;
　　I came to feast too, but I digged for food　　　　　25
　　In a much richer mine than gold or stone
　　Of any value balanced; 'tis a heart,
　　A heart, my lords, in which is mine entombed:
　　Look well upon't; d'ee know't?

VASQUES
　　What strange riddle's this?　　　　　　　　　　30

GIOVANNI
　　'Tis Annabella's heart, 'tis; why d'ee startle?
　　I vow 'tis hers: this dagger's point ploughed up
　　Her fruitful womb, and left to me the fame
　　Of a most glorious executioner.

FLORIO
　　Why, madman, art thyself?　　　　　　　　　　35

GIOVANNI
　　Yes, father; and that times to come may know
　　How as my fate I honoured my revenge,
　　List, father, to your ears I will yield up
　　How much I have deserved to be your son.

FLORIO
　　What is't thou say'st?

GIOVANNI　　　　　　Nine moons have had their changes　　40
　　Since I first throughly viewed and truly loved
　　Your daughter and my sister.

FLORIO　　　　　　　　　　How!—Alas,
　　My lords, he's a frantic madman!

GIOVANNI　　　　　　　　　　Father, no.
　　For nine months' space in secret I enjoyed
　　Sweet Annabella's sheets; nine months I lived　　45
　　A happy monarch of her heart and her.
　　Soranzo, thou know'st this; thy paler cheek
　　Bears the confounding print of thy disgrace,
　　For her too fruitful womb too soon bewrayed
　　The happy passage of our stol'n delights,　　　　50
　　And made her mother to a child unborn.

CARDINAL
　　Incestuous villain!

FLORIO　　　　　　O, his rage belies him.

GIOVANNI
  It does not, 'tis the oracle of truth;
  I vow it is so.
SORANZO   I shall burst with fury.
  Bring the strumpet forth.   55
VASQUES
  I shall, sir.   *Exit* VASQUES
GIOVANNI   Do, sir.—Have you all no faith
  To credit yet my triumphs? Here I swear
  By all that you call sacred, by the love
  I bore my Annabella whilst she lived,
  These hands have from her bosom ripped this heart.   60

                  Enter VASQUES

  Is't true or no, sir?
VASQUES   'Tis most strangely true.
FLORIO
  Cursed man!—Have I lived to—   *Dies*
CARDINAL   Hold up, Florio.—
  Monster of children, see what thou hast done,
  Broke thy old father's heart. Is none of you
  Dares venture on him?
GIOVANNI   Let 'em.—O, my father,   65
  How well his death becomes him in his griefs!
  Why, this was done with courage; now survives
  None of our house but I, gilt in the blood
  Of a fair sister and a hapless father.
SORANZO
  Inhuman scorn of men, hast thou a thought   70
  T'outlive thy murders?
GIOVANNI   Yes, I tell thee, yes;
  For in my fists I bear the twists of life.
  Soranzo, see this heart, which was thy wife's;
  Thus I exchange it royally for thine,   [*Stabs him*]
  And thus and thus. Now brave revenge is mine.   75
VASQUES
  I cannot hold any longer.—You, sir, are you grown insolent
  in your butcheries? Have at you!   [*They*] *fight*
GIOVANNI
  Come, I am armed to meet thee.

  72 *twists of life.* The Parcae, in Greek mythology, spun the threads of
  mortal life, and cut them at the moment appointed for death.

VASQUES

    No, will it not be yet? If this will not, another shall. Not yet?
    I shall fit you anon.—Vengeance!   80

            Enter BANDITTI [*and fight* GIOVANNI]

GIOVANNI

    Welcome, come more of you whate'er you be,
    I dare your worst—
    O, I can stand no longer! Feeble arms,
    Have you so soon lost strength?

VASQUES

    Now you are welcome, sir!—Away, my masters, all is done, 85
    shift for yourselves. Your reward is your own; shift for
    yourselves.

BANDITTI

    Away, away!   *Exeunt* BANDITTI

VASQUES

    How d'ee, my lord; see you this? How is't?

SORANZO

    Dead; but in death well pleased that I have lived   90
    To see my wrongs revenged on that black devil.
    O Vasques, to thy bosom let me give
    My last of breath; let not that lecher live—O!—   *Dies*

VASQUES

    The reward of peace and rest be with him, my ever dearest
    lord and master.   95

GIOVANNI

    Whose hand gave me this wound?

VASQUES

    Mine, sir, I was your first man; have you enough?

GIOVANNI

    I thank thee; thou hast done for me but what
    I would have else done on myself. Art sure
    Thy lord is dead?   100

VASQUES

    O impudent slave! As sure as I am sure to see thee die.

CARDINAL

    Think on thy life and end, and call for mercy.

GIOVANNI

    Mercy? Why, I have found it in this justice.

CARDINAL

    Strive yet to cry to Heaven.

   80 *Vengeance*. This is the watchword mentioned at V.iv, 14.
  101 *thee* ed. the Q

GIOVANNI   O, I bleed fast.
Death, thou art a guest long looked for; I embrace   105
Thee and thy wounds; O, my last minute comes!
Where'er I go, let me enjoy this grace,
Freely to view my Annabella's face.   *Dies*

DONADO
Strange miracle of justice!

CARDINAL
Raise up the city; we shall be murdered all.   110

VASQUES
You need not fear, you shall not; this strange task being
ended, I have paid the duty to the son which I have vowed to
the father.

CARDINAL
Speak, wretched villain, what incarnate fiend
Hath led thee on to this?   115

VASQUES
Honesty, and pity of my master's wrongs; for know, my
lord, I am by birth a Spaniard, brought forth my country
in my youth by Lord Soranzo's father, whom whilst he lived
I served faithfully; since whose death I have been to this
man as I was to him. What I have done was duty, and I   120
repent nothing but that the loss of my life had not ransomed
his.

CARDINAL
Say, fellow, know'st thou any yet unnamed
Of counsel in this incest?

VASQUES
Yes, an old woman, sometimes guardian to this murdered   125
lady.

CARDINAL
And what's become of her?

VASQUES
Within this room she is; whose eyes, after her confession, I
caused to be put out, but kept alive, to confirm what from
Giovanni's own mouth you have heard. Now, my lord, what   130
I have done you may judge of, and let your own wisdom be
a judge in your own reason.

CARDINAL
Peace!—First this woman, chief in these effects:

125 *sometimes* formerly

---

133 *this woman.* Ambiguous; the reference might be either to Putana, or the
    dead body of Annabella.

My sentence is, that forthwith she be ta'en
Out of the city, for example's sake,   135
There to be burnt to ashes.
DONADO   'Tis most just.
CARDINAL
  Be it your charge, Donado, see it done.
DONADO
  I shall.
VASQUES
  What for me? If death, 'tis welcome; I have been honest to
  the son as I was to the father.   140
CARDINAL
  Fellow, for thee, since what thou didst was done
  Not for thyself, being no Italian,
  We banish thee forever, to depart
  Within three days; in this we do dispense
  With grounds of reason, not of thine offence.   145
VASQUES
  'Tis well; this conquest is mine, and I rejoice that a Spaniard
  outwent an Italian in revenge.   *Exit* VASQUES
CARDINAL
  Take up these slaughtered bodies, see them buried;
  And all the gold and jewels, or whatsoever,
  Confiscate by the canons of the church,   150
  We seize upon to the Pope's proper use.
RICHARDETTO [*discovers himself*]
  Your grace's pardon: thus long I lived disguised
  To see the effect of pride and lust at once
  Brought both to shameful ends.
CARDINAL
  What, Richardetto whom we thought for dead?   155
DONADO
  Sir, was it you—
RICHARDETTO   Your friend.
CARDINAL   We shall have time
  To talk at large of all; but never yet
  Incest and murder have so strangely met.
  Of one so young, so rich in nature's store,
  Who could not say, 'tis pity she's a whore?   *Exeunt* 160

FINIS

[The Printer's Apology]

The general commendation deserved by the actors in their presentment of this tragedy may easily excuse such few faults as are escaped
in the printing. A common charity may allow him the ability of
spelling whom a secure confidence assures that he cannot ignorantly
err in the application of sense.

FURTHER READING

General Books

1 Eric Bentley, *The Life of the Drama* (1965)
2 M. C. Bradbrook, *Themes and Conventions of Elizabethan Tragedy* (1935, rev. ed. 1980)
3 Fredson T. Bowers, *Elizabethan Revenge Tragedy* (1940, rev. ed. 1959)
4 J. R. Brown and Bernard Harris, ed., Stratford-upon-Avon
5 Studies vol. I, *Jacobean Theatre* (1960), vol. 9, *Elizabethan Theatre* (1966)
6 T. S. Eliot, *Selected Essays* (3rd ed. 1951)
7 R. J. Kaufmann, ed., *Elizabethan Drama: Modern Essays in Criticism* (1961)
8 J. W. Lever, *The Tragedy of State* (1971)
9 C. Ricks, ed., *The Sphere History of Literature in the English Language* vol. 3, *English Drama to 1700* (1971)

Some Essential Articles

10 William Empson, Double Plots (chapter 2 in *Some Versions of Pastoral* 1935)
11 Alfred Harbage, Intrigue in Elizabethan Tragedy (in R. Hosley, ed., *Essays . . . in Honour of Hardin Craig* 1962)
12 G. K. Hunter, Seneca and the Elizabethans (in *Shakespeare Survey* 20 1967)
13 M. C. Bradbrook, Shakespeare and the Multiple Theatres of Jacobean London (in *The Elizabethan Theatre* vol. VI, ed. G. R. Hibbard, 1978)

Individual Dramatists

Kyd: Arthur Freeman, *Thomas Kyd: Facts and Problems* (1967)
G. K. Hunter, Ironies of Justice in *The Spanish Tragedy* in *Renaissance Drama* VIII, 1965, 89-104
Scott McMillin, The Figure of Silence in *The Spanish Tragedy, English Literary History*, 1972
Michael Hattaway, Chapter 4, *Elizabethan Popular Theatre*, 1982
See also 2, 3, 5, 7, 9, 10, 11, 12 above.

Marlowe M. C. Bradbrook, Marlowe's *Dr Faustus* and the Eldritch Tradition (in R. Hosley, ed., *Essays . . . in Honour of Hardin Craig* 1962)

J. P. Brockbank, *Marlowe: Dr Faustus* (1962)

Helen Gardner, The Tragedy of Damnation (in 7 above)

Harry Levin, *The Overreacher* (1954)

Brian Morris, ed., *Christopher Marlowe* (1968)

Judith Weil, *Christopher Marlowe, Merlin's Prophet* (1977)

Michael Hattaway, Chapter 7, *Elizabethan Popular Theatre* (1982)

See also 3, 6, 7, 9 above.

Jonson E. M. T. Duffy, Jonson's Debt to Renaissance Scholarship in *Sejanus* and *Catiline*, (MLR 1974)

A. Richard Dutton, The sources, text and readers of *Sejanus* (*Studies in Philology* 1978)

Ray L. Heffner Jr., Unifying Symbols in the Comedy of Ben Jonson (1954, repr. in Jonas Barish, ed., *Ben Jonson, Twentieth Century Views*, 1963)

G. Hill, The World's Proportion: Jonson's dramatic poetry in *Sejanus* and *Catiline* (in 4 above)

C. Ricks, *Sejanus* and Dismemberment (*MLN* 1961)

See also 6, 8, 9 above.

Webster M. C. Bradbrook, *John Webster* (1980)

Ralph Berry, *The Art of John Webster* (1972)

Inga-Stina Ekeblad, The Impure Art of John Webster (repr. in 7 above)

Brian Morris, ed., *John Webster* (1970)

See also 2, 3, 4, 6, 7, 8, 9 above.

Middleton Arthur Kirsh, *Jacobean Dramatic Perspectives* (1972)

J. R. Mulryne, *Thomas Middleton* (1979)

C. Ricks, Word-play in *Women Beware Women* (*RES* 1961)

See also 2, 3, 4, 6, 7, 9 above.

Ford Arthur Kirsh, *Jacobean Dramatic Perspectives* (1972)

Donald K. Anderson, Imagery in Ford's *'Tis Pity She's a Whore* and *The Broken Heart* (*SEL* II)

Una Ellis Fermor, *The Jacobean Drama* (rev. ed. 1958)

C. Leech, *John Ford and the Drama of his Time* (1957)

See also 2, 3, 6, 7, especially Kaufmann's article in 7 above.

More extensive reading lists can be found in the annual *Year's Work in English Studies* and in the Renaissance Drama issue of *Studies in English Literature*, also annual. The annual volumes of *Renaissance Drama* (new series ed. L. Barkan, Northwestern Univ. Press) and of *The Elizabethan Theatre* (ed. Galloway, Hibbard; Waterloo, Ont. & London) contain good articles on the plays.

New Mermaids

New Mermaid drama books
Paperback drama texts from Ernest Benn

New Mermaids present modern-spelling, fully annotated
editions of classic English plays, including works by Marlowe,
Jonson, Webster, Congreve, Sheridan, and Wilde. Each volume
includes a biography of the writer, a critical introduction to
the play, discussions of dates and sources, and a bibliography.

Arden of Faversham

edited by Martin White,
University of Bristol

160 pages
0 510-33508-X £3.25

Three Late Medieval Morality Plays

(Everyman, Mankind, Mundus et Infans)

edited by Geoffrey Lester,
University of Sheffield

204 pages
0 510-33505-5 £3.50

Francis Beaumont

The Knight of the Burning Pestle

edited by Michael Hattaway,
University of Kent

144 pages
0 510-33202-1 £3.25

George Chapman

Bussy D'Ambois

edited by Maurice Evans

160 pages
0 510-33202-1 £3.25

Chapman, Jonson and Marston

Eastward Ho!

edited by C. G. Petter

192 pages
0 510-33311-7 £3.25

William Congreve

The Double Dealer

edited by John Ross, Massey
University

168 pages
0 510-33504-7 £3.25

Love for Love

edited by Malcolm Kelsall,
University College, Cardiff

158 pages
0 510-33662-0 £3.25

The Way of the World

edited by Brian Gibbons,
University of Zurich

152 pages
0 510-33672-8 £3.25

Thomas Dekker

The Shoemakers' Holiday

edited by David Palmer, University of Manchester

128 pages
0 510-33721-X £3.25

John Dryden

All for Love

edited by N. J. Andrew

144 pages
0 510-33711-2 £3.25

Sir George Etherege

The Man of Mode

edited by John Barnard, University of Leeds

200 pages
0 510-33500-4 £3.25

George Farquhar

The Beaux' Stratagem

edited by Michael Cordner, University of York

160 pages
0 510-33781-3 £3.25

The Recruiting Officer

edited by John Ross, Massey University

184 pages
0 510-33731-7 £3.25

John Ford

'Tis Pity She's a Whore

edited by Brian Morris, University College, Lampeter

128 pages
0 510-34145-4 £3.25

Oliver Goldsmith

She Stoops to Conquer

edited by Tom Davis, University of Birmingham

132 pages
0 510-34142-X £3.25

Jasper Heywood/Seneca

Thyestes

edited by Joost Daalder, Flinders University

144 pages
0 510-39010-2 £3.95

Ben Jonson

The Alchemist
edited by Douglas Brown

176 pages
0 510-33606-X £3.25

Bartholmew Fair
edited by G. R. Hibbard,
University of Waterloo,
Ontario

216 pages
0 510-33710-4 £3.25

Epicoene
edited by R. V. Holdsworth,
University of Manchester

224 pages
0 510-34154-3 £3.25

Every Man in his Humour
edited by Martin Seymour-Smith

160 pages
0 510-33636-1 £3.25

Volpone
edited by Philip Brockbank,
Shakespeare Institute,
University of Birmingham

208 pages
0 510-34157-8 £3.25

Thomas Kyd

The Spanish Tragedy
edited by J. R. Mulryne,
University of Warwick

176 pages
0 510-33707-4 £3.25

Christopher Marlowe

Doctor Faustus
edited by Roma Gill,
University of Sheffield

128 pages
0 510-33821-6 £3.25

Edward the Second
edited by W. Moelwyn
Merchant, University of Exeter

144 pages
0 510-33806-2 £3.25

The Jew of Malta
edited by T. W. Craik,
University of Durham

128 pages
0 510-33836-4 £3.25

Tamburlaine Parts I & II
edited by J. W. Harper,
University of York

208 pages
0 510-33851-8 £3.25

Thomas Middleton and William Rowley

The Changeling
edited by Patricia Thomson, University of Sussex

128 pages
0 510-34106-3 £3.25

A Fair Quarrel
edited by R. V. Holdsworth, University of Manchester

176 pages
0 510-34108-X £3.25

George Peele, Nicholas Udall, etc.

Three Sixteenth Century Comedies
(The Old Wife's Tale, Gammer Gurton's Needle, Roister Doister)

edited by Charles Whitworth, University of Birmingham

240 pages
0 510-33509-8 £4.95

Richard Brinsley Sheridan

The Rivals
edited by Elizabeth Duthie, University College, Cardiff

160 pages
0 510-34141-1 £3.25

OD   O level Eng Lit 1983-4-5-6
SU   A level Eng Lit 1983

The School for Scandal
edited by F. W. Bateson

200 pages
0 510-34364-3 £3.25

J. M. Synge

The Playboy of the Western World
edited by Malcolm Kelsall, University College, Cardiff

128 pages
0 510-33771-6 £3.25

Cyril Tourneur

The Atheist's Tragedy
edited by Brian Morris, St Davids University College, & Roma Gill, University of Sheffield

144 pages
0 510-33751-1 £3.25

The Revenger's Tragedy

edited by Brian Gibbons,
University of Zurich

144 pages
0 510-34206-X £3.25

Sir John Vanbrugh

The Provoked Wife

edited by James L. Smith,
University of Southampton

160 pages
0 510-34252-3 £3.25

The Relapse

edited by Bernard Harris,
University of York

160 pages
0 510-34262-0 £3.25

John Webster

The Devil's Law-Case

edited by Elizabeth M.
Brennan, University of
London

192 pages
0 510-34296-5 £3.25

The Duchess of Malfi

edited by Elizabeth M.
Brennan, University of
London

160 pages
0 510-34306-6 £3.25

The White Devil

edited by Elizabeth M.
Brennan, University of
London

208 pages
0 510-34321-X £3.25

Oscar Wilde

The Importance of Being Earnest

edited by Russell Jackson, The
Shakespeare Institute,
University of Birmingham

192 pages
0 510-34143-8 £3.25

Lady Windermere's Fan

edited by Ian Small, University
of Birmingham

176 pages
0 510-34153-5 £3.25

Two Society Comedies

(An Ideal Husband, A Woman of No Importance)

edited by Russell Jackson, Shakespeare Institute, University of Birmingham & Ian Small, University of Birmingham

336 pages
0 510-33511-X £4.95

William Wycherley

The Country Wife

edited by John Dixon Hunt, University of London

160 pages
0 510-343521-X £3.25

The Plain Dealer

edited by James L. Smith, University of Southampton

216 pages
0 510-33503-9 £3.25